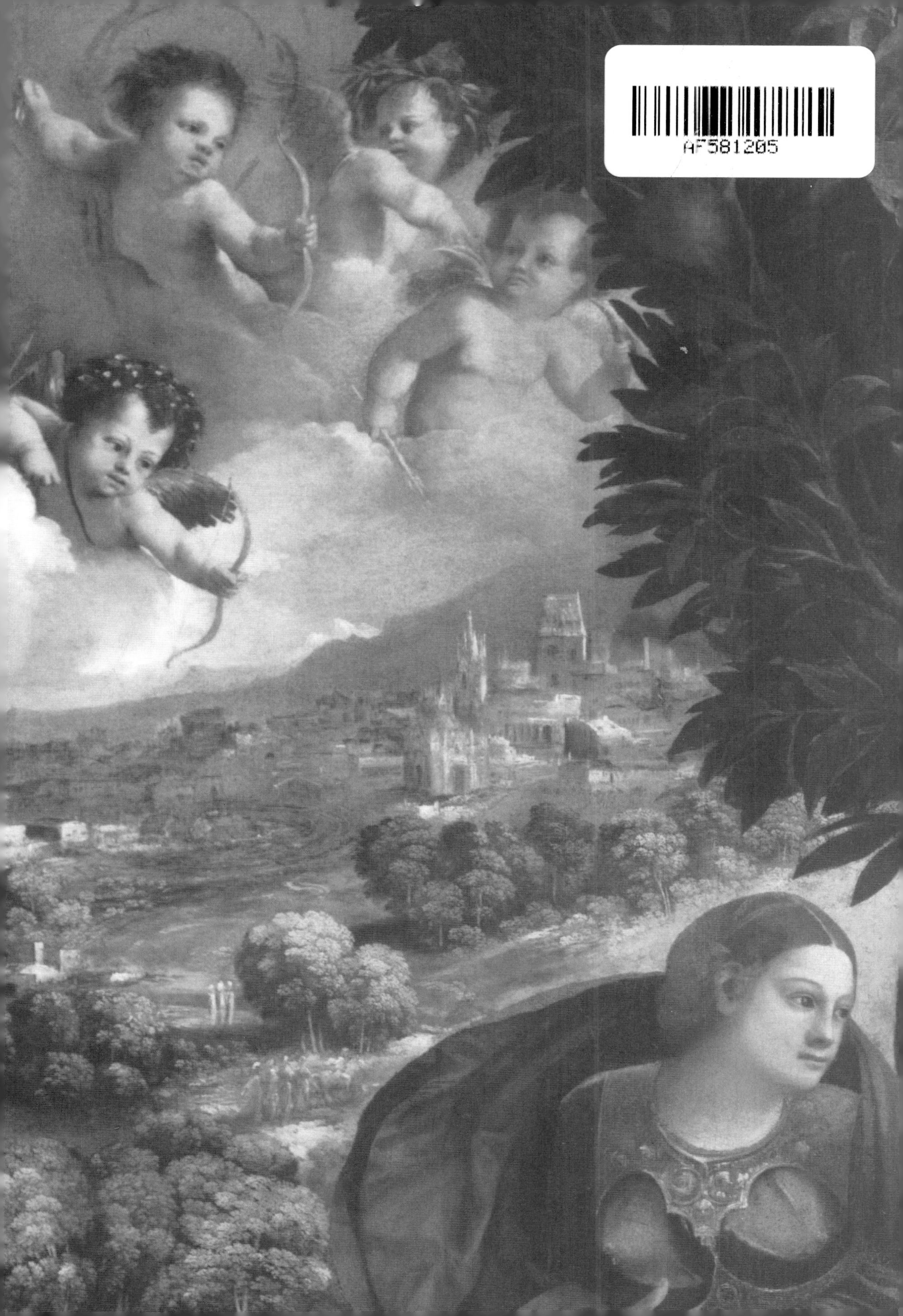

sso's

Fate

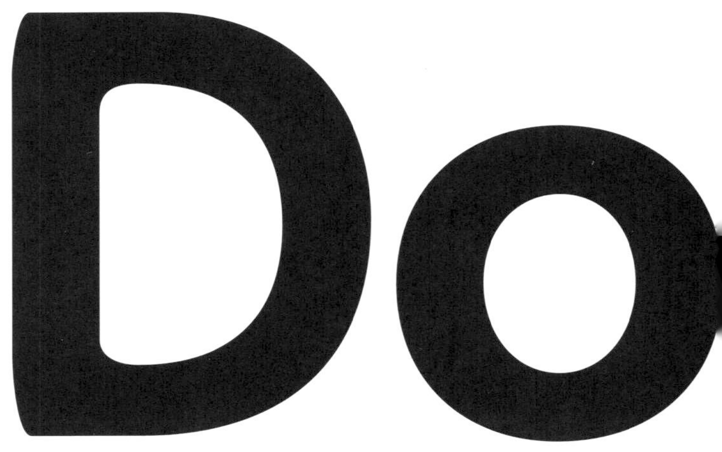

Published by the Getty Research Institute for the History of Art and the Humanities

ssos Fate

Dosso's Fate: Painting and Court Culture in Renaissance Italy

Edited by Luisa Ciammitti, Steven F. Ostrow, and Salvatore Settis

Issues & Debates

The Getty Research Institute Publications and Exhibitions Program

Issues & Debates
Julia Bloomfield, Thomas F. Reese, Michael S. Roth, and Salvatore Settis, *Editors*

Dosso's Fate: Painting and Court Culture in Renaissance Italy
Edited by Luisa Ciammitti, Steven F. Ostrow, and Salvatore Settis
Rebecca Frazier, *Senior Manuscript Editor*
Michelle Bonnice, *Manuscript Editor*
Translation of French and Italian essays by Jon R. Snyder

This volume, the fifth in the series Issues & Debates, evolved from two symposia organized by the Getty Research Institute for the History of Art and the Humanities in collaboration with the J. Paul Getty Museum, the Soprintendenza per i Beni Artistici e Storici, Bologna, and the Provincia Autonoma di Trento. The first, "Dosso Dossi and His Age," was held 9–11 May 1996 at the Getty Research Institute in Santa Monica, California; the second, "Dosso Dossi e il suo tempo, II" was held 3–5 April 1997 at the Castello del Buonconsiglio in Trent, Italy.

Published by The Getty Research Institute for the History of Art and the Humanities
Los Angeles, CA 90049-1688

Printed in the United States of America

03 02 01 00 99 98 7 6 5 4 3 2 1

Frontispiece: Dosso Dossi, *Mythological Scene* (detail). Los Angeles,
The J. Paul Getty Museum

Library of Congress Cataloging-in-Publication Data
Dossi, Dosso, d. 1542.
Dosso's Fate: Painting and Court Culture in Renaissance Italy /
edited by Luisa Ciammitti, Steven F. Ostrow, and Salvatore Settis.
p. cm. – (Issues & Debates)
Based on two symposia held in May 1996 and April 1997 organized by the
Getty Research Institute for the History of Art and the Humanities.
Includes bibliographical references and index.
ISBN 0-89236-505-6 (paper)
1. Dossi, Dosso. d. 1542 – Criticism and interpretation. 2. Alfonso I d'Este,
Duke of Ferrara. 1476–1534 – Art patronage.
I. Ciammitti, Luisa. II. Ostrow, Steven F. III. Settis, Salvatore. IV. Getty Research
Institute for the History of Art and the Humanities. V. Title. VI. Series.
ND623.D65D68 1998
759.5 – dc21 98-4758
CIP

Contents

Preface

Dosso Dossi, *Court Painter in Renaissance Ferrara*—an unprecedented exhibition of the work of Dosso and his brother Battista—will open in the Palazzo dei Diamanti in Ferrara, Italy, in September of 1998, and then travel to the Metropolitan Museum of Art in New York in January of 1999, and to the J. Paul Getty Museum in Los Angeles in April of that same year. From the very beginning of its planning, a scholarly conference was intended to accompany and complement the exhibition. To this end John Walsh, director of the J. Paul Getty Museum, and Salvatore Settis, director of the Getty Research Institute for the History of Art and the Humanities, contacted Luisa Ciammitti, of the Soprintendenza per i Beni Artistici e Storici di Bologna, to plan a symposium devoted to Dosso. After many meetings and much deliberation, four basic points were decided upon: the symposium would take the form of two separate meetings, at the Getty and in Italy; the two conference meetings would precede the exhibition, rather than coincide with it, in order to generate discussion that might inform the exhibition catalog; the conference would be designed to go beyond a strictly monographic approach to Dosso's artistic development by exploring the wider social, intellectual, and historical context in which he lived; and a book drawn from material presented at the two meetings would be published in the Getty Research Institute's "Issues & Debates" series.

This volume is that publication—one which grew out of a two-part international conference entitled "Dosso Dossi and His Age," organized by Luisa Ciammitti with the assistance of Amy Morris. The first meeting took place in May 1996 at the Getty Research Institute (then in Santa Monica, California) and the J. Paul Getty Museum in Malibu; the second, almost one year later, in April 1997, at the Castello del Buonconsiglio in Trent, Italy. Less than half of the papers presented in California and Trent appear here as essays, however, the remaining having been committed to publication elsewhere. Several of the papers, moreover, have been substantially rewritten and refined, two have been expanded from brief symposium "remarks" into fully developed essays, and one has been commissioned specifically for this volume. This book does not, therefore, constitute the "acts" or "proceedings" of the Dosso conference, but it has been conceived in such a way as to reflect the breadth and depth of inquiry that marked the two meetings and to stimulate further discussion and debate about Dosso and his fate.

The editors of this volume are much indebted to George R. Goldner and David Jaffé, former and present curators of painting at the J. Paul Getty Museum, Kurt Forster, former director of the Getty Research Institute, Andrea Emiliani, Soprintendente per i Beni Artistici e Storici di Bologna, Ferrara, Forlì, Rimini e Ravenna, and the Provincia Autonoma di Trento for their imagination, inspiration, and generous support at various stages in this project. We also gratefully acknowledge Jon Snyder and Nicholas Goodhue for their translations from the Italian and Latin.

To all those who have assisted and encouraged me in my role in this enterprise, most especially Amy Morris, Luisa Ciammitti, Salvatore Settis, Rebecca Frazier, Michelle Bonnice, Rachel Bindman, and Noriko Gamblin, I express my warmest thanks.

—S.F.O.

Introduction

Steven F. Ostrow

Among the more than one hundred extant paintings generally accepted as the work of Dosso Dossi, only one bears the artist's signature, his *Saint Jerome* in the Kunsthistorisches Museum in Vienna (p. 94). Rather than taking the form of the artist's name spelled out with letters, however, the signature appears in the form of a rebus, with a *D* stuck through by a large bone, a visual pun on the Italian word for bone (*osso*). With its play of verbal and visual elements, Dosso's only signature is reminiscent of the culture of emblematics that flourished in sixteenth-century Italy. It was a culture in which the artist—and the Estense court in Ferrara—was deeply immersed: Dosso drew upon the emblems in Andrea Alciati's *Emblematum libellus,* the earliest and most important emblem book of the Renaissance, for several of his paintings, and in 1543 Alciati himself was called to Ferrara by Ercole II d'Este.[1] Although unusual, it was not unprecedented for a rebus to appear in a sixteenth-century Italian painting.[2] As an Italian artist's signature, however, as Dosso's *only* signature on a work, his rebus is both unconventional and remarkable—at once learned, whimsical, and deeply reflective of the humanist culture in which it was produced.[3] And like a true *impresa,* as defined by Paolo Giovio, Dosso's rebus-signature is "not so obscure as to require a Sybil to interpret it, nor so obvious as to allow every plebeian to understand it."[4]

The qualities of Dosso's entire oeuvre mirror those of his rebus. His art—both formally and iconographically—remains elusive and difficult to categorize, which underscores why he continues to be such a compelling and endlessly challenging artist to study. Thanks to the wealth of documents that chronicle his life and career as a court artist, we know a great deal about Dosso.[5] Unfortunately, however, very little of the work he executed for the court of Ferrara survives, and owing to an almost complete lack of documentation for his extant paintings, many critical questions remain unanswered about his life and work. What we are certain about can be summarized as follows: Dosso Dossi was born Giovanni Lutero (or Luteri) in about 1487; his younger brother Battista was born between about 1490 and 1495. Their father, Nicolò, came from the Trentino and served as the bursar (*spenditore*) at the Ferrarese court of Ercole I d'Este. In 1512 Dosso is recorded as working in Mantua at the court of the Gonzaga, and by early 1514 he is documented as being in the service of Alfonso I d'Este in Ferrara—a position in which he would remain his entire life. Along with Battista, who is first recorded at the Ferrarese court in 1517, Dosso fulfilled all the duties expected of a court artist: adorning the ducal palaces and villas with frescoes and easel pictures, painting portraits, and designing theater sets, tapestries, festival decorations, fountains, arms and armor, banners, medals, prints, and majolica. We know that Dosso traveled on behalf of the duke to Venice in 1516, to Florence in 1517, to Venice again in 1518, and to Mantua (with Titian) in 1519. When permitted by Alfonso, he also produced altarpieces and secular works for the Ferrarese nobility and other patrons, and on two occasions the Dossi brothers were "lent" by Alfonso to other princely patrons to undertake large decorative projects. These consisted of frescoes adorning the Villa Imperiale near Pesaro, which they carried out for Francesco Maria I della Rovere, the duke of Urbino, in 1530, and, from 1531 to 1532, the decoration of a suite of rooms in the Castello del Buonconsiglio in Trent, for Cardinal Bernardo Cles, prince-bishop of that city. Following his return to Ferrara, Dosso resumed his duties as court painter to Alfonso and, among other activities, from 1532 on produced a number of altarpieces and votive paintings for Parma, Modena, and Faenza. In 1534, upon the death of Alfonso, his son Ercole II succeeded him as duke of Ferrara, and by about 1540, Battista had replaced Dosso as the leading court artist. In 1541 the two brothers traveled to Venice, and late that same year, or more probably early the next, Dosso died.

These "facts," all of them documented, provide an outline of Dosso's career as an artist. But so much more remains uncertain. We know little, for example, about his early years in Mantua, or about what other artists were doing there at the time. It is also unclear how to reconcile certain inconsistencies among the early sources. Giorgio Vasari, for example, reports that Dosso was a pupil of Lorenzo Costa in Ferrara; according to Lodovico Dolce, he studied in Venice; and Girolamo Baruffaldi, his seventeenth-century biographer, suggests that he spent time in both Venice and Rome. More recently, the impact on Dosso's development of Giorgione and Venetian art, of Raphael, and of northern European painters such as Joachim de Patinir and Albrecht Altdorfer has been widely debated, as have his contributions to the development of landscape and genre painting. The overall chronology of his oeuvre has yet to be established, and the precise subjects and meanings of many of his most complex paintings and the relationship between his art and the larger court culture in Ferrara are subject to continued discussion.

The conference that gave rise to this volume was conceived as a means to explore these and other issues in the hope of expanding our knowledge of Dosso's art within the wider intellectual and historical context in which he lived. A fortunate coincidence provided exceptional impetus to this effort: the publication, soon after the conference had been organized, of a new two-volume monograph on Dosso Dossi by the eminent scholar of northern Italian painting, Alessandro Ballarin.[6] Monumental in size, and rich in critical apparatuses and illustrations, Ballarin's work examines the art of Dosso in relation to the broader artistic context of Venetian, Mantuan, and Ferrarese painting in the first half of the sixteenth century. In addition to Dosso, Battista Dossi figures prominently in this study, as do a number of other painters, among them Giorgione, Boccaccio Boccaccino, Lodovico Mazzolino, Garofalo, and Girolamo da Carpi. At the core of Ballarin's monograph, however, is its central feature and most distinguished contribution: a year-by-year, and, in some instances, month-by-month chronology of Dosso's oeuvre, beginning circa 1508–1510 and ending circa 1540. The guiding methodology of this chronology, what governs Ballarin's approach, is connoisseurship, the "thinking eye."[7]

Owing to its scope and its depth of inquiry into the formal aspects of Dosso's art, Ballarin's monograph, not surprisingly, had an immediate and direct impact on the papers presented at the first meeting of the Dosso conference.[8] It became, in essence, the touchstone and reference point for all considerations of Dosso's artistic development. Regardless of whether or not they agreed with Ballarin's conclusions, participants simply had to take into account his dating for all but the few documented paintings by the artist. This was especially the case in regard to Dosso's earliest working years, the most studied and, also, the most controversial period of his career, especially with respect to the so-called Longhi group—a number of paintings, primarily religious in subject matter, that were first attributed to Dosso by Roberto Longhi and dated by him to between 1512 and 1517.[9] Ballarin's chronology also figured prominently in discussions of Giorgione's and Raphael's influence on Dosso's art, as well as other aspects of his career.

If the appearance of Ballarin's monograph framed one end of the Dosso conference, and provided it with an important and provocative stimulus, the other end of the conference—the meeting in Trent—was framed by an equally extraordinary event—the publication (in the fall of 1996) by Adriano Franceschini of documents for the Costabili polyptych, one of Dosso's most important altarpieces, which was executed in collaboration with Garofalo (p. 142).[10] Originally painted for the high altar of Sant'Andrea in Ferrara (and now housed in that city's Pinacoteca Nazionale), this large altarpiece was, as Vasari first noted, commissioned by Antonio Costabili, a Ferrarese nobleman and diplomat with close ties to the ducal court and a member of the Comune of Ferrara. As to its date, it was generally assumed, on the basis of the maturity of its forms, to have been painted in the early 1530s. Upon the discovery (by Alessandra Pattanaro in 1989) that the altarpiece was already in place at the time of Costabili's death in 1527,[11] a new dating to between 1523 and 1524 had been proposed by Ballarin. Franceschini's publication, however (which appears in this volume in an expanded form), points to a very different conclusion: the documents he found prove that work on the painting was under way by July 1513.

The discovery that work on one of Dosso's major paintings had already commenced as early as 1513 (an entire decade earlier than any modern scholar had proposed) suggests the need to rethink the entire chronology of Dosso's oeuvre and, also, Garofalo's career. In light of the Raphaelesque qualities of the Costabili polyptych, and of Vasari's statement (in his life of Garofalo) that it was finished within Raphael's lifetime, it also raises other pivotal issues pertaining to Dosso's development, among them whether he had visited Rome in about 1512, prior to the execution of the altarpiece, perhaps in the company of Garofalo.[12] For this very reason, the "Franceschini documents," as they came to be called, dominated much of the discussion at the second meeting of the Dosso conference. Given the open-ended nature of the documents (they say nothing about when the altarpiece was completed or about what, exactly, Dosso and Garofalo painted in 1513), opinions varied greatly as to how to interpret them, and considerable debate focused on the matter of how to reconcile stylistic and documentary evidence in reconstructing the chronology of Dosso's works.[13]

The two events that framed the Dosso conference and helped to shape this volume—the publication of Ballarin's monograph just before the first meeting and of Franceschini's documents just prior to the second; the former providing a connoisseurship-based chronology of the artist's oeuvre, the latter archival evidence that suggests a radically earlier inception for one of the artist's most important altarpieces—reveal much about the state of Dosso scholarship and what might be generally referred to as "Dosso's fate." They tell us that Dosso Dossi, an artist who served one of Renaissance Italy's richest and most illustrious courts, who was renowned during his lifetime, and whose works were admired and collected long after his death, continues to challenge our ability to circumscribe his life and his work and that further study of his art is much needed. Indeed, despite the publication of five Dosso monographs (including Ballarin's) over the course of this century,[14] fundamental questions about his art remain to be answered. The most pressing among them concern his stylistic development and chronology, which, as Felton Gibbons wrote thirty years ago, "confront the historian with problems of the utmost difficulty." This situation certainly explains the monumental effort made by Ballarin to construct a comprehensive chronological sequence of Dosso's works. It also underscores why the discovery of documents pertaining to a surviving painting has the power to create such an upheaval within Dosso studies, forcing us to radically revise our assumptions about his artistic development and to embark once more upon the process of reconstructing his chronology.

The essays in this volume reflect this scholarly necessity by taking up a variety of subjects, including the artist's contemporaries in Mantua and Venice, his contributions to the development of new genres of painting, questions of style and chronology, his collaboration with his brother Battista, the court culture of Mantua and Ferrara in which he lived and worked, his visual and literary sources, his painting technique, and the collecting of his work. No less varied are the approaches brought to bear in the essays that follow, encompassing close visual analysis and connoisseurship, technical and conservational methods, musicology, hermeneutics, textual analysis, architectural archaeology, and costume studies.

Part I of this book, titled "Problems in Interpretation," brings together five essays that elucidate artistic practices and iconographic innovations among Dosso and his contemporaries from a variety of different perspectives. Giovanni Romano takes as his subject Antonio Allegri, better known as Correggio (ca. 1489–1534), focusing on a critical moment in the artist's early career when he began to move away from the style of Mantegna toward a Leonardesque pictorial mode. Analyzing a small number of key works from this period, Romano raises the larger question of artistic choices, contrasting Correggio's artistic development with that of Dosso during the same years.

Very different kinds of interpretative problems confront Alessandro Nova in his essay on two late and no longer extant works by Giorgione—the first reflected in Marcantonio Raimondi's enigmatic engraving of the *Dream,* the second known only from a brief description by Marcantonio Michiel. With regard to the former, Nova's concern is to read the bizarre night scene in terms of the sixteenth-century humanist culture for which it was produced. As to the latter, Nova's challenge is to reconstruct Giorgione's lost painting *Inferno with Aeneas and Anchises* and to interpret its iconography—a *"nocte"* with the fall of Troy—in light of its probable patron's classical interests and political ties to the Republic.

Michel Hochmann turns his attention to the origins and development of a new type of imagery, namely, "comic paintings," genre scenes with half-length figures. After establishing Giorgione's pivotal role in the invention of this new genre—especially in the last phase of his career—the author analyzes its evolution in the works of Dosso and other artists. He discusses the influence of Leonardo and northern European paintings and draws important parallels between "comic paintings" and theater, providing new insights into this "low" genre in relation to poetics (both ancient and contemporary) and as an intentional reaction against, or an alternative to, "high" classical art.

In contrast to Hochmann, who analyzes the development and meaning of a new genre, Luisa Ciammitti analyzes a well-established type of painting: the mythology. Taking as her primary focus Dosso's puzzling *Mythological Scene* in the J. Paul Getty Museum, Ciammitti reconstructs its original appearance and offers a novel interpretation of its subject and sources. She then expands her field of inquiry to a few other of Dosso's mythological works, analyzing the artist's particular ways of constructing narrative images. What emerges is a different way of reading Dosso's art, as well as a more lucid understanding of his sources.

Vincenzo Gheroldi's essay is concerned with interpreting the distinctive painting techniques and style employed by Dosso and Battista in the frescoes in the Camera delle Cariatidi in the Villa Imperiale at Pesaro. Through close visual scrutiny and technical analysis of the paintings, the author identifies in them the appearance of a peculiar feature—painting in wet lime (*a calce*)—aimed at a style characterized by a sketchiness and great fluency of brushwork. Noting that this style was also practiced by contemporary artists working in the eastern Po valley, and that it was especially appreciated by certain "perceptive" patrons, Gheroldi reads the style and technique of the Pesaro frescoes as a response to specific aesthetic and cultural tastes.

In part II of this volume, seven essays are united under the title "Dosso's Career: Chronology, Sources, and Style." First among them is Adriano Franceschini's presentation of the documents for the Costabili polyptych, a slightly expanded version of his publication discussed above. The documentation is incomplete: it records three payments to Dosso and Garofalo between July and November 1513, and an additional payment for pigments purchased by the artists in Venice, but it does not include a final payment for the completed work. At the very least, however, the documents clearly prove that the artists received several payments in a row for work already under way (*"che depinzono"*—that they are painting—the first payment states) in the second half of 1513.

Andrea De Marchi redirects our attention to the Mantuan context of Dosso's early years by analyzing the art of Lorenzo Leonbruno, court painter to the Gonzaga between 1506 and 1524. He contrasts Dosso's early acceptance of the *"maniera moderna"* with Leonbruno's resistance to it, and pursues this comparison through the duration of both artists' careers, emphasizing Dosso's continual development and Leonbruno's more-or-less ongoing conservatism. Although several new attributions to Leonbruno suggest that he was occasionally capable of producing works closer to the spirit of Dosso, the distance between the two painters only increased as time went by, as evidenced by their different reactions to Giulio Romano in Mantua in the 1520s.

The Longhi group—those paintings on which the entire Dosso chronology has been based—lies at the core of Jane Bridgeman's essay on costumes in painting and related problems of dating. Resting her argument upon the simple but inarguable premise that the appearance of dress and hair styles in paintings can never precede their appearance in the real world, she analyzes, in terms of male and female costume and coiffures, four of the seven paintings that Longhi had attributed to Dosso and had dated to before about 1515. What emerges from her study, if not a precise chronology, is nevertheless a surprising and highly controversial revisionist view of their probable dates.

Peter Humfrey directs our attention to Dosso as a painter of landscapes, focusing on two specific "moments" in the artist's career: one early, from about 1513 to about 1515, and largely Titianesque in style; one later, about 1528, characterized by a very different, more panoramic and Patinir-like style. By means of visual comparisons, Humfrey constructs and dates a corpus of Dosso's early and later landscapes and provides the means to distinguish his works from those of Battista's. What results from the whole of Humfrey's essay is a more refined view of Dosso as a painter of landscapes.

Andrea Bayer's essay on the role of prints in Dosso's art demonstrates that prints provided a constant source of inspiration to Dosso and that references to the work of numerous printmakers appear in his paintings. In analyzing his borrowings from engravings and woodcuts—for compositional and specific iconographical sources—and in illuminating the extent to which he altered and obscured his models, Bayer reveals Dosso to have been an artist who distinguished himself from his contemporaries in his use of prints, in being always more freely interpretive and much quicker to assimilate a variety of sources.

Craig Hugh Smyth's essay explores two fundamental issues pertaining to the frescoes in the Villa Imperiale at Pesaro: the identification of the Dossi brothers' contributions to the scheme and their precise dating. Concerning the latter, through a close reading of Vasari's account of when the frescoes were painted, and a reconsideration of a number of documents, Smyth establishes a specific window of time when Dosso and Battista could have carried out the work. Concerning the former, the author rejects Vasari's account of what the Dossi painted in the villa and identifies their frescoes in the Camera delle Cariatidi and the Camera dei Semibusti. So identified and dated, a new and rare "guidepost" in the Dosso chronology is established.

Mauro Lucco provides the final contribution to this section with an essay exploring the difficult matter of the Dosso *bottega* and the ascendance of Battista in the 1530s. By means of what he terms a "process of elimination," and through probing visual analyses of a number of paintings that have long posed problems of attribution (to Dosso, Battista, or both), he provides a vivid—if speculative—picture of their individual artistic personalities. Lucco then groups together, for the first time, a small number of Dossesque paintings that have defied attribution, and, in proposing they were painted by Sebastiano Filippi, a little-known artist in the *ambito dossesco,* he offers a suggestive addition to our knowledge about the Dossi's workshop.

Part III of this book, titled "Court Culture in the Age of Dosso," expands our field of inquiry to the wider social, intellectual, and historical context in which Dosso lived. In the first of the three essays that constitute this section William Prizer offers a richly documented historical overview of music and its patronage at the courts of Mantua and Ferrara in the sixteenth century, with particular emphasis placed on the central roles played in Mantua by Isabella d'Este and her husband, Francesco Gonzaga, and in Ferrara by Ercole I d'Este, his son Alfonso I, Alfonso's two brothers, and his wife, Lucrezia Borgia. Special attention is also given to the most innovative musicians and composers they employed, new and traditional types of music performed at court, and the exchanges between Mantua and Ferrara.

We move from the world of music to that of literature in Luca D'Ascia's essay—a probing discussion exploring the impact of Leon Battista Alberti and the Lucianic revival on literary culture in Renaissance Ferrara, a revival with moral, political, and artistic implications. By means of a close analysis of the writings of Pandolfo Collenuccio, a jurist from Pesaro, and of Celio Calcagnini, a poet, philosopher, mathematician, humanist advisor to Antonio Costabili, and ducal servant, he demonstrates the diversity of the *"genere lucianesco"* and, at the same time, presents a vivid picture of Ferrarese humanism at the court of Alfonso I.

Franco Bacchelli concludes part III with a sweeping essay on science, cosmology, and religion in sixteenth-century Ferrara. Among the protagonists of his discussion are the Ferrarese humanist Lilio Gregorio Giraldi, Pico della Mirandola, and, most especially, Calcagnini and the philosopher and physician Antonio Musa Brasavola. Bacchelli gives close scrutiny to the influence of Protestantism in Ferrara and analyzes in great detail both the various responses to Reform ideas by the leading humanists at court and the political implications of Ferrara's flirtation with Protestantism. The result is a more complete view of the context in which Dosso's career in the Este court was spent than we previously possessed.

The final part of this volume comprises three essays that explore different aspects of the collecting of Dosso. In the first essay Jadranka Bentini provides for the first time the precise location and sequence of *camerini* in the ducal apartments as modified by Alfonso I, offering thereby the original context of some of Dosso's most important Ferrarese paintings.

What happened to Dosso's works once the Este court was transferred from Ferrara to Modena in 1598? Albano Biondi's essay takes up this matter, focusing on Francesco I d'Este's exploitation of a series of paintings by Dosso and Battista in January 1637. To celebrate the election of Ferdinand III as Holy Roman Emperor, the duke installed the works in the great courtyard of his palace, which was transformed into a grand ceremonial "theater." In showing the extent to which the paintings of the Dossi were invested with an unprecedented political role, Biondi makes clear that their appeal continued well into the seventeenth century.

The enduring appeal of Dosso is the subject of the final essay in this volume, in which Burton Fredericksen offers a broad look at the collecting of Dosso's work from the late sixteenth century onward. The acquisition of Dosso's work by such collectors as Scipione Borghese, Carlo Emmanuele Pio di Savoia, Charles I of England, and Archduke Leopold Wilhelm is carefully traced. Most illuminating, perhaps, is what Fredericksen tells us about the ebb and flow of taste for Ferrarese painting, the degree to which a clear definition of Dosso's style fluctuated over time, and, ultimately, how little we actually know about the provenance of so many of his paintings.

In the foregoing précis I have endeavored to convey the range and depth of inquiry that characterizes the eighteen essays in this volume. As readers of the essays will discover, much progress has been made toward understanding the art of Dosso Dossi and the cultural context in which he worked. The essays by Romano and De Marchi have alerted us to the need to consider the various artistic paths open to painters in Mantua in the early sixteenth century and to balance our assessment of Dosso's career against those of his contemporaries. Ciammitti, Hochmann, and Humfrey have contributed much to our knowledge of Dosso's contributions to mythological, genre, and landscape painting, while Bayer has enriched our view of the extent to and ways in which the artist used prints as sources for his paintings. The essay by Gheroldi has underscored the interdependence of style and technique in Dosso's frescoes and has shown that the particular style of the Pesaro frescoes bore specific cultural meanings. Nova's essay has provided us with new readings of two lost works by Giorgione that left a lasting impression on Dosso, and Lucco's contribution has gone far in separating Dosso's artistic personality from that of Battista.

Many of the authors have reminded us of the ongoing challenge of establishing Dosso's chronology. Franceschini has presented controversial new documents for one of his most important altarpieces, Smyth has endeavored to date the Pesaro frescoes more precisely than has ever been done before, and Bridgeman has challenged widely accepted notions about Dosso's early work by introducing costume analysis to the enterprise. Prizer, D'Ascia, and Bacchelli have documented and analyzed the larger court culture in which Dosso worked, making us more aware of patterns of patronage, the religious climate, and the development of new styles in music and literature in Mantua and Ferrara during the first half of the sixteenth century. And, finally, Bentini's essay has clarified the vexing problem of the original location of the *camerini,* which contained some of Dosso's most important works produced for the Este court, while Biondi and Fredericksen have provided us with a sense of the steady appeal and continued collection of Dosso's paintings.

It is thus the shared hope of the three editors that readers of this volume will come away with a more profound knowledge of Dosso Dossi and his age. But it is also our hope that readers will recognize that these essays can only begin to address the myriad questions—both of a documentary and hermeneutic nature—that pose challenges to the Dosso scholar. The conference devoted to Dosso yielded much new information and many new insights, and the essays it engendered serve as a testament to the creative approaches that the study of this important but elusive painter demands. With all that we have learned, however, the enigma of Dosso that his rebus-signature embodies remains, perhaps unsurprisingly, largely intact; we have much to look forward to with respect to future Dosso studies. Continued research on his patrons and public, the iconography of his paintings, his artistic development, and the chronology of his oeuvre, will certainly provide new ways to look at his art, as will the discovery of additional archival material and further consideration of the meaning and implications of the Costabili documents. If the present volume helps to foster awareness of the richness and complexity of Dosso's art, the Dosso Dossi exhibition, the catalog that will accompany it, and the conference sponsored by the Istituto di Studi Rinascimentali of Ferrara, which will be held in conjunction with the exhibition's closing, will no doubt heighten that appreciation and contribute further to our understanding of one of Renaissance Italy's most intriguing painters.

Notes

1. On the rebus, see Jean Céard and Jean-Claude Margolin, *Rébus de la Renaissance: Des images qui parlent* (Paris: Maisonneuve et Larose, 1986); Lina Bolzoni, *La stanza della memoria: Modelli letterari e iconografici nell'età della stampa* (Turin: Einaudi, 1995), 90–95. On Dosso's use of emblems, see, among others, Luisa Ciammitti's essay in this volume, and Felton Gibbons, *Dosso and Battista Dossi: Court Painters at Ferrara* (Princeton: Princeton Univ. Press, 1968), 7–8, 111, 218, 226.

2. For example, Lorenzo Lotto, Dosso's slightly older contemporary, incorporated a rebus (as Ciammitti notes in her essay in this volume) into his portrait of Lucina Brembati (Bergamo, Accademia Carrara) of circa 1520. It is a play on the sitter's name, with the letters *CI* inscribed on a moon at the upper left corner of the painting. When read with the Italian (and Latin) word for moon—*luna*—the rebus spells out *lu-ci-na*. On this work and other instances of Lotto's use of the rebus, see most recently Peter Humfrey, *Lorenzo Lotto* (New Haven: Yale Univ. Press, 1997), 45–46, 66–69, 105, 110.

3. Although uncommon in Italy, in the north of Europe, from the fifteenth century on, artists frequently signed their work with a rebus. This was especially true among printmakers, but painters and illuminators also employed rebus-signatures, among them Matthijs Bril (the letter *M* superimposed on a pair of spectacles) and Joris Hoefnagel (the letter *G* superimposed on a horseshoe nail). I am grateful to Nicola Courtright and Lee Hendrix for discussing this matter with me.

4. Paolo Giovio, *Dialogo dell'imprese militari et amorose* (Rome: Antonio Barre, 1555; Lyons: G. Rovillio, 1574), 12: *"non sia oscura, di sorte, c'habbia mistero della Sibilla per interprete a volerla intendere; né tanto chiara, ch'ogni plebeo l'intenda."* As Bolzoni (see note 1), 94, notes, Giovio nevertheless disapproved of the rebus, deeming it a childish and overly simple thing.

5. See the "Digest of Documents" in Gibbons (see note 1), 275–91; and Alessandra Pattanaro, ed., "Regesto della pittura a Ferrara (1497–1548)," in Alessandro Ballarin, *Dosso Dossi: La pittura a Ferrara negli anni del Ducato di Alfonso I,* 2 vols. (Cittadella: Bertoncello Artigrafiche, 1994–1995), 1: 109–79.

6. See the previous note for the full citation. Volume 2 of Ballarin's work consists exclusively of 815 captioned black-and-white illustrations. It was published before volume 1, which comprises a number of essays, an extensive catalog (for the two Dossi and selected other painters), 204 color plates, 244 additional black-and-white illustrations, a *regesto* of documents (mentioned in note 5), bibliography, and index.

7. I borrow this phrase from the title of an essay by Hal Opperman, "The Thinking Eye, the Mind That Sees: The Art Historian as Connoisseur," *Artibus et historiae*, no. 21 (1990): 9–13, in which Opperman argues for the centrality of connoisseurship to the art-historical process.

8. Ballarin spoke at the first meeting of the conference, presenting an overview—drawn from his monograph—of his chronology of Dosso's work.

9. Roberto Longhi, "Un problema di Cinquecento ferrarese (Dosso giovine)" (1927), in idem, *Saggi e ricerche, 1925–1928,* 2 vols. (Florence: Sansoni, 1967), 1: 306–11.

10. Adriano Franceschini, "Dosso Dossi, Benvenuto da Garofalo e il polittico Costabili di Ferrara," *Paragone,* nos. 543–545 (1995): 110–15. Although dated 1995,

the journal volume was not published until fall 1996, after the first meeting of the conference.

11. Alessandra Pattanaro, "Il testamento di Antonio Costabili: Per il polittico di Dosso e Garofalo già in Sant'Andrea a Ferrara," *Arte veneta* 43 (1989–1990): 130–42.

12. On this matter, see the article by Peter Humfrey and Mauro Lucco, "Dosso Dossi in 1513: A Reassessment of the Artist's Early Works and Influences," *Apollo* 147 (1998): 22–30, in which the authors also discuss—in light of the documents discovered by Franceschini (see note 10)—the question of whether Dosso may have painted, or at least influenced, the landscape in Raphael's *Madonna di Foligno*.

Had Dosso visited Rome in 1512, he may well have met Paolo Giovio, who was then in the papal capital serving as physician to Julius II. Giovio's famous description of Dosso's landscapes (on which, see Peter Humfrey's essay in this volume) might then be understood as having been based on direct and early contact with his paintings.

13. On this issue, see Alessandro Nova, review of *Dosso Dossi: La pittura a Ferrara negli anni del Ducato di Alfonso I*, by Alessandro Ballarin, *Burlington Magazine* 139 (1997): 125–26.

14. Walter Curt Zwanziger, *Dosso Dossi* (Leipzig: Klinkhardt & Biermann, 1911); Henriette Mendelsohn, *Das Werk der Dossi* (Munich: Georg Müller & Eugen Reutsch, 1914); Amalia Mezzetti, *Il Dosso e Battista ferraresi* (Milan: Silvana, 1965); Gibbons (see note 1); and Ballarin (see note 5).

Part I

Problems in Interpretation

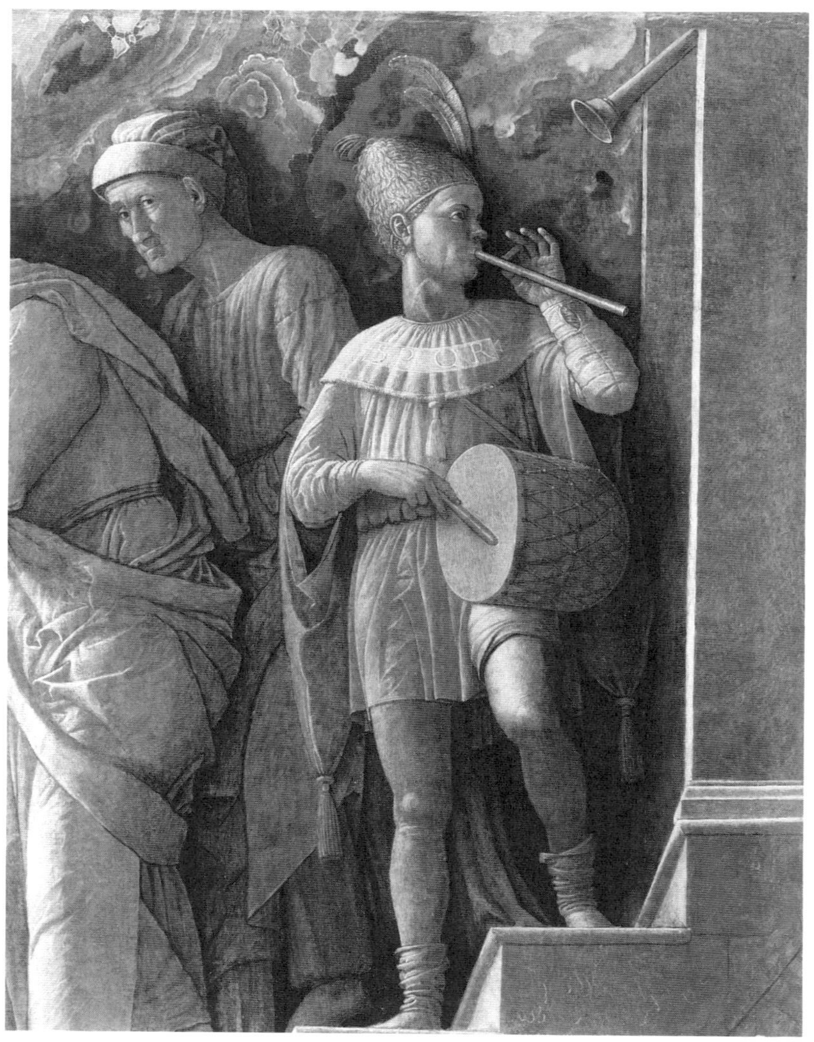

Fig. 1. Andrea Mantegna
The Introduction of the Cult of Cybele at Rome (detail)
London, The National Gallery

Correggio in Mantua and San Benedetto Po

Giovanni Romano

In memory of Laura Levi Petrazzini

According to the parish records of the city of Correggio, in January of 1511 "Antonius de Alegris" served as godfather at the baptism of Antonio Vigarini. This is the first known document to mention the artist and, based on what we know of the practices of the time, we may deduce that he had already distinguished himself in the city, most likely with his first works as a painter.[1] As far as we know, Correggio began his career in Mantua and, if we are to gauge more accurately the extent to which the early work of Dosso Dossi (who seems to have already been present as a painter in Mantua in 1512) departed from local traditions, it is important to establish the dates and level of quality of Correggio's own early output.[2]

If we accept that Correggio was born before 1490 and followed the normal course of development for a painter of his time, we must allow that there is nothing that would exclude an apprenticeship with Andrea Mantegna. Correggio would have entered into the master's workshop at around age fourteen and would have spent at least three and perhaps four years there. Assuming this to have been the case, the young Correggio might well have been a firsthand witness to the work of Mantegna, ranging from the *Minerva Expelling the Vices from the Garden of Virtue* (1502, Paris, Musée du Louvre), painted for Isabella d'Este's *studiolo,* to the *Introduction of the Cult of Cybele at Rome* (fig. 1), commissioned by the Corner family. The only surprising thing about such a hypothesis is that a young man with great artistic talent, born on the right bank of the Po River, would have turned to Mantua and to Mantegna's sponsorship—as did painters from Verona and their colleagues born on the shores of Lake Garda—rather than head for Parma (which later became the city that Correggio favored), where Francesco Marmitta offered brighter prospects.[3] In those years the pictorial traditions of Correggio's home territory were represented by two types of art: on the one hand, the frescoes of Lombard-Emilian inspiration in the Palazzo dei Principi in Correggio (1508) and, on the other hand, Mantegna's moving *Christ the Redeemer* (1493, Correggio, Congregazione di Carità). If Correggio had to make a choice between these two traditions, however symbolically, he could only have chosen to go to Mantua.[4]

A new piece of evidence has recently increased our understanding of this delicate moment in the history of Mantuan painting. According to notarial records, Francesco Mantegna, the master painter's son, appears to have received from "Antonio de Alegris de Corigio pictori," on a day perhaps preceding 29 (or 28) January 1512, a loan of ten ducats and an advance of six lire for certain expenses; this was repaid before 26 November 1512.[5] This amply confirms Correggio's personal authority and economic autonomy in 1511, which had seemed likely on the basis of his having been named a godfather in January of that year. The evidence also verifies his ties to the profligate painter-son of Mantegna and strengthens the hypothesis that Correggio participated in the work on the frescoes in Mantegna's chapel in the church of Sant'Andrea in Mantua and on the tondi in the church atrium. (This attribution has a long history that begins with the writings of Donesmondi toward the beginning of the seventeenth century.) Given the subtle chronological and stylistic distinctions that need to be made to evaluate this possibility, it is easy to foresee that consensus among specialists will not be easily attained. Nevertheless, it is my hope that a general agreement can be reached at least on the interpretation of the documents and in terms of reading the images themselves.

The fresco decoration in Mantegna's funerary chapel was conceived by the painter himself, but no definite documents concerning the work can be found for the period between 1506 and 21 October 1516, when the decoration of the chapel was completed with the installation of the bronze bust of the painter. Scholars and amateurs of the eighteenth and nineteenth centuries cite documents that concern the work and are now lost, but perhaps it is better not to count too heavily on these and instead squeeze the maximum amount out of the available undisputed facts. In 1504 the walls were still rough and unworked, and upon Mantegna's death in 1506 two paintings on canvas were ready to be installed in the chapel. According to the artist's will, the installation of these paintings was supposed to be completed within a year of Mantegna's death, that is to say, by 13 September 1507 (by this date Correggio would have been roughly twenty years old or slightly less, and he would have been on the threshold of an independent career as a painter in his own right).[6]

Recent criticism has tended to view the canvases that were prepared for the chapel and are still in situ (the *Families of Christ and Saint John the Baptist* and the *Baptism of Christ*) as having been executed in the two years prior to Mantegna's death. However, when they are compared to the refined *Introduction of the Cult of Cybele at Rome,* one becomes somewhat wary of such an enthusiastic conclusion.[7] This is not to suggest that I would attribute to Mantegna only those works done entirely by his own hand; after all, we are still not very well informed about the way in which works were carried out in Mantegna's studio. (Fifteenth-century workshops functioned in a variety of ways, and, in this regard, Giorgio Vasari's remark about Giovanfrancesco Caroto's contributions to Mantegna's works, starting with, for example, the Trivulzio altarpiece for the church of Santa Maria in Organo in Verona, has yet to be confirmed). The fact remains that the two canvases were the last ones to be executed under the master's control, and it would seem absurd to assume his indifference to their place within the larger scheme of frescoes in the chapel. Mantegna would never have exposed his finished works to the risks of a space still to be frescoed, and his death must have brought to a rapid conclusion at least that part of the decoration that had already been undertaken.

The double inscription of 1516 that appears in the chapel on the left wall and above Mantegna's bust concerns only the decorations below the pendentives, which are, stylistically speaking, more painstakingly detailed than the figures of the Evangelists in the pendentives. It could be said that the decorations were executed in the style of someone imbued with the work of Mantegna before his trip to Rome, and the biographical profile of his son Francesco, known from documents dating as far back as 1488, when he was already an adult and acting in his father's name, fits quite well with these gaunt images. Furthermore, Francesco's problems with the law, such as his struggles with his father's other heirs and his eventual exile from Mantua, together with his capricious distaste for the painter's profession, would suggest a series of delays before the chapel was completed. Logically, then, its decoration must have been carried out in two phases: the first of these, from about 1504 to 1507 or slightly later, includes the years in which the youthful Correggio may have participated in the work on the chapel; the second and final phase must have dragged on until 1516, when Francesco alone must have been involved in the work.

The confirmation—or, even, the evaluation—of these claims, however, is not easy to achieve because of the disastrous condition of the four Evangelists. In fact, recent restoration—done out of a desire for completeness—has obscured through in-painting what little remained of the original (and extraordinarily vivid) fresco surface.[8] Present-day scholars can now read these images only with effort if they lack clear memories of, or precise notes on, their state prior to preservation.

Despite the condition of these frescoes, it can be said that the idea of breaking through the surface of the four pendentives illusionistically, so that the chapel appears open to the sky, in a space in which Mantegna feared that little light would enter, was a new and brilliant idea. No less impressive are the four Evangelists, who lean on slender balconies and who appear to be hanging out into real space from a Paradise roof garden. The Evangelists, although physically imposing, occupy the available space with ease and do not impend upon the viewer. Saint Mark and Saint John seriously and quietly engage in reflection, while Saint Matthew is distracted by his angel's call. Saint Luke casts a glance below, almost as if he were portraying the Virgin and Child, drawing his inspiration from her appearance in Mantegna's altarpiece (an observation that supports the chronological contiguity between the frescoes and the canvases in the chapel). There is not much to say about the chromatic quality of these works, given their current condition. We can glimpse, however, a refined shifting of colors in Saint Luke's turban (a chromatic choice that seems related to *The Deposition* and the *Holy Family,* formerly in the atrium of Sant'Andrea and now in the Museo Diocesano, Mantua). The relationship between the head of Saint Mark and that of Saint Jerome in the *Mystic Marriage of Saint Catherine,* an early masterpiece by Correggio (ca. 1510, Detroit, Detroit Institute of Arts) which was originally in Mantua, has previously been pointed out by critics. This increases the temptation to consider the four Evangelists in the chapel as the work of Correggio, for they are at once solemn and humanly approachable in a way that Mantegna's individuals never are. Caution is warranted nevertheless because it is difficult to discern in these frescoes the Leonardesque and Giorgionesque elements found in the Detroit altarpiece. We should take account here, however, of a small chronological gap. It is a fact that Correggio, in order to be novel, relied upon a model available in Mantegna's workshop for the Detroit altarpiece (which, it is important to remember, was painted well before 1516). Thus it follows that the Evangelists in the funerary chapel were conceived prior to 1516.[9]

The critical fortune of the frescoed tondi formerly in the atrium of Sant'Andrea to a large extent parallels that of the frescoes in Mantegna's chapel: we know (from as highly a reputable source as Luigi Lanzi) that documents concerning the Sant'Andrea tondi have been lost and that this group of works is not homogeneous and poses significant difficulties for any analysis.[10] It is widely accepted that the tondo of *Christ in Glory* belongs directly to Mantegna's circle, even if it is not an autograph work. In fact, the fresco reveals the hand of an artist who humbles even the master's most heroic inventions (the basic idea can be traced to the drawing of *Christ between Saint Andrew and Longinus,* 1470s, now in the Staatliche Graphische Sammlung, Munich, or to the engraving derived from it, also executed in the 1470s and now in the Bibliothèque Nationale, Paris).[11] The possibility of Correggio's involvement has been taken into account only for *The Deposition* and the *Holy Family.*

Enduring problems with reading the surviving visual evidence has had a negative impact on the conservation of the tondi. Anyone able to remember clearly the way in which they appeared at the Mantegna exhibition held in Mantua in 1961, or even later, cannot avoid a sense of unease when first seeing them in their current state (figs. 2 and 3). In what had been the best-preserved parts, what once appeared as a precious but shadowy image glimmering through a fragmented surface now is a peremptory and rigidly defined form. Elsewhere, we see a kind of nebulous blur that obscures any distinction between the worn original and its watered-down simulation. Such faith in the miraculous powers of pictorial integration is astonishing, and art historians would do well to be guided by old photographs—two very beautiful examples of which, taken from old large-format glass negatives, can be found in the Gabinetto Fotografico Nazionale (figs. 4 and 5).[12] The current condition of the tondi is even more lamentable because the two of them, but especially the *Holy Family,* were an indispensable stylistic—and, in an indirect way, chronological—point of reference for any attempt to establish an order to Correggio's early independent works. Until very recently it still seemed possible to compare the *Holy Family* in Mantua with the *Nativity with Saint Elizabeth* (ca. 1512) in the Pinacoteca di Brera in Milan, in terms of both the similarity of emotions and the obvious distance that divides them. The Milan painting was badly damaged long ago. The Mantuan work offered a better view of the plush chromatic delicacy of the painter, which was most refined in the phosphorescent shroud of the dead Christ and the Virgin's headdress; the headdress is a silvery blue lavender that connects Correggio to Mantegna alone. The *Holy Family* and the *Mystic Marriage of Saint Catherine* now in Detroit once shared an even closer similarity. I have already discussed the latter in regard to the head of Saint Jerome, which was derived from a drawing that also served as the model for the head of Saint Mark in the Mantegna chapel.[13] The difference between them is found only in the imposing size of the figures in the fresco, an element lacking in the *Mystic Marriage,* but one that appears with a different sort of brutality in the tondo of *The Deposition.*

To speak of "brutality" today is perhaps insufficient, given that the restoration, which has reintegrated the fresco and the very rare sinopia, has transformed what was an expression of the highest and most intense dramatic power into something painfully shallow (fig. 6). From the sinopia we may discover, even more so than from the fresco itself, the source of the work's sudden surge of psychic and emotional energy. Mary, on the left (later altered), appears in the heavy garb of a nun; she seems of northern inspiration and was probably taken from one of the many images of a sorrowful Mary produced by Albrecht Dürer. A closer look at this might give us a firmer grasp on the chronology of the work, which cannot be later than 1510–1511.[14] The idea of a deposition in the sepulcher, with Christ's stiff corpse not yet in its tomb and its eyes wide open (the recent restoration exaggerates the painter's intentions), is far from the adolescent poetics that we expect to find in Correggio's work. It is precisely this dramatic masterpiece, following soon after Mantegna's death, that helps us to develop a less elegiac idea of the power of Correggio's genius. Fortunately we still have the extraordinary cartoon with a female head now in the Pierpont Morgan Library in New York to confirm the intensity and quality of this moment in Correggio's career. Who else could have evoked an image of such great pain, so reminiscent of Ercole de' Roberti, and modeled it upon one of the dancing muses in Isabella d'Este's *studiolo?*[15] These efforts to fix the quality and particular tone of Correggio's latent energy and his creative relationship with Mantegna's innovations are of help in uncovering the last part of Correggio's early career, and they assist us in approaching the new attribution that I will propose below.

Correggio's altarpiece for the church of San Francesco in Mantua (now in the Staatliche Kunstsammlungen, Gemäldegalerie Alte Meister, in Dresden) was commissioned on 30 August 1514, executed during the winter of 1514–1515, and completed by 4 April 1515. Despite the Mantegnesque derivation

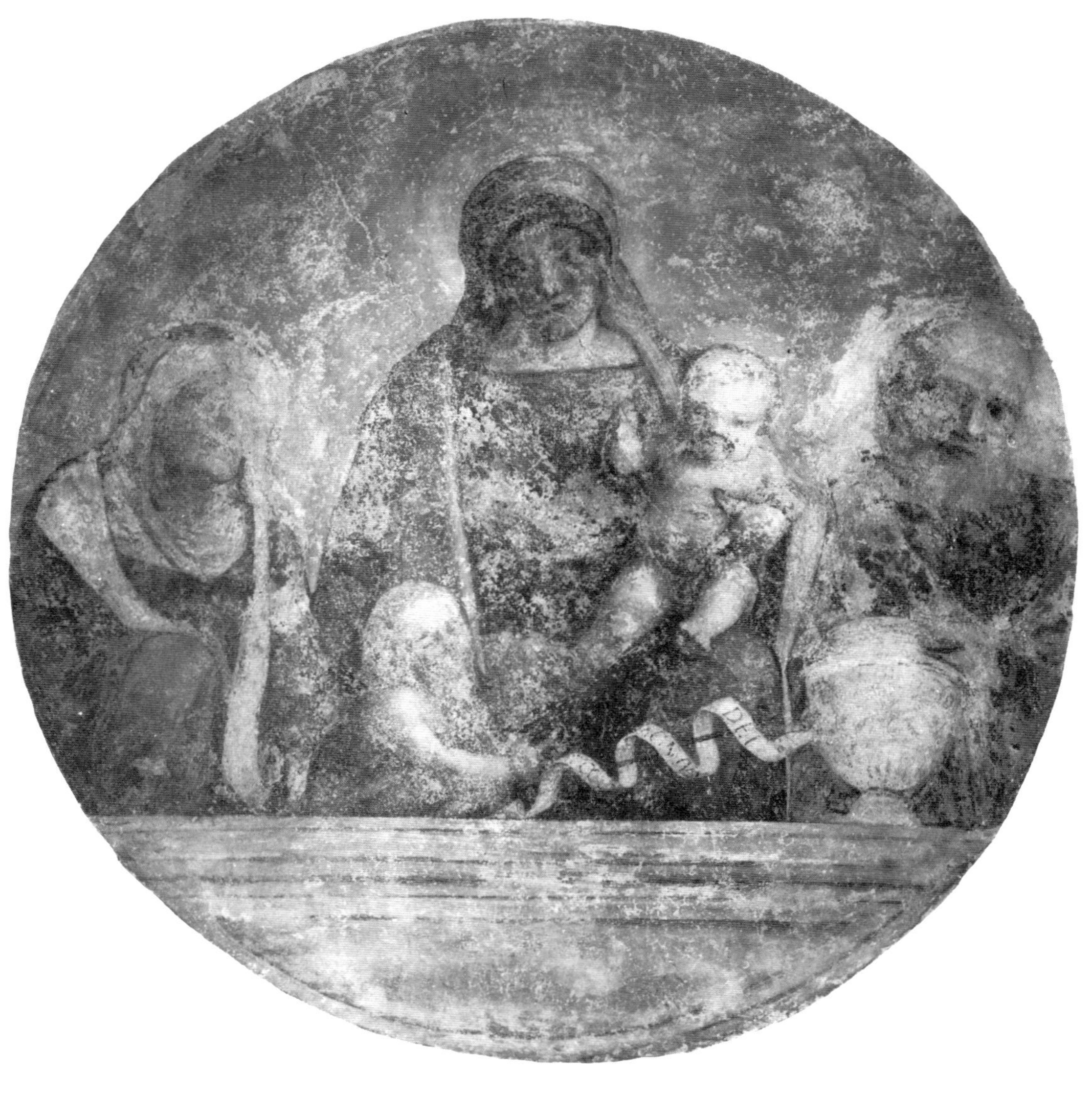

Fig. 2. Correggio
Holy Family (prior to the most recent restoration)
Mantua, Museo Diocesano

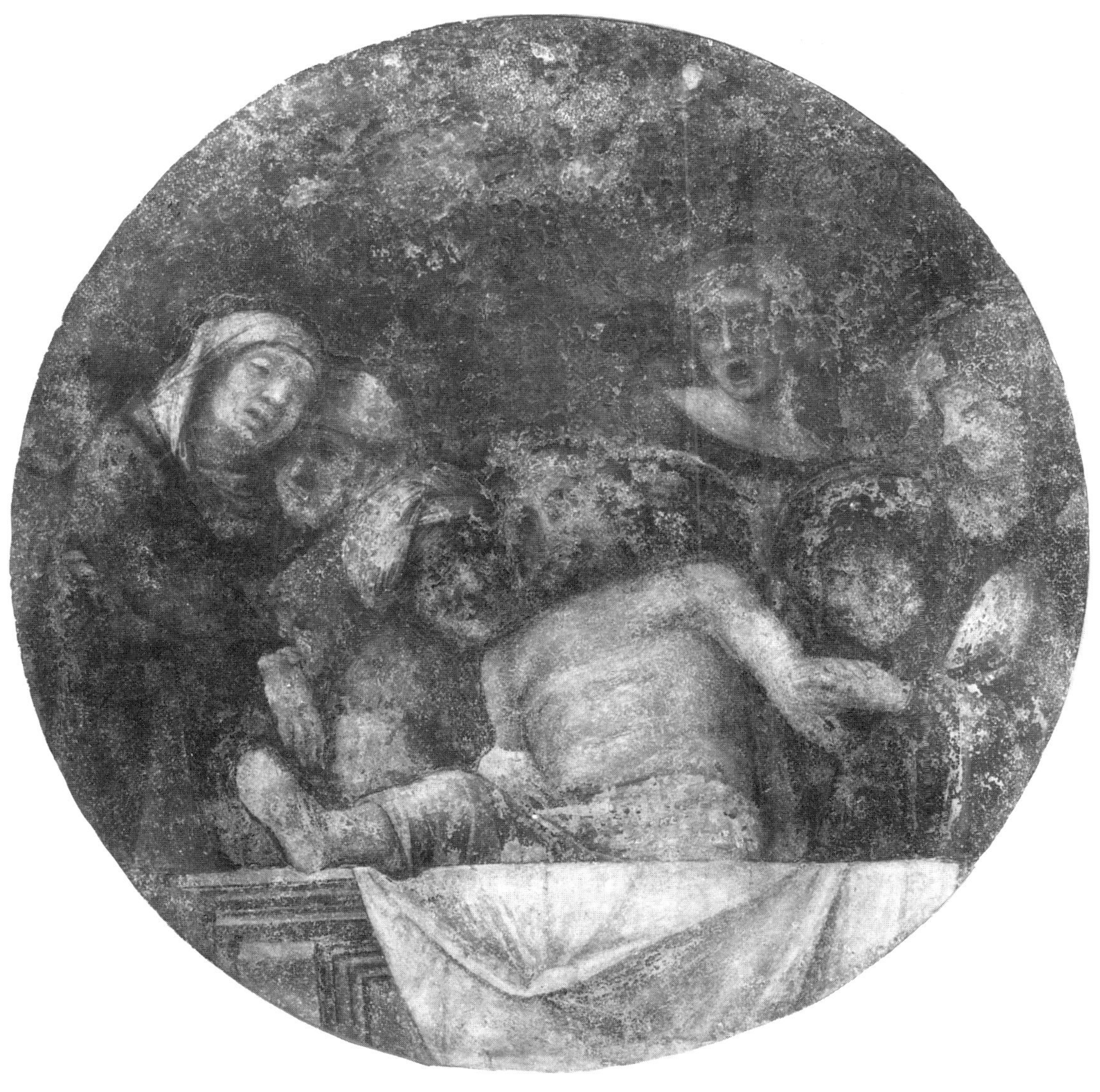

Fig. 3. Correggio
The Deposition (prior to the most recent restoration)
Mantua, Museo Diocesano

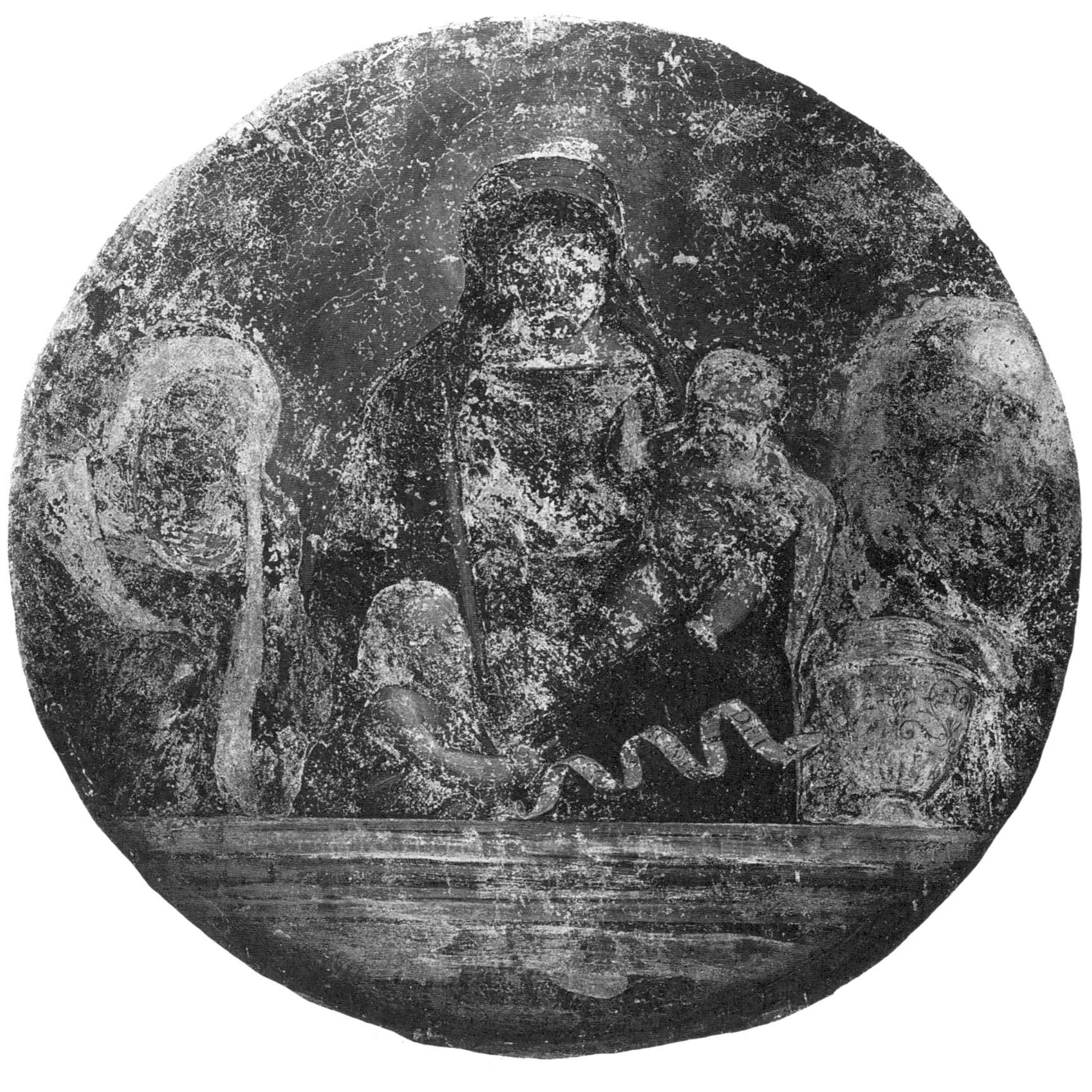

Fig. 4. Correggio
Holy Family (at the moment of its uncovering at Sant'Andrea in Mantua)
Mantua, Museo Diocesano

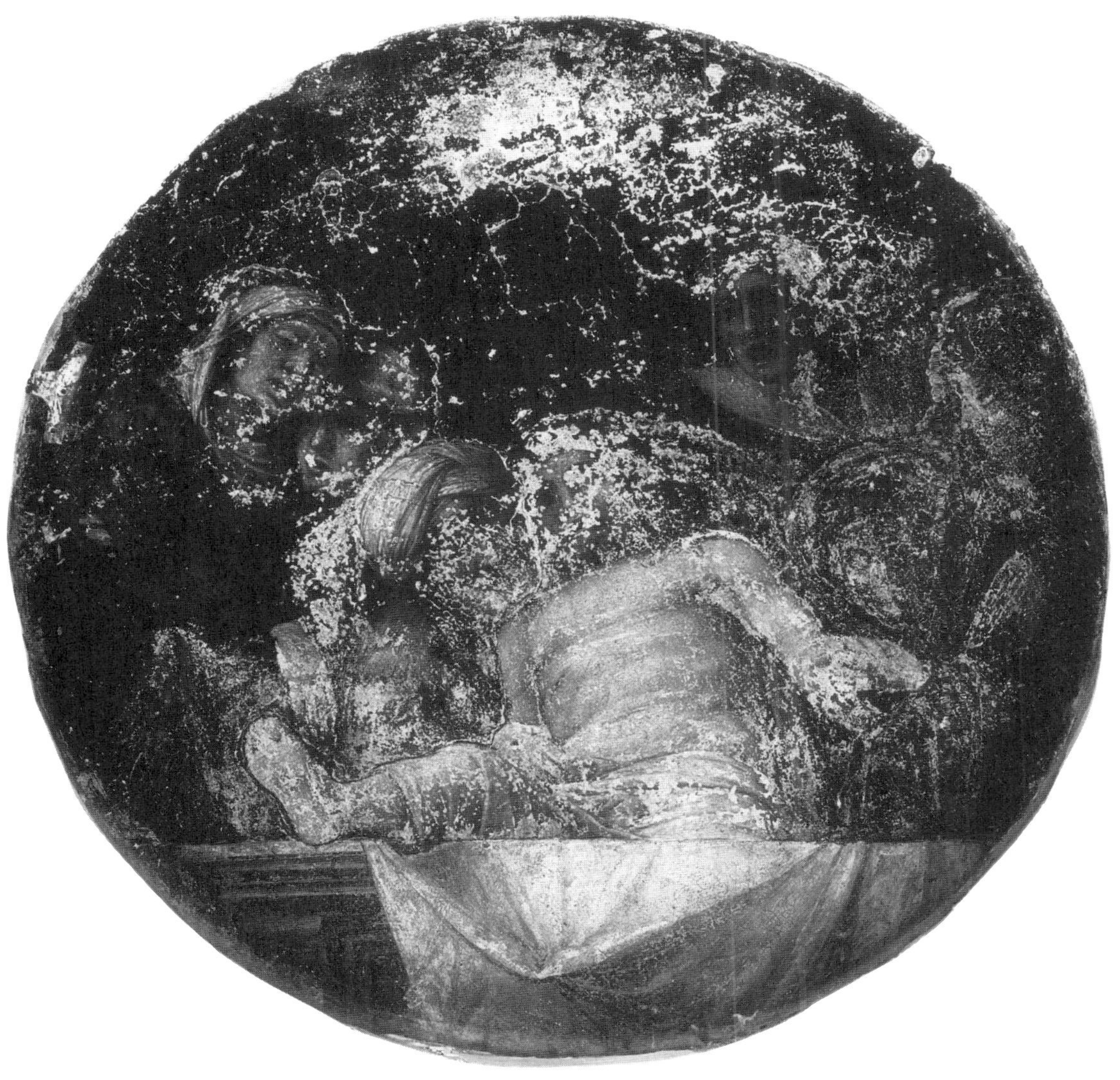

Fig. 5. Correggio
The Deposition (at the moment of its uncovering at Sant'Andrea in Mantua)
Mantua, Museo Diocesano

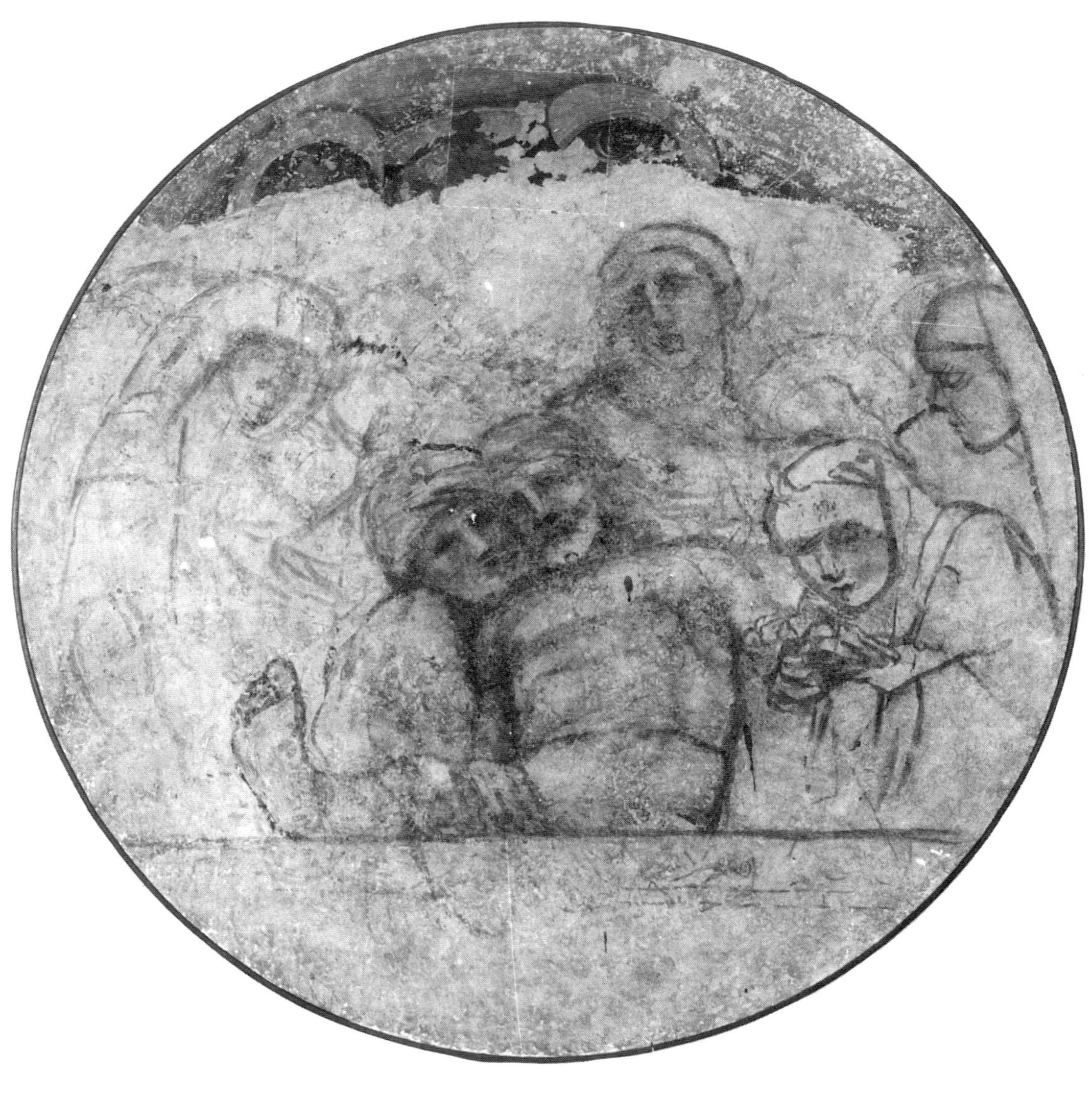

Fig. 6. Correggio
The Deposition (sinopia prior to the most recent restoration)
Mantua, Museo Diocesano

of the painting, Correggio appears open here to a broad range of other influences, as much from Emilia (and not only Lorenzo Costa and Francesco Francia) as from Leonardo (for which reason a quick trip to Milan around this time has been hypothesized by some).[16] The Dresden altarpiece marks the end of a phase in the history of Mantuan painting. The influence of Mantegna had been pushed to its limits, and the painting testifies to a precipitous updating to the modern manner by a painter intent on holding on to a market for himself.[17] It also marks the emergence, almost immediately thereafter, of new artists in the shadow of Correggio himself. This occurs with extreme rapidity at precisely the moment in which we would have expected a series of gradual steps in this direction.[18]

On 8 September 1514, immediately after signing the contract for the Dresden altarpiece, Correggio entered into an agreement with the Benedictine monastery at Polirone to paint the shutters of the organ and to decorate the baluster of the organ itself.[19] It is surprising that he would choose to commit himself to two rather large projects within a few days' time, and it is also surprising that he would ultimately succeed in completing them without delay (at least this is the case for the Dresden altarpiece). Hence there arises a special curiosity about the lost shutters, which I address, at least partially, in the following paragraphs.

A private collection in Turin has for many decades conserved a large unstudied canvas whose dimensions are appropriate for an organ shutter (fig. 7). It probably depicts the first part of the procession, headed by David, returning the Holy Ark to Jerusalem (Samuel 2:6).[20] Powerfully Mantegnesque in conception (it takes its inspiration from the master's *Triumphs of Caesar,* now in the collection of Queen Elizabeth II), Correggio could well have been responsible for the execution of this work, which seems to conform to one of the two paintings at San Benedetto Po described by Lanzi:

> it is believed that Carlo [del Mantegna] took part in the work on the [ducal] palace and the aforementioned chapel [Mantegna's chapel in Sant'Andrea] and in others that are ascribed to Mantegna's circle, including two stories of the Ark in the monastery of Saint Benedict in Mantua, where the manner of Andrea is somewhat broadened, even though the forms are less beautiful.[21]

Lanzi's remarks seem to correspond fully to the imposing foreground of the Turin painting, although he saw it when less damaged than it is today and without the widespread retouching added during an old restoration of the work. The attempt to recompose the surface of the painting, which has been corroded by craquelure and by the loss of colors, has had less effect on the faces in the middle ground, and on the basis of these we may guess about the condition of the least well preserved areas of the work (David's beard, the vegetation in the center, the face of the ox in the shadow, the feet of the young priest on the right). We also need to take into account the particularly rough grain of the canvas, as well as the methods likely employed to execute

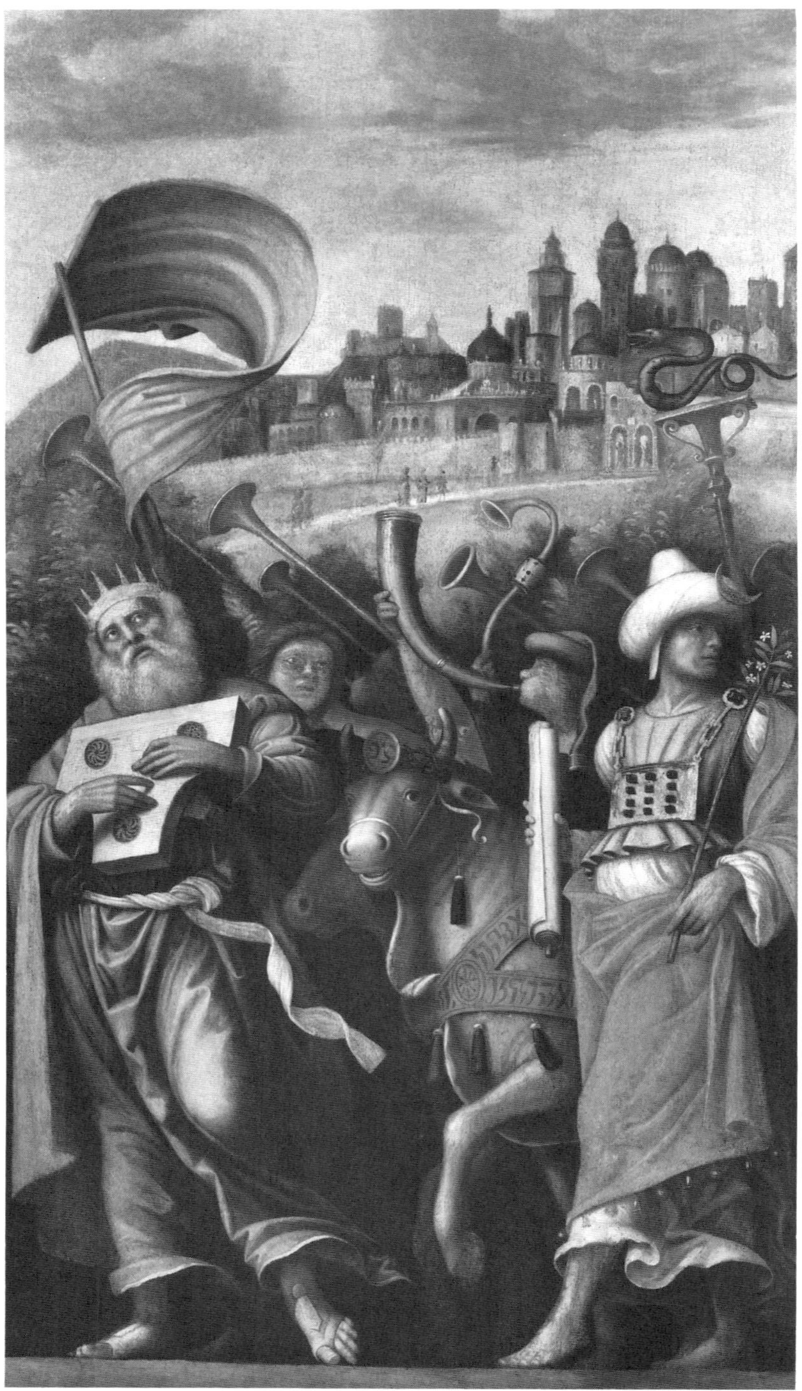

Fig. 7. Correggio
Triumph of David
Turin, private collection

the work. Since the shutters of the organ were furnishings to be seen from a distance, the artist did not apply with particular care the Leonardesque sfumato found in the Dresden altarpiece, which is, moreover, painted on wood.[22]

If we refrain from an overly sadistic closeup viewing of the work and instead look at the scene in its entirety, we see that the painting is sustained by its contradictory ambition, which is quite fascinating in its own right. The head of a crowded procession comes onto the scene obliquely, with the calm and deliberate gait suited to a sacred ceremony; even the ox at the center, looking attentively at the spectator, seems to be included in the solemnity. We have already mentioned the artist's reliance on Mantegna's *Triumphs,* but in comparing them, this procession quickly shows itself to be of more modest dimensions. There are only five figures, accompanied by two oxen, and the furnishings entirely lack the ornate and mysterious preciousness favored by the patriarch of Mantuan painting. The banner is little more than a "bedspread" (although it is the rose color of wine), and the numerous musical instruments seem suited for a country fair, even if they appear carefully cared for (the horn in the middle of the painting shines with silver and blue reflections). Moreover, the turban of the priest, with its half-moon, and his breastplate of solid gold, with large pieces of colored glass, are little different in their surprising naïveté from the way in which the ancient world of the Bible was portrayed in the parish theaters of earlier times. In the background, Jerusalem seems to be straight out of the scenographic excesses typically found in any Christmas crèche. When we look a little more closely, however, we can see the light-engulfing shadow of a still, cloudy sunset descending on the tall palaces and domes (fig. 8). Humidity seems to settle on the walls and soften them, releasing sugary vapors, as if the cardboard buildings were ready—through some magic—to transform themselves into palaces of crystal and glowing coals such as those that were, in these same years, blinding the viewers of Dosso's new landscapes. I know of no more explicit and meaningful pictorial farewell to the seductive archaeological apparatus of late humanism than this example of the new sixteenth-century painting. This painting offers the means with which to measure the distance and evaluate the mental impatience that lies between Correggio's slow development, open to the experiments of others but cautious about completely appropriating them for himself (indeed, he remained reticent to the point of dissimulation), and Dosso's lightning-quick embrace of the Venetian artistic avant-garde, of which he boldly made himself a chief figure and banner carrier.[23]

Despite these numerous clues, the attribution of this painting to Correggio might nevertheless seem overly hasty when it is considered in relation to the Dresden altarpiece. Let us try to keep in mind, however, not only the obvious technical gap between the two but also their different states of conservation and the radically divergent prestige of the two works in terms of their intended function. Let us also endeavor to take into account our own visual habits and our own hidden preference for avant-garde works. A rereading of the eighteenth-century sources, which belong to a period prior to

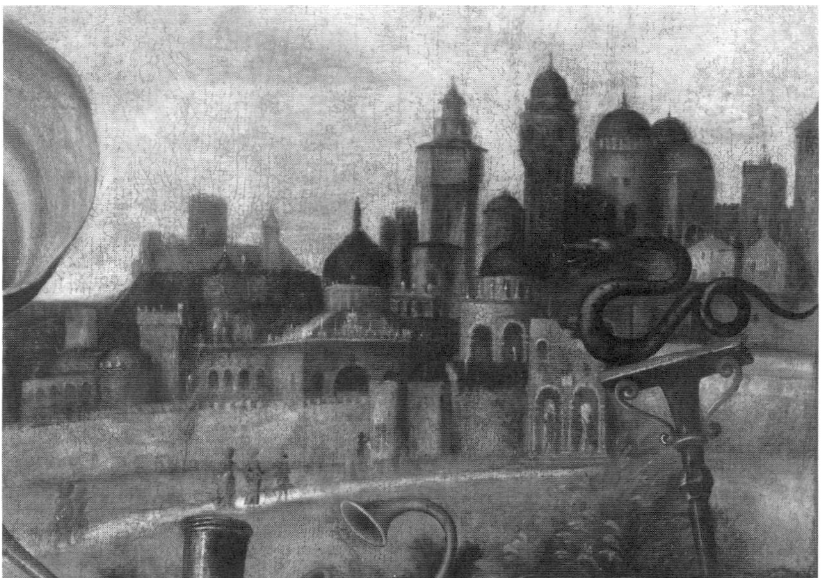

Fig. 8. Correggio
Triumph of David (detail)
Turin, private collection

the collapse of the technical skills taught in academies, may perhaps be able to lead us to a more balanced judgment. Lanzi already knew how to appreciate Correggio's shifting style in early works that are chronologically close to one another: "I hold to be true that which I once heard, namely that Correggio tried out many manners before settling on the one for which he is known."[24] A few years earlier, Carlo Giuseppe Ratti had—on the basis of Raffaello Mengs's remarks—evaluated the Dresden altarpiece in ways quite different from those in which we judge it today, but which are well suited to the painting of the *Triumph of David:*

> This work, although a bit stiff, and circumscribed by overly sharp contours, is nonetheless soft and of a very sweet mixture of colors; and the general tone of the colors (as far as can be ascertained) is in keeping with Mantegna's style and da Vinci's as well, especially the Virgin's head, which seems to be by Leonardo's hand, above all in the cheeks and in the sweetly smiling mouth. The folds rather clearly seem to be Mantegna's doing, especially in the way in which the limbs are too tightly wrapped with them; but these are rather less dry and much more grandiose. The composition, moreover, is utterly grandiose.[25]

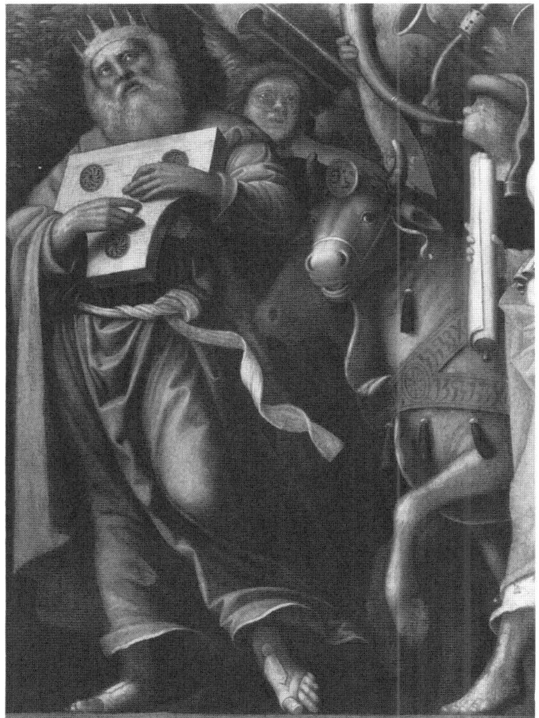

Fig. 9. Correggio
Triumph of David (detail)
Turin, private collection

Lanzi goes on to say that it is undeniable that, although damaged, the San Benedetto painting now in Turin displays "that grace and mirth . . . a certain rainbow of colors" that belong to Correggio alone.[26] Nowhere else can there be found the blue, blending into purple, of David's clothing (fig. 9), which seems to rework—in an inverse way, and by softening it—the sybil's clothing in the Mantegna painting (ca. 1485) now in the Cincinnati Art Museum. (Another debt to the master is found in the slow wavering of the clothes in the foreground, although here it is translated in musical terms.) Contrary to our expectations, the ox (fortunately well preserved) in the center of the painting is perhaps the detail of the painting most typical of Correggio's style. This is due to the dense, soft hair on his exquisite tobacco-brown hide and to the light that, starting from his head in the foreground, falls lazily along his neck, which is gracefully bridled with a magnificent blood-red strap.

Critics have correctly insisted on the relationship between the Dresden altarpiece and Raphael's *Sistine Madonna* (ca. 1513), which went to the Gemäldegalerie Alte Meister in Dresden from the Benedictine convent in Piacenza,[27] and I, too, wish to mention that masterpiece, without provocative intentions, but in comparison with the probable organ shutter from San Benedetto Po. Correggio, in bringing to completion with calculated simplicity his composition of an ancient "triumph," could only have felt comforted by Raphael's Virgin, who appears behind the open curtains of a modest proscenium. After being dumbfounded by the natural grace of the clothes and countenances, he would have also admired with particular approval Raphael's sublime idea of stripping the Virgin and Child of all ornament and capturing them in the more relaxed moment of strolling among the clouds. The two angelic half-figures behave nearly irreverently in the same way: they are idly drying themselves along the edge of a canal, waiting for a slightly more exciting sight to come along. For Correggio, the revelation of Raphael's intrinsic nobility, free of excessive ornamentation, cut forever the umbilical cord linking him to Mantegna and accelerated his backward assimilation both of Leonardo's work in Milan and of the work of Giorgione and his followers (although in the underhanded way that I mentioned earlier). At this point Correggio's road was well marked toward such experimental works as the *Four Saints* (ca. 1513–1514) now in New York at the Metropolitan Museum of Art, the *Adoration of the Three Kings* (1516–1517) in Milan at the Pinacoteca di Brera, the lost Albinea *Virgin* (1517–1519), and, ultimately, the amusing and heavenly decorations in the Camera di San Paolo (1519–1520) in Parma.[28]

Postscript

After I presented my paper at the Getty Research Institute on 9 May 1996, Adriano Franceschini published several documents in his essay "Dosso Dossi, Benvenuto da Garofalo e il polittico Costabili di Ferrara" that relate indirectly to the problems I discussed then.[29] It concerns a payment of 210 lire (taken from credit owed to Antonio Costabili by the city of Ferrara) to the painters Dosso and Garofalo for the large altarpiece once located on the high altar of Sant'Andrea and now in the Pinacoteca Nazionale in Ferrara. The payment was made in four installments during the period from 11 July 1513 to 21 November 1513. From the payment made on August 6 for colors bought by Dosso and Garofalo in Venice, we know that their work was just beginning during this period. It would be difficult to underestimate the significance of the archival material: the evidence shows that Dosso's youthful sojourn at court in Mantua was very brief; that Dosso was already documented as visiting Venice in the summer of 1513; and that guild custom made the association with Garofalo in Ferrara necessary given that Dosso was a foreigner and still not a salaried member of the Este court and that he therefore needed the guarantee of an authoritative local painter in order to work publicly.

Compared to the 100 *scudi* (excluding carpentry expenses) promised on 30 August 1514 to Correggio for the altarpiece now in Dresden (which is significantly smaller in dimension than the Costabili altarpiece), the 210 lire *ferraresi* seem a modest sum and, unfortunately, there is nothing more about successive payments. However, it is certain that at least by December 14 Dosso was lodging in the castle (*"alogia in castelo"*), and he immediately began to receive commissions for work from Alfonso I. How much time was he given to carry out the Costabili altarpiece? I do not want to enter into stylistic debates but, clearly, any solution must be equally valid for both artists; they cannot be treated in isolation. By this I mean to say that any disruption in Dosso's chronology—of which there had been no indication until now—would include a parallel upheaval in Garofalo's chronology, which had also been fairly steady.

Notes

1. This record, found in the registry of births of the parish of Correggio, refers to a date between 17 and 22 January 1511: Cecil Gould, *The Paintings of Correggio* (London: Faber, 1976), 188 (*"Antonius Vigarini... compater Antonius de Alegris, commater Angelica uxor magistri Bernardini de Bononia"* [Antonio Vigarini... godfather Antonio de Alegris, godmother Angelica, wife of the magistrate Bernardino of Bologna]—this Bolognese connection could be significant). The document assumes importance in establishing Correggio's date of birth: contrary to modern practice, in those days a godfather who was too young and lacking in prestige was not particularly well regarded. That no juvenile judge was present at the signing of the contract for the San Francesco altarpiece on 30 August 1514 also points in the direction of a birth date sometime just prior to 1490 (idem, 175). Still worthwhile are the observations made by Alessandro Luzio, *La galleria dei Gonzaga venduta all'Inghilterra nel 1627–28: Documenti degli archivi di Mantova e Londra* (Milan: L. F. Cogliati, 1913), 112. As for the father's consent, for this contract and other, similar contracts, it should be noted that emancipation for sons who had come of age was not legally obligatory and was avoided normally. The remarks found in Thomas Kuehn, *Emancipation in Late Medieval Florence* (New Brunswick, N.J.: Rutgers Univ. Press, 1982), likely hold true for northern Italy as well.

2. Carlo Giovannini, "Nuovi documenti sul Dosso," *Prospettiva,* no. 68 (1992): 57–60. Dosso was from Quistello, which is located on the south bank of the Po River and only thirty-odd kilometers (about eighteen miles) northeast of Correggio; Quistello is very close to the town of San Benedetto Po in Mantuan territory. The problem of Dosso's early career in Mantua revolves around the possible relationship between the payment made on 11 April 1512 for a large painting destined for the Palazzo di San Sebastiano and the *Bathers* of Castel Sant'Angelo in Rome. It is doubtful that such a large sum (more than 30 ducats) would have been paid to a painter who, although promising, was still young. Moreover, the Rome painting is not of such an extraordinarily large size as to warrant this sum. See Alessandro Ballarin, *Dosso Dossi: La pittura a Ferrara negli anni del Ducato di Alfonso I,* 2 vols. (Cittadella: Bertoncello Artigrafiche, 1994–1995), 1: 28–30, 295–96 (entry no. 333 by Vittoria Romani). The other payments made in 1512 (Adolfo Venturi says 1507; see his article cited below) to Matteo del Costa and/or Lorenzo Leonbruno for a painting, also destined for the Palazzo di San Sebastiano, representing a concert of vocal music by

the nine Muses and Apollo in the presence of Francesco Gonzaga, remain an open question because of problems with the documents. This painting contained eleven figures and was quite large, measuring approximately 3 × 2.4 meters. We may extrapolate what it looked from a painting in the Prince of Liechtenstein's collection: Metropolitan Museum of Art, *Liechtenstein, the Princely Collections,* exh. cat. (New York: Metropolitan Museum of Art, 1985), 199–202 (entry no. 127 by Keith Christiansen). Work on the Palazzo di San Sebastiano was carried out under the guidance of Lorenzo Costa, but there are doubts concerning the accuracy and even the authenticity of the copies of the original documents that have been lost. See Adolfo Venturi, "Lorenzo Costa," *Archivio storico dell'arte* 1 (1888): 253; Carlo Gamba, "Lorenzo Leombruno," *Rassegna d'arte* 6 (1906): 66; Clifford M. Brown, "The 'Camera del Mapamondo et del Caiero' in the Palazzo di San Sebastiano in Mantua," *Journal of Jewish Art* 10 (1984): 32–46, esp. 33 n. 2; Alessandro Conti, "Sfortuna di Lorenzo Leonbruno," *Prospettiva,* no. 77 (1995): 39. See, now, Clifford M. Brown with Anna Maria Lorenzoni, "The Palazzo di San Sebastiano (1506–1512) and the Art Patronage of Francesco II Gonzaga, Fourth Marquis of Mantua," *Gazette des beaux-arts,* ser. 6, 129 (1997): 131–80, which appeared just as this essay was going to press. If in fact it is a case of forgery, it is a very skillful one. The well-known letter of 22 November 1519 from Gerolamo da Sestola to Isabella d'Este would seem to show that Dosso had established himself quickly in Mantua: "Maestro Doso" is mentioned without any credentials, as if a well-known figure, while Titian (who is not called *"maestro"*) needs to be introduced as a *"bon pitore"* (good painter). See Luzio (see note 1), 218. An allusion to the elusive relationship between Dosso and Correggio can be found in Carlo Volpe, "Dosso: Segnalazioni e proposte per il suo primo itinerario," *Paragone,* no. 293 (1974): 22.

3. I refer the reader to the essay by Andrea Bacchi and Andrea De Marchi, "La Pala di San Quintino," in *Francesco Marmitta* (Turin: Umberto Allemandi, 1995), 253–88, for information on Marmitta's return to Parma, his fascinating altarpiece for the San Quintino convent, and the pictorial situation of the city in the decade around the beginning of the sixteenth century. Marmitta's drawings of small Virgins, now in the British Museum in London, prefigure the enchantment and the warmth of many of Correggio's Virgins. The appreciation shown for Marmitta's work by Correggio's circle extended beyond his own lifetime, as can be seen from Parmigianino's early portrait in the National Gallery in London (inv. no. 6441). The collector depicted in the painting displays the precious book of hours known as the *Uffiziolo Durazzo,* now in Genoa: Silvana Pettenati, "La biblioteca di Domenico della Rovere," in Giovanni Romano, ed., *Domenico della Rovere e il Duomo nuovo di Torino: Rinascimento a Roma e in Piemonte* (Turin: Cassa di Risparmio di Torino, 1990), 105–6.

4. There are good photographs of the frescoes and the wooden ceiling (in a style close to Cesariano and Araldi) in the Palazzo dei Principi in Correggio in Giuseppe Adani, Franca Manenti Valli, and Alberto Ghidini, *Il Palazzo dei Principi in Correggio* (Cinisello Balsamo: A. Pizzi, [ca. 1975]), 14, 26–27, 46–47. See also Massimo Pirondini, ed., *La pittura del Cinquecento a Reggio Emilia* (Milan: Federico Motta/Credito Emiliano, 1985), 17. More recently, the 1508 decoration has been considered, unaccountably, to be Mantuan in origin, close in style to Costa (one thinks of the

Lombard-Emilian artisans of Albi). See Massimo Pirondini, "La pittura a Reggio Emilia nel Cinquecento," in Giuliano Briganti, ed., *La pittura in Italia: Il Cinquecento,* 2 vols. (Milan: Electa, 1988), 248. See entry for Mantegna's *Christ the Redeemer* in Jane Martineau, ed., *Andrea Mantegna,* exh. cat. (London: Thames & Hudson, 1992), 231 (entry no. 54 by Keith Christiansen).

5. Rodolfo Signorini, "Un inedito su Francesco Mantegna e il Correggio," *Quaderni di Palazzo Te,* new ser., no. 3 (1996): 79–80, reads the document—which is somewhat ambiguous—in a completely different way. According to Signorini's reading, Francesco Mantegna loaned and advanced money to Correggio for expenses. From the published transcription, however, it seems evident to me that Correggio, in the document dated 26 November 1512, belongs to the group of creditors of Mantegna's son. It is apparent, from the few known documents, that Francesco Mantegna found himself in economic difficulty in the years following the death of his father, his half-brother Andrea, and his brother Ludovico (R. W. Lightbown, *Mantegna* [Milan: A. Mondadori, 1986], 278–80). This most recently discovered document does nothing to change my position; if anything, there emerges in it Francesco's pressing need to sell real estate to appease his creditors, including Correggio.

6. The basic documentation is still to be found in Paul Kristeller, *Andrea Mantegna,* trans. S. Arthur Strong (London: Longmans, Green, 1901). Various scholars, basing their work on these documents, have studied the Mantegna-Correggio connection: Gould (see note 1), 30, 283, is less than convinced by the evidence, and Lightbown (see note 5), 280–83, 300 n. 39, expresses a number of doubts. See also Paolo Piva, *Correggio giovane e l'affresco ritrovato di San Benedetto in Polirone* (Turin: Umberto Allemandi, 1988), 154–58. In the latter, however, the argument is fatally weakened by an absurd conception of Antonio Allegri's style. Piva contends that works such as the doubtful and damaged Los Angeles *Virgin,* the rough fresco that was taken to Modena from San Quirino di Correggio, and the frescoed wall in San Benedetto Po (which was painted by Gerolamo Bonsignori) are all by Correggio. They would have had to have been produced, along with all the painter's known works of the same period, within the space of a few years. Whatever limited success the last of these attributions has enjoyed represents, at its very worst, the crisis of methodological presumption into which our discipline has entered. Additional bibliography could be cited, although it would not be particularly useful to do so; noteworthy, however, is the article by Giovanni Agosti, "Su Mantegna, 4. (A Mantova, nel Cinquecento)," *Prospettiva,* no. 77 (1995): 70, 82 n. 114, where he proposes that Francesco Mantegna, whose work is mentioned in a 1506 document, must have worked on completing the fresco at the center of the Camera degli Sposi in the Palazzo Ducale in Mantua. There are good reasons to accept this hypothesis, for it allows us to grasp the predominant style in Mantegna's workshop immediately after his death. Agosti notes *"un sentore costesco"* (a Costa-like hint) in this fresco, but it would seem that the smile of the woman combing her hair is also already reminiscent of Leonardo; this is no small point to consider in trying to trace Correggio's early career. See also the dossier assembled in Giuse Pastore, ed., *La Cappella del Mantegna in Sant'Andrea a Mantova* (Mantua: Casa del Mantegna, 1986), for information on the condition of the frescoes in the Mantegna chapel and their most recent restoration. Unfortunately, the

pendentives of the four Evangelists were not documented during the course of the cleaning and appear (in restored condition) on pages 68–69 in a format the size of a postage stamp.

7. For the altar frontal with *The Families of Christ and Saint John the Baptist,* see Martineau (see note 4), 253–54 (entry no. 64 by Keith Christiansen). See also Andrea Rothe, "Mantegna's Paintings in Distemper," in Martineau (see note 4), 85, where he remarks on the techniques that link this work to the *Baptism* that hangs in the same chapel. On the *Baptism* itself, see Keith Christiansen, "Mantegna's Legacy," in *Studi di storia dell'arte in onore di Mina Gregori* (Milan: Silvana, 1994), 79–86.

8. See also the old Anderson photographs, previously used by Adolfo Venturi in his *La pittura del Quattrocento,* vol. 7 of idem, *Storia dell'arte italiana,* 11 vols. in 25 (Milan: U. Hoepli, 1901–1940), pt. 3, 253–54.

9. Giuse Pastore, "Gli affreschi," in Pastore (see note 6), 78, notes that John Shearman is willing to accept the attribution to Correggio for the years 1506–1507 and at least for Saint Mark and Saint Matthew. From a conversation in Santa Monica, California, I understand that Shearman has far fewer hesitations than I do regarding the attribution of the Evangelists in Sant'Andrea to the hand of Correggio.

10. See Luigi Lanzi's important remarks, originally published in 1809, in his *Storia pittorica della Italia dal risorgimento delle belle arti fin presso al fine del XVIII secolo,* ed. Martino Cappucci, 3 vols. (Florence: Sansoni, 1968–1974), 2: 226. For more recent contributions I refer the reader to note 6. I would, however, add here David A. Brown, *The Young Correggio and His Leonardesque Sources* (New York: Garland, 1981), 19, 117 n. 2, which contains further bibliography. The fate of the works up until 1961 can be followed by consulting the entries in Giovanni Paccagnini, ed., *Andrea Mantegna,* 2nd ed., exh. cat. (Venice: N. Pozza, 1961), 53–59. Here can be found remarks of considerable interest on the technique employed, although the interpretations are doubtful indeed:

> *La tecnica indica un lavoro rapidissimo che non appare neppure a buon fresco, e che ha piuttosto l'aspetto di una tempera grassa o di un olio, condotto con brevi superfici che si sovrappongono con larghe sbavature ai bordi, preparate sbrigativamente con un sottile strato di calce disteso sulle parti del disegno che, volta per volta, il pittore intendeva dipingere* (The technique used indicates extremely fast work that does not even seem to be true fresco, and that has rather the appearance of a greasy tempera or oil paint. The artist employed shallow surfaces superimposed with broad smudges along the edges, prepared hastily with a thin layer of lime spread on the parts of the drawing that, little by little, he planned to paint).

Although this would appear to be a rather slow technique, not a fast one, the description places *The Deposition* in the same line of experimentation as Leonardo's *Last Supper.* As for the *Holy Family,* Paccagnini sees it as a partial intervention by Correggio in an earlier work, which is doubtless the case for *The Deposition.* His claim, however, has been recently contradicted by a direct viewing of what is left of the work in situ—there is still quite a lot of it, even if we do not count the sinopia underneath it. See Marcello Castrichini and Leonilde Dominici, "Indagine sul tondo di destra nell'atrio della basilica di S. Andrea dove si trovava l'affresco strappato nel 1961 'Sacra famiglia e San Giovannino,'" in *Storia e arte religiosa a Mantova: Basilica Concattedrale di Sant'Andrea. L'atrio meridionale: Indagini, saggi e restauri dell'apparato decorativo*, exh. cat. (Mantua: Casa del Mantegna, 1991), 165–66. Castrichini and Dominici's quite plausible remarks are printed—in an unplanned act of provocation—facing a technical study of the detached (?!) fresco which tries to show that precisely the contrary is true. Here, as elsewhere, Correggio has been rather unlucky with his restorers, and it seems worthwhile to note that incidents such as this one cast a dark shadow on the abundant "technical and scientific" studies of restoration. Alessandro Conti, in Marina Romiti Conti, ed., *Manuale di restauro* (Turin: Einaudi, 1996), 275, expresses doubts about the restoration in Mantua.

In the most complex cases, a public discussion of planned restoration projects—well in advance of their undertaking—is greatly to be desired. Mauro Pellicioli's restoration work for the Camera degli Sposi in 1938, in consultation with Roberto Longhi, could be taken as an exemplary instance of this approach. See Antonio Paolucci, "Una inedita relazione di Roberto Longhi sul restauro di Mauro Pellicioli alla Camera degli Sposi del Mantegna," *Paragone*, nos. 419–421–423 (1985): 331–34. Unfortunately, Longhi's remarks on the two tondi from the atrium of Sant'Andrea were not included in this publication.

11. See Martineau (see note 4), 211 (entry no. 44 by David Ekserdjian), 213–17 (entry nos. 45–47 by David Landau).

12. Negatives C8445 (*Holy Family*) and C8446 (*The Deposition*), Istituto per il Catalogo e la Documentazione, Rome. These photographs were made immediately after the rediscovery of the tondi and published in Guglielmo Pacchioni, "Scoperta di affreschi giovanili del Correggio in S. Andrea di Mantova," *Bollettino d'arte* 10 (1916): 147–64, and in Adolfo Venturi, "Note sul Correggio," *L'arte* 18 (1915): 405–26. The remarks from 1914–1915 regarding the preservation of the chromatic film in the two tondi are of particular interest to us today, as are Pacchioni's remarks on the colors. Neither of the two scholars noticed in the *Holy Family* any work by others, and they had the opportunity to study it under optimal conditions.

13. Brown (see note 10), 35–38, 170–75 (entry no. 2), gives an approximate date of 1512, which could perhaps be moved backward a bit. His technical remarks on the emergence of the dark underlayers correspond to what can be seen today in the *Nativity with Saint Elizabeth* in the Pinacoteca di Brera (inv. no. 788). Brown insists that Giorgione mediates between Correggio and Leonardo; and thanks to a comparison with Giorgione's *Three Philosophers* (Vienna, Kunsthistorisches Museum), the Detroit *Mystic Marriage of Saint Catherine* found a place in the monumental photographic dossier that accompanies Ballarin (see note 2), 2: figs. 326–28, who gives circa 1510 as a plausible date for the Detroit altarpiece. I have not viewed the Correggio hanging in Detroit, but, judging from the small panel representing the same subject in Washington (National Gallery of Art, Kress Collection, inv. no. 194), which I have viewed and which is not chronologically remote from the former, I feel justified in claiming that Correggio explored, in the years following what seems to have been his apprenticeship with Mantegna, more than just Venetian art. The husked gold of the highlights, right up to the edge of the steps, the cherubs of the throne, and Saint

Catherine's shawl suggest a Lombard tone, while the diffuse shadows give off a warm and subtle frisson, as if Leonardo had been studied through the Milanese filter of Bernardo Zenale, Bramantino, and Giovanni Antonio Boltraffio.

14. Correggio's interest in Albrecht Dürer has been noted many times; see, for instance, Cecil Gould, "A Probable Adaptation by Correggio of Dürer's Iconography," *Burlington Magazine* 90 (1948): 286–89. The same engraving that Gould considers as a model for *Christ Taking Leave from His Mother,* at the National Gallery in London (inv. no. 4255), may have suggested the female figure on the left of the Mantuan tondo. See A. E. Popham, *Correggio's Drawings* (London: Oxford Univ. Press, 1957), 17, 19; in the latter passage, Popham identifies a citation from Dürer in the Detroit *Mystic Marriage of Saint Catherine,* which is chronologically not far from the Sant'Andrea tondi.

15. Popham (see note 14), 13, 78, 149; his hesitation in putting forward Correggio's name for the first time is less understandable in Mario Di Giampaolo and Andrea Muzzi, eds., *Correggio: I disegni,* 2nd ed. (Turin: Umberto Allemandi, 1989), unpaginated (entry no. 1), after forty years of studying the subject and developing a less univocal concept of Correggio's poetry. Some doubts also arise in Diane DeGrazia, ed., *Correggio e il suo lascito: Disegni del Cinquecento emiliano,* exh. cat. (Parma: Artegrafica Silva, 1984), 77–78. In the comparison photographs, the *Deposition* tondo, prior to the most recent restoration, is called a "sinopia." The recent claim for Dosso's authorship is a surprising one; see Andrea De Marchi, "Sugli esordi veneti di Dosso Dossi," *Arte veneta* 40 (1986): 28 n. 27.

16. Gould (see note 1), 174–76. I am convinced that, for his first altarpiece as an independent painter, Correggio would not have settled for aping Mantegna's *Madonna della Vittoria* altarpiece or the rather routine ideas of Costa and Francia. Francia's Mantuan *Annunciation,* now in the Brera museum (inv. no. 448) but originally from the Capilupi chapel in the church of San Francesco, is not particularly innovative. Costa's nonreligious painting for Isabella d'Este's *studiolo,* on the other hand, might have seemed exciting for its unusually successful chromatic scheme. The document recording the work's commissioning leads us to believe that the altarpiece now in Dresden was executed in the town of Correggio, very close to Modena (where Bianchi Ferrari's altarpieces could be seen) and not far from Parma, with its altarpieces by Marmitta and Giovanni Battista Cima da Conegliano. Correggio might have been seduced above all by Marmitta's formal choices, but we should also take into consideration a certain formal freedom in details such as those found in the *Annunciation* (the broach on Saint Quentin's breast) or the *Flight into Egypt* (at the base of the throne). These were painted with blurred contours of the sort employed by Correggio in his altarpiece, both in the oval with Moses and the base with stories of the Passion. See Brown (see note 10) for an authoritative discussion of Correggio's relationship to Leonardo's circle in Milan and its diaspora after 1499. One painting of excellent quality in the style of Leonardo, which has thus far remained marginal to the debate, seems to resemble Correggio's style in certain of its details: I am referring to the *Madonna of the Scales* in the Musée du Louvre (inv. no. 785), in which Saint Anne's head is clearly derived from Mantegna's late models (see the *Holy Family* paintings in Dresden and in the Kimbell Art Museum, Fort Worth, and the altar frontal for the

funerary chapel in Sant'Andrea). The other figures, in particular Saint Michael, seem to me related to the early Correggio in ways that I am unable to define. It is difficult to trace the work prior to its passing into the collection of Louis XIV (who obtained it from Jabach), but a careful review of Mantuan inventories might prove fruitful. W. R. Valentiner, "The Madonna of the Scales," *Gazette des beaux-arts*, ser. 6, 49 (1957): 129–48, resolutely attributes this work to Leonardo, thus confirming its quality. As far as is known today, the painting is not linked in any way to Cesare da Sesto.

17. This updating deserves a separate investigation, starting with Antonio da Pavia's surprising about-face visible in the altarpiece now found in the Pinacoteca di Brera (cat. no. 194, dated 1514) but originally from Santo Stefano di Novellara, about ten kilometers (six miles) from the town of Correggio. The painting exhibits a certain fascinating gloominess along the lines of Francesco Bonsignori's work, but certain parts of it are indirectly Leonardesque and reminiscent of Caroto's art. A drawing that Andrea Muzzi recently noted as attributed to Correggio—an attribution that spread by word of mouth at the opening of the show in Modena entitled *Disegno: Les dessins italiens du Musée de Rennes,* 27 May–29 July 1990—may be better understood in connection with the Brera painting. This drawing, *Face of the Redeemer,* or *Face of Saint John the Baptist,* appears in the exhibition catalog (Rennes: Le Musée, 1990), 30, as the work of Marco d'Oggiono. For the moment the attribution to Correggio remains a bit risky, although it is supported by comparisons with the *Youthful Christ* in the National Gallery of Art, Washington (inv. no. 1620), formerly in the Kress collection. See Mario di Giampaolo and Andrea Muzzi, *Correggio: Catalogo completo dei dipinti* (Florence: Cantini, 1993), 6. A shift similar to that of Antonio da Pavia can be seen in the early works of Zenone Veronese, beginning with the 1512 triptych in Cavriana, a town well to the north of the Po River and very near to Lake Garda but still in the diocese of Mantua. Zenone's involvement would seem to mean that Caroto takes precedence over Correggio as the point of origin of the crisis. There are, however, no up-to-date studies of Caroto's work. For new information about Antonio da Pavia and Caroto in Mantua, see Agosti (see note 6), 65, 66, 79 n. 73, 80 n. 86. For Zenone, see Federico Zeri, "Note su quadri italiani all'estero," *Bollettino d'arte,* ser. 4, 36 (1949): 26–30, reprinted in idem, *Giorno per giorno nella pittura,* vol. 4, *Scritti sull'arte italiana del Cinquecento* (Turin: Umberto Allemandi, 1994), 91–92; and Alessandro Ballarin, "Una 'Madonna del velo' di Zenone Veronese," *Prospettiva,* nos. 53–56 (1988–1989): 367–71. Finally, see also Isabella Marelli, *Zenone Veronese: Un pittore del Cinquecento sul lago di Garda* (Desenzano sul Garda: Lions Club, 1994).

18. Leonbruno has attracted relatively little attention. His crucial painting *Judgment of Midas* (Berlin, Staatliche Museen) displays a scalene composition reminiscent of Dosso's work. For the artist's personality and its contradictions, see Conti (see note 2), 36–50; we must keep in mind, however, that Conti died before he was able to revise his text and eliminate a few incongruities in it. Paolo Venturoli, "Lorenzo Costa," *Storia dell'arte* 1–2 (1969): 161–68, makes some interesting remarks about Leonbruno. A good deal of work has been done on the now-famous painting of *Saint Helen and Four Saints* in the collection of the Banca Popolare di Modena; this painting most likely came from the parish of Ostiglia on the north bank of the Po River. Longhi attributed this work to the early Correggio in his "Le fasi del Correggio giovane e

l'esigenza del suo viaggio romano," *Paragone,* no. 101 (1958): 41, now in idem, *Cinquecento classico e Cinquecento manieristico, 1951–1970* (Florence: Sansoni, 1976), 101. Longhi's article, full of welcome polemics concerning Correggio's journey to Rome, was less successful in treating the Mantua connection and has prompted more than one misunderstanding. See Renato Berzaghi, "Tre dipinti e un nome per il 'Maestro Orombelli,'" in Paolo Piva and Egidio Del Canto, eds., *Dal Correggio a Giulio Romano: La committenza di Gregorio Cortese* (Mantua: Casa del Mantegna, 1989), 171–92, for the status of current research on the subject, and the new contributions of Conti (see note 2) and Agosti (see note 6). We should mention two other significant studies of the problem. Carlo Volpe, "Il naturalismo di Giorgione e la tradizione critica: I rapporti con l'Emilia e con Raffaello," in *Giorgione: Atti del convegno internazionale di studio per il 5° centenario della nascita* (Castelfranco Veneto: Comitato per le Celebrazioni Giorgionesche, 1979), 223–24, fig. 178, attributes to Correggio another early masterpiece of the mysterious Maestro Orombelli, alias Giovan Francesco Tura. Massimo Ferretti, "Ai margini di Dosso (tre altari in san Pietro a Modena)," *Ricerche di storia dell'arte,* no. 17 (1982): 72 n. 20, establishes the chronology of Correggio's first success and points out the rapid response of the Master of Celano Pelumi. On the latter, see also Daniele Benati, *Francesco Bianchi Ferrari e la pittura a Modena fra '400 e '500* (Modena: Artiole, 1990), 134–38.

19. Emilio Menegazzo, "Contributo alla biografia di Teofilo Folengo (1512–1520)," *Italia medioevale e umanistica* 2 (1959): 383–84; and idem, "Marginalia su Raffaello, il Correggio e la Congregazione benedettina-cassinese," *Italia medioevale e umanistica* 3 (1960): 329–30. The seemingly endless (despite the good intentions of many critics) tragicomedy regarding the attribution to Correggio of the frescoed wall around Gerolamo Bonsignori's *Last Supper* was born from the contract for the Polirone organ. I have no illusions about this, and I am waiting for someone to attribute the painting that was recently on the market at Sotheby's in New York to Correggio as well (16 May 1996, no. 15: canvas, 88.9 × 95.3 cm, attributed to Girolamo da Treviso). This work, entitled *Adoration of the Shepherds,* is obviously by Gerolamo Bonsignori; indeed, it is his masterpiece. It is closely linked with the figurative part of the Polirone wall, and Andrea De Marchi has independently reached the same conclusion. The inscription near the bottom of the painting, "*Partus et integritas discordes tempore longo / Virginis in gremio federa pacis habent*" (Childbearing and chastity, which are at variance with each other, hold the covenants of peace in the bosom of the Virgin after a long time), can be traced to Jacopo Sannazzaro and could furnish a chronological link: the text of *De partu Virginis* was begun in 1504 and completed in 1513 but was not published until 1526 (with a dedication to Pope Clement VII). Another work has been attributed to Gerolamo Bonsignori by Alessandro Conti, "Osservazioni e appunti sulla 'Vita' di Leonardo di Giorgio Vasari," in *Kunst des Cinquecento in der Toskana* (Munich: Bruckmann, 1992), 27.

20. Oil on canvas, 260 × 153.5 cm; the central scene is surrounded by a grey band that runs along three edges (not the top) and ends in two (not easily explainable) brown rectangles. No one in the family that currently owns the picture is able to recall when and how the work was acquired by their grandparents.

21. Lanzi (see note 10), 2: 190: "*Credesi che Carlo [del Mantegna] avesse parte*

ne' lavori del palazzo [ducale] e della cappella riferita di sopra [quella del Mantegna in Sant'Andrea] e in altri che si ascrivono a mantegnesi; fra' quali son due istorie dell'Arca del monistero di San Benedetto, di Mantova, ove si rivede la maniera di Andrea ampliata alquanto, ancorchè di forme men belle."

22. A comparison of the Dresden altarpiece with the Turin painting leads us to think that Correggio, taking advantage of the varying amounts of time required for his two commissions, worked hastily on the organ shutters while awaiting the preparation of the wood for the altarpiece, work that had not been completed by 4 October 1514 (Gould [see note 1], 175).

23. If Correggio's date of birth is 1487, as seems likely, then Dosso's must be very shortly thereafter (1489–1490). The opposing artistic itineraries taken by these two masters, who were almost the same age and came from the same region, offer a good example of the openness of the situation for painters in the Po valley in the first decade of the sixteenth century. This area was, stylistically speaking, in upheaval in these years in which—however briefly—every painter was free to choose whatever career best accorded with his own preferences. Ariosto's famous 1536 octave provides double-edged proof of this phenomenon.

24. Lanzi (see note 10), 2: 230: "*Ho per vero ciò che udii un tempo, avere il Correggio tentate più e più maniere prima di fissarsi in quella che lo distingue.*"

25. Carlo Giuseppe Ratti, *Notizie storiche sincere intorno la vita e le opere del celebre Antonio Allegri da Correggio* (Finale: G. de' Rossi, 1781), 93:

> *Quest'opera, benche' un po' dura, e da troppo marcati contorni circoscritta, ella è ciò non pertanto morbida, e d'un impasto di colori molto soave; ed il tuono generale delle tinte (per quanto s'assicura) tien dello stile del Mantegna, e del Vinci, in particolare la testa della Vergine, che par di mano del Lionardo, principalmente nelle gote, e nel dolce sorriso della bocca. Nelle pieghe assai chiaro si scopre il fare del Mantegna, soprattutto nel fasciar troppo severamente con esse le membra; sono però queste assai meno secche, e molto piu' grandiose. La composizione poi è assolutamente grandiosa.*

Milizia's polemics concerning Ratti's plagiarism of Mengs's critical ideas about Correggio are well known. See Roberto Longhi, *Il Correggio e la Camera di San Paolo a Parma* (Genoa: Siglaeffe, 1956), 12, now in idem, 1976 (see note 18), 33–34, on Mengs's valuable work on Correggio.

26. Lanzi (see note 10), 2: 230: "*quella grazia e ilarità ... una certa iride di colori.*"

27. John Shearman, "Raphael's Clouds and Correggio's," in Micaela Sambucco Hamoud and Maria Letizia Strocchi, eds., *Studi su Raffaello: Atti del congresso internazionale di studi,* 2 vols. (Urbino: QuattroVenti, 1987), 1: 657–68; and idem, *Arte e spettatore nel Rinascimento italiano* (Milan: Jaka, 1995), 104.

28. I am of the opinion that Melchiorre Fassi's first will, dated 16 December 1517, takes for granted the existence of a family altar in the church of Santa Maria della Misericordia: "*in utilitate ipsius altaris situati in ecclesia dicti hospitalis*" (in the use of the altar itself situated in the church of the said house). The altarpiece on this altar, which had probably only recently been completed, was supposed to display the four saints to whom Fassi was particularly devoted (Saint Leonard, Saint Martha, Saint

Peter, and Saint Mary Magdalen, who appear in the painting now in the Metropolitan Museum in New York, inv. no. 12.211). At that date it would have been unthinkable to have had an altarpiece made for the church of San Quirino, which was still under construction. Various scholars put forward the correct date of the New York altarpiece immediately after Gould's monograph (see note 1) appeared; see John Shearman's review of this work, "Correggio and the Connoisseurs," *Times Literary Supplement,* 18 March 1977: 302. This review is fundamental—from a methodological perspective as well—yet it has not been translated into Italian. See also David A. Brown, "A New Book on Correggio," *Burlington Magazine* 119 (1977): 860–61. In this brief review of Gould's book, Brown also insists that the two Mantuan tondi and the fragmentary cartoon in New York belong to Correggio. After the *Four Saints* for Melchiorre comes the Brera *Adoration of the Magi* (cat. no. 427). The narrow window of time available for the production of the Albinea altarpiece and the Camera di San Paolo does not permit a later dating. See, for the relevant documents, Gould (see note 1), 176–80. There is a link between the idea of a dense, engulfing natural vegetation in the New York *Four Saints* and Costa's second painting for Isabella d'Este's *studiolo.*

I wish here to pay homage to two masters who guided my steps in approaching Correggio's poetic grandeur. Although parts of his arguments are no longer defensible and have been revised by others, Longhi's opinions on Correggio—from the early essays to the late work on the Camera di San Paolo and the journey to Rome—remain central for that part of art history concerned not only with attributions (always reasonable ones, we hope) but also with poetic individuals, each with his or her own specific human values to distinguish and place in a hierarchy that is moral but not moralistic (a danger that Correggio's work had to face). For the latter aspect of our discipline, which has lately been somewhat neglected for unworthy reasons, I refer the reader to the discussion of Correggio in Giuliano Briganti, "La natura lombarda, le idee romane, i demoni etruschi e l'antico, nella pittura emiliana del Cinquecento e del Seicento," in *Nell'età di Correggio e dei Carracci: Pittura in Emilia dei secoli XVI e XVII,* exh. cat. (Bologna: Nuova Alfa, 1986), xviii–xxii.

29. Adriano Franceschini, "Dosso Dossi, Benvenuto da Garofalo e il polittico Costabili di Ferrara," *Paragone,* nos. 543–545 (1995): 110–15 (the issue appeared after September 1996). Further discussion of the issues raised in this postscript can be found in the new and important contribution by Rodolfo Signorini, "New Findings about Andrea Mantegna: His Son Ludovico's Post-mortem Inventory (1510)," *Journal of the Warburg and Courtauld Institutes* 59 (1996): 103–18.

Giorgione's *Inferno with Aeneas and Anchises* for Taddeo Contarini

Alessandro Nova

Some of the most recent publications on Giorgione have punctiliously as well as convincingly reexamined his still controversial catalog and chronology.[1] This philological enterprise, however, seems to have been more concerned with organizing in a plausible chronological sequence the surviving paintings of the artist than with reconstructing and dating Giorgione's lost works and designs. The study of the copies after Giorgione has always been pursued, of course, but an analysis limited to the surviving visual material inevitably distorts our view of the historical picture. It must be conceded that we will probably never know what some lost works by Giorgione really looked like; this does not mean, however, that we have to ignore the rights and responsibilities of elaborating reasonable hypotheses about this no longer extant imagery.

The purpose of this paper is to reopen the debate surrounding two Giorgionesque works—works that have been neglected in the most recent philological overviews—because they help us visualize some of the most pressing issues that absorbed Giorgione's energies during the last three years of his life: the so-called *Dream,* once known as the *Dream of Raphael,* engraved by Marcantonio Raimondi (fig. 1),[2] and the *Inferno with Aeneas and Anchises,* a canvas seen by Marcantonio Michiel in the house of Taddeo Contarini in 1525.[3]

The fate of the *Dream* is very curious indeed. The attribution of the engraving's design to Giorgione is, as is well known, highly controversial. The majority of those who have tried to unravel its meaning have more or less tacitly agreed that it was designed by Giorgione or, at least, that it clearly reflects some of his most characteristic themes and motives. The best and most comprehensive philological reconstructions of Giorgione's career, however, have ignored this image, despite the fact that the view expressed by Johann David Passavant more than a century ago has been upheld correctly by Christian Hornig in his monograph on Giorgione's late works, Gianvittorio Dillon in the catalog of the Savoldo exhibition, Nicholas Penny in his essay on the depiction of night in Venetian painting, and Konrad Oberhuber in his entry for the catalog of the Venetian exhibition of 1993 in Paris.[4] There is little in Marcantonio's previous works to prepare us for such a revolutionary image, and although we cannot prove that the print reproduces a lost

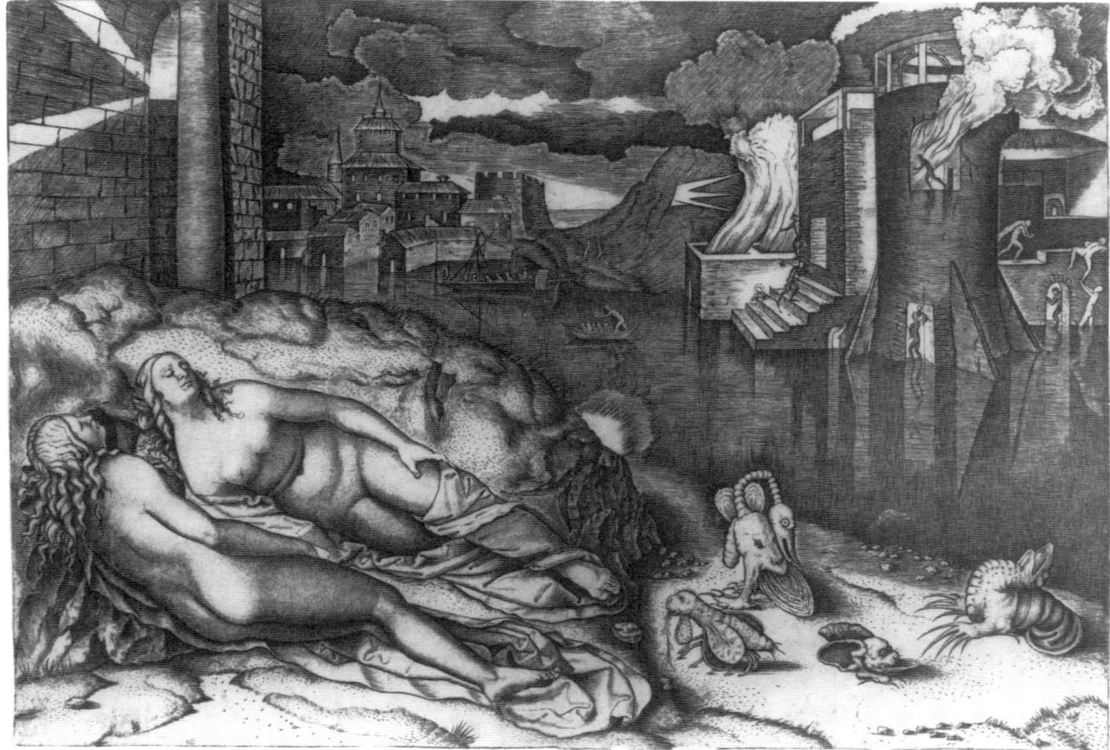

Fig. 1. Marcantonio Raimondi
The Dream
Vienna, Graphische Sammlung Albertina

painting by Giorgione (which is unlikely), it is a Venetian product profoundly influenced by, if not based on, Giorgione's designs.[5] It is possible that Marcantonio borrowed some elements of the background from other prints and that he rearranged some details of the composition according to his own artistic inclinations, and it is also possible that in so doing he created some puzzling iconographic aggregations that have tenaciously resisted interpretation. As we shall see, however, the most important parts of this mysterious engraving form a coherent design that was intended for a specific purpose. Before analyzing its formal structure, however, it is worth reviewing briefly the traditional as well as the most recent iconographic interpretations of this image, which continues to haunt our imagination.

Many if not most of the interpretations of early art historians incorporated Virgilian themes.[6] It is likely that this trend was consciously as well as unconsciously influenced by Michiel's *Notizia d'opere di disegno,* and more specifically by his reference to a canvas depicting the story of Aeneas and Anchises in the collection of Taddeo Contarini.[7] It should be noted, however, that no element of this composition identifies the burning city as Troy.

Another line of inquiry emerged from the wide-ranging research of Eugenio Battisti for his *L'antirinascimento.* The author did not discuss Marcantonio's engraving, but he did examine Battista Dosso's allegory in Dresden (*Night,* or *Dream,* 1544, Staatliche Kunstsammlungen, Gemäldegalerie Alte Meister), a painting that is often, albeit misleadingly, related to the *Dream* in the context of the early modern interest in magic.[8] This hermetic interpretation has prevailed in the most recent literature on the engraving, including not only Francesco Gandolfo's essay "Mistica, Ermetismo e Sogno nel Cinquecento,"[9] which developed the alchemic reading of the *Dream* suggested by Maurizio Calvesi, but also in the German reception of the problem. Heike Frosien-Leinz has discussed the print in the context of Agrippa von Nettesheim's *De occulta philosophia,*[10] and Horst Bredekamp has underlined the profane aspect of early modern dreams in his contribution to the exhibition catalog *Zauber der Medusa.*[11] More recently Louise Milne has unconvincingly suggested that the female nudes of Marcantonio's engraving seem to represent the human soul.[12]

The most plausible iconographic interpretation to date has been suggested in a short article by Guy de Tervarent.[13] He thinks that the key to the secret of Marcantonio's engraving is a verse by Statius, inaccurately transcribed by an absent-minded amanuensis. The text of the *Thebaid* available to early sixteenth-century artists would have read: "Vague dreams with innumerable faces are seen all around, the truthful ones mingled with untruthful ones and rivers with flames."[14] As to the fantastic creatures on the shore, de Tervarent pointed out a passage in *A True Story* by Lucian: "For as far as dreams go, these vary from one another, by their nature as well as by their appearance. Some bring before us figures which are beautiful and well proportioned, while others are small and ugly."[15] There are undoubtedly numerous affinities between these literary texts and Marcantonio's image, but they fail to explain all the elements of the puzzle. Moreover, it should be noted that in his edition of the *Thebaid,* Aldo Manuzio had already replaced the incorrect words *"flumina flammis"* with *"tristia blandis."*

Someone in the future may discover a more plausible literary source, but the great appeal of this engraving resides precisely in its intentional ambiguities. I wish to avoid any possible misunderstanding, however—one cannot retreat into the comfortable corner of the nonsubject. There is no question that this work is a virtuoso performance: as David Landau has pointed out, "the richness of texture of this early impression might indicate that it was intended as a demonstration of Marcantonio's mastery of line engraving to rival Giulio Campagnola's stipple-engraving."[16] It is unlikely, however, that Marcantonio was only interested in showing off his technical ability.

One crucial question has never been asked: For whom was such an image produced? That is, what kind of public would have bought or commissioned this engraving by Marcantonio, if it was ever on sale? One can safely assume that the ideal client for such a work would have been a humanist who would have enriched the abundant imagery offered by the engraving with his own personal and erudite associations. The name of Hieronymus Bosch has often been correctly mentioned in connection with the monsters on the shore, but the two animals on the far right seem even more related to the bizarre ink-wells and oil lamps that decorated the *studioli* of the time (fig. 2).

To come to the center of my argument, it is possible that this engraving was intentionally produced to challenge the technical as well as the iconographical knowledge of a learned viewer in order to create discussion and entertainment. The obvious ambiguities of the work seem to have been created deliberately, so that debate would ensue.[17] Some elements are immediately recognizable, others are difficult to identify, but the engraving is above all replete with polysemous elements such as fire, night, water, and ships. The enormous potential of this imagery for endless associations makes it difficult to propose a specific title for the work, but this does not mean that there is no subject. The alternative is not between subject and nonsubject, but between a closed, definite meaning and an open, flexible one. Let us pursue the most seductive element of the composition: the fire in the right background.

In his *Trattato dell'arte della pittura, scoltura, et architettura,* Giovanni Paolo Lomazzo discussed several themes that could be used as a pretext for representing a great fire. In chapter 7 of book 4 Lomazzo lists among his favorite themes the fire of Sodom and Gomorrah and the fall of Troy, two recurrent narratives in the pyrotechnic culture of the sixteenth century.[18] Chapters 24 and 37 of book 6 are also relevant. Chapter 24 deals with the subjects that should be painted *"in luochi di fuoco e patiboli"* (in places of fire and torment).[19] The number of suitable myths and biblical stories recorded by Lomazzo is amazing, but none can explain what we see in Marcantonio's engraving.

More to our purpose is perhaps the following passage from chapter 37, in which Lomazzo insists upon the effects of *varietà* in battle compositions:

> In such scenes of conflict and ruin, it adds great grace to show the city walls being knocked down, women crying aloud as they run with outstretched arms, and other women fleeing, as well as some men being bound, while others are killed and still others are stripped. Moreover, as at Troy and Carthage, the city is put to the torch and houses and palaces are destroyed, as has happened so many times to poor Rome, and many other cities of Italy as well, at the hands of barbarians. Filled with fear, some flee, just as Venus's son fled burning Troy with his aged father Anchises on his shoulders and his little son's hand in his. Some pass children down from balconies, others lower themselves down ropes, while still others leap; and one could, if one wished, count an infinite number of similar scenes of ruin and acts of desperation.[20]

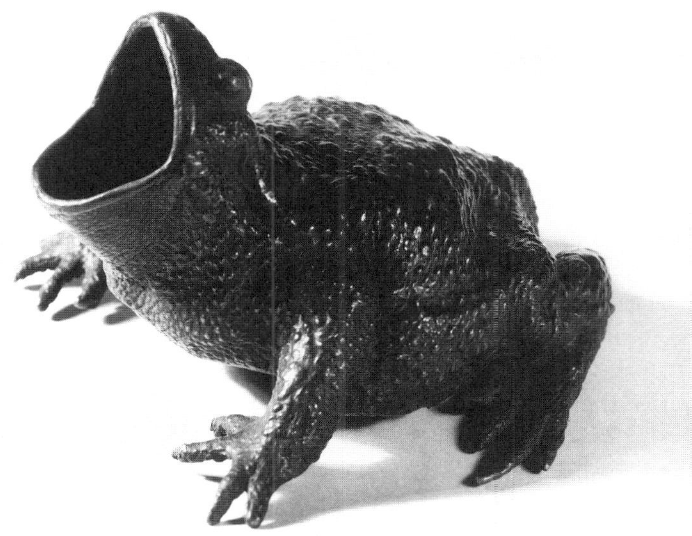

Fig. 2. Northern Italian (Padua?)
Inkwell in the Form of a Toad
Vienna, Kunsthistorisches Museum

None of the numerous narratives and compositions described by Lomazzo can be identified as *the* subject of Marcantonio's print, but this quotation reveals how these dramatic, indeed "fiery," episodes were greatly admired for their powerful narrative potential. Moreover, Lomazzo's list reveals the broad number of selections that were available by the end of the sixteenth century for an artist who wanted to paint such a work.

It may well be that the search for an accurate literary source is a futile enterprise and that a specific text will never clarify all the elements of the iconographic puzzle. Some elements of the composition seem to be meaningful: the gigantic ferryman steering the boat in the center of the landscape has been often identified with Charon, who is indeed a recurrent figure in sixteenth-century nightmares, as the autobiography of Benvenuto Cellini and the treatise on dreams by Girolamo Cardano show.[21] But if he really is Charon, who then is steering the ship that glides over the calm water of the river-lagoon? As I have already suggested, it is possible that such ambiguities are intentional.[22] One thing, however, is evident. The entire image is built around logically structured oppositions: the beautiful and the ugly in the foreground, the burning fortress on the right and the town beaten by the rain in the left background, the animated fortress and the deserted city, the

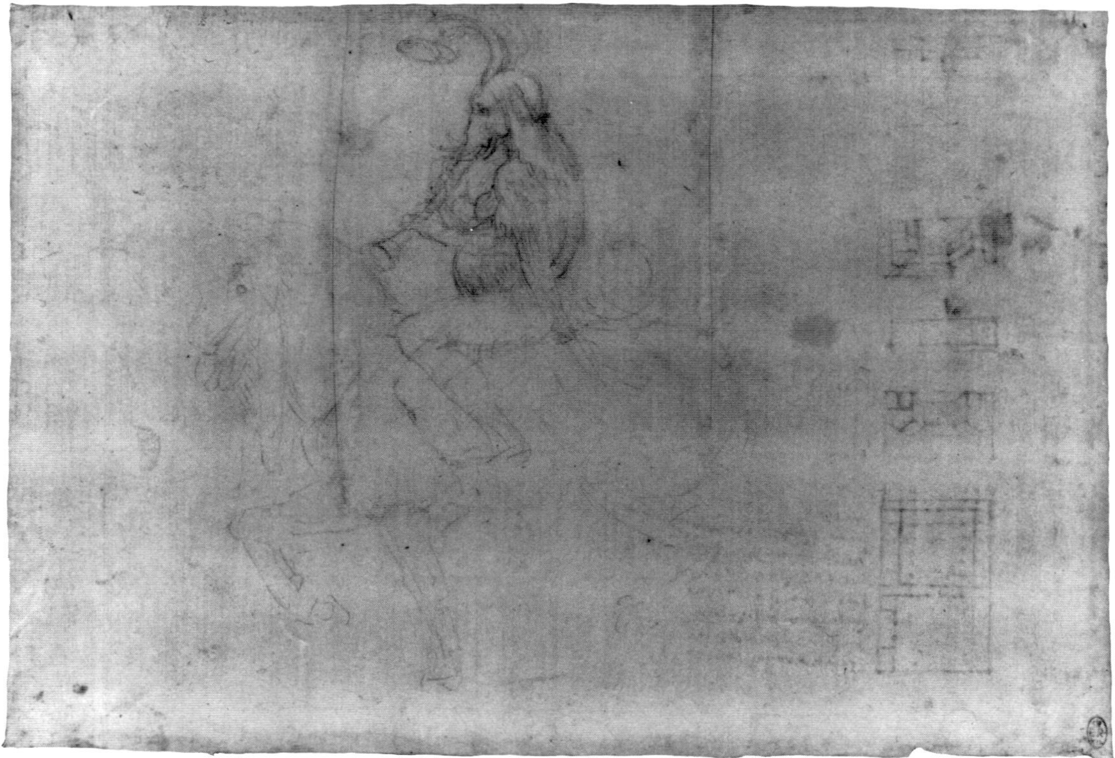

Fig. 3. Leonardo da Vinci
Masquerader Seated on a Horse
Windsor, Royal Library

flaming fire and the calm water. These are deliberate contrasts, which we can connect with a source that has not yet been discussed in this context: Leonardo's treatise on painting.

The two women in the foreground could be interpreted as an illustration of Leonardo's critique of sculpture in his celebrated passage on the *Paragone:*

> The art of painting [instead] embraces and contains within itself all visible things.... The painter shows to you different distances and...the rains, behind which can be discerned the cloudy mountains and valleys...; also the rivers of greater and lesser transparency...; also the polished pebbles of various hues, deposited on the washed sand of the river's bed.... Aerial perspective is absent from the sculptors' work. They cannot depict transparent bodies, nor can they represent luminous sources, nor reflected rays,... nor dreary weather.[23]

The remarkable affinities in tone and mood between text and image become even more persuasive when one considers that the most obvious theme of the engraving is the contrast between beauty and ugliness and, as Landau has noted, that this is "the first depiction of a dream in an Italian print and the first attempt to engrave a night scene."[24] Leonardo's interest in night scenes, dreams, and prophecies is well documented. One of his celebrated prophecies is dedicated to dreaming: "Men will seem to see new destructions in the sky.... They will see the greatest splendour in the midst of darkness. O! marvel of the human race! What frenzy has led you thus! You will speak with animals of every species and they with you in human speech."[25]

It is superfluous to quote Leonardo's famous passage in which the artist provides instructions on how to represent a night scene, but one cannot help quoting his words on the painter as the lord of all things: "If the painter wishes to see beauties that would enrapture him, he is master of their production, and if he wishes to see monstrous things which might terrify or which would be buffoonish and laughable or truly pitiable, he is their lord and god."[26]

The terrifying yet laughable metamorphic creatures on the shore of Marcantonio's *Dream* have always triggered a comparison with the grylli and *adynata,* or "impossibilities," to use the rhetorical term, created by Hieronymus Bosch. But we should not forget that Leonardo also designed similar freaks for the entertainment of his patrons, as shown by the drawing titled *Masquerader Seated on a Horse* (fig. 3).[27]

This monster with the head of an elephant who is playing its trunk as if it were a trumpet is actually an actor seated on horseback who wears a humorous costume. The drawing was once believed to be related to the masquerades organized by Galeazzo da Sanseverino in his Milanese palace in 1491, when Leonardo designed the costumes of certain *omini salvatici.* The most recent studies, however, date it to around 1508, which, by pure coincidence, is also the date of Marcantonio's engraving. In any case, this drawing and the masquerade remind us how the demonic and comic were intimately connected in the late medieval and early modern periods. Leonardo's instructions about how to make imaginary animals and monstrosities as well as Vasari's anecdotes about his early head of Medusa and about his later abstruse experiments or jokes in the garden of the Belvedere are both terrifying and humorous.[28]

These developments parallel those in the theater, as Milne notes: "By the second half of the fifteenth century, 'domestic' scenes in Hell, involving much comic banter between many... devils and increasingly elaborate special effects, had become the rule rather than the exception."[29] Similar spectacles were particularly popular during the carnival season, and a city like Venice could not but excel in the production of elaborate entertainments. Marino Sanudo's diaries are an inestimable source for our purposes. In 1515 a farce performed in the courtyard of Ca' Pesaro "opened with a scene of a flaming Hell peopled by actors in blackface."[30] Five years later "the Compagnia degli Immortali sponsored an evening *festa* in front of Ca' Foscari in which actors ... pantomimed the fall of Troy. The pageant ended with a devil emerging from a ball of fire, which ultimately consumed the set."[31]

These Venetian theatrical performances convey the medley of sacred and profane, of waning mystery plays and emerging classical aspirations, that must have characterized these pantomimes. To a large extent, the Hellmouth as a visual device had been demystified by the later Middle Ages, but the same portentous effects could be achieved by staging a debased and possibly disrespectful version of the classical drama.

Giorgione's lost *Inferno* did not fit into this scenario; it could not have been an "illustration" of a similar event. It is against this background, however, that we should place Giorgione's canvas: it embodied, so to speak, the other side of the same phenomenon, the revival of classical themes in Renaissance Venice.

We should ask first what Giorgione's canvas represented. In theory he could also have painted the meeting of Aeneas and Anchises in the Underworld. His canvas could have reproduced two passages of book 6 of the *Aeneid,* with the flaming Phlegethon on one side and the meeting in the Elysian Fields—the subject of Dosso's *Aeneas in the Elysian Fields* in the National Gallery of Canada in Ottawa—on the other side. Michiel's words, however (*"la tela ... de linferno cun Enea et Anchise"*), recall those he used to describe a painting by Bosch that he saw in the palace of Cardinal Grimani in 1521: *"La tela de linferno cun la gran diversità de monstri"* (the painting of the Inferno with a large assortment of monsters).[32] The most impressive element of Giorgione's composition, therefore, must have been the fire. Thus it is more likely that his *Inferno* depicted the fall of Troy, as has been often suggested, even if its design was influenced by the hellish Flemish imagery available in Venice.

Next we should ask what the picture looked like. According to Nicholas Penny, "some idea ... can probably be best obtained from a painting by Savoldo ... in which semitransparent demons assault a recumbent [figure] at sunset." At the right side a nude man carries on his shoulders the body of another man, whose head has assumed the features of a bird's skull in order to give a visible shape to a hallucination (fig. 4).[33] As is well known, these two figures are a reversed copy of the so-called Aeneas-Anchises group frescoed by Raphael in the Vatican's Stanza dell'Incendio and therefore cannot be a faithful record of Giorgione's heroes. The subject, however, requires that a younger man carry the body of an older man on his shoulders. If we imagine, moreover, that a similar group, possibly derived from one of those antique cameos or coins that a passionate collector of antiquities like Taddeo Contarini certainly possessed,[34] was set in a landscape dominated by the flames of a Boschian *Inferno* (fig. 5), like the one seen by

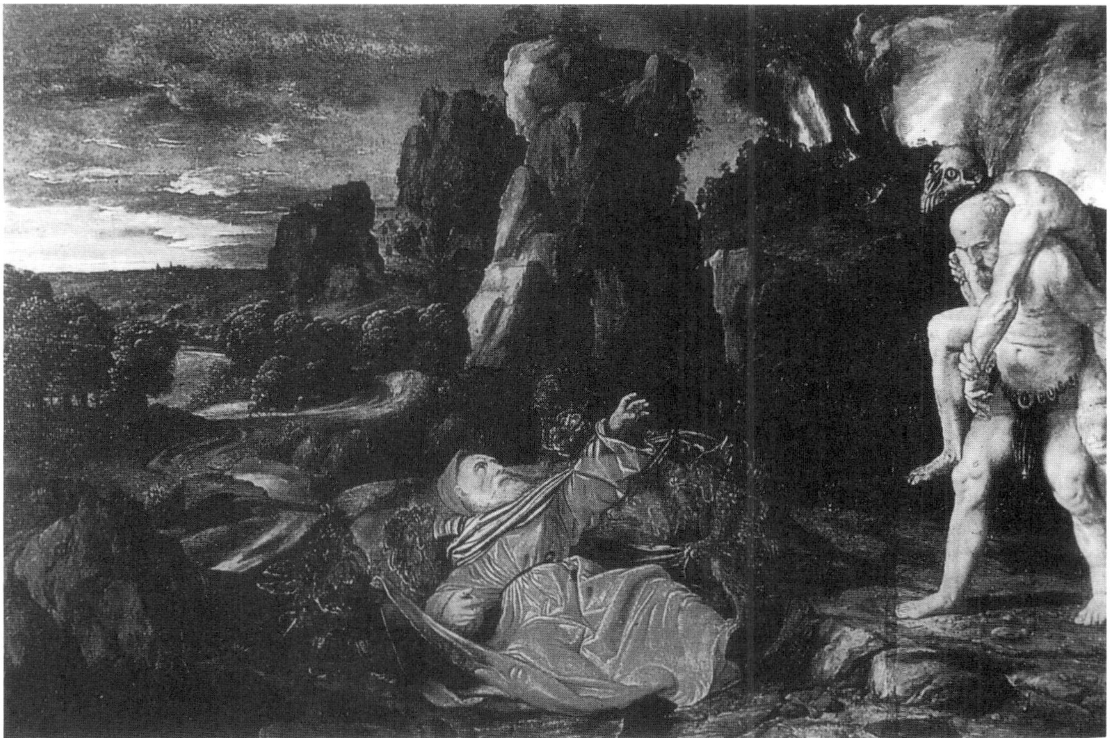

Fig. 4. Giovanni Girolamo Savoldo
Temptation of Saint Anthony
Moscow, Gosudarstvennyj Muzej A. S. Pushkina

Michiel in the Grimani collection, we can mentally, even if inaccurately, reconstruct Giorgione's lost canvas.

It is indeed puzzling that such an important work should have disappeared without trace, because it can be argued that Giorgione's *Inferno* was a very big picture. The reliable Michiel speaks of a "*tela grande a oglio*" (a large oil painting).[35] In the same collection, moreover, he saw among other things another big canvas painted in tempera by Girolamo Romanino and a small female portrait ("*el quadretto*") by Giovanni Bellini.[36] In other words, Michiel was very accurate in recording the sizes of the paintings he saw. Yet when he lists the so-called *Three Philosophers* (p. 203) in the same house he makes no comment on its size.[37] The fragmentary canvas in Vienna measures 1.23 by 1.44 meters.[38] The *Inferno* was probably bigger, certainly not smaller, than the *Three Philosophers,* and this means that the group of Aeneas and Anchises could have easily been eighty centimeters to one meter high, if not more.

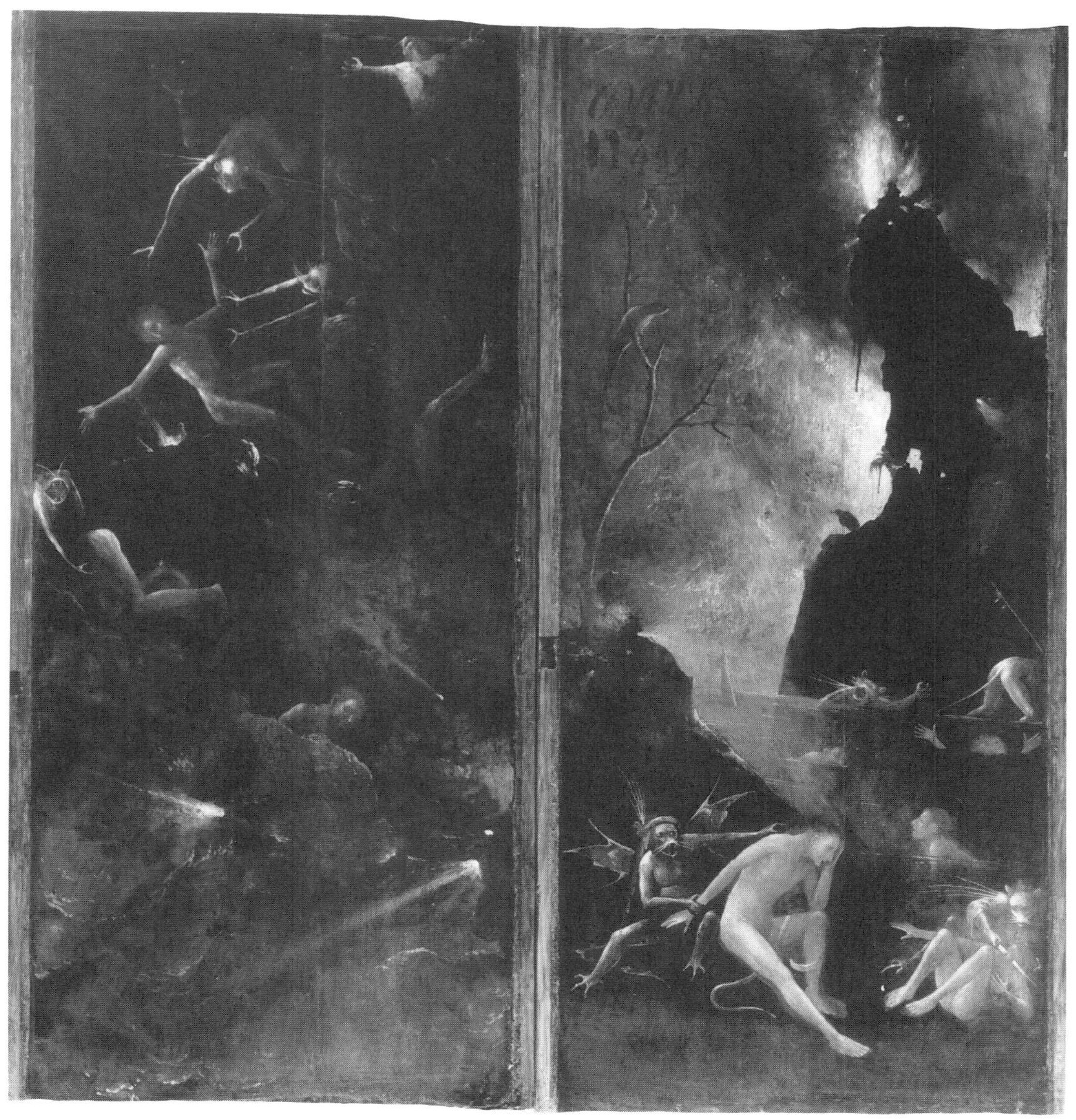

Fig. 5. Hieronymus Bosch
The Inferno
Venice, Palazzo Ducale

As far as I know, an almost life-size representation of the myth was unprecedented in Venice. (At this date I can only think of Girolamo Genga's fresco for the palace of Pandolfo Petrucci in Siena).[39] We should therefore ask why Giorgione selected this subject and who commissioned this large canvas.

As far as the latter question is concerned, two well-known, indeed celebrated, documents help us formulate the hypothesis that Taddeo Contarini himself commissioned the canvas. From a letter of Isabella d'Este to Taddeo Albano, her agent in Venice, dated 25 October 1510, we know that the marchesa wanted to purchase "a very beautiful and unusual 'nocte'" that had been painted by Giorgione and was apparently left in his studio after his death.[40] Albano replied on 8 November 1510 that such a painting did not exist in the artist's estate; moreover, both the *Nocte* owned by a certain Victorio Becharo and the *Nocte* owned by Taddeo Contarini were not on sale for any price because they had commissioned these paintings for their own enjoyment.[41] From these texts we learn three important facts: first, even if we do not know whether the term *nocte* referred to a specific iconography or to a genre, Isabella and Taddeo understood each other when they used it because they knew what this term meant; second, in November 1510 Taddeo Contarini owned a *Nocte* by Giorgione; third, Giorgione's patrons did not intend to sell their paintings because they wanted to enjoy them.

Fifteen years later, in 1525, Michiel visited Contarini's collection and listed in his notebook three paintings by Giorgione: the so-called *Three Philosophers, The Birth of Paris,* which is known through a copy by David Teniers, and the *Inferno with Aeneas and Anchises.* As we have seen, this canvas probably depicted the fall of Troy and was a night scene. It is therefore reasonable to suggest that the *Nocte* recorded by Taddeo Albano and the *Inferno* seen by Michiel were in fact the same picture. Indeed, this is the simplest solution, because if this were not so, one should assume that Contarini originally owned four and not three paintings by Giorgione and that Taddeo sold his *Nocte* between 1510 and 1525. Such a scenario has been implicitly suggested by some art historians who have identified the so-called *Allendale Nativity* (*Adoration of the Shepherds,* Washington, National Gallery of Art) and its unfinished replica in Vienna (*Adoration of the Shepherds,* Kunsthistorisches Museum), with the two *"nocti"* mentioned by Taddeo Albano.[42] This hypothesis has been accepted by many scholars.[43] As early as 1949, however, Hans Tietze and Erika Tietze-Conrat pointed out that at the beginning of the sixteenth century the term *nocte* could not have been used to describe a nativity.[44] Two more observations should be made. First, Giorgione's adorations do not take place at night. Second, if the *Nocte* was really a nativity or an adoration of the shepherds, namely the painting now in Vienna, Contarini should have sold it before 1525, before Michiel's visit to his collection. As we have seen, however, Contarini did not want to sell his *Nocte* to Isabella d'Este for any price. All in all, therefore, it is more reasonable to assume that the *Nocte* mentioned by Albano depicted the fall of Troy that Michiel saw fifteen years later in the same palace.

One possible objection to this reconstruction of the events is difficult to answer: we do not know of other sources from the early sixteenth century in which a time of the day (dawn, morning, afternoon, evening, sunset, night) is used to indicate the subject of a painting. Yet the impression is that Isabella d'Este, who was interested in collecting Flemish art,[45] and her agent used the term *nocte* to refer to a genre more than to a specific iconographic subject. Between the end of the fifteenth and the beginning of the sixteenth centuries, artists were keen on experimenting with the representation of atmospheric effects, and these interests were reflected in the writings of the time: not only in Leonardo's treatise on painting but also in Erasmus's *De recta Latini Graecique sermonis pronuntiatione* (1533), a dialogue that praises Albrecht Dürer's outstanding talent in reproducing what cannot be reproduced—that is, fire, rays of light, thunder, and lightning.[46] This was a *topos* based on Pliny the Elder and later repeated by Vasari in his life of Raphael, but this does not mean that these artists were not actually interested in these themes. This imagery was later "institutionalized" by Vasari, who was fond of night scenes,[47] yet the representation of atmospheric effects and in particular of night scenes was already a central issue at the turn of the century: indeed, this was one of the greatest achievements of the *maniera moderna,* which in this respect was deeply influenced by the Netherlandish paintings imported into Venice at the end of the fifteenth century.[48]

To conclude this part of the investigation, it is likely that the *Nocte* mentioned by Taddeo Albano in his letter to Isabella d'Este, dated 8 November 1510, and the lost *Inferno* seen by Michiel in 1525 were the same picture. It is therefore almost certain that Taddeo Contarini himself commissioned the canvas.

It would be superfluous to repeat all the important information on Taddeo Contarini gathered by Salvatore Settis in his book on Giorgione's *Tempest.*[49] Let us only mention that Contarini possessed an outstanding classical culture. There is perhaps no further need to explain why a man of his wide-ranging classical interests would have liked to see on the walls of his palace the story of Aeneas and Anchises, but the hypothesis that such an unusual commission was related to unusual historical circumstances is too tempting to resist.

The theme of Aeneas's flight from Troy with his father on his shoulders conveys the message of filial piety in the moment of danger, when the institutions and the country itself are collapsing, a moral that is depicted in Andrea Alciati's later *Emblematum libellus* (fig. 6). The motto of emblem 195 recites *"Pietas filiorum in parentes,"* but the text of the epigram also stresses the notion of *"patria."*[50] I am aware of the fact that the desire to connect the myth with the political realities of the Venetian republic and the military rout of Agnadello is based on no solid documentary evidence.[51] Skepticism over such direct political and contextual interpretations of works of art has grown louder in recent years[52]—imagine what can happen when the picture itself is lost or destroyed. Yet such a dramatic painting, a night illuminated by the

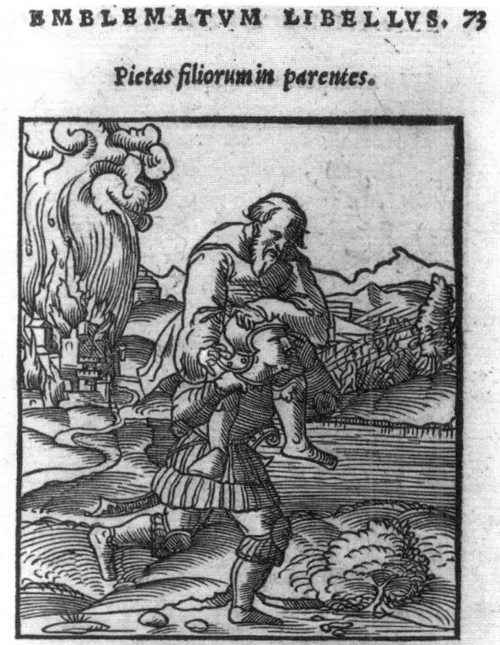
EMBLEMATVM LIBELLVS. 73

Pietas filiorum in parentes.

Fig. 6. "Pietas filiorum in parentes"
From Andrea Alciati, *Emblematum libellus,* emblem 73
(Paris: Christian Wechel, 1534)

burning Troy, a true Inferno, would have been a perfect metaphor for the collapsing Venetian state and would have well embodied the anxiety, sense of loss, and bewilderment that agitated Venetian society. It must be admitted that this interpretation is hard to defend: the late medieval tradition of the myth stresses its moral and private connotations, and there can be no doubt—as I have already suggested—that the painting had a very personal meaning for Taddeo Contarini. When I refer to the "political" implications of this commission, therefore, I do not intend to suggest that Giorgione's painting was an illustration or the direct reflection of a specific event, but that the unusual historical circumstances and the dark mood of those tragic days stimulated, almost subliminally, the recovery of the myth on a monumental scale. After May 1509 Venice's situation was so precarious that the troops of the League of Cambrai occupied Padua. This was not the appropriate time to commission a big canvas. By the following year, however, the situation had substantially improved.

The years between 1509 and 1511 are crucial for the history of Venetian altarpiece painting: Basaiti, Carpaccio, Buonconsiglio, Bellini, and Titian executed several altarpieces that, although intended as a petition for protection from the plague, also simultaneously celebrated the end of the worst of the political threats.[53] By a stretch of the imagination we could interpret the *Inferno* as a sort of secular ex-voto. If this were true, the lost canvas would belong to the last phase of Giorgione's career, a period characterized by the classical turn of his work from 1508.[54] The bodies of the two possibly seminaked figures were, then, possibly similar to the *ignudi* on the facade of the Fondaco dei Tedeschi.

There is at least one more clue that can be used to argue that the *Inferno* was a very late painting by Giorgione. As we have seen, Taddeo Albano wrote to Isabella d'Este that the *Nocte* owned by Becharo and the *Nocte* owned by Contarini were not for sale at any price. There was an important difference between these two pictures, however (which, incidentally, did not necessarily depict the same iconographic subject): the Becharo *Nocte* was a better finished painting, whereas the Contarini *Nocte* was "*non... molto perfecta.*" Albano's words might indicate that the big canvas was left unfinished because of the painter's sudden death. Indeed, it is unlikely that a demanding collector like Taddeo Contarini would have acquired an unfinished painting, if he did not have to succumb to exceptional circumstances. The letter of Isabella's agent was written only a few days after Giorgione's death: we must therefore assume that the painting entered Contarini's collection in the short time between the artist's death and the letter. If Taddeo Contarini had personally commissioned the work, as I have argued, such a scenario is plausible.[55]

The *Dream* engraved by Marcantonio and the *Inferno* are two very important works that help us reconstruct the last chapter of Giorgione's career between 1508 and 1510. If the *Three Philosophers* is not a late work and if we accept the proposal that what we see now in the *Venus* in the Staatliche Kunstsammlungen, Gemäldegalerie Alte Meister, in Dresden (ca. 1510) was painted mostly by Titian, as Alessandro Ballarin and Mauro Lucco have suggested,[56] then it is necessary to write a new profile of Giorgione's last works, a profile that must also take into account his lost or damaged compositions.

Giorgione's increasingly public role and his success is beyond dispute. This is proved not only by the frescoes on the facade of the Fondaco but also by his documented painting for the audience chamber of the Palazzo Ducale. The *Dream* engraved by Marcantonio Raimondi and the *Inferno* document a more private but equally important aspect of Giorgione's late phase: his love of night scenes, special light effects, and spellbinding, violent fires. His treatment of these themes, which were rooted in Leonardo's theoretical writings, was even more influential than his public works and had an enormous impact on western painting in the following decades and centuries, including the work of Dosso Dossi.

Leonardo was a constant point of reference for Giorgione, as the *Three Ages of Man* (Florence, Palazzo Pitti) and the so-called *Marcello* (Vienna, Kunsthistorisches Museum) show.[57] Here I have argued that this fascination endured until the very end of Giorgione's life. The flight of Aeneas and Anchises from the burning Troy demanded that Giorgione not only paint a great fire in the night, a quintessentially Leonardesque subject, but also portray the contrast between an older and a younger face. It is unlikely that in this lost painting Giorgione imitated the grotesque and idealized features of Leonardo's heads, which he had paraphrased five years earlier in the *Marcello*. The fragmentary surviving evidence confirms, however, that in his last works Giorgione continued to investigate themes and issues that had long concerned Leonardo.

Notes

I would like to thank Salvatore Settis for generously sharing his insights vis-à-vis some of the issues discussed in this essay and for providing numerous bibliographic references. My sincerest thanks also to David Ekserdjian, Victoria von Flemming, Jennifer Fletcher, and John Shearman. I am grateful to Luisa Ciammitti, who effectively organized the seminar, and to Mauro Natale, who chaired the session "Ferrara in the Age of Alfonso I."

1. Recent philological reconstructions of Giorgione's career are Alessandro Ballarin, "Une nouvelle perspective sur Giorgione: Les portraits des années 1500–1503" and "Le problème des œuvres de la jeunesse de Titien: Avancées et reculs de la critique," in *Le siècle de Titien: L'âge d'or de la peinture à Venise,* 2nd ed., exh. cat. (Paris: Editions de la Réunion des Musées Nationaux, 1993), 281–94, 357–66 (see also the important review by Mauro Lucco, "Le siècle de Titien," *Paragone,* nos. 535–537 [1994]: 26–47); and Mauro Lucco, *Giorgione* (Milan: Electa, 1995). Ballarin's texts are based on results achieved in the 1970s and partially published in three earlier articles: "Una nuova prospettiva su Giorgione: La ritrattistica degli anni 1500–1503," in *Giorgione: Atti del convegno internazionale di studio per il 5° centenario della nascita* (Castelfranco Veneto: Comitato per le Celebrazioni Giorgionesche, 1979): 227–52; "Giorgione: Per un nuovo catalogo e una nuova cronologia," in *Giorgione e la cultura veneta tra '400 e '500: Mito, allegoria, analisi iconologica* (Rome: De Luca, 1981), 26–30; "Giorgione e la Compagnia degli Amici: Il 'Doppio ritratto' Ludovisi," in *Storia dell'arte italiana,* 12 vols. (Turin: Einaudi, 1979–1982), 5: 479–541. The most recent monograph on the painter is Jaynie Anderson, *Giorgione: Peintre de la "Brièveté Poétique"* (Paris: Editions de la Lagune, 1996).

2. The extensive bibliography on the *Dream* is well summarized in Marzia Faietti and Konrad Oberhuber, eds., *Humanismus in Bologna, 1490–1510,* exh. cat. (Bologna: Nuova Alfa, 1988), 156–58 (entry no. 33 by Marzia Faietti). For further bibliographic references, see notes 4, 6, 10–13, 16, and 22 below.

3. [Marcantonio Michiel], *Notizia d'opere di disegno,* ed. Jacopo Morelli, 2nd ed., ed. Gustavo Frizzoni (1884; reprint, Bologna: Arnaldo Forni, 1976), 165; Marcantonio Michiel, *Der Anonimo Morelliano (Marcanton Michiel's* Notizia d'opere

del disegno): pt. 1, ed. and trans. Theodor Frimmel (Vienna: Carl Graeser, 1888), 88–89.

4. Johann David Passavant, *Le peintre-graveur,* 6 vols. (1864; reprint, New York: Burt Franklin, 1966), 35 (entry no. 218); Christian Hornig, *Giorgiones Spätwerk* (Munich: Wilhelm Fink, 1987), 26, 63–64 (as *The Dream of Hecuba*); *Giovanni Gerolamo Savoldo tra Foppa, Giorgione e Caravaggio,* exh. cat. (Milan: Electa, 1990), 240–41 (entry no. III.13 by Gianvittorio Dillon); Nicholas Penny, "The Night in Venetian Painting between Bellini and Elsheimer," in *Italia al chiaro di luna: La notte nella pittura italiana, 1550–1850,* 2nd. ed., exh. cat. (Rome: Il Cigno Galileo Galilei, 1990), 23–24; *Le siècle de Titien* (see note 1), 521 (entry no. 122 by Konrad Oberhuber).

5. For Marcantonio's earlier work, see Konrad Oberhuber, "Marcantonio Raimondi: Gli inizi a Bologna ed il primo periodo romano," in Faietti and Oberhuber (see note 2), 51–88; and Marzia Faietti, in idem, 89–156 (entry nos. 1–32).

6. In 1895, Franz Wickhoff, "Giorgiones Bilder zu römischen Heldengedichten," *Jahrbuch der königlich preußischen Kunstsammlungen* 16 (1895): 38, suggested that Servius's (fourth-century) commentary on Virgil's *Aeneid* 3.12 might be its literary source. Servius tells of two virgins who were surprised by a storm and took refuge in the temple of the gods at Lavinium; as they were sleeping, *"ea quae minus casta erat fulmine exanimatur, alteram nihil sensisse"* (the one who was less chaste was killed by lightning, while the other felt nothing). This interpretation was challenged by Gustav Friederich Hartlaub, *Giorgiones Geheimnis: Ein kunstgeschichtlicher Beitrag zur Mystik der Renaissance* (Munich: Allgemeine Verlagsanstalt, 1925), 63, who pointed out that the two virgins do not rest in a temple and that neither is being or has been struck by lightning. Later, Hartlaub suggested that the engraving represents Hecuba's dream, which foretold the fall of Troy; see Hartlaub, "Giorgione und der Mythos der Akademieen," *Repertorium für Kunstwissenschaft* 48 (1927): 241; and idem, "Zu den Bildmotiven des Giorgione," *Zeitschrift für Kunstwissenschaft* 7 (1953): 76. As Francesco Gandolfo, *Il "dolce tempo": Mistica, ermetismo e sogno nel Cinquecento* (Rome: Bulzoni, 1978), 80, noted, however, this episode had a well-established and very different iconography: according to the traditional iconography of Hecuba's dream, the pregnant queen dreams that a gigantic torch comes out of her abdomen and burns the town. In 1970, Maurizio Calvesi, "La 'morte di bacio': Saggio sull'ermetismo di Giorgione," *Storia dell'arte,* no. 7/8 (1970): 186, suggested that the engraving might represent the nightmares of Dido, here flanked by her sister Anna Perenna, who dreams about Aeneas's imminent departure. According to this interpretation, the engraving brings together different moments of Virgil's poem. See also Anderson (see note 1), 184.

7. Michiel, 1976 (see note 3), 165; or Michiel, 1888 (see note 3), 88–89: *"La tela grande a oglio dell'Inferno con Enea e Anchise fu de mano de Zorzi de Castelfranco"* (A large oil painting of the Inferno with Aeneas and Anchises by the hand of Giorgione da Castelfranco).

8. Eugenio Battisti, *L'antirinascimento,* 2 vols. (Milan: Garzanti, 1989), 1: 195.

9. Gandolfo (see note 6), 77–112.

10. Heike Frosien-Leinz, "Antikisches Gebrauchsgerät—Weisheit und Magie in

den Öllampen Riccios," in *Natur und Antike in der Renaissance*, exh. cat. (Frankfurt am Main: Liebieghaus Museum Alter Plastik, 1985), 253–54.

11. Horst Bredekamp, "Traumbilder von Marcantonio Raimondi bis Giorgio Ghisi," in Werner Hofmann, ed., *Zauber der Medusa: Europäische Manierismen*, exh. cat. (Vienna: Löcker, 1987), 64–65.

12. Louise Shona Milne, *Dreams and Popular Beliefs in the Imagery of Pieter Bruegel the Elder, c. 1528–1569* (Ann Arbor: University Microfilms, 1990), 87–88.

13. Guy de Tervarent, "Instances of Flemish Influence in Italian Art," *Burlington Magazine* 85 (1944): 290–94.

14. Statius, *Thebaid*, 10.112–13: *"adsunt innumero circum vaga somnia vultu / vera simul falsis permixtaque flumina flammis"*; see de Tervarent, ibid., 293.

15. Lucian, *A True Story*, 2.34; see de Tervarent (see note 13), 293.

16. Jane Martineau and Charles Hope, eds., *The Genius of Venice 1500–1600*, exh. cat. (London: Royal Academy of Arts/Weidenfeld & Nicolson, 1983), 318–19 (entry no. P15 by David Landau).

17. It is not easy to find written evidence to support this rather bold hypothesis, but Salvatore Settis has kindly brought to my attention a comment by the Riminese humanist Giovanni Aurelio Augurelli on the complicated symbolism of the banner painted for Giuliano de' Medici in 1475 (Florence, Biblioteca Laurenziana, MS. Laurenziano plut. XXXIV 46, poem 17):

> *L'immagine è, con la sua immediatezza e pregnanza, non solo piacevole oggetto alla vista; ma spunto per discorsi sull'immagine, discorsi che, anche se allusioni o variazioni o descrizioni, saranno sempre, in un qualche senso,* interpretazione; *e, se nell'interpretare*
>
> multi multa ferunt, eadem sententia nulli est,
> pulchrius est pictis istud imaginibus:
>
> *cosí scriveva, e proprio a proposito dello stendardo di Giuliano [de' Medici] nella giostra del 1475, l'umanista riminese Giovanni Aurelio Augurelli, in un poemetto dedicato a Bernardo Bembo* (With its immediacy and pregnancy, the image is not only a pleasurable object for the eye but a stimulus for discourses on the image—discourses that are always, in some sense, *interpretations*, even if allusions or variations or descriptions, and if, in interpreting,
>
> many people express many opinions, nobody has the same opinion,
> this [fact] is more beautiful than the painted images.
>
> Thus wrote the humanist from Rimini, Giovanni Aurelio Augurelli, in a brief poem dedicated to Bernardo Bembo, precisely in reference to Giuliano [de' Medici's] banner in the 1475 tournament).

See Salvatore Settis, "*Citarea* 'su una impresa di bronconi,'" *Journal of the Warburg and Courtauld Institutes* 34 (1971): 143, 176–77. My argument is that this taste for nonexplicit imagery might have been shared by those who collected early Venetian prints. Although born in Rimini, Augurelli studied in Padua and died in Treviso in 1524; see Armando Balduino, "Un poeta umanista (G. A. Augurelli) di fronte all'arte contemporanea," in Michelangelo Muraro, ed., *La letteratura, la rappresentazione, la musica al tempo e nei luoghi di Giorgione* (Rome: Jouvence, 1987), 63.

18. Giovanni Paolo Lomazzo, *Scritti sulle arti,* ed. Roberto Paolo Ciardi, 2 vols. (Florence: Marchi & Bertolli, 1973–1974), 2: 194–95.

19. See Lomazzo, ibid., 2: 297–98:

> *Ne' camini, adonque, non vogliono vedersi dipinte altre istorie, o favole, o significazioni, che dove entrino fuochi e significanti ardenti d'amori e di desiderij. Di che i pittori ingeniosi possono da se stessi formarne molte composizioni. E quanto alle favole et istorie si potrebbe rappresentare... Ascanio con la fiamma intorno alla testa doppo la distruzione di Troia;... la colonna di fuoco che precede innanzi di notte, come scorta, il populo d'Israel fuggito d'Egitto; e l'istesso popolo, mentre che nell'Egitto lavorava intorno alle fornaci. Ma tuttavia pare che le favole et istorie de' gentili piacciano, non so come, piú, quasi che abbiano maggior vaghezza d'invenzione. E però conviene avere buona conserva di favole, come... di Didone quando col tesoro si getta nel fuoco;... di Medea che per ringiovenire Esone fa il bizzarro incanto* (On fireplaces, therefore, no story, fable, or myth should be painted except for those about fires and important figures burning with loves and desires. From these, skillful painters may on their own create many compositions. And as for the fables and stories, they might represent... Ascanius with flames around his head after the destruction of Troy;... the pillar of fire that by night went as an escort before the people of Israel who had fled Egypt; and the same people, while in Egypt as they worked around the kilns. But it nonetheless seems that fables and stories of the gentiles are more pleasing [I know not why], almost as if they had greater grace of invention. However, one needs a good store of fables, such as... Dido, when she threw herself in the fire with the treasure;... [and] Medea, when she cast her bizarre spell to rejuvenate Jason).

20. Lomazzo (see note 18), 2: 322:

> *In tali conflitti e rovine aggiungerà molta grazia il far veder gettar a terra le mura, le femine con le braccia aperte andar gridando, et altre fuggire et altri esser legati, altri uccisi et altri spogliati; appresso, come a Troia e Cartagine, accendere il fuoco e rovinar le case et i palazzi come già tante volte è avvenuto alla povera Roma per mani di barbari et a molte altre città d'Italia; alcuni colmi di paura fuggire, come ardendo Troia fuggí il figliuolo di Venere col vecchio padre Anchise su le spalle et il figliuolo piccioletto per le mani; altri porgere giú da' balconi i fanciulli, altri calarsi per le corde, altri saltar giú, e simili rovine e disperazioni, le quali infinito sarebbe a volere annoverare.*

Lomazzo's words could well be inspired by Raphael's *Fire in the Borgo.*

21. See Bredekamp (see note 11): 66 n. 31. See also Peter Burke, "Für eine Geschichte des Traumes," *Freibeuter,* no. 27 (1986): 50–65.

22. To be more explicit: it is possible that the iconographically meaningful elements of the composition were deliberately introduced in order to confuse the viewer: the viewer identifies Charon but cannot connect him to the other elements of the engraving; on the right-hand side the viewer sees a man carrying a body on his shoulders, but because their poses indicate that the man is carrying a dead body, they cannot represent Aeneas and Anchises; at the top of the burning tower, the viewer sees

two bodies tied to a turning wheel, an image that might refer to *Aeneid* 6.616–17. These details make the viewer believe that she or he has identified the subject of the engraving, but the figures and the animals in the foreground contradict this first impression or intuition. See also Patricia Emison, "Asleep in the Grass of Arcady: Giulio Campagnola's Dreamer," *Renaissance Quarterly* 45 (1992): 271–92; and Craig Harbison, "Meaning in Venetian Renaissance Art: The Issues of Artistic Ingenuity and Oral Traditions," *Art History* 15 (1992): 19–37.

23. For the limitations imposed on the artist by sculpture, see Martin Kemp, ed., *Leonardo on Painting: An Anthology of Writings by Leonardo da Vinci, with a Selection of Documents Relating to His Career as an Artist* (New Haven: Yale Univ. Press, 1989), 39. For the passage on painting, see idem, 40–42.

24. Martineau and Hope (see note 16), 318 (entry no. P15 by David Landau).

25. Jean Paul Richter, ed., *The Literary Works of Leonardo da Vinci,* 3rd ed., 2 vols. (London: Phaidon, 1970), 2: 293.

26. For a good translation of the celebrated passage on "how to represent a night scene," see Kemp (see note 23), 238. For the passage quoted in the text, see idem, 32.

27. Windsor no. 12585 recto; see Kenneth Clark, *The Drawings of Leonardo da Vinci in the Collection of Her Majesty the Queen, at Windsor Castle,* 2nd ed., 3 vols. (London: Phaidon, 1968), 1: 115–16.

28. Richter (see note 25), 1: 54: "Do you not see to what an abundance of inventions the painter may resort if he wishes to portray animals or devils in hell?" Also, idem, 1: 342: "HOW YOU SHOULD MAKE AN IMAGINARY ANIMAL LOOK NATURAL. You know that you cannot invent animals without limbs, each of which, in itself, must resemble those of some other animal. Hence if you wish to make an animal, imagined by you, appear natural—let us say a dragon, take for its head that of a mastiff or hound, with the eyes of a cat, the ears of a porcupine, the nose of a greyhound, the brow of a lion, the temples of an old cock, the neck of a water-tortoise."

29. Milne (see note 12), 185.

30. Edward Muir, *Civic Ritual in Renaissance Venice* (Princeton: Princeton Univ. Press, 1981), 172–73.

31. Ibid., 172.

32. Michiel, 1976 (see note 3), 165, 196; or Michiel, 1888 (see note 3), 102.

33. Penny (see note 4), 31–32. Penny and I reached our very similar conclusions independently. I completed the first draft of this essay before reading Penny's article. Our similar reasoning may indicate that the Giorgione-Savoldo connection should not be hastily discarded, even if the group on the right derives from Raphael's *Fire in the Borgo*.

34. Gabriele Vendramin, Taddeo's brother-in-law, assembled a greatly admired collection of antiquities; see Irene Favaretto, *Arte antica e cultura antiquaria nelle collezioni venete al tempo della Serenissima* (Rome: L'Erma di Bretschneider, 1990). Two silver coins of the Republican period (47–46 B.C.) in the Museo Archeologico in Venice reproduce a well-known Aeneas-Anchises group; unfortunately, no. 777 (inv. no. 3366) was found in the province of Venice only in 1937, while the provenance of no. 74 (inv. no. 181) is unknown, as Giovanna Luisa Ravagnan has informed me. In

any case, this group was known at the beginning of the sixteenth century, because it was engraved by Marcantonio Raimondi; see *The Illustrated Bartsch,* vol. 26, *The Works of Marcantonio Raimondi and of His School, Part 1,* ed. Konrad Oberhuber (New York: Abaris, 1978), 180 (entry no. 186 [152]).

35. Michiel made no corrections to his entry on the *Aeneas* in the original manuscript, now in the Biblioteca nazionale Marciana, Venice.

36. This information is reported without additions or corrections in Michiel's original manuscript.

37. Michiel himself added above the original text in the manuscript that *Three Philosophers* is painted in oil. In other words, he took the trouble to add information about the medium yet says nothing about the size of the canvas.

38. See Terisio Pignatti, *Giorgione,* 2nd ed. (Milan: Alfieri, 1978), 108.

39. On Genga's detached fresco, see Piero Torriti, *La Pinacoteca Nazionale di Siena: I dipinti dal XV al XVIII secolo* (Genoa: Sagep, 1981), 50–52; Fiorella Sricchia Santoro, "'Ricerche senesi': 2. Il Palazzo del Magnifico Pandolfo Petrucci," *Prospettiva,* no. 29 (1982): 24–31; Giovanni Agosti, "Precisioni su un *Baccanale* perduto del Signorelli," *Prospettiva,* no. 30 (1982): 70–77, who clarifies the marital-dynastic implications of the cycle painted for Pandolfo Petrucci in 1509; and *Domenico Beccafumi e il suo tempo,* exh. cat. (Milan: Electa, 1990), 260–62 (entry no. 49 by Fiorella Sricchia Santoro). Other late sixteenth-century examples are listed in Jane Davidson Reid, *The Oxford Guide to Classical Mythology in the Arts, 1300–1990s,* 2 vols. (New York: Oxford Univ. Press, 1993), 1: 43–44.

40. For a transcription of this famous letter, see Ruggero Maschio, "Per la biografia di Giorgione," in Ruggero Maschio, ed., *I tempi di Giorgione* (Rome: Gangemi, 1994), 203 (doc. no. 6, Lettera di Isabella d'Este a Taddeo Albano, Mantova, 25 ottobre 1510, initialed p. c. [Paolo Carpeggiani]).

41. For an accurate transcription of this celebrated letter, see ibid., 203 (doc. no. 7, Lettera di Taddeo Albano ad Isabella d'Este, Venezia, 8 novembre 1510, initialed p. c. [Paolo Carpeggiani]).

42. George Martin Richter, *Giorgio da Castelfranco, Called Giorgione* (Chicago: Univ. of Chicago Press, 1937), 257 (entry no. 99), identified the *Allendale Nativity* with the *Nocte* for Victorio Becharo. Giuseppe Fiocco, *Giorgione* (Bergamo: Istituto Italiano d'Arti Grafiche, 1941), 16; and Antonio Morassi, *Giorgione* (Milan: Hoepli, 1942), 66, both identify its replica in Vienna with the *Nocte* for Taddeo Contarini.

43. Most notably by Johannes Wilde, *Venetian Art from Bellini to Titian* (Oxford: Oxford Univ. Press, 1974), 60.

44. Hans Tietze and Erika Tietze-Conrat, "The *Allendale Nativity* in the National Gallery," *Art Bulletin* 31 (1949): 13–14.

45. Isabella's interest in Flemish art is well documented; see, for example, Lorne Campbell, "Notes on Netherlandish Pictures in the Veneto in the Fifteenth and Sixteenth Centuries," *Burlington Magazine* 123 (1981): 467–73; Clifford M. Brown, *Isabella d'Este and Lorenzo da Pavia: Documents for the History of Art and Culture in Renaissance Mantua* (Geneva: Libraire Droz, 1982), 169–71; and Sylvia Ferino-Pagden, *Isabella d'Este, "La prima donna del mondo": Fürstin und Mäzenatin der Renaissance,* exh. cat. (Vienna: Kunsthistorisches Museum, 1994).

46. See Erwin Panofsky, *Albrecht Dürer,* 3rd ed., 2 vols. (Princeton: Princeton Univ. Press, 1948), 1: 44.

47. Three passages come immediately to mind; they are in the lives of Piero della Francesca (the dream of Constantine), Correggio (the agony in the Garden), and Raphael. See Giorgio Vasari, *The Lives of the Artists: A Selection,* trans. George Bull (Harmondsworth: Penguin Books, 1971), 194–95, 281, 317.

48. In his recent discussion of Giorgione's *Tempest,* Paul Holberton reached similar conclusions: "Giorgione was . . . interested in an iconography introducing light and weather in sky and landscape. . . . Writers who singled out such effects (for instance, Summonte writing to Michiel on Colantonio, or even Vasari) do not suggest classical emulation; if anything such effects were to be associated with Netherlandish or German art"; see Paul Holberton, "Giorgione's *Tempest* or 'Little Landscape with the Storm with the Gypsy': More on the Gypsy, and a Reassessment," *Art History* 18 (1995): 398.

49. There were many Taddeo Contarinis in Venice. Giorgione's friend and collector is identified in Salvatore Settis, *La "Tempesta" interpretata: Giorgione, i committenti, il soggetto* (Turin: Einaudi, 1978), 139–41. This proposal has been confirmed by the inventory of 1556 found by Charles Hope and discussed by Anderson (see note 1), 148. Additional information on Taddeo appears in Giorgio Padoan, "Giorgione e la cultura umanistica," in *Giorgione* (see note 1), 25–36, esp. 33–34; Donata Battilotti, "Taddeo Contarini," in Maschio, ed. (see note 40), 205–6; Simona Cohen, "A New Perspective on Giorgione's *Three Philosophers,*" *Gazette des beaux-arts,* ser. 6, 126 (1995): 53–64.

50. Andrea Alciati, *Emblematum libellus* (Paris: Ex officina C. Wecheli, 1535), c. 73. See also Peter M. Daly, Virginia W. Callahan, and Simon Cuttler, eds., *Andreas Alciatus,* 2 vols. (Toronto: Univ. of Toronto Press, 1985), 1: emblem 195; 2: emblem 195.

51. For the political use of the figure of Aeneas in different contexts, see Bernice Davidson, "The *Navigatione d'Enea* Tapestries Designed by Perino del Vaga for Andrea Doria," *Art Bulletin* 72 (1990): 35–50, esp. 39, 48; and Marie Tanner, *The Last Descendant of Aeneas: The Hapsburgs and the Mythic Image of the Emperor* (New Haven: Yale Univ. Press, 1993).

52. For example, the political interpretation of Giorgione's frescoes on the facade of the Fondaco dei Tedeschi suggested by Michelangelo Muraro has been partly rejected by Charles Hope, who confines the political implications to the figure of Judith frescoed by Titian. See Michelangelo Muraro, "The Political Interpretation of Giorgione's Frescoes on the Fondaco dei Tedeschi," *Gazette des beaux-arts,* ser. 6, 86 (1975): 177–84; and Charles Hope, *Titian* (London: Jupiter, 1980), 12–14.

53. This extraordinary historical phenomenon needs to be properly investigated. For the individual altarpieces, see Peter Humfrey, *The Altarpiece in Renaissance Venice* (New Haven: Yale Univ. Press, 1993).

54. For this stylistic turn in the history of Venetian art, see Ballarin, 1981 (see note 1), 28.

55. It should not be forgotten that Taddeo Albano used the past tense in his letter: *"Zorzo ne feze una a messer Tadheo Contarini"* (Giorgione did one [a night scene] for

Taddeo Contarini). It is clear, however, that he did not know the painting and that he was reporting information obtained from Giorgione's friends. Indeed, it is even possible that by a curious coincidence Isabella's agent was inquiring about the canvas that Giorgione had been painting for Contarini and that the painter could not complete because of his untimely death. Contarini probably collected this unfinished painting immediately after Giorgione's death.

56. See Ballarin, 1981 (see note 1), 26, 30; and Lucco, 1995 (see note 1), 26, 30.

57. For these two paintings and their relationship with Leonardo, see *Le siècle de Titien* (see note 1), 309–13 (entry no. 21 by Alessandro Ballarin), 329–31 (entry no. 26 by Alessandro Ballarin); and Lucco, 1995 (see note 1), 22–23, 26.

Genre Scenes by Dosso and Giorgione

Michel Hochmann

Since Roberto Longhi,[1] art historians have constantly returned to the question of the relationship between sixteenth-century Venetian and Lombard painting, on the one hand, and Caravaggio's art, on the other. There is another domain in which the same question could rightly be posed, namely, the numerous paintings with half-length figures found in the oeuvres of Dosso Dossi and a great number of northern Italian and Flemish painters. Moreover, in recent years several studies have attempted to define the origins of this type of painting, emphasizing the fundamental role played by Giorgione and Dosso in the creation of the new genre—for these depictions of half-length figures do constitute a genre, or at least the beginning of the genre painting. I would like to examine these origins once again, turning first to a painting known as *Good Fortune,* found today in the Museo e Gallerie Nazionali di Capodimonte in Naples but acquired from the collection of Fulvio Orsini, where it was attributed to Giorgione. Such an attribution is, naturally, an implausible one, but the painting nevertheless allows us to reflect upon not only the development of the last phase of Giorgione's style but also Dosso's debt to him. I will also discuss the appearance and the success of these genre scenes, as well as the standing that they enjoyed until the seventeenth century.

Giorgione's Mature Style

The fact that I have spoken of the existence of genre painting from the beginning of the sixteenth century may at first seem surprising. It has often been remarked, however, that in this period a particular group of works displayed a certain number of mutually shared and very characteristic traits. There are, first of all, compositions with half-length figures that explore the expression of the passions almost to the point of caricature (this is the birth of what might be called the comic painting); these paintings possess, for the most part, an anecdotal content. Dosso executed such works throughout his career, from the *Buffoon* in the Galleria Estense (fig. 1) or the *Nymph and Satyr* in the Palazzo Pitti (fig. 2), both of which are unquestionably early works,[2] to the *Bambocciata* in the Galleria degli Uffizi in Florence.[3] The rhomboids in Modena (fig. 3), the painting of the young man with a basket of flowers, known as the *Laughing Youth,* in the Fondazione Roberto Longhi, Florence, and the *Poet and Muse* in the National Gallery in London

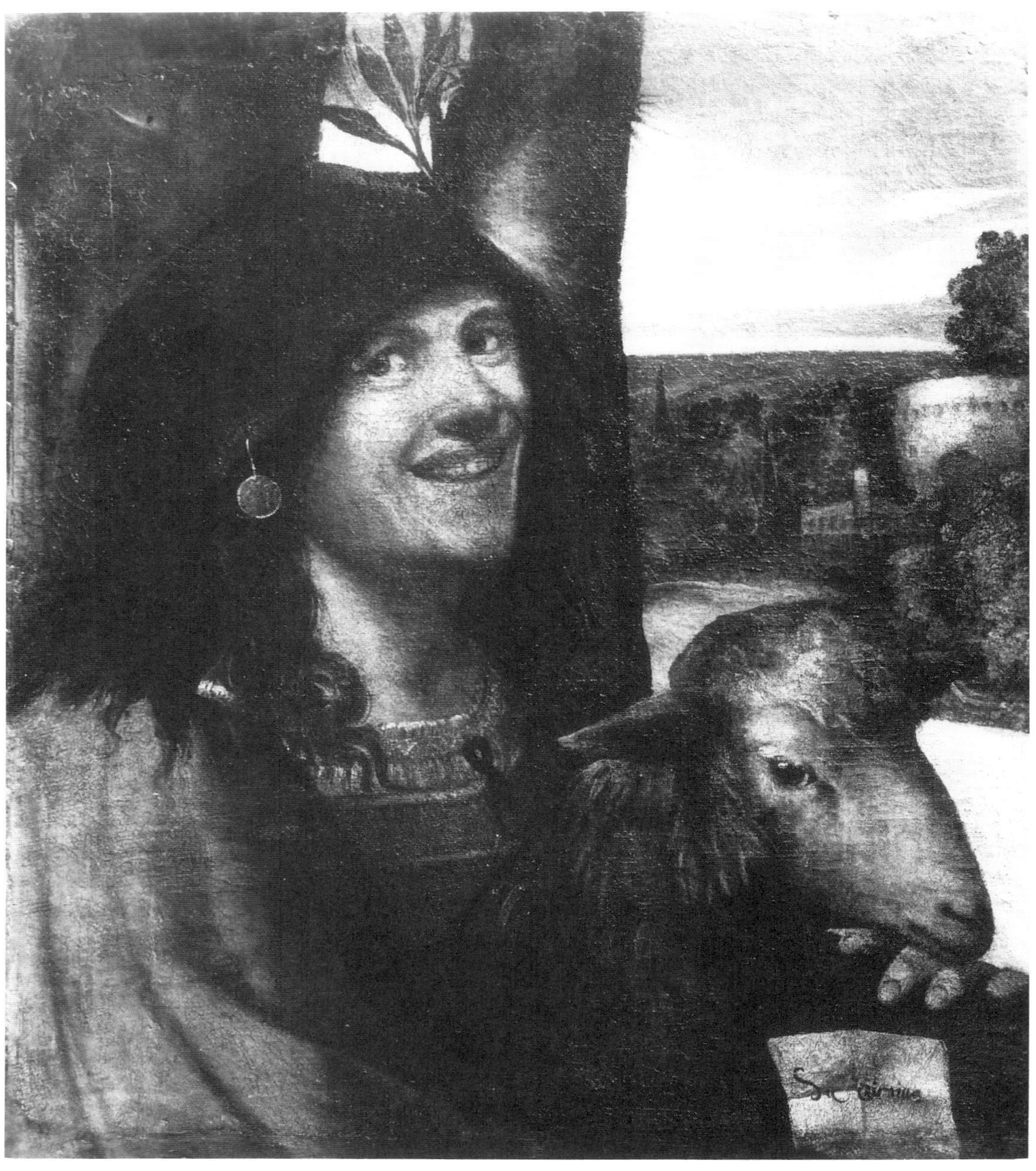

Fig. 1. Dosso Dossi
Buffoon
Modena, Galleria Estense

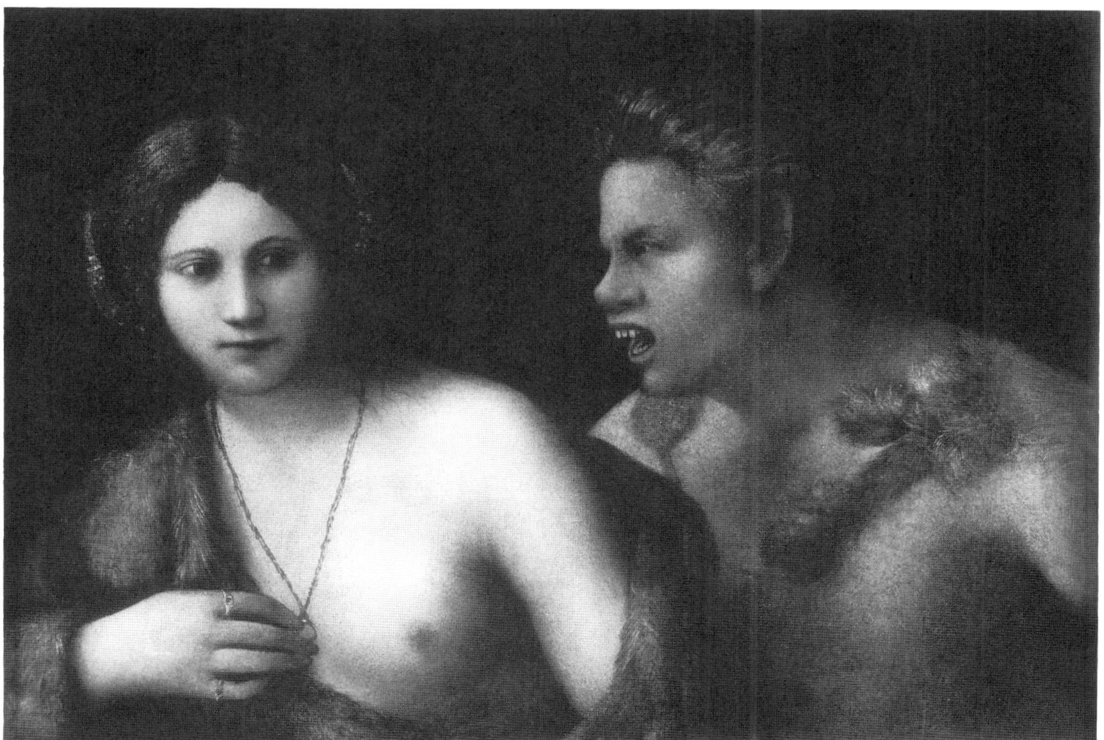

Fig. 2. Dosso Dossi
Nymph and Satyr
Florence, Palazzo Pitti

are fragments of the decoration that Dosso composed entirely in this new genre for the duke of Ferrara's palace. It has been shown that the latter two works are remnants of the great tondo that decorated the ceiling of the room called the Camera del Poggiolo.[4] This indicates the popularity that these subjects enjoyed with the greatest patrons of the period.

This quick definition remains deliberately vague. A large number of paintings do fit more or less into this category, and others that do not belong, at least *a priori,* to genre painting could also be included here. There are, for instance, religious paintings: half-length figures first became frequent in this domain, for the reasons established by Sixten Ringbom.[5] Looking at Dosso's work, *Saint John the Baptist* in the Palazzo Pitti and *Saint William* in the Royal Gallery, Hampton Court, are half-length figures, and their pained expressions testify to concerns comparable to those found in the rhomboids in the Galleria Estense.[6] Some portraits or paintings of the heads of imaginary figures, such as Dosso's *Dido* in the Galleria Doria-Pamphili in Rome, could also be connected to this group,[7] within which several subgroupings

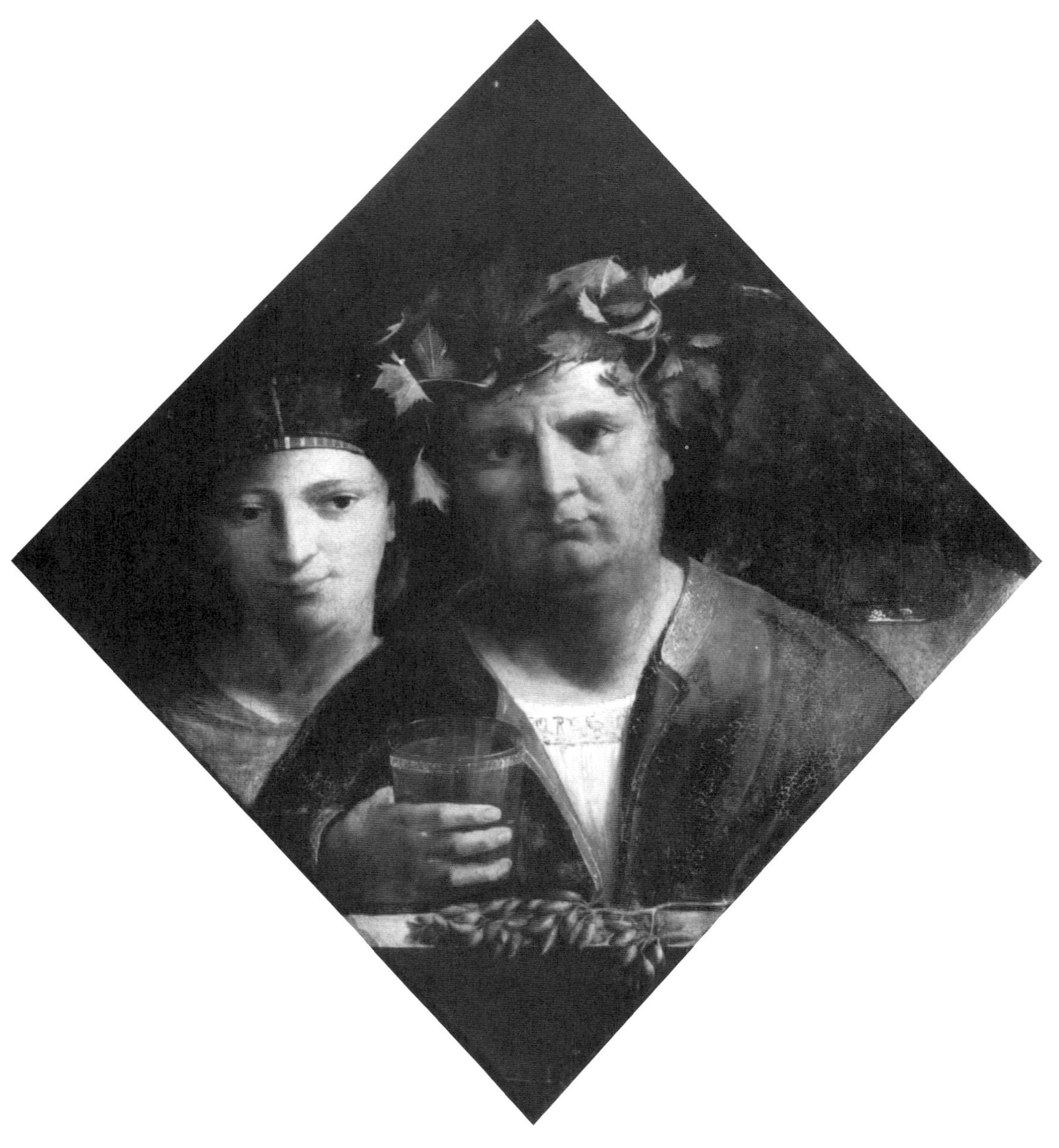

Fig. 3. Dosso Dossi
Rhomboid (Bacchus with two youths)
Modena, Galleria Estense

may be distinguished: concerts, *scènes galantes,* clowns and comic scenes, and so on. Thus the notion of genre must be rather elastic, and we must first concern ourselves with the origins of these forms and their exploration of the passions.

It is often said that Giorgione played a determining role in the development of this genre. Some of his works, such as the *Three Ages of Man* in the Palazzo Pitti, are—from this point of view—authentic archetypes. As are many of his paintings, these works stand at the beginning of a tradition that traverses all of modern painting. Even if the Florence painting is the only one that the majority of art historians accept as being in Giorgione's own hand, several works by the painter's circle or by his contemporaries show that this new formula was just as successful as were the pastoral scenes. Obvious examples are Titian's *Concert* in the Palazzo Pitti and the *Double Portrait* in the National Gallery of Art, Washington, sometimes identified with the portrait of Giovanni Borgherini and his tutor.[8] Although the cut of the figures as well as the somber background that reappear in all the paintings by his followers can already be seen in these works, there are none of the pained or laughing faces that are found in Dosso's art. On the contrary, the *Concert* or the *Three Ages* displays the sort of expressive suspense that is generally considered characteristic of Giorgione's style. Yet a break quite likely occurred in the last years of his career.

Unfortunately, here rather little is known about Giorgione's evolution in his very last years, apart from the consequences of his work, most notably its effect on Dosso. This is also the view that the seventeenth-century critics had of Giorgione's art, as witnessed in Pietro della Vecchia's pastiches, in which the exploration of expression and a taste for the genre scene predominate. Was not this view a deformed one, and should it not be called into question through what we know today of the master's authentic works? They all show, with differing shades of nuance, the same sort of reserve represented in the *Three Ages*. Those paintings tending toward a greater expressive violence are of debatable—and often debated—authenticity. This is obviously the case for the two heads of the *Singers* in the Galleria Borghese, which some still insist on attributing to Giorgione. These paintings illustrate my point extremely well, and they demonstrate in point of fact everything that the seventeenth century owed to Giorgione, as Longhi notes: "Caravaggio and Velázquez would have kept their distance or would have taken off their hats (Caravaggio his beret, Velázquez his sombrero) to this passionate artist, which ... helps ... us better to understand, a century later, upon which elements of Giorgione's style the renewers of painting were to call."[9]

Such highly evident relationships with the painters mentioned by Longhi ought to lead us to consider these works as belonging instead—in my opinion—to the category of seventeenth-century pastiches.[10] One may have the same doubts in regard to the *Singers* (also called *Samson*), found today in a private collection in Milan, which Longhi also attributed to the mature Giorgione. Alessandro Ballarin exhibited this painting in Paris in 1993, on the occasion of the great retrospective entitled *Le siècle de Titien,* under Giorgione's name. I find this attribution debatable, despite the work's undeniable qualities, including the virtuosity of the artist's rendering of the clothes of the central figure, the fringes of the sleeve, and the red and yellow bands of the vest. The expression and the execution of the faces, however, are rather crude. But this painting is surely a sixteenth-century work. Moreover, Ballarin plausibly proposed to identify it with the mention made in the inventories of Gabriele Vendramin and Nicolas Régnier, which indicates that the work should not be considered a pastiche like the *Singers* in the Galleria Borghese. If *Samson* is not in Giorgione's own hand, it nevertheless reflects—in spite of its awkwardness and the crudity of certain details—an aspect of his late work. Mauro Lucco, who so clearly revealed all that the youthful Dosso owed to paintings of this nature, has quite rightly emphasized this very point.[11]

Several of the works in the collection of Andrea Vendramin that were attributed by him to Giorgione also appear to belong to this same expressive current. Unfortunately, most of these are known only through the drawings in the catalog. Ballarin has recently identified one of these artworks as a seventeenth-century copy of an original work by Giorgione.[12] Other paintings and drawings seem to be connected with greater certainty to the works of the master. The self-portrait in the Herzog Anton Ulrich-Museum in Brunswick is one example; another is the drawing of Federico Zuccaro (Berlin, Staatliche Museen, Kupferstichkabinett), which—as Ballarin has correctly argued—must be a copy of one of the works by Giorgione that Giorgio Vasari saw in the Grimani collection.[13] The style of the drawing of Zuccaro is very close to that of the Milan *Singers* or to Dosso's works, primarily in terms of the figure's pose, which in some ways became a characteristic trait of a good many paintings in this genre. The head is thrust backward and turned toward the side (like Dosso's *Dido*); the mouth is half-open so that the teeth can be glimpsed. Finally, the *Old Woman* in the Gallerie dell'Accademia in Venice strikes me as being one of the works most incontrovertibly by Giorgione that can serve to document his final phase. The psychological climate of his work has changed completely: a kind of violence has supplanted the inner meditation that characterizes works that we know today to be in Giorgione's hand. I think, as does Ballarin, that the vision of Giorgione's style that the *Tempest* (Venice, Gallerie dell'Accademia) or the *Three Philosophers* (Vienna, Kunsthistorisches Museum) offers us cannot stand for his full oeuvre. A profound evolution must have taken place in the very last years of his life. It is from Giorgione's late phase that many of Dosso's, Girolamo Romanino's, and Giovanni Cariani's respective works take their inspiration. One example is Cariani's *Concert* (today in a private collection in Lugano), a work that Rodolfo Pallucchini and Francesco Rossi have dated as belonging to the period between 1518 and 1520.[14] The seventeenth century's vision of Giorgione was not, then, completely false, and it did not depend solely upon Pietro della Vecchia's pastiches.

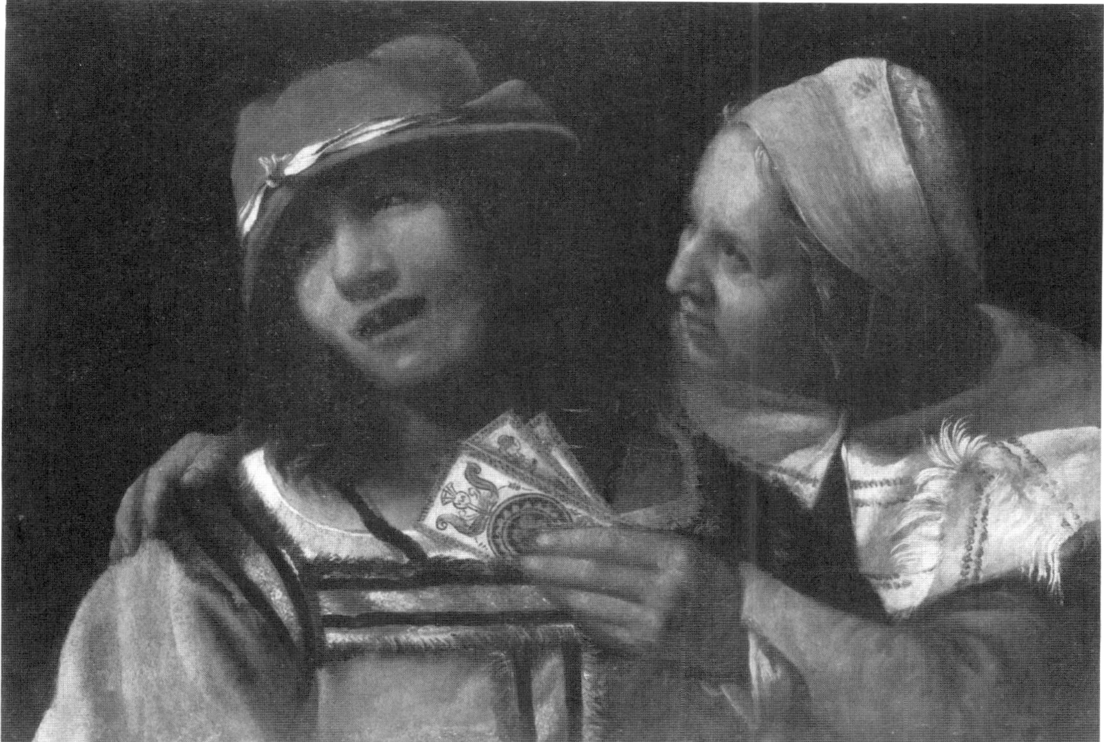

Fig. 4. Giuseppe Caletti
Good Fortune
Naples, Museo e Gallerie Nazionali di Capodimonte
Here attributed to an anonymous Giorgionesque painter

I would like to turn now to a work (fig. 4) that raises as many questions as the majority of those discussed above, but that also allows us to develop a new evaluation of the mature Giorgione's influence and of the context in which Dosso's genre scenes were executed. The painting's provenance is, moreover, an exciting one, for it once belonged to the collection of Fulvio Orsini; it was described in 1600 as "*due teste d'una vecchia et un giovine di mano del giorgione*" (two heads, by Giorgione, of an old woman and a young man). The painting reappeared later, together with many other works from the Orsini collection, in the 1644 inventory of the Palazzo Farnese. Here it had a more precise description—"*un quadro in tela con cornice di noce, dentro è depinto il ritratto d'una Donna di tempo che fa carezze ad un giovane*" (a painting on canvas with a walnut frame: in the painting there is a portrait of an old woman caressing a young man)—but no attribution.[15]

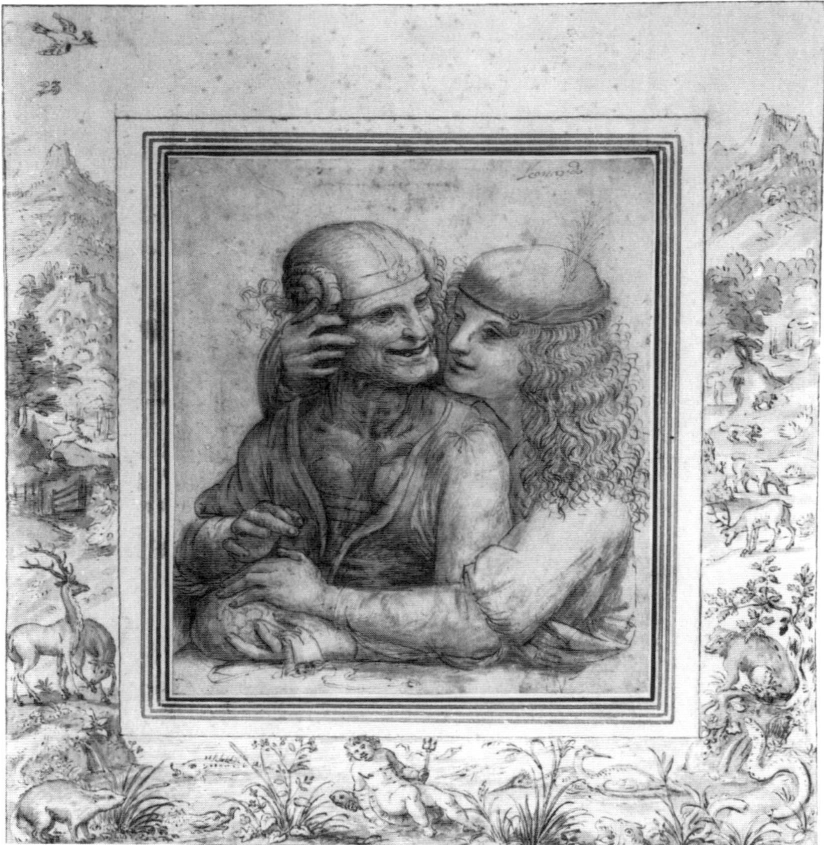

Fig. 5. Jacob Hoefnagel (after Leonardo da Vinci)
Old Woman with Young Man
Vienna, Graphische Sammlung Albertina

Orsini's view of Giorgione at the end of the sixteenth century was the view that would become standard in the century following. Orsini had, it seems, a passion for this painter, for he recommended that Cardinal Alessandro Farnese purchase a *Christ Bearing the Cross,* which Orsini attributed to Giorgione and which perhaps was a copy of the painting with the same title in the church of San Rocco.[16] The attribution of the Capodimonte painting to Giorgione is evidently absurd: the work instead recalls Pietro della Vecchia's pastiches. The authors of the recent catalog of the Museo e Gallerie Nazionali di Capodimonte must have thought the same thing, for they have attributed *Good Fortune* to Giuseppe Caletti, another imitator (and perhaps forger) of Giorgione and Dosso.[17] The presence of this work in the Orsini collection naturally excludes such a hypothesis, since Caletti was only two years old in 1600.

The *Good Fortune* certainly seems to have been repainted quite a bit, and it is currently in poor condition despite a recent cleaning. The old woman's face is especially crude, and her eyelids are emphasized by a red line. The young man's face, although of better quality, has components that are less satisfactory, such as the chin and the mouth, which also seem to have suffered deterioration. Nevertheless, the reflected light on the young man's clothing and the fringes of the old woman's shirt are reminiscent of Dosso's flamboyant palette, as well as of the *Concert,* now in a private collection in Milan. Could this be an imitation dating from the end of the sixteenth century? We have no examples of forgeries of Giorgione's works in this period, although we cannot exclude the possibility that it could be the work of a very late imitator like Niccolò Frangipane.[18] If this is not the case, the painting must date from the early decades of the sixteenth century. This is what the costumes worn by the figures in the painting would indicate, since the red hat and shirt collar without lace are found only in works dating from the late 1510s or the 1520s. On the other hand, the style of the work is likewise reminiscent of the *Pastoral Concert* (Paris, Musée du Louvre) or the *Portrait of a Young Man* (New York, Frick Collection), despite its weaknesses, which are perhaps due to considerable repainting. We are quite far from the quality of these masterpieces in the case at hand. If, however, this work does indeed date from this period, it bears eloquent witness to the consequences brought on by Giorgione's late style.

Good Fortune would represent, in effect, one of the first appearances of a theme that would later become widely popular, namely, the fortune-teller. The woman in the painting is presenting three cards to the young man, in which he must read his destiny. Unfortunately we see only the backs of the cards and can neither say what they predict nor define exactly the young man's reaction. All the same, however, this work goes beyond the Concerts and other genre paintings by Giorgione and his circle. A real narrative—a comedy-like scene—is working in the picture. If the character types that appear in this work are less broadly drawn than those in the Milan *Concert,* the dramatic relationship between the figures is more marked. The contrast between the old woman and the young man is part of a well-established literary and figurative tradition that is most notable in works from northern Europe.[19] Leonardo da Vinci himself took up this theme in a drawing, of which we have a copy by Jacob Hoefnagel (fig. 5) and an engraving by Wenzel Hollar, and explained its attraction in his *Trattato della pittura,* in which he recommended that contrasting figures be placed side by side, such as an ugly figure next to a lovely one, a young one next to a old one, and so on.[20] It is precisely its narrative content that constitutes the most original aspect of this work: this fortune-teller, if indeed *Good Fortune* belongs to the beginning of the sixteenth century, was evidently at the origin of a significant tradition, and it illuminates Zuccaro's famous statement about Caravaggio's art: "What is all the fuss about? I do not see anything here other than the thought of Giorgione."[21] Its presence in the Orsini collection could, moreover, lead us to wonder if Caravaggio himself did not know it and if it was not one of his sources of inspiration.

Comic Painting

In these works are to be found the first elements of what might be called comic painting. The expression of the passions is strongly accented. Behind this development is, quite naturally, all the influence that Leonardo's studies of physiognomy must have had. The Italians and the Flemish were fascinated by these studies. The Milan *Concert* has been studied in comparison to Leonardo's famous drawing in the Royal Collection at Windsor Castle, the group of *Five Grotesque Heads*. Here are already to be found nearly all the elements of the new genre, and the group is already treated as half-length figures. It was widely known, and it was imitated very early on by Quinten Massys, another important innovator in the history of the genre scene with half-length figures. He was inspired by Leonardo's drawing to paint the heads of some of the executioners in the *Martyrdom of Saint John* in the altarpiece now in the Koninklijk Museum in Antwerp (dated between 1508 and 1511).[22] Imitations of the figure in the background, who opens his mouth wide and throws his head back, are to be found in several anonymous paintings that were undoubtedly executed in Lombardy in the sixteenth century. These paintings are also inscribed in the tradition of the comic painting.[23] It is therefore not at all improbable that Giorgione and his circle might also have known the Windsor drawing.

On the other hand, the composition with half-length figures derives from an evolutionary process that affected religious painting over the course of the entire fifteenth century and in which Venice played a leading role. Mantegna and Giovanni Bellini were among the first creators of religious scenes with half-length figures.[24] This type of visual organization was clearly conceived as a means of drawing spectators into the painted scene and allowing them to experience the emotions expressed by the figures. In Venice, as in Flanders, this new format was therefore incorporated into all experimentation in the expression of the passions. Leonardo's ideas must have been very influential from this point of view as well, as is shown especially by the *Christ Bearing the Cross* by Giorgione (or Titian) in the church of San Rocco (or the *Christ among the Doctors* that Albrecht Dürer perhaps painted in Venice).[25] The San Rocco work, like Dürer's, displays the desire to accentuate the dramatic character of the scene while setting Christ's suffering beauty in violent contrast to the ugliness of his executioners. This contrast is, moreover, reinforced in other versions of the same theme, such as Cariani's *Christ and Saint Veronica,* now in the Pinacoteca Tosio Martinengo in Brescia.[26] Once again, the passage from works such as these to the comic paintings must have been an easy one. The spectator's sympathy for Christ's suffering could thus be transformed into empathy with the emotions expressed by the figures' laughter.

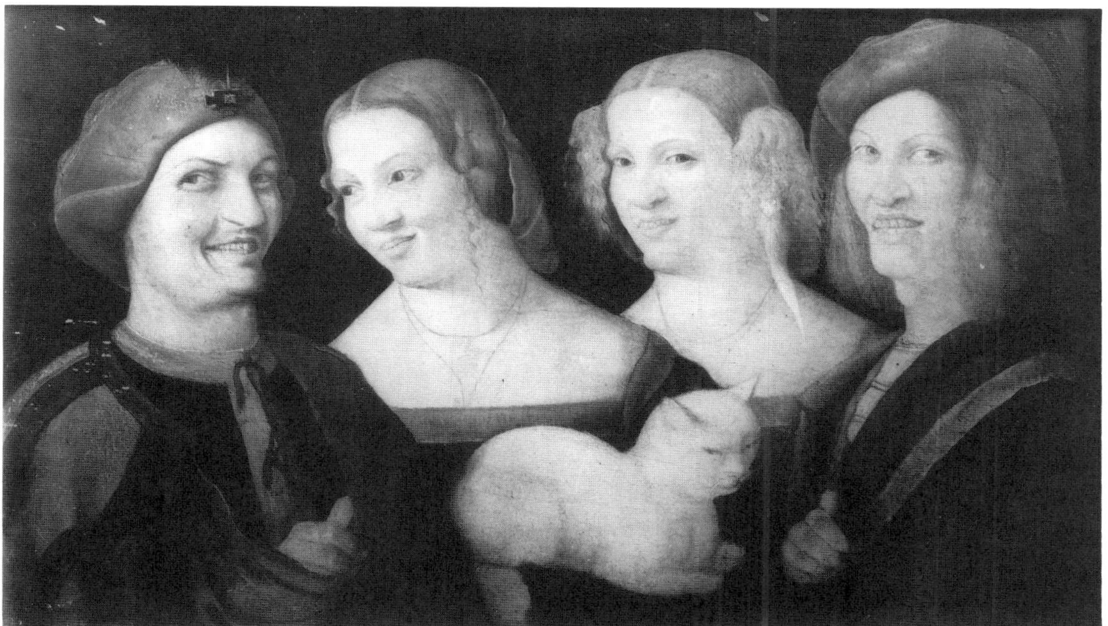

Fig. 6. Niccolò Frangipane
Four Laughing Figures with a Cat
Angers, Musée des Beaux-Arts

At the end of the sixteenth century, Giovanni Paolo Lomazzo consecrated this genre by giving it its first definition when, in his *Trattato dell'arte della pittura, scoltura, et architettura,* he mentioned those paintings that make us laugh: "Among all the parts that we look for in order to compose well a history of happy or comic things, the first and foremost is seeing the cause for which happiness, laughter or cackling occur . . . ; for example, in a love story, joking, teasing, and other games of love, and, in a funny story, certain things that by their nature cause all those watching to laugh."[27] Lomazzo insists, that is to say, on the narrative content. There must be a story because, if there were none, "if one were to see someone having fun and laughing without a motive, that would certainly be insanity worthy of a beating."[28] One of the essential resources of the comic is, precisely, caricature (fig. 6). The comic needs "to show happy faces, turned upward, or to the side, or in another manner, which gaze at each other and laugh, breaking their jaws [with laughter] and showing their teeth in throwing open their mouths indecently in a new and different act of laughter, flaring their nostrils and hiding their eyes in their heads."[29] He too refers to the role played by Leonardo in the creation of the comic painting: Leonardo "took delight in drawing old men and deformed peasant men and women laughing."[30] Bert Meijer also refers in this regard to the chapter that Gabriele Paleotti devotes in his treatise to "ridiculous paintings."[31] Even though he does not offer a true definition of what he means by this term, his reflections—like Lomazzo's—are clear testimony to the fact that this genre was fully consecrated as such by the end of the century.

As Meijer clearly indicates, the genre painting and the comic painting are not to be confused with each other. But, although these works do not all share the same taste for satire, the figures in some of the paintings that have been mentioned here appear to represent actors or clowns. This is clearly the case of Dosso's *Buffoon*. According to Ballarin, this painting must date to the period 1508–1510, and the laughing face it portrays is thus one of the first appearances in Dosso's work of this characteristic trait. In the 1650 inventory of the Villa Borghese collection, the figure in the large tondo in the Camera del Poggiolo is called a "portrait of Gonella."[32] Unfortunately, nothing is known about the overall program for the cycle painted in the apartment in the Via Coperta, and I have not been successful in attempting to discover it. The titles usually given to these rhomboids are purely conventional. From 1530 on, paintings with clowns or "Bergamasque figures" appear in Venetian inventories.[33]

In the case of the painting in the Orsini collection, its relationship with comedy is perhaps even more evident: the theme of the odd couple was frequently employed in the theater of the period and, to remain with the example of Venice, Tommaso Mezzo's *Fabella Epirota* (first published in 1483) tells the story of the love of the old woman Panfila for the youth Clitifon.[34] Let us not forget, finally, that in Pliny's description of what could be called ancient genre painting, he speaks of a certain Calates who painted comic subjects in miniature and of an Antiphilus who painted a ridiculously dressed figure.[35] Eugenio Battisti has pointed out in his study of Renaissance genre painting that there was a "coincidence between the 'comic' and genre painting,"[36] and Jean Adhémar has shown the influence that comic actors and scenes from comedies exercised on the genre painting in France in the sixteenth century.[37]

We know, moreover, that Ferrara and Venice played a central role in the development of Renaissance comedy. The complete works of Plautus and Terence were staged at the court of Ercole I starting in 1486.[38] In Venice, Cherea presented translations of Terence and (above all) Plautus precisely in the 1507–1508 period.[39] So great was his success that the Council of Ten was put out of sorts and published a decree on 29 December 1508 that banned all theatrical performances. At this same time the *momarie* had become extraordinarily popular and appeared at the majority of great patrician feasts and celebrations.[40] Obviously genre paintings did not always represent scenes or characters taken from the comedies, but the polemics during these years between comic authors (in poetry as well as theater) and Pietro Bembo, who was in the process of codifying his linguistic and literary rules, perhaps find their equivalent in the opposition of these first genre paintings to the first great classical works by Titian or Giorgione. In the comedies, dialect was used in a multiplicity of ways, before Bembo's *Prose* vigorously condemned its use. In *Pastoral* (1517–1518), the first of Ruzzante's plays, the Paduan dialect used by peasants is set in opposition to the Tuscan spoken by shepherds, who imitate the arcadian taste of Jacopo Sannazaro or of Bembo's own *Gli Asolani.*[41] This clash escalated in *Betia* (1524–1526), in which whole passages from *Gli Asolani* are parodied and ridiculed and Bembo himself becomes the object of mockery.[42]

In his recent book on Romanino, Alessandro Nova has explored the origins of what he terms the anticlassical and heterodox style of this painter. He notes, in particular, that Romanino's *Resurrection* in Capriolo is a sort of parody of Titian's Averoldi altarpiece.[43] Nova has carefully compared this painter's development to the debates between the humanists concerning the *questione della lingua,* or debate over the vernacular, in Italy. Bembo, he remarks, probably was greatly influential in the artistic milieu, and scholars have long sought to link Giorgione's work to the atmosphere of *Gli Asolani.* However, Nova recognizes (as I have) that dialect literature was extremely vital in Padua during this period.[44] It thus seems to him that Romanino's development might run parallel to the work of Teofilo Folengo, the greatest macaronic poet. According to Nova, both artists sought to call into question the certitudes of the classical canon which, in northern Italy, was incarnated by Bembo and by Titian.[45] While not all of Nova's hypotheses regarding the relationship between Folengo and Romanino need to be taken into account here, the path that he takes is invaluable for understanding the cultural climate in which genre painting appeared. In fact, it may be that genre painting was a sort of reaction against the high classicism that Titian and Giorgione had begun to develop in the early years of the sixteenth century, as well as a figurative equivalent of the satire found in the theater and in dialect poetry.

The notion of genre appears at the same time as does the hierarchical classification of the different subjects to be treated by painters. Aristotle, in the *Poetics,* illustrated the superiority of tragedy to comedy through a comparison between painters like Polygnotus, who painted men as better than they are, and Pauson, who painted them as worse.[46] A few years after Giorgione's death, Aristotle's translator Giovanni Giorgio Trissino took up this idea, replacing Polygnotus and Pauson with contemporary Italian painters: "Vinci imitated the best, Montagna the worst, and Titian as they are."[47] Even if Trissino's examples seem somewhat surprising, they show that the idea of a classification of genres in painting had reappeared in the sixteenth century. Montagna was evidently not chosen here for his talent as a caricaturist or comic painter, like Pauson, but rather because he belonged to the first phase of the Renaissance; his art must have seemed less perfect to Trissino than Titian's or Leonardo's. Still more revealing, however, is the opposition between Titian and Leonardo, which is situated at the origin of the commonplaces in art theory concerning Tuscan idealism and Venetian naturalism. The models supplied by poetics and rhetoric are thus essential for understanding the concepts and practices of amateurs as well as artists.

Although the "rediscovery" of the *Poetics* occurred some decades after Giorgione's death, the birth of a codification of literary language and, in a parallel fashion, the birth of classical painting must have encouraged reflection—and, sometimes, polemics—about comedy and comic painting. It is in this context that the genre painting was able to be reborn after having disappeared during the Middle Ages.[48] Paintings with half-length figures are the most exemplary instance of this development, inasmuch as these works favor comic scenes over mythological and historical subjects, as in the case of the Capodimonte painting. They may also parody fables, as does one of the rhomboids in the Galleria Estense. It is no longer only the form or the style that are opposed to the grand style of classical painting, for a new thematics appears here, one whose echoes are to be found far into the seventeenth century.

This opposition between the two styles must have been clearly visible at the time. Dosso's rhomboids, for instance, were placed in the Via Coperta apartment near the Bacchanals, in which Titian brought his own notion of mythological narrative to its most perfect expression. Although the boundary between the genres was not defined in a precise way (and would it ever be?), several of Dosso's religious paintings, as well as his portraits and even a work such as Romanino's *Salome* (Berlin, Staatliche Museen, Gemäldegalerie), could easily be linked—in terms of their visual organization and the treatment of figures—to the corpus that I have analyzed here. A new path had been discovered, and we should keep in mind that what really defines a genre is its growth over time and the stature of those who contribute, little by little, to its codification.

If Giorgione had not contributed to its origin, however, it is unlikely that this type of painting would have become so widespread. After having established—together with Titian—the foundations of classical painting in Venice, Giorgione explored a completely new direction for painting. Through his participation in the creation of the genre painting, the last phase of his career, he opened up an alternative to classicism for the artists of northern Italy. This was to have immense consequences and was to become one of the most profound sources of inspiration for an entire branch of European painting in the century that followed.

Notes

1. Roberto Longhi, "Quesiti caravaggeschi: I precedenti" (1929), in idem, *"Me pinxit" e quesiti caravaggeschi, 1928–1934* (Florence: Sansoni, 1968), 97–143.

2. Alessandro Ballarin dates these works as belonging to the second decade of the sixteenth century; see Alessandro Ballarin, *Dosso Dossi: La pittura a Ferrara negli anni del Ducato di Alfonso I,* 2 vols. (Cittadella: Bertoncello Artigrafiche, 1994–

1995), 1: 293 (entry no. 328). Felton Gibbons dates the *Nymph and Satyr* and the *Buffoon* as belonging to the 1520s; see Felton Gibbons, *Dosso and Battista Dossi: Court Painters at Ferrara* (Princeton: Princeton Univ. Press, 1968), 175–76 (entry no. 18), 189–90 (entry no. 43).

3. See Ballarin (see note 2), 1: 367 (entry no. 500). The work dates to the years 1536–1540.

4. See Allan Braham and Jill Dunkerton, "Fragments of a Ceiling Decoration by Dosso Dossi," *National Gallery Technical Bulletin* 5 (1981): 27–37.

5. Sixten Ringbom, *Icon to Narrative: The Rise of the Dramatic Close-Up in Fifteenth-Century Devotional Painting*, rev. ed. (Doornspijk, The Netherlands: Davaco, 1984).

6. According to Gibbons (see note 2), 176 (entry no. 19), the painting of *Saint John the Baptist* should be dated to "several years after 1520." According to Ballarin (see note 2), 1: 338–39 (entry no. 432), the painting of *Saint William* dates to around 1524.

7. See Gibbons (see note 2), 205–6 (entry no. 65), who dates *Dido* to the beginning of the 1520s. See also Ballarin (see note 2), 1: 315 (entry no. 378), according to whom the painting dates to circa 1519.

8. See Terisio Pignatti, *Giorgione* (Venice: Alfieri, 1969), 140 (entry no. A 67), concerning this painting, sometimes attributed to Giorgione himself.

9. Roberto Longhi, "Precisioni nelle gallerie italiane. R. Galleria Borghese. Domenico Mancini," cited and translated in *Le siècle de Titien: L'âge d'or de la peinture à Venise*, 2nd ed., exh. cat. (Paris: Editions de la Réunion des Musées Nationaux, 1993), 346 (entry no. 30 by Alessandro Ballarin).

10. Anna Coliva, "La Collezione Borghese: La storia, le opere," in idem, ed., *Galleria Borghese* (Rome: Progetti Museali, 1994), 56–58.

11. Mauro Lucco, "Le siècle de Titien," *Paragone*, nos. 535–537 (1994): 26–47:

> *Senza questo dipinto non sarebbe a mio avviso comprensibile un'opera giovanilissima del Dosso come il "Buffone" nella Galleria Estense di Modena, databile al 1510 circa; e senza quella mano dalla postura sforzata, col pollice all'insù, non si comprenderebbero i cambiamenti del Romanino dalla sua prima maniera di radice lombarda-bramantiniana a quella veneziana* (Without this painting an extremely early work of Dosso's such as the *Buffoon* in the Galleria Estense in Modena, which can be dated to circa 1510, would not—in my opinion—be understandable. And without the forced posture of that hand with its thumb pointed upward it would be impossible to understand Romanino's development from the early style rooted in Lombard and Bramantesque art to the later Venetian style) (37).

12. The work now hangs in the Palazzo Reale in Siena. See Ballarin (see note 2), 2: figs. 425–26.

13. See Alessandro Ballarin, "Une nouvelle perspective sur Giorgione: Les portraits des années 1500–1503," in *Le siècle de Titien* (see note 9), 293–94. It is worth citing here Vasari's description of this work: "*L'altra è una testona maggiore, ritratta di naturale, che tiene in mano una berretta rossa da comandatore, con un bavero di pelle, e sotto uno di que' saioni all'antica: questo si pensa che fusse fatto per un*

generale di eserciti" (The other is a large head, portrayed from life, holding a red commander's hat in hand, with leather lapels, and wearing one of those big old-style habits underneath: this painting is believed to have been made for an army general). In Giorgio Vasari, *Le vite de' più eccellenti pittori, scultori ed architettori,* ed. Gaetano Milanesi, 9 vols. (Florence: Sansoni, 1906), 4: 94.

14. See Rodolfo Pallucchini and Francesco Rossi, *Giovanni Cariani* (Bergamo: Silvana, 1983), 125 (entry no. 46).

15. See Bertrand Jestaz, ed., with Michel Hochmann and Philippe Sénéchal, *L'inventaire du palais et des propriétés Farnèse à Rome en 1644,* vol. 3, pt. 3, of *Le Palais Farnèse* (Rome: Ecole Française de Rome, 1994), 175 (entry no. 4370); and Michel Hochmann, "La collezione di dipinti di Palazzo Farnese a Roma secondo l'inventario del 1644," in Lucia Fornari Schianchi, ed., *I Farnese: Arte e collezionismo: Studi* (Milan: Electa, 1995), 118–19.

16. See, in this regard, Clare Robertson, *Il Gran Cardinale: Alessandro Farnese, Patron of the Arts* (New Haven: Yale Univ. Press, 1992), 147.

17. See Pierluigi Leone de Castris and Mariella Utili, "La Scuola emiliana: I dipinti del XVI e XVII secolo," in Museo e Gallerie Nazionali di Capodimonte, *La Collezione Farnese,* vol. 1, *La Scuola emiliana: I dipinti, I disegni* (Naples: Electa Napoli, 1994), 104. On the activities of Giuseppe Caletti (ca. 1598–ca. 1660) as an imitator of Dosso, Giorgione, and Titian, see Massimo Ferretti, "Falsi e tradizione artistica," in *Storia dell'arte italiana,* 12 vols. (Turin: Einaudi, 1979–1983), 10: 145–56.

18. This painting does not seem, in any case, attributable to Niccolò Frangipane himself. See Bert W. Meijer, "Niccolò Frangipane," *Saggi e memorie di storia dell'arte* 8 (1972): 151–91.

19. See Alison G. Stewart, *Unequal Lovers: A Study of Unequal Couples in Northern Art* (New York: Abaris, 1977).

20. Ibid., 140 (entry nos. 5–6).

21. See Giovanni Baglione, *Le vite de' pittori, scultori et architetti: Dal pontificato di Gregorio XIII del 1572. In fino a tempi di Papa Urbano Ottauo nel 1642* (1642; facs. reprint, Rome: E. Calzone, 1935), 137: "*Che rumore è questo?... Io non ci vedo altro, che il pensiero di Giorgione.*" This is doubtless one of the first times that this theme was treated. There is also a work by Lucas van Leyden, *The Card-Player,* now in the Musée du Louvre; see Elise Lawton Smith, *The Paintings of Lucas van Leyden: A New Appraisal, with Catalogue Raisonné* (Columbia: Univ. of Missouri Press, 1992), 164–66 (entry no. 35). The painting is generally dated 1508. On the tradition that influenced Caravaggio's *Fortune-Teller,* see Jean-Pierre Cuzin, *La diseuse de bonne aventure de Caravage* (Paris: Editions des Musées Nationaux, 1977), 16–34.

22. Larry Silver, *The Paintings of Quinten Massys, with Catalogue Raisonné* (Montclair, N.J.: Allanheld & Schram, 1984), 46, 204–5 (entry no. 11).

23. These works are reproduced in Bert W. Meijer, "Esempi del comico figurativo nel rinascimento lombardo," *Arte lombarda* 16 (1971): 264, figs. 7–8.

24. See Ringbom (see note 5), 104–6.

25. Ringbom (see note 5), 152.

26. See, on this work, Pallucchini and Rossi (see note 14), 117–18 (entry no. 31). According to them, the work ought to date to the 1525–1530 period.

27. Giovanni Paolo Lomazzo, "Compositione delle allegrezze, and risi," in idem, *Trattato dell'arte della pittura, scoltura, et architettura* (Milan: Per Paolo Gottardo Pontio, a instantia di Pietro Tini, 1584), bk. 6, chap. 32, 359–60: "*Frà tutte le parte che si ricercano per ben comporre una historia di cose allegre, & di riso, la principale è che si vegga la causa per cui l'allegrezza, il riso, & lo schiamazzo s'introduce, la quale sarebbe per essempio in una historia d'amore lo scherzare, lo stuccicare, & simili altri vezzi amorosi; & in una historia ridicolosa certe cose atte per sua natura à muovere il riso à chiunque le guarda.*" Bert W. Meijer was the first to analyze this text in his remarkable studies of sixteenth-century genre painting. See Meijer (see note 23), 259–66; Meijer (see note 18); and Bert W. Meijer, "Sull'origine e mutamenti dei generi," in *La pittura in Italia: Il Seicento,* 2 vols. (Milan: Electa, 1988), 2: 585–604.

28. Lomazzo (see note 27), bk. 6, chap. 32, 359: "*se si vedesse alcuno far festa & ridere senza causa, certo che sarebbe una pazzia da bastonate.*"

29. Lomazzo (see note 27), bk. 6, chap. 32, 359: "*facendo vedere quei volti spensierati, rivolti chi all'in sù, & chi per fianco, & altri in altre maniere che di rincontro guardandosi, ridano, & smascellino, mostrando i denti, aprendo sconciamente la bocca in nuovo, & diverso atto di ridere, allargando le narici, & nascondendo gli occhi nel capo.*"

30. Lomazzo (see note 27), bk. 6, chap. 32, 360: "*molto si dilettò di disegnare vecchi, & villani, & villane diformi che ridessero.*"

31. See Gabriele Paleotti, *Discorso intorno alle imagini sacre e profane,* in Paola Barocchi, ed., *Trattati d'arte del Cinquecento, fra manierismo e Controriforma,* 3 vols. (Bari: Laterza, 1960–1962), 2: 390–98.

32. See Ballarin (see note 2), 1: 331 (entry no. 421), 294–95 (entry no. 332), 342–43 (entry no. 440); and Braham and Dunkerton (see note 4). [Translator's note: *Gonnella* is a mask, or stock character, in the *commedia dell'arte*.]

33. See Archivio di Stato di Venezia, Giudici del Proprio, Mobili, reg. 8: fol. 119, inv. of Helisabet Pisani (15 January 1536, n. st.), "*un quadro con do buffoni in tela*" (a painting on canvas with two clowns); fol. 207, inv. of Catherina "relicta Domini Jacobi quondam s. Antonii a Serico" (3 August 1536), "*do quadreti picoli in tella cum do figure bergamasche cum el goffo*" (two small paintings on canvas with two Bergamasque figures with the clown [?]).

34. See Giorgio Padoan, "La commedia rinascimentale a Venezia: Dalla sperimentazione umanistica alla commedia 'regolare,'" in *Storia della cultura veneta,* vol. 3, *Dal primo Quattrocento al concilio di Trento,* ed. Girolamo Arnaldi and Manlio Pastore Stocchi, 3 vols. (Vicenza: Neri Pozza, 1981), 3: 387.

35. Pliny, *Natural History,* trans. H. Rackham (Cambridge: Harvard Univ. Press, 1952), 35.37.112, 114:

> *Namque subtexi par est minoris picturae celebres in penicillo.... [P]arva et Callicles fecit, item Calates comicis tabellis, utraque Antiphilus.... [I]dem iocoso nomine Gryllum deridiculi habitus pinxit, unde id genus picturae grylli vocantur* (For it is proper to append the artists famous with the brush in a minor style of painting.... Callicles also made small pictures, and so did Calates of subjects taken

from comedy; both classes were painted by Antiphilus.... He also painted a figure in an absurd costume known by the joking name of Gryllus, the name consequently applied to every picture of that sort).

36. Eugenio Battisti, *L'antirinascimento* (Milan: Feltrinelli, 1962), 288–89:

Soprattutto il sospetto di una coincidenza, notevolmente precisa e puntuale, fra "comico" e pittura di genere, si ha seguendo, da un lato, la storia della fortuna critica della commedia e della rappresentazione; e dell'altro, il contemporaneo penetrare nell'arte sacra di episodi, parerga, tipi a caratteri, tolti dalla vita reale.... Naturalmente, con ciò non intendiamo affatto sostenere che la tematica sia la stessa, cosicché la pittura non sarebbe che una illustrazione o documentazione di commedie. Tutt'altro. Però esistono singolari coincidenze, non tanto di carattere, quanto di situazione storica, che val la pena di sottolineare (If we follow, on the one hand, the history of the critical fortune of the comedy and of representation, and, on the other, the contemporaneous penetration of sacred art by episodes, parerga, types, and characters taken from real life, we begin especially to suspect the existence of a remarkably precise and timely coincidence between the "comic" and genre painting.... Naturally, we do not mean to claim that the thematics are the same, just as the paintings are not illustrations or documents taken from the comedies. Quite the opposite. There are, however, some striking coincidences, not so much in terms of character as of historical situation, which are worth emphasizing).

37. Jean Adhémar, "French Sixteenth Century Genre Painting," *Journal of the Warburg and Courtauld Institutes* 8 (1945): 191–95.

38. See Alessandro d'Ancona's classic study, *Origini del teatro italiano,* 2nd ed., 2 vols. (Turin: Ermanno Loescher, 1891), 2: 349–53: *"Se i primi accenni alla restaurazione del teatro antico si videro fra noi in Roma a' tempi di Paulo II e di Sisto IV... egli è pure bene assodato che la città ove esso veramente rinacque dalle sue ceneri fu Ferrara"* (If the first hints of a revival of ancient theater were to be found in Paul II's and Sixtus IV's Rome..., it is also well established that the city in which the theater was truly reborn from its ashes was Ferrara) (349). This work contains a number of descriptions of plays put on in Ferrara at the beginning of the sixteenth century.

39. Padoan (see note 34), 393.

40. [Translator's note: *Momarie* were complex masked entertainments staged in Venice from the fifteenth century on. A hybrid of Venetian masked revelries and French and Burgundian masked court balls (*mommeries;* or, in England, *mummings*), they were performed at the weddings and banquets of patricians and important citizens or as carnival parades. They could include court dances, mock battles, allegories, triumphs, or other events, and these often represented mythological or pastoral tales. See Raimondo Guarino, *Teatro e mutamenti: Rinascimento e spettacolo a Venezia* (Bologna: Il Mulino, 1995), 86–146.]

41. Giorgio Padoan, "Angelo Beolco, detto il Ruzante," in *Storia della cultura veneta,* vol. 3 (see note 34), 3: 345.

42. Ibid., 353–54.

43. Alessandro Nova, *Girolamo Romanino* (Turin: Umberto Allemandi, 1994), 36–37.

44. Ibid., 41.

45. Nova (see note 43), 47:

> *é infatti probabile che nei loro esperimenti eterodossi Folengo e Romanino abbiano condiviso lo stesso obiettivo intellettuale, nella misura in cui ambedue cercarono di screditare o quanto meno di mettere in dubbio le certezze del canone classicista incarnato, nell'Italia settentionale, dal Bembo e da Tiziano* (it is in fact likely that Folengo and Romanino, in their heterodox experiments, shared the same intellectual aim, inasmuch as both sought to discredit or at least place in doubt the certainties of the classicist canon incarnated by Bembo and Titian in northern Italy).

46. Aristotle, *Poetics,* trans. W. Hamilton Fyfe (Cambridge: Harvard Univ. Press, 1932), 1448a (II.3):

> Since living persons [*lit.* men doing or experiencing something] are the objects of representation, these must necessarily be either good men or inferior—thus only are characters normally distinguished, since ethical differences depend upon vice and virtue—that is to say, either better than ourselves or worse or much what we are. It is the same with painters. Polygnotus depicted men as better than they are and Pauson worse, while Dionysius made likenesses.... It is just in this respect that tragedy differs from comedy. The latter sets out to represent people as worse than they are today, the former as better. [Translator's note: I have modified slightly Fyfe's translation.]

47. Giovan Giorgio Trissino, *Le sei divisioni della poetica: Quinta divisione,* in *Tutte le opere di Giovan Giorgio Trissino,* ed. S. Maffei, 2 vols. in 1 (Verona: Presso Jacapo Vallarsi, 1729), 2: 94:

> *Essendo adunque tutti gli uomini per vizi o per virtù tra sé ne li loro costumi differenti, è necessaria cosa farli overo migliori, overo come sono quelli della nostra età, overo peggiori, come fanno alcuni pittori, de li quali il Vinci imitava i migliori, il Montagna i peggiori, e Tiziano gli fa simili.... In questa differenza ancora vedeon essere la Commedia con la Tragedia, che l'una vuole imitare i peggiori, e l'altra i migliori* (Since all men are different from each other in their customs, either through virtue or vice, it is necessary to make them either better than, or similar to, or worse than the men of our own time, as some painters do; Vinci imitated the best, Montagna the worst, and Titian as they are.... In this difference can be seen the difference between Comedy and Tragedy, because the former wants to imitate the worst men, and the latter the best).

48. On the reasons for the disappearance of genre painting in the Middle Ages, see Francesco Abbate, "Generi artistici," in Giovanni Previtali, ed., *Enciclopedia Feltrinelli—Arte* (Milan: Feltrinelli, 1971), 2.1: 188. Abbate also observes that this notion began to reappear in Alberti. See Leon Battista Alberti, *L'architettura (De re aedificatoria),* ed. Giovanni Orlandi and Paolo Portoghesi, 2 vols. (Milan: Edizioni il

Polifilo, 1966), bk. 9, chap. 4, 2: 804; idem, *On the Art of Building in Ten Books*, trans. Joseph Rykwert, Neil Leach, and Robert Tavernor (Cambridge: MIT Press, 1988), bk. 9, chap. 4, 299:

> *Ora, poiché la pittura, come la poesia, può trattare diversi argomenti: le gesta memorabili dei grandi monarchi, i costumi dei semplici cittadini, la vita dei contadini; il primo di questi tre generi, quello di maggior prestigio, si userà negli edifici pubblici e nelle case dei personaggi più ragguardevoli; il secondo si applicherà come ornamento alle pareti delle case private; l'ultimo meglio degli altri si attaglierà ai giardini, per essere di tutti il più piacevole* (Since painting, like poetry, can deal with various matters—some depict the memorable deeds of great princes, others the manners of private citizens, and still others the life of the simple farmer—those first, which are the most majestic, will be appropriate for public works and for the buildings of the most eminent individuals; the second should adorn the walls of private citizens; and the last will be particularly suitable for gardens, being the most lighthearted of them all).

Dosso as a Storyteller: Reflections on His Mythological Paintings

Luisa Ciammitti

Dosso never saw, as we see it today, the painting known as the *Mythological Scene* that was once in the Northampton collection and is now in the J. Paul Getty Museum. The present composition does not in fact correspond to the painter's final conception of the work. Rather, it is the result of an unfortunate restoration that, around 1850, brought back into view the cloaked woman on the left (fig. 1). X-ray photography reveals that this female figure, which was perhaps conceived by Dosso for a theme in which music was to play a central role, originally played a viola da gamba; she held a bow in her right hand and directed her inspired gaze toward her left hand, which held the instrument and fingered the strings (fig. 2). On the tree behind her hung some objects that are now difficult to identify.[1] On her right, the small figure of a man, who perhaps held a musical instrument, moved off through the landscape with a woman whose dress seems decorated with a long train. Dosso probably never even finished the viola da gamba, whose size seems incompatible not only with the sleeping nude but also with the old woman, who would have been too close to the instrument.[2]

As can be seen in X-ray photographs of other paintings by Dosso, the painter often changed his mind in the course of his work. On the basis of the recent restoration of the painting, it is possible to define two successive phases in Dosso's work on the *Mythological Scene*. First, after having painted the woman with the viola da gamba, Dosso replaced her with a field at the edge of a lake and, perhaps at the same time, eliminated the figures in the landscape and the objects hung on the tree. Second, he then painted the old woman and the nude sleeping on a bed of flowers near some books of music, and he also added the figure of Pan; last of all, he added the amphora on the grass.[3]

All the details in the painting were subjected to modification and revision by Dosso, including the position of the old woman's head and hands, a laurel wreath that was added to and then removed from the nude's hair, and the position of the syrinx in Pan's hands. Moreover, Dosso reworked the trees more than once, altering their nature and tangling their branches together. What at first seems to have been a laurel tree, or in any case a tree with long, pointed leaves, displayed at one point small flowers that looked like orange flowers or lemon flowers; it was subsequently transformed into a citron tree intertwined with an apple tree. Finally, the putti—whose figures were originally fully painted—were covered partially by clouds.

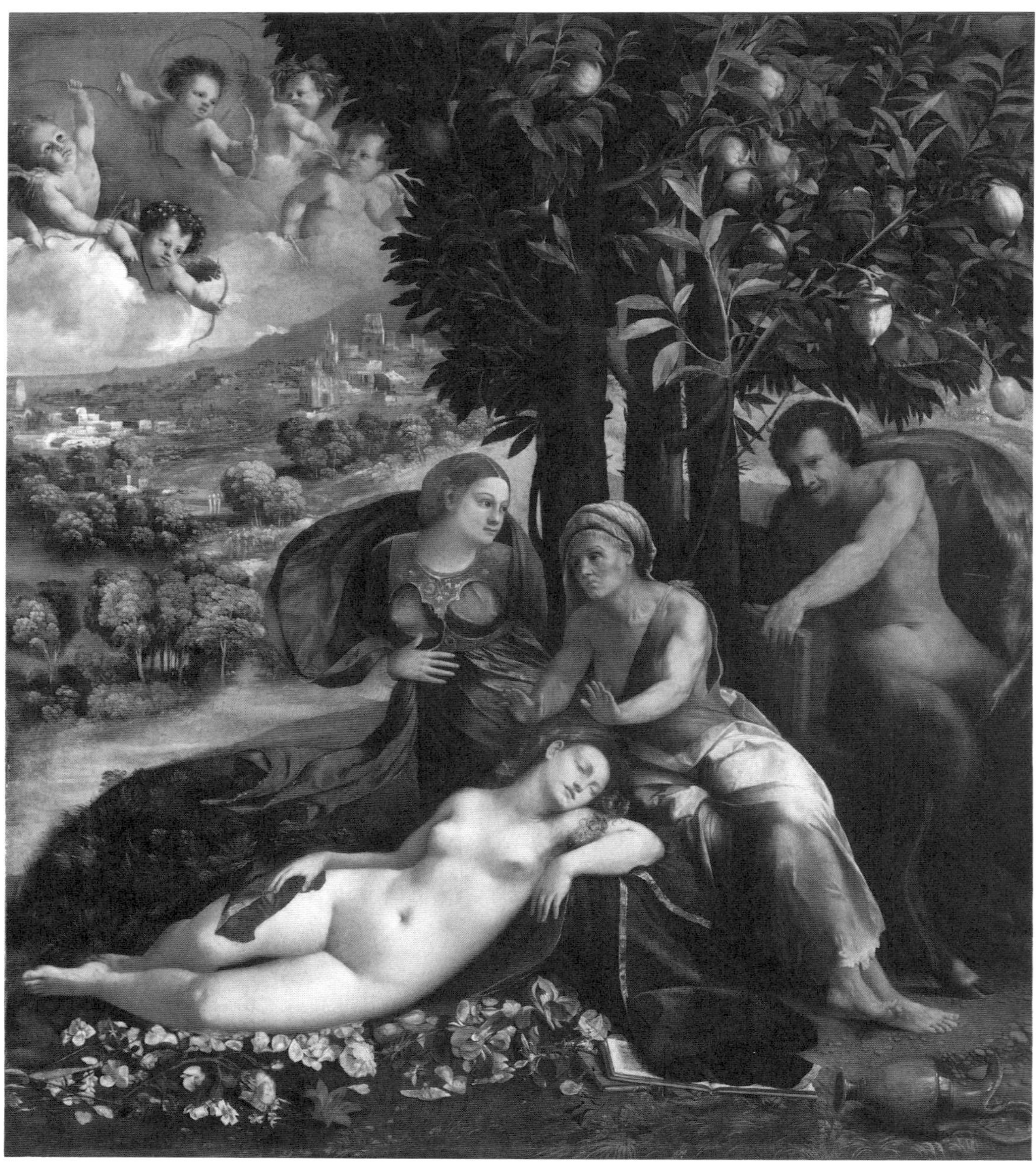

Fig. 1. Dosso Dossi
Mythological Scene
Los Angeles, The J. Paul Getty Museum

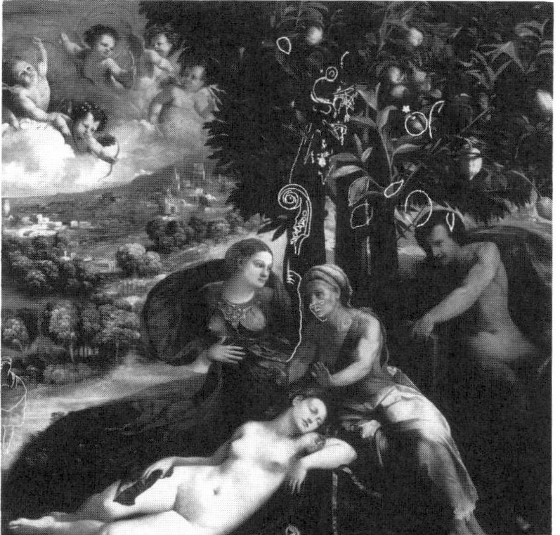

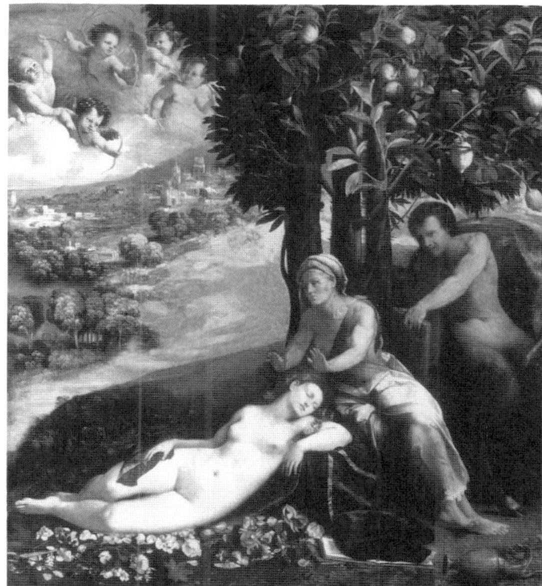

Fig. 2. Dosso Dossi
Mythological Scene (computer reconstruction with changes evident in X-ray marked in white)
Los Angeles, The J. Paul Getty Museum, Paintings Conservation Department

Fig. 3. Dosso Dossi
Mythological Scene (computer reconstruction with cloaked woman removed and background reconstructed)
Los Angeles, The J. Paul Getty Museum, Paintings Conservation Department

The composition that Dosso submitted to his patron was, then, totally different and much more harmonious than the one we see today. It was organized in terms of two triangular wedges, one of which contained the figures and the other of which contained the landscape (fig. 3).[4] In the lower right-hand section the three figures were stretched out along a slightly arching diagonal line indicated by the gestures of Pan's hands and those of the old woman and in the elongated body of the sleeping nude. In the other half of the painting, the light in the expanse of landscape counterbalanced the colored mass of the figures.

Two sorts of interpretations of the painting that we see today have heretofore been offered by scholars. Some have sought to justify the presence of the woman on the left, but without knowing that she originally held a viola da gamba that had been painted over; others have chosen to ignore her altogether. Some have seen her as Artemis coming to the aid of Echo or as Lyda, one of the nymphs loved by Pan. Some have even seen her as Pandora, the bringer of evil into the world: Evil is personified by the lecherous Pan, who threatens Innocence, lying naked and asleep; the old woman raises her hands in an attempt to protect Innocence.[5] In general, scholars have focused almost exclusively on the old woman and the sleeping nude. But all interpretations that include the woman on the left are necessarily wrong, since she is the result of a mistaken nineteenth-century restoration.

The enigmatic figure of the old woman in front of a tree heavy with fruit has attracted comparisons with the myths of Vertumnus and Pomona or Jupiter and Antiope. The former involves Pan only marginally as one of Pomona's many suitors (and she is not asleep in the myth); in the latter Pan does not appear at all. Felton Gibbons has rightly noted that Pan is the only character in the painting who can be identified with certainty, thanks to his syrinx. Because of this, and because of the explicit allusions to music, Gibbons interprets the painting's subject as the satyr's unhappy love for Echo; here the passion for music that might have united them instead tragically separated them. According to this interpretation, the old woman would be Mother Earth trying to protect the nymph from Love's arrows.[6]

Gibbons also briefly considered alternative hypotheses and wondered if the bed of flowers on which the nude young woman lies sleeping, together with the fruit trees behind her, might not allude to a similar episode involving the nymph Nicaia told by Nonnus of Panopolis in his *Dionysiaca,* which presumably dates from the fifth century.[7] Gibbons rejected this possibility on the grounds that it merely contains the generic ornaments of an amorous encounter. I wish here to propose anew the myth of Nicaia as the subject of the painting, because one can show that the bed of flowers and the fruit trees, apart from their undeniably decorative appearance, are such conspicuous elements in the general economy of this painting that their role in relation to the content of the tale must be a significant one. I maintain that in recognizing its subject as the myth of Nicaia one can provide a more exhaustive explanation of every element in the painting than Gibbons was able to offer.

In the course of this essay, I will concentrate exclusively on the final three-figure composition that Dosso submitted to his patrons. In this way I will attempt to generate a new interpretation of the subject of the work, namely an old woman with one breast bared who gestures with her hands, a young woman asleep on a bed of flowers, and, last of all, Pan with his pipes. Although this scene is recondite, there is a way to explain all its elements. Putti, fruit trees, an overturned amphora, musical notes, a river, a city in the background—all of these features play important roles in this painting, which has thus far frustrated every attempt at interpretation.

> If the words which a writer uses have in them a little, I will not say difficulty, but subtlety that is hidden, and thus are not so familiar as the words that are commonly used in speaking, they do give a certain greater authority to the writing and cause the reader to proceed with more restraint and concentration, to reflect more, and to enjoy the talent and doctrine of the writer; and, by judiciously exerting himself a little, he tastes that pleasure which is had when we achieve difficult things.

Thus did Baldassare Castiglione, in his *Il libro del cortegiano,* emphasize the special complicity that binds together and extols the skillful writer and the refined reader and that distinguishes them from commoners. In fact, he added that "if the ignorance of the one who reads is so great that he cannot overcome these difficulties, that is no fault of the writer."[8] In endorsing the writer's "subtlety that is hidden" for the benefit of those who truly know how to read, Castiglione made a point that was equally of concern to those patrons who, in wishing to commission a painting with a rare and erudite subject, either sought or had others seek the subject in rare texts.[9]

The myth of Nicaia is extremely rare: only Nonnus was to recount it, drawing on a text by Memnon of Heraclea, who had dealt with it briefly.[10] In his *Dionysiaca,* Nonnus devoted nearly two cantos to the myth, namely the fifteenth and sixteenth cantos (the fourteenth, devoted to the triumph of Dionysus over the Indians, is a preparation to the episode of Nicaia).

A proposal to connect the myth of Nicaia to the central scene of Lorenzo Costa's *Myth of Comus* was advanced on the occasion of the outstanding exhibition of 1975 at the Musée du Louvre concerning Isabella d'Este's *studiolo* (whose curator was Sylvie Béguin). In this painting a young woman is asleep in Dionysus's arms, the latter figure being clearly identifiable by the grape leaves encircling his brow and his little horns (fig. 4). This hypothesis was later developed by John Schloder, but in both cases Costa's familiarity with the *Dionysiaca* was simply taken for granted.[11] The *Dionysiaca,* however, was published only in 1569 and, during the 1510–1515 period to which Costa's painting belongs, its circulation was confined to a single manuscript.[12] Its history is worth recounting briefly.

The manuscript tradition of the *Dionysiaca* is composed of two branches, one of which mentions the author's name and the other of which omits it.

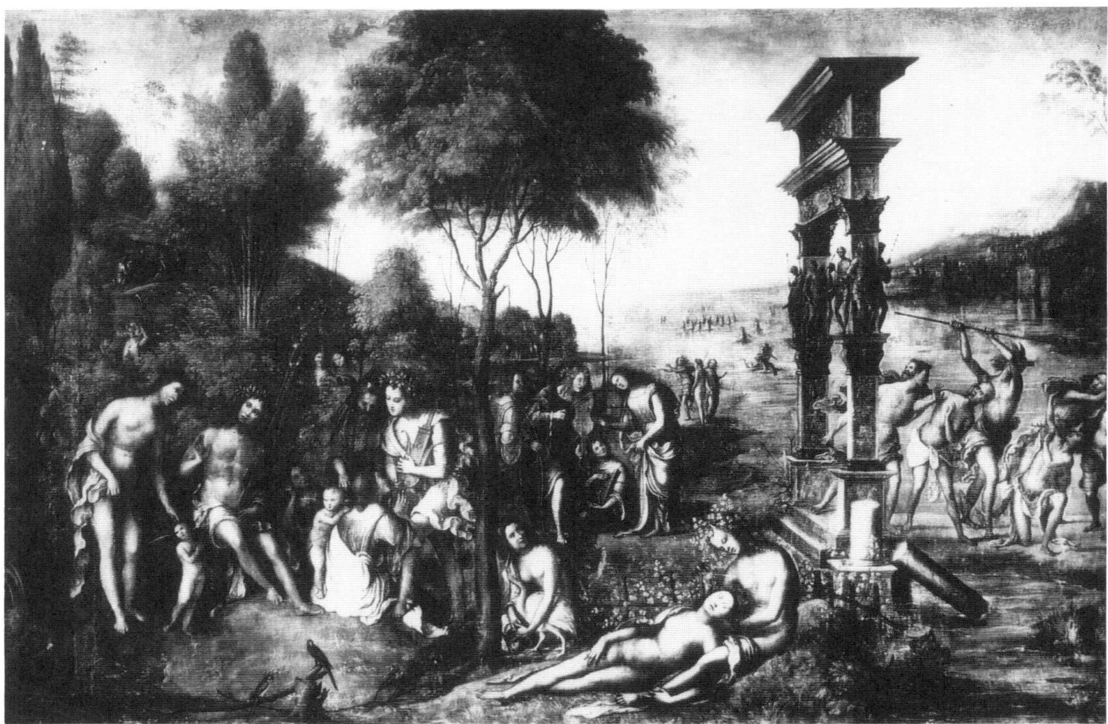

Fig. 4. Lorenzo Costa
Myth of Comus
Paris, Musée du Louvre

This first group is today represented only by the "Papirus Berolinensis 10567," which probably dates from the seventh century and is composed of only five fragmentary leaves, as well as by the "Vaticanus Latinus 5250" codex, in which there appear *excerpta* of notes taken by Ciriaco D'Ancona from a (now lost) manuscript that he read in the Lavra monastery on Mount Athos. All the other manuscripts belong to the "anonymous" tradition that begins with the manuscript "Mediceo-Laurentianus XXXII, 16," which is today in the holdings of the Biblioteca Laurenziana in Florence. Transcriptions began appearing only in the sixteenth century.[13]

The manuscript in the Biblioteca Laurenziana is a paper codex, dated 1280, that contains a miscellany of texts. In an owner's note, Francesco Filelfo states that he bought it in Constantinople in 1423 from his own mother-in-law, the wife of Giovanni Crisolora.[14] The codex ended up in Lorenzo de' Medici's library after Filelfo's death. Angelo Poliziano studied it there and, through one of his typical insights, was able to identify the author as Nonnus of Panopolis on the basis of a reference by the sixth-century Byzantine historian Agathias of Myrina. His attribution of the *Dionysiaca* to Nonnus appeared in the *Miscellanea Prima* of 1489, and in 1508–1510, Fabio Vigili, in his inventory of Greek manuscripts in Italy, was able to list the *Dionysiaca* as a work by Nonnus. In the meantime the codex had been taken to Rome by Cardinal Giovanni de' Medici, the future Pope Leo X.[15]

In those same years, the Greek Janus Lascaris pressed Aldus Manutius to devote himself to the printing of unpublished Greek texts.[16] The Venetian printer accepted enthusiastically the project of publishing the *Dionysiaca* and spoke of it as an imminent project in his dedicatory letter to the *Rhetores graeci,* addressed to Lascaris himself, dated November 1508.[17] By April 1507 some twenty cantos of the *Dionysiaca* had been transcribed, as we learn in a letter from Scipione Forteguerri (nicknamed Carteromachus) to Aldus Manutius. In the letter Forteguerri explained that after stopping in Bologna with his friend Piero Candido, who was an erudite humanist Camaldolese friar, he traveled with him to Rome. Forteguerri added, "Even our Don Piero has become a courtier and lives in Rome and has brought Nonnus with him and writes steadily and has already written twenty books."[18] In March 1508 the transcription was clearly complete: Forteguerri complained that he had not been able to check for any eventual "mistakes... in several passages." He noted that the only revision permitted by Candido was to check "the sum of the books, and they are all there," and he also remarked on the "way in which he kept the same number of lines that were in the original."[19]

The start of the war with Venice in December 1508, following the formation of the League of Cambrai, evidently interrupted the publishing of the work. Lascaris nonetheless traveled to the court of Mantua in February 1509, leading us to suppose that he may have had something to do with the insertion of the myth of Nicaia into the already complicated project of the *Myth of Comus* for Isabella. It should be recalled here that Janus Lascaris's family, which came from the Rhyndacus region (where Nonnus sets the episode in which the nymph is seduced by Dionysus), had set four of its members as emperors on the throne of Nicaia.[20]

It is more difficult to determine who might have suggested this theme to Dosso toward the end of the 1520s.[21] In this same period, Lascaris is known to have revised a Greek text belonging to Isabella d'Este which Federico Gonzaga had recommended to Giulio Romano for the frescoes in the Sala di Troia in the Palazzo Te, namely the commentaries on the *Iliad* written by Eustathius, the archbishop of Thessalonica, in the twelfth century.[22] It would certainly be of great help to know the provenance of the Getty painting, but unfortunately there is not the slightest clue. If Dosso's patrons were from the Ferrara area, it would be conceivable to think that Alfonso I, having finally abandoned his plans to have Raphael paint a depiction of Bacchus's triumph in India, fell back on the next episode in Nonnus's poem, namely the defeat of Nicaia.[23] Even the duke's reiterated requests to Raphael between 1513 and 1517 for a rendering of Bacchus's triumph in India could perhaps be explained by the interest in the *Dionysiaca* and the presence in Rome, in those same years, of the Biblioteca Laurenziana codex. As is well known, Raphael abandoned the project when he learned that the drawing that he had sent to the duke had been executed by Pellegrino da San Daniele.[24]

The nymph Nicaia was a follower of Artemis and, as such, was sworn to virginity. In a fit of rage, she killed the shepherd Hymnos who had fallen in love with her and followed her wherever she went.[25] Eros was angered by the violence of this gesture and decided to revenge himself upon the nymph. He thus arranged for Dionysus to fall in love with her. The god started his lengthy pursuit of the nymph almost immediately after his triumph over the Indians, whom he had conquered by transforming the transparent waters of the river into sweet wine. Dionysus sought in vain to convince Nicaia to marry him. He implored this lovely being, with her delicate cheeks like rose petals, to marry him as he followed her through the forest, saying several times that she had stolen her beauty from the flowers, in particular the rose, the anemone, the lily, and the iris. He invited her to lay down beside him on a bed of roses and hyacinths, but she continued to flee from him and to despise his entreaties. Only if he succeeded in marrying Artemis or Athena, she told him, could he have her as well. Finally she warned him not to lay a hand on her arrows or her bow, or she would see to it that he met the same fate as the shepherd Hymnos: she would wound the untouchable Dionysus.

Suddenly, the old woman Melía—daughter of Oceanus, born from the drops of blood from the castrated Uranus—began to mock Dionysus from an ancient ash tree, contrasting his stupid pleading with the nymph to the ingenious stratagems of his father Jupiter, who always knew how to overcome the resistance of the young girls with whom he fell in love. Having said this, Melía disappeared once again into the ash tree. Thirsty from the long chase, Nicaia stopped at a spring to drink. When she lifted her head, her eyes saw double from fatigue and she fell fast asleep. Out of compassion for Hymnos, Eros showed Dionysus where she lay, while Nemesis laughed at the scene. Noiselessly, the god—who had changed the water into wine—tiptoed toward her and then away again, possessing her without having been seen or heard. To please Dionysus, the Earth released a sweet scent of vines and grape leaves.

In the forest, the notes of the wedding song rang out. Hymnos's voice in the wind sarcastically compared the eternal sleep into which Nicaia had plunged him with the sleep that had led to the loss of her virginity. Pan himself, the lord of music, played the wedding song on his pipes, while he hid his envy in the depths of his heart and lamented the nymph's forced union with the god. One of the satyrs, gone mad with love, began to tease him, suggesting that he give up his flocks and become a gardener instead, so that he might plant a vineyard that would finally gain him a marriage of love. With a sigh, Pan recalled his loves that had fled and thought of Syrinx, who, weeping an unrequested melody, had just accompanied the forced union of nymph and god. With bitterness, he then expressed his envy of Dionysus, who always used wine as a trick when he was in trouble, for wine was an aid in love and helped to bring about marriages.

The unhappy nymph awoke to the sound of the Hymenaea, and, after giving birth to her daughter Telete, she committed suicide by hanging herself. Telete was consecrated at her father's orgiastic festivals. In order to celebrate this triumph and his triumph over the Indians whom he had conquered with the same trick, Dionysus built a city called Nicaia on the shores of the lake.

In the *Myth of Comus,* Lorenzo Costa chose a very specific detail from Nonnus's text to represent the culminating moment of the tale. The drunken young woman lies near a pergola, on which vines and grape leaves grow: Earth (as was mentioned above) had filled the air with their fragrance in order to please Dionysus at the moment of his union with the nymph. Dionysus, "unseen and unheard," is seated behind her. In the *Mythological Scene,* Dosso depicted the bed of flowers—anemones, roses, irises, and lilies—on which the god invited Nicaia to couple with him, the flowers from which the nymph had stolen her tender beauty.[26] Nicaia lies in a drunken sleep. Instead of painting Dionysus, who is invisible, Dosso painted an overturned amphora.

Whereas Costa simply inserted the episode of Nicaia into a mix of elements taken from various texts, Dosso stuck to a single text. Another element of agreement with Nonnus's text is the figure of Pan, who seems to clutch at his syrinx almost with a grimace of pain: he had blown on his reeds and taken part in the wedding song despite his envy. More generic but still significant elements include the books containing the music that awakened Nicaia, the distant city on the shores of the lake, and the small cupids who carried out Eros's plan for revenge, which was seconded by all the other gods.

There are, however, features of the painting that do not seem to fit fully with the story, namely the old woman and the trees behind her. Nonnus described an old woman, Melía, who emerged from an old ash tree, but no such trees can be seen. Dosso painted at least two types of trees with unusual botanical precision. Judging from the fruit hanging from their boughs, the painting displays an apple tree and a citron tree, so tightly interwoven with each other as to seem a single tree.

The Greek term for *ash tree* is μελία, written with the ε and, as we have already noted, this is also the name of the old woman in Nonnus's text; ultimately she is the embodiment of the tree. The Greek terms for *apple* and *citron,* respectively, are μηλέα and μηλέα μηδική, both with the η. *Melía* and *meléa* are undoubtedly two different words, but it may be supposed that whoever explained the content of the tale to Dosso made an effort to preserve the identity between the name of the old woman who had come out of the tree and the tree itself. The fruit hanging behind Melía represents her attributes.[27]

Let us now consider the gesture of her hands, which are directed toward the sleeping young nymph. Until now this gesture has been interpreted as a protective one. It is, instead, a gesture of grief, and this explains the pained expression on the old woman's face. This gesture is proleptic, for it anticipates Nicaia's fate—she is destined to kill herself after the birth of her daughter Telete.

A similar hand gesture is often found in reliefs of funeral scenes. For example, on the sarcophagus decorated with the story of Creusa (fig. 5), Medea's children offer Creusa the garment that will set her body on fire as soon as she puts it on, killing her in the most excruciating pain. Two men and an old woman, perhaps a wet-nurse, look on. The latter has bared one breast and displays a sorrowful look that seems to foresee the tragedy to come; she stands across from Creusa and is raising her hands. The male figure behind the old woman is perhaps a personification of death, as the upside-down flame that he holds in his hands would suggest, and thus he reinforces the proleptic value of the old woman's gesture. On another sarcophagus displaying the myth of Creusa (fig. 6), a scantily clad old woman stands behind a young woman on whose shoulders her hands almost rest.[28] Wet-nurses and mothers lamenting tragic deaths are often shown bare-breasted on sarcophagi and in funeral reliefs; in general, scantily clad women — whether young or old—play the role of mourners in scenes like this.[29] In Dosso's painting, the funereal nature of the scene is proleptically expressed by sleep, which presages the imminent death of the nymph, and by the clothing and gesture of the old woman.

Who knows what Dosso and Titian said to each other when together they paid a visit to Isabella d'Este's collection in Mantua in 1519?[30] It is certainly hard to imagine two artists with more divergent approaches to the painting of ancient myths. In his *Bacchus and Ariadne* (London, National Gallery), for instance, Titian includes a liberal helping of details taken from a number of different texts and concentrates his narrative on the climax, in which Dionysus leaps from the chariot (a gesture that Catullus captured in a single verb, *desilit*).[31] Dosso's painting, on the contrary, does not correspond to any specific moment in Nonnus's text. The painting itself is a mosaic of different motifs. The reclining nymph was a topos that had been revived by Jan Goritz and Angelo Colocci's literary circle (which included Lascaris himself). The figure of Pan seems to have been adapted from two engravings, Marco Dente's *Pan and His Syrinx* and Giulio Campagnola's *The Young Shepherd*. The old woman Melía, as was said above, seems to derive from ancient sarcophagi.[32] The figures do not seem fully integrated; the link between them remains elusive. But this may well be one of the general characteristics of Dosso, who often employs a "nonnarrative" strategy. For Dosso, a painter of *parerga*, the *parergon* of the bed of flowers contained the distinctive element of the narrative itself.[33] The amphora, which represents the absent god, and the fruit, which allude to the name of the old woman, constitute other salient moments of the narrative.

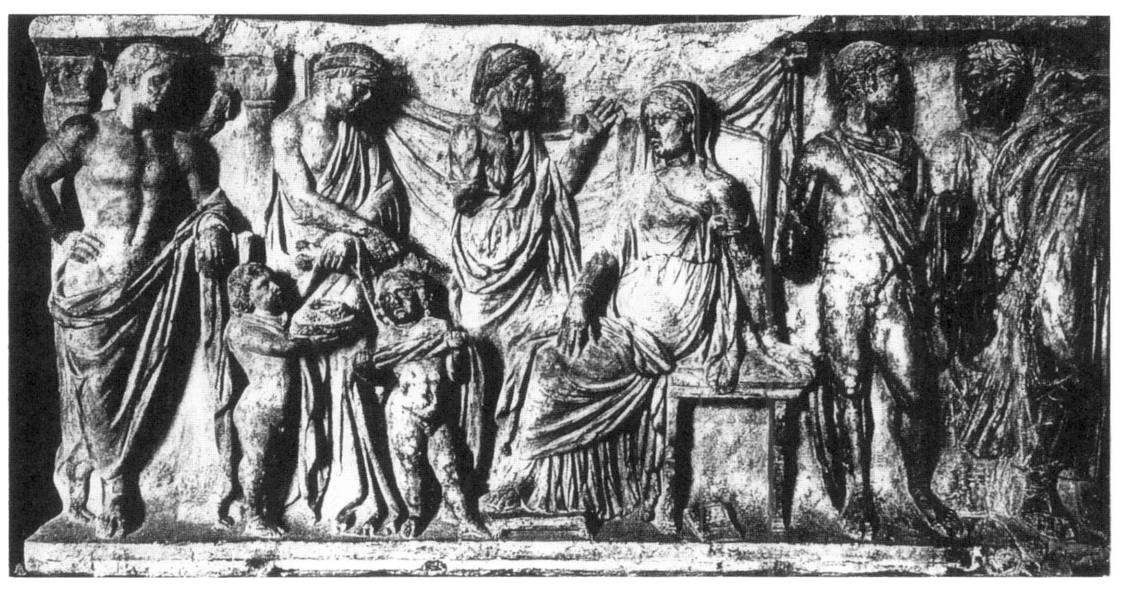

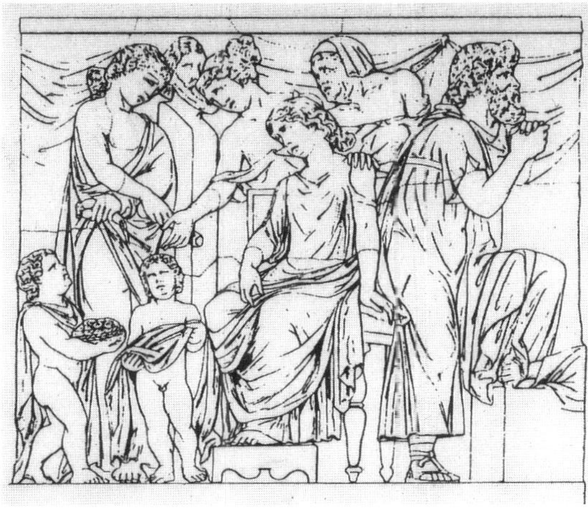

Fig. 5. Sarcophagus depicting the story of Creusa (detail)
Mantua, Palazzo Ducale

Fig. 6. Ernst Eichler
Drawing of sacrophagus fragment depicting the story of Creusa. From Carl Roberts, *Mythologische Cyklen* (Rome: "L'Erma" di Bretschneider, 1968)

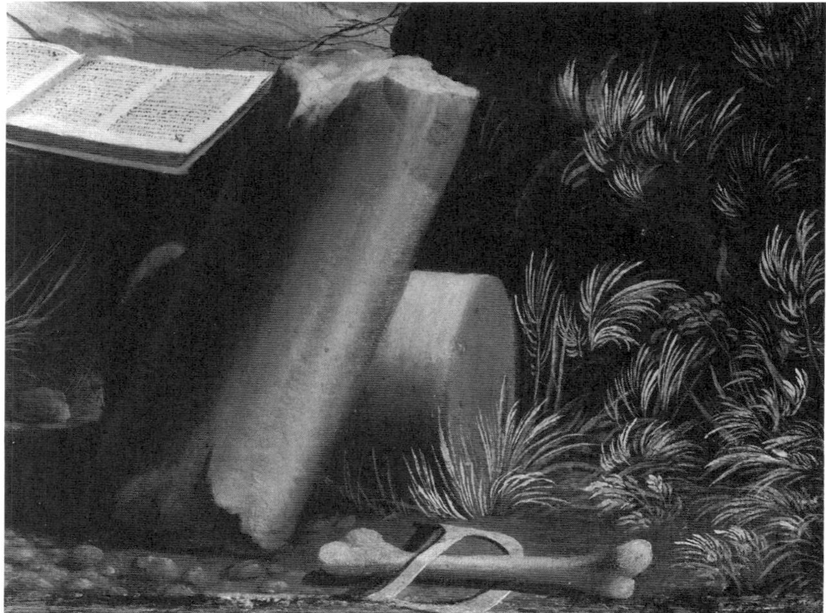

Fig. 7. Dosso Dossi
Saint Jerome (detail)
Vienna, Kunsthistorisches Museum

This idea of narrating a story through objects recalls the fad for figural rebuses, hieroglyphics, riddles, and emblems, which was widespread in court society and even beyond it. Dosso himself was certainly deeply interested in such matters, as his signature on the Vienna *Saint Jerome* shows (fig. 7). In this painting, the letter *D* is crossed by a bone (*osso* in Italian); echoing Saint Jerome's ascetic meditations, Dosso alludes to human vanity while revealing his name.[34] The only other signature by Dosso (as deciphered by Giovanni Morelli) is the inscription "ONTO D" on the pharmacist's jar in his painting *Saint Cosmas and Saint Damian,* now in Rome at the Galleria Borghese, which was done for the Sant'Anna hospital in Ferrara.[35] It expresses the spirit of "witty games," as Castiglione called them, in which all competed to discover who was hiding "allegorically... beneath several veils."[36] Significantly, Dosso is one of only a few painters to play a role in Sigismondo Fanti's *Triompho di Fortuna,* a lavish book based on a parlor game with astrological implications, published in Venice in 1527 (fig. 8).[37]

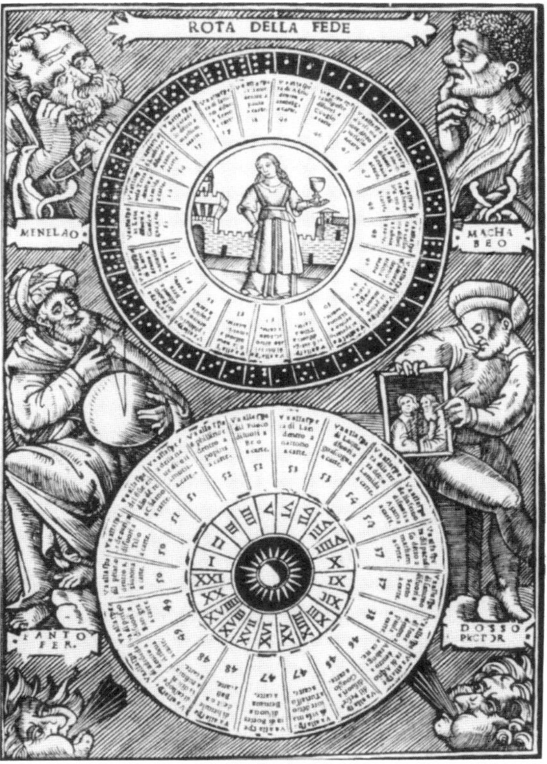

Fig. 8. "Rota della fede"
From Sigismondo Fanti, *Triompho di Fortuna,* carta 34
(Venice: Agostin da Portese, 1527)

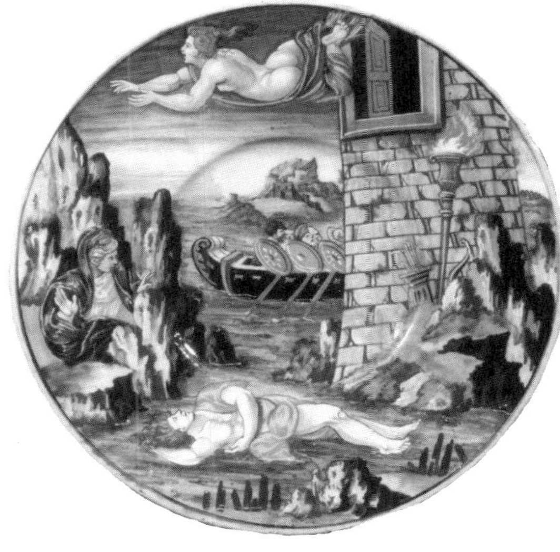

Fig. 9. Francesco Xanto Avelli
Story of Hero and Leander
Modena, Galleria Estense

The pharmacist's jar in *Saint Cosmas and Saint Damian* serves to remind us that Dosso, as is known from documents, was also active in the art of majolica. In fact, his way of composing his subjects recalls the modus operandi of the *istoriato* majolica painters, who used gestures from more than one source, mainly engravings.[38] Single figures could then be composed and recomposed in different ways, a technique of scissors-and-paste pastiche that enabled the artist to use the same gesture for even diametrically opposed meanings. Such was the method of Francesco Xanto Avelli, one of the most talented majolica artists. In his plate representing the story of Hero and Leander, the gesture of the old woman mourning over the body of the dead Leander closely resembles the gesture used by Dosso for Melia (fig. 9).[39]

In the Galleria Borghese's so-called *Story of Callisto* (fig. 10), we find two of the figures employed by Dosso in the Getty painting, namely the old woman and the sleeping nude. The two paintings also have in common the same relationship between landscape and figures; this similarity, however, which scholars have long recognized, is strictly formal and does not correspond to content. The subject of the painting in the Galleria Borghese

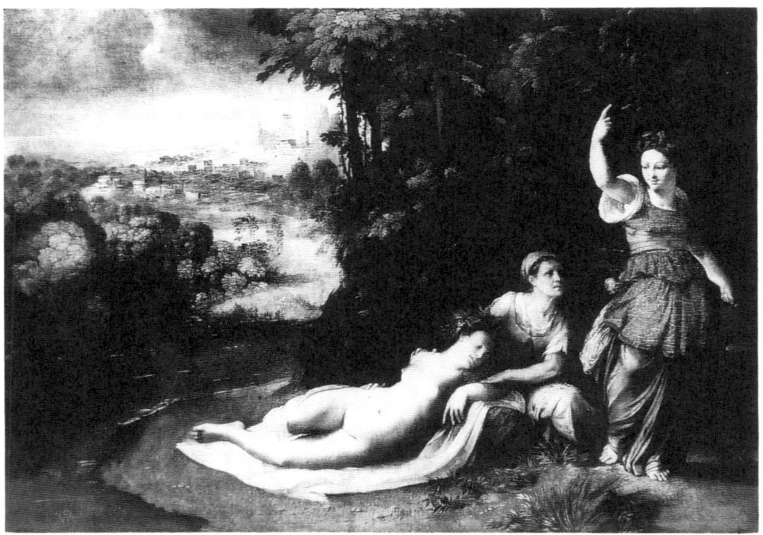

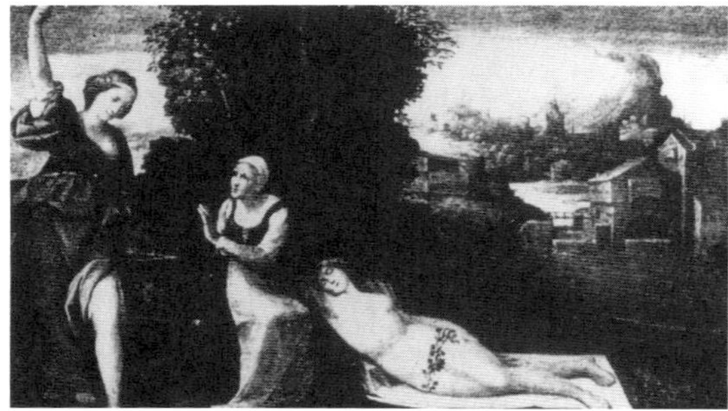

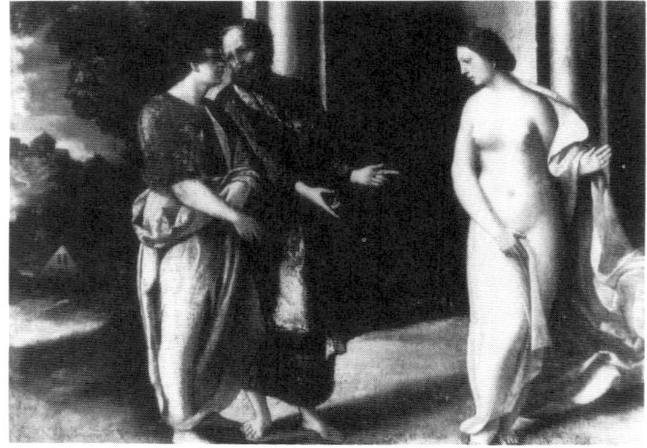

Fig. 10. Dosso Dossi
Story of Callisto
Rome, Galleria Borghese

Fig. 11. Garofalo
Mythological Allegory
Whereabouts unknown

Fig. 12. Dosso Dossi
Gyges, Candaules, and Rhodope
Rome, Galleria Borghese

remains, for the time being, obscure, but it seems connected to another painting (whose current location is unknown) that appeared on the art market in 1933 and was at that time attributed to Garofalo (fig. 11).[40] In this painting the composition is reversed, as if a print had mediated between the two works. The old woman turns in alarm toward the woman who is lifting the lid of the amphora, as if she wants to protect the sleeping figure from imminent danger. In spite of the dramatic emphasis placed on the old woman's gesture in the work attributed to Garofalo, the two paintings seem to allude to the same subject. This subject currently eludes us, but it is certainly not the story of Nicaia.

From the beginning of his career, Dosso had to reckon with the problems inherent in synthesizing the plot of a narrative. An early work titled *Gyges, Candaules, and Rhodope,* with its three small figures clumsily aligned like actors on a stage, is a case in point (fig. 12). Dosso did not try to cast the dramatic crescendo of Herodotus's tale into bold relief, nor did he attempt to create a spatial backdrop that could suggest the emotional content of the plot and the succession of its events.[41] Instead he abbreviated the plot, employing only the old man's gesture in pointing out the woman to the youth as a means of unifying the characters in the scene. Rather than narrate, Dosso limited himself to hinting at the role of each of the characters through the depiction of their respective attributes: the king wears a crown, the youth is indeed young-looking, the woman is half-naked. Dosso thus managed to characterize the respective protagonists of this profane scene, just as he would have done if they were saints to be identified through the instruments of their martyrdom.

The relationship between painting and text is more complex in the case of *Jupiter, Mercury, and Virtue* (fig. 13). Julius von Schlosser[42] linked this work to Leon Battista Alberti's "Virtus," one of the *Intercenales,* which is presented as a work by Lucian, namely a dialogue between Virtue and Mercury. Virtue explains that, while waiting for Jupiter to receive her (and she has already been waiting for a month), she has tried to complain to all the other gods who have passed that way. The other gods, however, have put her off with the most absurd excuses: there is the flowering of the gourds to attend to, or the birth of butterflies to watch over, to ensure that the new generations are born with well-painted wings. The gourds have already all flowered, however, and the butterflies are all already flying about and spreading their magnificent wings. Only Virtue is left alone, forgotten by god and man alike, after having been mistreated by Fortune, who cast her down into the mud and then stripped her of her clothes while she was strolling in the Elysian Fields in the company of learned men. Virtue has therefore decided to ask Mercury to intercede on her behalf with Jupiter. However, once Mercury hears the tale of her misfortunes, he tells her only that her case is a most difficult one, for it is well known that even Jupiter depends upon favors from Fortune. Mercury therefore counsels Virtue to hide herself, if she is truly wise, amid the vulgar and plebeian gods, until Fortune's hatred for her has weakened.[43]

Dosso's approach here is unquestionably very different from his paratactic presentation of the scene in *Gyges, Candaules, and Rhodope.* The characters, although unquestionably more lively than those in Dosso's very early paintings, are still lined up side by side, as if they were playing cards laid down on the table to tell a story. Some variations in regard to the text are worthy of notice. J. H. Whitfield has pointed out Dosso's transformation of the gods caught up in their useless tasks into the single figure of Jupiter, the great creator. The figure of Virtue is even more surprising. In Alberti's text she describes herself as filthy and dressed in rags; in Dosso's painting she is an elegant woman who graciously speaks with Mercury. Dosso thus chose to ignore, or at least not to employ, one of the crucial points of the narrative, namely the very reason for Virtue's request for an audience with Jupiter.

Virtue appears with torn garments in an illustration for the dialogue published in the Venice edition of 1525 by the Ferrarese publisher Nicolò di Aristotile, called Zoppino (fig. 14).[44] The image is quite crude. Just as Dosso did in his *Gyges, Candaules, and Rhodope,* the illustrator here simply lined up the characters, employing the figure of Fortune—balancing between the sphere at her feet and the sail pushing her—to evoke the earlier stage of the narrative. He concentrated on the fate of Virtue, summarizing the dialogue in Mercury's gesture, which appears as a sort of expulsion from Paradise, hustling the tattered figure of Virtue out of Jupiter's realm. Dosso takes the dialogue literally: if you are wise, Mercury tells Virtue, you will keep silent.[45]

Behind Mercury's gesture one can detect a written source: Marsilio Ficino's *In Mercurium Trismegistum,* especially chapter 13, titled "Mercurii . . . de impositione silentii," which inspired the Ferrarese scholar Celio Calcagnini, who allegedly interpreted the figure as an image of Harpocrates, the Egyptian god.[46] Dosso was presumably also familiar with Andrea Alciati's *Emblematum libellus,* first published in 1531, but circulating in Italy by 1521. In the emblem "In silentium," the sage, his finger raised to his lips, urges the fool to transform himself into Haprocrates.[47] Virtue's crowns of flowers are also possibly inspired by another Alciati emblem, "Anteros sive Amor Virtutis."[48]

Dosso returned to Alberti's "Virtus" once again, supplying a much more faithful interpretation of the text. One of the monochrome frescoes in the Sala del Camin Nero in Trent (works that so far have defied interpretation) shows Mercury in the act of stopping on the threshold of a room *from which butterflies are flying away.* With him is a young woman who, with an animated gesture, seems to be asking to speak (fig. 15). Virtue is not dressed in rags, but she is half-naked, covered only by a length of cloth draped over her shoulders. The butterflies are flying out the open doorway, their wings having been carefully painted by Jupiter. In the aforementioned passage, Virtue exclaimed disconsolately that the gourds have all flowered and that the butterflies are flying away. A group of old men observe the scene from a position behind Virtue: they are clearly the learned men of antiquity with whom she was strolling in the Elysian Fields when she was first assaulted by Fortune. We immediately notice that Dosso gave Virtue the same eloquent and imploring gesture that

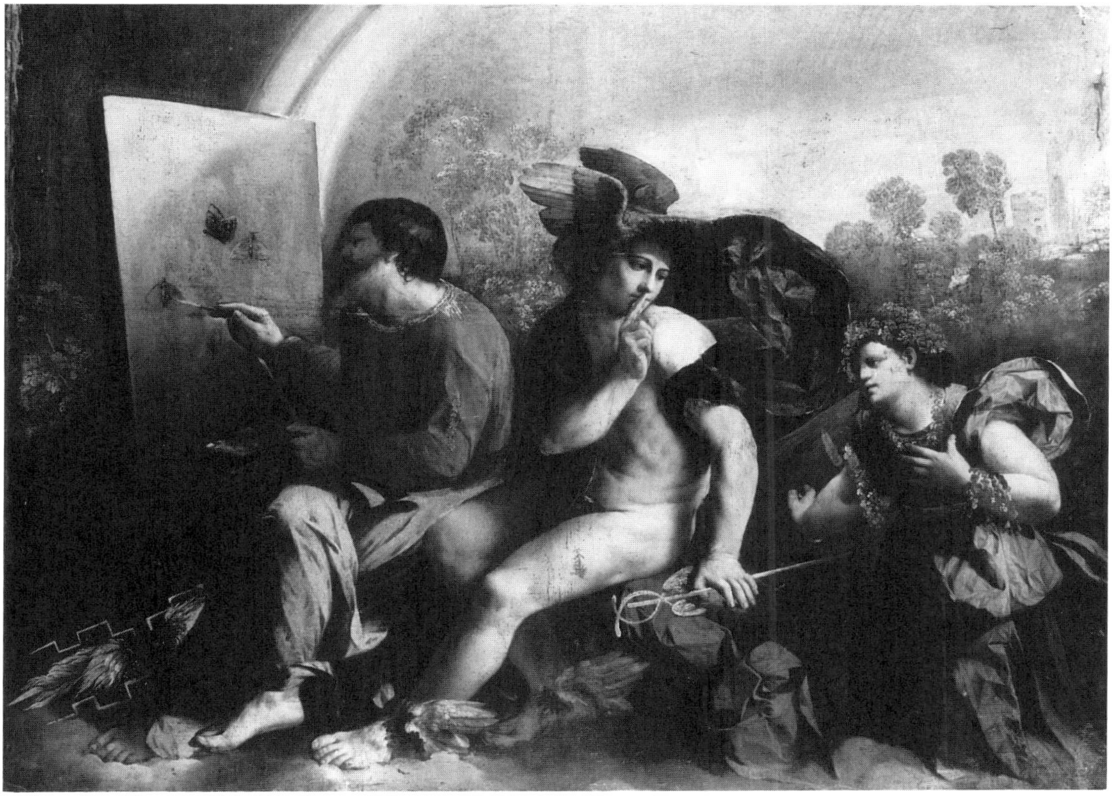

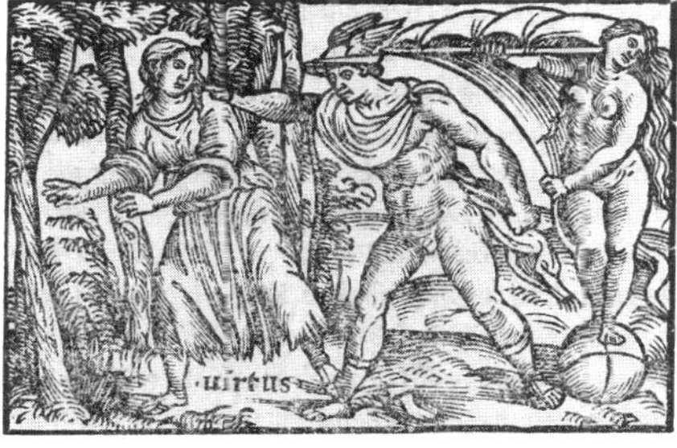

Fig. 13. Dosso Dossi
Jupiter, Mercury, and Virtue (or *Virgo*)
Vienna, Kunsthistorisches Museum

Fig. 14. "Virtus"
From Lucian, *I dilettevoli dialoghi*, 23r
(Venice: Nicolò di Aristotile detto Zoppino, 1525)

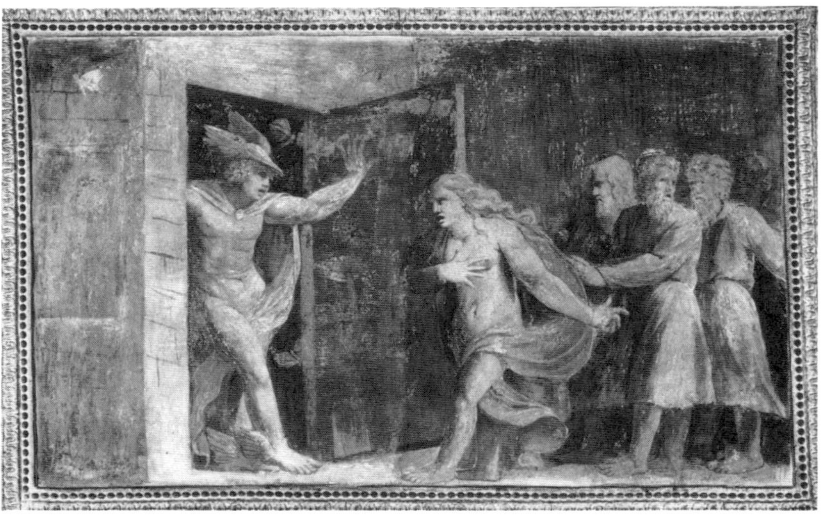

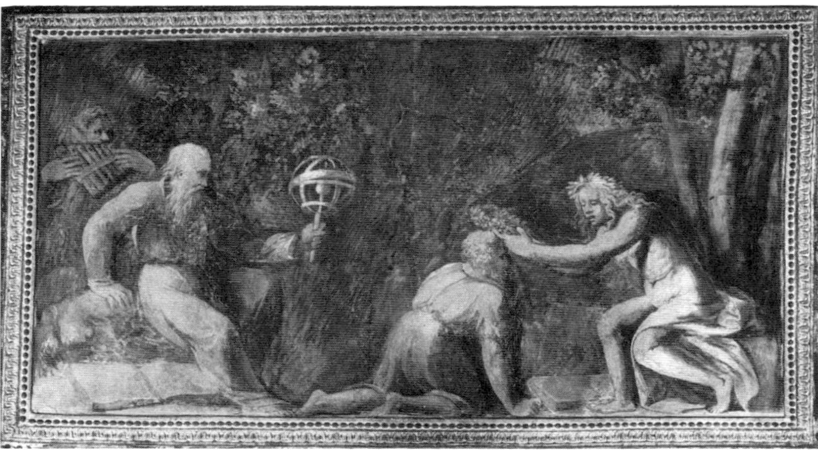

Fig. 15. Dosso Dossi
Jupiter, Mercury, and Virtue
Trent, Castello del Buonconsiglio, Sala del Camin Nero

Fig. 16. Dosso Dossi
Triumph of Virtue
Trent, Castello del Buonconsiglio, Sala del Camin Nero

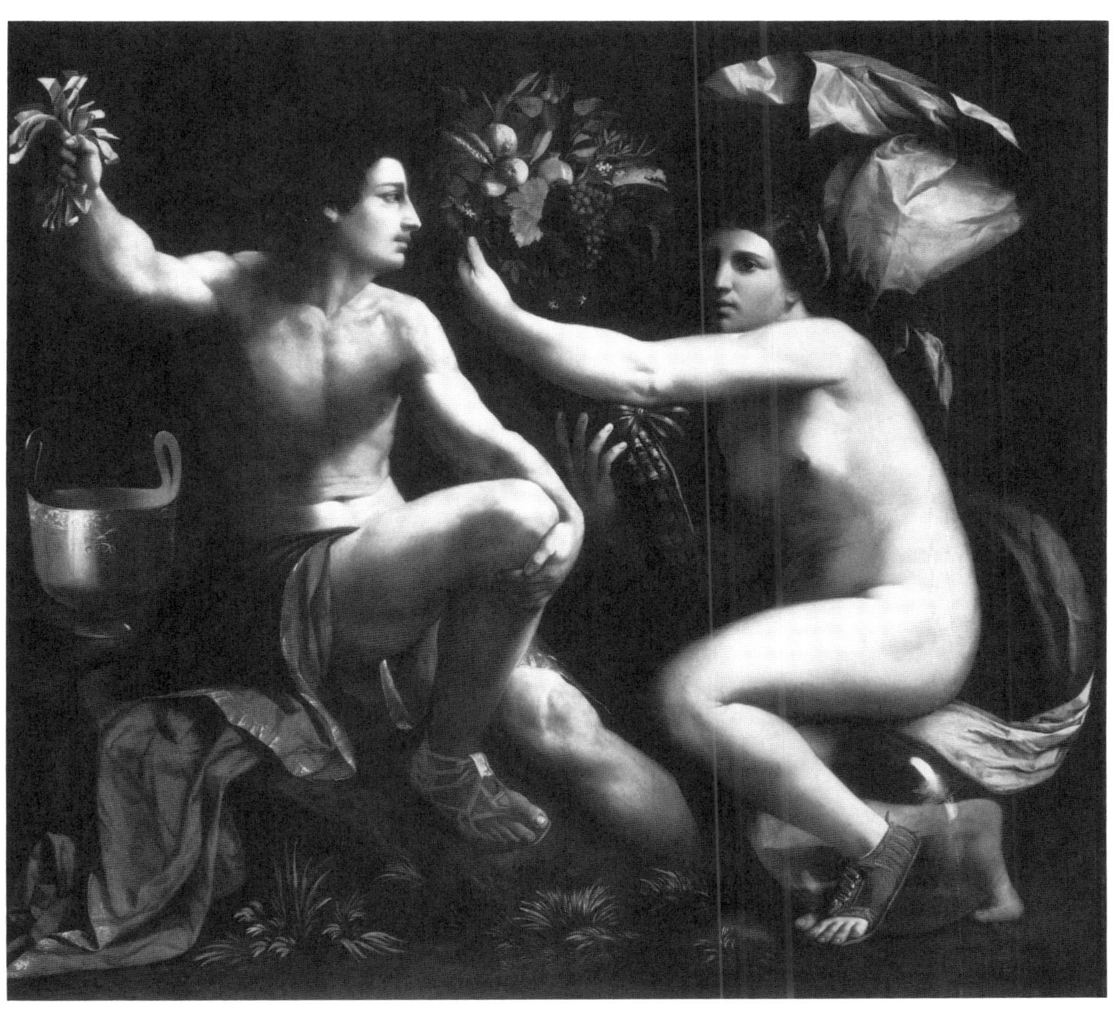

Fig. 17. Dosso Dossi
Allegory of Fortune
Los Angeles, The J. Paul Getty Museum

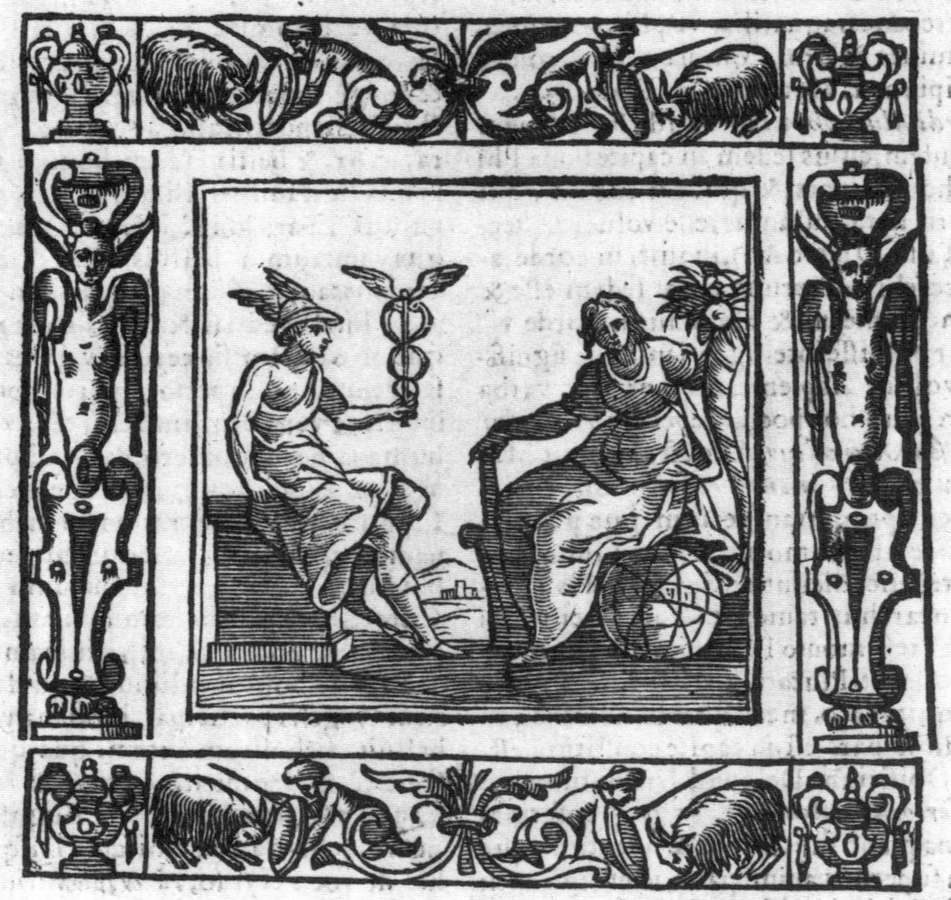

Fig. 18. "Ars naturam adiuvans"
From Andrea Alciati, *Emblemata,* emblem 99
(Padua: Peter Paul Tozzi, 1621)

he employed in the Vienna painting, but in reverse. Mercury seems to be in a hurry, and his gesture resembles that which appears in the print in the Zoppino edition. In the text, Mercury claims that he has left the room because he received a letter from Virtue, but that he must soon return to Jupiter.

Alberti's "Virtus" was a suitable text for emphasizing in monochrome the themes of an entire room devoted to the celebration of the cardinal virtues—Justice, Temperance, Prudence, and Fortitude—who are frescoed in the corners of the vaults—as well as the liberal arts as embodied by leading practitioners of them. Bernardo Cles had wished to devote the Sala delle Udienza to Fortune, and she appears there among famous men as the personification of Occasio. He had wished nonetheless to celebrate those virtues that light the fires of culture in the Sala del Camin Nero, which was to be used for less solemn occasions.[49]

The interpretation of the subject of the first monochrome helps us to decipher the other one, which appears to be a scene of triumph. Indeed, here we are shown the triumph of Virtue, in clear opposition to her humiliation when the gods indifferently left her standing on the threshold of Olympus. Virtue, crowned, confers the same honor on the old learned man prostrate at her feet (fig. 16). Also present are an astrologer—perhaps Beroso-Atlas, who appears on the facing wall—and Pan with his syrinx, who appears elsewhere as well. This second monochrome does not appear to depend upon a written text, but is the moralizing conclusion of the previous scene. In depicting Virtue in the act of putting a crown on the sage's head, however, Dosso might have recalled the four crowns representing the cardinal virtues, which adorned "Anteros, sive Amor Virtutis" in Alciati's emblem.

In conclusion, I would like to point out that the relationship between Dosso and Alciati, as we have thus far defined it, seems to be reversed in the *Allegory of Fortune* (fig. 17). The emblem "Ars naturam adiuvans" changes in the 1621 edition: Mercury raising his staff is clearly derived from the young man in Dosso's painting who clutches lottery tickets in his upraised hand, and the figure of Fortune-Abundance closely mirrors Dosso's Fortune, who is seated on a transparent sphere (fig. 18).[50] This is the only known trace of the reception of this painting by Dosso, about whose provenance we—once again—know nothing.

Notes

1. Andrea Rothe, who supervised the restoration of the painting when it entered the J. Paul Getty Museum collection, interprets these objects as a sword and a coat of mail. In numerous compositions with a sleeping nude near a tree, the objects hanging in the tree are a bow and a quiver. See, for example, illustrations in Millard Meiss, "Sleep in Venice: Ancient Myths and Renaissance Proclivities" (1966), in idem, *The Painter's Choice: Problems in the Interpretation of Renaissance Art* (New York: Harper & Row, 1976), 212–239, esp. figs. 234 (Paris Bordon, *Venus and Cupid*), 239 (Pomedelli, engraving of Quiet), 237 (Titian, *The Pardo Venus*). A quiver and finger

cymbals appear in Bonasone's engraving *Pan and Pomona,* described by Malvasia, for which I refer the reader to Stefania Massari, *Giulio Bonasone,* 2 vols., exh. cat. (Rome: Quasar, 1973), 1: 94–95 (entry no. 121). For the report on the restoration of Dosso's painting, see Alessandro Ballarin, *Dosso Dossi: La pittura a Ferrara negli anni del Ducato di Alfonso I,* 2 vols. (Cittadella: Bertoncello Artigrafiche, 1994–1995), 1: 102, 348 (entry no. 453).

2. Ultraviolet rays do not show the instrument's acoustic chamber. According to Andrea Rothe, that part of the instrument probably was damaged in the restoration carried out circa 1850 by Raffaello Pinti, who had arranged for the sale of the painting to the Marquess of Northampton. I wish to thank Andrea Rothe for generously providing me with copious photographic records and for discussing with me all of the restoration work he supervised.

3. The length of time separating the phases cannot be determined precisely, but it is certain that the woman with the viola da gamba was not in the final composition.

4. By completing the cupid now cut off on the upper left, it can be shown that the painting was twenty or even thirty centimeters wider, which makes the composition perfectly divisible along a diagonal line with the three characters on one side and the landscape on the other.

5. Felton Gibbons, *Dosso and Battista Dossi: Court Painters at Ferrara* (Princeton: Princeton Univ. Press, 1968), 86–89, 170 (entry no. 11), suggests that the figure on the left is Artemis coming to protect Echo from the attentions of Pan, or the Lyda who appears in a fragment from Moschus ("Pan loved his neighbour Echo; Echo loved a frisking Satyr; and Satyr, he was head over ears for Lydè; see *The Greek Bucolic Poets,* trans. J. M. Edmonds, rev. ed. [Cambridge: Harvard Univ. Press, 1928], 459–60). Amalia Mezzetti, *Il Dosso e Battista ferraresi* (Milan: Silvana, 1965), 45–46, 76 (entry no. 25), with some doubts refers to the hypothesis that the subject is the myth of Pandora, which had been suggested verbally to Henriette Mendelsohn by R. Föster. On the conflicting opinions about the subject of the painting, see—in addition to the aforementioned works—Ballarin (see note 1), 1: 348 (entry no. 453). The hypothesis that the subject is an allegory on the theme of Pan and his syrinx deriving from Leone Ebreo's *Dialoghi d'amore* is unfounded; see Augusto Gentili, *Da Tiziano a Tiziano: Mito e allegoria nella cultura veneziana del Cinquecento* (Milan: Feltrinelli, 1980), 78–81, 207–8.

6. Gibbons (see note 5), 86–89.

7. Gibbons (see note 5), 88.

8. Baldassare Castiglione, *The Book of the Courtier,* trans. Charles S. Singleton (Garden City, N.Y.: Anchor/Doubleday, 1959), bk. 1, chap. 30, 49; and, idem, *Il libro del cortegiano, novamente rivisto* (Venice: Giouanni Paduano, 1538), 27–28:

> *ché se le parole che usa il scrittore, portan seco un poco, non dirò di difficultà, ma d'acutezza recondita, e non cosí nota come quelle che si dicono parlando ordinariamente, dànno una certa maggior autorità alla scrittura, e fanno che il lettore va piú ritenuto e sopra di sé, e meglio considera, e si diletta dello ingegno e della dottrina di chi scrive; e col bon giudicio affaticandosi un poco, gusta quel piacere, che s'ha nel conseguir le cose difficili. E se la ignoranzia di chi legge è tanta, che non possa superar quelle difficultà, non è la colpa dello scrittore.*

9. On the *"soggetto nascosto"* (hidden subject), see Salvatore Settis, *La "Tempesta" interpretata: Giorgione, i committenti, il soggetto* (Turin: Einaudi, 1978), esp. 121–52; and, idem, *Giorgione's Tempest: Interpreting the Hidden Subject*, trans. Ellen Bianchini (Chicago: Univ. of Chicago Press, 1990), esp. 126–159.

10. This is Memnon of Heraclea Pontica, the historiographer who was perhaps Plutarch's contemporary; see Nonnus of Panopolis, *Les dionysiaques*, vol. 6, *Chants XIV–XVII*, ed. and trans. Bernard Gerlaud (Paris: Les Belles Lettres, 1994), 50.

11. Sylvie Béguin, ed., *Le Studiolo d'Isabelle d'Este*, exh. cat. (Paris: Editions des Musées Nationaux, 1975), 44–46 (entry no. 128 by John Schloder). The hypothesis, which is briefly treated in the catalog, is considered at greater length in John Schloder, "Les Costa du Studiolo d'Isabelle d'Este: Sources iconographiques," *Revue du Louvre* 25 (1975): 230–33; and has recently been discussed by Sylvia Ferino-Pagden, *Isabella d'Este, "La prima donna del mondo": Fürstin und Mäzenatin der Renaissance*, exh. cat. (Vienna: Kunsthistorisches Museum, 1994), 235–39 (entry no. 86).

12. Nonnus of Panopolis, *Nonni Panopolitae Dionysiaca, nunc primum in lucem edita, ex bibliotheca Ioannis Sambuci Pannonii. Cum lectionibus et conjecturis Gerarti Falkenburgii Noviomagi, et indice copioso* (Antwerp: Ex officina Christophori Plantini, 1569). Giovanni Romano, "Verso la maniera moderna: Da Mantegna a Raffaello," in *Storia dell'arte italiana*, 12 vols. (Turin: Einaudi, 1979–1983), 6: 31, dates the *Myth of Comus* at 1511 *"solo con qualche margine di incertezza"* (with some slight room for doubt).

13. On the Berlin papyrus, see Wilhelm Schubart and Ulrich von Wilamowitz-Moellendorff, "Nonnos, *Dionysiaka* 14, 15, 16, Papyrus 10567," in idem, *Berliner Klassikertexte*, vol. 5, *Griechische Dichterfragmente*, pt. 1, *Epische und elegische Fragmente* (Berlin: Weidmann, 1907), 94–106. Francis Vian dates the papyrus, with some doubts, to the sixth century; see Nonnus of Panopolis, *Les dionysiaques*, vol. 1, *Chants I–II*, ed. and trans. Francis Vian (Paris: Les Belles Lettres, 1976), lxi–lxx, esp. lxi. On all the extant manuscript codices, see Vian's comments in idem, lxi–lxv.

14. Alexander Turyn, *Dated Greek Manuscripts of the Thirteenth and Fourteenth Centuries in the Libraries of Italy*, 2 vols. (Urbana: Univ. of Illinois Press, 1972), 1: 36–39, supplies a rich bibliography concerning the history of the manuscript and the studies devoted to it.

15. Nonnus of Panopolis, *Nonni Panopolitani Dionysiaca*, vol. 2, *Libros I–XXIV*, ed. Arthur Ludwich (Leipzig: B. G. Teubner, 1909), vi–viii, esp. 159–228. On the history of the Medici library, see E. B. Fryde, *Humanism and Renaissance Historiography* (London: Hambledon, 1983), 160–214, esp. 179–82. The Medici library was stored in the San Marco convent in Florence from 1494 to 1508, when Cardinal Giovanni de' Medici reacquired the part belonging to the family and took it with him to Rome. Clement VII brought it back to Florence in 1523. On Politian's method, see Anthony Grafton, "On the Scholarship of Politian and Its Context" (1977), in idem, *Defenders of the Text: The Traditions of Scholarship in an Age of Science, 1450–1800* (Cambridge: Harvard Univ. Press, 1991), 47–75. Marie-Hyacinthe Laurent provides a great deal of information on the interesting case of Fabio Vigili in *Fabio Vigili et les bibliothèques de Bologne au début du XVIe siècle, d'après le MS. Barb. Lat. 3185*, ed. M. H. Laurent (Rome: Città del Vaticano, 1943), viii–xx.

16. Pierre de Nolhac, *Les correspondants d'Alde Manuce* (1887–1888; reprint, Turin: Bottega d'Erasmo, 1961), 24–26 (letter no. 24), written from Blois in 1501. In this letter, Lascaris complains that Aldus is no longer publishing Greek works and is more interested in Latin and vernacular texts.

17. Emile Legrand, *Bibliographie hellénique des XVe et XVIe siècles,* 4 vols. (1885–1906; reprint, Paris: G. P. Maisonneuve & Larose, 1962), 1: 83–85. On Lascaris as a poet, see Janus Lascaris, *Epigrammi greci,* ed. Anna Meschini (Padua: Liviana, 1976).

18. Nolhac (see note 16), 44 (letter no. 37): "*Don Piero nostro ancor lui è fatto cortigiano et vivit Romae, et ha portato seco el Nonno et scrive continuamente et di gia ha scritto venti libri.*" On Piero Candido, see the entry by Paolo Orvieto in *Dizionario biografico degli italiani* (Rome: Istituto della Enciclopedia Italiana, 1960–   ), 17: 785–86.

19. Nolhac (see note 16), 45 (letter no. 38): "*scorrettioni... in qualche dittioni*"; "*la somma de libri e sono tutti*"; "*modo [che] lui ha tenuto di far tante righe quante erano nello exemplare.*" This information on the method employed by Candido suggests that his transcription may be what is now known as the "Palatino Heidelbergensis gr. 85" described in 1909 by Ludwich; see Nonnus (see note 15), xi: "*optimum apographon Laurentiani, cuius vel etiam dispositionem versuum et correcturas fere semper fidelissime repraesentavit*" (the best copy of the Laurentian [manuscript], whose arrangement of verses and whose corrections it almost always exhibited). I will attempt to verify this as soon as possible. On the history of the "Palatino Heidelbergensis" manuscript, which was given along with a group of codices to Heidelberg by Pius VII after 1815, see Friedrich Wilken, *Geschichte der Bildung, Beraubung und Vernichtung der alten heidelbergischen Büchersammlungen* (Heidelberg: A. Oswald, 1817), 291–303.

20. Pierre Chuvin, *Mythologie et géographie dionysiaques: Recherches sur l'œuvre de Nonnos de Panopolis* (Clermont-Ferrand: ADOSA, 1991), 148–54. Some further remarks on Janus Lascaris are in order. He fled Constantinople at age eight, along with his father. He later studied in Venice with Bessarione and in Padua with Demetrio Calcondila. In 1494 he edited, together with Bartolomeo Ciai, the inventory of the Medici's books, and on that occasion he perhaps personally annotated Nonnus's text in a number of places. He served as the French ambassador to Venice during the period of the League of Cambrai, and remained in the service of Louis XII until Pope Leo X summoned him to Rome soon after elected to the papacy. Leo X wanted him to establish the Greek school at the Palazzo del Quirinale. Pietro Bembo and Marco Musuro were also—at Lascaris's suggestion—asked to take part in this same project. Lascaris died in 1534. A lengthy and excellent biography on Lascaris appears in Legrand (see note 17), 1: cxxxi–clxii. See also Vittorio Fanelli, "Il ginnasio greco di Leone X a Roma," *Studi romani* 9 (1961): 390–93. On Lascaris's hand, see Turyn (see note 14), 36. See also Vian's comments on the various revisions of the Biblioteca Laurenziana codex in Nonnus (see note 13), 202ff.

21. A similar case happens for the *Allegory of Music* (Florence, Museo del Fondazione Horne), which dates to the mid-1520s: Dosso employs the notes of Josquin Desprez, the famous *maestro di capella* in Ferrara who died in 1504. See H.

Colin Slim, "Dosso Dossi's Allegory at Florence about Music," *Journal of the American Musicological Society* 43 (1990): 43–98 (and the corrections published in the summer 1990 issue), in which Slim identifies the two canons and the music of Josquin Desprez.

22. On this subject, see Bette L. Talvacchia, "Homer, Greek Heroes and Hellenism in Giulio Romano's Hall of Troy," *Journal of the Warburg and Courtauld Institutes* 51 (1988): 235–42. The pope, obviously on Lascaris's recommendation, asked Federico to loan him the text. On the provenance of the painting now in the J. Paul Getty Museum, see the essay by Burton Fredericksen in this volume.

23. The close ties between the theme of Nicaia and the *Triumph of Bacchus in India* suggest that the J. Paul Getty Museum's painting might be identified with the Bacchanal that was taken, along with four other paintings, from Alfonso's *camerino* by the papal legate Pietro Aldobrandini in January 1598. Some months later, Annibale Roncaglia, Cesare d'Este's agent, recorded its disappearance and noted that it used to be hung next to Titian's *Worship of Venus* in Alfonso's *camerino*. The theme of the celebration of love and wine clearly connects it to the other paintings. There are, however, at least two problems with this identification. The first is the problem of size: even if we take into account the later cutting down of the canvas (at least along the left side), Dosso's painting was smaller than the others, presumably measuring 163.8 × 145.4 cm (Bellini, *Feast of the Gods,* 170 × 188 cm; Titian, *Worship of Venus,* 175 × 175 cm; Titian, *The Andrians,* 175 × 193 cm; Titian, *Bacchus and Ariadne,* 175 × 190 cm). A more serious problem is posed by the fact that this painting (as Dosso completed it) had only three figures in it, while the others are crowded compositions. For the time being, then, we must reject this hypothesis. On the issues related to the arrangement of the paintings in Alfonso's *camerino,* see the recent work by Grazia Agostini and Anna Stanzani, "Pittori veneti e commissioni estensi a Ferrara," in Jadranka Bentini, Sergio Marinelli, and Angelo Mazza, eds., *La pittura veneta negli stati estensi* (Verona: Artioli, 1996), 21–56, and bibliography.

24. On the backdating of the project for the *Triumph of Bacchus in India* and Raphael's commission, see John Shearman, "Alfonso d'Este's Camerino," in *"Il se rendit en Italie": Etudes offertes à André Chastel* (Rome: Edizioni dell'Elefante, 1987), 209–29, esp. 210–14. Shearman focuses on the animals in Raphael's drawing and notes that these could certainly have been derived from ancient sarcophagi and reliefs, for they did not often appear in literary texts. It is worth noting here that serpents and elephants play an important role in the triumph of Bacchus narrated by Nonnus in *Dionysiaca* 15.119–68. See Nonnus (see note 10), 47.

25. Memnon completely omits the episode of Hymnos's love for Nicaia. Nonnus instead fails to mention Sangarius, the father of the nymph, while naming Cybil as one of those who turned against Nicaia after she killed the shepherd. See Nonnus (see note 10), 50.

26. On the comparison of female beauty to flowers, along with other metaphors used repeatedly by Nonnus, see Daria Gigli Piccardi, *Metafora e poetica in Nonno di Panopoli* (Florence: Università degli Studi di Firenze, Dipartimento di Scienze dell'Antichità "Giorgio Pasquali," 1985), 63–69.

27. In 1545, after Dosso's death, Battista Dossi represented a young nymph named Melia who, having fallen in love with Libanus, was transformed—as he was—

into a tree. One of them became an ash and the other a citron tree, and their branches are entangled in the tapestry executed by Nicholas Karcher and now in the Musée du Louvre. See Felton Gibbons, "Ferrarese Tapestries of Metamorphoses," *Art Bulletin* 48 (1966): 409–11. I wish to thank Grazia Stussi for discussing with me the problem of the fruit in the painting.

28. Carl Robert, *Mythologische Cyklen,* vol. 2 of *Die antiken Sarkophag-Reliefs,* (1890; reprint, Rome: "L'Erma" di Bretschneider, 1968), 211 (entry no. 197). Concerning the sarcophagus now in Mantua, see idem, 210 (entry no. 196); and Helmut Sichtermann and Guntram Koch, *Griechische Mythen auf römischen Sarkophagen* (Tübingen: E. Wasmuth, 1975), 41–42.

29. I wish here to thank warmly Maria-Luisa Catoni, who helped me to understand this crucial issue in my study.

30. Alessandro Luzio, *La galleria dei Gonzaga venduta all'Inghilterra nel 1627–28: Documenti degli archivi di Mantova e Londra* (Milan: L. F. Cogliati, 1913), 218.

31. Erwin Panofsky, *Problems in Titian, Mostly Iconographic* (New York: New York Univ. Press, 1969), 139–71, esp. 141–44. Carlo Ginzburg, "Tiziano e Ovidio," in idem, *Miti, emblemi, spie: Morfologia e storia* (Turin: Einaudi, 1986), 133–57, has demonstrated Titian's dependence on vernacular translations, for he clearly did not know Latin.

32. On the theme of the sleeping nymph, see Elisabeth B. MacDougall, "The Sleeping Nymph: Origins of a Humanist Fountain Type," *Art Bulletin* 57 (1975): 357–65; Phyllis Pray Bober, "The *Coryciana* and the Nymph Corycia," *Journal of the Warburg and Courtauld Institutes* 40 (1977): 223–39; and Yvonne Hackenbroch, "An Early-Renaissance Cameo 'Sleep in Venice,'" in *Studi di storia dell'arte in onore di Mina Gregori* (Milan: Silvana, 1994), 92–95. On the engraving by Marco Dente (called "Marco da Ravenna"), see Stefania Massari, *Giulio Romano pinxit et delineavit: Opere grafiche autografe di collaborazione e di bottega,* exh. cat. (Rome: Fratelli Palombi, 1993), 34–36 (entry no. 32 by Stefania Massari); and Adam Bartsch, *Le peintre graveur,* 21 vols. (Vienna: J. V. Degen, 1803–1821), 14: 245–47 (entry no. 325). On Campagnola's engraving, see Mark J. Zucker, *Early Italian Masters,* vol. 25 (commentary) of *The Illustrated Bartsch* (New York: Abaris, 1984), 476–77 (entry nos. .009 S1, .009 S2).

33. On the meaning of the *parerga* and Giovio's debt to Pliny, see E. H. Gombrich, "The Renaissance Theory of Art and the Rise of Landscape" (1950), in idem, *Norm and Form: Studies in the Art of the Renaissance* (London: Phaidon, 1966), 107–21, esp. 113–14. See also Creighton Gilbert, "On Subject and Not-Subject in Italian Renaissance Pictures," *Art Bulletin* 34 (1952): 202–17, in which Gilbert uses the passage in Giovio referring to Dosso as a painter of *parerga* in order to argue for the existence as early as 1527 (the year in which the text was written) of a subjectless and nonnarrative painting. See also Salvatore Settis, "Soggetto e non-soggetto," in Settis (see note 9), 3–18; and, idem, "Subject and Not-Subject," 1–14.

34. In this same period another instance of a figurative rebus may be found in Lorenzo Lotto's *Lucina Brembati* (dated 1525). The figurative rebus was popularized in print by Antonio Baiardo, *Philogyne* (Parma: Per A. Viotto, 1508); and by Giovanni Giorgio Alione, "Rondeaux d'amour composé par signification," in idem, *Opera*

jocunda Joannes Georgii Alioni Astensis, metro maccheronico materno et gallico composita (Asti: Per F. Silva, 1521). Baiardo was the father of Francesco and Elena, who were Parmigianino's patrons. A rich bibliography on the rebus may be found in Lina Bolzoni, *La stanza della memoria: Modelli letterari e iconografici nell'età della stampa* (Turin: Einaudi, 1995), esp. chap. 3, "I giochi delle memorie," 87–134 (with thanks to the author).

35. See Gibbons (see note 5), 196 (entry no. 56), who lists other opinions on this issue which we may safely disregard here. The *onto d('osso)* (bone grease) in the pharmaceutical jar playfully points to what the painter has managed to squeeze out of himself, while also alluding to the medical cure that will presumably result from the analysis that the saints are about to perform on the contents of the glass that the woman has brought to them. The patient is an onlooker in this scene.

36. Castiglione, 1538 (see note 8), bk. 1, 20: *"giochi ingeniosi"; "allegoricamente ... sotto vari velami."*

37. Sigismondo Fanti, *Triompho di Fortuna* (1527; reprint, Modena: Edizioni Aldine, 1983), pl. XXXIV. This is the facsimile reprint (with a modern introduction by Albano Biondi) of the edition that appeared in Venice in 1527. On Dosso's presence in this text, see Giovanni Agosti, "Su Mantegna, 3. (Ancora all'ingresso della 'maniera moderna')," *Prospettiva,* nos. 73–74 (1994): 131–43, esp. 137.

38. Mezzetti (see note 5), 62–63.

39. Xanto took this gesture from a print by Gian Jacopo Caraglio (Bartsch [see note 32], 15: 68 [entry no. 4]), which in turn was derived from a *Nativity* by Parmigianino (Bartsch [see note 32], 16: 7 [entry no. 3]), and he used it again in a plate illustrating the birth of Christ now in the Museo Correr in Venice. See Francesco Liverani, *Le maioliche della Galleria Estense di Modena* (Faenza: Faenza, 1979), 37–40; and Alison Holcroft, "Francesco Xanto Avelli and Petrarch," *Journal of the Warburg and Courtauld Institutes* 51 (1988): 225–34. See also John V. G. Mallet, "La biografia di Francesco Xanto Avelli alla luce dei suoi sonetti," *Faenza* 70 (1984): 384–402. On the method of the majolica painters, see Bertrand Jestaz, "Les modèles de la majolique historiée: Bilan d'une enquête," *Gazette des beaux-arts,* ser. 6, 79 (1972): 215–40. Dosso also employs Melía's gesture in the so-called *Zingarella,* who reaches out her hands to dry the Holy Child's swaddling clothes by the fire.

40. I wish to thank Burton Fredericksen for pointing out this connection.

41. Lionello Venturi, "Note sulla Galleria Borghese," *L'arte* 12 (1909): 33–37, first established the subject of this painting. The Greek manuscript translated by Matteo Maria Boiardo around 1480 is now in the Biblioteca Estense in Modena. The only visual representation of Gyges, Candaules, and Rhodope prior to Dosso's painting was much more faithful to the letter of the text; I am referring to a miniature on page 36 of a copy of Boccaccio belonging to Jean Sans Peur, duke of Burgundy (died 1419). See Henry M. R. Martin and Philippe Lauer, *Les principaux manuscrits à peintures de la Bibliothèque de l'Arsenal à Paris* (Paris: Pour la Société Française de Reproductions de Manuscrits à Peintures, 1929), pl. XLVII. See also Andor Pigler, *Barockthemen: Eine Auswahl von Verzeichnissen zur Ikonographie des 17. und 18. Jahrhunderts,* 2nd ed., 3 vols. (Budapest: Akadémiai Kiadó, 1974), 2: 317. The Braunschweigisches Landesmuseum in Brunswick, Germany, owns a ceramic work from 1551, perhaps originating

in Pesaro, which represents the theme of Gyges, Candaules, and Rhodope. In 1581 Jeremias Reusner moralized the myth of Gyges and Candaules in his emblem "Coniugij Arcana non revelanda"; see Arthur Henkel and Albrecht Schöne, eds., *Emblemata: Handbuch zur Sinnbildkunst des XVI. und XVII. Jahrhunderts* (Stuttgart: Metzler, 1976), 1603–4.

42. Julius von Schlosser, "Jupiter und die Tugend: Ein Gemälde des Dosso Dossi," *Jahrbuch der königlich preußischen Kunstsammlungen* 21 (1900): 262–70; and Julius Schlosser, "Der Weltenmaler Zeus: Ein Capriccio des Dosso Dossi" (1918), in idem, *Präludien: Vorträge und Aussäße* (Berlin: Julius Bard, 1927), 269–303. On the provenance of the painting and the various interpretations of its subject, see Gibbons (see note 5), 212 (entry no. 78); and Ballarin (see note 1), 1: 339 (entry no. 433). An astrological interpretation has been formulated by Friderike Klauner, "Ein Planetenbild von Dosso Dossi," *Jahrbuch der kunsthistorischen Sammlungen in Wien* 60 (1964): 137–60. J. H. Whitfield, "Leon Battista Alberti, Ariosto and Dosso Dossi," *Italian Studies* 21 (1966): 16–30, has reviewed the competing claims about the subject of the painting. Here I should add that the dates provided by Klauner—1489 for Dosso's birth and 1529 for the execution of the painting in question—represent an arbitrary choice on her part; other dates also saw the conjunction of the planets Jupiter and Mercury with the Virgin. See the astrological note by Ferrari d'Occhieppo published by Klauner as an appendix (159–60). An astrological interpretation would not in fact be incompatible with an interpretation derived from the dialogue, but Klauner's arguments are less than convincing. She accepted the proposed date of Dosso's birth put forward by Longhi on the basis of quite different criteria (Longhi is explicitly mentioned by Klauner on p. 158), and then constructed her astrological interpretation on that specific date. See Roberto Longhi, *Officina ferrarese, 1934: Seguita dagli ampliamenti, 1940, e dai nuovi ampliamenti, 1940–55* (Florence: Sansoni, 1956), 80–91, esp. 81, 157–59. There is, however, a typographical error in the date of Dosso's birth (it should read 1489, not 1479, on p. 157 of Longhi).

43. See Leon Battista Alberti, "Virtue," in idem, *Dinner Pieces,* trans. David Marsh (Binghamton, N.Y.: Medieval & Renaissance Texts & Studies, 1987), 21–22. Five Latin editions of the text were published between 1494 and 1504; see Whitfield, ibid., 18–19. Whitfield overlooked, however, the first vernacular edition, which was printed in Venice in 1525 by Nicolò di Aristotile, called Zoppino; see Prince d'Essling, *Les livres à figures vénitiens de la fin du XV*[e] *siècle et du commencement du XVI*[e], pt. 1, vol. 2, *Ouvrages imprimés de 1491 à 1500 et leurs éditions successives jusqu'à 1525* (Florence: L. S. Olschki, 1908), 211 (entry no. 748).

44. The life and works of the Ferrarese Nicolò di Aristotile, called Zoppino, are quite interesting. See Mario Emilio Cosenza, *Biographical and Bibliographical Dictionary of the Italian Printers and of Foreign Printers in Italy* (Boston: G. K. Hall, 1968), 676–77; and Donatella Paradisi Maltese and Lelia Sereni, eds., *Arte tipografica del secolo XVI in Italia: Bibliografia italiana* (1850–1979) (Rome: Istituto Centrale per il Catalogo Unico delle Biblioteche Italiane e per le Informazioni Bibliografiche, 1979), 50 (entry no. 506), 55 (entry no. 567).

45. See Whitfield (see note 41), 30.

46. See Edgar Wind, *Pagan Mysteries in the Renaissance* (New Haven: Yale Univ.

Press, 1958), 20. See also the quite different interpretation put forward by Giorgia Biasini, "Giove pittore di farfalle: Un'ipotesi interpretativa del dipinto di Dosso Dossi," *Schifanoia* 13–14 (1992): 9–18, with which I do not agree, although she too thinks that Calcagnini played an influential role. See Luca D'Ascia's essay in the present volume for more on Calcagnini's importance in Ferrarese culture.

47. Maria Antonietta De Angelis, *Gli emblemi di Andrea Alciato nella edizione Steyner del 1531: Fonti e simbologie* (Salerno: M. A. De Angelis, 1984), 60–63.

48. De Angelis, ibid., 269–71. In the text accompanying the image of "Anteros sive Amor Virtutis," the following questions are posed: *"Tres unde corollas fert manus? Unde aliam tempora cincta gerunt?"* (Whence the three garlands in your hand? Whence the fourth wreathing your brow?) The fourth crown linked to Virtue, Anteros answers, is the chief crown because it stands for wisdom (or prudence) and, as such is placed on her temples. The other three crowns indicate Justice, Fortitude, and Temperance. On the iconographic imprecisions in regard to the emblem of Anteros, see John Manning, "A Bibliographical Approach to the Illustrations in Sixteenth-Century Editions of Alciato's *Emblemata,*" in Peter M. Daly, ed., *Andrea Alciato and the Emblem Tradition: Essays in Honor of Virginia Woods Callahan* (New York: AMS, 1989), esp. 129–34. On the relationship between text and image in the emblems, see William S. Heckscher, "Renaissance Emblems: Observations Suggested by Some Emblem-Books in the Princeton University Library" (1954), in idem, *Art and Literature: Studies in Relationship,* ed. Egon Verheyen (Durham: Duke Univ. Press, 1985), 111–24. A different approach is taken by Hessel Miedema, "The Term *Emblema* in Alciati," *Journal of the Warburg and Courtauld Institutes* 31 (1968): 234–50. See also Guy de Tervarent, *Attributs et symboles dans l'art profane, 1450–1600: Dictionnaire d'un langage perdu* (Geneva: E. Droz, 1958), 20; and Erwin Panofsky, *Studies in Iconology: Humanistic Themes in the Art of the Renaissance* (New York: Oxford Univ. Press, 1939), 126.

49. Pietro Andrea Mattioli's description of the Trent frescoes has been republished in Michelangelo Lupo, "Il Magno Palazzo annotato," in Enrico Castelnuovo, ed., *Il Castello del Buonconsiglio,* vol. 1, *Percorso nel Magno Palazzo* (Trent: Temi, 1995), 67–231, esp. 145–56. Gibbons (see note 5), 52ff., regards the first monochrome as a depiction of the marriage of Mercury and Philology.

50. Peter M. Daly, Virginia W. Callahan, and Simon Cuttler, eds., *Andreas Alciatus,* 2 vols. (Toronto: Univ. of Toronto Press, 1985), 1: emblem 99. On the painting *Allegory of Fortune,* see Dawson Carr, "The *Allegory of Fortune* in the Getty Museum" (paper presented at the conference "Dosso Dossi and His Age," Malibu, Calif., May 1996). See also Ferino-Pagden (see note 11), 420–25 (entry no. 144).

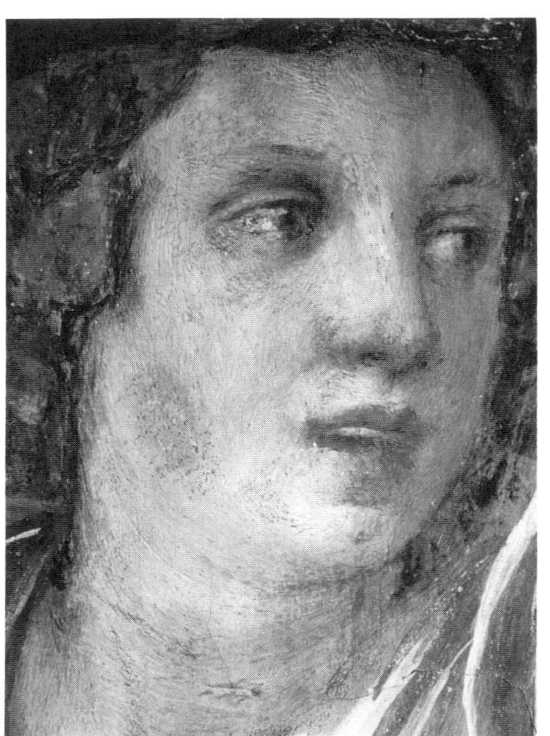

Fig. 1. Dosso Dossi and workshop
Head of a caryatid on the west wall (photographed with diffused light)
Pesaro, Villa Imperiale, Camera delle Cariatidi

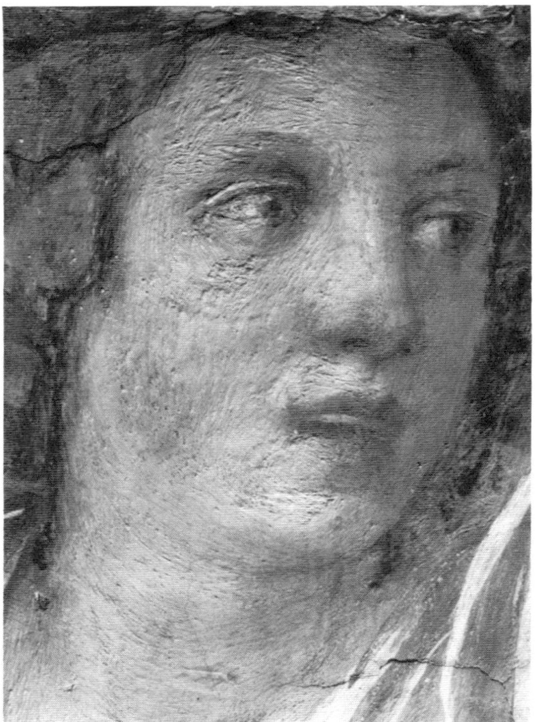

Fig. 2. Dosso Dossi and workshop
Head of a caryatid on the west wall (photographed with strong raking light)
Pesaro, Villa Imperiale, Camera delle Cariatidi

Painting *A Calce* and *Sprezzatura* in the 1530s: A Technical Context for Dosso

Vincenzo Gheroldi

This essay examines the experiments in wall painting *a calce* (with wet lime) carried out by Dosso's workshop. Focusing on the paintings in the Camera delle Cariatidi in the Villa Imperiale in Pesaro, its aim is to explain the practices of Dosso and Battista Dossi in light of the technical traditions and technical experiments with wet lime painting among artists in the eastern Po valley during the 1530s. I will begin with some observations on the procedures employed by Dosso and his circle, then attempt to reconstruct the cultural context that led to the development of these procedures. I will show how the adoption of a particular painting technique could be shaped by complex cultural values. In particular, I will describe the link between experiments in painting *a calce* and the taste for *sprezzatura* (nonchalance, or ease) found in the eastern Po valley during the years in which Dosso and his associates were active there.

A comparison may be useful in defining the principal theme of this study. The subject in question is a detail of the head of one of the plant-shaped figures in the Camera delle Cariatidi.[1] This detail was photographed first in soft light (fig. 1) and then in strong raking light (fig. 2), in order to bring out some of the characteristics of the plastering and, especially, in order to show the direction of the brushstrokes and the thickness of the mixture of colors in the various coats of paint. This is clearly a work in which wet lime painting is predominant. A macrophotograph of another face, taken in strong raking light, serves to reveal immediately the distinctive ways in which the flesh tones were executed (fig. 3): the artist began with a more fluid application of paint and subsequently mixed increasingly dense color with wet lime directly onto the surface of the plaster, dragging his brushstrokes and leaving thick lumps in the paint.

The few examples of wall paintings from the 1530s that have survived in Ferrara—from Girolamo da Carpi's work of 1530 in San Francesco to Garofalo's and Girolamo da Carpi's tondi of about 1535 in San Giorgio—reveal a technique that cannot be compared in any way to either the thick layering of paint or the brushwork that is found in the paintings by the Dossi in Pesaro and Trent. In the works of Girolamo da Carpi and Garofalo, for example, the paint is normally absorbed by the *intonaco* and highlighted

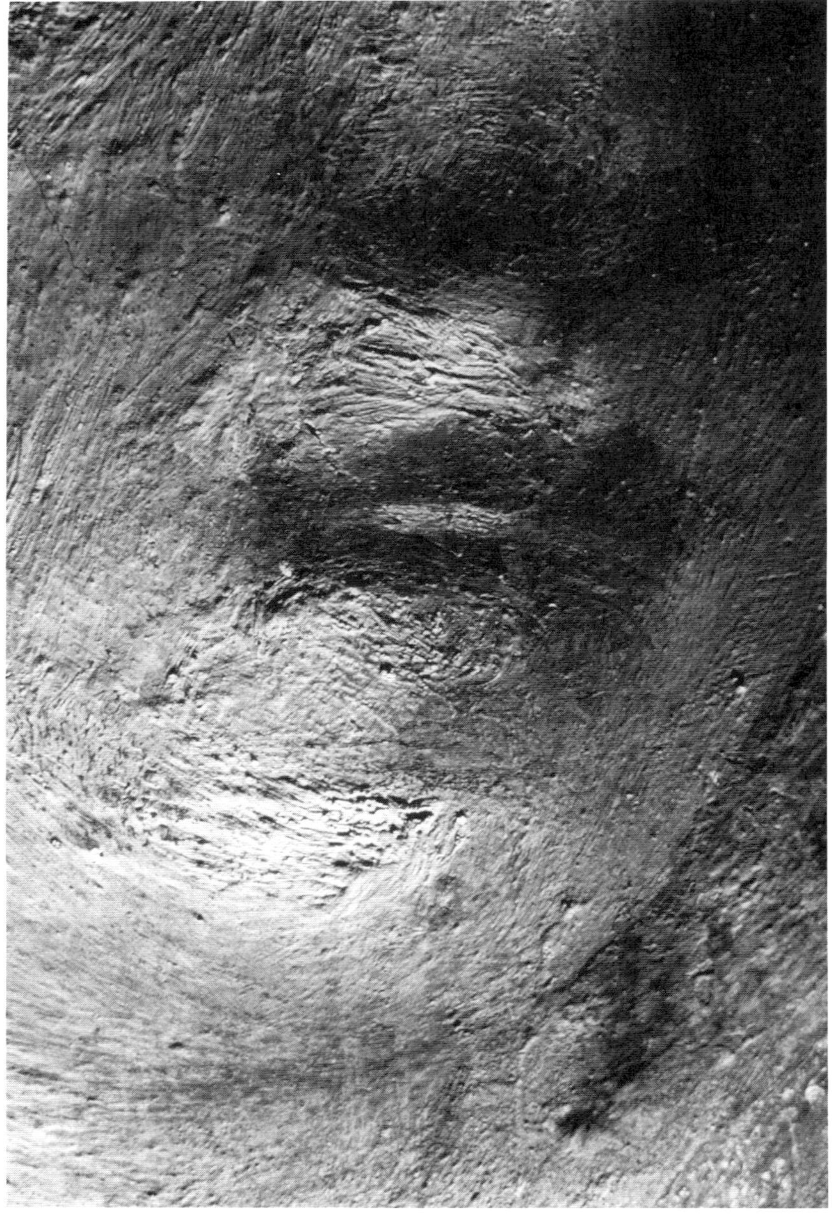

Fig. 3. Dosso Dossi and workshop
Mouth and chin of a caryatid on the west wall
(photographed with strong raking light)
Pesaro, Villa Imperiale, Camera delle Cariatidi

with whitewash. Garofalo tended to modulate his rather liquid mixtures of paint, whereas Girolamo da Carpi preferred uniform coats of paint which he then highlighted with highly diluted touch-ups, applied in slender sinuous strokes. Both artists produced paintings with smooth and regular surfaces, which, as can be seen in Garofalo's *Saint Catherine* and Girolamo da Carpi's *Redeemer* (both of which come from San Giorgio), display a considerable uniformity when removed from the wall by means of a *strappo* (pulled away) technique.

Judging from these examples, Ferrara is not the most suitable context for discussing the Dossi's wall paintings. We must therefore look elsewhere. But before beginning this search, it is necessary to enrich our view of painting *a calce* as practiced by Dosso and his associates, inasmuch as the generic definition of painting *a calce* is inadequate for the complex sets of practices that distinguished individual approaches to the use of this bonding agent in the eastern Po valley during the 1530s.

These practices may be reconstructed only by direct study of the wall paintings themselves. In fact, the available written sources usually have only a normative or rhetorical value, and for this reason the technical literature of the sixteenth century contains nothing of any specific interest on practices connected to the technique of painting *a calce*. The few available sixteenth-century remarks on the topic tend in fact to present this technique as a short cut of fresco painting, employed when depicting highlights, or as a low-level technique suitable primarily for the creation of decorative works. Only a brief remark by Giovanni Battista Armenini on the practice of mixing some pigments with a bit of quicklime (*bianco di calce*) and applying them to a preexisting coat of almost dry plaster provides an interesting perspective for the study of the practices of sixteenth-century painters in the Po valley. These painters applied colors containing whitewash or slaked lime both when working on drying plaster (which could absorb very little and could therefore allow only a surface carbonation), and when working on plaster that had been given a preliminary whitening with lime (*scialbatura*).[2]

This brings into focus a set of practices that is incompatible with any overly schematic distinction between painting *a fresco* and painting *a calce*.[3] And although Armenini's remark dates from the 1580s and thus is rather late in regard to the chronological limits of this study, it is nevertheless worth observing that the technical problems mentioned by this late sixteenth-century writer are nonetheless very close to those that we seek to analyze in the technique of Dosso and his associates. An examination of the material sources in fact allows us to see how Armenini's comment on the use of mixing pigments with lime and subsequently applying them on nearly dry plaster in no way refers to a technical innovation of his time. Rather, it describes a far older practice, one that had been resumed on specific occasions in the eastern part of the Po valley during the late 1520s and the 1530s. The practice of wall painting in Dosso's workshop, which developed precisely in this geographical and chronological context, can thus easily be included as a part of this trend, in which new attention was paid to the technical possibilities offered by painting *a calce*.

The reconstruction of the working organization at Pesaro immediately brings us face-to-face with a distribution of *intonaci* that is typical of a context in which painting *a calce* played an important role. The *intonaci* do not follow the outlines of the figures, but are instead applied in sections following the architectural elements in this order: ceiling, spandrel, lunette, wall. On the walls, the large layers to the left are almost always cut vertically, while to the right they are brought virtually to the edge of the caryatids.[4] Some areas of the plaster display signs of remodeling: the small rectangles of plaster over the caryatids (fig. 4)—superimposed over the plaster of the spandrel but set beneath the plaster on the wall—covered areas where protruding corbels had been removed. They were removed, most likely, because their presence interrupted the continuity of the illusion created by the figures in the wall paintings, which the Dossi obviously planned for the room only after it had already been laid out. The stratigraphic sequence of the edges of the *intonaci*, together with the placement and filling in of the openings in the walls, lead me to believe that the holes where the corbels were inserted were subsequently used for the props that supported the scaffolding necessary for painting the ceiling. When strong raking light is cast on the left-hand portion of the plaster on the wall to the left of the entryway, the uneven surfaces that are visible in the Dossi's work seem to correspond to the preexisting openings in the wall that had been filled in.

This last supposition could be verified through a thermographic examination of the wall, but the study of the plaster in strong raking light and the reconstruction of the positioning of the holes for the scaffolding allow us to define the chronological sequence of the work (fig. 5; see also p. 242). The first phase, realized with the use of scaffolding, proceeded from the ceiling to the spandrels to the lunettes; subsequently, in a second phase, in which only a small freestanding scaffold (perhaps two meters in width) was employed, the walls were painted. The vertical and rather irregular pieces of the plaster on the walls and the figurative continuity between the walls, lunettes, and spandrels, however, were hardly suited to the fresco technique. Once dry, the frescoes would have shown the inevitable dissimilarities caused by the different applications of paint absorbed by the various sections of the plaster. (This occurred, for example, in the water painted on the left area of the west wall of the Sala di Psiche in the Palazzo Te in Mantua.) The wall painters of this period either hid these variations with slight retouching or with systematic retouching with tempera *a secco*, or they overcame it by making ample use of painting *a calce*, first on a nearly dry *intonaco*, in part already frescoed, and then on a fully dry *intonaco*.

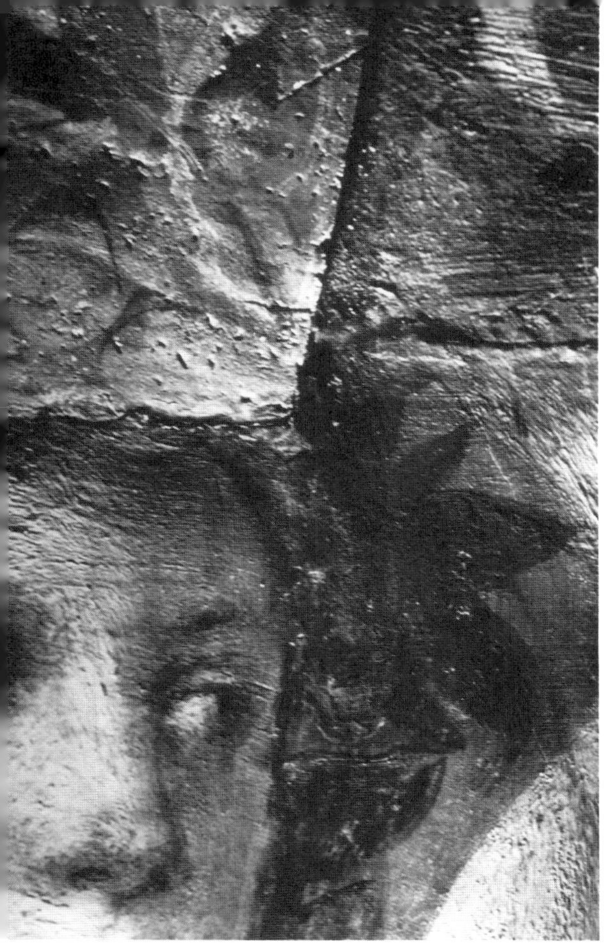

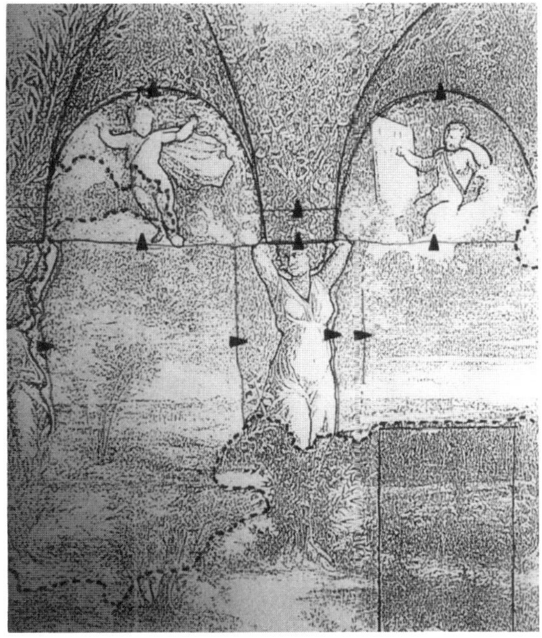

Fig. 4. Dosso Dossi and workshop
Upper part of the head of a caryatid on the west wall (photographed with strong raking light)
Pesaro, Villa Imperiale, Camera delle Cariatidi

Fig. 5. Graphic reconstruction
Chronological sequence of the layering of the plaster on a section of the north wall
Pesaro, Villa Imperiale, Camera delle Cariatidi

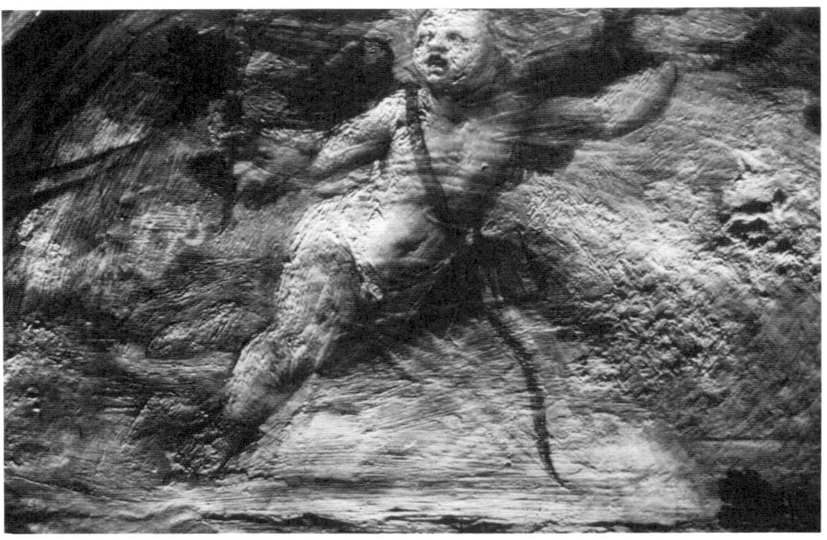

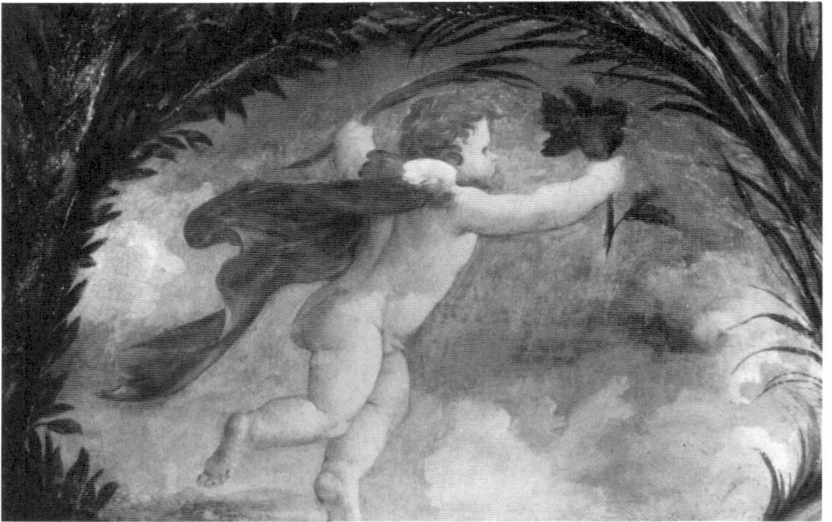

Fig. 6. Dosso Dossi and workshop
Putto on the west wall (photographed with strong raking light)
Pesaro, Villa Imperiale, Camera delle Cariatidi

Fig. 7. Dosso Dossi and workshop
Lunette on the east wall (photographed with diffused light)
Pesaro, Villa Imperiale, Camera delle Cariatidi
Here attributed to Battista Dossi

The Dossi's workshop used this latter approach, as can be seen in the bonding of the sky to the lunette representing a putto with bow and quiver (fig. 6). The sky is superimposed precisely in the area of connection between the plaster of the lunette and that of the wall beneath it. The execution of the lunette belonged to the first phase of the work, which was carried out with scaffolding, whereas the wall was done with the free-standing scaffold at a later point. The sky, which was painted *a calce* and superimposed upon both, was therefore done starting from the wall, when the lunette was already dry. This simple deduction helps us reconstruct with greater precision the order in which the artists and their assistants worked. All of the surfaces were treated in the same way as the one described above, and therefore the process bears witness to the practice of Dosso's workshop. What had already been painted on fresh or drying plaster was retouched with ample and elaborate applications of wet lime paint. The recognition of this practice is fundamental for our technical reconstruction, but we must not overlook the fact that such an organization of the work site could call into question efforts to distinguish the work of Dosso from that of Battista Dossi, inasmuch as the superimposed applications of paint could point to a tightly interwoven—and hence inextricable—collaboration between the two. A layer painted by Battista, in other words, could have been entirely repainted *a calce* by Dosso himself, or vice versa. Either of the two artists, moreover, could have intervened later to refine the work. Prior to the retouching, however, the work was divided according to the individual sections of the lunettes, and here we can note differences between slightly granular surfaces of paintings executed with a very diluted mixture of colors, on the one hand, and plaster surfaces trowelled smooth and painted more vigorously with abundant thick mixtures of wet lime, on the other. A comparison between the two putti over the door in the back wall and the two putti to the right of the door in the entry wall reveals this difference. The putti in the lunettes executed with the rougher plaster and a more limited use of the *a calce* technique are associated with the style of Battista Dossi between the end of the 1520s and the first three or four years of the 1530s (fig. 7). They are reminiscent of, for example, the Christ Child in the *Flight from Egypt* in the Niedersächisches Landesmuseum in Hannover, or the Christ Child in the *Virgin Enthroned with Saint Jerome and Saint John the Baptist,* now in Ferrara in the Pinacoteca Nazionale. To Dosso, then, could be attributed the work executed with a more lively use of the *a calce* technique on the smoother plaster surfaces, which constitutes the largest part of the wall painting in the Pesaro villa. If, as I have hypothesized, there was scaffolding set up at the height where the corbels had been removed in order to paint the vault, the spandrels, and the lunettes, then we may imagine that the two painters worked at the same time on the scaffolding. Once the ceiling scaffolding had been dismantled, the holes in the walls filled in, and the walls painted with the help of a freestanding scaffold, however, then all of the frescoes were retouched and made homogeneous *a calce* chiefly by Dosso himself.[5]

The study of the surfaces, moreover, allows us to reconstruct a series of special techniques for the use of the wet lime. Under strong raking light, the lunettes with thicker paint display the arched traces of having been flattened and smoothed with a trowel. This operation was performed to make the plaster denser and therefore less absorbent, but it also served to break the veil of surface carbonation and to draw the limewater back to the surface of the plaster. An examination of the depth of penetration of the colors into the plaster allows us to measure the binding between colors and plaster: it takes place at the surface level. Therefore this technique was normally used to produce paintings that were not fully absorbed by the plaster and were therefore chromatically more intense.

A lacuna in the area near the toes of the putto permits us to observe in strong raking light a stratification of layers of painting *a calce* that look like a peeling-off of superimposed films (fig. 8). We can see that, in this case, painting *a calce* was executed with brushstrokes that were then repeated when the surface was dry (that is, in an *a secco* technique). In this case too the application of paint on the lunette was superimposed over the bonding of the *intonaco* that separated the lunette from the wall beneath it. This therefore confirms that not only was the sky painted *a calce* over the dry plaster in order to link the two sections of the plaster, but that even the detail of the putto was executed in the same phase, when the portion of the wall below had already been painted.

With a movable scaffold it would have been easy to return to the already painted parts of the work to add the final linking, mask over the bondings between the sections of plaster with painting *a calce,* and execute parts of the figures. A study in strong raking light of the places where plaster has fallen or where there are abrasions confirms in every instance this procedure. In the area of the sky, for instance, many places can be seen in which the base layer of *smaltino* (enamel-like blue paint) has been exposed, over which were superimposed several layers of color bonded with whitewash.[6] The long brushstrokes in these fields of *smaltino* bonded with whitewash can easily be followed in strong raking light as they lead beneath the areas of landscape. Raised surfaces are visible in various other areas of the work, evidencing the directions and superimpositions of broad vertical brushstrokes and long horizontal applications of *smaltino* bonded with whitewash that form the background for further *a calce* applications. The same procedure of painting *a calce* may be seen in the execution of the clouds in the lunettes of the "Volto avanti la chapela" in the Castello del Buonconsiglio of Trent, where, exactly as in the Villa Imperiale in Pesaro, we find the same broad and rapid brushstrokes of *smaltino,* with the mixed pigments of the colored clouds superimposed over them. This allows us to recognize immediately that the technical approach of the Dossi was based upon a desire to display the brushstrokes and mixes of pigments that were brought into bold relief by a repeated application of painting *a calce.*

In those damaged parts of the Pesaro paintings in which it is possible to

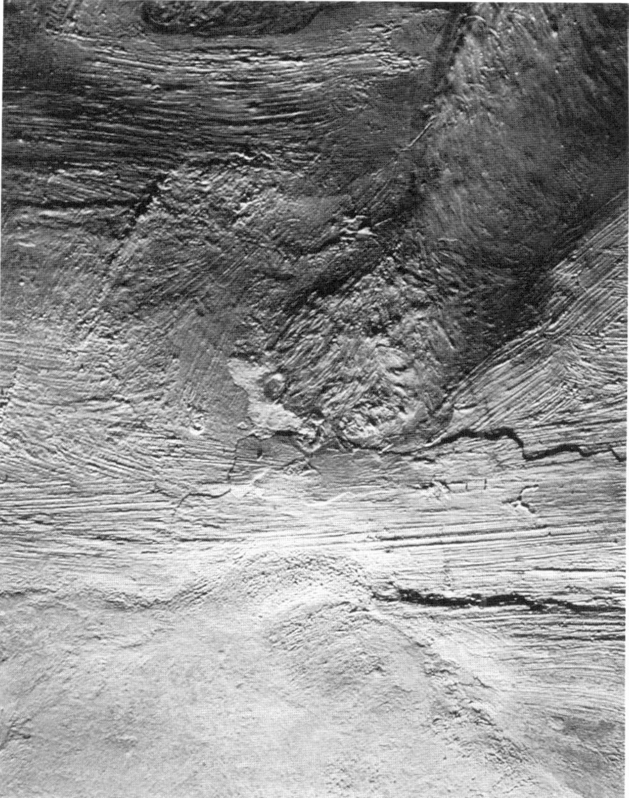

Fig. 8. Dosso Dossi and workshop
Foot of a putto on the west wall (detail of fig. 6)
Pesaro, Villa Imperiale, Camera delle Cariatidi

observe closely with a magnifier a cross section of the painted plaster, it is clear that the first, more liquid coats of paint always penetrated only slightly into the plaster. Subsequent layers of brushstrokes *a calce* always appear over them in filmlike layers. The frescoes in Trent also contain some useful clues for assessing the interest of Dosso's workshop for working with plaster that was not very absorbent and for painting *a calce* on smooth plaster. By looking in strong raking light at the lunette with the figure of Minerva in the "Volto avanti la chapela," we can detect the presence of whitewash under the layers of painted surface, recognizable by the raised edges of several long horizontal strokes executed with a brush approximately four centimeters in diameter. The lunette displaying Apollodorus in the Sala del Camin Nero was done instead on whitewash in a more regular fashion: an examination of the surface in strong raking light shows that the flesh tones were executed upon a

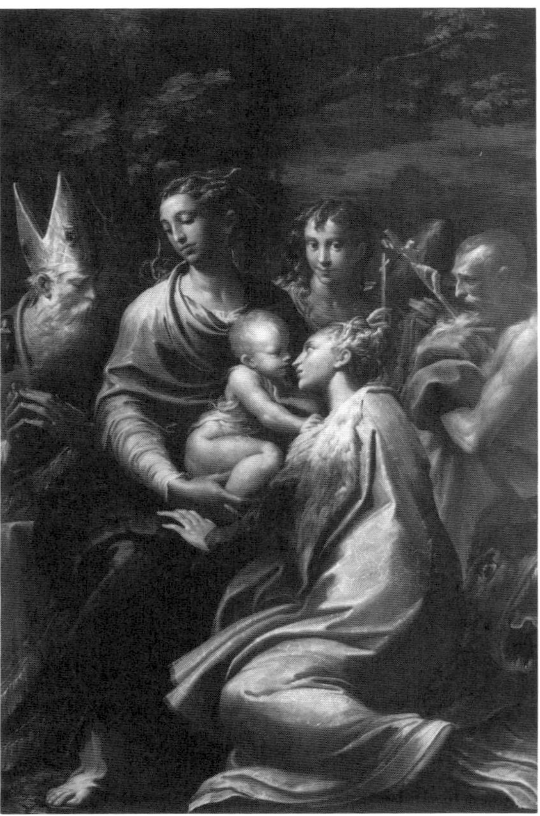

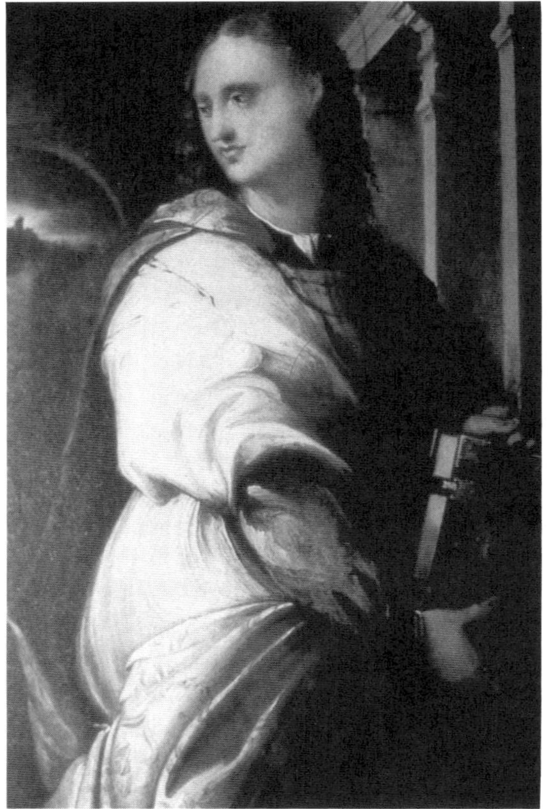

Fig. 9. Altobello Melone
Saint Damian (detail)
Whereabouts unknown

Fig. 10. Parmigianino
Madonna and Child with Saint Margaret, Saint Peter, Saint Jerome, and an Angel
Bologna, Pinacoteca Nazionale

rather thick base of lime. In this room the holes produced by the pressure of the handrest on the fresh *intonaco* are extremely shallow, which indicates that this instrument—used to support the hand holding the brush—did not sink into fresh plaster but rested on an already drying and compacted plaster.

The amount of attention paid by Dosso's workshop to the technique of painting *a calce* on drying plaster would seem therefore to have been motivated by an interest in the fluency of brushstrokes and the display of colors. It would have been impossible to produce these effects through the traditional fresco technique, but the use of drying plaster and the addition of a little lime to the pigments made it possible to achieve lively colored applications of paint and the superimposition of veils of liquid hues, while leaving visible the thick mixtures of pigment and the artists' brushstrokes.

The majority of the details in the Pesaro cycle that I have examined are located approximately two meters above the floor. This means that they were easily visible and that the thick applications *a calce*—intensely and repeatedly applied, with their evident brushwork and colored mixtures of pigment—were deliberate and were meant to be seen by the viewer as a specific trait characterizing the quality of the painting. The development of this mode of painting by the Dossi thus depended upon choices and ideas that were concerned with much more than simply the instrumental use of a technique.

A taste for this kind of painting existed in the 1530s. Its free style of execution and its thick mixtures of colors were very likely disturbing to the more conservative members of the public, but more discerning viewers admired these traits and interpreted them as a form of cultural renewal. Indeed, there are remarks dating from the late 1530s and the early 1540s that tend to associate a free or even sketchlike execution with the expression of an individual personality reacting against the hypocrisy of "diligence." Pietro Aretino, for example, polemically attacked the carefully constructed writing of classicizing literary circles and referred to very sketchy paintings in order to justify his own "antidiligent" approach to literature: "I attempt," he wrote in a letter to Bernardo Valdura, "to depict the natures of others with the same liveliness with which the admirable Titian portrays this or that face; since good painters greatly appreciate a group of sketched figures, I let my things be printed as they are, and do not try at all to craft carefully my words."[7]

The characteristic techniques that we have seen in the paintings by the Dossi belong therefore to a particular cultural orientation of which their contemporaries were well aware. The most interesting evidence of this is furnished by a series of paintings that belong to the second half of the 1520s and the early 1530s, in which incomplete and sketchy execution was deliberately displayed in the most visible areas. In Altobello Melone's *Saint Damian*, for example, the figure in a large yellow robe is sketched with broad brushstrokes (fig. 9); Melone dated the painting in December 1529.[8] In the same year Parmigianino submitted his *Madonna and Child with Saint Margaret*,

Saint Peter, Saint Jerome, and an Angel (fig. 10), a large-scale painting that was intended to serve as an altarpiece and was completely done in the style of a sketch. Another painting by Parmigianino from the same Bolognese period, the *Adoration of the Magi* in San Domenico a Taggia, is also characterized by a very free style of execution. Roberto Longhi dated this work as belonging to the painter's Bolognese period[9] on the basis of Giorgio Vasari's remark (found only in the 1550 edition of the *Lives*) about the "small, colorful, and sketchlike paintings" done by Parmigianino in that city.[10] It is a description that may also be applied to the artist's *Virgin and Child* (fig. 11), now in the Courtauld Gallery in London, whose style is also sketchy. Two or three years earlier, however, Girolamo Romanino had painted the panels for the organ loft in the parish church of Asola with a radically sketchlike technique in which the bare wood support remains visible, and at the same time he intentionally left several areas of his frescoes in the spandrels and the lunettes in the choir of San Francesco in Brescia in a sketchlike state with the *intonaco* exposed and long brushstrokes evident.

The value attributed to this type of painting is attested to by the fact that Parmigianino's "sketched" paintings attracted widespread approbation and, as a consequence, a market. Vasari himself stated that he had purchased a painting by Parmigianino that had been done in this "sketched" style, writing that the artist "sketched the painting of another Virgin, which was sold in Bologna to Giorgio Vasari from Arezzo."[11] The decisive proof of this interest for painting marked by *sprezzatura* is found in the fact that it was reserved for the most visible parts of paintings. Romanino's *Resurrection* (ca. 1526) in Capriolo, for example, displays a free style of execution, consisting of long oily brushstrokes, that is mostly used in the soldier's large sleeve (fig. 12), which is located at the center of the painting in the foreground. The *Scenes from the Passion* (1534) in Santa Maria della Neve in Pisogne were painted by Romanino with rapid strokes, colors mixed with lime, and with portions of the plaster left visible, all of which were at the height of the viewers' eyes. His approach was largely sketchlike and was counterposed to that of the more finished works in the other parts of the cycle that were higher on the walls.[12]

These cases define a context that allows us to understand the technique used for the Dossi's Pesaro paintings as expressing a cultural choice; it was not a chance event or the product of personal whimsy. From the names of the artists mentioned above, it is clear that, toward the end of the 1520s in a specific geographical region, there was a clearly defined group of painters who very consciously adopted this technique of "sketched" painting. Significantly enough, the artists who tended to employ it were those who some fifteen years earlier had begun to work in an anticlassical vein. Lorenzo Lotto, Altobello Melone, Girolamo Romanino, and Amico Aspertini represent the leading figures in this "antidiligent" group of artists from the eastern Po valley. Gianfrancesco Bembo should also be added to this group, for he, in the very same years, chose to adhere to this same style in his predellas known as

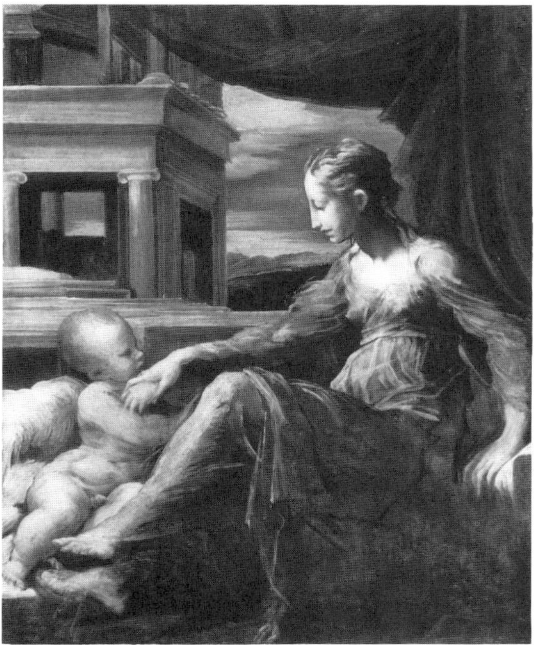

Fig. 11. Parmigianino
The Virgin and Child
London, The Courtauld Gallery

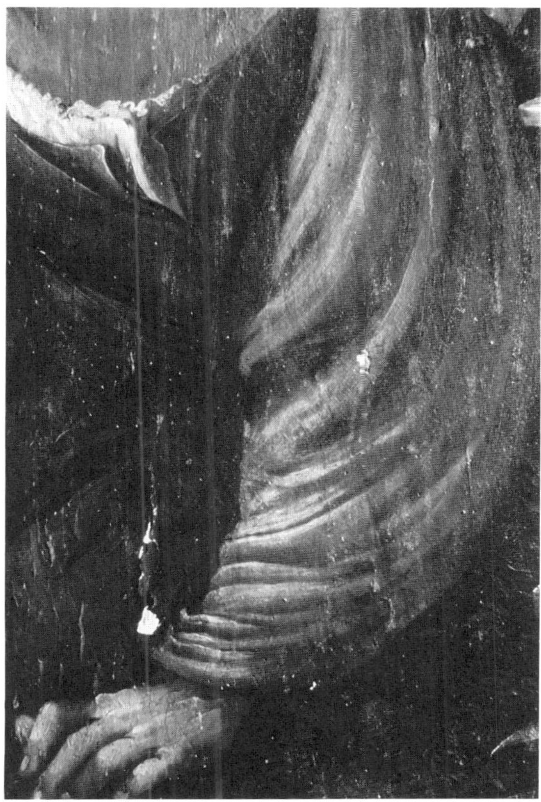

Fig. 12. Girolamo Romanino
Resurrection (detail)
Capriolo, Chiesa Parrocchiale

the *Stories of Saint Stephen* (now in the Pinacoteca Carrara in Bergamo).[13] Whereas Boccaccino employed highly meticulous outlining in his wall paintings of 1514 and 1515, Gianfrancesco Bembo began to employ the "nonchalant" style by 1516; Romanino used lively sketching everywhere in his work of 1519; Pordenone added the finishing touches to his work in Cremona with a loose brush in 1520. This technique may already have been present in the latter's Mantuan paintings from 1519, which happen to have been done when Romanino and Dosso were also both present in Mantua.[14]

Between 1515 and 1517 Dosso was already tending toward displaying thick mixtures of paint that were then touched up with quick strokes of the brush (as can be seen in small- and medium-sized works such as the *Standard Bearer* in the Allentown Art Museum, the *Rest on the Flight into Egypt* in the Galleria degli Uffizi in Florence, and the *Virgin and Child with a Bishop Saint and a Donor Presented by an Angel* in the Szépmüvészeti Múzeum in Budapest). He seems to have been one of the pathbreaking figures of this trend. There are also sections of larger paintings executed with this technique in this period, as, for example, in the right-hand part of the *Adoration of the Magi* in the National Gallery in London.

We can measure the novelty of this "antidiligent" trend against the success in Ferrara, between 1510 and 1515, of more traditional, highly finished, "diligent" paintings. Lodovico Mazzolino produced works whose surfaces were smooth and show no traces of brushwork, such as the *Nativity* in the Pinacoteca Nazionale in Ferrara, or his *Saint Anthony* and his *Saint Mary Magdalen* in the Staatliche Museen, Gemäldegalerie, in Berlin; the Master of the Assumption of Mary Magdalen, whose *Assumption of Mary Magdalen* is now in the Pinacoteca Nazionale, worked in a slow technique; Ortolano used subtly fused colors in his paintings *Saint Nicholas* and *Saint Sebastian* in the Pinacoteca Capitolina in Rome and in his *Nativity*, which formerly belonged to the Loeser collection in Florence; and Garofalo painted in a highly controlled style, evident in his *Adoration of the Magi* in the Staatliche Museen, Gemäldegalerie, in Berlin. Although there are clear individual differences, the execution of these works describes with great precision the stylistic unity of the "diligent" painters of Ferrara and thus indicates the predominate taste in this context around the year 1515. It is interesting to compare all this with the cultural components that emerged from the freer style of painting that Dosso was already employing around 1512. A small work like the *Virgin with Child and Saints* (43.5 × 35 cm), now in the Glasgow Art Gallery and Museum, allows us to see very well the first "antidiligent" hints in Dosso's work, and to see how he produced them by emphasizing and distorting the typical practices of Venetian painting.

Was Venice then the starting point for the "antidiligent" painting of the eastern Po valley? It would seem so, especially considering the fact that in these very same years Altobello Melone, Girolamo Romanino, Lorenzo Lotto, Amico Aspertini, and Dosso himself passed through Venice.[15] If Dosso's Glasgow *Virgin* can be dated to approximately 1512, then we have a preliminary basis for thinking about the development of the "antidiligent" direction of his art, which would lead to the crucial period between 1516 and 1517.[16] Around 1519 to 1520 his work passed through another crucial phase, which was likely linked to the appearance in Bologna of the streaked, thick, and tormented brushwork of Amico Aspertini in works such as the *Marsili Pietà* of 1519 in San Petronio in Bologna and, slightly after 1520, his *Holy Family and Saints* (now in Saint Nicholas des Champs in Paris) and *Madonna and Child with Saint Helena and Saint Francis* (fig. 13). These approaches to painting did not go unnoticed by seventeenth-century writers. Malvasia, for instance, remarked on Aspertini's particular technique of painting in a "*sfregazzi*" (scrawllike) manner, while Francesco Paglia saw in Romanino's brushwork the choice of a technique that "*sprezza la diligenza*" (disdains diligence).[17]

In spite of the spread of this phenomenon over the following fifteen years (with its high point reached around 1528–1529, when these "antidiligent" techniques tended to be identified with "sketched" painting), several hints point to a reluctance to accept a similar style of painting during the 1530s and 1540s. The polemical edge with which Aretino defended his "antidiligent" position could be taken as evidence of this. Above all, however, we ought to consider the resistance posed by the Dossi's patrons of the cycle in the Villa Imperiale and recorded by Vasari. Vasari surely did not possess any firsthand information about this, but his remarks probably were derived from a well-informed source such as Bartolomeo Genga, the son of Girolamo Genga and a friend of Vasari's. For this reason Vasari's remarks possess an element of truth—in spite of the obvious reach he made in order to transform a mere episode into a moral example—concerning the very real difficulties that the Dossi's patrons had in accepting these wall paintings.

Furthermore, it is important to observe that Vasari's criticism of these wall paintings was expressed in a more emphatic version in the second edition of the *Lives*, in which, perhaps not by chance, Vasari took the rejection of the Pesaro cycle as an occasion for treating the theme of the need to control one's own artistic inclinations through study and diligence, without, however, falling into affectation.[18] Significantly enough, in the second edition of the *Lives*, Vasari eliminated from his biography of Parmigianino his remarks concerning the painter's sketchlike works.

These are clues to the shift in attitude toward painterly *sprezzatura* in the second half of the sixteenth century. As far as the patrons of the Dossi's works are concerned—including their possible surprise when confronted with the artists' "antidiligent" mode of painting—it is worth noting that, just a few years before the Dossi's arrival in Pesaro, Raffaellino dal Colle had carried out, on the other side of the entrance in the Camera delle Cariatidi, a painting that was executed in the very controlled technique against which the Dossi were reacting.

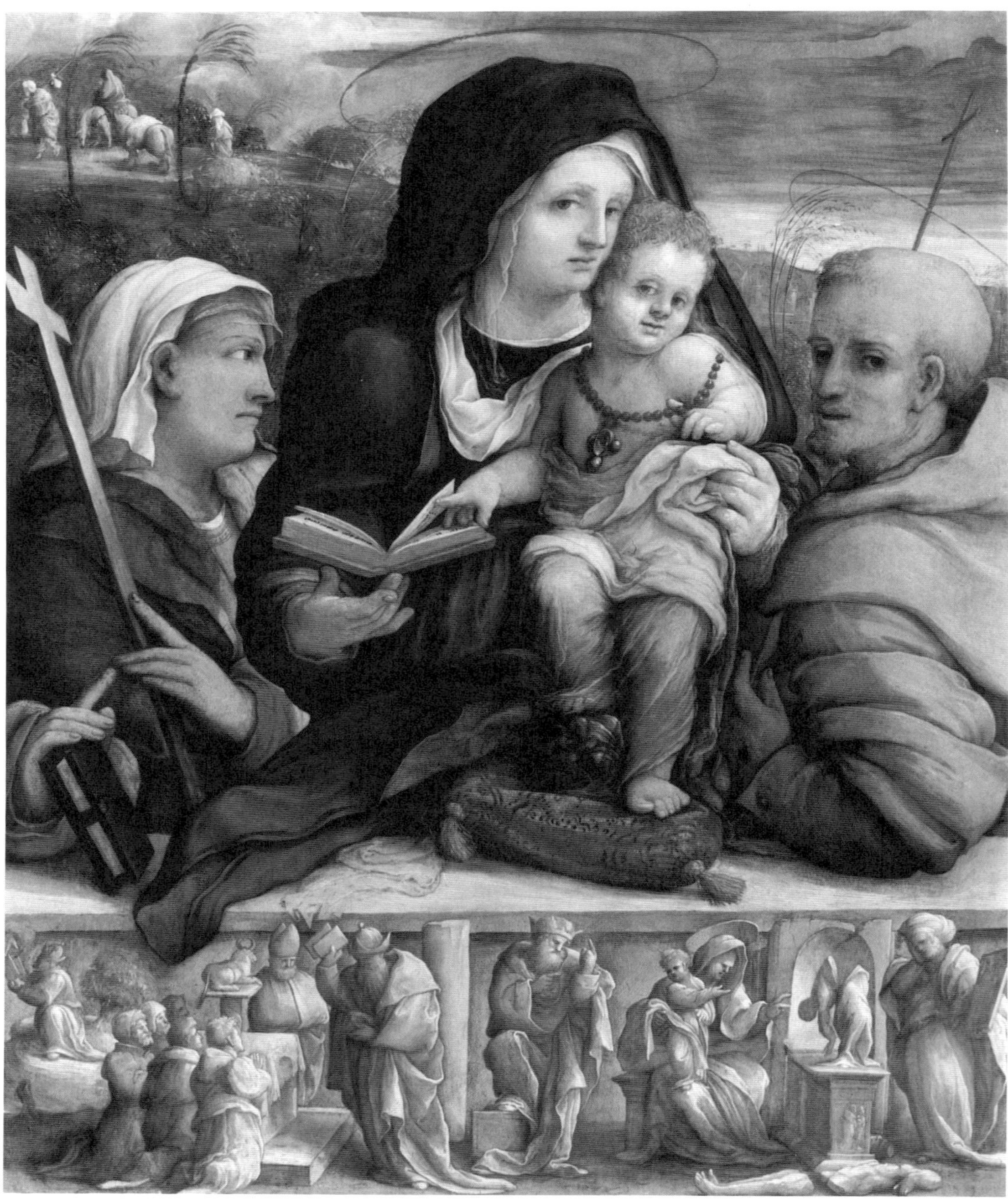

Fig. 13. Amico Aspertini
Madonna and Child with Saint Helena and Saint Francis
Cardiff, National Museum of Wales

There are also, however, clues about the resistance around 1530 to the "antidiligent" style that can be found within the paintings themselves. It is possible, in fact, to trace several artists' wavering, even within a single work, between the use of the new technique and the use of older procedures. This is evidenced, for example, in the final touches applied by Romanino to wall paintings in Trent precisely during the period in which the Dosso workshop was active in the city. In the Loggia del Buonconsiglio, the head of the musician playing the lute in the lunette known as the *Concert with String Instruments* displays the kind of flaking typical of paintings made with whitewash over drying plaster. The final touches for the flesh tones were executed with the tip of the brush, chiefly with extremely short and highly fluid red dashes. This was a typical technique for finishing wall paintings that had been fashionable some ten years earlier, and it stands in sharp contrast to the practice of painters toward the beginning of the 1530s, who used long strokes of a soft brush for a fluid application of finishing touches that followed the flow of the volumes of the fleshy figures. This technique was frequently applied to paintings in Trent, as can be seen in the lunette with the *Flute Concert* and in the flesh tones of Lucretia and Virginia in the lunettes. Along with this approach another sort of finishing was employed, which involved quicker long strokes and, at times, required the use of a wider and looser brush, as in the head of the figure above the lunettes displaying Cleopatra and the Graces. This practice was clearly derived from Pordenone's method of finishing wall paintings.[19]

Interest in the "antidiligent" approach favored a return to the particular chromatic liveliness achieved by painting on drying plaster and by employing thick mixtures of pigments and the kind of brushstrokes used in painting *a calce*. It was therefore natural for "antidiligent" practices and experiments in painting a calce to come together in the eastern Po valley region during the mid-1520s and the early 1530s.

The details of the Dossi's work that we have observed allow us to make some remarks about this experimental phase involving the use of painting *a calce*. In the Camera delle Cariatidi in Pesaro, for instance, there are no cracks in the plaster of the sort caused by drying, but the plaster has widely fragmented into sharp angular lines that do not follow the underlying brick structure. These breaks in the plaster are chiefly to be found in the Dossi's plasterings on the entry wall, and they are not present in the lunettes. Nor are there any fractures on the other side of the entrance on the same wall, which a few years earlier had been plastered over for Raffaellino dal Colle's paintings. Surely these breaks, and the consequent separation of the plaster from the wall at these points, are due to the elastic vibration of the wall, which is only eleven centimeters thick, as well as to the rigidity of the Dossi's *intonaco*. The lack of cracks from the drying process seems to indicate that the plaster did not contain too much lime and that it dried rather slowly.

When taken together, these elements suggest that an additive was mixed into the plaster. Most likely this was milk, which slows the drying of plaster and creates a certain hardness in dry plaster. Casein also has this same effect, but whereas plaster becomes more absorbent when casein is added to it, adding milk to the plaster markedly lowers the ability of the plaster to absorb the paint, owing to the increased fat content of the mixture. The result is a livelier look with more visible brushstrokes, as in the work of the Dossi. There exist numerous sixteenth-century documents concerning the use of milk as an additive,[20] and the practice of adding it to the plaster mix continued until the early twentieth century.[21]

The use of these types of plaster can be connected to the implementation of pictorial practices more complex than simple fresco painting. In the case of painting *a calce,* it is even possible that the wet lime was mixed with the same additive used in treating the *intonaco.* The absence of cracks even in the thicker whites applied *a calce* in the Pesaro cycle certainly suggests the use of a perfectly slaked lime, but it also suggests that some sort of protein-based substance may have been added to the mixture.

Over and beyond the possibility of mixing substances such as milk, glue, or eggs into the lime, I should also mention that there was a tendency to create polymaterial substances for wall paintings in which the *a calce* technique was used extensively. The Sala di Psiche in the Palazzo Te in Mantua, which Dosso himself surely knew, was executed with ample use of paint added to the wet lime and applied over the drying plaster. This was, however, a technique favored by Giulio Romano's collaborators, whereas the artist himself employed thinner applications of paint finished with fluid strokes analogous to those of Raphael's workshop. The area that Vasari attributed to Giulio—"Bacchus, Silenus, and the two cherubs being nursed by a she-goat"[22]—is in fact different from areas executed by his collaborators, who worked from Giulio's cartoons (in some cases the artist himself retouched the paintings by his collaborators). The Sala di Psiche displays, in the ribbed vaulting and the ceiling panels, thick oily layers of paint, while the walls—which were largely done with the various techniques of painting *a calce*—not only possess the opacity typical of the wet lime procedure but also have been finished in a number of places with tempera and oil paint. In more than one case, the reds were finished with layers of lacquer mixed with an oily bonding agent (identified as a saponific substance). The shimmering draperies of the figure stretched out on Apollo's left were executed with ochre yellow *a calce,* but the figure's violet shadows were subsequently finished with cinnabar, whose bonding agent also shows traces of saponific substances.[23] There are highly visible brownish-violet shifts in the highlighting of some of the draperies, which would indicate the use of lead white (obviously not applied *a calce*). There were, moreover, black glazings done with oily tempera that radically deepened the leaves of the pergola, painted *a calce.*

This approach is analogous to the one commonly used in painting on canvas or wood, in which foliage painted with verdigris was then shaded with dark brushstrokes.[24] These additions in oil, which were surely done at the very end of the work, together with the corrections done in whitewash and the retouchings with limewater, were therefore the retouchings described by Vasari as follows: "the work was then almost entirely retouched by Giulio, so that it is as if it had been wholly done by him."[25] For the sixteenth-century mentality, retouching painting *a calce* with oil paint was not a mere expedient, but an intervention that could determine in a decisive manner the identity of the author of the work.

Keeping in mind this perception of the practice of retouching wall paintings with oil paint, let us return to the Dossi's work in Pesaro and Trent, for in both cycles there are traces of oil-based paint over the *a calce* layers. Many of these traces obviously should be attributed to subsequent restorations of the works. Let us not forget, however, that (for instance) the frieze that completes the cycle of paintings by the Dossi in the "Volto avanti la chapela" in Trent, and which has been interpreted as the base of lost stucco work,[26] was in fact painted with oil paint or greasy tempera. Its very smooth surface (absolutely unsuited for supporting stucco) is flush with the surrounding stucco cornices and could not therefore lend itself to holding a stucco work. It displays some traces of penetration by colors that, when viewed under ultraviolet light, reveal the fluorescence typical of oily substances. Doubtless the applications of gilding in the paintings were adapted to the figures represented through retouching with oil paint or with colored varnish. The problem therefore is to determine whether these retouchings were also done within the paintings themselves, and whether the removal of these oil-based retouchings would allow us to separate with certainty the original retouchings from later ones, which may have been done with the same bonding agents. The fine threading in the thickest black shadows in both the Trent and Pesaro paintings certainly could not have been realized with a thick but whitening bonding agent such as lime. The fact that Giulio Romano retouched the details of his work in the Palazzo Te with oil-based lacquer ought to lead us at least to consider the hypothesis that some details in the red draped cloths and the shimmering violet colors in the cycle in the Sala del Camin Nero and the "Volto avanti la chapela" might have been completed with a similar finishing technique.

The ample use of cinnabar in these two rooms would in any event indicate that complex retouching techniques were employed there. As is well known, cinnabar darkens quickly on the surface[27] and cannot be applied and retouched *a calce* except through the use of complicated and rather unreliable preliminary treatments.[28] When applied on a wall, then, cinnabar must be protected with a veiling of oil paint or varnish, and in late-medieval painting it was sometimes covered with a final layer of lacquer bonded with oil or with an oleoresin-based varnish.[29] For this reason the various applications of cinnabar in Trent, which have been whitewashed and unwhitened, are visible with brown surfaces. This is due both to the cinnabar's having come into contact with the lime used in the whitewashing process and to the removal of the protective veiling which occurred during the work of unwhitening the painting, which once again exposed the cinnabar to the air. In the lunette in the vestibule with the figure of Ceres, the cloth swirling behind the figure has this appearance, and the original surface can still be seen in the parts protected by the fragments of the threads of gilded highlighting. All of the gray halos that are visible around the cinnabar in the vestibule and (especially) in the Sala del Camin Nero indicate the penetration of an oily substance through capillarity. These traces might therefore point to the use of a bonding agent containing oil, but more likely they should be interpreted as the residue of a protective retouching with oil paint, oily varnish, or a thin oil-based lacquer similar to the ones used by Serafino dei Serafini over the cinnabar in the details in the Gonzaga chapel in San Francesco in Mantua.

Furthermore, some greens show browning that is similar to that characteristic of verdigris, copper resinate, or copper acetate, whether applied to canvas or wood. In Pesaro, for example, the caryatid with the green dress on the wall to the right of the entryway displays slight traces of such a color change. It is important to note here that the stratigraphic position of these fragments testifies to their belonging to the original painting, inasmuch as they are found not only under the most recent restoration using *tratteggio* (hatching), but are covered by the retouchings done by Giuseppe Gennari in 1880. The written documents do not mention the use of verdigris in wall paintings, but the material documents, which should be the preferred source of information for the type of research being carried out here, demonstrate that it was customary to add final touches in verdigris to those wall paintings that had been executed *a calce* with green and yellow earth colors. This is clear from the leaves painted by Giovanni Pietro da Cemmo in 1493 in Bienno, which were found under an old coat of whitewash and display the absorption of altered copper resinate.[30]

These facts concerning the finishing of wall paintings with oil or varnish gain in importance when they are set in the context of the Dossi's preference for complicated chromatic development in more famous works on canvas and wood. The influence of Venetian painting, along with the emergence of a taste for *sprezzatura* in the eastern Po valley, are the two ingredients of the development of this particular technique. Both the former and the latter allow us to grasp the ways in which the practices connected to painting *a calce* were the result of an intersection between a taste for complex color schemes and an interest in the "antidiligent" freedom of the brushstroke.

Notes

1. For the bibliography on the Camera delle Cariatidi in the Villa Imperiale in Pesaro, see Alessandro Ballarin, *Dosso Dossi: La pittura a Ferrara negli anni del Ducato di Alfonso I,* 2 vols. (Cittadella: Bertoncello Artigrafiche, 1994–1995), 1: 350 (entry no. 458). Ballarin dates this room to about 1530. For more on the dating, see the essay by Craig Hugh Smyth in this volume. Any reference to Dosso as the sole author of this work must be discussed in terms of the technical data, which allow us to see the division of labor between Dosso and Battista Dossi and thus to conclude that Dosso made the greater contribution, even in the phase of retouching the work. For the Trent frescoes, see the bibliography in Ezio Chini, "Dosso Dossi al Castello del Buonconsiglio: L'Atrio e la Sala Grande del Magno Palazzo dopo il restauro del 1990," in Laura Dal Prà, ed., *Un museo nel Castello del Buonconsiglio. Acquisizioni, contributi, restauri,* exh. cat. (Trent: Castello del Buonconsiglio, 1995), 201–38. I would append to Chini's bibliography the recent article by Stefano Tumidei, "Dosso (e Battista) al Buonconsiglio," in Enrico Castelnuovo, ed., *Il Castello del Buonconsiglio,* vol. 2, *Dimora dei Principi Vescovi di Trento: Persone e tempi di una storia* (Trent: Temi, 1996), 131–57.

2. See, for Armenini's remarks on painting *a calce,* and (more specifically) on the practices mentioned in the text, Giovanni Battista Armenini, *De' veri precetti della pittura* (Ravenna: F. Tebaldini, 1586), bk. 2, chap. 8, 107–8 (on lime white and its mixing with other pigments), 114 (the use of drying plaster to paint *"mentre che la calcina si mostra fermissima"* [while the plaster is extremely firm] and painting on whitewash).

3. The lack of a firm distinction between fresco and painting *a calce* in the early sources, which is due to a practice in which one method presupposed the other, is rightly noted by Alessandro Conti, "Affresco, pittura a calce, pittura a secco," in Regina Poso and Lucio Galante, eds., *Tra metodo e ricerca: Contributi di storia dell'arte* (Galatina: Congedo, 1991), 159–77. On lime white and painting *a calce,* see Rutherford J. Gettens, Elisabeth West Fitzhugh, and Robert L. Feller, "Calcium Carbonate Whites," *Studies in Conservation* 19 (1974): 157–84; Edgar Denninger, "What Is 'Bianco di San Giovanni' of Cennino Cennini?" *Studies in Conservation* 19 (1974): 185–87; Bruno Zanardi, Luca Arcangeli, and Lorenzo Appolonia, "'Della natura del bianco sangiovanni': Un pigmento e la lettura delle fonti," *Ricerche di storia dell'arte,* no. 24 (1984): 62–74; Andreina Costanzi Cobau, "La pittura a calce: Osservazioni," in Guido Biscontin, ed., *L'intonaco: Storia, cultura e tecnologia* (Padua: Libreria Progetto, 1985), 123–31.

4. This figurative typology is well suited for scaffold painting. See, for example, the Camera delle Cariatidi in the Belriguardo residence, located near Voghenza, which can be dated circa 1537, in which a horizontal scaffold platform cut the figures in half. The cracks in the plaster of the Belriguardo Camera delle Cariatidi indicate shrinkage during the drying process, which suggests excessive lime in the mixture. On this room, see Vittorio Sgarbi, "Testimonianze inedite del raffaellismo in Emilia: Garofalo, Gerolamo da Carpi e Battista Dossi a Belriguardo," in Micaela Sambucco Hamoud and Maria Letizia Strocchi, eds., *Studi su Raffaello,* 2 vols. (Urbino: QuattroVenti, 1987), 1: 595–601.

5. Recent studies waver between attributing the work to Dosso alone—for example, S. J. Freedberg, *Painting in Italy, 1500 to 1600,* rev. ed. (Harmondsworth, Middlesex: Penguin, 1975), 320–21; *Le siècle de Titien: L'âge d'or de la peinture à Venise,* 2nd ed., exh. cat. (Paris: Editions de la Réunion des Musées Nationaux, 1993), 474 (entry no. 81 by Alessandro Ballarin); and Ballarin (see note 1), 1: 350 (entry no. 458)—and seeing Dosso's contribution as more substantial than that of Battista—for example, Paolo Dal Poggetto, "Il cantiere della Villa Imperiale," in Maria Grazia Ciardi Duprè dal Poggetto and Paolo Dal Poggetto, eds., *Urbino e le Marche prima e dopo Raffaello,* exh. cat. (Florence: Salani, 1983), 381–97. Still others regard the work as the result of a full-fledged collaboration between the artists. See Amalia Mezzetti, *Il Dosso e Battista ferraresi* (Milan: Silvana, 1965), 32–35; Bernard Berenson, *Italian Pictures of the Renaissance: A List of the Principal Artists and Their Works, with an Index of Places: Central Italian and North Italian Schools,* rev. ed., 3 vols. (London: Phaidon, 1968), 1: 113; and Felton Gibbons, *Dosso and Battista Dossi: Court Painters at Ferrara* (Princeton: Princeton Univ. Press, 1968), 76–85.

6. *Smaltino* is easily identifiable under a 30-power microscope; it displays a granular structure of ground particles with sharp, angular fissures and is translucent. On this artificial blue pigment (created from powdered glass colored with cobalt oxide), see Bruno Mühlethaler and Jean Thissen, "Smalt," *Studies in Conservation* 14 (1969): 47–61. On the use of *smaltino* in wall paintings in the 1520s and 1530s, see Vincenzo Gheroldi, "Finiture murali di Paolo da Caylina il Giovane: Tre note tecniche sull'*Adorazione di Cristo eucaristico* del Coro delle Monache di Santa Giulia a Brescia," *Museo bresciano* 5 (1995): 47–62, esp. 61 n. 21.

7. Pietro Aretino, *Lettere sull'arte,* ed. Ettore Camesasca, 3 vols. (Milan: Edizioni del Milione, 1957–1960), 1: 108: *"E per ciò io mi sforzo di ritrarre le nature altrui con la vivacità con che il mirabile Tiziano ritrae questo e quel volto, e perchè i buoni pittori apprezzano molto un bel groppo di figure abozzate, lascio stampare le mie cose così fatte, né mi curo punto di miniar parole."* See also Aretino's letter to Paolo Manuzio from Venice, dated 9 December 1537 (1: 100–101). Giorgio Vasari's *Le vite de' più eccellenti pittori, scultori ed architettori,* ed. Gaetano Milanesi, 9 vols. (Florence: Sansoni, 1906), includes various passages on the practice of painting in sketches (*a bozze*), which was presented as a Venetian tradition. About Andrea Schiavone, Vasari writes, *"[una figura] è fatta con una certa pratica, che s'usa a Vinezia, di macchie ovvero bozze, senza esser finita punto"* ([a figure] is made with a certain practice that is used in Venice, employing blotches or rather sketches without being retouched at all) (4: 596). He also notes that Titian's late works are *"condotte di colpi, tirate via di grosso e con macchie, di maniera che da presso non si possono vedere"* (executed in bold strokes, very quickly and sketchily and with blotches, in such a manner that they cannot be viewed from up close) (7: 452), and remarks of Tintoretto that *"Ha costui alcuna volta lasciato le bozze per finite, tanto a fatica sgrossate, che si veggiono i colpi de' pennegli fatti dal caso e dalla fierezza"* (he sometimes left sketches as finished works, after having toiled at stripping them down, so that the brushstrokes are seen as random and proud) (6: 587). In these descriptions, the traces of the artist's tools are the most visible features in their sketched works. Vasari links these to his favorable remarks about the signs left by the sculptor's chisel on the surface of a

roughly worked piece of sculpture: *"[gli scultori] vanno per tutto con gentilezza gradinando la figura con la proporzione de' muscoli e delle pieghe, e la tratteggiano di maniera per la virtù delle tacche o denti predetti, che la pietra mostra grazia mirabile"* ([sculptors] gently work with a gradine [toothed chisel] on their figures with the proportions of muscles and folds, and with the aforesaid tool rough out the work so that the stone displays admirable grace); cited in Giorgio Vasari, *Le vite de' più eccellenti architetti, pittori, et scultori italiani: Da Cimabue insino a' tempi nostri: Nell' edizione per i tipi di Lorenzo Torrentino, Firenze 1550,* ed. Luciano Bellosi and Aldo Rossi (Turin: Einaudi, 1986), 47. This treatment is recognized in Michelangelo's *Madonna* for the Medici Chapel, *"rimasta abozzata e gradinata, nella imperfezione della bozza, la perfezione dell'opera"* (left roughed out and gradined, so that the perfection of the work is found in the imperfection of the rough sketch) (7: 195). See, on these remarks by Vasari, Paola Barocchi, "Finito e non-finito nella critica vasariana," *Arte antica e moderna,* no. 3 (1958): 221–35. See, on the relationship between Vasari's appreciation of chiseling and the taste for the "rustic," Luciano Bellosi, "Linguaggio della critica d'arte," in Giovanni Previtali, ed., *Enciclopedia Feltrinelli—Arte* (Milan: Feltrinelli, 1971), 2.1: 292–93. Painting in the *sprezzante* style was seen not only as a reaction to the meticulous "diligent" approach but as proof of the painter's facility and as evidence of his individuality. Let us not forget that the term *sprezzatura* was used for the first time by Baldassare Castiglione in his *Il libro del cortegiano* (written between 1508 and 1518, but first published in Venice in 1527), bk. 1, chap. 26, to define a way of behaving in social interactions that aimed at avoiding affectation, which was thought to make all one's gestures appear false and impersonal.

8. Altobello Melone's *Saint Damian* (oil on wood, 154.5 × 53 cm, sold at Sotheby's in London on 5 July 1989) bears the inscriptions: "S. DAMIANVS" (below the figure) and "ANO SANITIS 1529 / DIE 20 DECB 152[9]" (on a painted cartouche). For the attribution, see Sotheby's, *Old Master Paintings, London, Wednesday, 5th July 1989,* lot 61. A good photographic reproduction may be found in Mina Gregori, ed., *Pittura a Cremona dal Romanico al Settecento* (Milan: Cassa di Risparmio delle Provincie Lombarde, 1990), pl. 70; see also, in the same volume, the entry for this plate by Francesco Frangi on page 264.

9. Roberto Longhi, "Un nuovo Parmigianino," *Paragone,* no. 99 (1958): 33–36; and idem, "L'inizio dell'abbozzo autonomo," *Paragone,* no. 195 (1966): 25–29.

10. Giorgio Vasari, *Le vite de' più eccellenti pittori, scultori e architettori: Nelle redazioni del 1550 e 1568: Testo,* ed. Rosanna Bettari and Paola Barocchi, 6 vols. (Florence: Sansoni, 1966–1971; Studio per Edizioni Scelte, 1976–1987), 4: 541: *"quadri piccoli coloriti e bozzati."* It should be noted that Vasari eliminated the remarks about Parmigianino's sketchy style that appear in the 1550 edition when he rewrote his life of the painter for the second edition, published in 1568.

11. Vasari (see note 9), 4: 541: *"abbozzò il quadro d'un'altra Madonna, il quale in Bologna fu venduto a Giorgio Vasari aretino."*

12. On Romanino's *sprezzatura,* see Vincenzo Gheroldi, "Una ricerca sui livelli del finito," in *Romanino in Sant'Antonio a Breno* (Breno: Commune di Breno, 1992), 77–105; and idem, "Romanino: Un percorso ravvicinato," *Franciacorta Magazine* 13 (1992): 15–43.

13. For Gianfrancesco Bembo's predellas, see *I Campi: Cultura artistica cremonese del Cinquecento* (Milan: Electa, 1985), 104–5 (entry no. 1.9.2 by Mina Gregori), which brings into focus his relationship with Lotto and Aspertini. For a parallel with Grammorseo, see Giovanni Romano, *Casalesi del Cinquecento: L'avvento del manierismo in una città padana* (Turin: Einaudi, 1970), 33–34.

14. Contacts between Dosso and Pordenone could have occurred not only in Venice but in Mantua as well. Dosso was in Mantua in 1519—according to documents, he accompanied Titian on a visit to the collection of Isabella d'Este; see Alessandro Luzio, *La galleria dei Gonzaga venduta all'Inghilterra nel 1627–28: Documenti degli archivi di Mantova e Londra* (Milan: L. F. Cogliati, 1913), 218—while Pordenone was executing a cycle of exterior wall paintings for Paride da Ceresara's villa after having taken over the commission from Romanino (who must also have been present in Mantua during 1519). The importance of these wall paintings is confirmed by the fact that they are cited as a qualitative model for imitation in the contract between Pordenone and the administrators of the Duomo di Cremona dated 20 August 1520 in which Pordenone was awarded his commission; see *I Campi* (see note 13), 112 (biography of Pordenone by Caterina Furlan). The fragment of fresco with the head of Diana (Mantua, collection of the Banca Agricola Mantovana) has been identified variously as a fragment by Pordenone from this cycle (Mina Gregori, ed., *Pittura a Mantova dal Romanico al Settecento* [Milan: Cassa di Risparmio della Provincie Lombardo, 1989], 229 [entry by Chiara Tellini Perina]) or as a work by Gerolamo da Treviso (Marco Tanzi, "Gli esordi di Bernardino Campi e gli affreschi di Pizzighettone," in Alberto Fontanini, Vincenzo Gheroldi, and Marco Tanzi, *Bernardino Campi a Pizzighettone: La crocefissione in San Bassiano e il suo restauro* [Pizzighettone: San Bassiano, 1991], 8). Gerolamo da Treviso worked as a collaborator of Giulio Romano's on the Sala dei Venti in the Palazzo Te in Mantua; see Vincenzo Mancini, "Un insospettato collaboratore di Giulio Romano a Palazzo del Te: Gerolamo da Treviso," *Paragone*, no. 453 (1987): 3–21.

15. Aspertini and Dosso could have met not only in Bologna but in Venice, where Aspertini was present in 1515 and (especially) in 1518, the same period in which Dosso was there; see Marzia Faietti and Daniela Scaglietti Kelescian, *Amico Aspertini* (Modena: Artioli, 1995), 42, 57. On Dosso's continued presence in Venice between 1515 and 1519, see Andrea De Marchi, "Sugli esordi veneti di Dosso Dossi," *Arte veneta* 40 (1986): 22. Altobello Melone was educated as an artist in this setting, in which Romanino was also present; see Francesco Frangi, "Sulle tracce di Altobello giovane," *Arte cristiana* 76 (1988): 392. On the relationship between Romanino and Melone, see Alessandro Ballarin, "Corso di lezioni sulla giovinezza del pittore bresciano: La *Salomè* del Romanino" (University of Ferrara, 1970–1971, lecture notes).

16. The technical context that I have outlined here for the Dossi's "antidiligent" approach corresponds to the description of the artistic scene in the eastern Po valley around 1517 provided by Ballarin (see note 1), 1: 64:

> *[Dosso, sul 1517, è al centro] di quella breve ma intensa stagione di diversioni eccentriche condotte sul corpo del classicismo romano e lagunare, di moti di fronda*

propriamente anticlassici, che attraversa la pianura padana, dalla Cremona di Bembo e di Altobello alla Brescia di Romanino e di Moretto, alla Bergamo di Lotto, al Friuli di Pordenone, alla Padova di Domenico Campagnola, alla Bologna di Aspertini ([Dosso, around 1517, was at the center] of that brief but intense period of eccentric experiments carried out on the body of Roman and Venetian classicism; an anticlassical revolt spread across the Po valley from Bembo and Altobello in Cremona to Romanino and Moretto in Brescia, from Lotto in Bergamo to Pordenone in Friuli, from Domenico Campagnola in Padua to Aspertini in Bologna).

17. For Aspertini's works of this sort, as discussed by Malvasia, see Daniele Benati, "Reintegrazione della *Pietà Marsili* di Amico Aspertini," in Mario Fanti and Deanna Lenzi, eds., *Una basilica per una città: Sei secoli in San Petronio* (Bologna: Istituto per la Storia della Chiesa di Bologna, 1994), 297–306. See also Gheroldi, "Romanino" (see note 12), esp. 21–24, which discusses Paglia's interest in Romanino's *sprezzatura.*

18. The passage concerning the Dossi's works in Pesaro is found in different versions in the 1550 and 1568 editions of the *Lives*. In the second edition, Vasari no longer considers Dosso and Battista Dossi individually, shunting them to the margins along with other painters, and he strengthens his negative opinion of the Pesaro cycle. See Vasari (see note 9), 4: 422:

> [1550 edition]: *Condussero a fine una delle dette stanze della Imperiale, la quale fu poi gittata in terra per non piacere al Duca, e rifatta dagli altri maestri che erano quivi* (They brought to completion one of the aforementioned rooms in the Villa Imperiale, which was later torn down because it did not please the Duke, and was redone by other artists who were found there).
> [1568 edition]: *Scopertasi dunque l'opera dei Dossi, ella fu di maniera ridicola che si partirono con vergogna da quel signore; il quale fu forzato a buttar in terra tutto quello che avevano lavorato e farlo da altri ridipignere con il disegno del Genga* (Once the Dossi's work was shown, it was of such a ridiculous manner that they parted with shame from the Duke, who was compelled to destroy everything that had been done and to have it all repainted by others, following Genga's drawings).

In the second edition, Vasari wrote that the Dossi's error was

> *dal troppo volere sforzare l'ingegno; essendo che nell'andar di passo e come porge la natura, senza mancar però di studio e diligenza, pare che sia miglior modo che il voler cavar le cose quasi per forza dell'ingegno dove non sono: onde è vero che anco nell'altre arti, e massimamente negli scritti, troppo bene si conosce l'affettazione, e per dir così, il troppo studio in ogni cosa* (that they desired too greatly to employ their intellect to the full; for it seems better to proceed step by step with nature, without, however, lacking in studiousness and diligence, than to want to wrest things [from nature] almost by a force of the intellect, where they are not to be found. Thus it is true, that in the other arts as well—especially in writing—affectation is all too familiar a defect, as is too much study in anything).

19. The details mentioned here are visible in some of the photographs in Ezio Chini, *Il Romanino a Trento: Gli affreschi nella Loggia del Buonconsiglio* (Milan: Electa, 1988), 31 (photo 23), 27 (photo 17), 41 (photo 41), 81 (photo 92).

20. On adding milk, eggs, glue, and oil to the binding agent for plaster, see Gettens et al. (see note 3), 157–84. A table with the additives for plasters used from antiquity to 1850 appears in Ferruccio Micocci and Giorgio Pulcini, *Gli intonaci: Materiali, tipologie, tecniche di posatura e finitura, degrado e recupero* (Rome: NIS, 1992), 28. Unfortunately, Micocci and Pulcini only sporadically document the sources they consulted.

21. See my *Tradizione e innovazione: Due seminari sui comportamenti tecnici dei decoratori fra storia, industria e artigianato senza tempo* (Milan: Studio Miky Degni, 1997), for a discussion of the continued use of additives such as milk and casein in plaster.

22. Vasari (see note 7), 5: 539: *"il Bacco, il Sileno, ed i due putti che poppano la capra."*

23. On the ceiling of the Sala di Psiche, see also Giuseppe Basile, "Il restauro della volta della Sala di Psiche," *Quaderni di Palazzo Te,* no. 8 (1988): 49–67. On the use of oil paints in the Sala di Psiche, see Fabio Talarico and Giuseppina Vigliano, "Contributo alla conoscenza della tecnica di esecuzione ed allo stato di conservazione dei dipinti murali della Sala di Psiche," *Bollettino d'arte,* spec. issue, *L'Istituto centrale del restauro per Palazzo Te* (Rome: Istituto Poligrafico e Zecca dello Stato, 1994), 75–84. The retouching of the walls with lacquer, and the presence of saponific substances, cannot be attributed solely to the need to protect and touch up the work (Talarico and Vigliano, 79). Sample 19 displays traces of lacquer taken from the red fabric on the woman carrying the game to the left of the *Banquet* on the south wall (an organic microchemical analysis reveals traces of proteins and the presence of saponific substances). Sample 22 contains malachite (probably a chemically altered version of azurite) and cinnabar (i.e., red mercuric sulfide), while sample 23 contains ochre yellow, and sample 22 contains traces of substances that could be used for soap.

24. On this usage, see Alessandro Conti, *Manuale di restauro* (Turin: Einaudi, 1996), 191–97; see also Lorenzo Lazzarini et al., eds., *Giorgione: La Pala di Castelfranco Veneto* (Milan: Electa, 1978), 51 (sample N).

25. Vasari (see note 7), 5: 539: *"l'opera fu poi quasi tutta ritocca da Giulio, onde è come fusse tutta stata fatta da lui."*

26. Chini (see note 1), 209, considers them *"schizzi per una decorazione mai realizzata, forse a stucco"* (sketches for an unrealized decorative scheme, perhaps in stucco).

27. Cinnabar, whether artificial or natural, tends to blacken, especially if not protected by an oily final coat or if used without a great deal of binding agent. This chemical alteration is fairly frequent in unprotected wall paintings. Cennini (chap. 40) notes, *"piu sostiene in tavola che in muro; peró che per lunghezza di tempo, stando all' aria, vien nero quando é lavorato e messo in muro"* (it stands up better on panel than on the wall; because, in the course of time, from exposure to the air, it turns black when it is used and laid on the wall); see Cennino Cennini, *Il libro dell'arte,* ed. and trans. Daniel V. Thompson Jr., 2 vols. (New Haven: Yale Univ. Press, 1932–1933), 1: 24, 2: 24.

28. One of these practices is discussed in Andrea Pozzo, "Breve instruttione per dipingere à fresco," in idem, *Prospettiva de' pittori e architetti* (Rome: J. J. Komarek, 1700), pt. 2, sec. 14, "Cinnabar":

> *Questo colore è il più vivace di tutti; [e] è affatto contrario alla calce, particolarmente quando è esposto all'aria; quando però la pittura stà al coperto, io l'hò spesso adoperato in molti panneggiamenti; avendolo però prima purgato col secreto, che ora dirò. Prendasi cinabro puro in polvere, e postolo in una scodella di majolica vi s'infonde sopra que ll'acqua che bolle, quando in essa si disfà la calce viva, ma sia l'acqua quanto più chiara si può, poi si getti l'acqua, e più volte allo stesso modo vi si rifonda della nuova: in questa maniera il Cinabro s'imbeve della qualità della calce, nè le perde già mai* (This color is liveliest of all, and is completely unsuited to use on plaster, especially when it is exposed to air; when the painting is covered, however, I have often used it in cloth, first having purged it with a secret that I shall now reveal to you. Take pure cinnabar in powdered form, place it in a ceramic bowl and mix it with some boiling water. When the quicklime has dissolved in the water, but the water is as clear as possible, then throw out the water and repeat this same procedure a number of times. In this way the cinnabar absorbs the quality of the plaster and never loses it).

On this problem, see Gheroldi (see note 6), 51–56, esp. 56.

29. I verified the veiling of thick cinnabar with oil-based lacquer in the wall paintings by Serafino dei Serafini in the Gonzaga Chapel in San Francesco in Mantua. In this case, the original lacquer coat was protected by the superimposition of details in tin and gilded tin. Visible around the lacquer-coated areas are grey halos, which are typical indications of the penetration and diffusion through capillarity of oil into the plaster or into the surrounding painting *a calce*.

30. I discuss this detail in my *Esibizioni polimateriche di Giovanni Pietro da Cemmo: Per la ricostruzione dell'aspetto originario dei dipinti murali di Santa Maria Annunciata a Bienno* (Brescia: in press). Mirella Simonetti has informed me that she found verdigris in the finishing of the foliage of the Montefiore wall paintings by Jacopo Avanzi.

Part II

Dosso's Career: Chronology, Sources, and Style

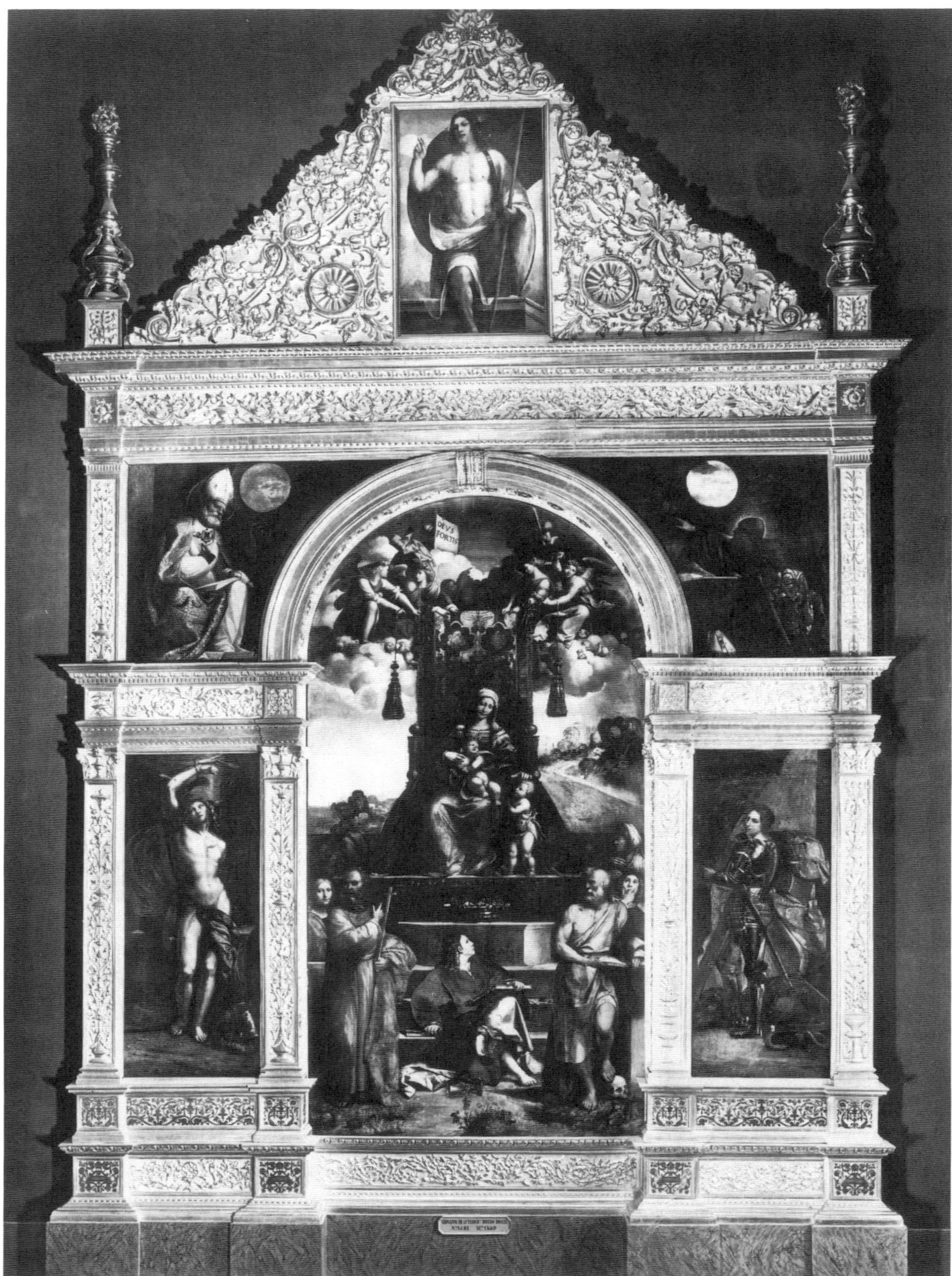

Fig. 1. Dosso Dossi and Garofolo
Costabili altarpiece
Ferrara, Pinacoteca Nazionale

Dosso Dossi, Benvenuto da Garofalo, and the Costabili Polyptych in Ferrara

Adriano Franceschini

The large polyptych (fig. 1) formerly on the high altar in the chapel of Antonio Costabili in the church of Sant'Andrea in Ferrara (and now in the Pinacoteca Nazionale, Ferrara) is considered one of the masterpieces of the northern Italian Renaissance. Over the years it has been variously attributed to Dosso, to Dosso and Garofalo (in collaboration or in succession), and to Dosso and Garofalo with additions by Girolamo da Carpi.[1] As for the date of its execution, Vasari claimed that the polyptych was commissioned from Garofalo by Costabili, who was, according to him, a judge of the Dodici Savi of the municipality of Ferrara during the third and fourth decades of the sixteenth century. Based on this claim, nearly all historians and art critics have argued that the altarpiece must be dated to about 1530, supporting this date with philological evidence and stylistic comparisons with other works by the same artists during the period from 1530 to 1531, along with a few works dating from the years 1523, 1525, and 1527. Some have even fixed the date of Dosso's contribution to the altarpiece as 1531, during a period in which Garofalo was suffering from blindness (or worse). Only Longhi, in analyzing Titian's *Saint George* of 1511 (Venice, Collezione Vittorio Cini), noted that this could have been a source for the figure of Saint George in the Ferrara polyptych. He was on the right track, but he went no further than this observation. All Dosso scholars have, in any event, agreed that the altarpiece displays the work of the fully mature Dosso.

Likewise, the many scholars of the work of Garofalo have maintained the same position, although the most recent, Anna Maria Fioravanti Baraldi, has prudently remarked that rather than affirm that Girolamo da Carpi participated in the painting of the altarpiece, as might seem possible on the basis of its stylistic similarity to his Bologna paintings from the years 1524 to 1525, it would be more appropriate to discern the influence of Dosso in those very same paintings. This marked a new direction in studies of the polyptych, although it was limited to the figure of Girolamo da Carpi.

There are no archival documents regarding the work. Documents pertaining to the two painters collected in Modena by Adolfo Venturi and Maria Grazia Antonelli Trenti allow us to confirm Dosso's presence in Ferrara starting in June 1514. As for Ferrara, the documents on Dosso and Garofalo first mentioned by Luigi Napoleone Cittadella are still valid today, but no one has ever thought to try to track down those documents that eluded the grasp of that great scholar. The key to the problem, however, is to be found precisely in the documents that he did not see, starting with those that pertain to the place of origin of the painter Giovanni Luteri, the son of Nicolò da Trento, who is known to us as Dosso Dossi. Dosso has been variously thought to be Ferrarese, Mantuan, or from the Trentino. He, in turn, referred to himself as coming from Mirandola, but here at least the disagreement is more a matter of terminology than anything else.

Having been asked to elucidate this point, in order to eliminate any doubt that it might be a matter of a different person, I have therefore carried out research on the subject in the Archivio Notarile Antico in Mirandola, taking the surname "Luteri" and the name "Nicola da Trento" as the focus of my investigation. Although neither systematic nor exhaustive, my study has ascertained that during the last quarter of the fifteenth century in Mirandola and its surrounding district there were numerous individuals named Luteri, with someone named Nicolò in at least three branches of the family, distinguished by different fathers. The first of these, identified as *"Nicolaus filius quondam Togni de Luteriis,"* in 1475 declared to have purchased a house in the Borgo di Vigona (called Borgofranco) in Mirandola.[2] He appears again, and is more clearly identified, in a notarial document dated 18 August 1481, when he gave his son-in-law his daughter's dowry: *"Nicolaus filius quondam Antonii de Lucteriis, alias dicto Bazino, de villa Vigone districtus Mirandulae, habitator in dicta terra Mirandulae."*[3] He had no connection with Trent, however, and seems to have been too old to have been the painter's father, who was still alive in 1532. The second of these was Nicolò, son of the late Iacobo Luteri, who, along with his brothers Giovanni and Iacobo, signed a contract to rent lands in Verzola, in the district of Mirandola, on 16 September 1482.[4] The three brothers had been regularly meeting with one another and would continue to do so, but this particular Nicolò was already dead by 5 January 1503, and left a sole male heir named Pietro.[5] He cannot therefore have been the father of the painters Dosso and Battista. The third of these relatives was identified as *"Nicolao filio quondam Alberti Luterii de Trento,"* a resident in Tramuschio di Mirandola, a town on the border between Mirandola and the Mantuan districts of Quistello and Revere.[6] He was present in Tramuschio (which was part of three districts, including Mirandola) on 15 January 1485, for the reading of the will of Stefano Smereri. The presence of this branch of the family (Luteri di Trento) is confirmed by a document dated 13 November 1487, concerning the renting of land found *"in villa Tramuschii"* in the Mirandola district; one of the neighbors of this property was a certain "Luterius de Trento."[7]

It is most likely that this latter individual was the father of Dosso dalla Mirandola, although further research into the matter would be desirable. I would add here that near Roncole in the territory of Mirandola (and not far from Tramuschio) we find mention of a place called *"la via del Dosso"* in 1479[8] and 1489,[9] as well as a *"villa Dossi districtus Mirandulae"* in 1480.[10] These are details to keep in mind, independent of the known (if rather later) links between the Luteri and the town of Dosso di Quistello, a place also situated not far from Tramuschio.

Taking for granted that Dosso lived in the Mirandola area at least during his childhood and early youth, we ought to consider the fact that Mirandola was a cultural and artistic center of some note that was not without local painters who may have influenced Dosso and Battista Luteri as youths.[11] It is plausible to assume that Dosso lived in Ferrara in his youth and that part of his training took place in that city, before he matured as an artist elsewhere, but there are no documents connecting him to the city before 1513. On 11 July of that year, records show that Dosso, an already experienced painter, was engaged with Garofalo in painting the polyptych for the high altar of the church of Sant'Andrea, which had been commissioned by Antonio Costabili, who at that time was already serving as a judge of the Dodici Savi in the municipal administration of Ferrara. It is recorded in the municipal ledger for expenses and payments that on this date in 1513 a first installment charged against Costabili's salary as a judge was paid to Dosso *"da Mirandola"* and Garofalo for the *"tavola"* (altarpiece) upon which they were already at work.[12]

Even earlier the two painters had gone together to Venice to purchase the colors for the *"tavola"* upon which they were about to begin work. At that time they might in fact have seen Titian's *Saint George*. The funds were drawn from Costabili's salary only on 6 August 1513 and transferred to bankers who had advanced the money needed by the two painters after having arrived in Venice: the payment amounted to the sum of 120 lire.[13] Other collective payments to Dosso and Garofalo for the work in the course of its execution were made on 15 November[14] and 21 November.[15] In these records, which cover at least six months of labor, no other painter is mentioned alongside Dosso and Garofalo; in particular, there is no mention of Girolamo da Carpi, who was in 1513 quite young and inexperienced. It has in any case never been absolutely certain that the latter should be identified as the "Girolamo" mentioned as Garofalo's apprentice in 1520.[16]

The payments specifically refer to the early phase of the work. The largest one was for the purchase of colors in Venice, to which the two painters had traveled together precisely for this purpose. The colors were fine and costly and were rarely to be found for sale in Ferrara, especially after the recent war. They were paid for in advance by Costabili, a patron who never disbursed funds without sufficient assurance that the work would be completed within the period of time called for in the contract. The other three payments fall perfectly within the norm for distributing the sum due to the artists in several installments during the course of work. With the final payment the completed work was to be delivered; the final phase of the project, in which the gilding was added, did not involve the two painters.

Each one of the final three installments was in the amount of 30 lire, but it is unthinkable that there could have been a mistake in their recording, either in terms of their all being for the same sum or for the proximity of the dates of the payments (which were in any case a week apart). The municipal ledger, or *Zornale,* was cross-referenced with other city records (the *Memoriale,* the *Libro Mastro,* and so on) which used double-entry bookkeeping and would have exposed such an error. The entry for each installment makes reference to chapter 44 of the *Libro Mastro,* which contained the records of what was earned by and paid to Costabili.

The period of time in which the work occurred must have been contemporaneous with these records (to judge from the phrase *"che depinzono,"* [that they are painting]), and thus work on the altarpiece must have been in progress during the dates 11 July, 15 November, and 21 November 1513, with the intent being to continue after this last date, but certainly not to delay the completion of the work for a further seventeen years.

The phrase *"che fano, on dano prenzipio a fare"* (that they are doing, or starting to do) is found in the document relating to the acquisition of the colors for the altarpiece, and it indicates that the preparatory phase of the work was underway. It is dated 6 August 1513, but it refers to purchases previously made when Dosso and Garofalo were preparing to paint the altarpiece with those colors. The transfer of funds from one banker to another between Venice and Ferrara delayed the recording of the charges against Costabili's account, although the work was already underway.

The woodwork was carried out by carpenters and wood-carvers, with whom Costabili dealt separately. Documentation of their contribution has not been found thus far. For the forms and carving of the decoration, such artisans normally relied upon drawings supplied by the painters. They worked ahead of the painters; thus we may assume that the wooden support structure of the polyptych was set up at the site by at least the beginning of 1513, and that Dosso and Garofalo (or at least one of the two) already had a clear idea of the dimensions, form, and content of the work, as agreed upon with Costabili and in accordance with the requirements of the site for which the work was destined.

We do not know how much an altarpiece of this kind cost in Ferrara at the time. There are contracts and expense accounts for polyptychs that are closely related to the work under consideration, and some of these have been previously published. On 24 January 1494, Clara Clavel signed contracts for a large altarpiece (560 × 240 cm) with the wood-carver Bernardino da Venezia for 58 lire *marchesane* and with the painter Ercole de' Roberti for 100 ducats (about 300 lire), gilding excluded. Perhaps it was never finished, but delays in the completion of the work led to a large number of documents that have survived in the archives (this did not occur in the case of the Costabili polyptych, for which there is no trace of any disagreement with the painters). The dimensions were less than half those of the Costabili polyptych.

In 1517 Garofalo was paid 80 lire, 12 soldi for the ancona for the high altar of the church of San Guglielmo (198 × 208 cm; now in the National Gallery in London), but not without litigation. He finally reached an agreement through the intercession of Antonio Costabili. The wood-carver Giovanni da Carpi was paid 30 lire for the cost of wood and his labor.

In the same months of 1513–1514, during which the work on the Sant'Andrea altarpiece was being executed, Niccolò Pisano painted an altarpiece (now in the Pinacoteca di Brera in Milan) for the Confraternita della Morte (a work that was transferred onto canvas in the nineteenth century). Niccolò Pisano requested 50 ducats for his work (about 157 lire) and received 40 (about 124 lire); he wrote off the other 10 ducats as his gift *"amore Dei"* (for the love of God). The wood-carver, Stefano da Modena, received 46 lire for the cost of wood and his labor. Bernardino Fiorini and Toneto received 38 ducats for the gilding (about 117 lire, 16 soldi). The total cost for the ancona, which measured 225 × 175 cm and was crowned by a lunette (now lost), amounted to 315 lire, 6 soldi. From these figures the proportional cost of the Costabili altarpiece can be easily established.

Concerning the painters' fees, it should be kept in mind that the best-paid painters in Ferrara in 1509 were Niccolò Pisano and Domenico Panetti (10 soldi per day), followed by Ettore Bonacossi, Tommaso da Carpi, and Garofalo (9 soldi per day). In 1510, Giovanni Maria Aventi and Pietro della Mirandola (but from Trent) received 10 soldi per day, followed by Giovanni Antonio dall'Argento, Tommaso da Carpi, and Cesare da Casale, who were paid 9 soldi per day. Pellegrino da Udine and Michele Costa earned more than the others, for they were given monthly stipends by the Estense family.

All this leads me to think that the 120 lire spent just for the colors for the Costabili altarpiece represent an adequate sum for such a large-scale work that was to be executed so quickly. The 90 lire paid in installments to the painters were no doubt only a small portion of their total fees, which must have been stipulated to be no less than 9 soldi per day, even though they so welcomed the opportunity to produce a magnum opus for Costabili. A master painter would have needed two hundred working days to earn 90 lire; thus Dosso and Garofalo both must have had to work hard from the very outset to complete the painting, even if we take into account the work contributed by their assistants and apprentices (who were undoubtedly part of the team), which must have consisted of at least the same number of working days if the painting was finished by the middle of March. Dosso, Garofalo, and Costabili were not inclined to waste time.[17]

The loss of the municipal registers for the year 1514 and the following years prevents us from knowing either how long Costabili continued to serve as a judge for the Dodici Savi (it is certain he was once again serving in this capacity in 1522) or whether the city continued to pay Dosso and Garofalo on his behalf; the work, however, must have been completed quickly. In the spring of 1514, Dosso was already working for the Estense court and was living in the castle. On March 14 he was given *"robe da letto e da tavola"* (things for bed and table),[18] and in early June he undertook work on three paintings for Alfonso I.[19] Garofalo, although still working intensively on the Costabili altarpiece, signed a contract for the *Virgin on Her Throne* for the

Celletta di Argenta in October 1513, and by the end of 1514 he had also completed the *Virgin of the Clouds* for the chapel of the Immaculate Conception in the church of Santo Spirito in Ferrara.[20] The Sant'Andrea altarpiece was clearly behind both painters at this point.

The documentation presented here thus demands a complete revision of the authoritative, but merely inductive, scholarship concerning the Costabili polyptych, and requires new perspectives on the problem of the artistic development and output of the young Dosso Dossi.

Notes

An earlier version of this essay, "Dosso Dossi, Benvenuto da Garofalo e il polittico Costabili di Ferrara," was published in *Paragone,* nos. 543–545 (1995): 110–15. The publisher wishes to thank the Fondazione di Studi di Storia dell'Arte Roberto Longhi, Florence, for permission to reprint portions of this article.

1. See Luigi Napoleone Cittadella, *I due Dossi, pittori ferraresi, del secolo XVI: Memorie* (Ferrara: Tip. dell'Eridano, 1870); Luigi Napoleone Cittadella, *Benvenuto Tisi da Garofalo: Pittore ferrarese del secolo XVI* (1872; reprint, Bologna: Arnaldo Forni, 1979); Adolfo Venturi, "I due Dossi," *Archivio storico dell'arte* 5 (1892): 440–43 and 6 (1893): 48–62, 130–35, 219–24; Roberto Longhi, *Officina ferrarese, 1934,* followed by *Ampliamenti, 1940,* and by *Nuovi ampliamenti, 1940–55* (Florence: Sansoni, 1956); Maria Grazia Antonelli Trenti, "Notizie e precisazioni sul Dosso giovane," *Arte antica e moderna,* no. 28 (1964): 404–15; Amalia Mezzetti, *Il Dosso e Battista ferraresi* (Milan: Silvana, 1965); Carlo Brisighella, *Descrizione delle pitture e sculture della città di Ferrara,* ed. Maria Angela Novelli (Ferrara: Spazio, 1990); Anna Maria Fioravanti Baraldi, *Il Garofalo, Benvenuto Tisi, pittore (c. 1476–1559)* (Rimini: Luisè, 1993); Alessandro Ballarin, *Dosso Dossi: La pittura a Ferrara negli anni del Ducato di Alfonso I,* 2 vols. (Cittadella: Bertoncello Artigrafiche, 1994–1995). Mezzetti, Brisighella, Fioravanti Baraldi, and Ballarin have extensive bibliographies.
2. Archivio di Stato di Modena (A.S.M.), Archivi Notarili Provinciali, Archivio Notarile di Mirandola: notary Francesco Sassoli Bergami, packet 12, c. 179, act dated 12 April 1475.
3. A.S.M. (see note 2), notary Bernardino Marini, packet 23, act dated 18 August 1481.
4. A.S.M. (see note 2), notary Bernardino Marini, packet 23, act dated 16 September 1482.
5. A.S.M. (see note 2), notary Bernardino Marini, packet 29, act dated 5 January 1503.
6. A.S.M. (see note 2), notary Bernardino Marini, packet 24, act dated 15 January 1485.
7. A.S.M. (see note 2), notary Borso Cavizzani, packet 18, fasc. 1487, act dated 13 November 1487.
8. A.S.M. (see note 2), notary Matteo Grossi, packet 19, act dated 23 November 1479.
9. A.S.M. (see note 2), notary Borso Cavizzani, packet 18, act dated 11 April 1489.

10. A.S.M. (see note 2), notary Giovanni Natali, packet 41, c. 25, act dated 4 May 1480.

11. Without getting into the problems of the history of Mirandola, I would like to mention the painters I found named in the notarial acts issued between 1465 and 1505 (they may be looked up under the date given): 21 October 1474: Bernardino, son of the late *"Magistri Ioannis de Revero pictoris"* (notary Bernardino Marini, packet 25); 2 June 1487: witnessing the change in the holding of a piece of land are *"Santo filio quondam Magistri Ioannis de Revere, pictore; Francisco filio Petri de Ferrariis, pictore,"* both from Mirandola (packet 24); 9 December 1490: *"Ioannes Maria pictor"* is one of the witnesses (packet 25); 9 November 1493: Giovanni Maria da Revere, son of the late painter Bernardino, is mentioned as a witness (packet 26); on 21 September 1495 *"magister Franciscus filius quondam Blanchi de Nicholis pictor de civitate Mutine"* signed a contract with Bianca d'Este, wife of Galeotto Pico della Mirandola, to paint an ancona by October, according to the drawing that he was to furnish her (packet 27); 9 August 1499: *"Petro filio Magistri Urbani de Pictoribus, de dicta terra Mirandule"* is listed as a witness (packet 27); 6 December 1499: *"Serafino filio quondam Ioannis Antonii de Pictoribus"* is named as a witness (packet 27); 7 January, 11 March, and 21 December 1503: *"Laurentio filio quondam Magistri Bartholomei dicti Rositi pictoris, de Mutina, pictore habitatore in dicta terra Mirandule"* is mentioned as a witness (packet 29).

I would like to note that Girolamo Baruffaldi, who always played with the true and the false, claimed that a certain Lorenzo was Dosso's master (and this might be true); he felt, however, that this was a reference to Lorenzo Costa, which remains to be confirmed. See Girolamo Baruffaldi, *Vite de' pittori e scultori ferraresi,* 2 vols. (1844–1846; reprint, Bologna: Arnaldo Forni, 1971), 1: 250–51.

12. Archivio di Stato di Ferrara (A.S.F.), Archivio Storico Comunale di Ferrara, Serie Finanziaria, sixteenth century, envelope 55, 1513 *Zornale,* c. 188:

> *Al Magnifico Messer Antonio di Costabili lire trenta de marchesani per compto de suo salario, et per Sua Magnificientia a Dosso da la Mirandola et Benvegnudo da Garofalo picturi contanti a buon compto de una tavola che depinzono alo altare grande de la chiesia de Santo Andrea in Ferrara, quale fa fare il prefato Magnifico Messer Antonio.... L. XXX* (To the magnificent Messer Antonio di Costabili 30 lire *marchesane* for his salary, and by His Magnificence [30 lire] in cash on account to the painters Dosso della Mirandola and Benvenuto da Garofalo in payment for an altarpiece that they are painting for the high altar of the church of Sant'Andrea in Ferrara, commissioned by the aforesaid magnificent Messer Antonio.... L[ire] XXX).

The *marchesano* is a silver coin issued by the Este of Ferrara. In October 1513 the gold ducat was worth 62 lire *marchesane.*

13. A.S.F. (see note 12), c. 194:

> *Al Magnifico Messer Antonio di Costabili lire centovinte marchesane per compto de suo salario, et per Sua Magnificientia a Piero d'Albertin e compagni banchieri in Ferrara contanti per tanti che loro ànno fato pagare in Venezia per le mane de li Sarazini al Doso dala Mirandola et Benvegnù da Garofalo depinturi per compto*

de la tavola de l'altaro grande de Santo Andrea che fano, on dano prenzipio a fare, per comprare coluri in Venezia.... L. CXX (To the magnificent Messer Antonio di Costabili 120 lire *marchesane* for his salary, and by His Magnificence [120 lire] in cash to Piero d'Albertin and his fellow bankers in Ferrara for what they have had paid through the Sarazini in Venice to the painters Dosso della Mirandola and Benvenuto da Garofalo on account for the altarpiece for the high altar in Sant'Andrea which they are doing, or are starting to do, in order to purchase colors in Venice.... L[ire] CXX).

14. A.S.F. (see note 12), c. 207:

Al Magnifico Messer Antonio di Costabili lire trenta de marchesani per compto de suo salario, et per Sua Magnificientia et di sua voluntà et commissione al Dosso da la Mirandola et a Benvegnudo da Garofalo picturi contanti per compto de loro mercede de depingere la tavola on sia anchona de lo altaro grande de la chiesia de Santo Andrea, la quale fa depingere per mane de li dicti il prefato Magnifico Messer Antonio.... L. XXX (To the magnificent Messer Antonio di Costabili 30 lire *marchesane* for his salary, and by His Magnificence upon his express wish and commission [30 lire] in cash to the painters Dosso della Mirandola and Benvenuto da Garofalo on account [and] in recompense for painting the altarpiece or ancona for the high altar of the church of Sant'Andrea in Ferrara, which the aforesaid magnificent Messer Antonio is having painted.... L[ire] XXX).

15. A.S.F. (see note 12), c. 208:

Al Magnifico Messer Antonio di Costabili lire trenta de marchesani per compto de suo salario, et per Sua Magnificientia al Dosso da la Mirandola et a Benvegnudo da Garofalo picturi contanti per compto de la mercede sua de depingere la anchona de lo altaro grande de la chiesia de Santo Andrea che fa fare Sua Magnificienta.... L. XXX (To the magnificent Messer Antonio di Costabili 30 lire *marchesane* for his salary, and by His Magnificence and his express wish [30 lire] in cash to the painters Dosso della Mirandola and Benvenuto da Garofalo on account for painting the ancona for the high altar of the church of Sant'Andrea in Ferrara, which the aforesaid magnificent Messer Antonio is having painted.... L[ire] XXX).

16. It is in fact believed that Girolamo da Carpi was born in Ferrara in 1503. When the polyptych was painted in 1513, he was barely ten years old, but in 1520, at age seventeen, he was certainly old enough to have been an apprentice. Thus, Girolamo might indeed have been Garofalo's apprentice, but not at the time of the painting of the Costabili altarpiece.

17. For all the documentation cited here, published and unpublished, see my *Artisti a Ferrara in età umanistica e rinascimentale: Testimonianze archivistiche,* pt. 2, vol. 2, *Dal 1493 al 1516* (Ferrara: Gabriele Corbo, 1997), with its photographic reproductions of the four entries regarding Dosso and Benvenuto (doc. 1013 u, z, bb, cc).

18. Archivio di Stato di Modena (A.S.M.), Archivio Estense, Camera Ducale: Guardaroba 129, c. 75, "Ordinario de drapamenti," 14 March 1514:

A Maistro Dosso depintore che alogia in castelo le infrascritte robe da leto et da tavola, de comision de Messer Girolimo Ziliolo:

Lenzoli da leto de teli 4 l'uno, dui	*lenzoli 2, n. 391646*
Lenzoli da cariola de teli 3 l'uno, dui	*lenzoli 2, n. 598213*
Coltra una da leto azura verde	*coltra 1, n. 159*
Coltra una da cariola azura biancha	*coltra 1, n. 27*
Sparaviero uno da leto grosso fornito	*sparav. 1*
Tamarazi dui da leto azuri, de lana, novi	*tam. 2*
Mantile de renso	*mantile 1*
Tovaia una da famia	*tovaia 1*
Truchabuchi	*truchabuchi 1*

(To Master Dosso the painter, who is living in the castle, the things for bed and table listed below, commissioned by Messer Girolimo Ziliolo:

Two bedsheets, each 4 cloth lengths	2 sheets, n. 391646
Two trundle-bed bedsheets, each 3 cloth lengths	2 sheets, n. 598213
One bedcover, blue [and] green	1 cover, n. 159
One trundle-bed bedcover, blue [and] white	1 cover, n. 27
One bedcanopy, large, furnished	1 canopy
Two bedmattresses, blue, wool, new	2 mattresses
Towel of Rheims linen	1 towel
Tablecloth	1 tablecloth
Cloth cover	1 cloth cover).

19. A.S.M. (see note 18), Munizioni e fabbriche 55, c. 106v, registration of credit on 3 June 1514 in order to issue payment *"A Mafie de Ranexe per doe ase mezane per lo telaro dali tapidi et per li telari tri dati a Mistro Doso dipintore, zoè una ase per fabrica.... L. 0.16.0"* (To Mafie de Ranexe for two medium-sized lengths of wood for the supports for the panels and for the three supports given to Master Dosso the painter, that is to say, one length for each work.... L[ire] 0.16.0).

20. Fioravanti Baraldi (see note 1), 11; Alessandra Pattanaro, ed., "Regesto della pittura a Ferrara (1497–1548)," in Ballarin (see note 1), 1: 128–29.

Dosso versus Leonbruno

Andrea De Marchi

Until recently it had always seemed entirely accidental that the first document to mention Dosso, dated 11 April 1512, should have come from Mantua. The references to his early days in Venice had long been known to be quite accurate, after all, and it was recognized that from the first he was profoundly rooted in the culture of Ferrara, where he was so close to Garofalo. We only know of the payment made to Dosso of thirty ducats and ninety-two lire for *"quadrum... magnum cum undecim figuris humanis"* (a large painting with eleven human figures), intended for the Camera Superiore del Sole in the new palace of San Sebastiano built for Francesco II, through a nineteenth-century transcription.[1] Its reliability has recently been confirmed, however, by the discovery of various documents closely linking Dosso's life to the city of Mantua.

Giovanni Francesco di Nicolò di Alberto di Costantino Luteri came from a family from Trent, but grew up in a remote village in the southern reaches of the duchy of Mantua, Dosso Scaffa (now known as San Giovanni del Dosso), located in the triangle of territory between Mirandola, Quistello, and Revere.[2] Dosso's father Nicolò lived there until his death in 1536, managing his landholdings at Villa Pentida and Poggio Rusco, which gradually grew in size (thanks most likely to his son's success). Dosso is mentioned in Ferrara for the first time in a document dated July 1513, where he undertook to work alongside Garofalo on the Costabili altarpiece for the church of Sant'Andrea; his own contribution to it would, however, come much later.[3] He was, significantly enough, referred to in the document as "Dosso da la Mirandola," whereas in 1518 another document—the contract for the San Sebastiano altarpiece in the cathedral of Modena (completed in 1522)—described him as being *"de Mantua, nunc vero habitator inclitae civitatis Ferrariae"* (from Mantua, but now truly an inhabitant of the celebrated city of Ferrara).[4] Dosso had been received at the court of Alfonso I, and it is in fact known that he was living in the castle from 15 March 1514 on.[5] The year before, when he and Garofalo had received payments from Antonio Costabili in Ferrara, he was described in a document (dated 30 August 1513) as *"civis et habitator Mantuae in contra Cornu"* (citizen and inhabitant of Mantua in the district of Cornu).[6]

Dosso started his career, then, in Mantua. Yet this is of little help in understanding his training, and it does not seem that Mantua was particularly generous to him during that long and difficult interval between Andrea Mantegna's death (1506) and Giulio Romano's arrival in the city (1524) under the aging Lorenzo Costa's ambiguous auspices.[7] It would be risky to attempt, as a historical novelist might, to find the reason for such seeming ostracism, or in any event a lack of initial momentum, in Dosso's career at the court of Isabella and Francesco II. Nonetheless, it may be instructive to compare the earliest work of Dosso with the work of Lorenzo Leonbruno, a painter favored by the Gonzagas, who seemed to be a rising star at this same time. Leonbruno was the adopted son of Giovanni Luca de' Liombeni of Mantua, who was a court painter. He was likely born between 1477 and 1479,[8] some ten years before Dosso, whose birth must have occurred sometime around or just prior to 1490.[9] Leonbruno had already been taken under Isabella's wing by 1504, when he was sent to Florence, where she warmly recommended him to the care of Perugino as a young man *"prono et inclinato a qualche virtù et maxime a questa dela pictura la quale sopra modo apreciamo"* (prone and inclined to some virtues, especially that of painting, which we so greatly appreciate).[10] Later, in 1512, we find him working by Dosso's side in the Palazzo di San Sebastiano under Costa's general supervision; there he decorated the oratory, two rooms, a *camerino*, the loggia, and many other places, and painted a large canvas with *"nove muse che chantino, Apolo che sona, cum lo illustrissimo Signor nostro che ascolta"* (nine muses singing, Apollo playing, and our most illustrious Lord listening to them).[11]

If Dosso's early career in the 1510s has been the subject of much debate, it is no less difficult to reconstruct the entire course of Leonbruno's career. It is certain that he decorated the Camera Grande (later called the *sala della Scalcheria,* the steward's apartment) in Isabella's apartment in the Corte Vecchia, where she lived as a widow; the decorations, which still exist, were reported in a document dated 1522.[12] He executed, moreover, four signed paintings, none of which seem to belong to the early phase of his career.[13] The most imposing of these is the *Judgment of Midas* (fig. 1) now in Berlin.[14] It has been dated to sometime around 1510, but if this were the case it would figure as decisive for the development of the young Correggio because of the softness of the flesh tones and, even more important, for its airy rendering of the landscape, which seems to be evaporating among swirling leafy branches.[15] It is currently impossible to determine clearly what Leonbruno's style might have been in the first decade of the sixteenth century.[16] We ought therefore to turn our attention to the painting most likely to have been executed before any of the others, although certainly its date must be fixed sometime well along in the second decade of the century: Leonbruno's *Allegory with Mercury and a Nude* (fig. 2), now in Florence.[17]

Leonbruno's intention must have been to paint a work in the style of Giorgione, but in the *Allegory* there are clear sympathetic references to the young Correggio's art as well: without the latter, the damp bluish haze into which the distant woods seem to dissolve would be unthinkable. Leonbruno also owed a debt in this painting to the Ferrarese school, as witnessed in the

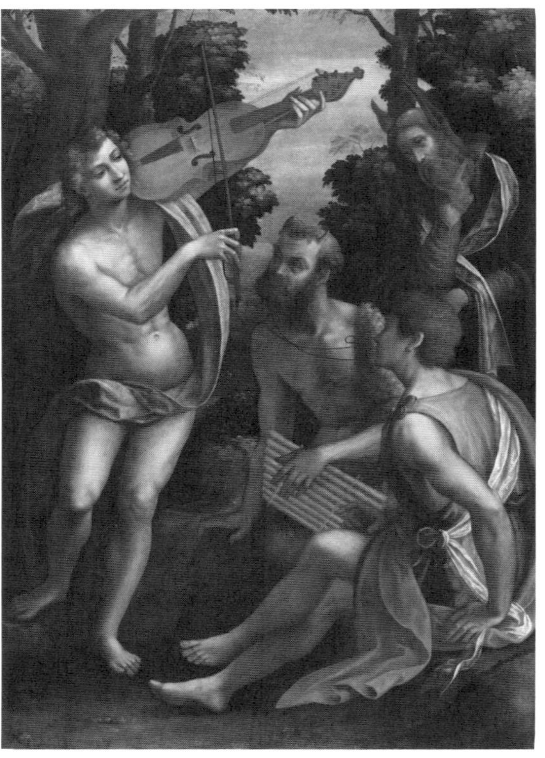

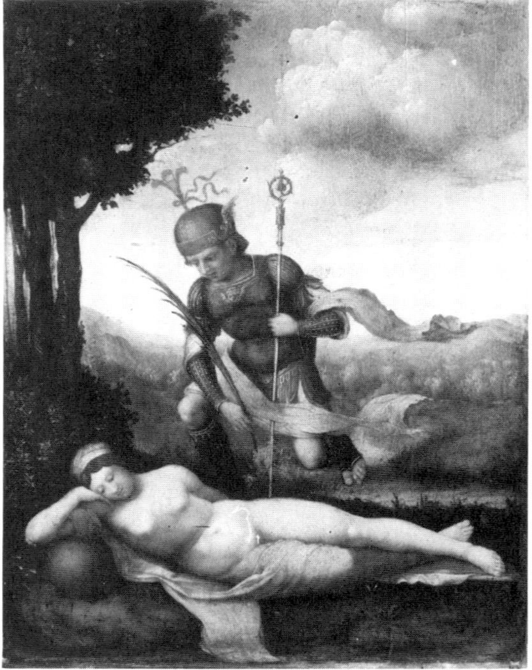

Fig. 1. Lorenzo Leonbruno
Judgment of Midas
Berlin, Staatliche Museen, Gemäldegalerie

Fig. 2. Lorenzo Leonbruno
Allegory with Mercury and a Nude
Florence, Galleria degli Uffizi

intense colors of the clothes, such as the dense yellow that seemingly changes into a reddish orange, which can be traced to the work of Lodovico Mazzolino or Dosso. These overtures were, however, disguised by his recourse to two figures drawn from Mantegnesque prototypes. His Mercury was derived from the engraving *Virtus deserta* (ca. 1500–1505) by Giovanni Antonio da Brescia, and the nude was derived from the monochrome *Allegory of Mantua* (ca. 1500) that came from Mantegna's workshop, or perhaps, even more precisely, from the *Metamorphosis of the Nymph Amymone* (ca. 1500) engraved by Girolamo Mocetto.[18] In Leonbruno's *Allegory* the new meanings of modern painting were filtered through a precious and educated sensibility, signaling a reassuring continuity with the splendors of the past. This stood in inevitable contrast with the scandalous naturalness of the young nude figures, who have just emerged from the water and are stretched out on the grass, found in Dosso's *Bathers* (p. 232), which can be identified as the painting commissioned by Francesco II for the Palazzo di San Sebastiano in 1512.[19] In Dosso's *Bathers,* there is no trace of the gold that, as imperceptible as a filigree, appears in endless details in Leonbruno's painting,[20] which range from Mercury's armor, to the fluttering cloth, to the leaves and even the bark on the tree trunk. This meticulous attention to detail, when compared to the pictorial informality favored by Dosso, must have been particularly appealing to Isabella, who in 1505 complained that Perugino's painting for her *studiolo* was not "*finito cum magior diligentia*" (finished with greater diligence) when compared to Mantegna's paintings, "*che sono summamente netti*" (which are supremely precise).[21] It is not surprising, then, that Leonbruno was favored by Isabella in the years to come, while Dosso had to follow another path that was to lead him far from Mantua. Dosso would return there to work only at the end of the 1520s, at that point as a famous artist highly praised in Paolo Giovio's *Elogia doctorum virorum ad avorum memoria.* By then Isabella's tastes—for she was a woman of the world—had probably changed in response to the radically different circumstances of the new era.

The subtle dialectic that set Leonbruno against the younger Dosso mirrored the crisis that had beset the entire system of values upon which the courtly world had been based in the late fifteenth and early sixteenth centuries. This world was at that time profoundly threatened by the discovery of a new sentimental reality in literature and in art, as Giovanni Romano has so convincingly shown.[22] We can grasp the antiheroic stance and modern sentiments with which Dosso approached religious themes as well by adding a new painting to the corpus of the young artist. This painting is the *Martyrdom of Saint Sebastian* (fig. 3), which I have unfortunately seen only in a poor photographic reproduction (apparently by a certain Henri Bron from Montpellier). It is clearly related to *Salome before Herod* (fig. 4) in its setting, which resembles a little papier-mâché theater, and in its small figures of staggering guards who are seemingly printed in soft silhouettes. It also seems linked to the *Virgin and Child with Saints* (ca. 1515) now in the Glasgow Art Gallery and Museum, because of the softened profiles in the

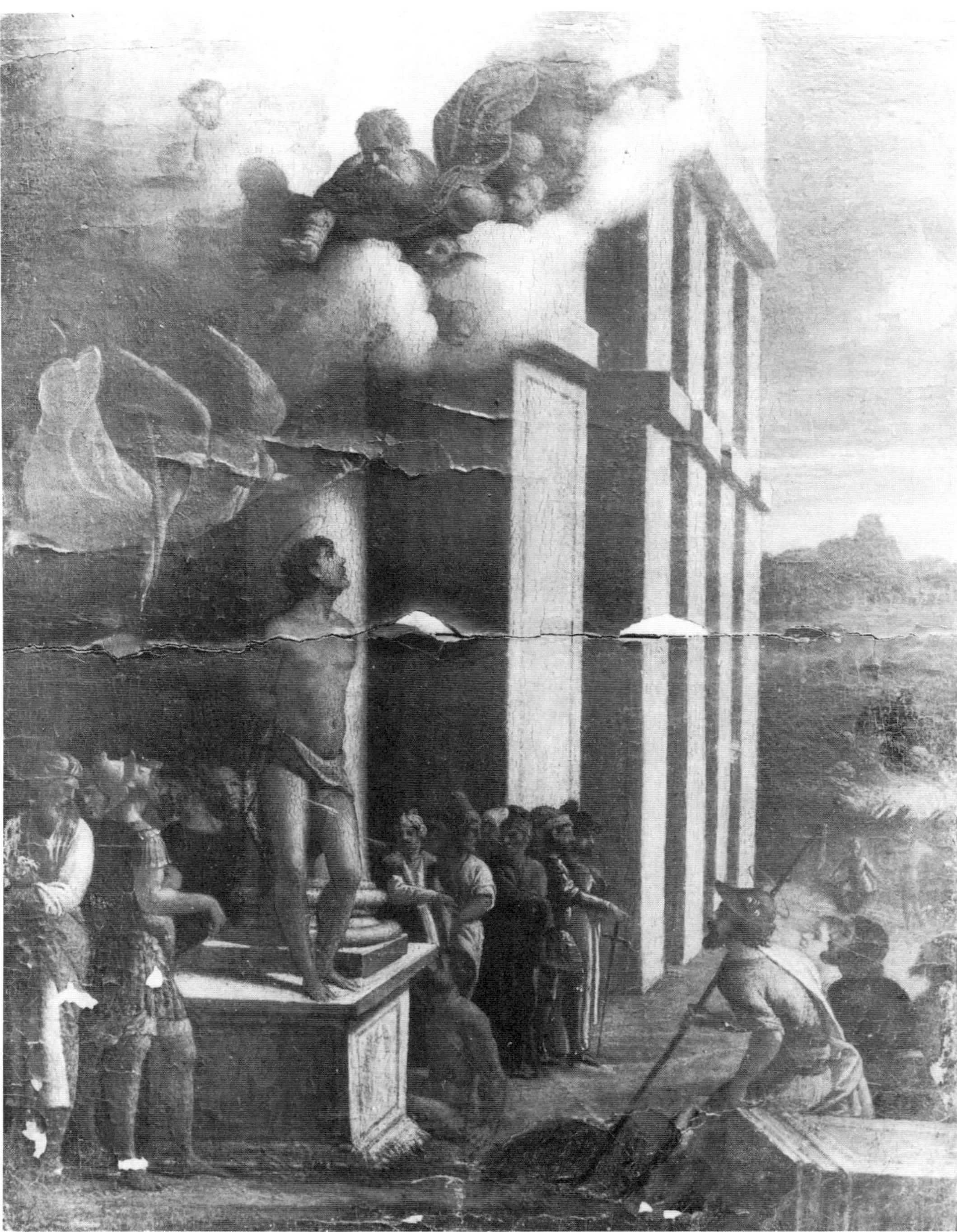

Fig. 3. Dosso Dossi
Martyrdom of Saint Sebastian
Whereabouts unknown

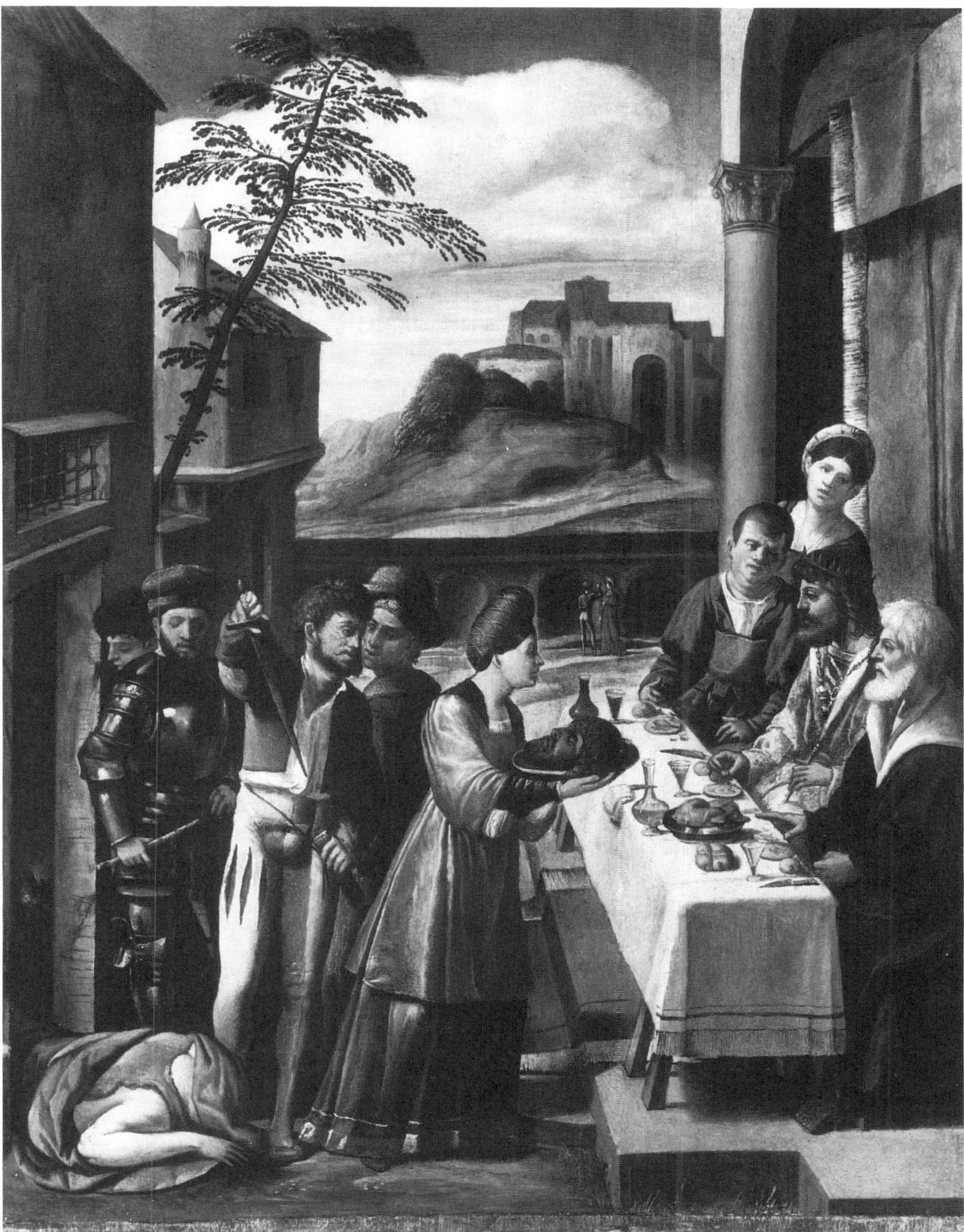

Fig. 4. Dosso Dossi
Salome before Herod
Milan, private collection

shadows and its Saint John the Baptist, who leans forward like Saint James in the foreground on the right side of the painting. Saint Sebastian's naked body seems already reminiscent of Titian's art, but the pose is quiet and relaxed rather than heroic, like the bathers in the Castel Sant'Angelo painting or the figures in *Gyges, Candaules, and Rhodope* (p. 96), now in the Galleria Borghese. An angel floats down from on high with the palm and crown, and God the Father blesses the adolescent martyr: his sharp shadow is imprinted on the clouds, only to dissolve, while behind them we barely glimpse abstract buildings almost resembling those of the *Metafisica* school of painting. The height of the action eludes the spectator and becomes indefinite in this seemingly suspended atmosphere; this represents an intelligent, emotionally more exposed and melancholy response to the moving *poesie* that the most daring young painters—Titian and Sebastiano del Piombo—were painting in Venice in the wake of Giorgione. The more ordinary tone of this painting, especially in the surrounding small figures, seems to converse from a distance with certain details in the young Correggio's work, such as the young men seated, collapsing with exhaustion, between a resting horse and a dog curled up at their feet in the background of the *Adoration of the Magi* (ca. 1515, Milan, Pinacoteca di Brera). Their point of intersection could only have been Mantua.

The *Martyrdom of Saint Sebastian* is clearly linked with the group of works centered around the Philadelphia *Holy Family and Donors* (p. 178) and the altarpiece for the church of Santa Maria in Vado (Ferrara, Arcivescovado). Several scholars, however, reject both the attribution of the entire group to the young Dosso and its early dating.[23] Until now no one has, however, been able to develop a more plausible (or less controversial) explanation of these works. Their early dates, however, are confirmed by the style of Calzolaretto's altarpiece for the church of San Francesco (Ferrara, Pinacoteca Nazionale), which is quite distinct from his Arivieri altarpiece of 1522 (Ferrara, Arcivescovado). On the contrary, the San Francisco altarpiece clearly depends upon the controversial works of the early Dosso and therefore cannot be dated beyond the last years of the second decade of the sixteenth century.[24] Moreover, any attempt to call into question this reconstruction would have to explain in other terms and with other works the first steps in the painter's career during a period of radical change for virtually all of the most advanced painters in the eastern Po valley. Unlike Minerva, Dosso was not born from the head of Jupiter, already in possession of the perfectly formed language of the Costabili altarpiece!

This is certainly not the place to discuss in a satisfactory manner the conclusions drawn by Adriano Franceschini in this regard.[25] According to him, the altarpiece must have been completed shortly after the payments made to Dosso in July through November of 1513. But this would call into question not so much Roberto Longhi's reconstruction of Dosso's early years as the whole history of northern Italian painting in the early sixteenth century. Dosso's informality of execution was quite deliberate, of course; it was a gesture of *sprezzatura* (nonchalance) and not a sign of haste. This, however, related him to the new visual sensibility that in the early part of the 1520s linked Girolamo Romanino, Dosso, and Parmigianino, and whose precursor was Amico Aspertini. Ten years earlier these would have been forward-looking efforts not yet isolated from the eccentric experimentation that later took place in the central part of the Po valley, and they would have anticipated even the freedom of means that Titian achieved only later, in the *Assumption of the Virgin* (ca. 1516–1518) in the church of Santa Maria Gloriosa dei Frari, Venice. Given all the complex and controversial ramifications of this problem, the ease with which many scholars have ascribed the whole execution of the Costabili altarpiece to the year 1513, without allowing for a realistic amount of time necessary for the completion of a commission of this kind, is very surprising. Yet this was probably the most imposing altarpiece to have been painted in Ferrara in the course of the entire sixteenth century, and we know that Dosso spent four years—between the signing of the contract and the delivery of the painting—to complete the much smaller altarpiece for the cathedral of Modena, as has been well documented.

The 1513 advance payments for the Costabili altarpiece ought nevertheless to lead us to reconsider seriously other problems raised by this work. Garofalo was the first to work on the picture, and Dosso followed later, and their contributions interfered with one another in a way that is inconsistent with any division of roles that would have been agreed upon in advance. It is surprising that this has not been noticed before by scholars. I am convinced that the structure of the drawing, as well as a broad area of the whole central composition, may be attributed to Garofalo, including the figures of Saint John (which pays homage to ideas like those of Vittore Carpaccio's altarpiece for the church of San Giobbe, *The Presentation in the Temple,* dated 1510 and now in the Gallerie dell'Accademia in Venice) and Saint Jerome, whose chiastic stance is typical of Garofalo's style but quite alien to Dosso's explosive vitalism (which can be seen clearly in the altarpiece for the cathedral of Modena, the work that stands closest to the Costabili altarpiece in pictorial terms). If we look carefully at the regular and pyramidal grouping of the Virgin and Child in the Costabili painting (see fig. 5), its drawing does not seem to result from the creative deviations used by Dosso in his construction of human figures. Dosso transformed the work with his pictorial treatment of the surfaces. If we were to strip it of the paint that he added, it would seem reminiscent of Romanino's "architectural" approach, which can be found in the *Virgin and Child with Saints* (ca. 1512) in the church of San Pietro in Tavernola Bergamasca and the *Last Supper* painted for the church of Santa Giustina in Padua (1513–1514, now in the Musei Civici in Padua). The perspectival construction of the throne presents a contradiction between the view from above of the throne's base and the view from below, looking upward at the seat. This contradiction is found as well in, for example, Giorgione's Castelfranco altarpiece from about 1500 (Castelfranco Veneto, Duomo), but had been overcome by Garofalo, who preferred a coherent

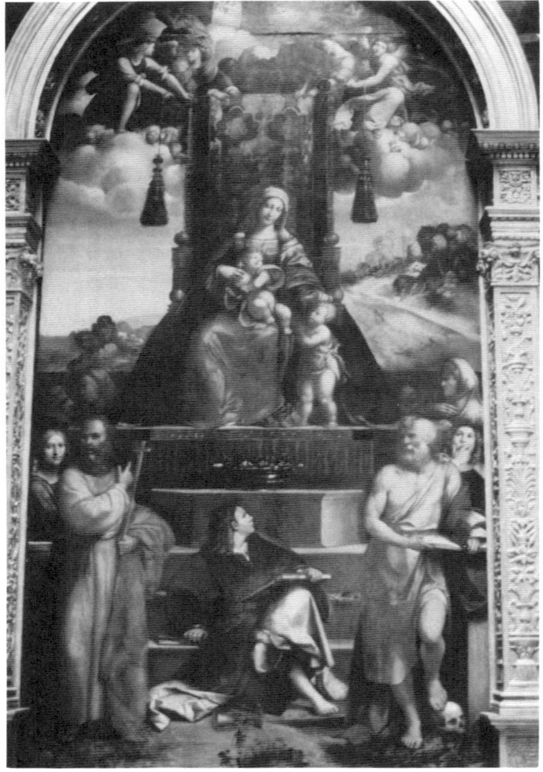

Fig. 5. Garofalo and Dosso Dossi
Costabili altarpiece (central panel)
Ferrara, Pinacoteca Nazionale

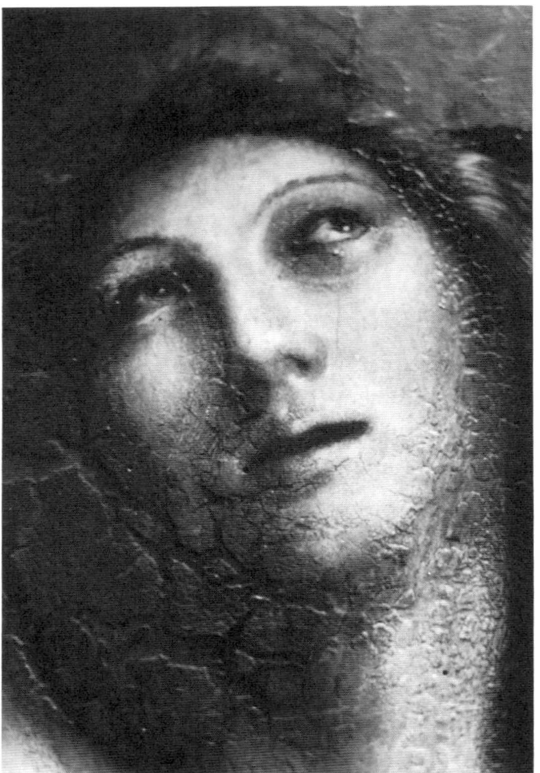

Fig. 6. Garofalo and Dosso Dossi
Costabili altarpiece (detail of Saint Sebastian)
Ferrara, Pinacoteca Nazionale

view from below. This more classical approach was also less difficult for the viewer, and Garofalo began to employ it with the Trotti altarpiece of 1517 (Ferrara, Pinacoteca Nazionale). Garofalo also contributed, exclusively in his own hand, the broad swaths of cloth around the angels in the upper part of the work and Saint John's pink and carmine cloak; these may instantly be recognized as one with the figure of Saint Jerome in the Suxena altarpiece, dated December 1514 (Ferrara, Pinacoteca Nazionale), which forms the basis of Garofalo's own turn toward Dosso's style. In short, we should probably revise the chronology of Garofalo's contribution to the work and assign to it a date between 1514 and 1515.

The imposition of work in Dosso's hand over the parts already sketched out by Garofalo signals what must have been a traumatic interruption in the painting of the altarpiece, which was only resumed some time later. The reasons for this are unknown, but light might be shed on the matter by looking at the political ups and downs of Antonio Costabili. In 1513 he was judge for the Dodici Savi in Ferrara, and he once again served in this capacity in 1522 (the advance payments to Dosso and Garofalo were charged against his salary while employed as a judge). A careful analysis of Dosso's contributions to the Costabili altarpiece still needs to be done; he certainly executed the shadows made of *bitume* that have been discussed by Vincenzo Gheroldi, for Garofalo experimented with this medium only in the 1530s and only to a degree. The veiled flesh tones painted over Garofalo's delicately nuanced work may be glimpsed through the fine craquelure, as can be seen quite clearly, for instance, in the figure of Saint Sebastian (fig. 6). Another proof of this technique of superimposition may be found in Saint Andrew's robe, in which the violently orange and Dossesque tones correct a more delicate mallow coloring. The only components that are entirely in Dosso's own hand are the panels representing Saint Augustine and Saint George. Dosso repainted the face and backside of Saint Ambrose, whereas the steps and the saint's garb were done by Garofalo. The Costabili altarpiece was not, in short, an organic collaboration between the two artists: Dosso completed and transformed an unfinished work by Garofalo.

In 1522 Leonbruno created his elegant grotesques for the vault of the Camera Grande (fig. 7), with their fine white and gold stucco work and refined citations from antiquity. In that same year Dosso completed his stunning altarpiece for the cathedral of Modena: it possessed a vital tension that derived from a simultaneous explosion of color and light effects, as if Dosso sought to challenge Titian himself while at the same time pushing to an extreme Raphael's most daring innovations in the *Madonna di Foligno* (ca. 1512, Vatican, Pinacoteca Vaticana) and the Vatican's Stanza d'Eliodoro (1511–1514). The paths that the two artists had taken could not have been more different. Only the year before, Leonbruno had been sent by the new marquis of Mantua, Federico II, "*vedere quelle cose antiche et moderne belle di Roma*" (to see those lovely ancient and modern things in Rome) and to update his own cultural perspective. The letter that Baldassare Castiglione sent back with him to Mantua, however, expressed some perplexity: "*per haver piena notitia delle cose di Roma bisognerebbe starvi molto più*" (to come to know fully the things of Rome, one ought to stay there much longer).[26] Some details in Leonbruno's stuccoes and grotesques from 1522 were unthinkable without the Vatican loggias, but their overall arrangement remained traditional, as can be seen in their homogenous and carefully delimited color fields, which seem indifferent to Raphael's provocative and decorative illusionistic effects. He instead paid homage to Mantegna, in the illusionistic tondo at the center of the vault and in the sculptural busts set against gilded mosaics. This was the crowning touch of Leonbruno's sense of nostalgia, expressing the mental reservations of an artist who was still linked

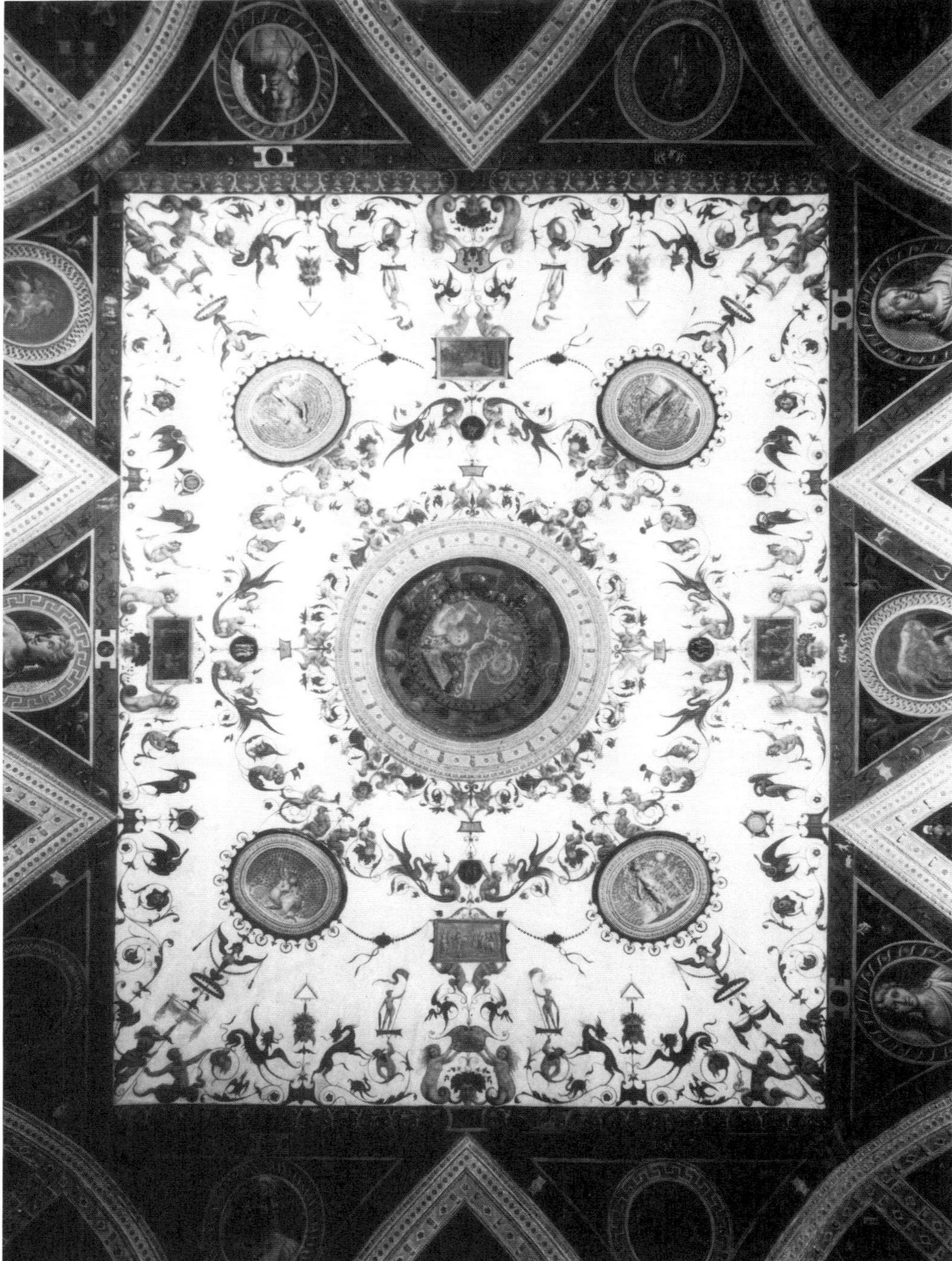

Fig. 7. Lorenzo Leonbruno
Ceiling
Mantua, Palazzo Ducale, Camera Grande

to the premature classicism of an earlier period but who was torn between timid naturalistic gestures and a by now overly detailed antiquarianism.[27]

Because of his ambiguity, Leonbruno serves as a paradigm of the artistic atmosphere in Mantua, where Mantegna's unmatched artistic mastery had had a hypnotic effect. Now, in spite of—or perhaps thanks to—Isabella, Mantuan art was relegated to the sidelines, and interest focused on the more lively developments that were taking place in other cities of the central part of the northern Italian plain, such as Ferrara and Cremona. Nevertheless, rebellious groups in Mantua, as well as elsewhere, sympathized with the experiments being made by young painters such as Correggio and Dosso. Their work was interpreted in the light of a larger and multiform artistic movement centering on the eccentrics, such as Gian Francesco Tura;[28] the latter, indeed, was to remain linked to this movement for the rest of his career. Despite the fact that Leonbruno was part of the official coterie of the court in Mantua, he experienced some ups and downs, so that it is rather difficult to establish a coherent sense of his activity there. He did not, however, fail to be affected by Dosso's work, if only to a degree and in a strangely delayed way.

In 1957 a painting, titled *Saint John the Baptist* (fig. 8) and attributed to Girolamo da Carpi, was donated to the parish of San Paolo della Croce in the town of Port'Ercole on the Argentario peninsula in southern Tuscany.[29] The bottom part of the painting is very Dossesque, and Alessandro Bagnoli has pointed out to me that this painting could be related to Dosso's work. I think that it is among the paintings most clearly comparable to the Berlin *Judgment of Midas*. The figure's pose—unstable and slipping—is similar, as is the broad sweep of red cloth, which falls to earth with its hem dragging on the ground, as does the cloth on Tmolus's legs. The two paintings also represent light in a similar way, at once delicate and shifting. The idea of a figure emerging against the half-light of a mossy ruin, which in turn contrasts with the bright light in the distance, is reminiscent of Leonardo but is filtered through Correggio's style. The movement of the figure's legs, as if they were coming apart and collapsing, is a trait common to Leonbruno's works; for instance, it is found in the huntress-nymph who is seated with two female companions and faces a pair of hunting dogs in a lunette in the Camera Grande and in the painting of the youth with a dog in another lunette of the same cycle (fig. 9). It can also be seen in the figure of Suspicion in the *Calumny of Apelles* (1524–1525), now in the Pinacoteca di Brera. In this latter work, in which Leonbruno laments his misfortune after the arrival of Giulio Romano in Mantua in 1524—"*hec* [*sic*] *si in adversa quid in prospera Lionbrunus pinxiset* [*sic*] *fortuna*" (if Leonbruno painted these things in adverse fortune, what would he have painted in good fortune)[30]—his imitation of Mantegna's final stylistic phase is programmatic. Perhaps this was due to his dependence on an older prototype,[31] or to a polemical intent in recalling the continuity between his own work and the glorious figurative tradition that Mantua had known and, now, had definitively been abandoned.

Quite a different softness of the senses, seemingly incompatible with such a work, emanates from the Port'Ercole *Baptist* and the *Judgment of Midas.* In this case the common point of reference seems, reassuringly enough, to be Lorenzo Costa, who was a significant figure in Mantua until his death in 1535. Costa represented the continuity of the transition that historiography terms *antico-moderno,* and he was respected and employed by Federico II himself.[32] The intensity with which Leonbruno alludes to Costa's work would seem to suggest, first of all, that the painting predates his trip to Rome in 1521 and the partial shift that ensued in his work. Confirmation of this may be found by comparing the painting with Costa's altarpiece of 1518 for the Pio chapel in the church of San Niccolò in Carpi, which represents Saint Catherine, Saint Anthony of Padua, and Saint Ursula (now in the Fondazione Severi in Carpi).[33] I think it preferable, however, to opt for a more challenging interpretation resulting from a later dating of the work.[34] Leonbruno's return to Costa's work would thus be the result of a consciously reactionary stance in regard to the upheaval caused by Giulio's arrival in Mantua.

The *Nativity* (fig. 10) in the National Museum of Western Art in Tokyo, signed by Leonbruno, displays a different approach, and it should be considered one of Leonbruno's earliest known works.[35] The youthful works of Garofalo are often mentioned as somehow parallel to Leonbruno's painting, but this is a rather generic claim and does not suffice to explain the unusual contamination evident in the *Nativity:* the painting makes reference to Mantegna's art in its vague residues of his graphic style (the group of the Virgin nursing the Child), to Costa's *Myth of Comus* (p. 88) in the rustle of the fluttering robe of the adoring angel, and to Correggio's fuzzy shadows in, especially, the figure of Saint Joseph; it even makes a nod toward Lorenzo Lotto's works in Bergamo in the group of shepherds and the angel beyond the fence.[36] Over the whole scene there is a splendid sense of atmospheric clarity, executed with the meticulous care worthy of a Flemish painter. All this leads me to conjecture that the painting's date must not be prior to 1515. Once again this picture displays a delicately enamelled touch that would have appealed to Isabella's capricious taste. As Keith Christiansen has pointed out, she had Leonbruno modernize the background of *Parnassus* (Paris, Musée du Louvre) with a Flemish-style landscape comparable to the one visible in the Tokyo painting.[37]

On the other hand, it is precisely the pictorially informal and cluttered landscape in the Port'Ercole *Saint John the Baptist* that suggests a later dating. By this I mean to suggest that in this work Leonbruno went beyond the lunettes in the Camera Grande, where the backgrounds are tersely luminous and articulated by trees seemingly as light as fans, and thus this painting falls somewhere between Costa's style and the Venetian manner of painting. The stormy sky, with its threatening clouds and patches of sudden brightness, refers specifically to Dosso's work. I would prefer, however, to see the *Saint John the Baptist* as referring in particular to the youthful Dosso, who painted the stupendous harbor scene in the background of the Philadelphia

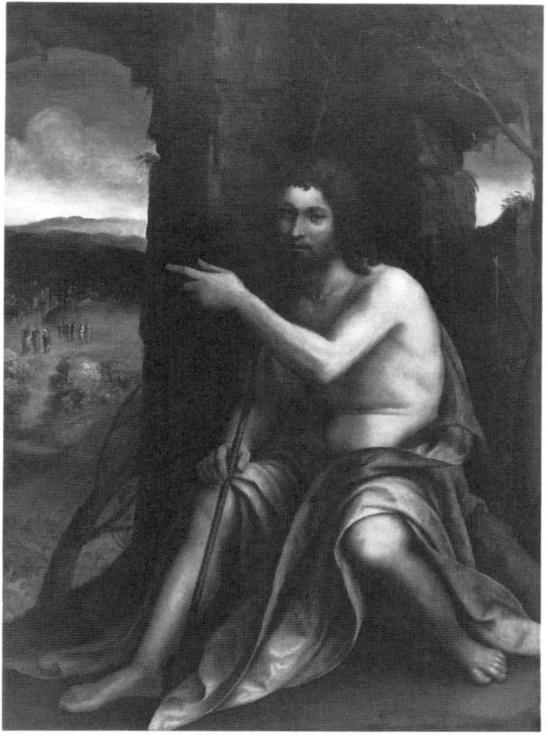

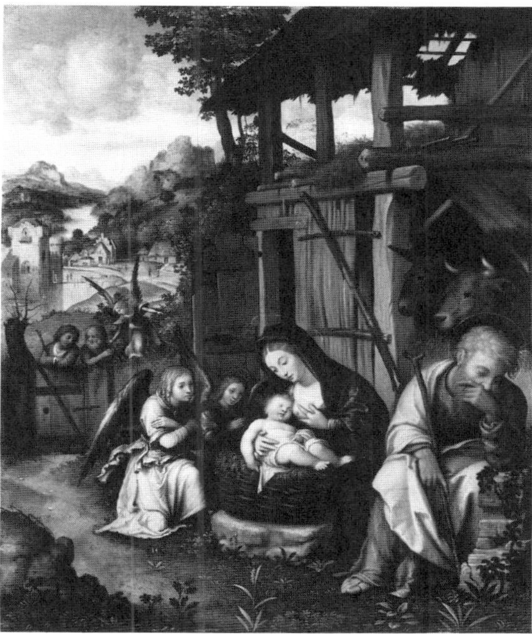

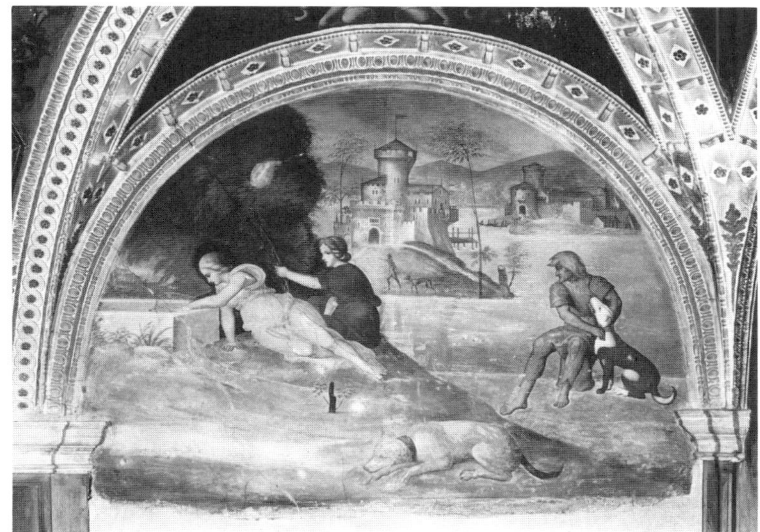

Fig. 8. Lorenzo Leonbruno
Saint John the Baptist
Port'Ercole, San Paolo della Croce

Fig. 9. Lorenzo Leonbruno
Nymph Fishing and a Youth Hunting
Mantua, Palazzo Ducale, Camera Grande

Fig. 10. Lorenzo Leonbruno
Nativity
Tokyo, The National Museum of Western Art

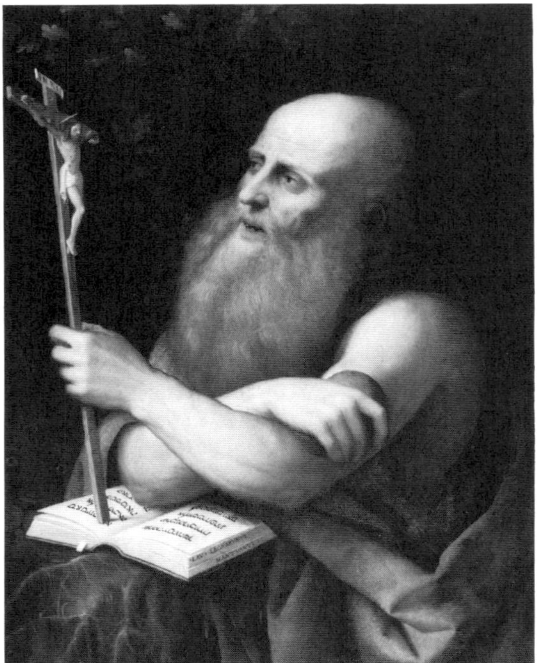

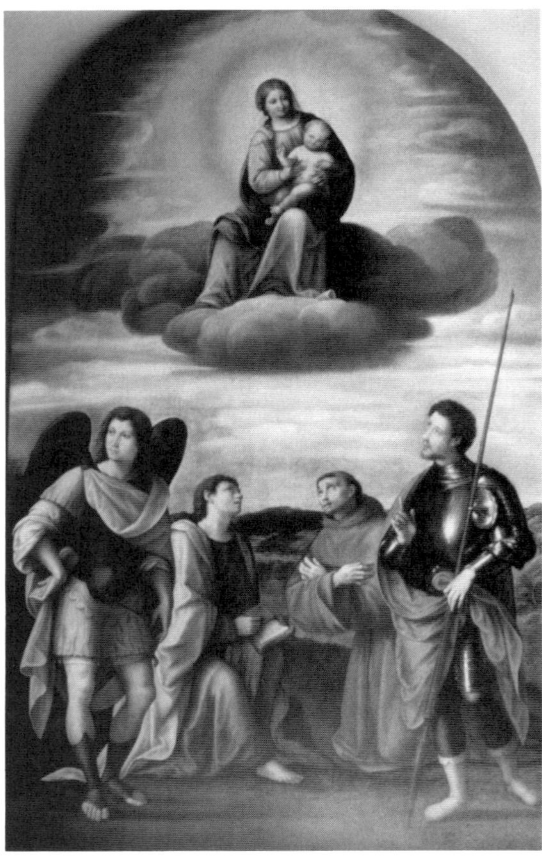

Fig. 11. Lorenzo Leonbruno
Saint Jerome
Mantua, private collection

Fig. 12. Lorenzo Leonbruno (?)
Madonna and Child in Glory with the Archangel Michael, Saint John the Evangelist, Saint Francis, and Saint Longinus
Mantua, Palazzo Ducale

Holy Family, rather than to the mature Dosso. If we look carefully at the frescoes in the Camera Grande, the flowing robes contain traces of the nervousness, *"a punta come ali di drago"* (pointed like dragon's wings),[38] which was typical of Mantegna's final phase (for example, *Minerva Expelling the Vices from the Garden of Virtue,* ca. 1499–1502, Paris, Musée du Louvre) and which in *The Judgment of Midas* and *Saint John the Baptist* is reabsorbed by softer and more continuous curves. In particular, we can see this in Leonbruno's huntress-nymphs and in the chimney painting representing Venus, Love, and Vulcan, which reads well when set side-by-side with Leonbruno's signed *Saint Jerome* (fig. 11), an intense study that shows the influences of Correggio, Costa, and Lotto.[39]

We can find confirmation of this chronological hypothesis—which I nonetheless am putting forward with all due caution while awaiting the discovery of more decisive proof—if we assign three Mantuan paintings to the final phase of Leonbruno's artistic career (he was still active as a painter in 1533, as we know from the documents). The unstable poses and the clothing in Costa's style, although more swollen and woolly, together with the full fleshiness of the figures in the *Judgment of Midas* and *Saint John the Baptist,* all seem to point to a link with the altarpiece in the Palazzo Ducale, *Madonna and Child in Glory with the Archangel Michael, Saint John the Evangelist, Saint Francis, and Saint Longinus* (fig. 12). This work has traditionally been attributed to Francia,[40] and the idea of attributing it to Leonbruno instead was suggested to me by Andrea Bacchi. Here too the landscape is animated by trees waving their fronds which shine with frothy light, and this signals the same superficial influence of Dosso's work. This makes it easier to see Leonbruno's connection to another altarpiece, namely the *Madonna and Child Enthroned with Saint Lawrence, Saint Peter, and Saint Louis of Toulouse* (fig. 13),[41] which was commissioned in 1531 by Benedetta Gonzaga for an as yet unknown altar. Alessandro Conti has attributed this altarpiece, as well as the former work, to the very last phase of Costa's career,[42] and Andrea Ugolini has attributed it to Leonbruno.[43] The group of figures with the Virgin seems similar to the group in the Palazzo Ducale altarpiece, both in the arrangement of the figures and the structure of the clothing, and the landscape has become an even more sulfurous yellow.

Usually this altarpiece is attributed to Lorenzo Costa's son, Ippolito, during the first part of his career. Ippolito Costa is known to us in an entirely different and decidedly mannerist vein, as can be seen in his *Saint Agatha,* painted in 1552 for the cathedral of Mantua. Even if the altarpiece were to prove to be the work of one of Leonbruno's close followers, rather than by his own hand, the date of 1531 would remain important and constitute a point of chronological centrality for the works by Leonbruno under discussion here. The matter remains open to debate. To the discussion should be added consideration of the lovely altarpiece (sorely in need of restoration) on the first altar on the left in the church of Sant'Apollonia in Mantua, *Saint Peter, Saint Anthony of Padua, and Saint Paul* (fig. 14).[44] The landscape in the background was redone in the late sixteenth century, and the angels bearing the emblem of Christ were added at around the same time in order to transform Saint Anthony of Padua into Saint Bernardino of Siena. In spite of its poor condition, the wavy, quick silhouettes of the figures, the way in which the clothing hangs from them, and the barest hint of emphatic gesture—like a timid memory of Rome!—all recall the *Judgment of Midas* tondo and the *Saint John the Baptist,* although in a diminished context.

Like a strange chiastic game, Leonbruno's decline as an artist intersected with the "Mantuan" Dosso Dossi's steady and inexorable ascent. Dosso left the hothouse atmosphere of Isabella's court—his work was probably met initially with incomprehension in Mantua—but he continued to visit the area, if for no other reason than to deal with his father's business affairs.[45] Finally, Dosso was recalled to the court of the Gonzaga. Isabella was interested in a view of Ferrara executed by Dosso, which she had wished to have copied in 1523.[46] Dosso's presence at court is confirmed by the Mantuan provenance of the so-called *Holy Family with Rooster* (ca. 1525), now in the Royal Collection at Hampton Court,[47] and the *Allegory of Fortune* (p. 101) at the J. Paul Getty Museum.[48] Isabella's tastes had evolved since Dosso's early years in Mantua, and she had become an advocate of the modern manner. In 1525 Costa, then in Mantua, paid an unexpected and moving homage to Dosso and his *Saint Sebastian* (Milan, Pinacoteca di Brera) in painting the Saint Sylvester altarpiece now found in the church of Sant'Andrea.[49] In the second half of the 1520s Dosso was working for Mantuan patrons, but he was not the painter that they had known earlier. Alessandro Ballarin has rightly described Dosso's new look in the following terms:

> forms arise from the artificial movements [...] which, in the context of his previous experience as a painter, appear beautiful through their being grounded above all in concerns for decorum. The figures are subjected to a process of refinement in this sense; the very heads of the figures, which once had seemed wild and frightened by their own inner visions and by the violence of their own feelings, are now idealized according to the canons of classical aesthetics. They thus attain a generic sort of beauty and express a register of conventional sentiments.[50]

In spite of, or perhaps thanks to, this decisive change, Dosso (who was Titian's friend, as by now even Leonbruno, faced with Giulio Romano's extraordinary power in Mantua, wished to appear to be)[51] became a very free interpreter of the modern manner. Unlike Leonbruno—who, thanks to the ambiguities of Isabella's somewhat archaic ideals, had once cast a long shadow over Dosso's early career in Mantua—Dosso knew how to keep up with the times.

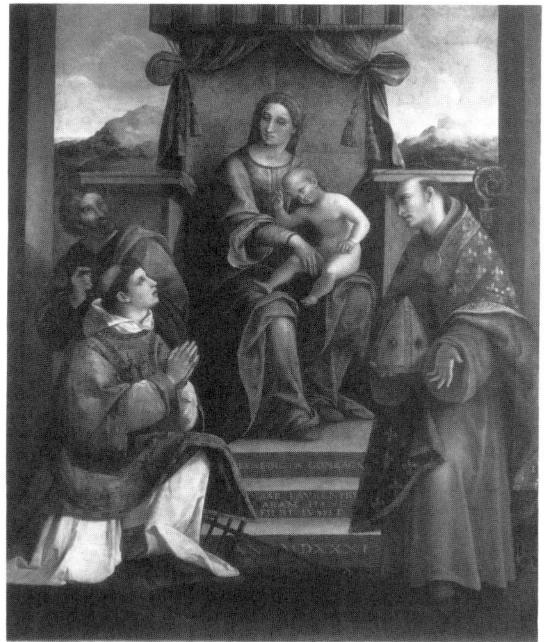

Fig. 13. Ippolito Costa
Madonna and Child Enthroned with Saint Lawrence, Saint Peter, and Saint Louis of Toulouse
Milan, Museo Poldi Pezzoli
Here attributed to Lorenzo Leonbruno

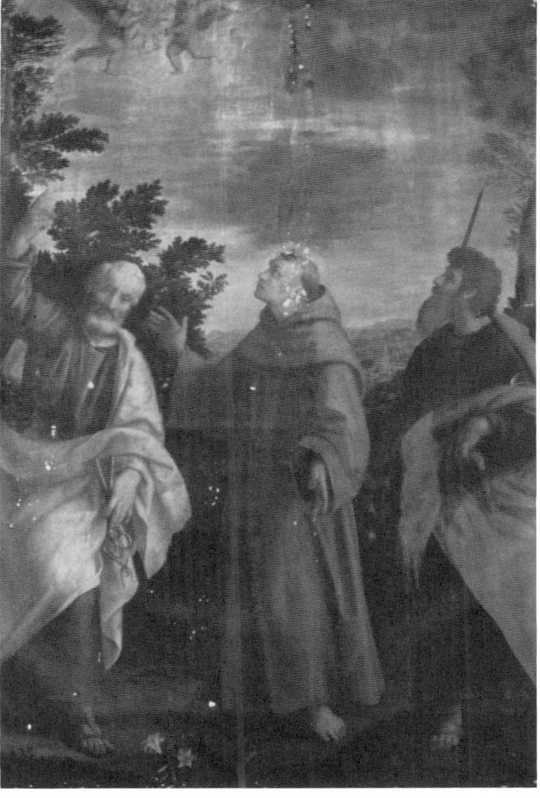

Fig. 14. Lorenzo Leonbruno
Saint Peter, Saint Anthony of Padua, and Saint Paul
Mantua, Sant'Apollonia

Notes

An expanded version of this essay is forthcoming in *Bollettino d'arte.*

1. Carlo d'Arco, *Delle arti e degli artefici di Mantova,* 2 vols. (Mantua: Tipografia G. Agazzi, 1857–1859; reprint, Bologna: Arnaldo Forni, 1975), 2: 79 (doc. 101 n. 3); Alessandro Ballarin, *Dosso Dossi: La pittura a Ferrara negli anni del Ducato di Alfonso I,* 2 vols. (Cittadella: Bertoncello Artigrafiche, 1994–1995), 1: 295 (entry no. 333); and see note 11 below.

2. Carlo Giovannini, "Nuovi documenti sul Dosso," *Prospettiva,* no. 68 (1992): 57–60.

3. Adriano Franceschini, "Dosso Dossi, Benvenuto da Garofalo e il polittico Costabili di Ferrara," *Paragone,* nos. 543–545 (1995): 110–15, and see his essay in this volume. Prior to Franceschini's essay, no one had placed Dosso in Ferrara before 1514.

4. Giovannini (see note 2), 57, 59 (doc. 8), made this point in correcting a surprising "*de Mutina*" reading by Orianna Baracchi.

5. On 15 March 1514 he received *"robe da letto e da tavola"* (things for bed and table); Franceschini, 1995 (see note 3), 115 n. 17. The new document discovered by Franceschini thus allows us to use an earlier date for the start of Dosso's work for the court of Alfonso. Until now it had been known that payments were made on 7 and 14 June 1514 for three frames for oil paintings and portraits to be sent to Rome, and that in December there was placed *"una stua in castelo ale stanzie nove dove sta m*[*aestr*]o *Dosso"* (a stove in the castle in the new rooms where Master Dosso is staying). Alessandra Pattanaro, ed., "Regesto della pittura a Ferrara (1497–1548)," in Ballarin (see note 1), 1: 128–29.

6. Giovannini (see note 2), 58 (doc. 3); but on 23 June 1512, he was instead described as living with his father in Dosso Scaffa (idem, 58 [doc. 1]).

7. For a general overview of the situation of Mantuan painting during those eighteen years, see Giovanni Agosti, "Su Mantegna, 4. (A Mantova, nel Cinquecento)," *Prospettiva,* no. 77 (1995): 58–83; and Alessandro Conti, "Sfortuna di Lorenzo Leonbruno," *Prospettiva,* no. 77 (1995): 36–50, which also furnishes an accurate study of the eclipse of Leonbruno's fame among art historians, starting with Vasari's silence.

8. Mara Pasetti, "Lorenzo Leombruno in un documento del 1499," *Civiltà Mantovana* 12 (1978): 237–44; and Leandro Ventura, *Lorenzo Leonbruno: Un pittore a corte nella Mantova di primo Cinquecento* (Rome: Bulzoni, 1995), 31–34, 241 (doc. 1; the date of 1489 found on the copy of the original baptismal document in the San Barnaba parish is probably an erroneous transcription of the date 1479).

9. Giovannini (see note 2), 58, speculates that he was born in 1487 or a little earlier, given that he should have been twenty-five years old when first mentioned in a notary's document dated 23 June 1512, in which he figures as *"coniuncte persone"* with his father Nicolò; see also Ballarin (see note 1), 1: 58–59.

10. This letter of recommendation, dated 16 April 1504, was published in its entirety in Ventura (see note 8), 246–47 (doc. 8).

11. See Ventura (see note 8), 250–52 (docs. 19–21). The payment for the painting of the Muses was made on 8 May 1512; it is known to us only through a transcription

by Carlo d'Arco, who seems to be referring to this document while relating it to a mysterious Matteo Costa; d'Arco (see note 1), 2: 79 (doc. 101 n. 3). This confusion may have been caused by the fact that Lorenzo Costa is recorded as the supervisor of the project. On this intricate question, see Clifford M. Brown with Anna Maria Lorenzoni, "The Palazzo di San Sebastiano (1506–1512) and the Art Patronage of Francesco II Gonzaga, Fourth Marquis of Mantua," *Gazette des beaux-arts,* ser. 6, 129 (1997): 131–80, esp. 151–58. (I do not, however, understand how one can assume that Dosso's painting had to have had the same dimensions as the *Apollo and Nine Muses* by Lorenzo Leonbruno and Matteo Costa.)

12. Carlo Gamba, "Lorenzo Leombruno," *Rassegna d'arte* 6 (1906): 65–70, 91–96; Ventura (see note 8), 262–64 (docs. 55–56; the *mandato di pagamento* is dated 22 April 1523 but refers to work begun on 2 April 1522 and completed on 14 December 1522).

13. These are the Tokyo *Nativity,* the former Rizzini *Saint Jerome,* the Brera *Calumny of Apelles,* and the Berlin *Judgment of Midas.* A fifth painting, a *Lamentation over the Dead Christ,* which belonged to Francesco Rizzini in the nineteenth century and recently was acquired by the Italian government for the collection of the Palazzo Ducale in Mantua, displays a signature in purpurin (Conti [see note 7], 46 n. 5) that reads "Laur(...)nbrunus." When examined up close, the signature is obviously inauthentic (the gilded decorations are also fake, and they are indeed preserved only in the same area where the artist's signature is found). It is likely that this was done by the restorer Sigismondo Belluti; see Massimo Ferretti, "Falsi e tradizione artistica," in *Storia dell'arte italiana,* 12 vols. (Turin: Einaudi, 1979–1983), 10: 170 n. 21, who casts similar doubts on the *Saint Jerome.*

14. See Ventura (see note 8), 150–53. The signature is legible on the ground near Tmolus's left hand. The high quality and Correggio-like traits of this work seem to have made Longhi wonder whether it might have been by Correggio himself, according to Conti (see note 7), 39. I wish to thank Eric Schleier for generously supplying me with this photograph.

15. Ventura (see note 8), 81, proposes a date circa 1510. The opening up of the landscape between fronds arranged like the wings of a stage in the *Judgment of Midas* presupposes at least some knowledge of Correggio's *Noli me tangere* (now in the Museo del Prado, Madrid), which dates to about 1518.

16. It is easy to imagine that the beginning of Leonbruno's career took place in proximity to Mantegna, given the later reemergence of traces of Mantegna's influence, but it is by no means certain. In any event, given the current state of scholarship, it is delusory to attribute to him the *Allegory of Mantua* that was formerly in the Rey-Spitzer collection. See Adolfo Venturi, "Vendite d'opere d'arte e i loro nomi," *L'arte* 7 (1904): 393; Gamba (see note 12), 91–92; and Ventura (see note 8), 87, who goes so far as to propose a date circa 1522 for the painting. See also, on this painting, Giovanni Agosti, "Su Mantegna, 1. (All'ingresso della mostra del 1992, a Londra)," *Prospettiva,* no. 71 (1993): 46.

17. Ventura (see note 8), 176–77; Sylvia Ferino-Pagden, *Isabella d'Este, "La prima donna del mondo": Fürstin und Mäzenatin der Renaissance,* exh. cat. (Vienna: Kunsthistorisches Museum, 1994), 402–4 (entry no. 138 by Leandro Ventura).

18. These derivations were noted by Carlo Gamba, the first to attribute the work to Leonbruno: "Un nuovo dipinto del Leonbruno," *Rassegna d'arte* 9 (1909): 30–31, for the model of the nymph; and "Un'allegoria del Leonbruno agli Uffizi," *Bollettino d'arte* 4 (1910): 199, for the model of Mercury.

19. Lionello Puppi, "Dosso al Buonconsiglio," *Arte veneta* 18 (1964): 20; Andrea De Marchi, "Sugli esordi veneti di Dosso Dossi," *Arte veneta* 40 (1986): 24; Ballarin (see note 1), 1: 30; and the essays by Giovanni Romano and Peter Humfrey in this volume.

20. A valuable point of comparison is to be found in the small painting of about 1510 depicting the *Mystic Marriage of Saint Catherine* by a very young Correggio (Washington, National Gallery of Art, no. 194); Correggio does not use gold in his later works.

21. Fiorenzo Canuti, *Il Perugino,* 2 vols. (Siena: Editrice d'Arte "La Diana," 1931), 2: 236 (the letter is dated 30 June 1505). Isabella's partiality toward Leonbruno is documented in various sources, from her warm recommendation of Leonbruno to Perugino in 1504 to her letter dated 23 February 1523 to the treasurer Girolamo Arcari in which she asks for better treatment for Leonbruno; Ventura (see note 8), 246–47 (doc. 8), 261–62 (doc. 54).

22. Giovanni Romano, "Verso la maniera moderna: Da Mantegna a Raffaello," in *Storia dell'arte italiana,* 12 vols. (Turin: Einaudi, 1979–1983), 6: 3–85, esp. 63–85.

23. For the reconstruction of Dosso's youth, see Roberto Longhi, "Un problema di Cinquecento ferrarese (Dosso giovine)" (1927), in idem, *Saggi e ricerche, 1925–1928,* 2 vols. (Florence: Sansoni, 1967), 1: 306–11; Roberto Longhi, "Officina ferrarese" (1936), in idem, *Officina ferrarese, 1934: Seguita dagli ampliamenti, 1940, e dai nuovi ampliamenti, 1940–55,* 2nd ed. (Florence: Sansoni, 1968), 81–82; Carlo Volpe, "Dosso: Segnalazioni e proposte per il suo primo itinerario," *Paragone,* no. 293 (1974): 20–29, and Carlo Volpe, "Una pala d'altare del giovane Dosso," *Paragone,* nos. 383–385 (1982): 3–14; De Marchi (see note 19), 20–28; and Ballarin (see note 1), 1: 23–32, 53–59. In the Philadelphia *Holy Family,* the entire landscape is painted over a sky-blue undercoat, which is exposed around the fronds of the trees, an expedient clearly visible in other typical works by Dosso. How can we explain that one of his followers, although having assimilated even this technical procedure, nonetheless insistently employed approaches that the master had long since left behind?

24. Ballarin (see note 1), 1: 375–76 (entry no. 511), who for this reason dates the San Francesco altarpiece toward 1515.

25. Franceschini (see note 3).

26. See Girolamo Prandi, *Notizie storiche spettanti la vita e le opere di Lorenzo Leonbruno* (Mantua: Tip. Virgiliana de L. Caranenti, 1825), 76–77; and Ventura (see note 8), 259 (doc. 47).

27. Romano (see note 22), 83–84, perfectly describes the ambiguities of the decoration of the Camera Grande for Isabella. See also Agosti (see note 7), 68–69.

28. On the phenomenon of "regional proto-Mannerism," which Longhi analyzed, see the crucial essay by Giovanni Romano, "Gli eccentrici del Cinquecento, tra classicismo e 'maniera,'" in Giovanni Previtali, ed., *L'arte di scrivere sull'arte: Roberto Longhi nella cultura del nostro tempo* (Rome: Editori Riuniti, 1982), 184–91. For a

complete reconstruction of the activities of Gian Francesco Tura, see the expanded version of this chapter forthcoming in *Bollettino d'arte.* For general information and the identification of Tura with the Orombelli Master, see Renato Berzaghi, "Tre dipinti e un nome per il 'Maestro Orombelli,'" in Paolo Piva and Egidio Del Canto, eds., *Dal Correggio a Giulio Romano: La committenza di Gregorio Cortese* (Mantua: Casa del Mantegna, 1989), 171–92.

29. This painting on canvas, measuring about 120 × 180 cm, was donated in 1957 by the Cornaggia Medici Castiglioni family. It is cited as the work of Girolamo da Carpi by Cristina Gnoni Maravelli, "Monte Argentario," in Bruno Santi, ed., *Guida storico-artistica alla Maremma: Itinerari culturali nella provincia di Grosseto* (Siena: Nuova Immagine, 1995), 258. The painting's landscape is in excellent condition, but the figures have rather deteriorated and display impoverished and flattened flesh tones in the reinforced parts of the canvas.

30. See Ventura (see note 8), 162–64; Ferino-Pagden (see note 17), 404–7 (entry no. 139 by Leandro Ventura).

31. Various artists derived works from this composition, a Mantegnesque pastiche that in any case should be credited to Leonbruno. These derivatives, summarized by Ventura (see note 8), 162–64, include an engraving by Giulio Sanuto and a painting by Giovanni Battista Moroni (Nîmes, Musée des Beaux-Arts), an artist from Bergamo.

32. Let us recall here at least the grandiose painting for the Palazzo di San Sebastiano, entitled *The Investiture of Federico II as a Captain of the Church,* now in the Národní Galerie in Prague. Andrea Bacchi (personal communication, 1995) has added a *Virgin and Child* from the collection of the Galleria Nazionale, Parma (inv. no. 394, in storage), to the catalog of Costa's Mantuan works, with a date placing it near the altarpiece of 1525 now in Sant'Andrea. I believe that this work has not been published previously; the Galleria Nazionale classifies it as belonging to the "sixteenth-century Lombard school."

33. Clifford M. Brown, *Lorenzo Costa* (Ann Arbor: University Microfilms, 1967), 277–78, 382; and Graziano Manni, Emilio Negro, and Massimo Pirondini, eds., *Arte emiliana: Dalle raccolte storiche al nuovo collezionismo* (Modena: Artioli, 1989), 32 (entry no. 14 by Emilio Negro).

34. One argument in favor of a later date depends upon the work's possible reliance on Raphael's *Saint John the Baptist,* painted for Cardinal Adrien Gouffier. This painting is now in the Musée du Louvre; see *Raphael dans les collections françaises,* exh. cat. (Paris: Editions de la Réunion des Musées Nationaux, 1983), 88–89 (entry no. 8 by Sylvie Beguin). Leonbruno might have known something about this painting from his stay in Rome in 1521. This reliance was suggested to me by Alessandro Ballarin, who assumes that Dosso also knew about this work. This would be demonstrated by his *Saint John the Baptist* (published by Longhi when it was a part of the Gnecco collection in Genoa and never again seen), which appears to be very close to the Modena altarpiece of 1522. See Roberto Longhi, *Officina ferrarese, 1934: Seguita dagli ampliamenti, 1940, e dai nuovi ampliamenti, 1940–55,* 2nd ed. (Florence: Sansoni, 1968), 158, fig. 377; and Ballarin (see note 1), 1: 333–34 (entry no. 425), 2: figs. 625, 626.

35. Inv. no. P.1979-1: Francis Russell, "Saleroom Discoveries: A 'Nativity' by

Lorenzo Leonbruno," *Burlington Magazine* 119 (1977): 601; *Shin shuzo kaiga mokuroku, showa 54 nen–heisei 1 nen/Catalogue of Painting Acquisitions, 1979–1989* (Tokyo: Koruritsu Seiyo Bijutsukan/National Museum of Western Art, 1990), 41–42; and Ventura (see note 8), 149–50. I wish to thank Michiaki Koshikawa from the National Museum of Western Art, Tokyo, for having furnished me with the documentation regarding the painting.

36. Russell, ibid., 601.

37. Keith Christiansen, "The Studiolo of Isabella d'Este and Late Themes," in Jane Martineau, ed., *Andrea Mantegna,* exh. cat. (London: Thames & Hudson, 1992), 421, 425 n. 22, 426 n. 23. Michel Laclotte, "Mantegna et Crivelli," *L'œil* 85 (1962): 92, proposed the name of Lorenzo Costa after studying the retouchings of the work which probably occurred on the occasion of Isabella's move to the Corte Vecchia; but see also Conti (see note 7), 41, 49 n. 21. Leonbruno himself amply retouched the faces of several of the muses.

38. Gamba (see note 12), 70, 94.

39. Ventura (see note 8), 165–67.

40. Inv. no. 6810: Leandro Ozzòla, *La Galleria di Mantova, Palazzo ducale,* 2nd ed. (Mantua: Ente Provinciale per il Turismo, 1953), 9–10 (entry no. 55), figs. 59–60. Renato Berzaghi pointed out to me that the altarpiece is described in an inventory from the Napoleonic era as a work "of the school of Giulio Romano" coming from the "Franciscans," likely San Francesco (Mantua, Archivio di Stato, Scalcheria, b. 90, "Inventario generale de' mobili, quadri, arredi sagri," after 1803). Given the presence of Saint Longinus, the iconography of the work is doubtless Mantuan.

41. Inv. no. 60/54: Museo Poldi Pezzoli, *Dipinti* (Milan: Electa, 1981), 132–33 (entry no. 140 by Mauro Natale).

42. Conti (see note 7), 48 n. 17.

43. Andrea Ugolini, "Lorenzo Costa da Bologna a Mantova," *Prospettiva,* no. 48 (1987): 81.

44. *Inventario degli oggetti d'arte d'Italia,* vol. 6, *Provincia di Mantova* (Rome: Libreria dello Stato, 1935), 10 (see *S. Bernardino fra S. Pietro e S. Paolo*), lists it as belonging to the "sixteenth-century Venetian school" and includes a reproduction. The fact that this altarpiece comes from a Franciscan building, like the two altarpieces previously discussed, is most significant. Renato Berzaghi has informed me that during the eighteenth century the painting was recorded as being in the church of San Francesco in Mantua (Giovanni Cadioli, *Descrizione delle pitture, sculture, ed architetture che si osservano nella città di Mantova e de' suoi contorni* [Mantua: Per l'Erede di Alberto Pazzoni, 1763], 59) and that only in the nineteenth century did it end up in Sant'Apollonia, as Gaetano Susani mentioned in his *Nuovo prospetto delle pitture, sculture ed architetture di Mantova* (Mantua: Fr. Agazzi, 1818), 60. Susani calls it a "*pregiato lavoro di uno degli scolari di Tiziano*" (skilled work by one of Titian's students).

45. Dosso is almost always mentioned as being at his father's side in the acts registering the lands acquired by his father, but this does not necessarily mean that he was physically present. His physical presence is explicitly noted in two rental contracts signed on 22–23 September 1529 *("Johannes filius m*[*agist*]*ri Nicolai de Costantino de*

Luterio habitator Ferrarie nunc moram trahens in suprascripta villa dossi"). See Giovannini (see note 2), 59–60 (docs. (19–20).

46. Alessandro Luzio, *La galleria dei Gonzaga venduta all'Inghilterra nel 1627–28: Documenti degli archivi di Mantova e Londra* (Milan: L. F. Cogliati, 1913), 26 n. 2; and Pattanaro (see note 5), 1: 142–43.

47. John Shearman, *The Early Italian Pictures in the Collection of Her Majesty the Queen* (Cambridge: Cambridge Univ Press, 1983), 87–89 (entry no. 81); and Ballarin (see note 1), 1: 104, 344–45 (entry no. 444). The work can be identified in the Gonzaga inventory of 1627, when it was sold to Charles I of England. I concur with the early dating proposed by Shearman and Ballarin which would place it at about the same time as the Della Sale altarpiece of 1527 (Rome, Galleria Nazionale di Palazzo Barberini).

48. Inv. no. 89.PA.32: Ferino-Pagden (see note 17), 420–25 (entry no. 144 by Sylvia Ferino-Pagden); Ballarin (see note 1), 1: 349–50 (entry no. 456); and Dawson Carr, "The *Allegory of Fortune* in the Getty Museum" (paper presented at the conference "Dosso Dossi and His Age," Malibu, Calif., May 1996).

49. For Lorenzo Costa's altarpiece, which depicts the Virgin and Child with Saint Sebastian, Saint Sylvester, Saint Augustine (?), Saint Roche, Saint Elizabeth, Saint John, and Saint Paul and bears the inscription "LAURENTIUS COSTA FECIT ET DONAVIT MDXXV," see Ranieri Varese, *Lorenzo Costa* (Milan: Silvana, 1967), 72 (entry no. 58). For Dosso's *Saint Sebastian,* which was originally located in the church of Santissima Annunziata in Cremona but is now in the Brera collection, see Ballarin (see note 1), 1: 344 (entry no. 443).

50. Ballarin (see note 1), 1: 103:

> Questi movimenti artificiosi [...] dànno luogo a delle forme che a fronte della sua storia trascorsa appaiono di una bellezza fondata soprattutto su delle preoccupazioni di decoro. Le figure sono sottoposte a un processo di raffinamento in questo senso; le teste stesse, una volta selvatiche e impaurite dalle proprie visioni interiori, dalla violenza dei propri sentimenti, sono ora idealizzate secondo i canoni dell'estetica classica, acquistano una bellezza generica ed esprimono un registro di sentimenti convenzionali.

51. The allusion here is to the letter dated 20 January 1525, in which Leonbruno defended himself against the insulting attacks of Equicola. See Giovan Battista Intra, "Lorenzo Leonbruno e Giulio Romano," *Archivio storico lombardo* 36 (1887): 573; Ventura (see note 8), 271–72 (doc. 73); and Agosti (see note 7), 66–67.

Dates, Dress, and Dosso: Some Problems of Chronology

Jane Bridgeman

In the first three decades of the sixteenth century many rapid changes in the style of clothing in Italy were recorded in the visual arts and discussed in contemporary literature. These changes were regarded as unusual and were ascribed to various causes, not least the influx of foreigners and the chronic state of war that afflicted northern Italy between the League of Cambrai in 1508 and the Congress of Bologna in 1530.

Foreign influences in dress, and the changing design of Italian clothes, were discussed by contemporary authors, notably the writer and diplomat Baldassare Castiglione in *Il libro del cortegiano*[1] and the historian Benedetto Varchi in his *Storia fiorentina*. Varchi emphasized the contrast between the clothes worn by himself and his contemporaries and those that they had worn only a few years before: "And there is no doubt that between 1512 and today [1527] men's dress, like women's, has become a good deal brighter and more elegant. Men no longer wear, as they used to, ample overtunics that have a bodice and sleeves so wide that they hang down beyond the knees, or hats three times bigger than those worn now with brims tucked upright, or pumps [slipperlike footwear] awkwardly made with low backs."[2]

These alterations in the appearance of clothing happened throughout Italy, although, as Castiglione observed, regional characteristics were preserved.[3] Parallel changes in style are seen in armor (of which many examples survive), and these too are clearly depicted in the many contemporary representations of warrior saints, particularly George, who were quite naturally the subjects of popular devotion in wartime.[4]

The speed of change during this period makes it relatively easy to analyze dress in visual sources, in contrast to other centuries in which the process of change was so slow that different strategies for interpreting the evidence must be sought. The extant written evidence from the early sixteenth century furthermore corroborates the chronology of stylistic change in dress and clarifies many aspects of contemporary iconography in the visual arts.

Very distinct differences in shape and style developed within only forty years, from 1490 to 1530, but were most noticeable between 1506 and 1518 and again during the years 1524 to 1530—that is, during the time that Dosso Dossi was active as a painter. The record of these changes and their geographical, social, and historical contexts have to be taken into account when studying the depiction of dress in undated paintings.[5] At the beginning of the sixteenth century, in what is today Emilia and Lombardy, it is safe to assume that clothing had a reasonable similarity of style that would naturally be illustrated in paintings associated with Ferrara and the other cities of the Po valley. In fact, the attire of the rulers and their courtiers at Ferrara, Mantua, and Milan was very much the same, partly because of close personal ties between the Este, the Gonzaga, and the Sforza. When in November 1515 Francis I of France requested that Isabella d'Este send him a doll dressed like the ladies of Mantua, Isabella was happy to oblige. She warned him, however, that the doll would probably be a disappointment: "we will have the doll made with the clothes and hairstyle that we wear, although Your Majesty will not see anything new, *because what we wear is also worn in Milan by the Milanese ladies.*"[6]

From about 1505 onward, and especially between 1510 and 1530, when Dosso was painting, there were noticeable alterations in the shape of male and female clothing and in hair arrangements.[7] Men's hair was long and shoulder length around 1506, but by 1530 it was cut very short above the ears. Women's hair, which lay over the shoulders in a net or was braided in a long plait falling down the back between about 1506 and 1510, was by 1530 pinned up and often covered by a decorative cap. The shape of sleeves also changed. In the first decade of the century women's gowns had very big triangular or baglike sleeves, embellished with hanging ribbons and ties, that completely hid the shape of the arms. By 1530, sleeves, although having a small globular puff at the shoulder, were narrow and straight, with ruffles showing beneath the cuff at the wrist.

Over seventy years ago Roberto Longhi suggested that a group of seven paintings, all previously of uncertain or disputed authorship, were early works by Dosso Dossi and dateable on stylistic grounds to before about 1515.[8] In four of these works it is possible to identify significant features of contemporary attire: the Philadelphia *Holy Family and Donors* (fig. 1), the Naples *Holy Family with Saint John the Baptist, Saint Barbara, and a Donor* (fig. 2), the Rome *Virgin and Child with Saint John the Baptist, Saint Jerome, Saint Paul, and Donor* (fig. 3), and *Salome before Herod* (p. 157). The secular civilian dress portrayed in these paintings will be discussed here, and I will show that none of them displays features commonly found before about 1515.

Of the four paintings ascribed to Dosso by Longhi as having been painted before 1515, and with which this essay is concerned, the most useful from the point of view of dress is the Philadelphia *Holy Family.* Longhi generally relied upon stylistic criteria for dating and rarely referred to other methodologies, but, in this instance, he rather surprisingly stated that the dress of the kneeling donors "in truth, is more appropriate for 1515 than 1530."[9] His opinion of both the date and the authorship of the *Holy Family* conflicted with that of Bernard Berenson, who thought the work was painted in about 1530 and was attributable not to Dosso but to a Bergamasque painter in the circle of Lorenzo Lotto (although he originally cataloged it as "Venetian about 1530").[10]

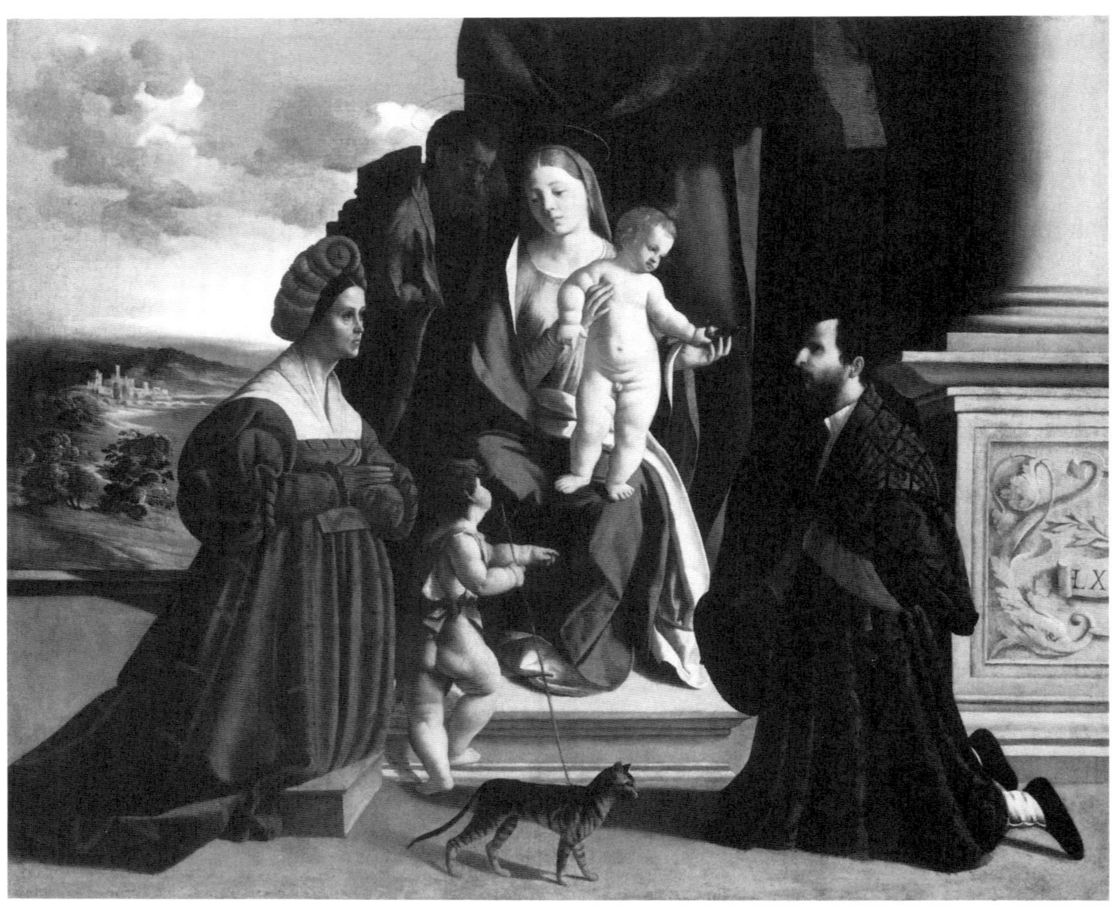

Fig. 1. Dosso Dossi
Holy Family and Donors
Philadelphia, Philadelphia Museum of Art

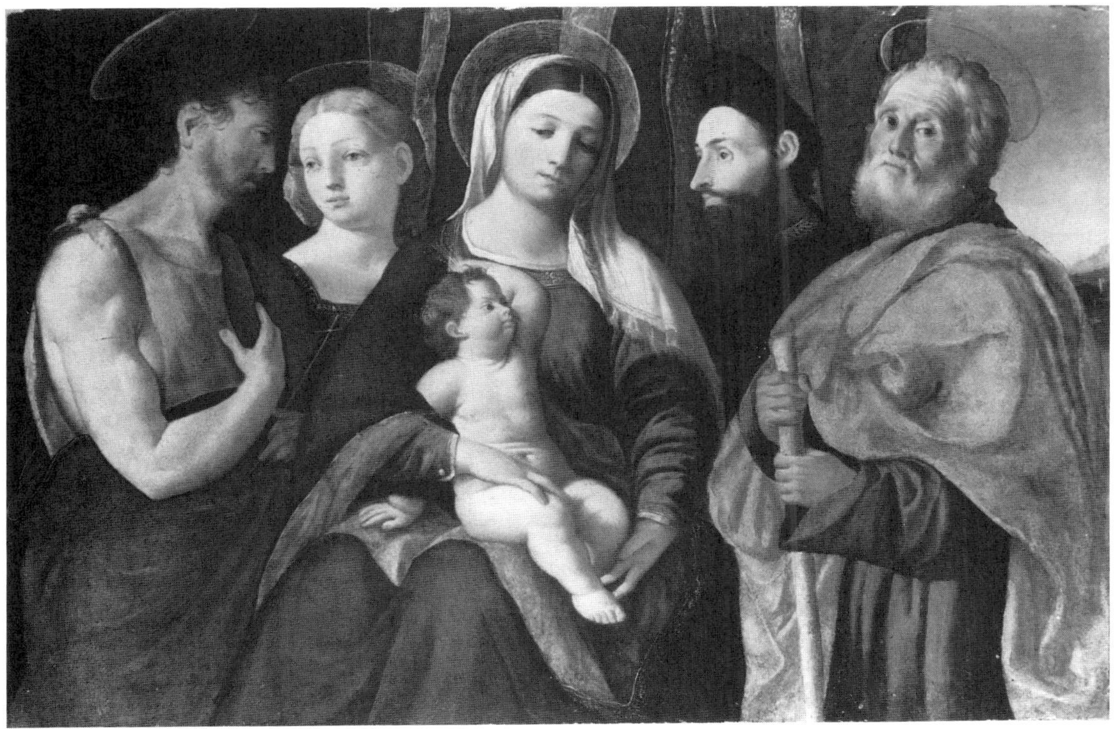

Fig. 2. Dosso Dossi
Holy Family with Saint John the Baptist, Saint Barbara, and a Donor
Naples, Museo e Gallerie Nazionali di Capodimonte

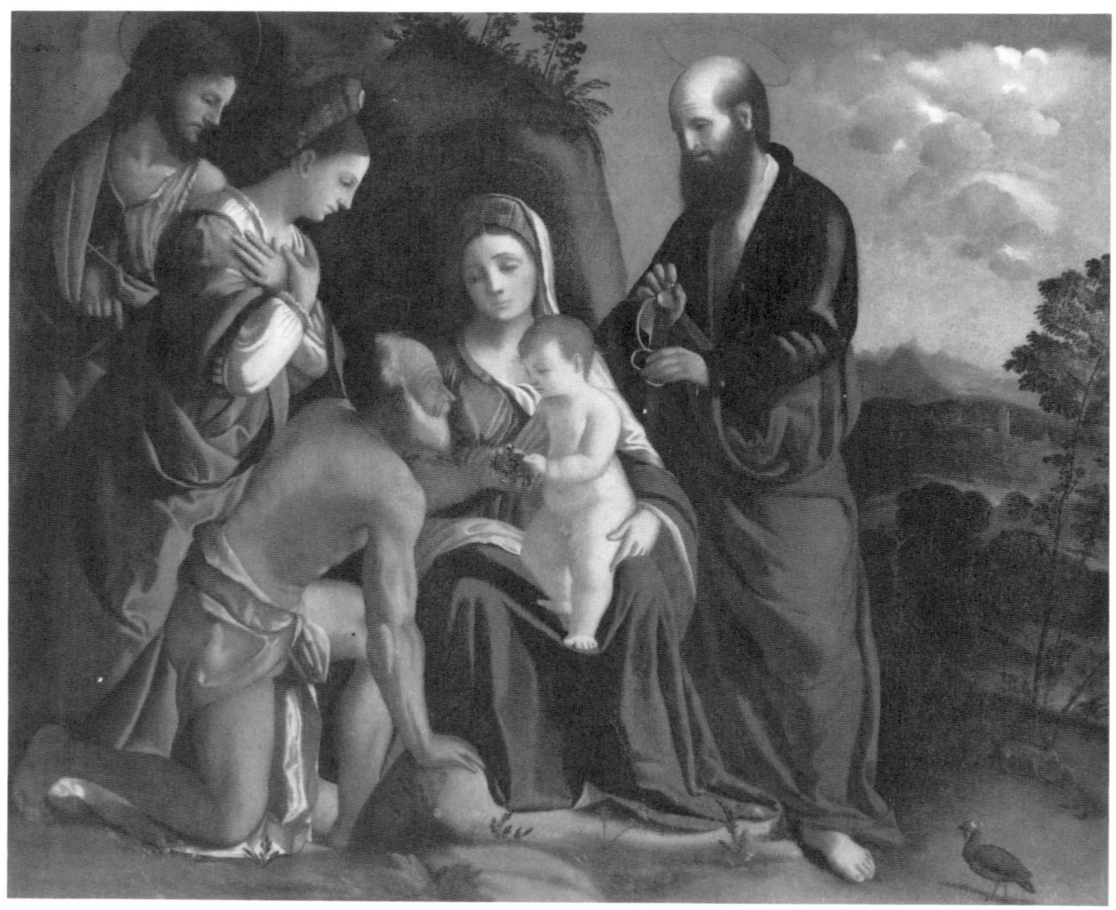

Fig. 3. Dosso Dossi
Virgin and Child with Saint John the Baptist, Saint Jerome, Saint Paul, and Donor
Rome, Pinacoteca Capitolina

It is certainly difficult to recognize the donor's attire in the *Holy Family* as typical of male dress in Italy in 1515. Gowns with elbow-length sleeves, a shirt with a high ruffled collar, a beard, and short hair revealing the ears and neck are not a combination of elements found in male dress at that time. Boccaccio Boccaccino's fresco *Meeting at the Golden Gate* of 1514–1515 (fig. 4) includes typical examples of male dress worn in northern Italy at the end of the first decade of the sixteenth century. Men are shown wearing square (not round) hats with flat crowns and wide brims tied or turned up and hair cut in a pageboy or bobbed style that covers the ears.[11] The fresco cycle of 1510–1511 in the Scuola del Santo at Padua illustrating the Miracles of Saint Anthony—for example, Titian's *Miracle of the Talking Babe* (fig. 5) and Francesco Vecellio's *Miracle of the Usurer's Heart* (fig. 6)—includes examples of contemporary male attire, including striped and checked *saioni* (overtunics), *robe* or *veste* (gowns), and hats and shoes of design almost identical to those illustrated by Boccaccino.

Other representations are seen in Giovanni Buonconsiglio's *Saint Catherine with Saint Bernardino and the Archangel Gabriel with Tobit,* 1513, in the cathedral of Montagnana, and in two silver panels of a reliquary chest by Giovanni Antonio Leli da Foligno, the court silversmith and jeweler at Ferrara. In the Buonconsiglio painting, Tobit, shown as a small boy with long hair holding the hand of the Archangel Gabriel, wears a *saione* of the same sort as the young Ercole d'Este in the first silver panel (fig. 7). In the second panel (fig. 8), Alfonso d'Este, who kneels before Saint Maurelius, also wears a *saione*. He is bearded and has shoulder-length hair. His dress and hairstyle are like those worn by the members of the papal guard in Raphael's *Mass at Bolsena* of 1512–1514 in the Vatican's Stanza d'Eliodoro, and by Saint Faustinus and Saint Giovitas on the organ shutters painted by Moretto da Brescia and Floriano Ferramola in 1518 for the church of Santa Maria in Valvendra, Lovere.[12]

Romanino's *Ecce Homo* fresco in the cathedral of Cremona, completed in 1519, portrays civilians in dress of a similar style (fig. 9). The most prominent figure, in the left foreground, wears a loosely fitting sleeveless gown of black damask over a red *saione* that has a low square-cut neck, straight sleeves, and a pleated knee-length skirt. The *saione* (which was worn over a doublet, shirt, and hose) is ornamented with white bands around the hem and neck, and the open sleeves have cuffs edged with brown. The shirt, seen above the neck of the *saione,* does not have a high collar. This man has grey hair, which hides his ears and rests on his shoulders, and he wears a hat with an upturned brim tied across the forehead. These clothes are similar to those recorded in the frescoes at the Scuola del Santo, which were painted nine years earlier: the black slip-on shoes worn by the man depicted by Romanino are, for example, identical to those worn by the father in Titian's *Miracle of the Talking Babe.*[13]

The shoes of the donor in the Philadelphia *Holy Family* also look later than 1515. Shoes with rounded toes were still worn in 1515, but square toes

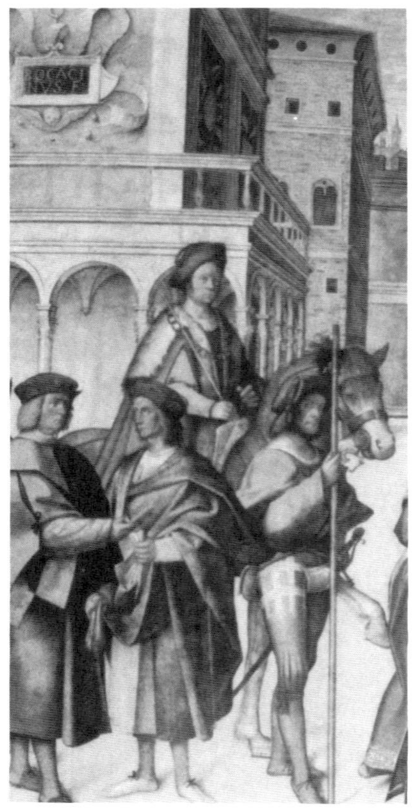

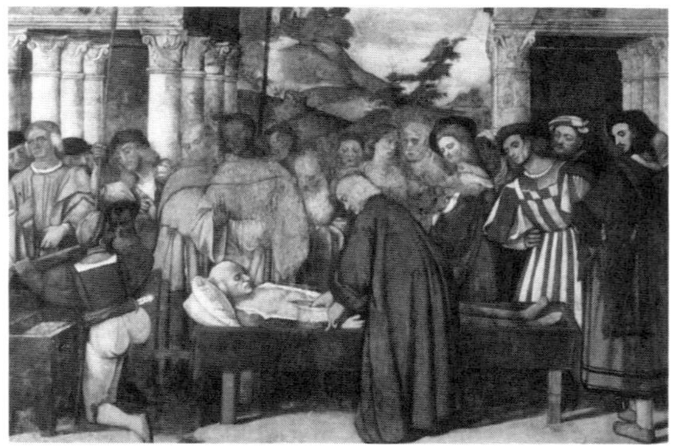

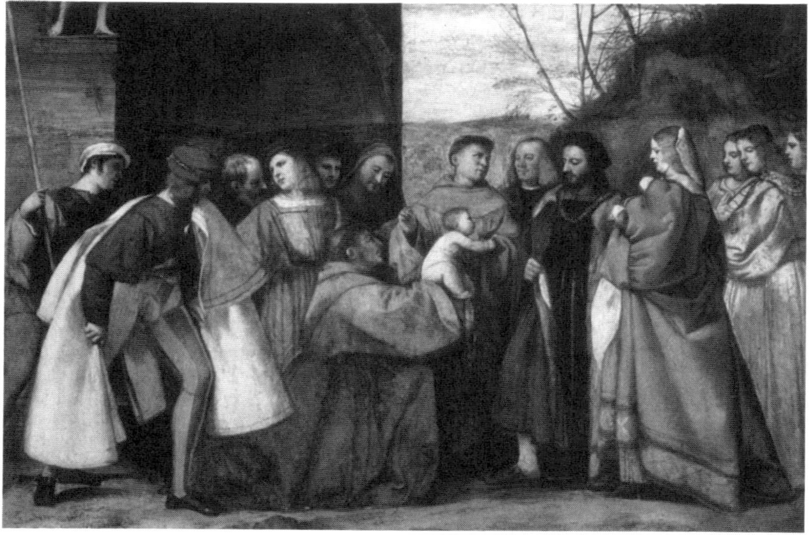

Fig. 4. Boccaccio Boccaccino
Meeting at the Golden Gate (detail)
Cremona, Duomo

Fig. 5. Titian
Miracle of the Talking Babe
Padua, Scuola del Santo

Fig. 6. Francesco Vecellio
Miracle of the Usurer's Heart
Padua, Scuola del Santo

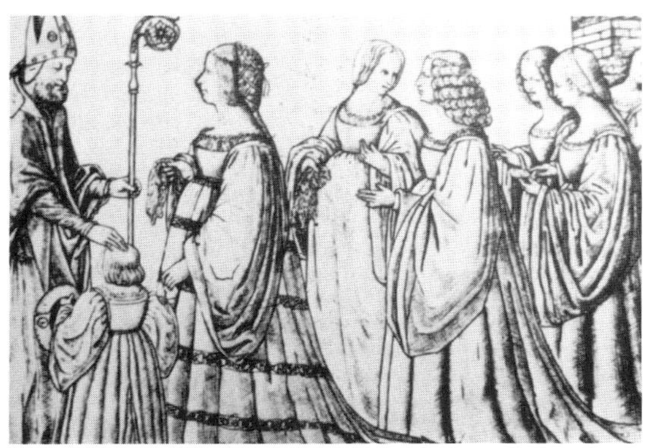

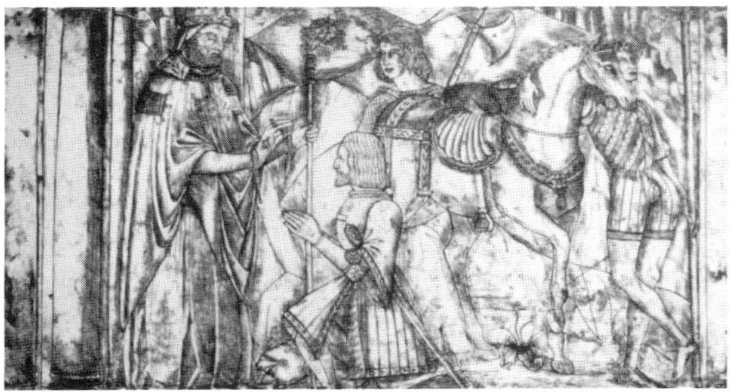

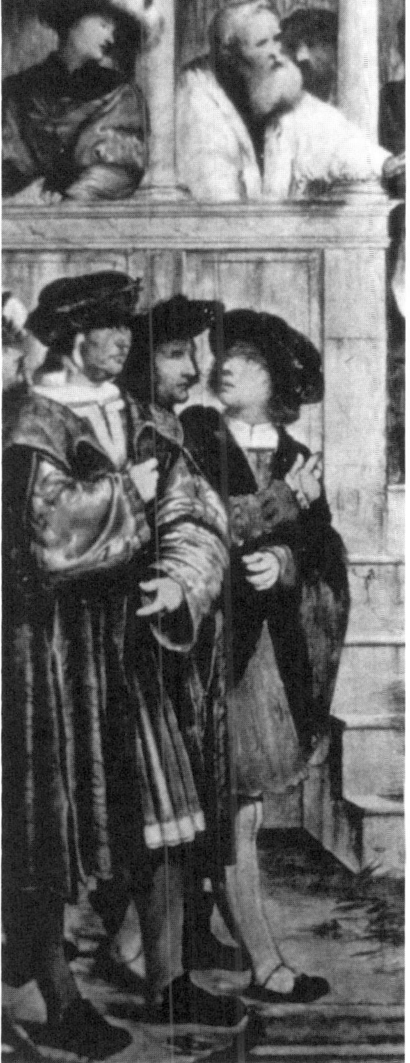

Fig. 7. Giovanni Antonio Leli da Foligno
Lucrezia Borgia, Duchess of Ferrara, Presenting Her Son Ercole d'Este to Saint Maurelius (detail)
Ferrara, San Giorgio

Fig. 8. Giovanni Antonio Leli da Foligno
Duke Alfonso I d'Este Kneeling before Saint Maurelius
Ferrara, San Giorgio

Fig. 9. Gerolamo Romanino
Ecce Homo
Cremona, Duomo

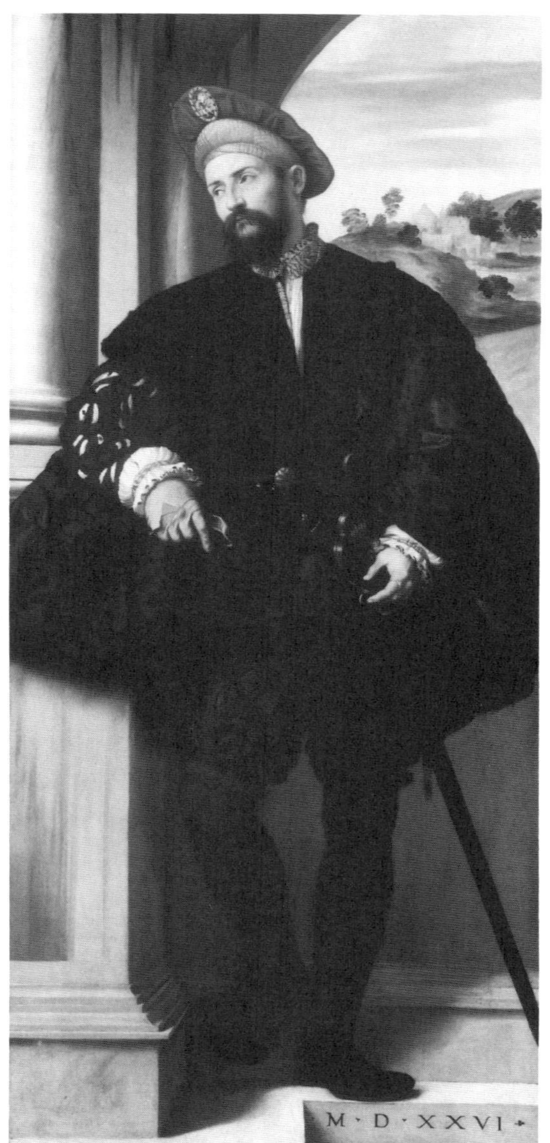

Fig. 10. Moretto da Brescia, also called Alessandro Bonvicino
Portrait of an Unknown Gentleman
London, National Gallery

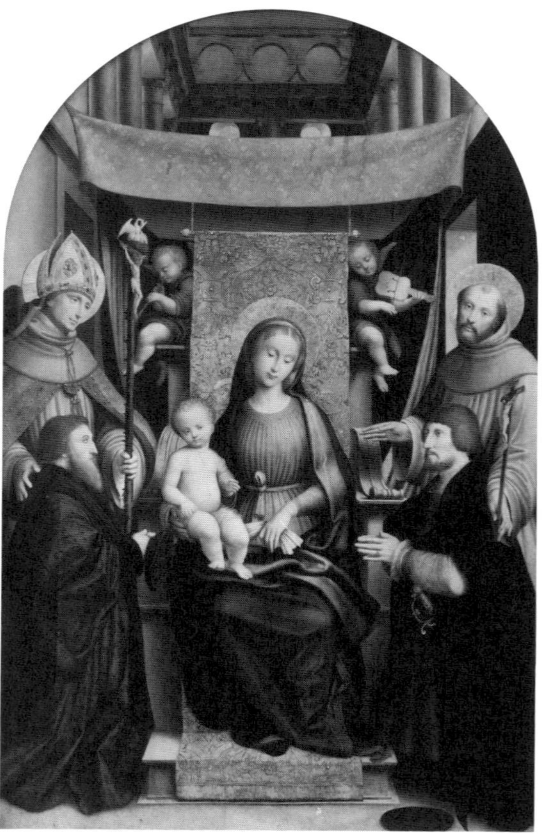

Fig. 11. Gerolamo Giovenone
The Virgin and Child with Saint Francis and Saint Bonaventure and Two Kneeling Donors
London, National Gallery

were more common; the older style of shoes with rounded toes were also usually fastened by laces over the instep or at the top of the foot. Two very clearly depicted examples of this type of shoe are seen in Boccaccino's *Meeting at the Golden Gate.*[14] The donor's very short hair and high, pleated collarband are equally unusual for 1515. At that date a few soldiers wore shirts with an embroidered collarband and ruffled edge; these shirts were worn with a *sciuffiotto* (bonnet), under which the hair was concealed. An example is seen in the *Portrait of a Condottiere,* attributed to Dosso (Cambridge, Massachusetts, Fogg Art Museum) and probably painted about 1515.[15] These shirts were introduced into Italy by German soldiers. In April 1516 the young Federigo Gonzaga, then in Lyons in the entourage of Francis I of France, wrote to his mother, Isabella d'Este, with a request for such shirts, "because here people wear shirts in the German style, with high collarbands, and bonnets.... I pray Your Excellency be pleased to have some made for me, with the collar and sleeves worked like those belonging to Signor Luigi Gonzaga, who can show them [to you] there, and to send them to me, so that I too may dress like everyone else."[16]

Shirts with a low neck and long hair that concealed the ears were worn by many men until the late 1520s. In the Philadelphia painting, the donor's collar (at least 6 mm high) and shirt, seen beneath an open doublet, thus suggest a date after 1525. By then it was the custom sometimes to leave the doublet (and the short tunic or jerkin worn over it) unbuttoned to show off the shirt, as depicted in Moretto's full-length *Portrait of an Unknown Gentleman,* which was painted in 1526 (fig. 10). Moretto's subject wears a shirt with an embroidered collarband as well as wrist ruffles. The same style is seen in Titian's *Portrait of a Man with a Glove,* about 1520–1522 (Paris, Musée du Louvre) and Bernardino Licinio's *Portrait of Stefano Nani,* 1528 (London, National Gallery), although Nani wears a low-necked shirt and has ear-length hair.

No less difficult to reconcile with any depictions that date from about 1515 is the donor's hair. Even soldiers did not wear their hair like this then. In Dosso and Garofalo's Costabili altarpiece (p. 142), for example, Saint George's hair, although short for 1513, nevertheless hides the ears.[17] The hair of civilians, until at least 1524, was (unless they were elderly or balding) cut in a pageboy that covered both the ears and the neck. In the late twenties it was shorter. Comparisons with male hairstyles and dress from about 1520—for example, those worn by the two kneeling donors in Gerolamo Giovenone's *Virgin and Child with Saint Francis and Saint Bonaventure and Two Kneeling Donors* of 1520 (fig. 11), by the husband in Lotto's *Double Portrait* of about 1523–1524 (St. Petersburg, Hermitage), and by various men in Lotto's *Vesting of Saint Bridget* of 1524 (fig. 12)—demonstrate that 1520 is an unlikely date for the portrait of the donor in the Philadelphia painting. By the late 1520s men's hair was shorter. Titian's *Federico Gonzaga* (Madrid, Museo del Prado) of about 1523–1524 depicts clothing, hair, and beard much like that of Saint Nazarus in Giulio Campi's *Madonna and Child with Saint Nazarus and Saint Celsus* of 1527 (fig. 13). The head of the donor, however,

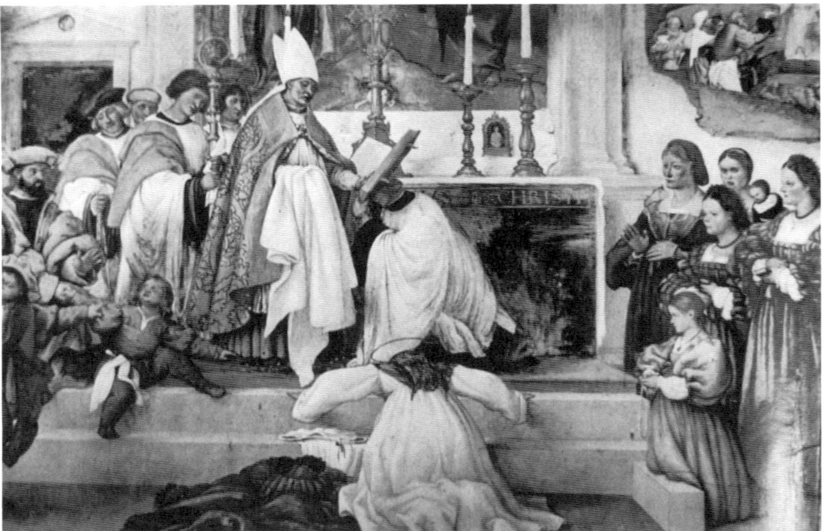

Fig. 12. Lorenzo Lotto
Vesting of Saint Bridget
Trescore, Villa Suardi, Oratorio Suardi

more closely resembles male heads in Callisto Piazza's *Saint John the Baptist Preaching,* 1530 (fig. 14), in Romanino's frescoes in the Castello del Buonconsiglio, Trent, 1530–1532, or in Gaudenzio Ferrari's various *Scenes from the Life of the Virgin,* 1532–1534, at San Cristoforo, Vercelli.

The donatrix in the Philadelphia *Holy Family* kneels in profile facing her husband. Her hair is parted in the center and covers the ears, but it is scarcely visible under an orange-brown turbanlike head covering. Her gown, perhaps a heavy grey silk, is ornamented with a geometric arrangement of orange stripes. Its square neckline has a serrated or tabbed edge filled by an opaque partlet of white linen embellished with faint, broad horizontal bands of yellow embroidery. It completely covers the shoulders and has a V-shaped neck opening. The sleeves of the gown are bulbous between shoulder and elbow but straight from elbow to wrist. The cuffs, which partly cover the hand, have a serrated edge to match the neckline.

What is depicted here does not look like other examples of gowns worn in the first decades of the sixteenth century, which had a low square neckline (above which the frilled edge of a linen smock was displayed), a short bodice with a high waistline, very full skirts, and enormous sleeves that completely concealed the shape of the arms from shoulder to wrist. These features are seen in the silver panel by Leli that depicts Lucrezia Borgia and her son Ercole d'Este. They are also found in the frescoes painted between about 1506

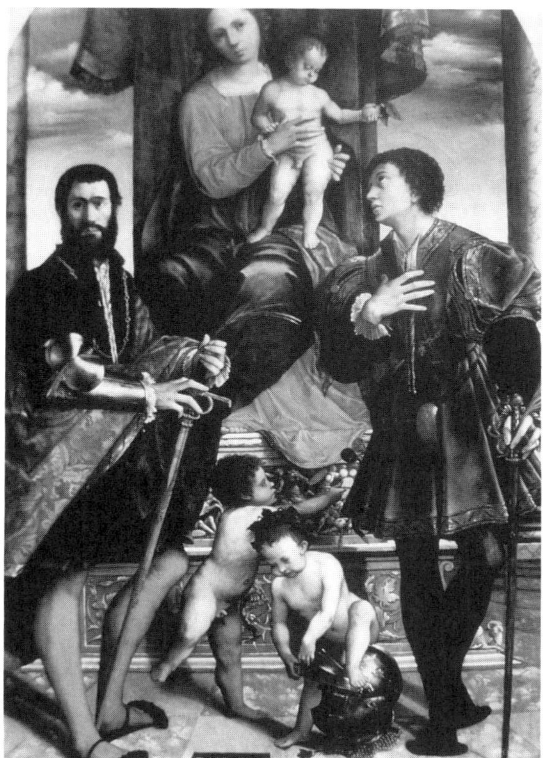

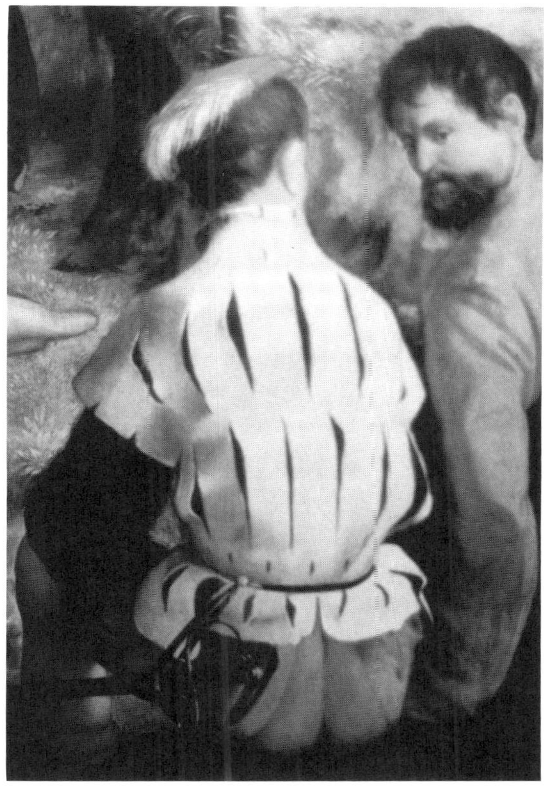

Fig. 13. Giulio Campi
Madonna and Child with Saint Nazarus and Saint Celsus
Cremona, Sant'Abbondio

Fig. 14. Callisto Piazza da Lodi
Saint John the Baptist Preaching (detail)
Lodi, Incoronata

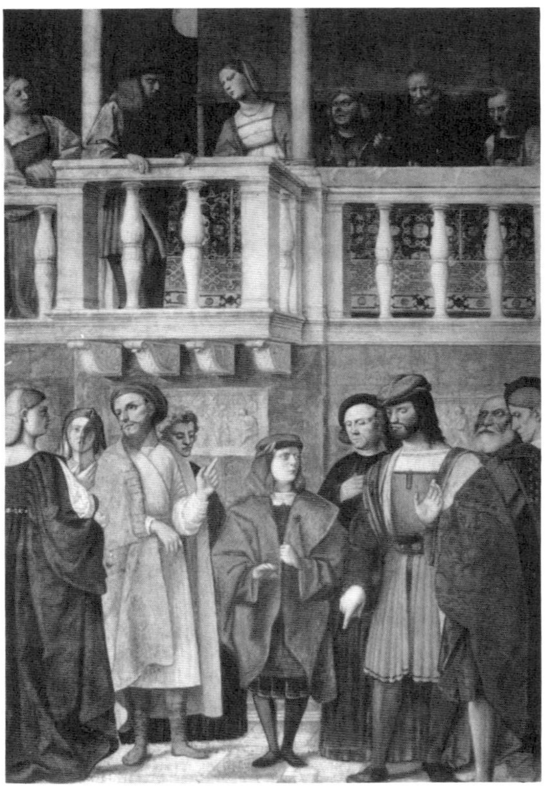

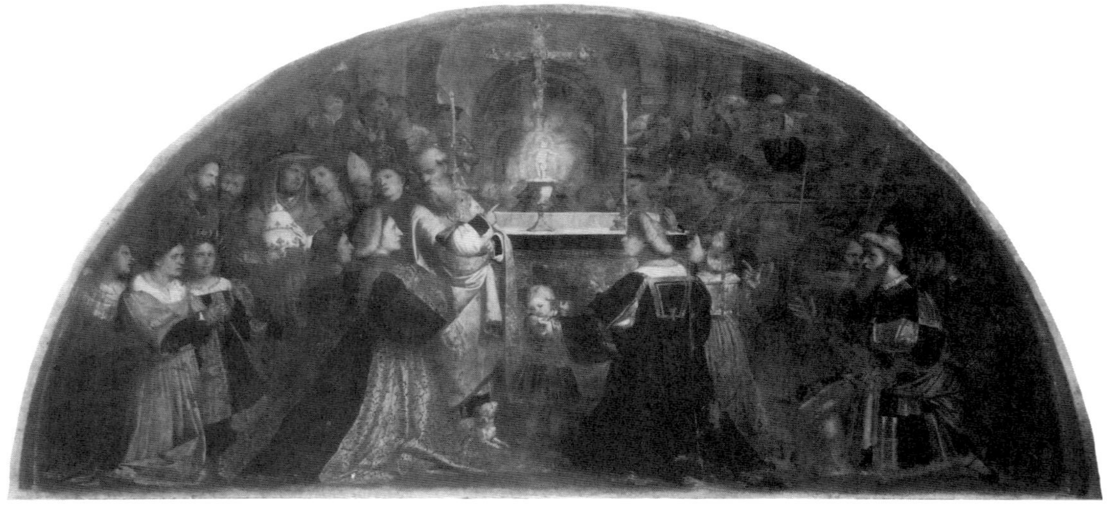

Fig. 15. Girolamo Tessari
Miracle of the Glass
Padua, Scuola del Santo

Fig. 16. Girolamo Romanino
Mass of Saint Gregory (or *Miracle of the Holy Sacrament*)
Brescia, San Giovanni Evangelista

and 1512 by Ferramola for the Casa Borgondio della Corte (Palazzo Calini) in Brescia, notably the *Meeting of the Bride and Bridegroom* (Brescia, Pinacoteca Civica Tosio Martinengo), and in frescoes painted between about 1510 and 1511 in the Scuola del Santo, Padua.

In Leli's panel, the duchess of Ferrara and two of her ladies are shown with their hair in a long plait *(coazzone)* hanging down the back; this was a Spanish style popular in Lombardy and Emilia.[18] Another contemporary style seen here shows the hair resting on the shoulders and enclosed by a light net that was kept in place by a cord around the head.[19] An alternative worn between about 1508 and 1520 was a snood worn on the back of the head, such as that depicted by Giovanni Bellini in the *Young Woman with a Mirror,* 1515 (Vienna, Kunsthistorisches Museum) and in Titian's *"La Schiavona,"* from about 1511–1515 (London, National Gallery). These styles are seen too in Lotto's predella panel of 1508, *A Saint Preaching,* for the Recanati altarpiece (Vienna, Kunsthistorisches Museum), in Girolamo Tessari's *Miracle of the Glass* of 1511 (fig. 15), and in Romanino's *Mass of Saint Gregory* of 1521–1524 (fig. 16). In Parma and Milan, versions of this style are seen in Francesco di Bosio Zaganelli's portrait *Domicilla Gambara Pallavicini,* commissioned in 1518 (Parma, Santissima Annunziata), and the portrait of Giulia Trivulzio by Paolo Morando (Il Cavazzola), signed and dated 1519 (Milan, Biblioteca Trivulziana).

The head covering and hair arrangement of the donatrix in the Philadelphia *Holy Family* do not resemble any of those in the above-mentioned works of art. Her hair is not braided in a plait hanging down the back nor does it lie on the shoulders contained by some form of covering, as is usual in contemporary representations of women in northern Italy from about 1508 to 1519. Examples of a *balzo* (turbanlike headdress) are found in Ferrarese art from about 1519—for instance, on the far left-hand side of Garofalo's *Massacre of the Innocents* (1519, Ferrara, Pinacoteca Nazionale), and they are worn by Saint Agatha and Saint Apollonia in Michele Coltellini's *Enthroned Madonna and Child with the Young Baptist, Two Donors, and Saints* (1512 or 1513, Ferrara, Pinacoteca Nazionale). Another is seen immediately behind Joseph in the background of Boccaccino's *Circumcision* of 1518, in Cremona. These stiffened cylinders or rolls worn on the back of the head were sometimes ornamented with ribbons or a circular medallion in the center. They may have been worn slightly earlier, but are certainly rare before about 1515 in secular representations.[20] On the other hand, more ornamented versions of this head covering are recorded in Lotto's *Double Portrait* of about 1523–1524 (St. Petersburg, Hermitage), in Romanino's *Virgin Appearing to Augustus* of 1524–1525 in the cathedral of Asolo, in Bernardino Licinio's *Family Group* of 1524 (Hampton Court, Royal Collection), and in Callisto Piazza's *Visitation* of 1525 in the church of Santa Maria in Calchera, Brescia.

The geometric patterning on the donatrix's gown suggests a date in the mid-1520s. Nonfigurative decoration was popular at this time. Contrasting areas of checkered and striped color can be seen on male and female garments in Romanino's *Mass of Saint Gregory,* and a woman in a gown ornamented with stripes (combined with stylized petals) is seen standing behind Saint Sigismund in Bernardino Luini's *Saint Sigismund of Burgundy Offers the Church to Saint Maurice* of 1522–1524 (Milan, San Maurizio). But a later dating seems even more likely because of the shape of the donatrix's sleeves. By the mid-1520s some gowns had elbow-length sleeves showing off the white linen smock below the elbow. Excellent representations of this sort of sleeve are seen in Luini's *Ippolita Sforza with Saint Scolastica, Saint Agnes, and Saint Catherine of Alexandria,* which dates to 1522–1524 (fig. 17), and in Lotto's *Torture of Saint Barbara,* 1524 (Trescore, Oratorio Suardi), where in the left background a line of women are dressed in gowns with the same style of sleeves. An alternative was a sleeve bulbous above the elbow and narrow from elbow to wrist, as seen in Licinio's *Family Group* of 1524. After 1525 and certainly by 1530, this upper sleeve had shrunk to an onion-shaped mass of fabric between shoulder and elbow. This is seen quite clearly in Romanino's lunette *Tarquin and Lucretia* (Trent, Castello del Buonconsiglio) of 1531–1532 and in Lotto's *Lady as Lucretia* (London, National Gallery) of about the same date.

To be dateable to about 1515, the donatrix in the Philadelphia *Holy Family* would have to resemble in her dress and hair arrangement the Ferrarese ladies accompanying Lucrezia Borgia in 1512–1514 (see fig. 7) or at least share some similarities with the female dress shown in the frescoes of the Scuola del Santo in Padua. This is clearly not the case. As it is highly unlikely that any painter could anticipate styles in dress by some fifteen years, the combination of hairstyles and clothing worn by the two kneeling donors in the Philadelphia *Holy Family* suggests that it was painted in the very late 1520s or in the 1530s.

Longhi thought the Naples *Holy Family* to have been painted by Dosso in about 1510, although both the profile portrait of the donor in the right background between Saint Joseph and the Virgin and Child and the head of Saint Barbara suggest a date in the following decade.[21] The donor's hair is concealed in a *sciuffiotto,* revealing his left ear and the back of his neck. His shirt collar is embroidered with gold. As previously noted, the ensemble of high collarband and bonnet was mentioned as a new style by Federico Gonzaga in April 1516. It would not have been worn by Italians in 1510. By 1527, as Varchi noted, it was usual to wear a shirt with ruffles at the wrist and neck.[22] Moreover, in the first decade of the century, most men wore their hair long and were clean-shaven, since "anyone who wore long hair and did not shave his beard was held [to be] a ruffian and criminal."[23] The Scuola del Santo frescoes in Padua, of 1510–1511, show mostly clean-shaven men, except, significantly, for the protagonists in the *Miracle of the Talking Babe,* the *Jealous Husband Murdering His Wife,* and the *Miracle of the Glass.* Fuller or bushy beards seen after about 1514 were chiefly worn by soldiers, although they were beginning to be usual also for civilians. Boccaccino depicts two

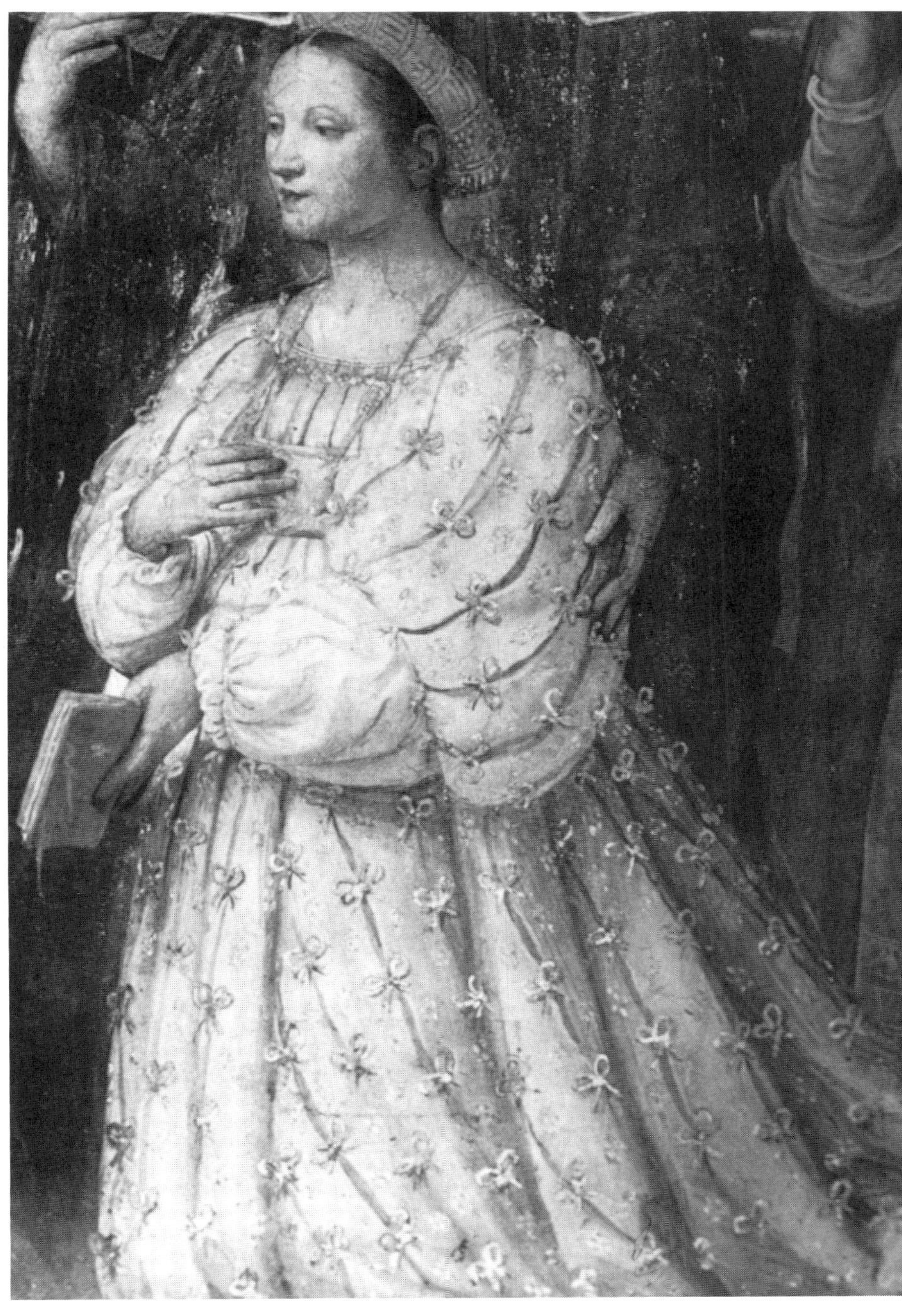

Fig. 17. Bernardino Luini
Ippolita Sforza with Saint Scolastica, Saint Agnes, and Saint Catherine of Alexandria (detail)
Milan, San Maurizio al Monastero Maggiore

bearded horsemen in the extreme left background of the *Marriage of the Virgin* of 1514–1518 in the cathedral of Cremona. By the 1520s beards were more common.[24] The donor on the left in Giovenone's *Virgin and Child*, 1520, has a long beard, as does the kneeling man on the right in Romanino's *Mass of Saint Gregory*, 1521–1524.

The development of headwear is an important indicator of date in the first half of the sixteenth century. From about 1495 through about 1506, men's hats evolved from the small, brimless berets seen in paintings by Domenico Ghirlandaio and Vittore Carpaccio into what might be termed "proper" hats with crowns and brims. Good examples dating from about 1506 are seen in Andrea Solario's *Giovanni Cristoforo Longoni* (1505, London, National Gallery) and the better-known *Agnolo Doni* (1506, Florence, Palazzo Pitti) by Raphael. About 1510, men's hats developed wide brims that had a gap over the forehead and were often tied or pinned up with tassels, bows, and badges. Some were worn at an angle, whereas others sat square on the head. Various examples are depicted in Boccaccino's *Marriage of the Virgin*, 1514–1518, and *Meeting at the Golden Gate*, 1515. Large hats with wide circular serrated brims tended to be worn by soldiers, as shown in Ferramola and Moretto's organ shutters depicting Saint Faustinus and Saint Giovitus of 1518, and they are seen in Romanino's *Christ before Caiaphas* and *Ecce Homo*, both in the cathedral of Cremona and both of 1519. Sometimes these were worn over *sciuffiotti*.

Bonnets are depicted by Luca Signorelli in his *Apocalypse* and *Sermon and Deeds of the Antichrist*, 1501–1504, in the cathedral of Orvieto. Later examples are worn by the kneeling soldier opening the chest in Vecellio's *Miracle of the Usurer's Heart* of about 1511 and by one of the papal guard in Raphael's *Mass at Bolsena* of 1512–1514. Those worn in the 1520s were more structured and larger than those of the first decade, as depicted in Romanino's *Christ before Caiaphas*, 1519, and his *Mass of Saint Gregory*, 1521–1524. In the latter, the kneeling, bearded man on the right, who is dressed in a blue-and-gold-checkered *saione*, wears a bonnet very similar to that worn by the donor in the background of the Naples *Holy Family*. In Moretto's exactly contemporary lunette fresco depicting the Last Supper, in the same Brescian chapel, two more bearded men wearing bonnets can be seen at the extreme left and right. The man on the left, seen in profile as he places a carafe of wine in front of the drowsy Saint John, makes a good comparison with the donor in the Naples painting.

Saint Barbara, standing between the Baptist and the Virgin, wears a red gown with a square neck above which the white linen of her smock is seen. Her blond hair is parted in the center and pulled back behind the ears into a blue snood embellished with gold embroidery. As mentioned above, this hair covering is depicted in Tessari's *Miracle of the Glass* of 1511 and in Bellini's *Young Woman with a Mirror* of 1515. As it was the convention to portray female saints (other than Saint Catherine of Alexandria) in clothing that was contemporary but not startlingly stylish, it has to be assumed that Saint

Barbara is shown wearing conservative, but not outmoded, dress of about 1511 to 1515, although a version of the hair covering seen here may have come into use between about 1504 and 1508.[25] A dating previous to 1515, however, conflicts with the dating evidence offered by the donor's shirt. As Romanino's *Mass of Saint Gregory* shows, the snood was worn into the 1520s—one is worn by the woman in a blue-and-white-quartered gown kneeling just in front of the bearded man on the right; it thus seems reasonable to suggest that the Naples *Holy Family* may be dated to about 1519–1526.

In Dosso's *Virgin and Child* in Rome, the only secular dress to be seen is worn by the woman in profile who stands with her arms crossed over her breast. Her brownish gown has elbow-length sleeves. Its neckline is not completely visible, but the smock with its ruffled neckline can be seen covering the shoulders. Its sleeves are visible from elbow to wrist, and both the edge of the neckband and the cuffs (also ruffled) are embroidered in gold. The woman's hair, pulled back tightly behind the ears, is covered by a cylindrical roll with a decorative medallion in the center. These features do not suggest a date before 1510. The style of gown displaying the smock at the neck and arms is typical of the mid-1520s, as exemplified by Luini's *Ippolita Sforza.* In contrast, the cylindrical headdress, although reminiscent of those seen in Romanino's *Mass of Saint Gregory,* much more closely resembles the headdress worn by the donatrix holding a child in an *Annunciation* by Vicenzo Pagano da Monterubbiano, which is signed and dated 1532 (Urbino, Galleria Nazionale delle Marche). Another head covering with about the same height above the crown, although of a slightly different design, is seen in Romanino's *Two Women Fighting over Cupid* of 1531–1532 (Trent, Castello del Buonconsiglio). The dress is certainly of a later date than Longhi suggested for this painting.[26]

In 1940 Roberto Longhi attributed the *Salome before Herod* to Dosso, associating it stylistically with the three paintings in Naples, Rome, and Philadelphia, as well as with the *Virgin with Child and Saints* in the Glasgow Art Gallery and Museum.[27] He suggested that it had been painted in about 1511. From what has already been noted about dress between 1510 and 1530, it should be clear that neither the male nor the female clothing in this painting is of the first decade of the sixteenth century. The hair of the men (excluding Herod and a counselor) is far too short for 1511, and the head coverings of the women look closer to those of 1530.

The clothing and appearance of the executioner, the man in armor, and Salome, all in the foreground, are significant. The attire of the executioner, who is sheathing his sword, should be compared with that of the soldiers seen on the left in Titian's *Miracle of the Talking Babe,* with that of the pikeman standing in front of the horseman in Boccaccino's *Meeting at the Golden Gate* or soldiers depicted in Lotto's *Stoning of Saint Stephen,* 1516, in the Pinacoteca dell'Accademia Carrara, Bergamo. All are dressed in doublet, codpiece, and hose. Boccaccino's pikeman has decorative slashing around the knees of his hose, and his codpiece and sword belt compare well with those seen in Titian's fresco. The pikeman's grey doublet has a low neck displaying the shirt; the sleeves are large and puffy above the elbow and wide but straight in the lower arm and have open cuffs. It looks very like the green doublet worn by the man with gold-and-red-striped hose on the left in the *Miracle of the Talking Babe.* Even allowing for a disparity in the quality of Titian's fresco and the much less competent (and smaller) *Salome,* one must question the powers of observation of *Salome's* artist. The sleeves of the executioner's doublet are the wrong shape for a date between 1511 and 1520, and the painting lacks the contemporary details usual in the depiction of an unfastened doublet, such as a few eyelet holes, laces, or buttons. For a date of circa 1510, this man's hair is also far too short—his neck and ears are clearly visible.[28] In addition, his weapon is atypical of blades used for decapitation in the sixteenth century—a two-handed sword or a falchion, examples of which are seen in Pordenone's *Beheading of Saint Paul* (1525–1526, Treviso, San Paolo) and Piazza's *Beheading of the Baptist* (1526, Venice, Gallerie dell'Accademia).

The soldier in armor at the extreme left carries a commander's baton in his right hand. He has short hair (his ears are visible), is bearded, and wears a round brimless hat with a high crown. The comments I have made earlier about hairstyles and beards of about 1510 are relevant here, but, more pertinently, the rounded breastplate he wears was not in use in 1511, and the armor shows other features that suggest the artist is recording armor dating after 1525 rather than before 1510.[29]

Salome is seen in profile to the right carrying a platter with the head of the Baptist, which she offers to Herod. She wears a golden yellow gown with a square neckline and a knee-length hem. It is worn over a dark green undergown that has a decorative horizontal gold line and wide gold band running around the ankle-length hem. The bodice of the undergown can be seen at the shoulders above the neckline of the gold gown. The neckline of the smock with its slightly frilled edge rising above a band of embroidery is also visible, and its sleeves are seen hanging out in festoons below the elbow. Salome's hair is parted in the center and pulled behind the ears. She wears a roll headdress of dark red fabric that stands up approximately ten centimeters above the crown of the head; it is diagonally ornamented with ribbon. She has an earring in her left ear.

Traditionally Salome was nearly always portrayed in recognizably "exotic" or "foreign" garments. Here her dress is somewhat fanciful: the gown's skirts have been shortened to display the undergown. The only visible sleeve, however, does not relate to shapes usual from about 1511 to 1520, even as a point of departure for a theatrical interpretation of exotic clothes. The sleeve has wide cuffs and is elbow length, showing off an extraordinary amount of fabric in the smock sleeve. Similar, although not so exaggerated, smock sleeves are found in paintings dating from about 1480 to 1507. For instance, in Ferramola's *Birth of Adonis* (ca. 1506–1512, Brescia, Pinacoteca Civica Tosio Martinengo), the woman taking Adonis from the myrtle has a gown with similar but narrower sleeves and a turbanlike roll worn over a veil, but these elements are not exaggerated and are consonant with her gown; this is not true of Salome's attire, especially her gown and headdress, which are more reminiscent of the 1530s. Salome's earring may also suggest a date after 1515. Italian women did not pierce their ears in the early sixteenth century, this practice becoming common only from about 1525 onward (probably because ears were no longer hidden by shoulder-length hair or by a head covering).[30] It was known, however, that Moorish women wore earrings, and perhaps Salome is thus shown to give her a more "foreign," Middle Eastern appearance.

Of the other figures in this work, the woman standing at the table appears to be dressed in a style more typical of 1530 than 1510. Her hair is pulled back behind the ears and covered by a roll headdress worn on the back of the head, and the neckline of her gown looks considerably later as well. The attire of the young man seated at Herod's right has features dating from the first decade of the century, such as the doublet with a low neck and wide bodice, but the sleeves are the wrong shape for that period, as is evident from a comparison with the above-mentioned works by Boccaccino and Titian. The most striking evidence for a later dating is the young man's very short, cropped hair, which was not worn in Italy before 1510. The male and female dress in the *Salome* presents little convincing evidence that it could have been painted between 1510 and 1515. Some of the discrepancies noted may perhaps be due to paint loss or repainting, but based on the evidence available at present, this work should be dated well after 1524 and possibly in the 1530s.

This paper was completed before Adriano Franceschini's discovery of documentary evidence that shows that the Costabili altarpiece was painted between 1513 and 1514. His work reinforces the argument that there is a need for further investigation to resolve the contradictions between the hitherto perceived evolution of Dosso's painting style and the dating evidence offered by a study of dress and armor. Such an investigation should combine the skills of various disciplines—of archivists and painting conservators as well as historians of art, dress, and armor.

Notes

1. Baldassare Castiglione, *Il libro del cortegiano* (1516), ed. Ettore Bonora (Milan: Mursia, 1972), bk. 2, chap. 26, 132.

2. Benedetto Varchi, *Storia fiorentina* (1538), ed. Lelio Arbib, 3 vols. (Florence: Società Editrice delle Storie del Nardi e del Varchi, 1838–1841), 2: bk. 9, 113–14: "*E non è dubbio che il vestir così degli uomini, come delle donne dal dodici in qua s'è forte ripulito e fatto leggiadro, non sì portando più come allora si faceva, nè saioni con pettini e colle maniche larghe, i quali davano per giù che a mezza gamba, nè berrette che erano per tre delle presenti, colle pieghe rimboccate all'insù, nè scarpette goffamente fatte con calcagnini di dietro*" (translation mine).

3. See, for instance, Castiglione (see note 1), bk. 2, chap. 27, 133–34; idem, *The Book of the Courtier,* trans. Charles S. Singleton (New York: Anchor/Doubleday, 1959), 122:

> *Pur qual è di noi che, vedendo passeggiar un gentilomo con una robba adosso quartata di diversi colori, o vero con tante stringhette e fettuzze annodate e fregi traversati, non lo tenesse per pazzo o per buffone?— Né pazzo né buffone—disse messer Pietro Bembo, sarebbe costui tenuto da chi fosse qualche tempo vivuto nella Lombardia perché cosí vanno tutti* ("Yet who of us, on seeing a gentleman pass by dressed in a habit quartered in varied colors, or with an array of strings and ribbons in bows and cross-lacings, does not take him to be a fool or a buffoon?" "Such a one would be taken neither for a fool," said messer Pietro Bembo, "nor for a buffoon by anyone who had lived for any time in Lombardy, for there they all go about like that").

4. Saint Maurelius and Saint George were the patron saints of Ferrara. Saint George was also the patron of soldiers, knights, armorers, and archers.

5. In the context of sixteenth-century Italy, terms such as *provincial* or *local* are confusing, unless a relationship between center and periphery is quite obvious. It is appropriate for dress associated with, but found at a distance from, large, clearly defined urban centers with rural hinterlands common in centralized kingdoms such as France, Spain, and England.

6. Alessandro Luzio and Rodolfo Renier, "Il lusso di Isabella d'Este marchesa di Mantova," *Nuova Antologia,* ser. 4, 63 (1896): 466 (emphasis mine): *"faremo fare la puva [pupattola] con tutti li acconciamenti di dosso et testa che portamo nui, anchora che Sua Maestà non vederà cosa alcuna nova,* perchè quelli che portamo nui si usano anche lì in Milano *da le gentildonne milanese"* (translation mine). It was common practice at this time for rulers to exchange small dolls dressed in the styles worn at each other's courts. It was the easiest means of satisfying curiosity about the clothes worn by their peers in foreign countries.

7. For a brief overview of changes at the turn of the century, see Grazietta Butazzi, "Elementi 'italiani' nella moda sullo scorcio tra il XV e il XVI secolo," in Chiara Buss, Marina Molinelli, and Grazietta Butazzi, eds., *Tessuti serici italiani, 1450–1530,* exh. cat. (Milan: Electa, 1983), 56–63.

8. The seven paintings are *Holy Family and Donors,* Philadelphia, Johnson Collection, Museum of Art (fig. 1); *Holy Family with Saint John the Baptist, Saint Barbara, and a Donor,* Naples, Museo e Gallerie Nazionale di Capodimonte (fig. 2); *Virgin and Child with Saint John the Baptist, Saint Jerome, Saint Paul, and Donor,* Rome, Pinacoteca Capitolina (fig. 3); *Virgin with Child and Saints,* Glasgow, Glasgow Art Gallery and Museum (see Felton Gibbons, *Dosso and Battista Dossi: Court Painters at Ferrara* [Princeton: Princeton Univ. Press, 1968], fig. 10); *Salome before Herod,* Milan, private collection (p. 157); *The Bathers,* Rome, Museo Nazionale di Castel Sant'Angelo (p. 232); and *The Bacchanal,* London, National Gallery (see Gibbons, fig. 19). Roberto Longhi, "Un problema di Cinquecento ferrarese (Dosso giovine)" (1927), in idem, *Saggi e ricerche, 1925–1928,* 2 vols. (Florence: Sansoni, 1967), 1: 309–11; and Roberto Longhi, *Officina ferrarese, 1934: Seguita dagli ampliamenti,*

1940, e dai nuovi ampliamenti, 1940–55 (Florence: Sansoni, 1956), 80–83, 157–59. For the most recent bibliography, see Alessandro Ballarin, *Dosso Dossi: La pittura a Ferrara negli anni del Ducato di Alfonso I,* 2 vols. (Cittadella: Bertoncello Artigrafiche, 1994–1995).

9. Longhi, 1956 (see note 7), 82: *"in verità, conviene più al '15 che al '30."* In 1927, Longhi disagreed with both Berenson's attribution and dating: *"S'intende che la data proposta dal Berenson è certamente troppo inoltrata e non sorretta da alcuna prova decisiva, né di costume né di stile; tutto ciò che abbiam detto collima anzi a rettificarla non oltre il secondo decennio del Cinquecento"* (The date proposed by Berenson is certainly too late, and is unsupported by any decisive evidence of costume or style. Rather, everything that we have said instead tallies with an adjusted dating no later than the second decade of the sixteenth century); Longhi, 1967 (see note 7), 1: 309–10 (translation mine).

10. Bernhard [*sic*] Berenson, *Italian Paintings,* vol. 1 of John G. Johnson Collection, Philadelphia, *Catalogue of a Collection of Paintings and Some Art Objects,* 3 vols. (Philadelphia: John G. Johnson, 1913–1914), 122–23 (entry no. 197). Berenson noted that this work recalled Lotto, but "the picture as a whole is somehow too serious, at once too monumental and compact for Lotto. The folds of the draperies are far too functional and too linear for him. The ears are not his shape; the hands of the Donoress [*sic*] are far too long; the infant Baptist is too Raphaelesque; and, in general the modelling is too firm and the painting too solid."

11. Titian's *The Sick Man* of 1514 (Florence, Galleria degli Uffizi), although showing the sitter in Venetian dress, shows hair of similar length and a beard.

12. Three engraved silver panels were commissioned immediately after the battle of Ravenna (1512) by Alfonso I from the court silversmith and jeweler Giovanni Antonio Leli da Foligno. Probably intended as a votive gift to the patron saint of Ferrara, they were inserted into the sides of a bronze casket holding the relics of Saint Maurelius in 1514. See Jadranka Bentini, ed., *Signore cortese e umanissimo: Viaggio intorno a Ludovico Ariosto,* exh. cat. (Venice: Marsilio, 1994), 216. The influence of military styles on civilian dress at this date is discussed by Grazietta Butazzi, "Le pompe et superflue vesti di huomini et donne," in *Alessandro Bonvicino, il Moretto,* exh. cat. (Bologna: Nuova Alfa, 1988), 253–57.

13. Possibly the *"scarpette goffamente fatte con calcagnini di dietro"* (pumps awkwardly made with low backs), mentioned by Varchi (see note 2), 2: bk. 9, 114.

14. The square toe remained popular until about 1540. It is possible that there has been some loss of detail from the shoes, although this is not specifically noted in the Philadelphia Museum of Art Conservation Department Examination and Treatment Report of March 1992, which notes paint losses in the lower left arm of the kneeling male donor and overall abrasion of paint layers. I am grateful to Professor Peter Humfrey for forwarding this report to me. A puzzling feature is the distinctive fold in the hose along the donor's left leg, which seems to be fastened at two places by buckles. This is not a feature of sixteenth-century hose and suggests intervention at some point in the eighteenth century when gaiters were developed as leg coverings. Another problem is the end of the dagger or belt hanging below the donor's left arm. A dagger was always worn on the right and the longer sword on the left, both attached

to a belt around the waist of the tunic *beneath* the gown. If this is a belt, it is inexplicable since the gown was never belted. Possibly these are later additions, although there is nothing in the 1992 examination report to suggest this.

15. My dating. See Gibbons (see note 7), fig. 78. This German shirt is illustrated in Albrecht Altdorfer's *Lovers in a Field of Grain* of 1508 (Basel, Öffentliche Kunstsammlung) and in works by other contemporary German artists.

16. Raffaele Tamalio, *Federico Gonzaga alla corte di Francesco I di Francia nel carteggio privato con Mantova (1515–1517)* (Paris: Champion, 1994), 241: "*perché qua si usa portar camise alla tedescha col colaro alto portando il scuffiotto* [*sic*].... *prego Vostra Excellentia sia contenta farmine far qualcuna lavorata il colaro et maniche come sono quelle dil Signor Loys da Gonzaga che la si potrà far monstrar, et mandarmele, acioché possa anch'io usar quel che si usa dali altri*" (translation mine).

17. For the date of the Costabili altarpiece, see Adriano Franceschini, "Dosso Dossi, Benvenuto da Garofalo e il polittico Costabili di Ferrara," *Paragone*, nos. 543–545 (1995): 110–15, and his contribution to this volume. For an alternative dating of Dosso's contribution to this work, see Andrea De Marchi's essay in this volume.

18. This style was worn by Beatrice d'Este, duchess of Milan, as portrayed in 1494 by an anonymous painter in the *Pala Sforzesca* (Milan, Pinacoteca di Brera), and by Elizabetta Gonzaga, duchess of Urbino, in the medal by Adriano Fiorentino from about 1495 (Washington, National Gallery of Art, Kress Collection).

19. Other examples are seen in Leonardo da Vinci's drawing of Isabella d'Este, circa 1499–1500 (Paris, Musée du Louvre); Giancristoforo Romano's portrait of Lucrezia Borgia (reverse *Medal of Alfonso I d'Este,* of 1502, Modena, Medagliere Estense); Lorenzo Costa's *Allegory,* of 1505–1506, painted for Isabella d'Este (Paris, Musée du Louvre); and Giovanni Antonio Boltraffio's *Portrait of a Lady* (Milan, Museo Civico d'Arte Antica, Castello Sforzesca), possibly painted circa 1506–1507.

20. In Ferramola's *Birth of Adonis* (1506–1512, Brescia, Pinacoteca Civica Tosio Martinengo), the woman taking Adonis from the myrtle wears a turbanlike roll over a veil, but the subject suggests the use of theatrical or fantastic dress, rather than everyday garments.

21. This painting is recorded as originating from the Palazzo Farnese. Until the nineteenth century it was attributed to Perugino, and then subsequently to Titian, Bellini, and, when Longhi was writing in 1927, to Cariani. He noted that it was "*un'opera orrendamente guasta dai ridipinti*" (a work horribly damaged by repainting). See Longhi, 1967 (see note 7), 1: 309; and Longhi, 1956 (see note 7), 82.

22. Varchi (see note 2), 2: bk. 9, 116: "*colla camicia, la quale oggi usano increspata da capo e dalle mani*" (with the shirt, which is worn today ruffled at the neck and wrists).

23. Varchi (see note 2), 2: bk. 9, 113: "*chi portava i capelli e non si radeva la barba, era tenuto sgherro, e persona di mal affare*" (translation mine).

24. Varchi (see note 2), 2: bk. 9, 113: "*oggi [1538] di cento, novantacinque sono zucconi e portano la barba*" (today [1538] out of one hundred men, ninety-five are close-cropped/shorn and wear a beard).

25. Early examples are worn by Saint Catherine in Andrea Previtali's *Virgin and Child with Saints* (1504, London, National Gallery) and by Saint Giustina and the

donatrix in the *Madonna and Child with Saint Giustina and Saint Barbara* (ca. 1508–1510, Rome, Galleria Borghese) attributed to Palma Vecchio. Examples more like that worn by Saint Barbara in the Naples *Holy Family* are worn by the two female saints in Cariani's *Virgin and Child Enthroned with Saints* (undated, Venice, Gallerie dell'Accademia).

26. Longhi, 1956 (see note 7), 82: "*Qui è una freschezza prativa di toni; una spositura cromatica tutta sotto il pensiero di Giorgione e di Tiziano giovanissimo*" (Here is a meadow freshness of tone; and a display of color entirely influenced by the concepts of Giorgione and the very young Titian) (translation mine). Berenson attributed this work to Girolamo da Carpi and then to an unknown Brescian artist. It originated, unattributed, from the collection of Cardinal Emmanuele Pio of Savoy (1578–1641).

27. Longhi, 1956 (see note 7), 157. At that time it was in the Lazzaroni collection, Rome. Its previous provenance is unknown.

28. Compare for example the long shoulder-length hair and low-necked doublets worn by soldiers and young men in Pinturicchio's frescoes from 1505–1507, which depict scenes from the life of Pius II (Siena, Libreria Piccolomini).

29. The multiple lames of the tasset were an innovation of the second decade. The artist does not seem to have had great familiarity with armor: the arm lames here are too accentuated, there are no points on the couter (elbow defence), and no rivets are portrayed on the lames. I am indebted to Karen Watts, Senior Curator of Armour, The Royal Armouries London and Leeds, for this information. We shall shortly be publishing a study of the representation of armor in works attributed to Dosso.

30. F. Stefani, ed., *I diarii di Marino Sanudo* (Venice, 1883; reprint, Bologna, 1970), vol. 40, col. 425, 6 Dec. 1525.

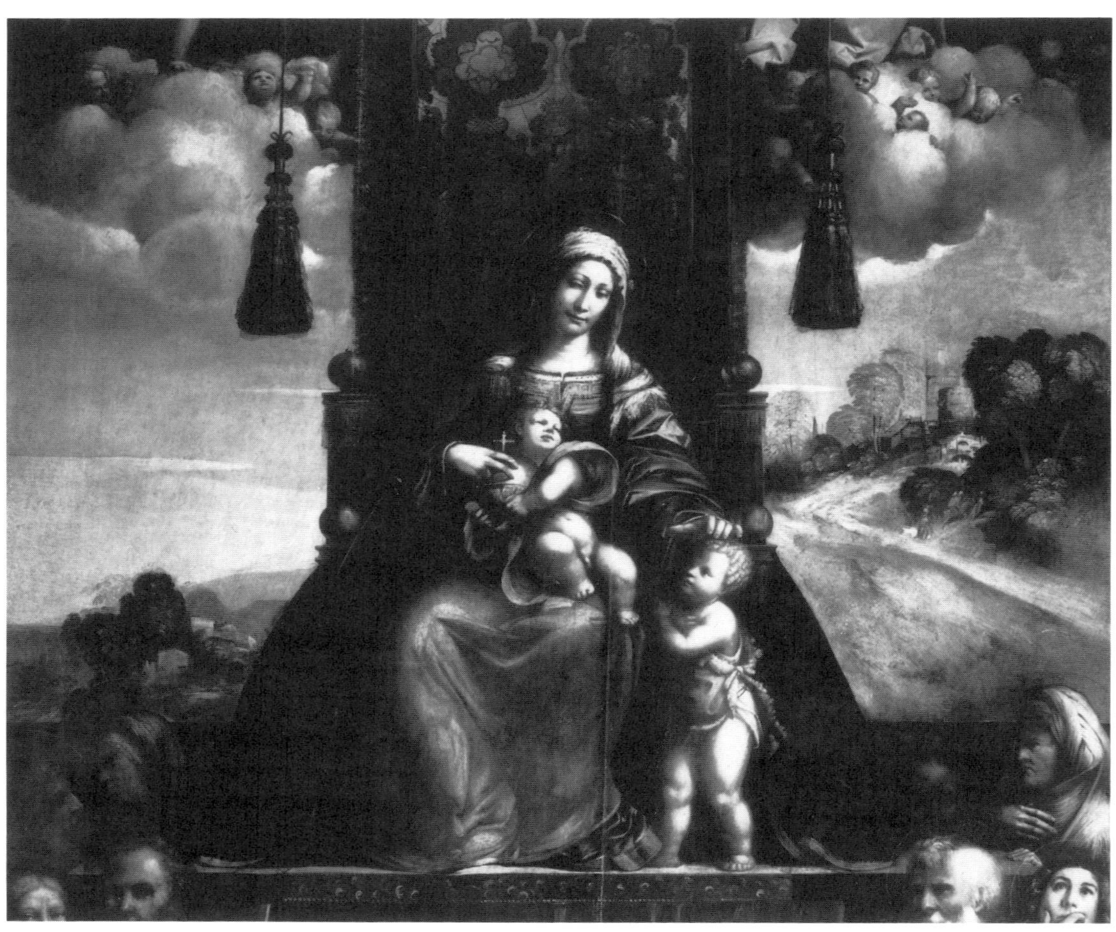

Fig. 1. Dosso Dossi and Garofalo
Costabili altarpiece (detail)
Ferrara, Pinacoteca Nazionale

Two Moments in Dosso's Career as a Landscape Painter

Peter Humfrey

As has often been pointed out, Dosso's genius as a landscape painter was already recognized by his contemporaries Paolo Giovio and Giorgio Vasari.[1] It is true that by emphasizing his proficiency in an aspect of art that both writers regarded as relatively unimportant, both were implicitly—and to our eyes unjustifiably—denigrating Dosso's abilities as a painter of human figures. Further, Giovio modeled his comments so closely on those made by Pliny the Elder about the Augustan landscape painter Studius that one wonders how carefully he had looked at Dosso's work. Thus Giovio's words—"jagged rocks, green groves, the firm banks of traversing rivers, the flourishing work of the countryside, the gay and hard toil of the peasants, and also the far distant prospects of land and sea, fleets, fowling, [and] hunting"[2]—are in many ways more evocative of Flemish painters such as Joachim de Patinir than of Dosso, whose background figures tend to be idly sitting or conversing, or mysteriously ambiguous in their actions, but never employed in seasonal toil or field sports. Yet, on balance, Giovio's choice of Dosso to represent a modern Studius was not an unreasonable one, since landscape painting does indeed constitute a major and highly original aspect of Dosso's artistic achievement. As is evident from a masterpiece of his early maturity, the *Melissa* (or *The Enchantress Circe*) in the Galleria Borghese (p. 235), Dosso succeeded in creating his own, immediately recognizable morphology of landscape, characterized by dense, suddenly illuminated thickets—what Giovanni Paolo Lomazzo perceptively called "receding woods illuminated from within by rays of sunlight."[3] Furthermore, Dosso typically invests his landscape backgrounds, as here, with a mood of poetic enchantment so powerful and so pervasive that it frequently verges on becoming the true subject of the picture.

A comprehensive discussion of Dosso's character and development as a landscape painter is beyond the scope of this essay, which will focus instead on two particular moments, both of which have been illuminated by important recent archival discoveries. The first concerns Dosso's early career, before about 1515, during which he created the kind of fecund, thickly wooded landscape still seen in the *Melissa* (which I would date to about 1515–1516).[4] Crucial to an understanding of this early phase is the discovery by Adriano Franceschini that the Costabili altarpiece in Ferrara (p. 142), traditionally thought to date from the 1530s and previously never dated before about 1523, was in fact largely executed a whole decade earlier, by Dosso and Garofalo together, within the year 1513.[5] The second embraces Dosso's career after about 1528, during which he regularly worked in collaboration with his younger brother Battista, albeit according to procedures that remain to be satisfactorily clarified. Relevant for this phase (although unfortunately only moderately relevant for the present purpose, since the work in question was destroyed in 1945) is the discovery by Claudia Cremonini that the *Immaculate Conception* altarpiece for the cathedral of Modena (formerly Dresden, Staatliche Kunstsammlungen, Gemäldegalerie Alte Meister) was commissioned in January 1527[6] and was probably executed soon afterward—a few years earlier, in other words, than the previously accepted date of 1532.

The new date of 1513 for the Costabili altarpiece throws into disarray all previous reconstructions of Dosso's early career.[7] In particular, it means that the group of works first attributed by Roberto Longhi to the young Dosso, including the *Holy Family and Donors* in the Philadelphia Museum of Art (p. 178) and the *Bathers* in the Museo Nazionale di Castel Sant'Angelo (p. 232), now has to be eliminated from the painter's oeuvre.[8] (For many external reasons, these pictures cannot be dated much before 1513, and in fact they probably date from considerably later; if later, they can no longer be plausibly fitted into Dosso's chronology.) Yet surprising as the 1513 date may seem at first, there is no stylistic argument against it, and the already maturely Dossesque landscape in the main panel (fig. 1) is perfectly comprehensible in terms of existing Venetian models by both Giorgione and Titian. The picturesquely irregular grouping of rustic buildings on a hilltop, accompanied by lush vegetation, is obviously generically Giorgionesque, and relevant prototypes can be found in such works as Giorgione's altarpiece in the cathedral of Castelfranco and the *Adoration of the Shepherds* (Washington, National Gallery of Art), as well as in landscape drawings such as the *Two Men on the Edge of a Wood* (Paris, Musée du Louvre), traditionally attributed to Giulio Campagnola, but recently given by Konrad Oberhuber to Giorgione.[9]

Yet, as is clear from these examples or by the background of the *Three Philosophers* (fig. 2), Giorgione's treatment of landscape is characterized by a delicacy of touch and minutely stippled highlights in the foliage that differ from Dosso's much broader treatment. Dosso seems to owe more to very contemporary works by Titian such as the *Noli me tangere* (fig. 3), which is usually and convincingly dated to 1511–1512.[10] Titian provides a model not just for the rustic hilltop buildings, but also for the dynamic upward sweep of Dosso's road, for his thrusting bushes and tree trunks, and for his drastically abbreviated human figures. Dosso's foreground plants are also very close to those of the *Noli me tangere* and of other early works by Titian such as the *Christ and the Adulteress* (Glasgow, Glasgow Art Gallery and Museum). At the same time, it may be observed that Dosso has already gone somewhat further than Titian in the misty disintegration of form in the middle ground and in a freedom of brushwork that leaves thick blobs of impasto in the highlights.

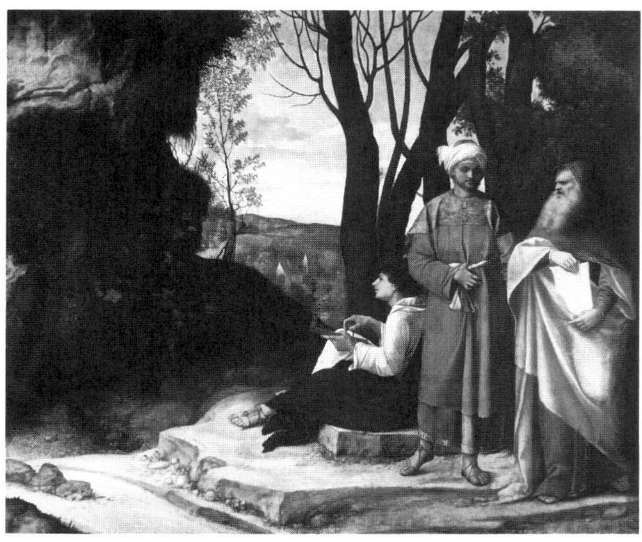

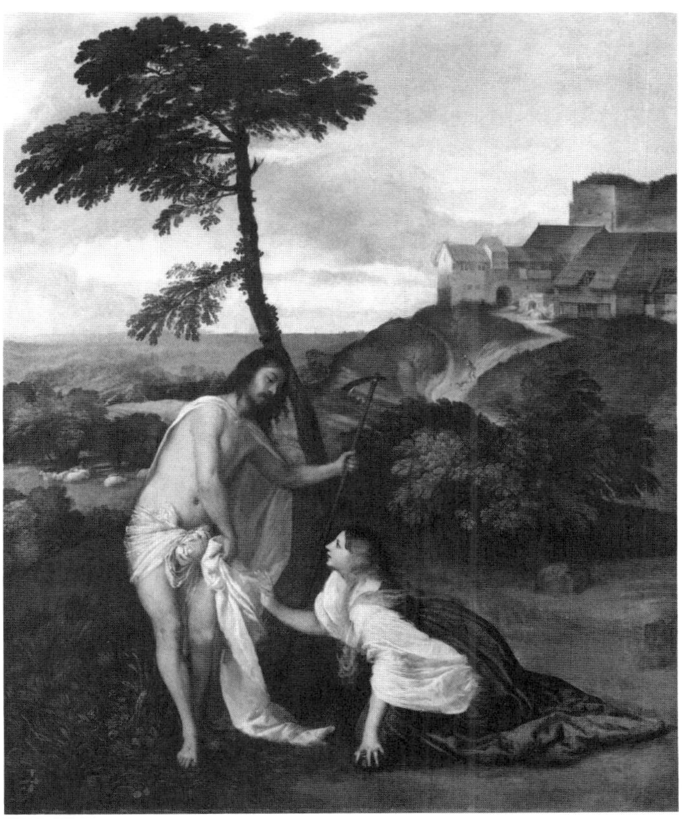

Fig. 2. Giorgione
The Three Philosophers
Vienna, Kunsthistorisches Museum

Fig. 3. Titian
Noli me tangere
London, The National Gallery

If Dosso painted like this in 1513, which of his landscapes may be judged to have preceded his arrival in Ferrara? As plausibly suggested by Alessandro Ballarin, a strong candidate for one of his earliest works, painted in Venice in Giorgione's lifetime, is the *Buffoon* (p. 64).[11] Dosso's deep indebtedness here to the example of Giorgione as a landscape painter is particularly evident from the comparison, already made by Ballarin, with the *Three Philosophers*—for instance, in the silhouetting of the dark tree trunks against a luminous sky; in the picturesque buildings with Gothic spires, similarly nestling in a thickly wooded valley; and in the creation of recession by means of a gentle superimposition of planes, and without as yet the dynamic thrust of the early work of Titian or of the Costabili altarpiece. Unfortunately the surface of Dosso's *Buffoon* is severely abraded, so the full extent of his debt to Giorgione here cannot be properly assessed; but again, as in the *Three Philosophers,* the background foliage is likely to have been evoked with little points of light.

Another candidate for a date previous to 1513, one that arguably forms a stylistic bridge between the landscape of the *Buffoon* and that of the Costabili altarpiece, is the *Circe and Her Lovers in a Landscape* in the National Gallery of Art, Washington (p. 235). It has been assigned widely differing dates in Dosso's career, partly, no doubt, because until very recently this picture had been covered in extensive overpaint. Before Longhi published his attributions, it was always seen as a very early work because of its manifest Giorgionism; thereafter, it was generally placed immediately after the putative early group, between about 1515 and 1520; more recently, Amalia Mezzetti's idea that it is a late work, because of the complication of the pose and the quality of *disegno* in the figure, has won some support.[12] But as pointed out long ago by Tancred Borenius,[13] Circe's pose is based on that of Giulio Campagnola's *Young Shepherd* engraving of about 1509; moreover, Dosso must also have known a drawing after Leonardo's lost *Standing Leda* of about 1506. X-rays have now shown extensive *pentimenti* in a once much slimmer figure, suggesting that it may have been reworked at a later date, perhaps in the 1520s. In any case, Dosso's extensive and rather literal use of graphic sources—not just those of Giulio and Leonardo, but also obviously of Albrecht Dürer's engraving of the stag and the greyhound in *Saint Eustace* (ca. 1501, p. 235)—lend the picture a strongly additive character, implying an early and not yet fully mature work.[14] Indeed, there is little sign as yet of the vigorous Titianism of the Costabili landscape, and although the gracefully curving tree trunks still closely resemble those of Giorgione's *Three Philosophers,* the gentle serpentine progression from foreground, to middle ground, to background remains comparable to that of the *Sunset Landscape* (ca. 1503–1505, London, National Gallery). With the elimination of the Castel Sant'Angelo *Bathers* as a candidate for the documented Mantuan commission of 1512,[15] the *Circe*—as already suggested by Peter Dreyer[16]—may be seen as providing the closest point of stylistic reference for the lost work.

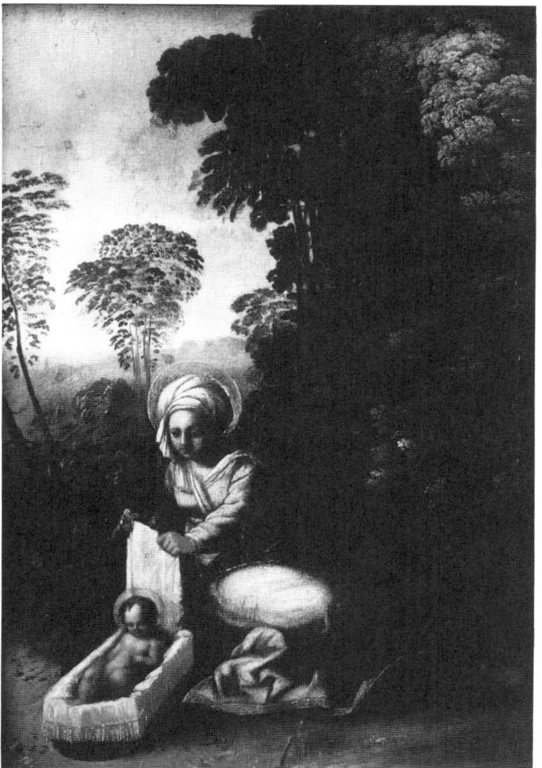

Fig. 4. Dosso Dossi
Madonna and Child in a Landscape (La Zingarella)
Parma, Galleria Nazionale

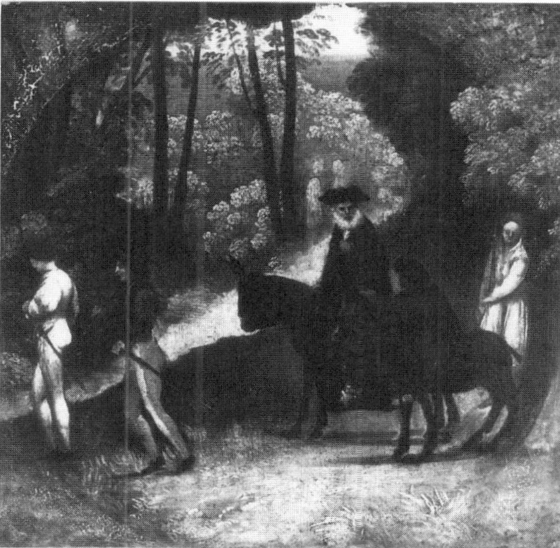

Fig. 5. Dosso Dossi
Travelers in a Wood
Besançon, Musée des Beaux-Arts et d'Archéologie

Contemporary with or slightly later than the Costabili altarpiece is, to my mind, a group of works dated by Ballarin to a few years later (about 1515–1516): *Madonna and Child in a Landscape* (*La Zingarella*) (fig. 4), *Three Ages of Man* (p. 236), *Travelers in a Wood* (fig. 5), and *Rest on the Flight into Egypt* (Florence, Galleria degli Uffizi).[17] In all of these, the treatment of the elements of landscape show the post-Giorgionesque freedom of handling already seen in the altarpiece, but perhaps even more important, they continue the development toward autonomous landscape painting, already initiated by Giorgione in such works as the *Tempest* (ca. 1505–1506, Venice, Gallerie dell'Accademia) and the *Sunset Landscape*. The subjects—or indeed, in some cases, nonsubjects—seem to have been chosen for the opportunities they present for an enveloping landscape, and any devotional or moralizing intention appears quite secondary. In the aptly nicknamed *Zingarella*, for example,

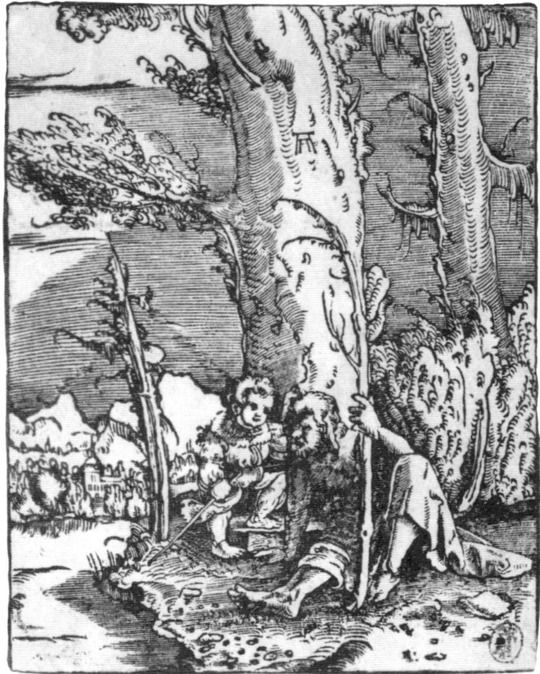

Fig. 6. Albrecht Altdorfer
Saint Christopher Seated by a River Bank
Washington, National Gallery of Art

which appears to be the earliest of the group, the Madonna and Child seem not to have come out from their house into the countryside, as they do in similar works by Raphael, Garofalo, and even Titian, but seem to resemble inhabitants of the woods and meadows, no less than Giorgione's "gypsy" in the *Tempest*. In comparison with traditional devotional images, they are rather small in relation to the field, which is also unusually vertical in its proportions, as if to accommodate the tall, luxuriant, swaying trees. In this respect, Dosso may again have been inspired by German prints, but this time less literally, and perhaps less by Dürer than by Albrecht Altdorfer. A woodcut such as the *Saint Christopher Seated by a River Bank* of about 1512, for example (fig. 6),[18] shows similarly vertical proportions and a composition also consisting of tall trees in the foreground, extending beyond the confines of the field at the upper edge, and of a distant vista on the left.

Dosso's energetic treatment of his trees and bushes in the *Zingarella,* and his bold use of impasto, is very close to that of the Costabili altarpiece and also of the New York *Three Ages of Man*. Neither of the two smaller works shows the carefully graduated recession of the *Circe*, and in the *Three Ages* there is an abrupt jump from the screen of plumed trees and bushes in the middle ground to the distant blue of the horizon. The remarkable conceptual novelty of the latter picture is that, perhaps even more than in Giorgione, the subject of the picture has now moved from the figures to the landscape itself. It is not impossible that the three groups of figures were chosen to refer to the three ages of man—childhood, maturity, and old age—yet this is surely no bittersweet allegory on the passage of time and the inevitability of death. The figures are considerably smaller relative to the field than are those in Titian's much more assertive allegory (loaned by the Duke of Sutherland to the National Gallery of Scotland, Edinburgh), and although Erika Tietze-Conrat was probably incorrect to suppose Dosso's picture to be a fragment of a larger composition,[19] her mistake usefully reveals the extent to which the figures appear more as aspects of, or as incidents in, the landscape than as the principal bearers of the picture's meaning. As early as about 1514, therefore, Dosso was painting a type of work that Paolo Giovio, on the basis of Pliny, was later to call a *parergon:* that is to say, a relaxing and diverting complement to proper or serious pictures, one in which the viewer could take simple pleasure in contemplating the countryside, with its green groves, its riverbanks, and its rustic inhabitants.[20] This then raises the question as to how far Dosso, his literary colleagues at court, and his patron—presumably in this case Duke Alfonso—might already have been aware of Pliny's concept of the *parergon* and of his account of the landscapes of Studius. Although this question cannot be answered with any certainty, it is worth recalling that it was only about three years earlier, in 1511, that Isabella d'Este's court humanist Mario Equicola had devised a program of six subjects for Alfonso's *camerino,* two or three of which were based on Philostratus's descriptions of paintings that had existed in classical antiquity.[21] In other words, the *Three Ages* may have been painted in the same conscious spirit of classical re-creation of Titian's later Bacchanals.

Certainly this vision of a sylvan arcadia, with its luxuriantly uncultivated vegetation and its uninhibited rustic lovers, would have been intended to provide the duke with the same pleasant relief from the formality of court life as did his real *delizie,* or country retreats. The same is true of the Besançon *Travelers,* the landscape of which remains close to that of the Costabili altarpiece, and which, even more than the *Three Ages,* has moved in the direction of pure genre and pure landscape.[22] Although the canvas presumably originally formed part of some larger decorative ensemble, it is difficult to imagine that its former companion pieces helped provide any more definite information about the identity of these figures. Moreover, although the picture was perhaps conceived as a sort of secular "Flight into Egypt," with its landscape inspired by the dense primeval forest of Dürer's *Flight into Egypt* (fig. 7), a woodcut from the *Life of the Virgin,* Dosso's figures were probably always intended to be no more than what they seem: anonymous travelers, the natural inhabitants of a delightfully mysterious *parergon.*

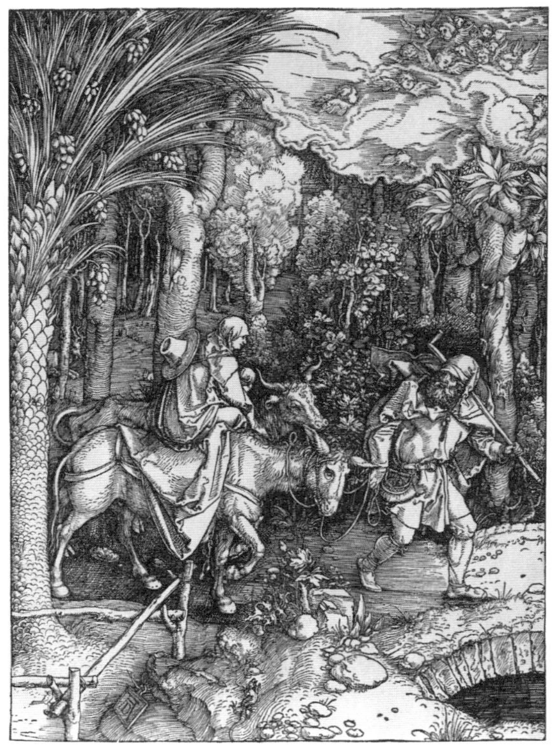

Fig. 7. Albrecht Dürer
The Flight into Egypt
Washington, National Gallery of Art

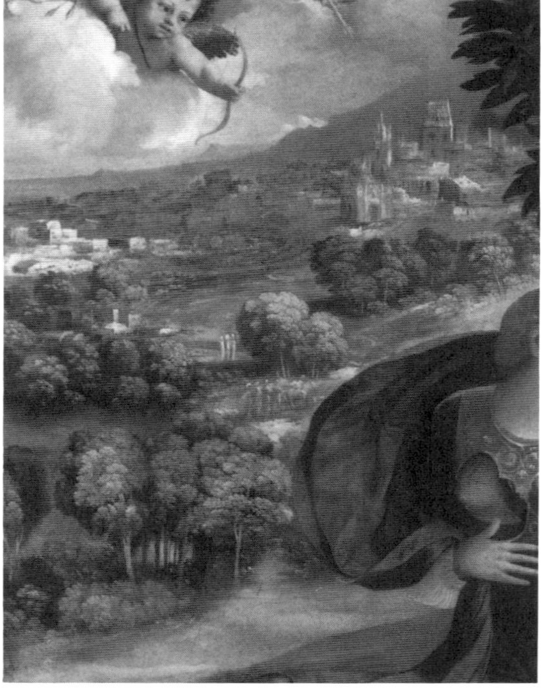

Fig. 8. Dosso Dossi
Mythological Scene (detail)
Los Angeles, J. Paul Getty Museum

In his *parerga*, Dosso may be said to have created a highly original blend of the iconographical and compositional freedom of German Renaissance prints and the chromatic richness and pictorial expressiveness of the Venetian *maniera moderna*. Perhaps it was only in the sophisticated culture of a court that their nonutilitarian purpose of refreshing the mind and delighting the senses could be fully appreciated. Dosso seems, however, not to have pursued the type further after about 1520 (at least, in the form of small-scale easel pictures),[23] although he did continue to use throughout the 1520s a style of landscape very similar to the one he had created in the phase around 1513. For example, in the *Jupiter, Mercury, and Virtue* of the earlier 1520s (p. 99), which is now in Vienna,[24] the figures dominate the picture field, and the landscape is reduced to a distant backdrop; yet the form and handling of the trees, bushes, and buildings do not differ significantly from those of the Costabili altarpiece of a decade earlier. Perhaps the only discernible novelty is the particular effect of placing bright yellow dabs of foliage against a dark sky, one that appears to derive from the right background of Titian's *Bacchanal of the Andrians* (Madrid, Museo del Prado), which was delivered to Ferrara in early 1524 (or 1523?).[25] But by the end of the third decade, in an iconographically comparable picture such as the J. Paul Getty Museum's *Mythological Scene* (p. 84), Dosso can be seen to have developed a different type of landscape (fig. 8). The terrain is no longer presented as seen from a normative viewpoint, sloping gently uphill, but rather as seen from a high viewpoint, sloping downhill toward sea level. A broad panorama is thereby created, comprising a shimmering view of a maritime city, with towers, spires, and gables rising up from its center, and lower buildings huddling around the inlets that form the port. Although the light is fractured and poetically suggestive, as always in Dosso, the foliage on the trees in the middle ground is treated more minutely than in the earlier works, with finer brushstrokes, in a way that complements the now much sharper and more precise rendering of the details in the foreground. The Getty *Mythological Scene* is not, of course, dated, and like most of Dosso's works it has been variously assigned by different critics to most stages of his career. Among the many reasons for agreeing with the dating to the late 1520s proposed by Ballarin is that of the treatment of the landscape.[26] Here a new point of reference is provided by the previously mentioned discovery by Claudia Cremonini of the contract dated 1527 for the *Immaculate Conception with Saint Bernadino, Saint Jerome, Saint Gregory, Saint Ambrose, and Saint Augustine* for the cathedral of Modena (fig. 9). The destruction of this picture in Dresden in 1945 and our necessary dependence on a prewar photograph unfortunately make detailed comparisons difficult, but it may be noted that here, too, the landscape consisted of a panoramic view of a seaport, with its towers and roofs seen from above, as if from the top of a long descending slope.

This kind of panoramic landscape did not appear in Dosso's previous work—although we do already seem to be looking down from above on the background of the Della Sale altarpiece (Rome, Galleria Nazionale di Palazzo

Barberini), a picture that is more likely to have been painted in 1526 than in 1527, the date always assigned to it on the basis of an inscription, recorded by Girolamo Baruffaldi,[27] above its altar. Two separate sources of inspiration may be suggested for Dosso's new approach. The first, which has already been emphasized by Ballarin and others with respect to the figure style of the *Immaculate Conception* and the *Mythological Scene,* is that of Giulio Romano. Thus, in the banquet scene in the Sala di Psiche at the Palazzo Te (ca. 1526–1528), the foreground plateau dips away to a distant bay flanked by steep hills, as in the *Immaculate Conception;* similarly, the Sala dei Giganti includes glimpses of a distant seascape, with a port jutting into the water at the edge of descending mountains, as in the *Mythological Scene.* Perhaps Dosso was no less responsive here to the world landscapes of Patinir and his school, which are known to have been much in demand in the courts of both Ferrara and Mantua.[28] The effect of these on Battista is particularly evident if one compares, for example, his *Flight into Egypt* (fig. 10) to a representation of the same subject attributed to Patinir's follower, the Master of the Female Half-Lengths (fig. 11) (a picture of a known Italian provenance),[29] with its farmhouses with pointed gables in the right middle ground, its exaggeratedly steep, jagged mountains, and its distant port and seascape. Battista's picture is dated by Ballarin to about 1527–1530, the very moment we are considering,[30] and although in this case I feel his dating is somewhat too early, another of Battista's panoramic landscapes, the *Battle of Orlando and Rodomonte* (Hartford, Wadsworth Atheneum),[31] does indeed appear to be close in date to Dosso's *Immaculate Conception,* thereby confirming a knowledge of and interest in Patinir on the part of both brothers by the later 1520s. As recently emphasized by Stefano Tumidei, Dosso's development toward increasingly extensive landscapes would then have been further stimulated by his experiences as a fresco painter in Pesaro and Trent in 1530–1532.[32] Thus at Pesaro, the illusionistic scheme devised by Girolamo Genga stimulated the representation of rolling plains, extending from the foreground to the distant background, and at Trent, the various fables depicted in the lunettes of the Stua della Famea are similarly unified by being placed in extensive panoramas that are bounded by a continuous distant horizon and are unobscured by the trees and dense thickets previously characteristic of Dosso. Paradoxically, in no other landscape does this painter so vividly evoke the watery expanses and misty atmosphere of the Po valley and, in particular, of the Po delta near Ferrara.

A comparison between the generically similar landscapes of Dosso's *Mythological Scene* and Battista's *Flight into Egypt* may usefully serve as a basis for distinguishing between the landscape backgrounds of the works produced by the brothers in the 1530s, a period in which regular close collaboration between them often makes specific attributions hazardous. Characteristic of Battista, in addition to the jagged rocks, are the greater number of more precisely represented buildings and, especially, the treatment of recession in terms of parallel stata, or coulisses. Dosso, by contrast, unites middle ground

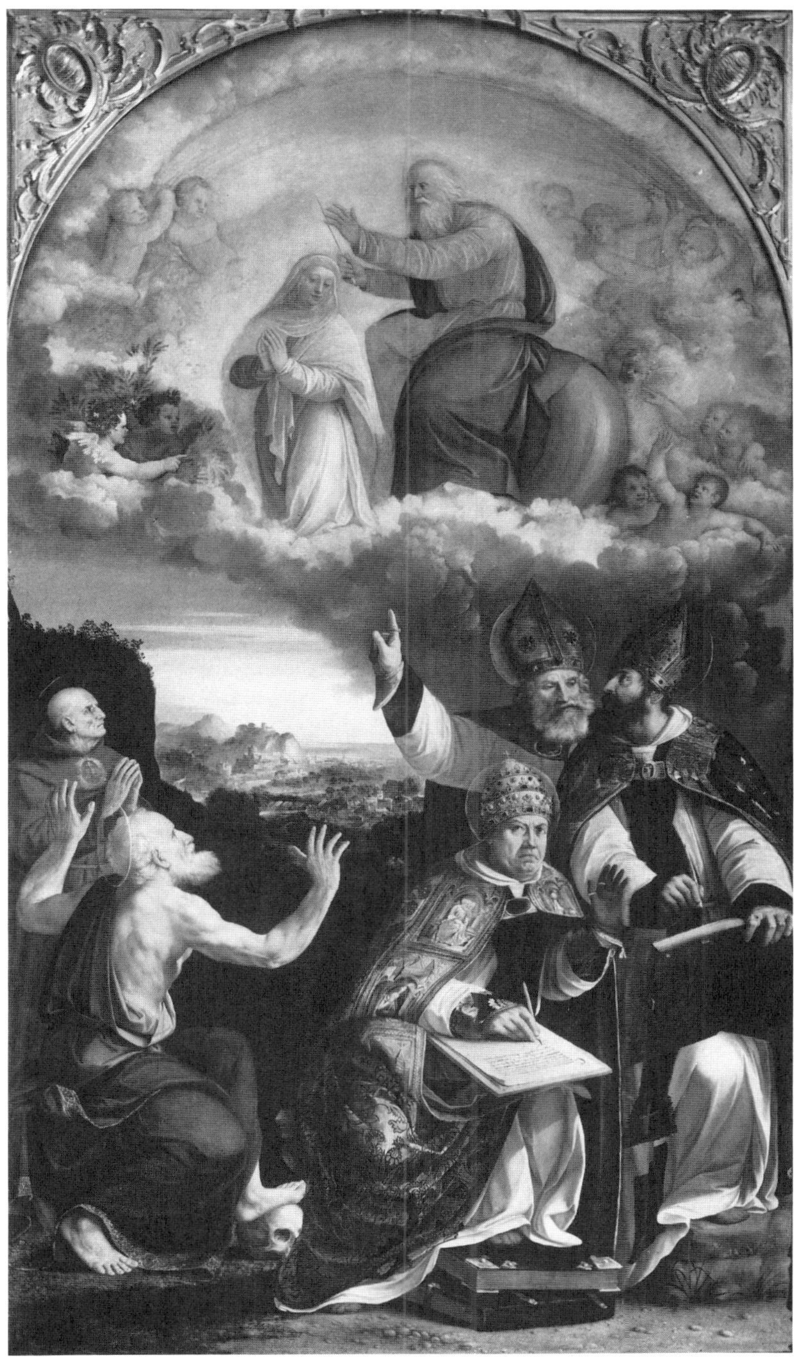

Fig. 9. Dosso Dossi
Immaculate Conception with Saint Bernadino, Saint Jerome, Saint Gregory, Saint Ambrose, and Saint Augustine
Destroyed (formerly Dresden, Staatliche Kunstsammlungen, Gemäldegalerie Alte Meister)

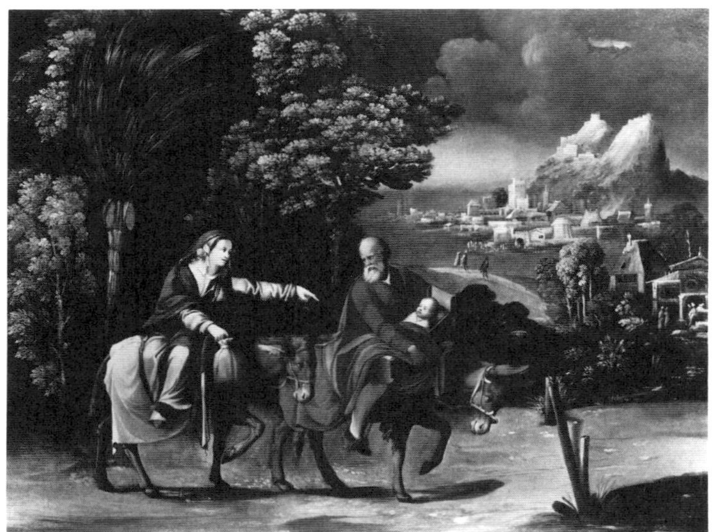

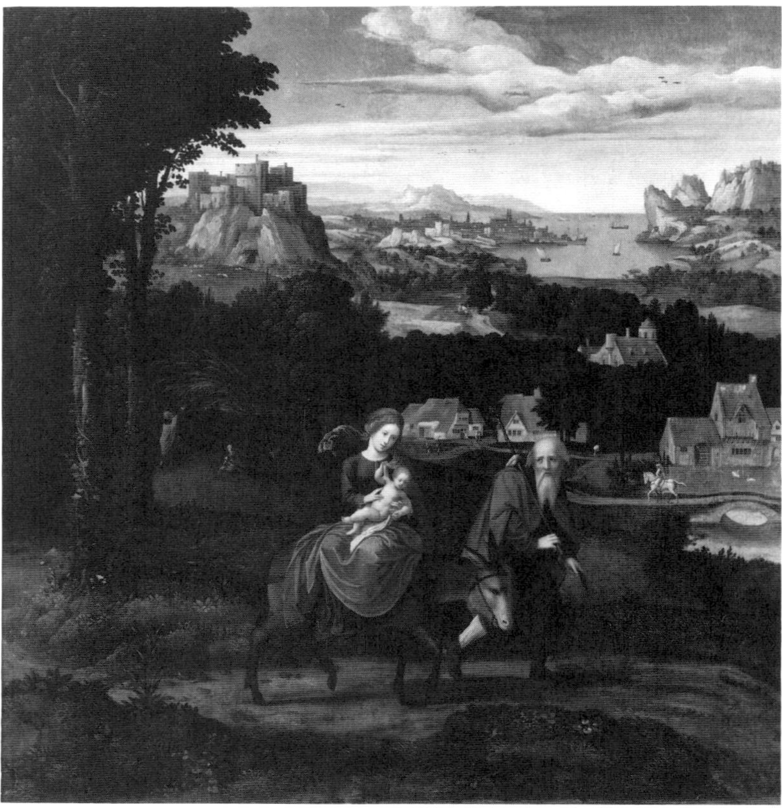

Fig. 10. Dosso Dossi and Battista Dossi
The Flight into Egypt
Coral Gables, Lowe Art Museum
Here attributed to Battista Dossi

Fig. 11. Master of the Female Half-Lengths
The Flight into Egypt
Raleigh, North Carolina Museum of Art

to background by dynamic snaking rhythms, as in the sweeping curve of the coastline, which endows the landscape with a vitality lacking in Battista's more additive formula. For this reason, I believe that Battista was probably chiefly responsible for the landscape backgrounds of a number of pictures datable to the late 1520s or early 1530s, which have traditionally been associated with Dosso alone. The *Story of Callisto* (p. 96), the Borghese variant of the Getty picture, for example,[33] shows a mistily evocative but much quieter type of landscape, with recession created by parallel horizontals, balanced against the verticals of buildings and steep crags. Very similar is the background of the *Hercules and the Pygmies* (Graz, Landesmuseum Johanneum), a picture that is usually and reasonably dated soon after the accession of Ercole II in 1534,[34] and which may be seen as a later development by Battista of the same type. Here, too, the cityscape and nearby crags, now more detailed, are composed according to a vertical-horizontal grid, unanimated by sweeping curves or diagonals.

This is not to say that the figure of Hercules, and indeed the basic conception of the picture, may not be by Dosso; in other pictures of the mid-1530s the brothers may not only have worked in collaboration, but may have divided their separate tasks differently. In the *Saint Michael and the Devil,* for example (fig. 12), documented to the years 1533–1534,[35] Battista was probably responsible for the group of apostles at the left, for the glory above, and for the group of buildings on the right, but I would give to Dosso not only the magnificent foreground figures but also the resplendent verdant landscape (in conception, even if not in every detail of the execution). It is true that this broad panorama, with its distant cities and lake and its rolling plain leading back to a chain of high mountains, is by now very different from the earlier type of landscape that we associate most readily with Dosso. Although the details are now rendered in much sharper focus than in the Getty painting, the rhythmical structure of the landscape remains similar and is quite different from the compositional habits of Battista. In the pendant altarpiece to the *Saint Michael,* the exactly contemporary *Nativity* (p. 268) in Modena, the distribution of work was evidently different, and I would accept Lancillotti's information that the picture—including the foreground figures—is essentially by Battista.[36] Yet, the landscape background, with its antiquarian, Giuliesque vision of Bethlehem,[37] is much more like that of the *Saint Michael* than of the Graz *Hercules,* and, again, I would attribute at least the design to Dosso. It may seem paradoxical that in the *Hercules* Dosso should execute the figure and Battista the landscape, while in the *Nativity* the reverse should be the case, but I believe that the visual evidence points this way. The rhythmic energy of the landscapes of the two pendant altarpieces may then be seen to reach a climax in the Dresden *Archangel Michael* (p. 264) of 1540,[38] with its swirls of infernal vapor mingling with the huge banks of cloud and the sudden glimpse of a mountain chain very similar to that of the Parma *Saint Michael.* By now, Dosso has created a type of landscape background almost unrecognizably different from that of the *Jupiter, Mercury,*

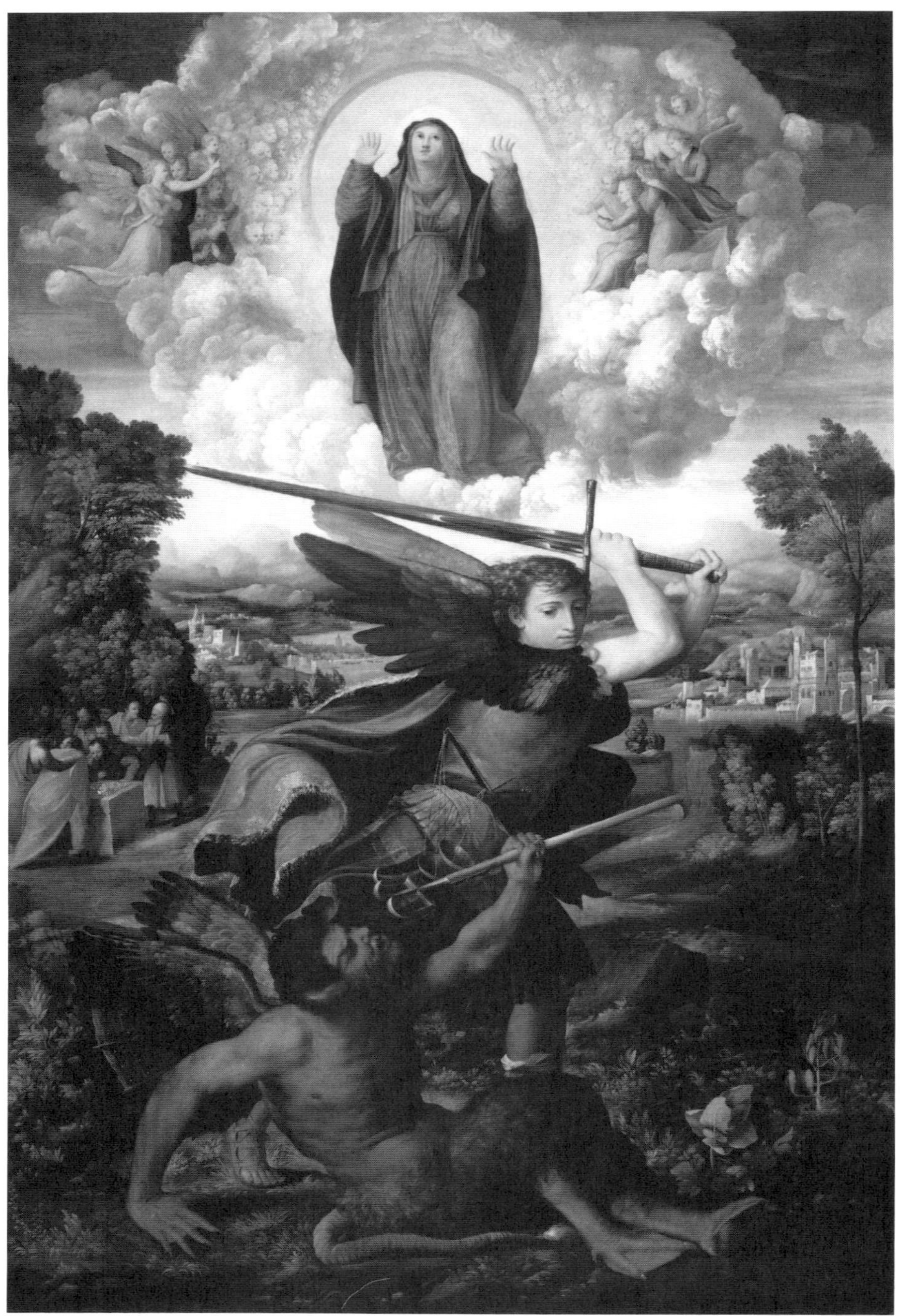

Fig. 12. Dosso Dossi and Battista Dossi
Saint Michael and the Devil; on High, the Assumption of the Virgin
Parma, Galleria Nazionale

and Virtue and other works of his middle career. Yet one only has to look at the background of the Dresden *Allegory of Justice* (p. 267), painted by Battista two years after Dosso's death[39] but remaining essentially similar to the landscapes of a decade or more earlier, to see that such a development was beyond the capacity of the younger brother. Ever since the publication of Vasari's tale that Dosso gave up painting at the end of his life to live on a pension granted by Alfonso I,[40] the 1530s have been seen as a period of decline in his art; in the present context, it probably has to be admitted that his later landscapes lack the peculiar magic of the earlier ones, from the *Zingarella* to the Getty *Mythological Scene*. At the same time, it should also now be clear that contrary to what Vasari suggested, Dosso's extraordinary powers as a landscape painter continued to evolve until his death in 1542.

Notes

1. Paolo Giovio, *Pauli Iovii opera*, vol. 8, *Elogia virorum illustrium*, ed. R. Meregazzi (Rome: Istituto Poligrafico dello Stato, Libreria dello Stato, 1972), 232; Giorgio Vasari, *Le vite de' più eccellenti pittori, scultori e architettori: Nelle redazioni del 1550 e 1568: Testo*, ed. Rosanna Bettarini and Paola Barocchi, 6 vols. (Florence: Sansoni, 1966–1971; Studio per Edizioni Scelte, 1976–1987), 4: 420, 422: "*Ebbe in Lombardia titolo da tutti i pittori di fare i paesi meglio che alcuno altro che di quella pratica operasse, o in muro o in olio o a guazzo.... La principalissima laude sua fu il dipingere bene i paesi*" (He held title among all painters in Lombardy to making landscapes better than anyone else who worked in that practice, either on walls, in oil, or in gouache. His greatest commendation was that he painted landscapes well).

2. Giovio (see note 1), 232. The passage reads in full: "*Doxi autem Ferrariensis urbanum probatur ingenium cum in justis operibus, tum maxime in illis, quae parerga vocantur. Amoena namque picturae diverticula voluptario labore consectatus, praeruptas cautes, virentia nemora, opacas perfluentium ripas, florentes rei rusticae apparatus agricolarum laetos fervidosque labores, praeterea longissimos terrarum marisque prospectus, classes, aucupia, venationes, et cuncta id genus spectatu oculis jucunda, luxurianti ac festiva manu exprimere consuevit*" (The gentle manner of Dosso of Ferrara is esteemed in his proper works, but most of all in those which are called *parerga*. For devoting himself with relish to the pleasant diversions of painting he used to depict jagged rocks, green groves, the firm banks of traversing rivers, the flourishing work of the countryside, the gay and hard toil of the peasants, and also the far distant prospects of land and sea, fleets, fowling, hunting, and all that *genre* so pleasing to the eyes in a lavish and festive style). English translation by E. H. Gombrich, "The Renaissance Theory of Art and the Rise of Landscape Painting" (1950), in idem, *Norm and Form* (London: Phaidon, 1966), 113–14. Gombrich's classic essay draws attention both to Giovio's dependence on Pliny and to the writer's identification of landscape pictures, or *parerga*, as an artistic genre distinct from "proper works" (*justis operibus*). For the latter aspect, see also Creighton Gilbert, "On Subject and Not-Subject in Italian Renaissance Pictures," *Art Bulletin* 34 (1952): 204–5; and recently, Marzia Faietti, "1490–1530: Influssi nordici in alcuni artisti emiliani e romagnoli," in Vera Fortunati,

ed., *La pittura in Emilia e in Romagna. Il Cinquecento* (Milan: Electa, 1995), 1: 32–33. As pointed out by T. C. Price Zimmermann, *Paolo Giovio: The Historian and the Crisis of Sixteenth-Century Italy* (Princeton: Princeton Univ. Press, 1995), 49, Giovio would have seen Dosso's work on the occasion of his brief visit to Ferrara in November 1522, but he composed the *Elogia* more than twenty years later, in 1545.

3. Giovanni Paolo Lomazzo, *Trattato dell'arte della pittura, scultura ed architettura* (1584), 3 vols. (Rome: Presso S. Del-Monte, 1844), 2: 434–44: *"I due Dossi nello sfuggimento di boschi con raggi del sole che per entro lampeggino."*

4. The picture has usually been dated to the earlier 1520s. See the survey of opinions in Alessandro Ballarin, *Dosso Dossi: La pittura a Ferrara negli anni del Ducato di Alfonso I*, 2 vols. (Cittadella: Bertoncello Artigrafiche, 1994–1995), 1: 312 (entry no. 372). Ballarin dates it to about 1518.

5. Adriano Franceschini, "Dosso Dossi, Benvenuto da Garofalo e il polittico Costabili di Ferrara," *Paragone*, nos. 543–545 (1995): 110–15, and his essay in this volume. For earlier opinions, see Ballarin (see note 4), 1: 336–37 (entry no. 431; with a dating to about 1523–1524).

6. Claudia Cremonini, "La pala dell'*Immacolata Concezione* di Dosso Dossi nel Duomo di Modena: Un contributo per la cronologia," *Dialoghi di Storia dell'Arte* 4–5 (1997): 250–57. According to Lancellotti, 1532 was the date when the picture was installed above its altar in the cathedral; see Tommasino de' Bianchi detto de' Lancellotti, *Cronaca modenese*, 12 vols. (Parma: Pietro Fiaccadori, 1862–1884), 4: 114.

7. Some of the wider implications of the discovery are discussed in Peter Humfrey and Mauro Lucco, "Dosso Dossi in 1513: A Reassessment of the Artist's Early Works and Influences," *Apollo* 147 (1998): 22–30.

8. Roberto Longhi, *Officina ferrarese, 1934: Seguita dagli ampliamenti, 1940, e dai nuovi ampliamenti, 1940–55* (Florence: Sansoni, 1956), 81–84. The group, to which a number of related pictures have been added over the years, was accepted by all three of the postwar monographs on Dosso: Amalia Mezzetti, *Il Dosso e Battista ferraresi* (Milan: Silvana, 1965); Felton Gibbons, *Dosso and Battista Dossi: Court Painters at Ferrara* (Princeton: Princeton Univ. Press, 1968); and Ballarin (see note 4). The group has never, however, won unanimous critical acceptance, and it was rejected, for example, by Peter Dreyer, "Die Entwicklung des jungen Dosso: Ein Beitrag zur Chronologie des Meisters bis zum Jahre 1522," *Pantheon* 22 (1964): 220–32, 363–75; 23 (1965): 22–30. See also the evidence of costume considered by Jane Bridgeman in her essay in this volume.

9. *Le siècle de Titien: L'âge d'or de la peinture à Venise*, exh. cat. (Paris: Editions de la Réunion des Musées Nationaux, 1993), 454–55 (entry no. 93 by Konrad Oberhuber).

10. Ibid., 355–59 (entry no. 46 by Alessandro Ballarin; with a slightly earlier dating).

11. *Le siècle de Titien* (see note 9), 321 (entry no. 40 by Alessandro Ballarin); Ballarin (see note 4), 1: 302–3.

12. See the survey of opinions in Fern Rusk Shapley, *Catalogue of the Italian Paintings* (Washington: National Gallery of Art, 1979), 167–68. Ballarin (see note 4), 1: 348 (entry no. 452), considers it to be a relatively late work of about 1528 executed in collaboration with Battista.

13. Tancred Borenius, review of *Das Werk der Dossi,* by Henriette Mendelsohn, *Burlington Magazine* 25 (1914): 360–61.

14. Certain compositional and stylistic resemblances to Giovanni Bellini's *Feast of the Gods* (Washington, National Gallery of Art, inv. no. 597) might encourage one to interpret Dosso's *Circe* as a response to the arrival of Bellini's picture in Ferrara in 1514. However, the picture had been under way since 1511, and perhaps earlier, and Dosso could have seen it at that time in Bellini's workshop in Venice. Furthermore, the *Feast* resembled the *Circe* much more closely after Dosso himself had altered it than it would have done when completed by Bellini. For Dosso's alteration, see David Bull, "Conservation,Treatment, and Interpretation," in *The Feast of the Gods: The Conservation Treatment and Reexamination* (Washington: National Gallery of Art, 1990), 41–43.

15. As proposed by Ballarin (see note 4), 1: 28–31, 295–96 (entry no. 333), following a more tentative suggestion by Lionello Puppi, "Dosso al Buonconsiglio," *Arte Veneta* 18 (1964): 20.

16. Dreyer, 1964 (see note 8), 230.

17. Ballarin (see note 4), 1: 303–4 (entry no. 349), 310–11 (entry no. 368), 311 (entry no. 369), 303 (entry no. 347), respectively, with further references.

18. F. W. H. Hollstein, *German Engravings, Etchings, and Woodcuts, ca. 1400–1700,* 43 vols. (Amsterdam: Menno Hertzberger, 1954–1996), 1: 258.

19. Erika Tietze-Conrat, "Two Dosso Puzzles in Washington and New York," *Gazette des beaux-arts,* ser. 6, 33 (1948): 129–36. For the technical evidence, see Federico Zeri with Elizabeth E. Gardner, *Italian Paintings: A Catalogue of the Collection of the Metropolitan Museum of Art, North Italian School* (New York: Metropolitan Museum of Art, 1986), 11–12.

20. See note 2.

21. See John Shearman, "Alfonso d'Este's Camerino," in *"Il se rendit en Italie": Etudes offertes à André Chastel* (Rome: Edizioni dell'Elefante, 1987), 213; Paul Holberton, "The Choice of Texts for the Camerino Pictures," in Görel Cavalli-Björkman, ed., *Bacchanals by Titian and Rubens* (Stockholm: Nationalmuseum, 1987), 59.

22. Gilbert (see note 2), 204. The painting was originally circular, and the four spandrels are later additions. See Matthieu Pinette and Françoise Soulier-François, *De Bellini à Bonnard: Chefs-d'œuvre de la peinture du Musée des beaux-arts et d'archéologie de Besançon* (Paris: Le Temps Apprivoisé, 1992), 34.

23. He may well, however, have executed nearly pure landscapes in his many lost frescoes painted in Ferrara and its surroundings, as indeed he did in the Camera delle Cariatidi in the Villa Imperiale, Pesaro, probably in 1530. For the date, see the essay by Craig Hugh Smyth in the present volume.

24. Ballarin (see note 4), 1: 339–40 (entry no. 433). The author's date of about 1524 is convincing.

25. Charles Hope, "The Camerino d'Alabastro: A Reconsideration of the Evidence," in Cavalli-Björkman (see note 21), 26.

26. *Le siècle de Titien* (see note 9), 420–22 (entry no. 81 by Alessandro Ballarin); Ballarin (see note 4), 1: 348 (entry no. 453).

27. The inscription, according to Girolamo Baruffaldi, *Vite de' pittori e scultori ferraresi* (1697–1722), ed. Giovanni Boschini, 2 vols. (Ferrara Domenico Taddei,

1844–1846), 1: 277, recorded that the corresponding altar was endowed by the Della Sale family in March 1527. If this was the installation date of the altarpiece, it is likely to have been begun at least a year earlier.

28. Rezio Buscaroli, *La pittura di paesaggio in Italia* (Bologna: Società Tip. Mareggiani, 1935), 56–58; Victor Lasareff, "A Dosso Problem," *Art in America* 29 (1941): 129–38; A. Richard Turner, "Garofalo and a 'capriccio alla fiamminga,'" *Paragone,* no. 181 (1965): 60–69.

29. See Robert A. Koch, *Joachim Patinir* (Princeton: Princeton Univ. Press, 1968), 85.

30. Ballarin (see note 4), 1: 32, with a suggested date of about 1527–1530. The attribution to Battista is generally accepted, although some critics give Dosso some hand in the work.

31. Ballarin (see note 4), 1: 335–36 (entry no. 429; with a rather too early dating to about 1523).

32. Stefano Tumidei, "Dosso (e Battista) al Buonconsiglio," in Enrico Castelnuovo, ed., *Il Castello del Buonconsiglio,* 2 vols. (Trent: Temi, 1995–1996), 2: 131–57.

33. Ballarin (see note 4), 1: 349 (entry no. 454; as Dosso, about 1529).

34. Ballarin (see note 4), 1: 363 (entry no. 488; as both brothers in collaboration).

35. Documents in Elio Monducci, "Documenti," in Massimo Pirondini, ed., *La Pittura del Cinquecento a Reggio Emilia* (Milan: Federico Motta/Credito Emiliano, 1985), 251–53 (with payments to both brothers). For the Parma *Saint Michael* and its companion piece, the Modena *Nativity,* see Ballarin (see note 4), 1: 361–62 (entry nos. 485–86; with attributions to both brothers in collaboration).

36. Lancellotti (see note 6), 5: 195: *"La ditta ancona seu tavola d'altare fatta da mane de M.ro . . . fratello de M.ro Dosso ex.mo depintore"* (The said ancona or altarpiece made by M[ast]er . . . brother of M[ast]er Dosso most excellent painter).

37. Tumidei (see note 32), 142, claims, on the contrary, that antiquarian details are characteristic rather of Battista's approach to landscape. Although this is true of his late *Cleopatra* (private collection), painted for Laura de' Dianti in 1546, Battista may well have been elaborating here on the earlier example of Dosso—or the landscape is by a collaborator. See the essay by Mauro Lucco in the present volume.

38. Payment of March 1540, published by Adolfo Venturi, "I due Dossi. Documenti—Prima serie," *Archivio storico dell'arte* 6 (1893): 131–32; Ballarin (see note 4), 1: 368–69 (entry no. 502; with attribution to both brothers in collaboration).

39. Payment of March 1544, published by Amalia Mezzetti, *Girolamo da Ferrara detto da Carpi: L'opera pittorica* (Milan: Silvana, 1977), 58.

40. Vasari (see note 1), 4: 422.

Dosso Dossi and the Role of Prints in North Italy

Andrea Bayer

The subject of this essay was broached at the round table of the first symposium devoted to Dosso Dossi and his Age. An examination of the role of prints in Dosso's art, previously unstudied, promised to be of considerable potential interest, especially as prints had demonstrably served an important function for neighboring artists with connections to Dosso. It therefore seemed pertinent to determine whether they might not have had similar resonance for him and his contemporaries in Ferrara. My inquiry unfolded along two lines: the identification of Dosso's employment of prints as compositional and, possibly, iconographic sources, followed by closer analysis of the uses to which they were put. For reasons that will become clear, I concentrated on prints after central Italian artists, with side glances at those by northern Italian and German artists.

It has long been recognized that northern Italian painters of the sixteenth century were often inspired by prints. However, as Cecil Gould once said about the impact of Albrecht Dürer's prints on Italian art, "Like the Common Law of England it has never been codified, and it is not difficult to see why," given the ubiquitousness of the influence.[1] Therefore only recently has the true extent of the influence of prints begun to be defined and its purposes investigated. This realization has grown concurrently with our knowledge of the strength of print collections in the region by the first half of the sixteenth century and of the availability of prints to artists.

The former can be demonstrated with a good deal of contemporary evidence in which prints are listed in collections alongside other objects, such as antiquities. For example, the inventory of the collection of Francesco Baiardo (the brother of Elena Baiardo), who died in Parma in 1561, lists sixty-three items in three "*camerine,*" including seventeen prints by Marcantonio Raimondi and Dürer.[2] Gabriele Vendramin's spectacular collection in the Palazzo Vendramin a San Fosca was inventoried about a decade following his death in 1552. He too owned many prints, a number of which have been identified: they included engravings and woodcuts by Dürer, prints by Domenico Campagnola, and other prints after Raphael and Perino del Vaga. The collection of the Benavides family in Padua, most of it put together by Marco Benavides, who died in 1582, was rich in prints. A seventeenth-century inventory lists prints by Lucas van Leyden, Dürer, Andrea Mantegna, Marcantonio, Caraglio, and others.[3] The Paduan historian Bernardino Scardeone noted in his biography of Mantegna, published in 1560, that he owned nine diverse prints by the artist.[4] Coinciding with Dosso's years of activity, Marcantonio Michiel's notes of collections from the 1520s include several references that must be to prints: to works by Jacopo de'Barbari and Dürer in the collection of Cardinal Grimani in 1521, and the mention of a "book of prints by several hands"' in Antonio Foscarini's house in 1530.[5]

We are also increasingly aware of the pervasive presence of prints in artists' studios. Baiardo most likely obtained his print collection directly from Parmigianino, either as surety for the Steccata frescoes or after the artist's death.[6] Enea Vico proclaimed their importance for other artists in his application for a printmaker's privilege in 1546, in which he states that his engravings are "for the benefit and use of all the painters and sculptors." According to Lodovico Dolce, "Raphael himself kept Dürer's engravings pinned up in his studio"; we are not surprised then to remember that the artist also turned to Mantegna's engravings for the *Entombment* now in Rome in the Galleria Borghese.[7] Lorenzo Lotto bought prints in Venice in 1542 (unfortunately we do not know which), on the eve of his departure for Treviso as part of the artistic materials he would need for work in a new location.[8] Through Carlo Cesare Malvasia we know that several Bolognese artists were collectors of prints. Denys Calvaert used them as teaching aids (something Vasari recommends too, especially for poor draftsmen), likewise tacking them up on the walls, while Bartolomeo Passerotti, followed by his son Tiburzio, owned "all the most famous prints."[9]

This latter assertion is intriguing because it implies an ongoing creation of a canon of "famous prints." Scardeone, not surprisingly given his bias toward Mantegna, stressed that his prints were held in the highest esteem; the ubiquitousness of prints by Dürer and Marcantonio in the collections noted above also speaks for their special status. In the passage on Calvaert, Malvasia has a long aside in which he lists the *carte famose* that appeared in the artist's studio: the great Germans; the printmakers working after Raphael; Parmigianino's etchings and Ugo da Carpi's chiaroscuro woodcuts. Recently, Michael Bury has gone into this issue, analyzing the frequency with which specific printmakers appear in various writings by mid-century. Although a certain number of names appear sporadically, the core group is clear: Mantegna, Dürer, Lucas van Leyden, Marcantonio, Agostino Veneziano, Jacopo de'Barbari, and Caraglio.[10] Knowledge of this emerging canon is of great assistance in seeking out print sources in paintings and in understanding why certain prints have been singled out by artists.

In northern Italy in the first half of the sixteenth century it seems to have been crucial to many an artist's working method to have a carefully selected group of engravings "pinned up in [the] studio." In the paintings of Moretto da Brescia we can follow the myriad ways in which he made use of them, especially of engravings after Raphael. Although Moretto most probably made the journey to Rome at least once rather early in his career, his most lasting source of information about Raphael and central Italian art was through the works of Marcantonio and his school. The tale of how Moretto became known as "Il Raffaello Bresciano" is a fascinating one, studied in its nineteenth-century incarnation by Bruno Passamani; it dates back in its origins to Vasari, who commented favorably on the Raphaelesque quality of Moretto's work.[11] Of significance in the present context is the degree to which Moretto actually relied on prints after Raphael and others in the *invenzione* of his own paintings.[12]

The following two examples will suffice to document the numerous instances of quotations from print sources that are so close to the original that some degree of audience recognition may have been expected. In these cases, even if the subject matter is altered, the original intention of the figures or composition is taken over. In his organ shutters depicting the fall of Simon Magus (fig. 1), Moretto adapts the figures of the bystanders crowded under a portico found in Marcantonio's print titled *Martyrdom of Saint Cecilia* (fig. 2),[13] which itself is based on a drawing in Dresden likely to be by Raphael and related to the decoration of the chapel of the papal villa at Magliana. Although the torso of the foremost figure is somewhat rotated and some other modifications made, Moretto has captured the atmosphere of astonishment, generated by the figure pressing himself against the column, that already figured largely in the engraving's impact. The other example is limited to a single figure, the beautiful sleeping Elijah, which is a detail from Moretto's decoration of the Chapel of the Sacrament in San Giovanni Evangelista, Brescia. The figure type and pose are based on those of the river god Peneus being consoled for the loss of his daughter, Daphne, in an engraving by the anonymous Master of the Die after a drawing by Baldassare Peruzzi, *Neighboring River Gods Consoling Peneus on the Loss of His Daughter,*[14] which, in turn, derives from an ancient relief. In these cases, and many others, imitation and emulation combine, and Moretto presents himself as flowing along with the dominant current emanating from Rome.

In other examples, however, Moretto disregards the original intent of his print source, with results that could almost be considered subversive. Two examples are based on Marcantonio's *Judgment of Paris* (fig. 3), that most quoted of all prints.[15] In Moretto's *Gathering of Manna,* also from San Giovanni Evangelista, the sharply cropped figure to the far right is either an imaginative adaptation of the river god at the left of the triad to the right of the print, or reverses another small engraving, *Seated Nude,* which isolates that figure, supplying him with an urn.[16] The two river gods also provide the basis of figures of servants in Moretto's *Sacrifice of Isaac,* painted for the Chapel of the Sacrament in the cathedral in Brescia (fig. 4).

In both these cases Marcantonio's figures have been completely transformed: the two nude gods with leaves in their hair and carefully articulated anatomies are now rough peasants with bundles and donkeys. The aspects of the composition that would have seemed essential to Raphael—the recreation of the antique, ideal human proportions, even the importance of *disegno*—have been ignored by Moretto, as they do not suit his purposes. The

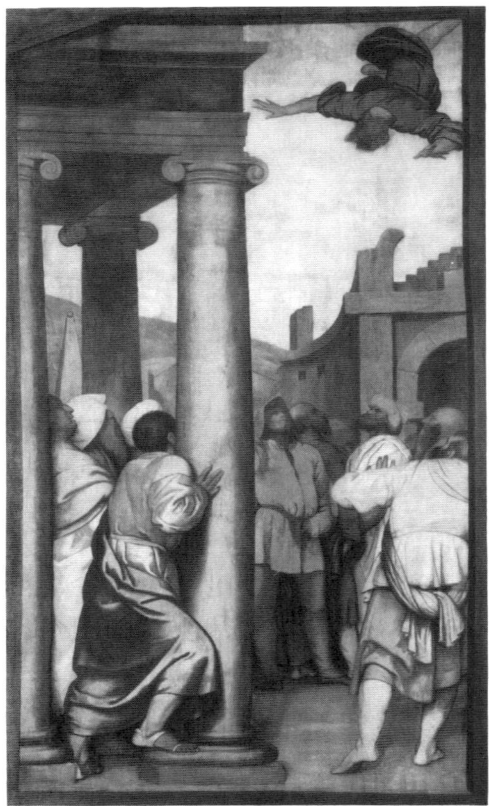

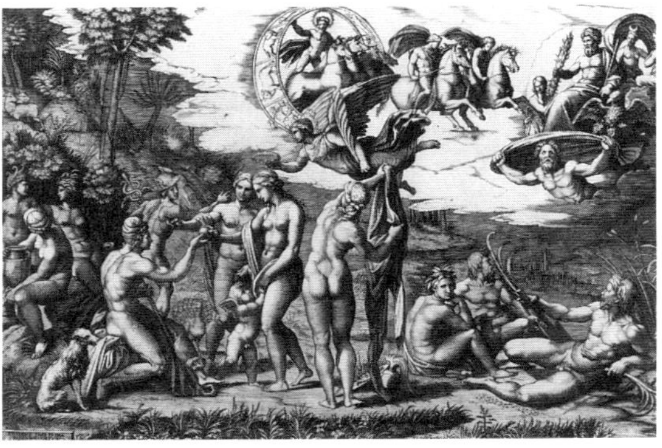

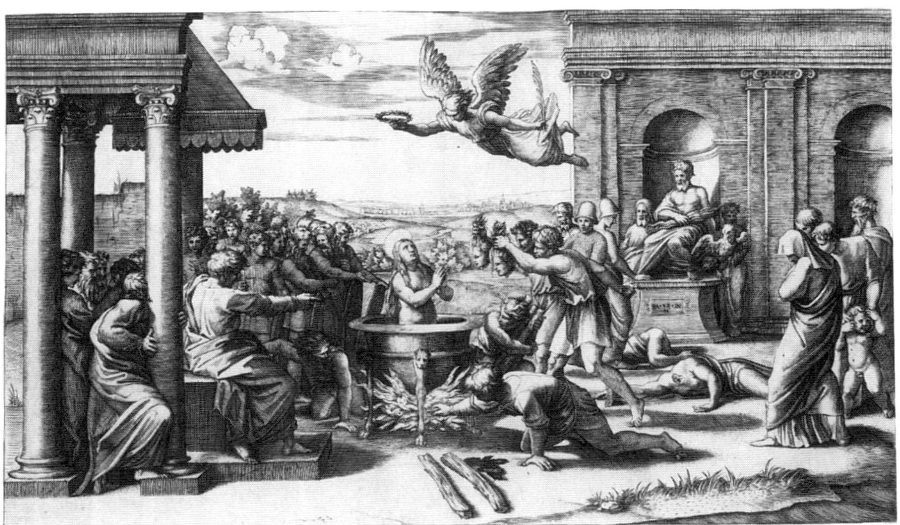

Fig. 1. Moretto da Brescia, also called Alessandro Bonvicino
Fall of Simon Magus
Brescia, Seminario Diocesano

Fig. 2. Marcantonio Raimondi (after Raphael)
Martyrdom of Saint Cecilia
New York, The Metropolitan Museum of Art

Fig. 3. Marcantonio Raimondi
Judgment of Paris
New York, The Metropolitan Museum of Art

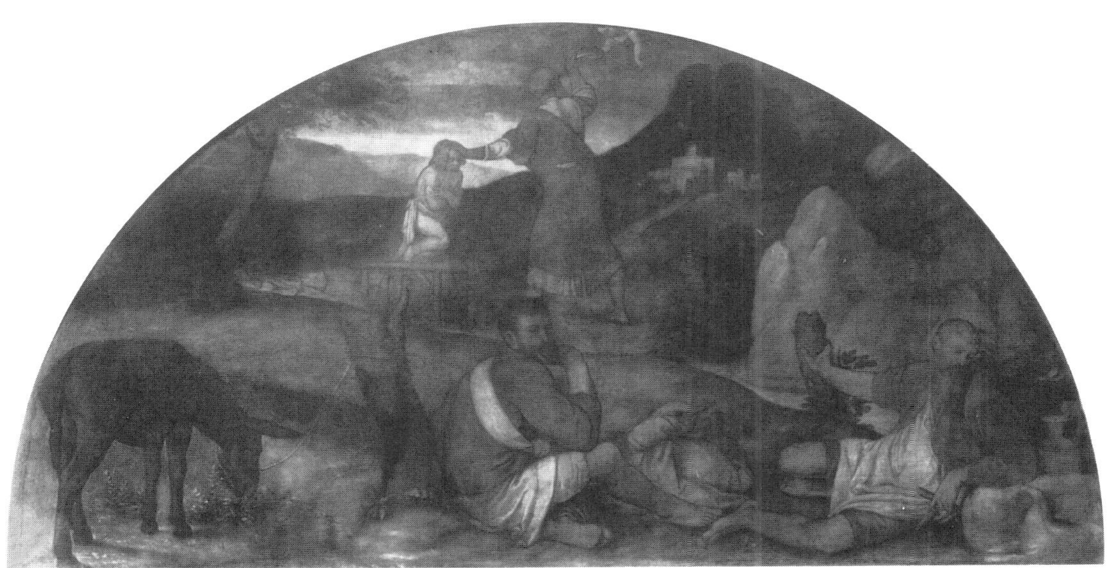

Fig. 4. Moretto da Brescia, also called Alessandro Bonvicino
Sacrifice of Isaac
Brescia, Duomo Nuovo

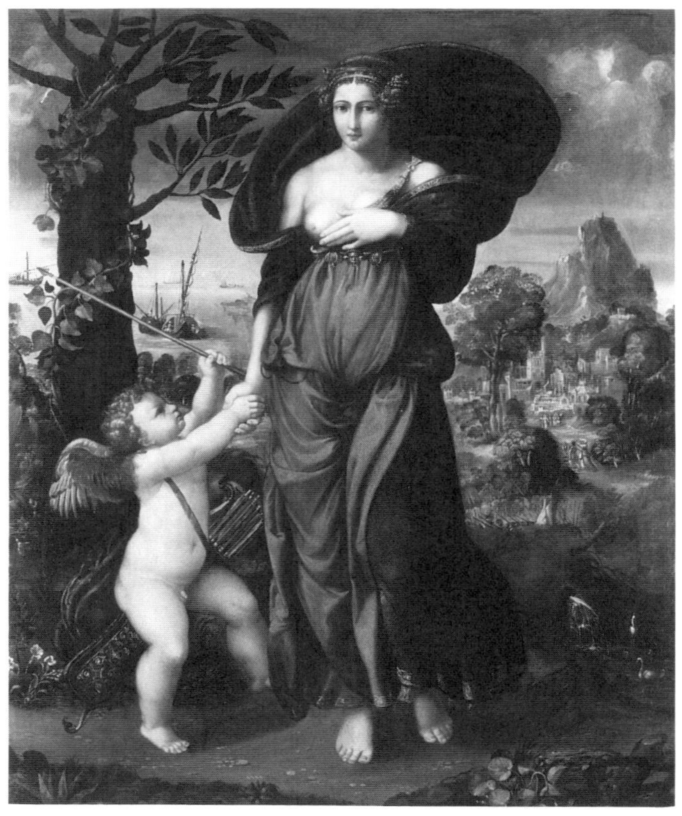

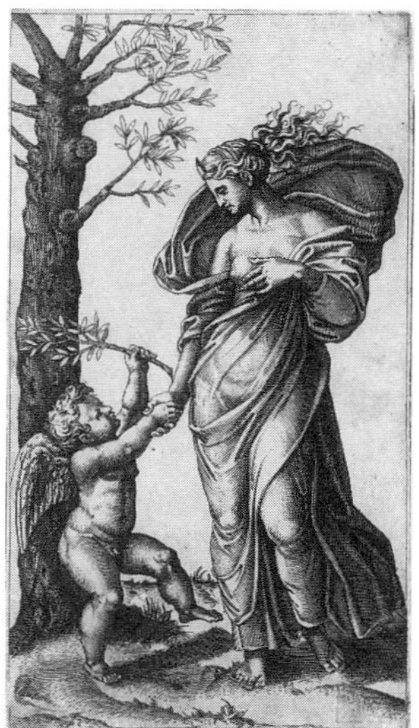

Fig. 5. Battista Dossi
Venus and Cupid
Philadelphia, Philadelphia Museum of Art

Fig. 6. Marcantonio Raimondi (after Raphael)
Reconciliation of Minerva and Cupid (or *Peace*)
New York, The Metropolitan Museum of Art

engravings have been used as a visual template for a group that was then drawn from life, probably from models in the studio, and little altered subsequently. The two characters in the *Sacrifice of Isaac* continue to look remarkably like *contadini* from the Brescian countryside; more startling still is the sensation, in the *Gathering of Manna*, of gazing at a blond, grimacing studio model rather than an idealized river god.

Keith Christiansen has shown that Caravaggio too was in the habit of moving from prints through study of a studio model to painting. One case is Caravaggio's *Bacchino Malato* (ca. 1593–1594, Rome, Galleria Borghese), which looks back to the same small engraving of the youth with an urn after Marcantonio. Simone Peterzano too studied a figure from life in this precise pose and then used it in his frescoes at Garegnano.[17] Taken together, this evidence suggests that the practice of frequently drawing on print sources was another link in that thick chain binding the *"Precedenti"* to Caravaggio, as first defined by Roberto Longhi.[18] These artists seem to have turned from prints to the study of the model, and it is this additional step that can so distance the final painting from its source. As nicely put by Valerio Terraroli in regard to Moretto, the artist is "play[ing] within the classical lexicon, seen anew in the light of the 'natural.'"[19] Nevertheless, the engraved source remains embedded in the picture; it is the evidence for the artist's interest in Raphael, however interpreted or, indeed, manipulated. In the discussion above I measured the proximity or distance between Moretto's image and the engraving, but this assessment assumes that the viewer has recognized the source. Indeed, it assumes that the painter has dipped quite naturally into the visual encyclopedia that prints offered him, both for individual figures and more complex compositional elements. He then has put them to use in various and even contradictory ways.

It is not surprising to find that in Ferrara, artists like Battista Dossi and Garofalo were equally attentive to engravings after central Italian art. Given their documented early and direct exposure to Raphael's art, and subsequent long years of working in northern Italy, prints after Raphael figure naturally in their repertories. In their choices and uses of engravings Vasari would have recognized the Battista who worked alongside Raphael, or the Garofalo who promised Raphael that he would return to Rome and was prevented from doing so only by the force of circumstances.[20] The painting that probably shows Venus and Cupid (fig. 5), attributed by Henriette Mendelsohn and Felton Gibbons to Battista, is quite openly indebted to the print by Marcantonio after Raphael that is traditionally titled *Peace* (fig. 6).[21] The painter's adherence to the general composition is self-evident, but Battista also maintains the statuesque figure type and the flowing classical drapery—indeed, all of the aspects of the print that were recognizably part of a classicizing aesthetic.

Garofalo's study of the works of Raphael and derivations from them is a complex subject, but he approached print sources in a similarly partisan manner. For example, the Minerva in *Neptune and Minerva* (fig. 7), dated November 1512—about the date of Garofalo's trip to Rome discussed by

Vasari[22] — may not be a strict derivation from the famous *Lucretia* (fig. 8) by Marcantonio after a lost original by Raphael,[23] but her stance, especially from the waist down, is directly indebted to it and certainly informed by the same concerns (both may be based ultimately on an antique sculpture discovered in Rome around 1500). The figure's balance and contrapposto, the position of the feet, the bunching of the drapery at the hips and under the breasts, and even the description of the sandals point to the connection between the two.

Even when Garofalo's principal source is elsewhere, as in his *Pagan Sacrifice* of 1526 (London, National Gallery), which is based on an illustration from Francesco Colonna's *Hypnerotomachia Poliphili*,[24] he has reinvented the figures so that they have less to do with those of the Venetian woodcut than with others of recognizably Roman inspiration. The young woman holding the overturned torch at the left, for example, has been rethought in a manner close to Marcantonio's *Venus* of 1512.[25] In his interpretation of this print, or of a figure very close to it, Garofalo captures the twist of the body and shoulder, the folds of the belly, the stiff supporting left leg, and the cast of the head. Each figure from the woodcut has been similarly rethought; the result gives a somewhat piecemeal character to the painting as a whole. While Moretto may have transcribed his Roman print sources more literally, Garofalo instead pointedly exploited them for their intrinsic stylistic character. As Fritz Saxl once said about this painting, Garofalo attempted to achieve "a general pagan sacredness, a general dignified behaviour, a general beauty of plastic form" and, in doing so, "[he] reshapes the early humanistic Venetian original."[26] Surely numerous instances like these could be found by a search through Garofalo's work; Alessandro Ballarin, for example, has pointed out his adaptation of Marcantonio's *Madonna of the Long Thigh*, which may be an illustration of the Ferrarese artist's intense interest in Giulio Romano after 1524.[27]

Having wandered across northern Italy from Milan on east, we finally arrive at Dosso's studio. Like Battista and Garofalo, Dosso's understanding of Roman art was based on firsthand knowledge; indeed, one of the most interesting implications of the new documentation on the Costabili altarpiece (p. 142), showing it to have been underway in 1513,[28] is that Dosso and Garofalo were probably both in Rome before it was begun. Vasari says as much about Garofalo, although he garbles the date, while numerous details of the altarpiece suggest an acquaintance with the current work of Raphael on the part of both artists. The subtlety with which Dosso was able to keep his sense of the Roman scene alive in his own later work in Ferrara is striking, and prints were one means of his doing so. They seem to have provided a starting point toward a more personalized imagery, or to have functioned as an aide-mémoire of a work studied in the original. Yet it is considerably less easy to glean print sources from his paintings than from any of those of the artists discussed above, and when they are readily identifiable they are apt to be for incidental motifs. I would suggest here that in his way of

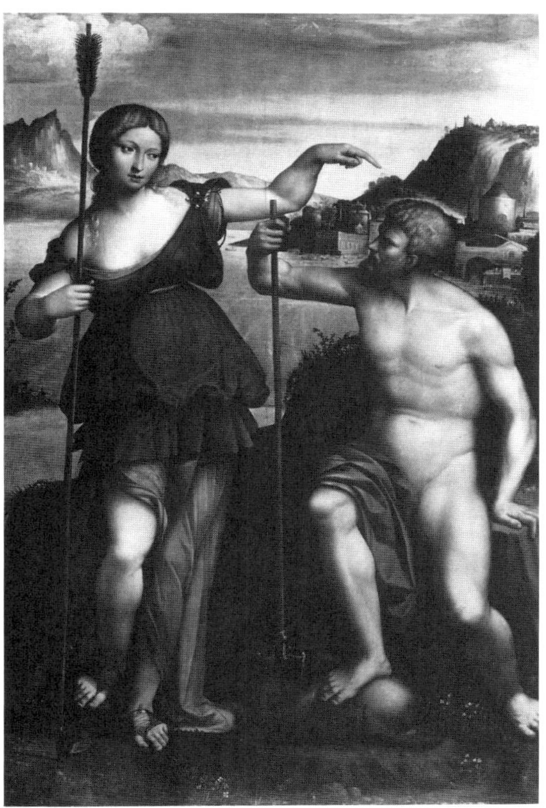

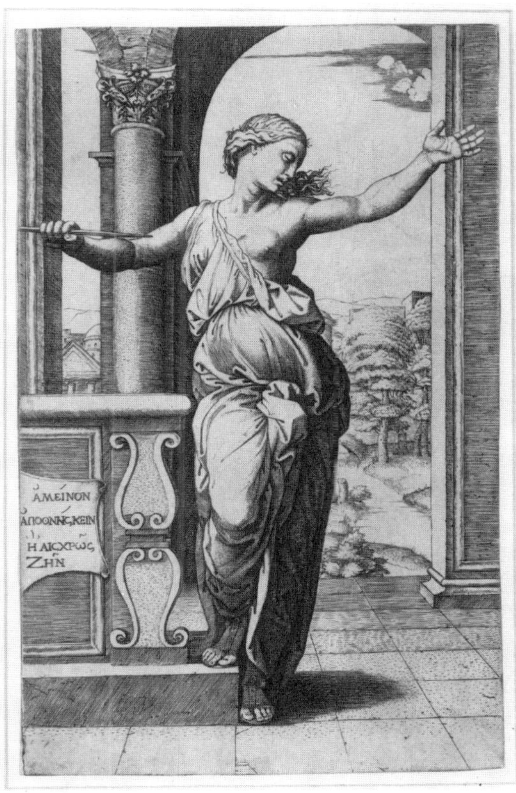

Fig. 7. Garofalo
Neptune and Minerva
Dresden, Staatliche Kunstsammlungen, Gemäldegalerie Alte Meister

Fig. 8. Marcantonio Raimondi (after Raphael)
Lucretia
Boston, Museum of Fine Arts

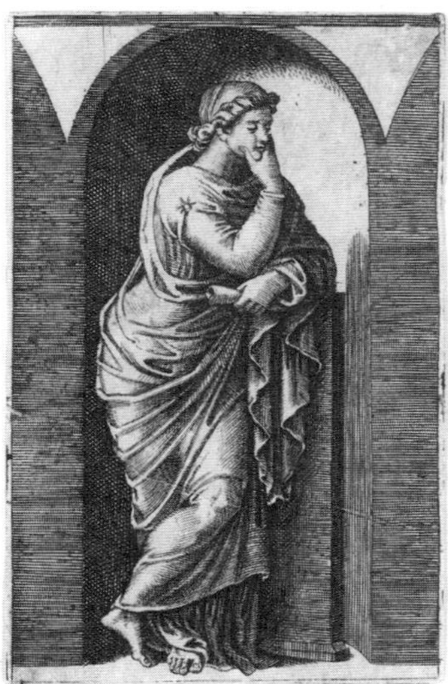

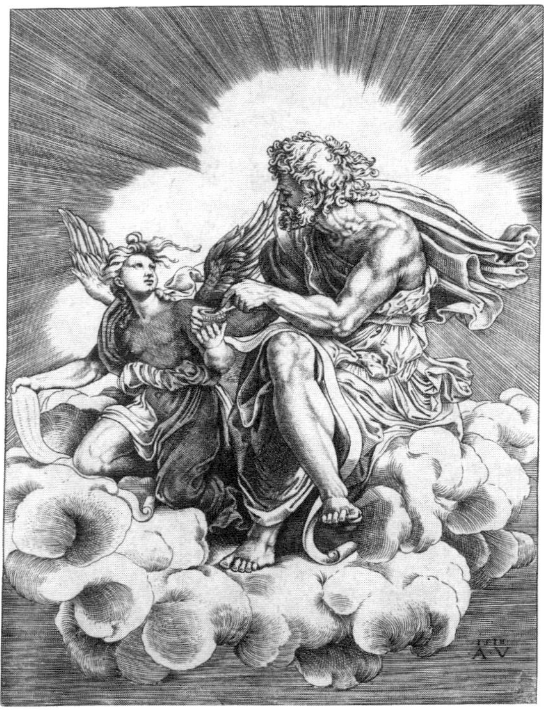

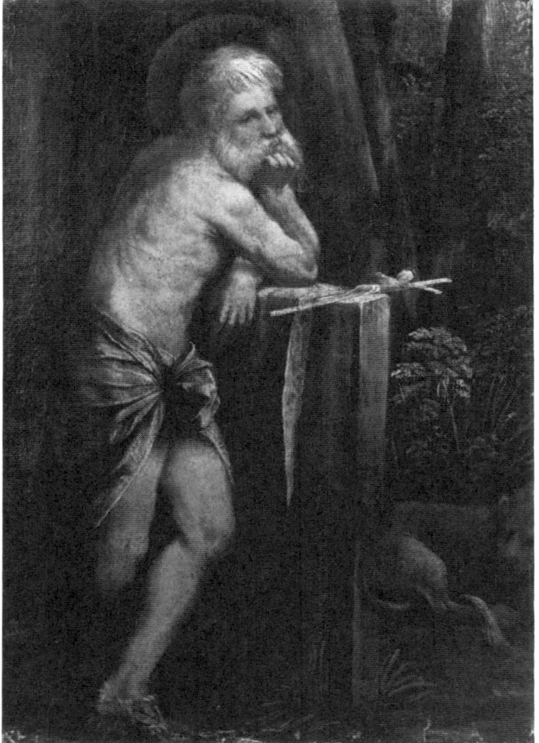

Fig. 9. Marcantonio Raimondi
Muse
New York, The Metropolitan Museum of Art

Fig. 10. Dosso Dossi
Saint Jerome
Whereabouts unknown

Fig. 11. Agostino Veneziano, also called Agostino Musi
Saint Matthew
New York, The Metropolitan Museum of Art

working with and from prints, Dosso exhibits the very complete and individual assimilation of central Italian art that is an important aspect of the sure-handed combination of various stylistic veins that is at the core of his painting's poetry. (David A. Brown has made a similar point about assimilation when contrasting Correggio's and the young Parmigianino's use of print sources, noting that "the younger artist [at Fontanellato] failed to fully assimilate them, so that they are easier to identify."[29])

The most transparent of the print derivations is Dosso's transformation of Marcantonio's *Muse* (fig. 9),[30] which is based on ancient prototypes, into a pensive Saint Jerome in a painting published by Longhi whose present location is unknown (fig. 10).[31] The figure's position is unchanged save for the arms, which are crossed more acutely, so that the elbow rests directly on the wooden support and the saint's chin on his knuckles. As it seems likely that this sharply observed rethinking of the pose was done from a model, it is interesting that the Muse is an image that Moretto worked from also for a *Saint Peter* (ca. 1550, Brescia, private collection) and more loosely for the *Eritrean Sybil* (ca. 1530) now in the Escorial in Madrid. From photographs, the *Saint Jerome* appears to be an early work (Ballarin has said about 1516), and the saint is shown set against the dense foliage, flecked with light, so characteristic of paintings of this period. Indeed, the concern with light is remarkable, as it picks out the crucifix and the folds of drapery tied across the saint's torso and spilling over the plinth. In this way Dosso brings together a figure directly based on a work by Marcantonio and a landscape and illumination of very differently oriented inspiration.

However, an even more typical pattern can be observed in the conception of the splendid figure of Jupiter in the *Jupiter, Mercury, and Virtue* in Vienna, generally dated about 1524 (p. 99). The position of this bearded figure—legs decisively crossed, left arm pulled across the waist, neck muscles bulging, the tug of the drapery under the thigh—has been compared to that of Raphael's frescoed Jupiter in the spandrel known as *Cupid and Jupiter* in the Villa Farnesina in Rome, a work commissioned by Agostino Chigi. As the date of the work by Raphael and his school in the Loggia di Psiche is about 1518, this comparison presupposes that Dosso made a trip to Rome sometime late in that decade or early in the next, which may very well be true.

Two engravings may have served as intermediaries for the artist some years later in Ferrara. One is Marcantonio's reproduction of the spandrel itself, sufficiently well known at the time to be singled out by Vasari, although incorrectly identified as a Ganymede.[32] The other is Agostino Veneziano's *Saint Matthew* (fig. 11),[33] one of the Four Evangelists (after the design of Giulio Romano?) also dated 1518, and itself a reinterpretation of the Jupiter. The introduction of this second engraving into the discussion is key because Dosso looked to it for certain inflections not found in the work for Chigi. Arm and leg have been brought closer together; Jupiter's hand holding the palette is stretched out in much the same way as Matthew's hand holding the pen; and the twist of the head, while not identical, thrusts back rather than forward. Dosso goes his own way entirely in dropping the exaggerated foreshortening of Jupiter's dangling right foot, an effect needed for the *di sotto in su* position of the original. More significant, he also changes Jupiter from Raphael's heroic, wavy-haired and muscle-bound god to a more lyrical personality. Although recognizably tied to its Roman prototypes, Dosso's Jupiter has been recast in the artist's own terms and set seamlessly within his own poetic conception. We witness Dosso moving from an original observation of a work in Rome, renewed and refined by a study of prints and perhaps restudied from a posed model, to a figure of extraordinary inventiveness.

A second instance is suggestive of a similar chain of events, but one that has to be put forward more tentatively, because Dosso is here more freely interpretive. Both Battista and Dosso seem to have been much impressed by Raphael's Sibyls and Angels, painted over the entrance of the Chigi Chapel in Santa Maria della Pace in about 1513, and comparable twisting figures, stretching as if their bodies curve over an arch, appear more than once in their work. In the *Sibyl* (ca. 1520) in the National Museum of Wales, Cardiff, Battista is looking to the figure at the far left of Raphael's fresco. He shifts the direction of her legs to achieve the desired effect of arching within a single figure, one that is actually more like a conflation of two of Raphael's sibyls. Dosso's Virgin in the *Holy Family* from about 1528 (now in the Pinacoteca Capitolina, Rome), who sprawls elegantly across an improbable stepped platform, probably goes back to the same source. Here too it seems likely that prints aided him in casting his mind back to the impressions left on him by Raphael's work. The anonymous engraving known as *Theology and Metaphysics*, which reproduces in reverse the figures to the left of the arch of the chapel, could have functioned as such an intermediary;[34] certain details such as the Virgin's pointing gesture are close to those found in the print. The gesture is actually an adaptation of the printmaker, as Raphael's sibyl is writing on a tablet. Clearly, however, the importance of any source here is as a point of departure, and the figural invention is palpably Dosso's own.

It is possible to move outside the sphere of prints inspired by works of art in Rome to find some examples of comparable adaptations from particularly significant contemporary northern Italian engravings.[35] The most striking of these is the enigmatic woman seen from behind in Dosso's *Allegory of Music* (fig. 12), who must have been inspired by the figure of Fame in Jacopo de'Barbari's engraving *Victory and Fame* of about 1500 (fig. 13).[36] We recall that prints by Barbari figured in Cardinal Grimani's collection in Venice and were certainly quite sought after. De'Barbari's engraving was inspired in turn by Dürer's *Four Naked Women* of 1497.[37] Dürer's print was also copied by Nicoletto da Modena very soon after it appeared,[38] so the appeal of this intriguing group of female figures seems to have been widespread throughout northern Italy (and the figure's genealogy is an impressive one). The rather flaccid body of Dosso's figure, with its slightly flattened buttocks,

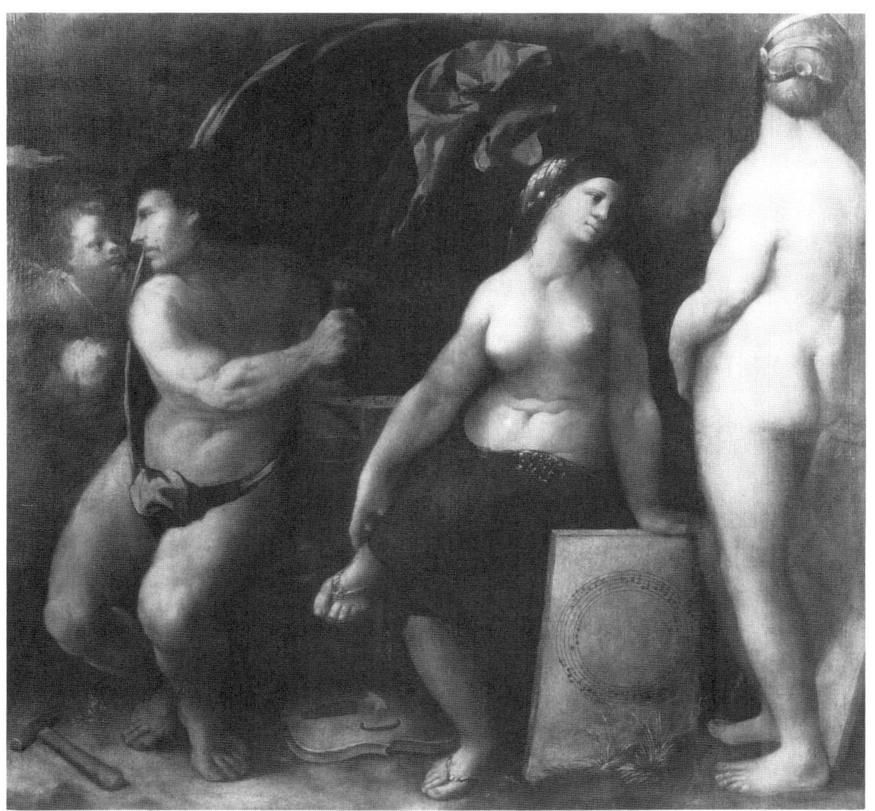

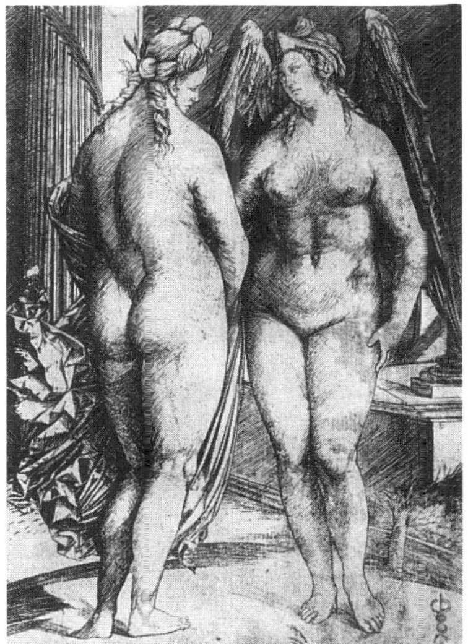

Fig. 12. Dosso Dossi
Allegory of Music
Florence, Museo della Fondazione Horne

Fig. 13. Jacopo de'Barbari
Victory and Fame
Oxford, Ashmolean Museum

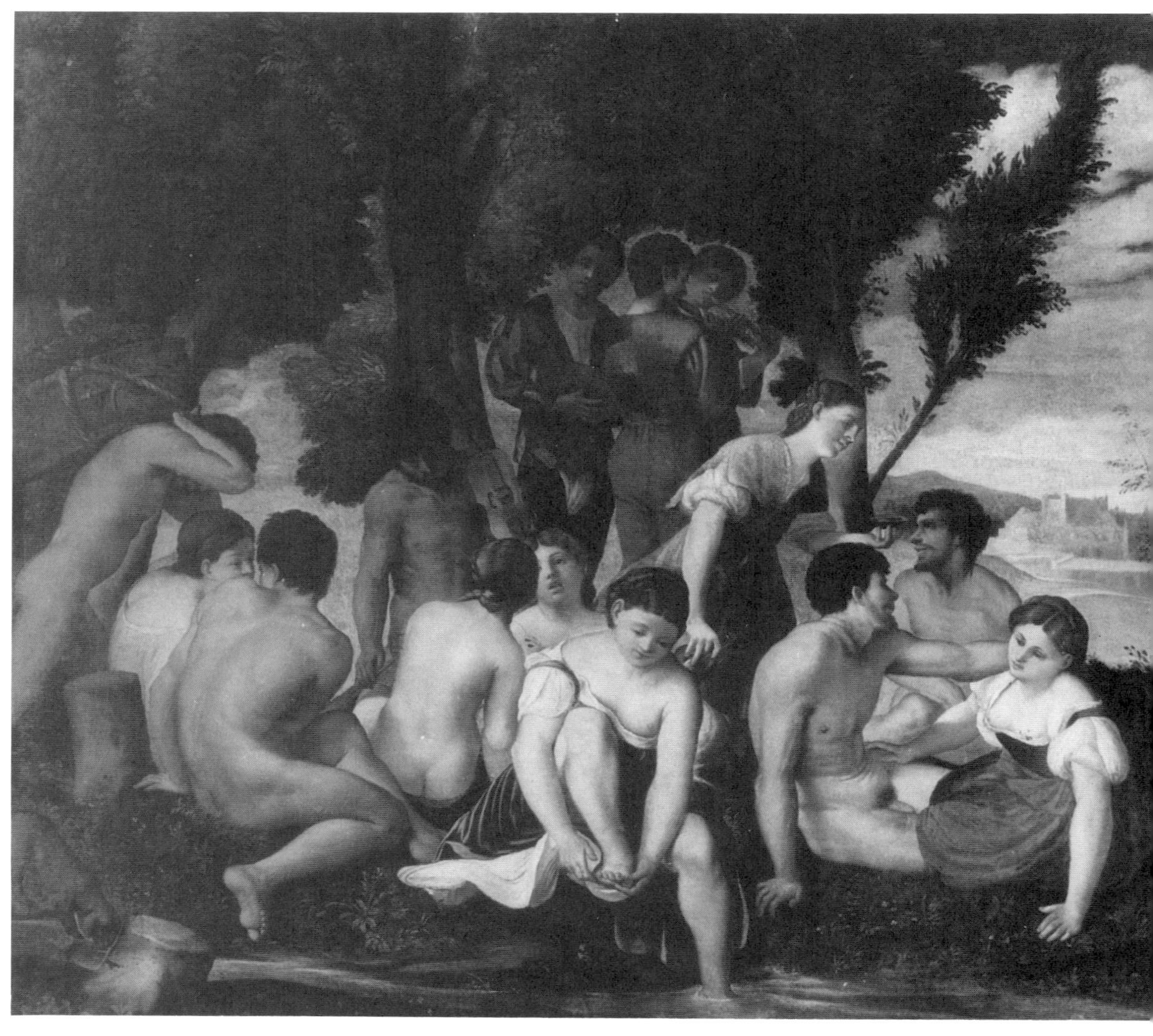

Fig. 14. Dosso Dossi
The Bathers
Rome, Museo Nazionale di Castel Sant'Angelo

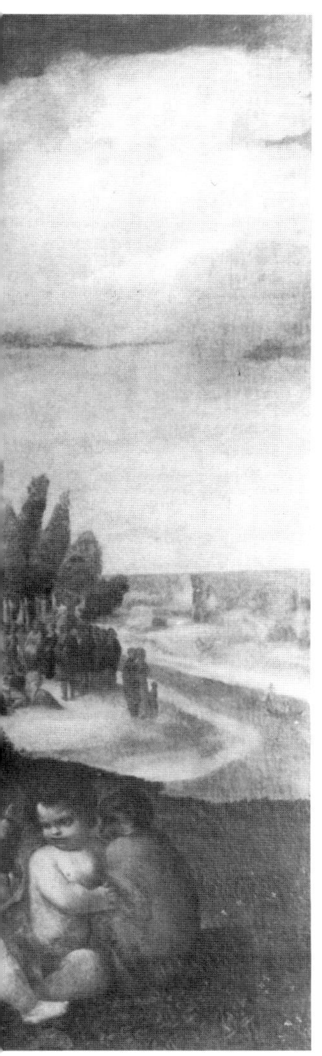

sloping shoulders and small head, and the arm wrapped around the midsection, all come from the print source, but as always, elements have been rethought. Here, it is the angle of view, the tilt of the head, and the shift of weight on the legs that have been slightly altered.

The fluidity of this adaptive process, which is a natural part of Dosso's working method, needs to be stressed. To be fair, in many instances prints seem not to have played any role in Dosso's mental repertory of images. The Saint Bartholomew in the Della Sale altarpiece of around 1527 (now in the Galleria Nazionale di Palazzo Barberini, Rome) represents another way of working. Does the pose of this majestic figure ultimately go back to Raphael's Sappho in the fresco known as *Parnassus* (Vatican, Stanza della Segnatura)? If so, it cannot have been Marcantonio's engraving of the composition that brought it to mind, as it is precisely the Sappho that is excluded from the print, which reproduces an earlier compositional study rather than the final work.[39] Likewise, the many personalized interpretations of figures from the Sistine Chapel, such as the series of Astronomers or Learned Men (1520–1522), demonstrate Dosso's remarkable absorption of Michelangelo's imagery, almost certainly without the intervention of a reproductive print.[40] Prints were just one of the ingredients that united in Dosso's mind to form his understanding of art in Rome, which came first and foremost from direct study. In this he was very unlike Moretto, for example, and this accounts for that seamless assimilation of print material, of which I have spoken, on the occasions when it was of use.

Dosso's approach, that of rarely pillaging prints of their identifiable compositions and figures, should be kept in mind in discussing the controversial painting known as *The Bathers*, now in the Museo Nazionale di Castel Sant'-Angelo (fig. 14). Most recently it has been hypothesized that this picture is identical with the one commissioned in Mantua for the Palazzo di San Sebastiano, payments for which were made in 1512.[41] Clifford Brown has shown this hypothesis to be practically untenable, reopening questions of authorship, date, and the original location of the painting.[42] This Bacchanal is liberally studded with synecdochic references to other works of art, including Marcantonio's prints: repeated torsos and legs, as well as figural groupings, are close to those found in the *Judgment of Paris*,[43] while the man struggling under the burden of the basket of grapes may be partly inspired by Marcantonio's engraving of a *Man Carrying the Base of a Column*.[44] Both of these prints are usually dated between 1515 and the end of the decade. If one considers that the couple to the right alludes both to Titian's *Three Ages of Man* (ca. 1516, Edinburgh, National Gallery of Scotland) and to the female figure reclining on the ground in the *Andrians* (ca. 1523–1525, Madrid, Museo del Prado), the painting begins to read as an additive compilation of preexisting characters, rather later in date than has generally been supposed. It remains open to question whether Dosso composed in this manner.

Dosso's use of German prints raises other questions and issues. On the one hand, he seems on at least one occasion to have approached Dürer's prints—as so many artists did—as a grab bag of motifs that could be appropriated at will, especially for animals or minor characters. On the other hand, it is clear that he studied northern prints principally for their expressive power without resorting to direct quotation of them in his paintings, a point demonstrated by Peter Humfrey in his discussion of Dosso's landscapes.[45] Here Dosso's method is not unlike that of the Brescian artist Girolamo Romanino, for example.

The best known of all Dosso's print citations, pointed out as early as 1911, is of the stag and greyhound from Dürer's *Saint Eustace* of about 1501 (fig. 15).[46] This print was of sufficient interest in the Veneto that the section including the animals was copied by Agostino Veneziano early in his career for a print known as *Animals*.[47] Agostino had already secularized the image, removing both the saint and the crucifix from the stag's head (and adding the very Venetian landscape), and Dosso completed the process, inserting the stag and one of the dogs into the painting of a sorceress traditionally called *Circe and Her Lovers in a Landscape,* but possibly depicting Alcina, now in Washington (fig. 16). The hound seen frontally in Dürer's print was also the inspiration for the beautiful dog in the painting in the Borghese Gallery known as *The Enchantress Circe* (or *Melissa*) (fig. 17). These same dogs appear in Parmigianino's frescoes at Fontanellato as well.

All of the sorceresses proposed as subjects of Dosso's paintings transformed their victims: Circe, who appears in the Odyssey, turned hers into animals, principally swine; the Ariostan Alcina changed hers into trees and animals; and Melissa returned those unfortunates to human form. It has been suggested that Dürer's print was inspirational to Dosso principally for the idea contained within it of "transformation"—that is, that of Eustace the hunter into a Christian.[48] The appropriation may indeed have been purposeful in that way, especially in the case of the painting in Washington, given that the artificiality of the insertion pointedly calls attention to itself as a quotation. It is important to recall that the date of this painting has been much discussed, some critics placing it as early as 1512 and others as late as 1528.[49] While problems with the painting's state have contributed to the difficulty in arriving at a consensus about the date, surely the dilemma is also partly due to the awkwardness of the pattern-book-like animals within the composition: it is the directness of the imitation that has rightly led to questions concerning the artist's intent.

It is the other kind of influence, however, the indirect and evocative, that brings us closer to the Dosso we have seen until now. For example, Dosso's swaggering *Standard Bearer* (ca. 1515–1516, Allentown, Allentown Art Museum) has been compared to various German prints, including Dürer's engraving of the same subject[50] and two works by Albrecht Altdorfer, the etched *Foot-Soldier Playing a Flute,*[51] dated 1510, and the woodcut of a *Standard Bearer in a Landscape,* dated 1520.[52] None of these are precisely comparable, and to them could be added others such as Hans Sebald Beham's *Soldier Standing by a Tree* (1520)[53] and others by Altdorfer.

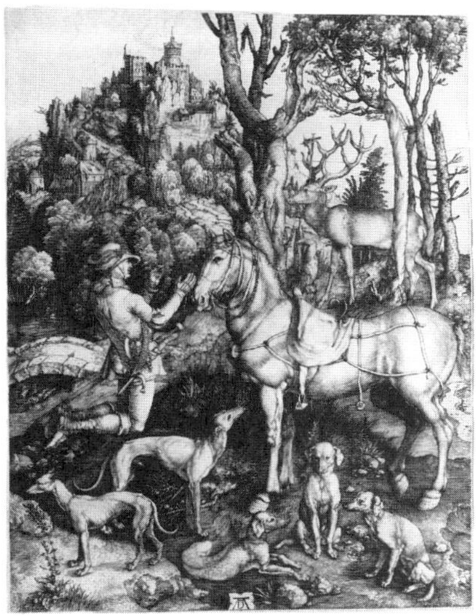

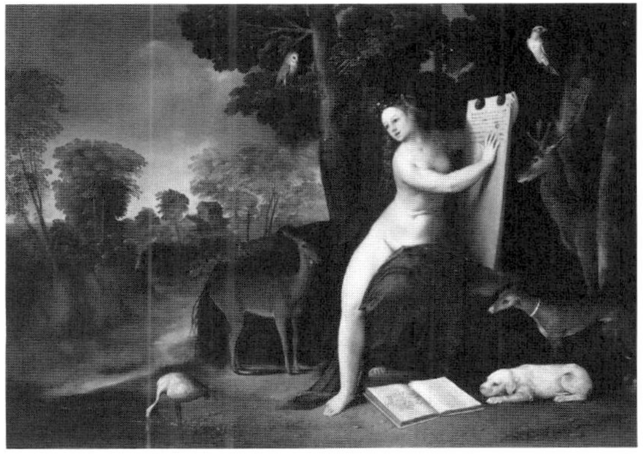

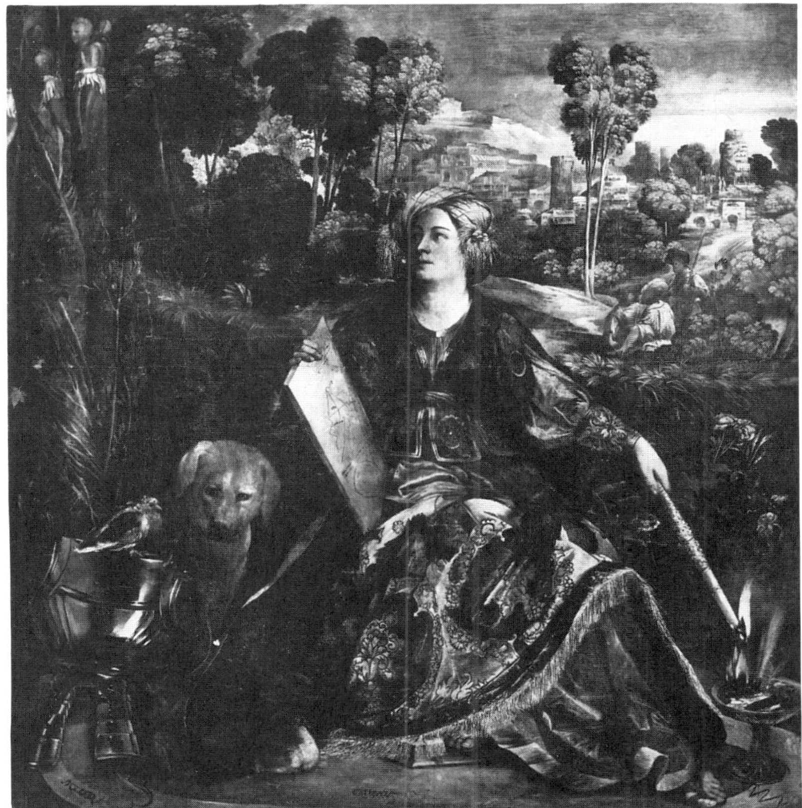

Fig. 15. Albrecht Dürer
Saint Eustace
New York, The Metropolitan Museum of Art

Fig. 16. Dosso Dossi
Circe and Her Lovers in a Landscape
Washington, National Gallery of Art

Fig. 17. Dosso Dossi
The Enchantress Circe (or *Melissa*)
Rome, Galleria Borghese

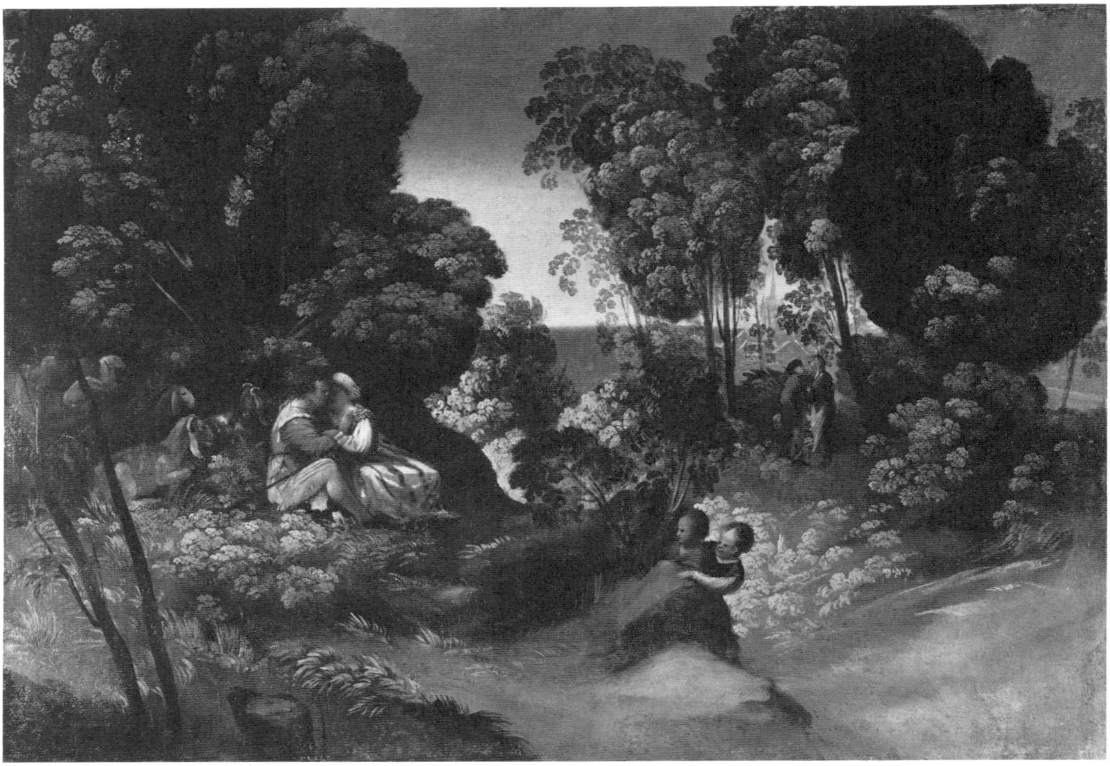

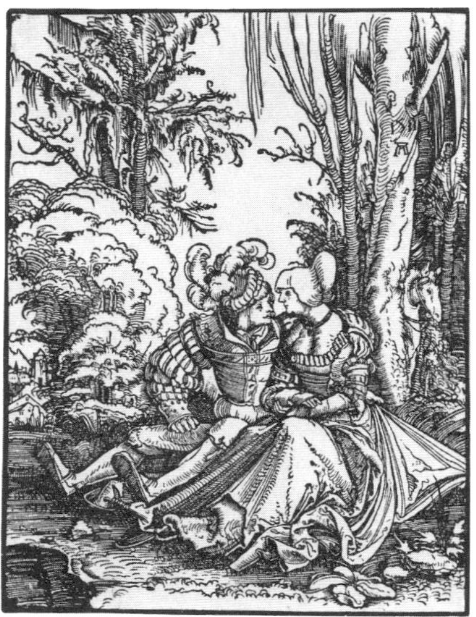

Fig. 18. Dosso Dossi
The Three Ages of Man
New York, The Metropolitan Museum of Art

Fig. 19. Albrecht Altdorfer
Couple of Lovers in the Forest
New York, The Metropolitan Museum of Art

Dosso is emulating specific effects found in these prints, but never follows any single one overtly.

German prints may likewise have been in his mind when he was painting the *Lamentation* (ca. 1517, London, National Gallery); their traces are seen in the roots slithering down the sides of the rocks and the pathos of the grieving women. Dosso may well have known Baldung Grien's woodcut of the same subject and approximately same date,[54] in which two dramatically gesturing women—one with outstretched arms—are stacked up over the sprawled figure of Christ. But here, too, this woodcut can only be considered a point of departure, one of the available and relevant sources (there are Italian prototypes for these gestures as well). The Metropolitan Museum's *Three Ages of Man* (fig. 18), with its unusual imagery of lovers hidden in a wood, may have been inspired by Altdorfer's wonderful woodcut of 1511 known as the *Couple of Lovers in the Forest* (fig. 19).[55] Dosso may have even had the opportunity to study drawings by Altdorfer, such as *Lovers in a Field of Grain* of 1508 (Basel, Öffentliche Kunstsammlung), which shows the lovers hidden in a field. Both print and drawing are examples of Altdorfer's potently expressive use of landscape, itself clearly fascinating to Dosso.

When I set out in this inquiry, I hoped it might prove possible to find in prints the explanation of some of Dosso's enigmatic imagery. This has not so far proven to be the case, and the reasons I arrived at this blank wall are not difficult to guess. Prints seemed to have played a role in Dosso's creative process that was neither direct nor facilely explanatory. They are there, but they are deeply embedded within his own inventions, and the original content of the print is infrequently adopted. So many things are brought together in his most personal imagery, including literary as well as visual sources and affinities. If we deviate from our principal theme for just one moment and return to the *Three Ages of Man,* we can see that Altdorfer's graphic works are not the only images that must be kept in mind when thinking of this sweetly oblivious couple, seated comfortably among their goats. Two drawings in the Devonshire Collection at Chatsworth, both titled *Alpine Village and Lovers Embracing,* reflect, at the least, a composition by Titian of about the same date (if one is not actually by him, as has often been suggested); the drawings include a diminutive amorous couple tucked against a hill and under a tree, showing that similar visual ideas were current in Venice.[56] Some years later such a couple appears again in a subsidiary role, in Domenico Campagnola's woodcut *Landscape with Wandering Family* (ca. 1535–1540),[57] further documenting the currency of the image in the Veneto. Although the scene's content, the ages of man, seems straightforward, the colloquy between the two men in the background, one white haired and bearded, may additionally refer to a passage in Pietro Bembo's *Gli Asolani* often invoked for such pastoral scenes.[58] X-ray photography shows that, unlike all the other figures whose shapes were left in reserve, these two were painted over the landscape and might have been a second thought on the artist's part, separately inspired. All (or none) of these things may have been present in

Dosso's mind; none, including the Altdorfer print, goes very far in explaining Dosso's painting in its entirety.

In a similar fashion, print sources for the J. Paul Getty Museum's great *Mythological Scene* (p. 84) provide us with the barest of entries into the world represented. No print known to me accounts either for the four figures we currently see or for the three in the composition as completed by the artist. Marco Dente's *Pan and Syrinx* (ca. 1516),[59] for example, could have been of importance in the genesis of the composition, but not to the allegorical meaning of the image as a whole.

Here, I am afraid, the task of elucidation still stretches before us.

Notes

1. Cecil Gould, "On Dürer's Graphic and Italian Painting," *Gazette des beaux-arts,* ser. 6, 75 (1970): 103.

2. A. E. Popham, "The Baiardo Inventory," in *Studies in Renaissance and Baroque Art Presented to Anthony Blunt on His 60th Birthday* (London: Phaidon, 1967), 26–29.

3. Michael Bury, "The Taste for Prints in Italy to c. 1600," *Print Quarterly* 2 (1985): 19–20.

4. Keith Christiansen, "The Case for Mantegna as Printmaker," *Burlington Magazine* 135 (1993): 607 n. 26.

5. Jacopo Morelli, ed., *Notizia d'opere di disegno* [attrib. to Marcantonio Michiel], 2nd ed., ed. Gustavo Frizzoni (1884; reprint, Bologna: Arnaldo Forni, 1976), 197, 199 for Grimani; 174 for Foscarini.

6. Popham (see note 2), 27.

7. Mark Roskill, *Dolce's* Aretino *and Venetian Art Theory of the Cinquecento* (New York: New York Univ. Press, 1968), 121; Christopher Lloyd, "A Short Footnote to Raphael Studies," *Burlington Magazine* 119 (1977): 113–14.

8. David Landau and Peter Parshall, *The Renaissance Print, 1470–1550* (New Haven: Yale Univ. Press, 1994), 295.

9. Carlo Cesare Malvasia, *Felsina pittrice: Vite de pittori bolognesi...,* 3 vols. (Bologna: Erede di D. Barbieri, 1678), 1: 238, 255.

10. Bury (see note 3), 24–25.

11. Bruno Passamani, "Il 'Raffaello bresciano': Formazione ed affermazione di un mito," in *Alessandro Bonvicino, il Moretto,* exh. cat. (Bologna: Nuova Alfa, 1988), 16–28; Andrea Bayer, "'If Only He Had Lived Closer...': Moretto and Painting in Brescia" (paper presented at the annual Sixteenth Century Studies conference, Atlanta, 1992).

12. For numerous examples, see Chiara Parisio, "Alcune indicazioni sulle fonti figurative del Moretto," in *Alessandro Bonvicino* (see note 11), 273–79; and Valerio Terraroli, "Moretto e alcune desunzioni iconografiche: Da Raimondi a Dürer," in idem, 280–86.

13. Adam Bartsch, *Le peintre-graveur,* 21 vols. (Vienna: J. V. Degan, 1803–1821), 14: 104, no. 117.

14. Ibid., 14: 198, no. 22.

15. Bartsch (see note 13), 14: 197, no. 245.

16. Bartsch (see note 13), 14: 207, no. 257.

17. Keith Christiansen, "Thoughts on the Lombard Training of Caravaggio," in Mina Gregori, ed., *Come dipingeva il Caravaggio* (Milan: Electa, 1996), 18.

18. Roberto Longhi, "Quesiti caravaggeschi: I precedenti" (1929), in idem, *"Me pinxit" e quesiti caravaggeschi, 1928–1934* (Florence: Sansoni, 1968), 97–143.

19. Terraroli (see note 12), 280.

20. For a summary of the information on Battista's presence in Rome, see Alessandra Pattanaro, "Regesto della pittura a Ferrara (1497–1548)," in Alessandro Ballarin, *Dosso Dossi: La pittura a Ferrara negli anni del Ducato di Alfonso I,* 2 vols. (Cittadella: Bertoncello Artigrafiche, 1994–1995), 138 [152]. On Garofalo's desire to return to Rome, see Giorgio Vasari, *Le vite de' più eccellenti pittori, scultori ed architettori,* ed. Gaetano Milanesi, 9 vols. (Florence: Sansoni, 1906), 6: 462–64.

21. Bartsch (see note 13), 14: 296, no. 393. For attributions to Battista, see Henriette Mendelsohn, *Das Werk der Dossi* (Munich: Georg Müller & Eugene Rentsch, 1914), 142; and Felton Gibbons, *Dosso and Battista Dossi: Court Painters at Ferrara* (Princeton: Princeton University Press, 1968). For the subject and the connection to the print, see Rudolf Wittkower, "Transformations of Minerva in Renaissance Imagery," in idem, *Allegory and the Migration of Symbols* (London: Thames & Hudson, 1977), 136–39.

22. Peter Humfrey and Mauro Lucco, "Dosso Dossi in 1513: A Reassessment of the Artist's Early Works and Influences," *Apollo* 147 (1998): 28 n. 17; Anna Maria Fioravanti Baraldi, *Il Garofalo, Benvenuto Tisi, pittore (c. 1476–1559)* (Rimini: Luisè, 1993), 112–13 (entry no. 40).

23. Bartsch (see note 13), 14: 155, no. 192.

24. Fritz Saxl, "A Scene from the *Hypnerotomachia* in a Painting by Garofalo," *Journal of the Warburg and Courtauld Institutes* 1 (1937–1938): 169–71.

25. Bartsch (see note 13), 14: 234, no. 311.

26. Saxl (see note 24), 171.

27. Bartsch (see note 13), 14: 64, no. 57. See the comparison in Ballarin (see note 20), 2: figs. 728–29; on the importance of Giulio Romano to Garofalo after 1524, see *Le siècle de Titien: L'âge d'or de la peinture à Venise,* 2nd ed., exh. cat. (Paris: Editions de la Réunion des Musées Nationaux, 1993), 470 (entry no. 80 by Alessandro Ballarin).

28. Adriano Franceschini, "Dosso Dossi, Benvenuto da Garofalo, e il polittico Costabili di Ferrara," *Paragone,* nos. 543–545 (1995): 110–15.

29. David Alan Brown, "A Print Source for Parmigianino at Fontanellato," in *Per A. E. Popham* (Parma: Consigli Arte, 1981), 43.

30. Bartsch (see note 13), 14: 211, no. 265.

31. Roberto Longhi, "Una favola del Dosso" (1927), in idem, *Saggi e ricerche, 1925–1928,* 2 vols. (Florence: Sansoni, 1967), 1: 158–61.

32. Bartsch (see note 13), 14: 256, no. 342.

33. Bartsch (see note 13), 14: 83, no. 95.

34. Bartsch (see note 13), 15: 49, no. 6.

35. For example, William E. Suida, "Lucrezia Borgia *in Memoriam,*" *Gazette des beaux-arts,* ser. 6, 35 (1949), 281, pointed out the relationship between the figure in the *Circe and Her Lovers in a Landscape* (Washington, National Gallery of Art) and Giulio Campagnola's engraving, *Young Shepherd.*

36. Arthur M. Hind, *Early Italian Engraving: A Critical Catalogue with Complete Reproduction of All the Prints Described,* 7 vols. (London: B. Quaritch, 1938–1948), no. 26.

37. F. W. H. Hollstein, *German Engravings, Etchings, and Woodcuts, ca. 1400–1700,* 43 vols. (Amsterdam: M. Hertzberger, 1954–), 7: 69.

38. Hind (see note 36), 98.

39. Bartsch (see note 13), 14: 200, no. 247. See Innis H. Shoemaker and Elizabeth Broun, *The Engravings of Marcantonio Raimondi,* exh. cat. (Lawrence, Kans.: Spencer Museum of Art, 1981), 155–56 (entry nos. 48a–48b by Innis H. Shoemaker).

40. For comparisons between Dosso's paintings and the *ignudi* of the Sistine Chapel, see Ballarin (see note 20), 2: figs. 570 vs. 576, figs. 599 vs. 597.

41. Ballarin (see note 20), 1: 295–96 (entry no. 333).

42. Clifford M. Brown with Anna Maria Lorenzoni, "The Palazzo di San Sebastiano (1506–1512) and the Art Patronage of Francesco II Gonzaga, Fourth Marquis of Mantua," *Gazette des beaux-arts,* ser. 6, 129 (1997), 151–58.

43. Bartsch (see note 13), 14: 197, no. 245.

44. Bartsch (see note 13), 14: 354, no. 476.

45. Peter Humfrey, "Two Moments in Dosso's Career as a Landscape Painter," in this volume.

46. Hollstein (see note 37), 7: 60.

47. Bartsch (see note 13), 14: 311, no. 414.

48. Brown (see note 29), 49.

49. For the range, see Ballarin (see note 20), 1: 348 (entry no. 452).

50. Hollstein (see note 37), 7: 92.

51. Hollstein (see note 37), 1: 67.

52. Hollstein (see note 37), 1: 87.

53. Hollstein (see note 37), 3: p. 118.

54. Hollstein (see note 37), 2: 53.

55. Hollstein (see note 37), 1: 88.

56. Konrad Oberhuber, ed., *Disegni di Tiziano e della sua cerchia,* exh. cat. (Venice: N. Pozza, 1976), 66 (entry no. 15), 67 (entry no. 16).

57. David Rosand and Michelangelo Muraro, *Titian and the Venetian Woodcut: A Loan Exhibition,* exh. cat. (Washington: The Foundation, 1976), 162, no. 28.

58. David Rosand, "Giorgione, Venice, and the Pastoral Vision," in Robert C. Cafritz, Lawrence Gowing, and David Rosand, *Places of Delight: The Pastoral Landscape,* exh. cat. (Washington: Phillips Collection, 1988), 53.

59. Bartsch (see note 13), 14: 245, no. 325.

On Dosso Dossi at Pesaro

Craig Hugh Smyth

Despite numerous advances in Dosso Dossi scholarship over the past several decades,[1] the extent to which problems of chronology continue is remarkable. For example, what is the date of the Getty *Allegory of Fortune*? Is this picture later than the Horne *Allegory of Music*, or earlier? And as for the Horne *Allegory of Music*, what, after all, is its date? So few of Dosso's works are datable by factual evidence that efforts to reconstruct their chronology continue to constitute an important part of Dosso scholarship, requiring the methods of the historian who is also connoisseur. Alessandro Ballarin's study of the early works of Dosso is an excellent example in point.[2]

Determining the chronology of Dosso's paintings is all the more demanding in that Dosso could work concurrently in more than one mode. Hence, differences among his paintings may not always and necessarily be indicative of differences in date. The propensity for painting in diverse modes, for changing expeditiously from one mode to another, came into clear view in Venetian painting with the early work of Giovanni Bellini.[3] An option from then on in Venetian painting, it is a development that was paralleled by a similar development in central Italy.

In this connection it may be useful to look at what remains of Dosso Dossi's work in the Villa Imperiale at Pesaro, because there one can see that Dosso used more than one mode at what was certainly one and the same time. Dosso's work in the villa is also worth noting because it is datable. It comes chronologically near the center of Dosso's maturity and at one of the turning points in his development.

My acquaintance with Dosso Dossi at Pesaro is due to my study of Agnolo Bronzino, who, as well as Dosso Dossi and Dosso's brother Battista, was among the painters who took part in decorating seven rooms in the Villa Imperiale at Pesaro, the property of Duke Francesco Maria of Urbino.[4] These seven rooms and an eighth room, not painted but panelled, constituted the private apartment of the duke and duchess.[5] Giorgio Vasari's life of Girolamo Genga, the duke's court architect for the villa (as well as a practicing painter), names Genga as in charge of the project to decorate these rooms.[6] Three surviving drawings by Genga for scenes on two of the ceilings confirm that Genga took an active role in their design.[7] In the same passage Vasari also gives the names of the painters who took part: Francesco Menzocchi, Raffaellino dal Colle, Camillo Mantovano—described as *"in far paesi e verdure rarissimo"*

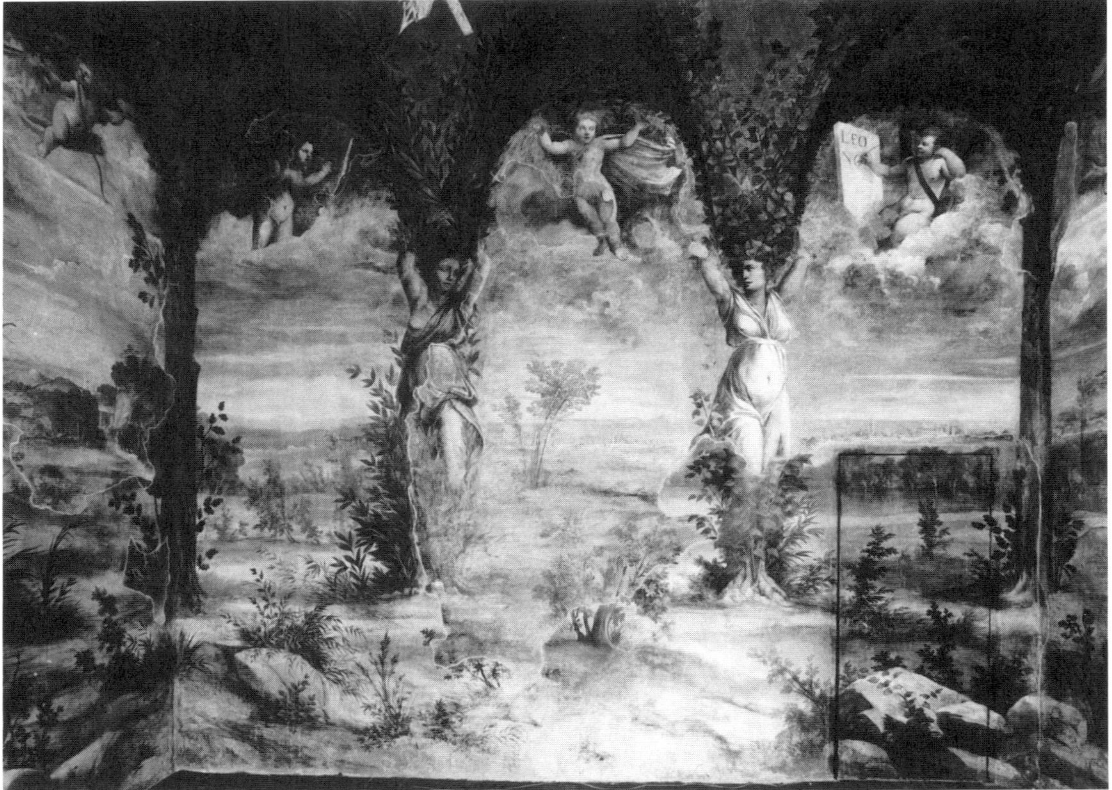

Fig. 1. Dosso Dossi and workshop
North wall
Pesaro, Villa Imperiale, Camera delle Cariatidi

(most rare in making landscapes and foliage)—as well as Bronzino and the Dossi.[8] Vasari, who had remarkably good sources of information about the decoration of the villa (as we shall see), says that the Dossi were assigned one room of their own to decorate and that their work there, having displeased, was destroyed. Nevertheless, scholars beginning with Henry Thode have long seen the existing decoration of the room now named the Camera delle Cariatidi as an invention of the Dossi (fig. 1),[9] even if no large amount of the execution can be said to show their own hands.[10] Vasari's story of the destruction has been thought, therefore, to be mistaken. The seeming contradiction between Vasari's account and the presence of the Dossi in the Camera delle Cariatidi can be explained, however, in the course of examining the Dossi's work in this room and in another as well. First, however, is the question of when the Dossi were at the Imperiale.

There exists a letter, dated 10 May 1530, from the duchess to the ducal agent in Venice that opens with these words: "Since we have made a beginning at having some rooms of ours here at the Imperiale painted and want them completed by the same master, who is Master Francesco from Forlì . . ."[11] The letter goes on to say that Master Francesco, namely Menzocchi, would not stay very willingly because of an obligation to finish works he had undertaken in Venice. The duchess asks the agent to intervene, so that Menzocchi "may stay here in our service for at least three months."[12]

The wording of the letter suggests Menzocchi had begun his work shortly before the date of the letter, but it does not say exactly when, nor does it enable us to deduce whether other painters were also working or had finished work in other rooms by the time the duchess wrote.[13] There has now come to be a consensus that the decorations were begun in 1530 or the year before;[14] this consensus is consonant with evidence cited below.

A recent examination of the archives of the confraternity at Borgo Sansepolcro, in which Raffaellino was an active, officeholding member, reveals that he would have been available for work at Pesaro during a one-year period from the autumn of 1529 to 11 November 1530 and during a two-year period from 1 May 1531 to the beginning of March 1533.[15] A letter written by Bronzino tells of his working with Raffaellino at Pesaro.[16]

According to Vasari, Bronzino went to the Villa Imperiale after the siege of Florence ended and the *accordo* was made (presumably the pact of August 12)[17]—that is to say, at least three months after the duchess wrote that Menzocchi's decoration of some rooms had begun. Bronzino must have stayed until some time after 2 April 1531, but very probably not later than 2 April 1532, because the inscription on his *Portrait of Guidobaldo,* the duke's son (Florence, Palazzo Pitti), puts the work on the portrait—or at least its completion—between these two dates.[18] To judge from Vasari's account, Bronzino was asked to paint the portrait soon after he arrived,[19] and as soon as the portrait was finished—following delays to await the armor to be worn in the portrait—he thereupon left for Florence (in response to much urging from Pontormo).[20] If Vasari is correct in adding that Bronzino would have done more work on the decorations had he not left when he did,[21] then not all seven rooms were finished at the time of his departure—that is to say, sometime after April 1531 and just possibly even as late as spring 1532. Much of Vasari's information about work at the villa would have come directly from Bronzino in 1533, when Vasari served as Bronzino's assistant at Florence,[22] and from Raffaellino dal Colle, whom Vasari called to be his assistant in Florence in 1536[23] and had with him as one of his assistants in Naples and at Rome in the mid-1540s.[24]

Henriette Mendelsohn proposed that the date of the Dossi's stay at Pesaro coincided with a gap in the documentation of their activity at Ferrara beginning 23 November 1532,[25] a gap of eight months that lasted until 21 August 1533.[26] I have pointed out elsewhere that there is an earlier gap in the documentation of the Dossi at Ferrara, from 4 December 1529 to 10 September 1530, which suits the circumstances.[27] The relevant data were only touched on there.[28] It is, therefore, worth examining in detail the evidence for the date of the Dossi's stay at Pesaro in 1530.

Turning first to the gap adduced by Mendelsohn and assuming, as one should, that the Dossi were not necessarily at Pesaro the whole time they were absent from the Ferrarese records and so might have been at Pesaro, despite winter weather, in only the earlier months of that absence—that is, in early 1533 rather than later—even then their work on the decorations would date approximately three years after work began. This is a long span of time for the decoration of seven rooms, five of them small,[29] given the number of painters involved and the expectation of the duchess in May 1530 that Menzocchi needed only three months to finish the rooms he had begun. One can imagine the impatience of the duke and duchess had prolongation of the work stretched to three years.[30]

On the other hand, the earlier gap in the documentation of the Dossi at Ferrara—from 4 December 1529 to 10 September 1530—is congruent both with data already cited and with key information in the rest of Vasari's account. In his life of Genga, Vasari states first that the villa was decorated by Menzocchi, Raffaellino, and Camillo Mantovano, and then adds in the same sentence that "among the others" the young Bronzino also worked there. It is in the next sentence that Vasari says that the Dossi, too, were brought to the villa and were assigned a room of their own, where their work proved unsatisfactory and was destroyed.[31] Elsewhere in the *Lives,* when telling of the Dossi's careers,[32] Vasari states clearly that the Dossi were called to Pesaro, especially to do landscapes, after work on the decorations had been begun, specifically stating that Menzocchi, Raffaellino, and others (he does not mention Bronzino) had made "many paintings" in the villa "much before" the Dossi arrived.[33] Thereupon, proceeding unamiably, he adds:

> Having arrived then at the Imperiale, Dosso and Battista, as is the custom of men made this way, disapproved of a large part of those things they saw and promised the duke that they wanted to make much better things, so that for this reason Genga, an acute man, seeing where the matter was likely to come out, gave them a room of their own to paint.[34]

After adding unfavorable words of his own about the Dossi, Vasari continues, "Then, when their work was uncovered, it was ridiculous in style, so that they departed in shame from the duke, who was compelled to destroy everything they had done and to have it repainted by others on the design of Genga."[35]

At the end of the passage recounting Genga's life, Vasari identifies those who did the repainting: "They [the Dossi] were assigned a room to paint, but because what they finished displeased the duke, it was destroyed and repainted by the above named."[36] Those "above named" were Menzocchi, Raffaellino, and Bronzino. This places the Dossi at Pesaro before Bronzino returned to Florence and Bronzino at Pesaro after they left. This, in turn, is in keeping with (a) Vasari's not having mentioned Bronzino as one of the painters who worked at the villa before the Dossi's arrival, (b) the date in early September 1530 when the Dossi reappear in the Ferrarese records, (c) the date Vasari gives for Bronzino's departure from Florence for Pesaro sometime after mid-August 1530 (the dates preclude the possibility that Bronzino and the Dossi overlapped), (d) Bronzino's presence at Pesaro well into 1531, as attested by his *Portrait of Guidobaldo*, and (e) visual evidence, described below, of Bronzino's share in continuing one part of the Dossi's work at the villa. In early 1533, however, during the later gap in the Ferrarese records, Bronzino was *not* available at Pesaro to share in the repainting. On 20 March 1533 he is documented at work in Florence on scenery for a comedy, with Vasari himself serving as his assistant.[37] It must have been at this point, just after the event, that Vasari heard most vividly about what went on at the Villa Imperiale, directly from Bronzino.

The information that we have places the Dossi at the Villa Imperiale in 1530. Without further documentation, however, we cannot know when between December 1529 and September 1530 the Dossi arrived. If they arrived late in May or early in June, a good season for this kind of work, the decoration of at least some of the rooms would have been underway, as we know from the letter of the duchess, and thus available to the Dossi for their criticism. It seems likely enough from the letter that some rooms had no decoration as yet, allowing the Dossi space of their own.[38] It is possible that they may have arrived somewhat earlier. In either case, three or more months would remain before the reappearance of the Dossi's names at Ferrara, a reasonable amount of time for what they appear to have painted. Now let us turn to a consideration of exactly what the Dossi did in the villa as a means of establishing one of the all-too-few guideposts to the chronology of their art.

Despite his sources, Vasari's account of what the Dossi did at the Villa Imperiale is inexact and insufficient. As explained below, there is reason to conclude that in at least two rooms the Dossi contributed work that was not destroyed and was continued by others. Any full destruction of their work must have occurred in still another room.[39] To judge by the long disapproving comment that Vasari added to his account (displaying something like disaffection of his own for the Dossi),[40] he evidently relished the episode of the destruction as he told it and could have stressed it in preference to anything else he may have been told about the Dossi's work at the villa. He did not mention at all the decoration in the room known now as the Camera delle Cariatidi, where scholars agree that the Dossi had much responsibility for the design and started to execute it. But neither did he mention the contributions of Raffaellino, Menzocchi, or Genga in *any* of the villa's rooms. In fact, he recorded no specific information about the work of the participants except, very sketchily, Bronzino's.[41] Wolfgang Kallab thought that Vasari must have failed to visit the Imperiale and see the decorations for himself when, many years later, he passed through the town of Pesaro, three miles away.[42]

On the basis of sixteenth- and seventeenth-century documents, Sabine Eiche has shown that the Camera delle Cariatidi was the *prima camera* (see fig. 1)—the room next to, and opening into, the duke's bedroom—and that in the sequence of rooms it came after the duke's *anticamera* (functioning also as a *sala*), known now as the Sala del Giuramento.[43] Mezzetti's words exemplify the praise that has been bestowed on the originality of the *prima camera*'s decoration: "Giving proof once more of his extraordinary capacity to project himself into the future, Dosso not only anticipates [...] the effects of illusionistic landscape painting, but pushes them to limits that would rarely be met even in later times."[44]

In each of the seven rooms of the apartment, the decorations painted on the walls incorporate distant landscapes; these are wide views in some cases, narrow views in others.[45] Doubtless this was planned by Genga with his patrons. Except in the *prima camera*, the landscapes are seen through illusionistic architecture. One can expect that Genga, both architect and painter, devised the architectural settings. In rooms that are vaulted, the decorative scheme has classical motifs in the lower part of the vaulting and a scene from the duke's career in the center of the vault.[46]

Vasari says the Dossi were called to the Imperiale "especially to do landscapes."[47] His wording sounds in keeping with the expectation that they would paint landscapes in settings determined for them, doubtless on Genga's designs—settings they may not have found congenial, given Vasari's report of their views about the decoration they found on arrival. The *prima camera* has the same scheme for the vault as other rooms, and landscape is seen through structure. But here illusionistic architecture is exchanged for structure of a different kind, made of caryatids growing like plants, with tree trunks at the room's corners and, above, garlands standing for ribs in the vault. Landscape is everywhere. Landscape was certainly the main task. The setting is an extraordinarily inventive adaptation of Genga's basic scheme,[48] and it is clear that much of the credit for the *adaptation* must go to Dosso Dossi or perhaps to both Dossi. In either case, Battista's later use of the same motif, caryatids and landscape, in tapestries testifies that the motif was originated by one or both of them.[49]

Giuseppe Marchini and Sydney Freedberg have suggested that the sense of space in the wall decoration of the *prima camera* could have been inspired by Genga and that something of the spatial effect was indeed "dictated" by him.[50] Although the vault decoration was described in 1844 as "very deteriorated"[51] and was restored by a local painter, Giuseppe Gennari, between 1880 and 1882,[52] scholars have seen the hands of other artists, in addition to those of the Dossi, in the original execution of the vault area.[53] Hence, even though the Dossi contributed greatly to the design of this room, it can appropriately be considered a collaboration, not a room of the Dossi's own—reason, therefore, why Vasari does not mention the Dossi's part in decorating the room any more than he is specific about Menzocchi's, Raffaellino's, or Genga's shares anywhere in the apartment and why Vasari's story of the destruction of the Dossi's work in a room of their own does not apply to the *prima camera.* The more-or-less prevailing view—that although the Dossi were occupied in painting the decoration of the *prima camera* at the beginning, the work was finished by others,[54] presumably after they left—only strengthens its status as a collaboration.

The caryatids have been aptly characterized as belonging to Dosso's classicizing mode under the influence of Rome,[55] having a notable "plastic force and a vigorous sense of organic growth"[56] and whose "deeper content is one of romantic fantasy."[57] This is the mode that has been seen as best exemplified elsewhere by Dosso's *Apollo* (Rome, Galleria Borghese).[58] One caryatid at the right of the north wall (the wall opposite the window wall) stands out as an excellent representative of this mode and as work most likely to be by Dosso's hand (fig. 2)—in particular, the head, arms, and torso, down as far as the hips. The figure was executed on a separate, rectangular area of plaster a little wider than the figure and including some of the sky on each side.[59] It seems that this caryatid could have served as a model to set a standard for the others, most of which have been judged not to be from Dosso's hand.[60]

In the room next to the *prima camera,* known as the Camera dei Semibusti (fig. 3)—recently shown by Eiche to have been the bedchamber of the duke[61]—the design of the figures on the spandrels of the vault is almost always attributed to Bronzino (an attribution first suggested by Thode); indeed, Bronzino is usually given the execution of at least one of the figures.[62] These attributions stem from Vasari's two references to Bronzino at the villa. One says that "having done a very beautiful nude cupid in the *peduccio* of a vault at the Imperiale and the cartoons for the others," Bronzino was ordered by Prince Guidobaldo, who had recognized his talent, to paint the prince's portrait;[63] Vasari's second reference says only that Bronzino did "some figures in oil in the *peduccio* of a vault."[64] (*Peduccio* normally is taken to mean a support, footing, or supporting bracket of a vault.[65])

In the duke's bedchamber there is one large nude Cupid in the spandrel of the vault (figs. 3 and 4), and it is in oil. It is consistently attributed to Bronzino. Nevertheless, it has never been possible for me to see Bronzino in this Cupid, especially because of its high, broad forehead and short face—its features look somewhat compressed—not to mention that there are no other putti in the room, as Vasari's words imply there should be. In my view, Bronzino's "cupid" and "the others" can be found in the duke's *anticamera,* while Vasari's two mentions of Bronzino's work refer not to one room but to two rooms: the duke's *anticamera* and the duke's bedchamber. Parts of the bedchamber (although not the Cupid) do indeed declare Bronzino to be their author, *continuing* work of the Dossi, as pointed out below.[66]

It is my conviction that the Cupid in the duke's bedchamber was painted by the Dossi, perhaps by Battista alone, judging from a comparison with the putti in the *Nativity in the Presence of Two Gentlemen* in the Galleria Estense,

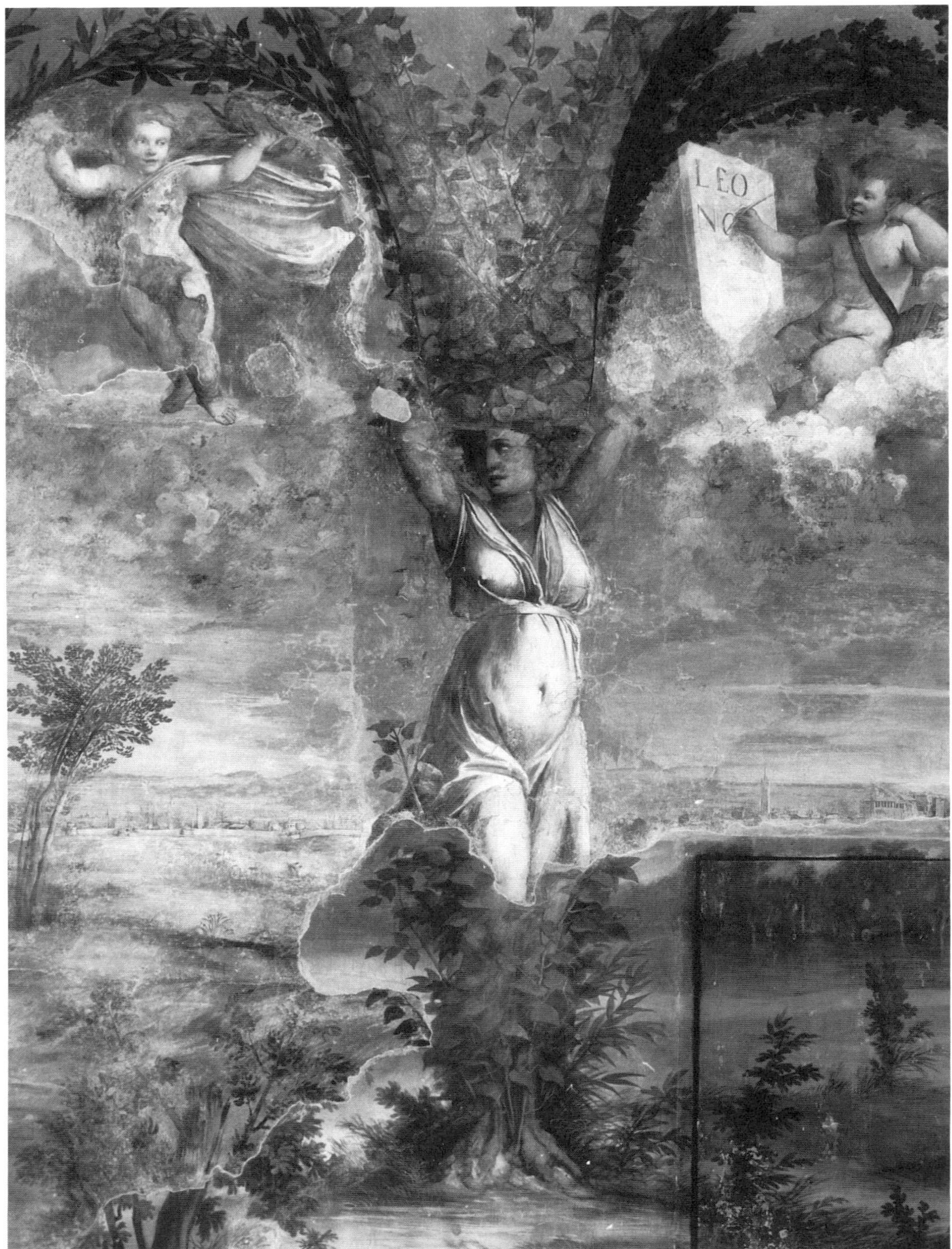

Fig. 2. Dosso Dossi and workshop
Caryatid and putti on the north wall
Pesaro, Villa Imperiale, Camera delle Cariatidi

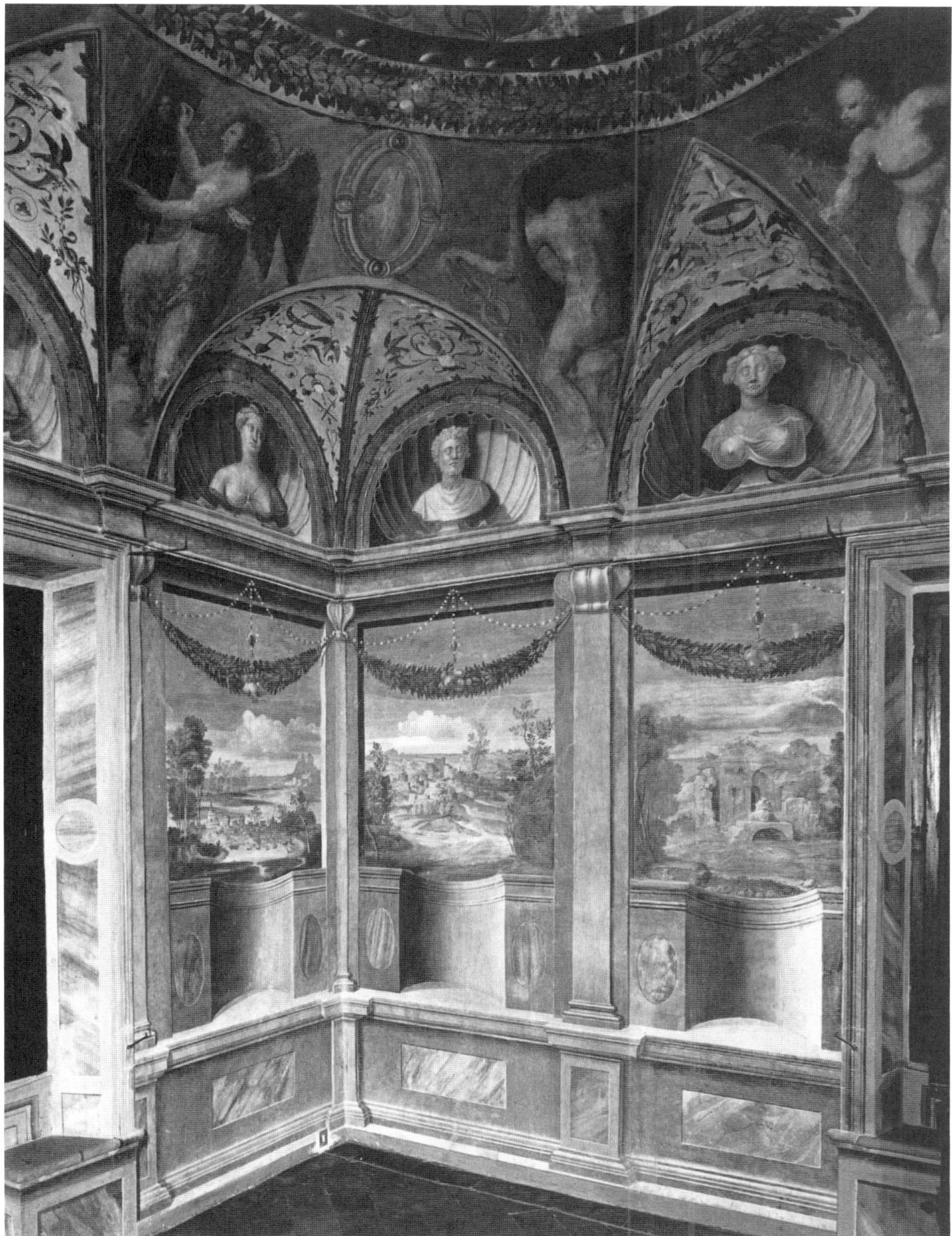

Fig. 3. Southeast corner with Painting, Mercury, and Cupid in the spandrels
Pesaro, Villa Imperiale, Camera dei Semibusti

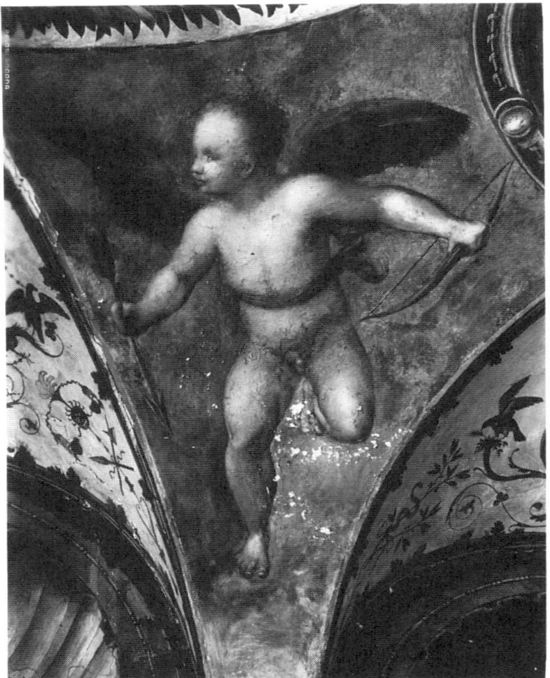

Fig. 4. Battista Dossi
Cupid (before restoration)
Pesaro, Villa Imperiale, Camera dei Semibusti

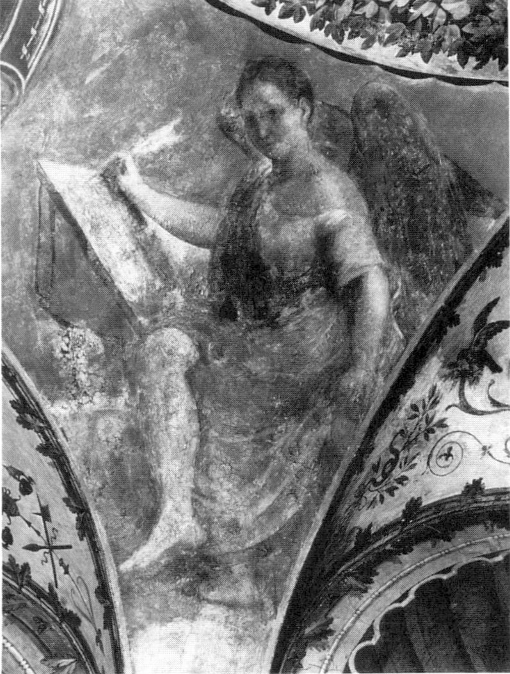

Fig. 5. Dosso Dossi
Architecture (before restoration)
Pesaro, Villa Imperiale, Camera dei Semibusti

Modena (p. 268), which is documented as Battista's and is dated to 1534–1536.[67] Next to the Cupid is a figure that clearly announces itself as theirs, one painted most likely by Dosso himself (fig. 5).[68] This second figure, costumed in an intense yet delicate blue, is the personification of an art, like the three other figures in corresponding positions on the vault, and probably represents Architecture.[69] This type of figure—distinguished especially by its fleshiness, singularly narrow shoulder, and the stubbiness of the upper part of the crossed leg—is the type evident in the Horne *Allegory of Music* (Florence, Museo del Fondazione Horne; p. 231), for which Roberto Longhi used the term *"deformazione."*[70] It belongs to what Freedberg has called the mode of Dosso that is "unclassical in essence."[71] Obviously this is not the classicizing mode of the caryatids.

It appears clear, then, that in the year 1530 the Dossi—or better, Dosso—painted in two very different modes in two adjacent rooms during one and the same short period of time.

The duke's bedchamber does not qualify as the room given to the Dossi for their own any better than does the *prima camera*. The scheme of the vault decoration conforms to the scheme in other rooms, and two drawings for the scene in the center of the vault are convincingly attributed to Genga.[72] This scene, depicting the coronation of Emperor Charles V at Bologna—an event in which Duke Francesco Maria took part—was described in 1844 as "worn and hardly recognizable."[73] In 1888 Thode reported it as much modified by the restorer Gennari.[74] Yet the coloring and some figures in the crowd are rather reminiscent of the Dossi. It is of much interest that Bernard Berenson attributed the coronation "and other scenes" in this room to Girolamo da Carpi "(with Dosso),"[75] thus introducing not only Girolamo's name (on no known external evidence) but also the name of Dosso (which was not, however, taken up by other observers, strange to say).[76]

It does seem possible that the Dossi were originally responsible for executing the coronation scene from Genga's design. That coronation took place on 24 February 1530, placing the execution of the scene thereafter. The likely months of 1530 for the Dossi's stay at the Imperiale locate them there when this scene could have been painted.[77]

Did the Dossi do more in this room? It seems to me that one of the antique busts painted in the lunettes of the vault to imitate sculpture might have been executed by one of the Dossi (perhaps again as a model?),[78] but in the spandrels, only the Cupid and the figure of Architecture can be seen as clearly theirs. While some of the other spandrel figures look as if they could well be based on the Dossi's designs, others do not—the figure of Victory, for example, appears more likely to be Raffaellino dal Colle's.[79]

At least one spandrel figure, that of Mercury (see fig. 3), has always had for me the mark of Bronzino.[80] Possibly it is an adaptation by him of a Dossi design,[81] but the pure, taut contours and surfaces, the shaping of shoulders and neck, and the lost profile put this Mercury close, for example, to Bronzino's drawing for the male nude who stands with his back to the viewer in the foreground of his *Crossing of the Red Sea* (Florence, Palazzo Vecchio).[82] Evidence that the Mercury is largely Bronzino's design, even if something of an adaptation, are the stability of the figure's adjustment to the area of the spandrel and the way the figure preserves the integrity of the picture plane. The Mercury looks toward the elegant secular style of Bronzino's maturity. In addition to the Mercury, a few other parts of the vault may be Bronzino's as well.[83]

It seems likely that the Dossi were involved from the beginning of the work in the duke's bedchamber and that it was finished by the others. (It is worth noting that here and elsewhere in the apartment the participants were evidently given the chance to make their own contribution to the style of the figures and even portions of the decoration, with the result that in much of the apartment the effect must have been rather like exhibitions of individual works of individual artists within an established scheme.) It also appears likely that the Dossi's participation both here and in the *prima camera* was interrupted by their departure from the villa, which made it necessary for the others to finish in their stead.[84]

A tantalizing question remains: which could be the room that Vasari says was assigned to the Dossi as their own, the room where, as he tells it, the duke "was compelled to destroy everything they had done," after which "he had it repainted by others on the design of Genga"?[85] My thought is that this room is likely to be the large room known now as the Sala Grande (fig. 6). Eiche has shown that this was the Sala Comune of the apartment, entered from both the duke's series of rooms and the duchess's two rooms (its ceiling was decorated with the initials of both),[86] yet it also has a separate entrance from the courtyard, suggesting that it could have served on occasion for receiving guests or as something of an audience chamber.

There appear to be no traces of the Dossi here. But it was in this room, in the context of its stately classicizing design, that Bronzino made his principal contribution to the decoration of the villa with two allegorical figures that are now recognized as significant examples of his art, especially because they show him beginning to move toward the mid-century central Italian *maniera*.[87] As soon as the layout of the apartment was decided, the Sala Comune had an importance that suited it for decoration by an artist of such high standing as Dosso's. By the same token, it was this room where the more eccentric aspects of the Dossi's art could have been regarded by the duke as out of place: witness the classicizing stateliness and dignity of the existing decoration.

Nevertheless, the duke clearly did not disapprove of the Dossi for the decoration of his own bedchamber and *prima camera*. What they began in those rooms, partly in the deformed mode, the duke retained and had other painters continue. If the Dossi's work was destroyed because the duke found it inappropriate for the most nearly public room of his private apartment, this could be one reason why the decorations that the Dossi began the next

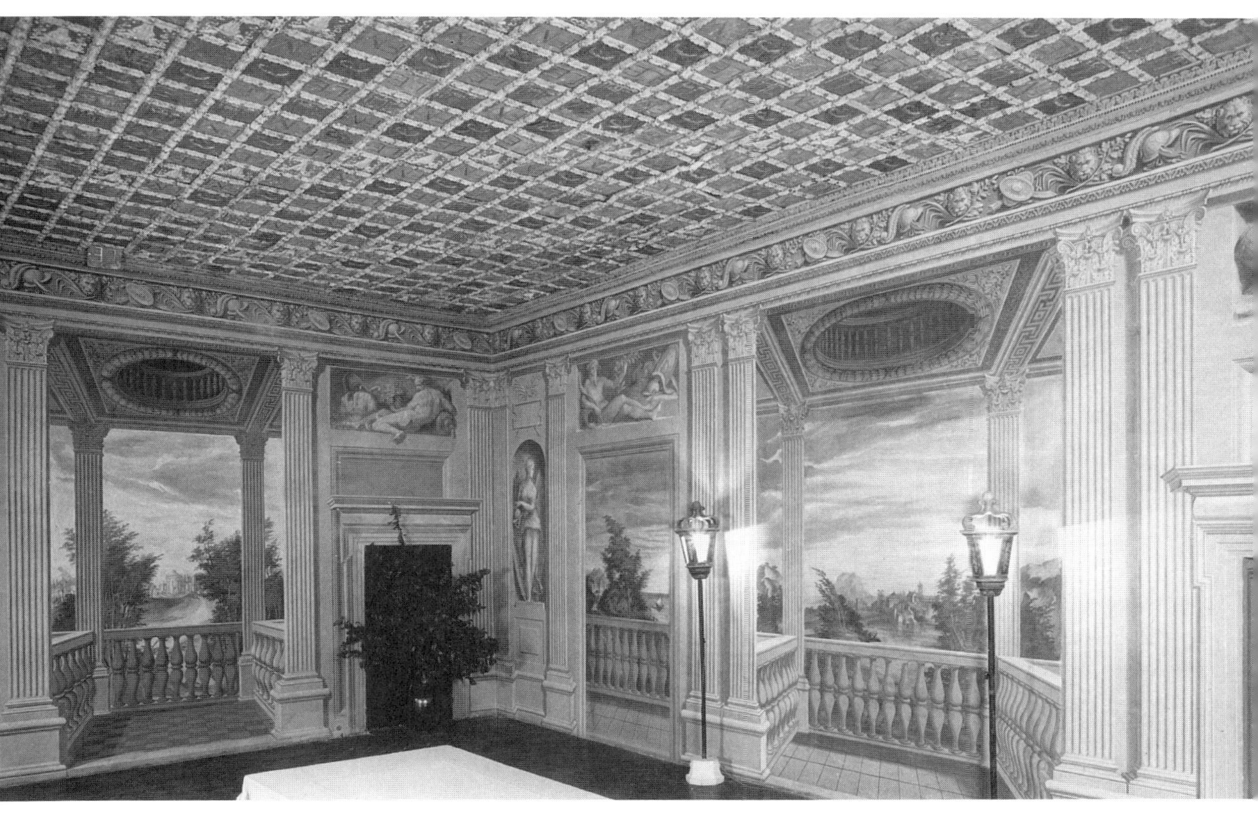

Fig. 6. South wall
Pesaro, Villa Imperiale, Sala Grande

year in the public rooms of the Castello del Buonconsiglio at Trent do not anywhere show the deformed mode.[88] The Trent decorations are seen as marking the beginning of a new period in the Dossi's work. The experience at Pesaro could have helped bring about what is recognized as an important turning point in their careers.

Notes

I want to record my profound thanks to Count and Countess Castelbarco Albani for permission long ago to study the decorations at the Villa Imperiale for extensive periods of time on numerous occasions. For the invitation that has resulted in this paper, I am very grateful to Salvatore Settis and his staff at the Getty Research Institute. I owe thanks for help in checking several references to Sabine Eiche, Valerie Lieberman, Henry Millon, and T. Barton Thurber, and for some helpful editorial suggestions to Andrew Morrogh. Not least, I am much indebted to Barbara F. Schuierer for her excellence in putting the manuscript into the computer and to Steven F. Ostrow, Rebecca Frazier, and Michelle Bonnice for their thoughtful editing.

1. See, for example, Amalia Mezzetti, *Il Dosso e Battista ferraresi* (Milan: Silvana, 1965); Felton Gibbons, *Dosso and Battista Dossi: Court Painters at Ferrara* (Princeton: Princeton Univ. Press, 1968); and Alessandro Ballarin, *Dosso Dossi: La pittura a Ferrara negli anni del Ducato di Alfonso I,* 2 vols. (Cittadella: Bertoncello Artigrafiche, 1994–1995).

2. Alessandro Ballarin, "Osservazioni sul percorso del Dosso," in Ballarin, ibid., 1: 25–50.

3. Craig Hugh Smyth, "Venice and the Emergence of the High Renaissance in Florence: Observations and Questions," in Sergio Bertelli, Nicolai Rubenstein, and Craig Hugh Smyth, eds., *Florence and Venice: Comparisons and Relations,* vol. 1, *Quattrocento* (Florence: La Nuova Italia, 1979), 229, 244 n. 164 (in the context of 219–220 on Bellini), with reference also to Giles Robertson, *Giovanni Bellini* (Oxford: Clarendon Press, 1968), 35–36, and Norbert Huse, *Studien zu Giovanni Bellini* (Berlin: Walter de Gruyter, 1972), 33–37.

4. To distinguish Bronzino's work at the Imperiale from that of the other painters engaged in the decoration was one purpose of my dissertation on Bronzino, written over forty years ago; this meant taking into consideration the shares of the other painters, including the Dossi. Except to those who study Bronzino, the results are unfamiliar. See Craig Hugh Smyth, *Bronzino Studies* (Ann Arbor: University Microfilms, 1955), esp. 135–86. In addition to what appears in the present essay, the results of my study, insofar as they are pertinent, are to be incorporated into a publication by Sabine Eiche. Conclusions in my dissertation concerning the Dossi's share in the decorations were taken into account approvingly by Mezzetti (see note 1), 32–33, 108 (entry no. 147), and cited by Gibbons (see note 1), 79, but they were not described by either since I was to present them in a book on the decorations of the Imperiale, which was then in preparation. Because of other obligations, to my regret the book was never completed for publication. In this essay, my previous conclusions regarding dating and Vasari's account of the Dossi at the Imperiale have been augmented. I have written

more about Bronzino at Pesaro in Craig Hugh Smyth, *Bronzino as Draughtsman: An Introduction* (Locust Valley, N.Y.: J. J. Augustin, for the Institute of Fine Arts, New York University, 1971), 80–86 (appendix 1); see also note 87 below. Another aspect of the contribution to the Imperiale made by Girolamo Genga, who figures in this essay, is stressed in Craig Hugh Smyth, "The Sunken Courts of the Villa Giulia and the Villa Imperiale," in Lucy Freeman Sandler, ed., *Essays in Memory of Karl Lehmann* (New York: Institute of Fine Arts, New York University, 1964), 304–13.

5. For the arrangement of the apartment, see Sabine Eiche, "Prologue to the Villa Imperiale Frescoes," *Notizie da Palazzo Albani* 20 (1991): 99–119. This article is invaluable for documentation, the identification of the rooms, the condition and restoration of the murals, and related matters.

6. Giorgio Vasari, *Le vite de' più eccellenti pittori, scultori ed architettori,* ed. Gaetano Milanesi, 9 vols. (Florence: Sansoni, 1906), 6: 318.

7. Eiche (see note 5), 104, 107, figs. 2, 8, 9.

8. Vasari (see note 6), 6: 318–19.

9. Henry Thode, "Ein fürstlicher Sommeraufenthalt in der Zeit der Hochrenaissance: Die Villa Monte Imperiale bei Pesaro," *Jahrbuch der königlich preußischen Kunstsammlungen* 9 (1888): 161–84, esp. 176ff. Scholars following Thode include, for example, Bernhard Patzak, *Die Villa Imperiale in Pesaro* (Leipzig: Klinkhardt & Biermann, 1908), 285ff., 320ff. (see also pp. 52ff. on the vicissitudes of the villa, including the whitewashing of decorations in the eighteenth century); Henriette Mendelsohn, *Das Werk der Dossi* (Munich: Georg Müller & Eugen Rentsch, 1914), 178ff., esp. 181ff.; Adolfo Venturi, *Storia dell'arte italiana,* vol. 9, *La pittura del Cinquecento* (Milan: Hoepli, 1932), pt. 5: 666–69, esp. 668 n. 1, which summarizes previous views concerning the attribution of the decorations in this and other rooms; Laura Filippini Baldani, "Francesco Menzocchi pittore forlivese e la Villa Imperiale a Pesaro, III: La Villa Imperiale di Pesaro," *Melozzo da Forlì* 16, no. 3 (1938): 136–45; Mezzetti (see note 1), 32–35; Gibbons (see note 1), 76–85.

10. Mezzetti (see note 1), 54 n. 102; Gibbons (see note 1), 79, 83–84; also Smyth, 1955 (see note 4), 155 n. 1.

11. Georg Gronau, *Documenti artistici urbinati* (Florence: Sansoni, 1936), 123 (doc. 127); republished in Eiche (see note 5), 118 (doc. 1).

12. Ibid.

13. As affirmed also by Eiche (see note 5), 118.

14. Ballarin (see note 1), 1: 350 (entry no. 458); Eiche (see note 5), 119.

15. David Franklin, "Raffaellino dal Colle: Painting and Patronage in Sansepolcro during the First Half of the Sixteenth Century," *Studi di storia dell'arte* 1 (1990): 159 (appendix B). Since Borgo Sansepolcro is not a great distance from Pesaro, it seems possible that Raffaellino could have been available for work at Pesaro during some of the time when he had obligations in Sansepolcro (as underlined by T. Barton Thurber in a brief discussion we had on this reference).

16. The letter is from Bronzino to Duke Cosimo in 1548; see Giovanni Gaye, ed., *Carteggio inedito d'artisti dei secoli XIV, XV, XVI,* 3 vols. (Florence: Presso Giuseppe Molini, 1840), 2: 368.

17. Vasari (see note 6), 7: 594.

18. Carl Justi, "Die Bildnisse des Kardinals Hippolyt von Medici in Florenz," *Zeitschrift für Bildende Kunst,* new ser., 8 (1897): 34–40; Arthur McComb, *Agnolo Bronzino: His Life and Works* (Cambridge, Mass.: Harvard Univ. Press, 1928), 57–58; Edi Baccheschi, *L'opera completa del Bronzino* (Milan: Rizzoli, 1973), 88.

19. Vasari (see note 6), 8: 276.

20. Vasari (see note 6), 6: 276.

21. Vasari (see note 6), 7: 595.

22. Giorgio Vasari, *Il libro delle ricordanze di Giorgio Vasari,* ed. Alessandro del Vita (Rome: Istituto d'Archeologia e Storia dell'Arte, 1938), 20, brought into the present context in Smyth, 1955 (see note 4), 129.

23. Vasari (see note 6), 6: 252–53.

24. Vasari (see note 6), 6: 228–29.

25. Mendelsohn (see note 9), 14, 178–83.

26. Mendelsohn (see note 9), 14, 178–83, gives the end date of this gap as 20 December 1533, but Mezzetti (see note 1), 64, showed that the gap extends only to 21 August 1533; see also Alessandra Pattanaro, ed., "Regesto della pittura a Ferrara (1497–1548)," in Ballarin (see note 1), 1: 157.

27. Smyth, 1955 (see note 4), 134.

28. The proposal convinced Amalia Mezzetti and became a strong possibility for Felton Gibbons. See Mezzetti (see note 1), 33, 64; Gibbons (see note 1), 79 n. 106. It was also accepted by Giuseppe Marchini, ed., *La Villa Imperiale di Pesaro* (Milan: Associazione fra le Casse di Risparmio Italiane, [1968?]), 21.

29. A plan of the apartment with the rooms labeled is given by Eiche (see note 5), 20.

30. In 1534 colors and gold were needed at the villa *"depingere alchune camere"* (for the painting of some rooms) by a certain recently arrived Fra Gregorio, but this, as Eiche says, does not mean work was still continuing on the mural decorations of the apartment, where there is no evidence of gold; see Eiche (see note 5), 119 (doc. 2). Although Eiche suggests that perhaps the document refers to work that was to have been done on ceiling ornaments (those in the Sala Comune or the duchess's *anticamera*), it might refer to decorative work in rooms of the remarkable new structure that Genga was then adding to the old building. Its construction was begun perhaps by 1528, but apparently began going forward mainly in 1531; see Smyth, 1964 (see note 4), 306 n. 11. For illustrations of the old and new parts of the Imperiale, see Marchini (see note 28), figs. 16, 17; pls. XXIV, XXIII.

31. Vasari (see note 6), 6: 318–19.

32. Vasari (see note 6), 5: 99–100.

33. Vasari (see note 6), 5: 99. Vasari's words are *"Francesco di Mirozzo da Forlì, Raffaello dal Colle del Borgo a Sansepolcro, e molti altri."* No other names have ever emerged in connection with the decoration of the apartment besides those listed by Vasari in his brief mentions of the work. His words here could be referring to anonymous assistants; certainly it is likely enough that there were such assistants, as past efforts to attribute various parts of the decoration have tended to assume.

34. Vasari (see note 6), 5: 99: *"Arrivati, dunque, il Dosso e Battista all'Imperiale, come è usanza di certi uomini così fatti, biasimarono la maggior parte di quelle cose*

che videro, e promessero a quel signore di voler essi fare cose molto migliori; perchè il Genga, che era persona accorta, vedendo dove la cosa doveva riuscire, diede loro a dipignere una camera da per loro."

35. Vasari (see note 6), 5: 100: *"Scopertasi dunque l'opera dei Dossi, ella fu di maniera ridicola, che si partirono con vergogna da quel signore; il quale fu forzato a buttar in terra tutto quello che avevano lavorato, e farlo da altri ridipignere con il disegno del Genga."*

36. Vasari (see note 6), 6: 319: *"fu allogata loro una stanza a dipignere; ma perchè finita che l'ebbero non piacque al duca, fu gittata a terra e fatta rifare dalli sopranominati."*

37. Vasari (see note 22), 20.

38. As mentioned in note 77, a letter from Genga of the same date as the duchess's letter refers to materials that could well have been needed specifically for starting the decoration in oil of one room where Dosso clearly did work, and where some evidence suggests that the participation of the Dossi dates from a time near the start of the decorating there (see below). If Genga's letter can be taken to refer to work in this room, it could indicate the Dossi's presence at the Imperiale at the beginning of May 1530.

39. As suggested by Mendelsohn (see note 9), 183.

40. Vasari (see note 6), 5: 99–100.

41. See notes 63 and 64. It is always assumed that Vasari was referring to just one place in the villa where Bronzino worked. Instead, it appears to me that he was referring to two places, as explained in note 66. Vasari did not, however, refer specifically to Bronzino's principal contribution to the decorations at the Imperiale, long overlooked (and cited below).

42. Wolfgang Kallab, *Vasaristudien* (Vienna: Karl Graeser, 1908), 386–87. Vasari visited the town of Pesaro in 1566, before finishing the second edition of the *Lives*, and saw monuments in the town itself. It is not recorded that he visited the villa.

43. Eiche (see note 5), 116–17.

44. Mezzetti (see note 1), 33: *"Dando prova ancora una volta delle sue straordinarie capacità di proiettarsi nel futuro, il Dosso non soltanto anticipa nella stanza dell'Imperiale, come già notarono il Thode (1888), la Mendelsohn (1914) e il Morassi (1929) gli effetti della pittura illusionistica di paesaggio, ma li spinge a limiti che raramente saranno raggiunti anche nei tempi successivi."* For illustrations, see especially Mezzetti (see note 1), figs. 40, 41a, 41b; Gibbons (see note 1), figs. 183–88; Marchini (see note 28), pls. V, VII–IX; Ballarin (see note 1), 2: figs. 792–94.

45. For illustrations, see especially Patzak (see note 9); Marchini (see note 28), pls. II, IV, X, XII, XIV, XV, XVIII, XXII; Eiche (see note 5), figs. 1, 6, 10–14, 16.

46. For succinct characterizations of the scheme in its variations from room to room, see Eiche (see note 5), 101ff.

47. Vasari (see note 6), 5: 99: *"massimamente per far paesi."*

48. For its character see, for example, Mezzetti (see note 1), 33–35; Gibbons (see note 1), 80–81; and Marchini (see note 28), 18. For an earlier bibliography on the decoration of this room, see note 9.

49. See Mezzetti (see note 1), 33–35, figs. 84a, 84b; Gibbons (see note 1), 82, figs. 234, 235. Mezzetti and Gibbons review the sources that have been adduced for this

invention, including the vault of Santa Costanza in Rome, suggested first by Patzak (see note 9), 300, fig. 212.

50. Marchini (see note 28), 18; and Sydney J. Freedberg, *Painting in Italy, 1500 to 1600* (Harmondsworth, Middlesex: Penguin, 1970), 211.

51. Pompeo Mancini, *L'Imperiale* (Pesaro: Esercitazioni dell'Accademia Agraria di Pesaro, 1844), 47–48, as reported in Eiche (see note 5), 104–5. Throughout her discussion of the condition of the decoration in the seven rooms, Eiche (100) stresses the importance of Mancini's "thorough and systematic report" about the rooms (as presented in Mancini, 41–61) as well as subsequent descriptions by others dating from 1881, 1888, 1905, and 1908.

52. Eiche (see note 5), 100. Eiche also refers throughout to what is known of Gennari's intervention in each room. For notes on the condition of the decorations in the *prima camera,* see Eiche (see note 5), 104–5, and Gibbons (see note 1), 81–82.

53. Laura Filippini Baldani, "Francesco Menzocchi pittore forlivese e la Villa Imperiale a Pesaro. La Camera degli Amorini," *Melozzo da Forlì* 16, no. 5 (1938): 253; Gibbons (see note 1), 84–85; Marchini (see note 28), 18. It is entirely likely that the Dossi had assistants with them at the Imperiale, given that in September and October 1530, just after their stay in Pesaro, they had seven assistants with them at Ferrara for *"depingere la navesella del giardinecto de castello"* (painting the boat in the castle garden); see Pattanaro (see note 26), 1: 152.

54. Patzak (see note 9), 285ff.; Mendelsohn (see note 9), 178ff.; Baldani (see note 53), 252ff.; Smyth, 1955 (see note 4), 155 n. 1; Mezzetti (see note 1), 54 n. 102; Gibbons (see note 1), 83; Marchini (see note 28), 18. Mindful of Vasari's account, Patzak and Baldani thought that here some *part* of the Dossi's work may have been destroyed.

55. Freedberg (see note 50), 211.

56. Gibbons (see note 1), 82.

57. Freedberg (see note 50), 211.

58. Freedberg (see note 50), 210. See also, for example, Mezzetti (see note 1), 38, 109–10 (entry no. 153), fig. 57. For a bibliography, see Ballarin (see note 1), 1: 343–44 (entry no. 442).

59. Baldani (see note 53), 255, singled out the head of this caryatid as Dosso's. Attribution of the major portions of the figure to Dosso as stated above is given in Smyth, 1955 (see note 4), 155 (where it is noted that there is a division in the plaster, just below the lunettes at the level of the foot of the spandrels, all around the room). See the attributions to Dosso in Gibbons (see note 1), 83. Mezzetti (see note 1), fig. 41a, chose this caryatid as the one to illustrate; see also Marchini (see note 28), fig. 1 (in color).

60. See note 54.

61. Eiche (see note 5), 116–17.

62. Marchini (see note 28), pls. X, XI, as well as fig. 18 (the Cupid in color). See also Patzak (see note 9), figs. 217–22.

Thode (see note 9), 178–79, considered Bronzino responsible for the design of the figures in the vault and the busts in the lunettes, but found it difficult to distinguish how much Bronzino himself executed. Patzak (see note 9) limited Bronzino's own execution to the figure of the Cupid (see below) and identified Genga and Raffaellino as the executants of the other figures on Bronzino's designs. Thereafter writers followed Patzak more or less closely—as described in Smyth, 1955 (see note 4), 138 n. 1—with Baldani (see note 53), 252, giving four other figures besides the Cupid to Bronzino (including the figure of Architecture, discussed below) and two figures to Raffaellino (including the figure of Victory, cited below). In his monograph on Bronzino, McComb (see note 18), 5–6, 77, saw the design of the spandrel figures as "most likely... Bronzino's, the execution Raffaelo dal Colle's."

63. Vasari (see note 6), 6: 276: *"però che avendo fatto nel peduccio d'una volta all'Imperiale un Cupido ignudo molto bello, ed i cartoni per gli altri, ordinò il prencipe Guidobaldo, conosciuta la virtù di quel giovane, d'essere ritratto da lui."*

64. Vasari (see note 6), 7: 595: *"alcune figure a olio ne' peducci d'una volta."*

65. As confirmed by Richard Krautheimer, when he defined it for me, and by the entry in Barbara Reynolds, gen. ed., *The Cambridge Italian Dictionary,* 2 vols. (Cambridge: Cambridge Univ. Press, 1962), 1: 552. Unfortunately, the *Vocabulario degli accademici della crusca* (1611; reprint, Florence: LICOSA, 1974) does not show whether the precise meaning might have been different in the sixteenth century, because its example is this same passage from Vasari.

66. The attribution of the Cupid in the duke's bedchamber to Bronzino is rejected in Smyth, 1955 (see note 4), 139, 145. For my attribution to Bronzino of at least one and perhaps two putti among other putti in the duke's *anticamera* (the Sala del Giuramento) and for the proposal that Bronzino could have designed some of the others that still remain from the original decoration, see Smyth, 1955 (see note 4), 140–44.

The two putti that I connect to Bronzino are on the east wall of the *anticamera,* one at the right of the door leading into the *prima camera,* the other (more striking) at the far left. They are in what might be referred to as the footing or support of the vault, being high on the wall just under where the vault begins. Neither is in oil. If one reads putto for "cupid," Vasari's reference to "a very beautiful nude Cupid in the *peduccio* of a vault at the Imperiale" and "the others" (see note 63)—not said by Vasari to be in oil—could apply to one of these putti (most likely, I think now, the one at the far left).

In the duke's bedchamber, however, at least one and probably two among the figures in oil on the spandrels have marks of Bronzino, as pointed out in Smyth, 1955 (see note 4), 145–46, and reiterated below. Both show signs of having been painted after the Dossi's figures. A small oval (with a cupid and a male figure seen from behind) at the corner of the vault has looked to me to be Bronzino's as well (147). Vasari's other mention of Bronzino's work—that he "did some figures in oil in the *peduccio* of a vault" (see note 64)—coincides satisfactorily.

If Vasari never visited the Imperiale, the vagueness of his account and the resulting confusion are more readily understandable.

67. Smyth, 1955 (see note 4), 148–49. Compare Ballarin (see note 1), 1: 361 (entry no. 485), fig. 222. Before the cleaning and restoration by Leonetto Tintori, the Cupid had suffered from retouching, and some paint was flaking.

68. Smyth, 1955 (see note 4), 149–50. For Bernard Berenson's early connection of Dosso's name with the decoration of this room, see note 75.

69. The spandrel figures are antique gods and personifications of the arts. Previously the figure designated here as Architecture was considered to be History; see Smyth, 1955 (see note 4), 150 n. 1.

70. See Smyth, 1955 (see note 4), 150 n. 1, in reference to Roberto Longhi, *Officina ferrarese, 1934: Seguita dagli ampliamenti, 1940, e dai nuovi ampliamenti, 1940–55,* 2nd ed. (Florence: Sansoni, 1968), 86: "*Anche nella* Allegoria della musica *. . . , le intenzioni più recondite dell'artiste s'illuminano in una deformazione*" (Also in the *Allegory of Music . . .* , the innermost intentions of the artist shine forth in a *deformazione*).

When writing his book around 1970, Marchini continued the tradition of seeing Bronzino as the painter of the Cupid and the designer of all the rest of the spandrel figures. He nevertheless added (without citing the figure of Architecture specifically) that they show "*un'attrazione delle deformazioni proprie del Dosso dettata evidentemente dalla vicinanza e dalla contemporaneità dell'opera sua*" (an affinity to Dosso's own *deformazione* that was evidently dictated by the proximity and contemporaneity of his work). Thereupon Marchini encountered the difficulty of not being able to see, as he noted, any relationship between his Bronzino of the spandrels and paintings Bronzino is held to have done while at the Imperiale, namely, the *Guidobaldo* and the *Apollo and Marsyas* (St. Petersburg, Hermitage); Marchini (see note 28), 21–22. The latter work is now accepted as the harpsichord cover that, according to Vasari, Bronzino painted there; see Vasari (see note 6), 7: 595, and Baccheschi (see note 18), 88.

It is obvious, in my view, that there is nothing in Bronzino's work, either before Pesaro or after, to permit the attribution of Architecture to Bronzino. For Bronzino's early work, see, for example, Craig Hugh Smyth, "The Earliest Works of Bronzino," *Art Bulletin* 31 (1949): 184–211; Elizabeth Pilliod, "Pontormo and Bronzino at the Certosa," *The J. Paul Getty Museum Journal* 20 (1992): 77–89; and Janet Cox-Rearick, *Bronzino's Chapel of Eleonora in the Palazzo Vecchio* (Berkeley: Univ. of California Press, 1993), which includes work of Bronzino before Pesaro as well as after.

71. Freedberg (see note 50), 210–11.

72. Eiche (see note 5), figs. 8, 9.

73. Eiche (see note 5), 106.

74. Eiche (see note 5), 74.

75. Bernard Berenson, *Italian Pictures of the Renaissance: A List of the Principal Artists and Their Works, with an Index of Places* (Oxford: Clarendon Press, 1932), 255. This attribution goes back to Berenson's early lists—it never changed. There are, in fact, no "other scenes" in the decoration of this room, only the spandrel figures, who are engaged in actions of their own, and the busts in the lunettes. The contents of the small ovals in the vault at the corners of the room can hardly have been scenes that Berenson was considering. In the list of all the works he attributed to Bronzino (114–116), Berenson did not include anything of this room—despite McComb's inclusion of the spandrel figures as being based on Bronzino's designs in his then new book on Bronzino (see note 18). In his preface, McComb recorded his gratefulness for "the benefit of Mr. Berenson's advice on a number of matters which came up in our conversations about Bronzino" while McComb was "working on this monograph" as a

guest in the Berensons' library at Villa I Tatti (ix). Yet McComb held to the connection with Bronzino, whereas Berenson held to his attribution to Girolamo da Carpi "(with Dosso)." An older attribution of the *Coronation* to Dosso had been denied by Thode in 1888 (see note 9), 178. (Girolamo's whereabouts in 1530 is documented only on 6 August in Ferrara, in a context that suggests his presence there in July, although not necessarily earlier; see Pattanaro [see note 26], 1: 152.)

76. The attribution to Girolamo da Carpi (but not "with Dosso") was continued in Giulio Vaccai, *Pesaro* (Bergamo: Istituto Italiano d'Artigrafiche, 1909), 47; and Luigi Serra, *Guida di Pesaro* (Pesaro, 1923), 72.

77. A letter from Genga dated 10 May 1530 (the same day the duchess wrote regarding Menzocchi) requests colors and fifty brushes for working in oil; see Gronau (see note 11), 123 (doc. 128). If this order should relate to work in the duke's bedroom, where oil is used, it would be in accord with the most likely time for the Dossi's presence at the villa, and it would reveal when work in the room began.

78. Smyth, 1955 (note 4), 152.

79. Smyth, 1955 (see note 4), 150–51, 159–60; Marchini (see note 28), pl. XI. See Baldani (see note 53), 252, on the figure of Victory. In recent publications Paola Dal Poggetto has given the Victory to Raffaellino, most recently in his "Precisazioni sull'influsso di Raffaello nelle Marche: L'Imperiale, Raffaellino del Colle e altro," in Micaela Sambucco Hamoud and Maria Letizia Strocchi, eds., *Studi su Raffaello,* 2 vols. (Urbino: QuattroVenti, 1987), 390. On the considerable possibility that the Dossi were responsible for the design of a number of the spandrel figures executed by others, see Smyth, 1955 (see note 4), 156–57, 159, 164–65.

80. Smyth, 1955 (see note 4), 145–46, 165–66. For an illustration in color, see Marchini (see note 28), pl. X.

81. Traces along the leg could be read, in my analysis, as showing a fatter silhouette and as apparently indicating the start by the Dossi of a different version of the figure underneath; see Smyth, 1955 (see note 4), 164–65.

82. Cox-Rearick (see note 70), pls. 6, 22.

83. See note 66. The figure of Music is a revision. To me it has seemed to be Bronzino's partial revision of something begun by the Dossi; see Smyth, 1955 (see note 4), 146–47. Baldani (see note 53), 252, attributed the figure of Music to Bronzino specifically—she has been the only one to single it out. One of the busts in the lunettes is also by Bronzino in my view; see Smyth, 1955 (see note 4), 147–48.

84. In my view a good case can be made for the Dossi having taken part in still another mode in the decoration of still another room, the *camerino appresso la camera del letto,* known in modern times as the *studiolo* or *gabinetto.* I refer to the ovals in the lower part of the vault that depict classical scenes painted in oil; see Marchini (see note 28), pls. XIII, XVI. This is a view that all might not share—that is to say, this point would need supporting discussion similar to that in Smyth, 1955 (see note 4), 163. If the Dossi worked in this room, then they participated in the decoration of all three of the rooms that form the innermost part of the duke's section of the apartment. The case for this view does not need to be included here in support of the point already stressed: that at the villa in 1530 Dosso worked simultaneously in very different modes.

85. See note 35.

86. Eiche (see note 5), 116–18, figs. 14, 15.

87. Smyth, 1955 (see note 4), 183–84; Craig Hugh Smyth, *Mannerism and* Maniera (Locust Valley, N.Y.: J. J. Augustin, for the Institute of Fine Arts, New York University, [1963]), 22, figs. 22, 23; rev. ed., with an introduction by Elizabeth Cropper (Vienna: IRSA, 1992), 80, figs. 81, 82. These figures have been accepted as Bronzino's: see Marchini (see note 28), 25, pl. XVI; Baccheschi (see note 18), 87–88 with illustrations; and Charles McCorquodale, *Bronzino* (London: Jupiter, 1981), 38, 40, fig. 25. Assuming the Sala Comune is the room where the Dossi's decoration was destroyed, Bronzino was indeed one of those who repainted it.

It can be added that, in my view, before the cleaning (but not studied by me afterward) there appeared to be well-preserved passages by Bronzino on two spandrels of the vault in the Camera delle Forze di Ercole (Eiche's *terzo camerino*); see Smyth, 1955 (see note 4), 167–69, and Marchini (see note 28), pl. XV. Raffaellino apparently worked here as well, as Marchini noted (24–25).

Bronzino's contributions to the decoration of the rooms in the Imperiale are in several different modes. The use of diverse modes more or less simultaneously by sixteenth-century artists of central Italy is a subject broached briefly in *Mannerism and* Maniera (24, 71, 76–77; rev. ed., 86, 126, 129). Examples in Cinquecento Italy reward our consciousness of them, all the more so if seen as presaging to some degree the Seicento's practice in respect to modes supported by theory.

88. Ballarin (see note 1), 1: 356–57 (entry no. 478), figs. 204–11.

Battista Dossi and Sebastiano Filippi

Mauro Lucco

According to Giorgio Vasari in the 1568 edition of his *Lives,* "having already reached old age, Dosso spent the last years of his life without working, for he was supported until the very end of his days by Duke Alfonso."[1] As Vasari reports this piece of information immediately after mentioning the completion of the (lost) Faenza altarpiece in 1536, one may presume that in Vasari's mind, Dosso's final phase of inactivity must have lasted six years, namely from 1536 to 1542, the year of his death. In the sixteenth century, the moment of passage into old age was conventionally held to occur between forty-five and fifty years of age.[2] For Dosso, then, who was born "almost at the same time as Heaven gave to Ferrara—or rather, to the world—the divine Ludovico Ariosto," this would have happened sometime between 1520 and 1525. Thus any attempt to explain Vasari's remark in these terms must be excluded on the basis of his reference to the Della Sale altarpiece in the cathedral of Ferrara (now in the Galleria Nazionale di Palazzo Barberini, Rome), which dates from about 1527.[3]

What led to Vasari's increased hostility, or open malevolence, toward Dosso and Battista Dossi in the years between the first edition of the *Lives* in 1550 and the second edition in 1568? I do not know the answer to this, but it seems clear that Vasari's remark about Dosso's complete inactivity—which is contradicted by the documents for the paintings that were completed in 1540 and are now found in Dresden—depends upon his idea about the ever-growing importance of the role played by Dosso's brother Battista, and Dosso's workshop, starting in the late 1520s. Battista Dossi's role became so significant in Vasari's eyes (and, after all, in the eyes of modern scholarship) that the entire team of artists at the service of the duke of the house of d'Este corresponded, in point of fact, to "Dosso's workshop."

The modest aim of this essay is, then, to define—within such a gigantic "workshop"—areas of close stylistic homogeneity, which can be assigned either conventional names or, in some rare lucky cases, those of the artists themselves, and, thus (through what may be termed a process of elimination), to arrive at a more accurate understanding of the art of Dosso himself. This way of approaching Dosso may appear to be quite banal and to offer no new methodological framework to support its conclusions, but an attempt to rationalize the artistic output in Ferrara in this period, which is still far from being definitively understood, seems necessary to me. A glance at the

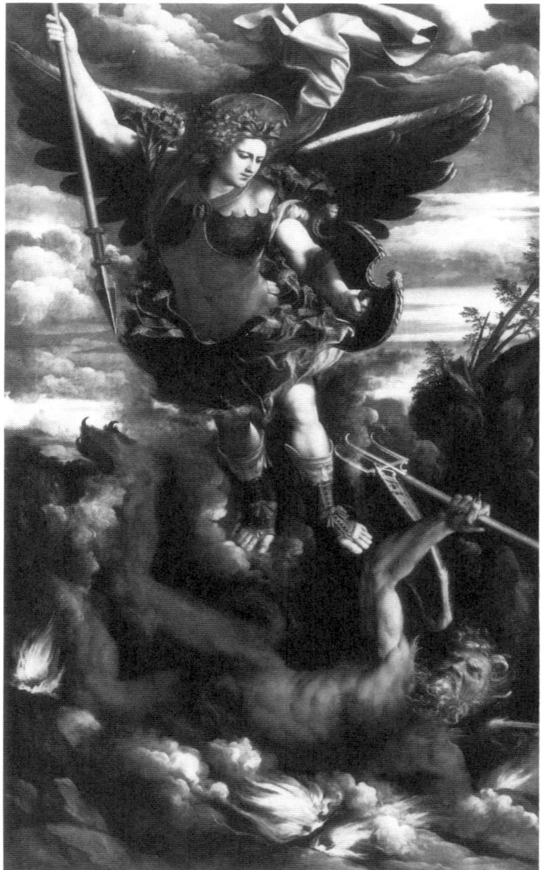

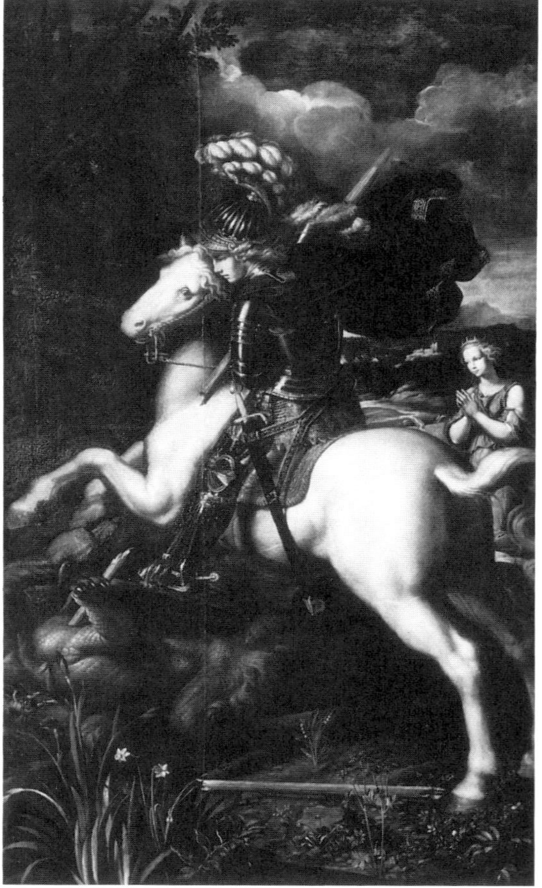

Fig. 1. Dosso Dossi
The Archangel Michael
Dresden, Staatliche Kunstsammlungen, Gemäldegalerie Alte Meister

Fig. 2. Dosso Dossi
Saint George
Dresden, Staatliche Kunstsammlungen, Gemäldegalerie Alte Meister
Here attributed to Battista Dossi

three modern studies of Battista Dossi — the monographs by Amalia Mezzetti and Felton Gibbons, as well as the recent monumental work by Alessandro Ballarin — shows that there is no consensus on the catalog of his works, for instance, and this seems a convincing argument for the approach taken in the present essay.[4]

I begin with the *Archangel Michael* and the *Saint George* in the Gemäldegalerie Alte Meister in Dresden (figs. 1 and 2). As is well known, a series of payments stretching from 28 February 1540 to 30 April 1540 was made by the Camera Ducale for these two paintings, with installments paid on 6 March and 13 March.[5] According to the document dated 13 March, these payments were made "to the painter Master Dosso for twelve working days [or hours] by him and his brother and for twelve by his apprentices, who were set to work on large paintings of Saint Michael and Saint George for our most illustrious Lord." The gilding of the frames was paid to Calzolaretto between February and June in installments.[6] The two paintings were executed for an unnamed room in the palace of Ercole II; it is likely that their being hung *"fra le finestre"* (between the windows) of the Galleria Ducale in Modena (as mentioned in an early seventeenth-century inventory published in the nineteenth century by Venturi)[7] was an effort to reproduce their original placement in Ferrara, for the two paintings are illuminated by opposite light sources, as if they had flanked a window, with the *Archangel Michael* on the left and the *Saint George* on the right. They are currently displayed in Dresden with an empty space — an imaginary window — between them. This serves to underscore, it seems to me, the fact that they were conceived as pendants, which is irrefutably confirmed by the documents transcribed by Venturi. Nevertheless, as early as the late seventeenth century or the very beginning of the eighteenth century, the two works began to appear to viewers as the work of different artists, with the *Saint George* attributed to Garofalo and, later, to Girolamo da Carpi. Henriette Mendelsohn was the first to attribute *Archangel Michael* to Dosso and *Saint George* to Battista, but this idea met with scant critical consensus. Bernard Berenson, who at one point thought that Girolamo da Carpi had painted the *Saint George,* imagined in the last edition of his *Indexes* that Battista Dossi had conceived the work and Sellari had actually painted it.[8]

More recent scholarship has tended to consider the *Saint George* a collaboration between Dosso and his brother, following the documents themselves. Ballarin instead has argued that Girolamo da Carpi was entirely responsible for its planning and execution.[9] This artist, however, is never mentioned in the registers of the Camera Ducale of Ferrara in 1540, although he did get married in Ferrara in 1538, have a son baptized there in 1539, and collaborate on painting the sets for Giambattista Cinzio Giraldi's *Orbecche tragedia* in 1541. Moreover, Vasari reports that in 1540 he saw in Ferrara a (now lost) nude *Venus* by Girolamo da Carpi, which was later sent to the king of France.[10] Thus the hypothetical possibility that he could have collaborated in the painting of *Saint George* must be left open. In my view only the face of the princess on the right-hand side (see fig. 2) seems to allude—but in a less than compelling way—to Girolamo's style of painting. There is some stylistic affinity with the face of Repentance in the allegorical painting of *Fate and Repentance* (1541, Dresden, Staatliche Kunstsammlungen, Gemäldegalerie Alte Meister) and the nymph on the extreme left of the *Venus on the Shell* (early 1540s, Dresden, Staatliche Kunstsammlungen, Gemäldegalerie Alte Meister), a painting that must have been, in my view, largely conceived and executed by Battista Dossi.[11] In comparing the *Archangel Michael* and *Saint George* paintings, the only way to overcome the radical difference between them is to attribute to Dosso the conception and execution of the *Archangel Michael.* The exciting quality of this painting, with its lucid formal definition, its refined manneristic depiction (reminiscent of Parmigianino) of Lucifer's wavy beard, the bursts of flame and bright flashes along the edges of the armor, the vapors joining together to form a dramatic cloud mass, and the extraordinary invention of the figure's pose bursting into the foreground of the work, find no comparable elements in the paintings of Battista. Indeed, Battista's *Allegory of Justice* and *Allegory of Peace* (figs. 3 and 4)—which were painted in 1544,[12] two years after Dosso's death, and thus serve as true mirrors of Battista's art—display none of the traits found in the *Archangel Michael.* Dosso and Battista could not, then, have collaborated on the *Archangel Michael,* as many scholars still believe; the work is in Dosso's hand alone. Let us then suppose that the division of labor between these two artists and their assistants, which is implicit in the documents, was made on the simplest and most ordinary basis. Each of two brothers, in other words, painted one canvas and provided stylistic unity to the work carried out by their "apprentices" by means of their finishing touches. In my view, in short, Dosso is the artist who painted the *Archangel Michael,* and Battista, with the help of some assistants, painted the *Saint George.*

These two paintings provide a good starting point for any attempt to distinguish Battista's style from Dosso's, for they are among their few existing documented works. Naturally, the two allegories in the same museum have even greater value, for they show Battista Dossi's art after he was free of supervision from his brother. So, too, does the Modena altarpiece titled *Nativity in the Presence of Two Gentlemen* (fig. 5), of which Lancillotti remarked in November 1536, at the moment of its completion, that it was "done by the hand of Master…, brother of that most excellent painter Master Dosso."[13] This is not to say, however, that Dosso himself might not have played a role in the conception of the work, at least in its lovely landscape, which seems rather different from what one would normally expect from Battista. A letter from Paolucci, who was Alfonso d'Este's agent in Rome, offers some additional information to the few facts we have for Battista's stylistic development. Written sometime after 20 January 1520, this letter states that Battista Dossi was in Rome in this period and in close contact with Raphael.[14] Based on this letter, scholars have always assumed—correctly and inevitably—that Battista Dossi was more open to Raphael's influence than Dosso was.

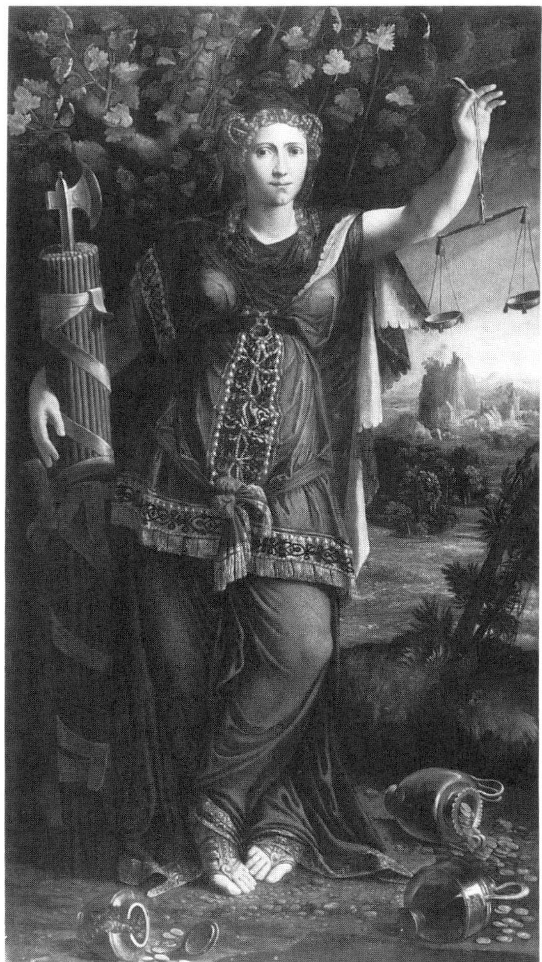

Fig. 3. Battista Dossi
Allegory of Justice
Dresden, Staatliche Kunstsammlungen, Gemäldegalerie Alte Meister

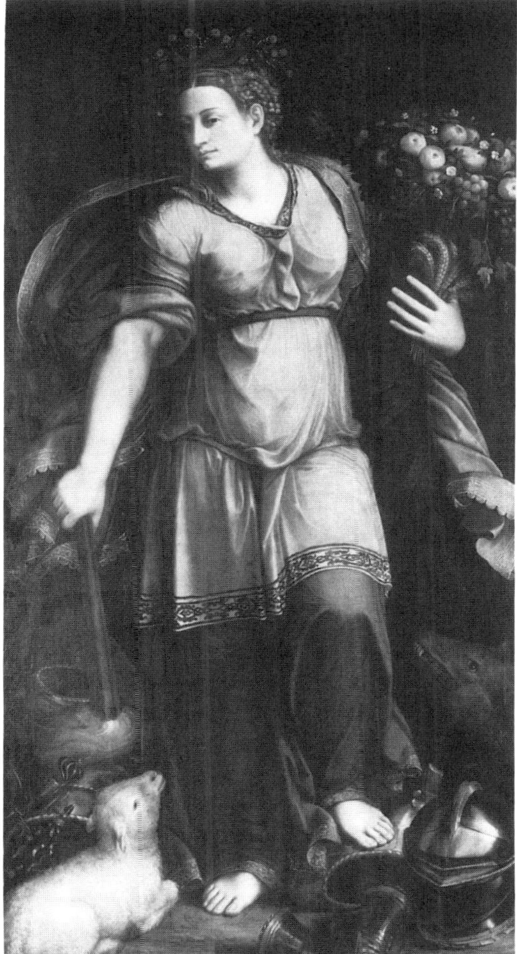

Fig. 4. Battista Dossi
Allegory of Peace
Dresden, Staatliche Kunstsammlungen, Gemäldegalerie Alte Meister

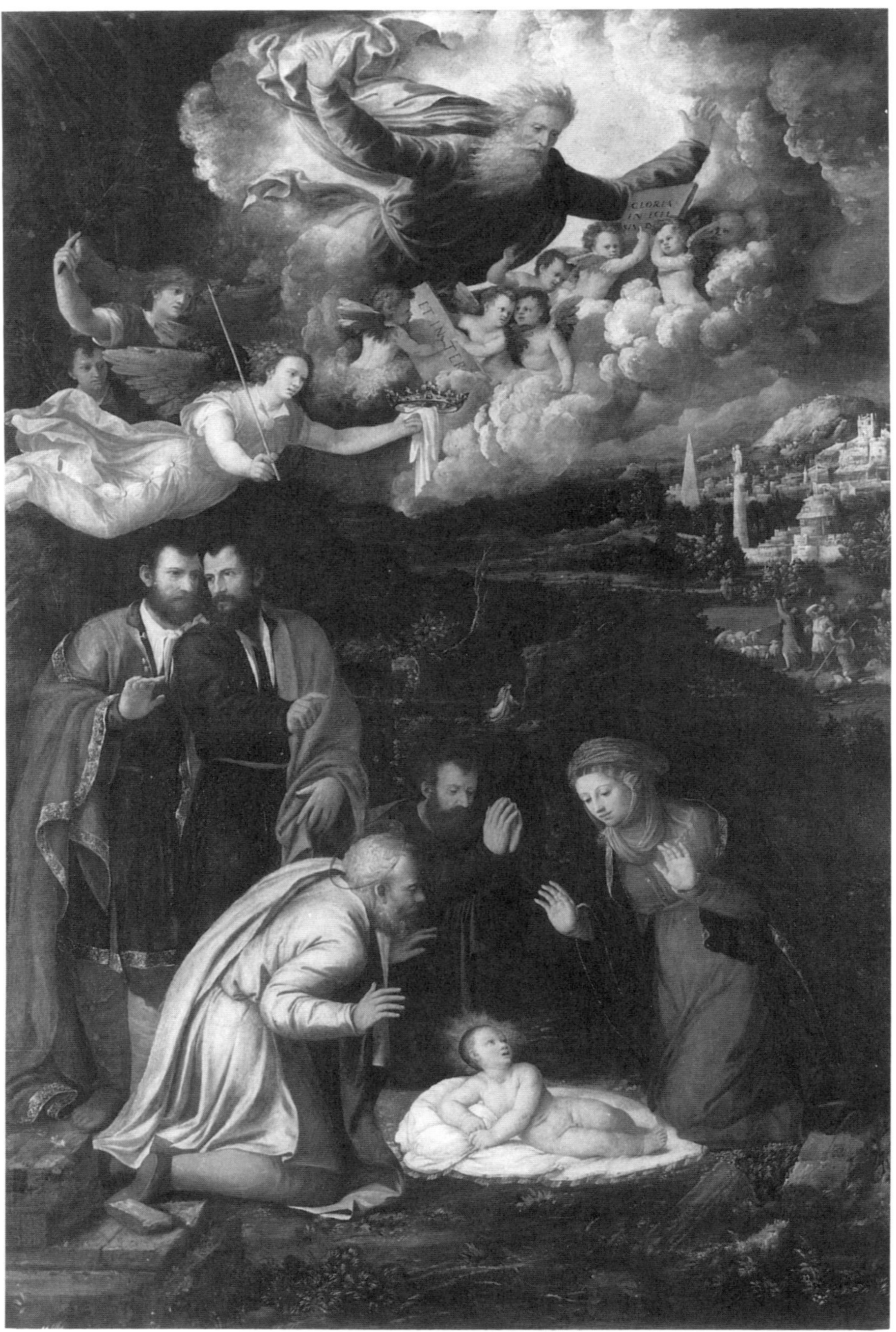

Fig. 5. Dosso Dossi
Nativity in the Presence of Two Gentlemen
Modena, Galleria Estense
Here attributed to Battista Dossi and Dosso Dossi

Nonetheless, the latter was also a friend of Raphael's, and thus the distinction has not held much importance for a number of scholars, who see Battista as almost always falling short of Dosso's standards of quality (which are never really defined). I seek to define Battista Dossi's art more precisely, on the basis of specific traits that can be localized in the paintings undoubtedly by Battista's hand: the morphology of the faces seen in these paintings, for example, and the specific aspects of their landscapes (increasingly linked to Joachim de Patinir's northern European models), are both distinctly opposed to those that appear in Dosso's works. The portrait of Battista Dossi resulting from this analysis is once again different from the one presented by earlier scholars. It naturally goes without saying that, because of limitations of space, it is not possible here to reconstruct exactly what Battista's art *is;* however, we may be able to say what his art *is not,* through a review of the work of others.

A fundamental question lies behind the need to reconstruct Battista Dossi's career starting from his final years of activity and working backward toward the early years: what is the first moment in which he may be identified as an autonomous artist? The fact that he was alone in Rome in 1520 would lead us to think that he had already achieved artistic autonomy some time before. It is, however, rather difficult (in my opinion) to identify any works dating from that period. Ballarin's revision of his own position in the interval between the publication of the first and second volumes of his study of Dosso show, beyond the shadow of a doubt, that the material evidence only acquires a certain consistency starting with the *Nativity in the Presence of Two Gentlemen,* that is to say, from about 1534 to 1548.[15] A document from Modena dated 6 May 1521, however, describes him as so young as to be mistaken for *"fiolo de magistro Dosso"* (Master Dosso's son) (Dosso was around thirty-five years old at this time).[16] This suggests that there was a significant age difference between the two; thus all attempts to identify those of his works that belong to the second decade of the sixteenth century are almost certainly doomed to failure.

This is not the place to discuss all the works thus far attributed to Battista Dossi. It is worth noting, however, that the *Nativity* formerly in the Collezione Bargellesi in Milan, the respective versions of the *Adoration of the Shepherds* (one of which was formerly in the von Fürstenberg collection in Herdringen Castle, and the other of which was formerly in the Lanfranchi collection in Santa Maria del Piano in Parma), and the *Calling of Zaccheus from the Tree* (formerly in London), all appear to have been painted in very different ways, if not by different hands.[17] It is difficult to attribute to the same artist two such different versions of the *Holy Family with a Shepherd* as the one in the Cleveland Museum of Art and the one formerly on the London market. It seems rather unlikely that the *Virgin and Child* and the *Infant Saint John and Saint Francis* (both on the art market in 1990), a variant of Raphael's idea for the *Madonna del Prato,* or the greatly damaged *Sybil* in the National Museum of Wales in Cardiff could belong to the period around 1520. The face and pose of the sybil in the latter work allude to the influence of Raphael and Giulio Romano, which would be impossible prior to about 1525.

Furthermore, in my view, the *Landscape with Soldier and Pair of Figures* (fig. 6), which Ballarin sees as a work by Battista from around 1518 to 1519, identifying it with a painting mentioned in Cesare Ignazio d'Este's Modena inventory of 1685, can in no way be attributed to the younger Dossi.[18] I have recently examined it in person twice, first in 1991 at the Ribolzi Gallery in Montecarlo and second in New York when it was auctioned in 1993. Undeniably the somewhat broad brushstrokes and feathery thickness of the trees are reminiscent of the Dossesque way of painting, but this work has a pendant, a *Landscape with Shepherds and Soldiers* (fig. 7), which has never been published, for it is an ugly work, and the details of its execution clearly demonstrate that it and its counterpart (in spite of the differences in "quality" between the two) are, at most, seventeenth-century copies of possible lost Dossesque prototypes of about 1517. The first of the two is, obviously, a collection of Dosso's motifs derived from the Besançon *Travelers in a Wood* (p. 205), the Metropolitan Museum of Art's *Three Ages of Man* (p. 236), and the Galleria Borghese's *Enchantress Circe* (or *Melissa*) (p. 235). But the secret of Dosso's touch, which was able to create phantasmagorically magic forms emerging in the fog and distant spaces, eluded the copyist. The mechanical rigidity with which the buildings on the right are set in the water, rather than rising like a magical spell from the mist on the great plain, absolutely proves that this is not a work by Dosso. Not even the structure of the ramshackle buildings really seems to belong to his hand. There is nothing comparable in the so-called *Departure of the Argonauts* (ca. 1517–1518) in the National Gallery in Washington or in the *Enchantress Circe* (or *Melissa*), to say nothing of the absolute immobility of the skies, which look like opaque, dense slabs rather than the supremely transparent heavens of Dosso's known works.

Nor does the *Hunt of the Calydonian Boar* (fig. 8) in El Paso belong to Battista Dossi. Roberto Longhi attributed this work to the painter and dated it to about 1520, and later scholars have unanimously agreed with him.[19] The execution of the fronds in the wooded landscape certainly reflects—although in a more generic way and with a less broad use of the *macchia* technique—Dosso's style between roughly 1517 and 1520. But it has nothing to do with the sinuous subtlety of the paintings undoubtedly by Battista, ranging from as far back as the *Battle of Orlando and Rodomonte* (Hartford, Wadsworth Atheneum), which dates from around 1528 to 1530 and is one of the artist's fundamental works, to the Dresden paintings.[20] In the El Paso panel there is a different sort of landscape with high rocks in the style of Patinir and buildings that have no equivalent in the rest of Ferrarese painting; the latter seem, if anything, to bear traces of Venetian influence. The only other painting that can be compared to the El Paso painting is the small *Judgment of Solomon* (fig. 9), which Vittorio Sgarbi published and attributed to Dosso himself.[21] I was able to examine this work in 1990 in the shop of an antiquities dealer in

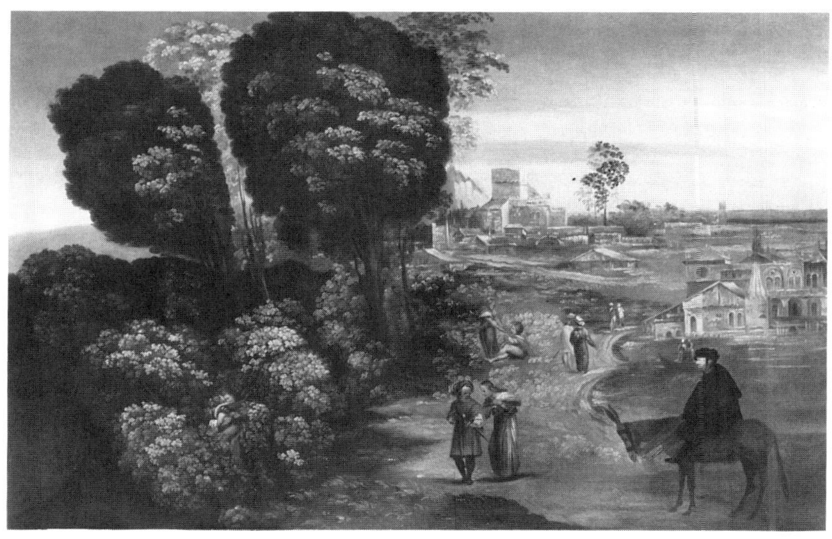

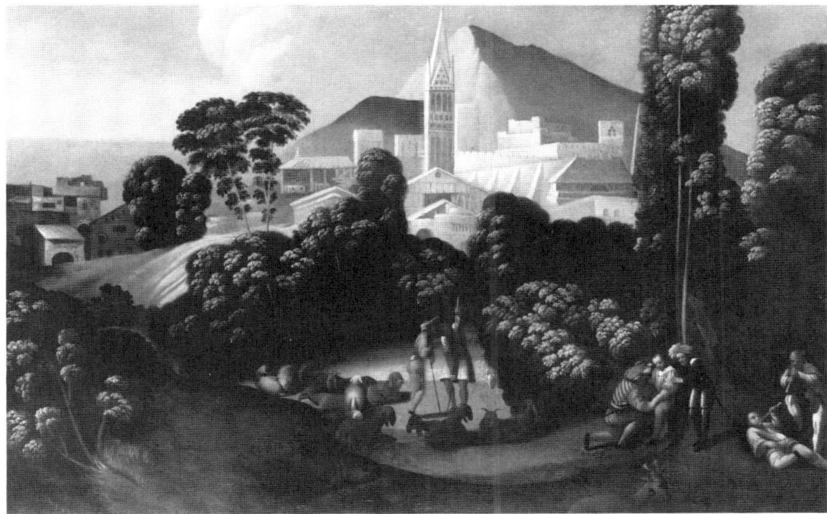

Fig. 6. Anonymous seventeenth-century imitator of Dosso Dossi
Landscape with Soldier and Pair of Figures
Whereabouts unknown

Fig. 7. Anonymous seventeenth-century imitator of Dosso Dossi
Landscape with Shepherds and Soldiers
Whereabouts unknown

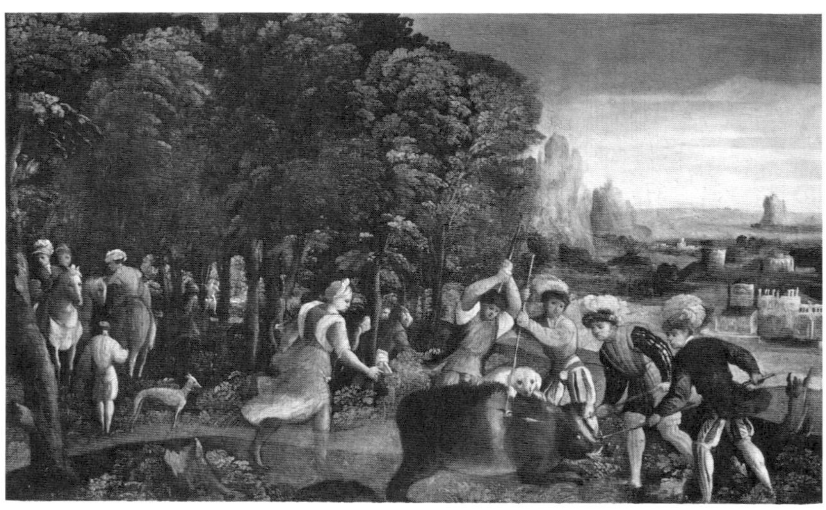

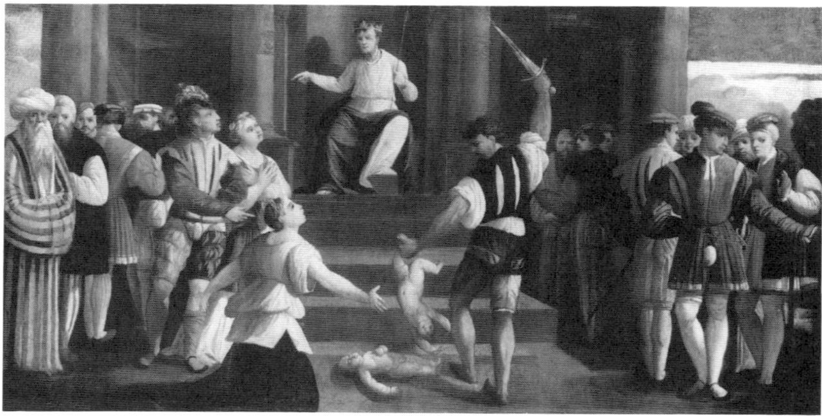

Fig. 8. Battista Dossi
The Hunt of the Calydonian Boar
El Paso, El Paso Museum of Art
Here attributed to Sebastiano Filippi

Fig. 9. Sebastiano Filippi
Judgment of Solomon
Rome, private collection

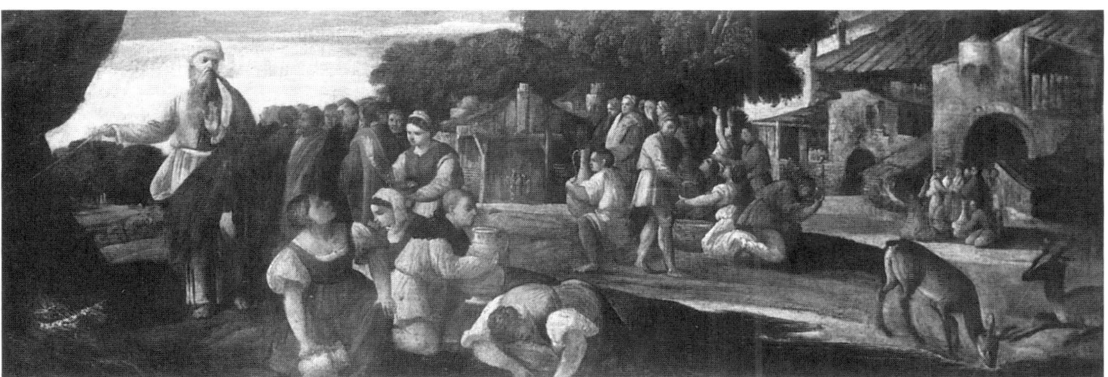

Fig. 10. Sebastiano Filippi
Moses Striking the Rock
Whereabouts unknown

Bologna. At almost the same time, Emanuele Mattaliano apparently told the owner of the painting that it was, in his opinion, a late work by Ortolano. The shared rustic motifs of these two works are so striking that it is pointless to emphasize them here. Judging from the photographs, the same hand seems to have also painted *Moses Striking the Rock* (fig. 10), which was sold at a Finarte auction in 1963 as a work by Battista Dossi, and which has since disappeared. Carlo Volpe republished the painting in 1974 and attributed it to Dosso, but wondered if—due to the impossibility of a direct study of the work—its apparent internal figurative contradictions were the result of its poor state of preservation and clumsy retouching, or if these instead indicated that it was merely a copy of a lost original by Dosso painted between 1515 and 1519.[22] The dimensions of this painting (45.5 × 125 cm) are quite similar to those of the *Judgment of Solomon* (42 × 105 cm), suggesting that both could belong to the same group of works, perhaps a frieze (although they are of different lengths).

Today it can be said that those departures from Dosso's characteristic style that Volpe saw in this painting derive from the fact that it is by another artist. The comparison between the figure of Moses and the "Oriental" man in the turban on the extreme left of the *Judgment of Solomon* could not be more eloquent. Inasmuch as I do not know where the painting is currently located, and have never seen it with my own eyes, I will limit myself to these brief remarks.

On the other hand, I wonder if the artist that painted the rear profile of the gentleman on the right in the *Judgment of Solomon,* whose nose and mouth jut out from the line defining the edge of his cheek, is not the same artist who created the female servant's face in the *Virgin and Child with Saint Anne and Saint Joseph and Attendant* now in Nottingham (fig. 11). Oliver Garnett has published and attributed this work to Dosso and dated it shortly after 1510; it was on display at the London exhibition in 1984 titled *From Borso to Cesare d'Este*.[23] The figure of the child, with its feeble Michelangel-esque traits and its open hand raised high over its head, seems similar to the two children and the good mother in the *Judgment of Solomon*. And it would seem almost automatic to compare these to the *Madonna and Child with Saint John the Baptist* (fig. 12) in Warsaw,[24] which shares with the Nottingham painting the same setting with stairs, a niche, and columns. The poses of the Virgin and the Holy Child seem rather similar in the two works as well. Finally, the Virgin's face in the Warsaw painting is reminiscent of the faces of the hunters on the right of the El Paso painting, as well as the face of Solomon; the figure of the latter, seated on his throne, appears in a setting whose architectural features resemble rather closely those visible in the Nottingham and Warsaw works.

Here I could be accused of a contradiction in methodology, because it is certainly not an established practice for art historians, at the moment in which they seek to establish the identity of a stylistic group, to choose works separated from one another by more than ten years' time. I nevertheless believe that a comparison with a detail from the San Biagio altarpiece in Lendinara, dated 1525 (fig. 13), will make it clear that the Nottingham painting could not belong to the years around 1510, as Garnett has claimed, nor to the years around 1517, as Ballarin has argued, nor, finally, to the period of 1530–1535, as Stefano Tumidei has asserted. In the Lendinara altarpiece, Saint Joseph leans with his hands on his stick in a peculiar pose; this pose is practically the same as that of Saint Joseph in the Nottingham painting, indicating that the Lendinara altarpiece belongs to the middle years of the 1520s. Both Gibbons and Ballarin date the Warsaw painting to about 1520,[25] and if we take this date as our point of reference, it becomes clear that the work must have been executed reasonably close in time to the *Hunt of the Calydonian Bear* and the *Judgment of Solomon,* which I have already dated to about 1520.

Although I have established that these five paintings constitute a unified group belonging to the period between 1520 (or slightly before) and 1525, I must confess that I have no definite proof that would allow me to link this group to any of the many artists who are known to have been associated with Dosso. Neither is any help offered by the recognition that the same painter seems to have had a hand in painting the altarpiece of the *Madonna with Child and Saints* (fig. 14) in the Pinacoteca dell'Accademia dei Concordi in Rovigo, which came from the parish church of Arquà Polesine.[26] Here what was seemingly one of Dosso's ideas was diminished first in its execution by Battista and his collaborators and then by its late eighteenth-century restoration by Baldassini. The faces of Saint Benedict and Saint Nicholas of

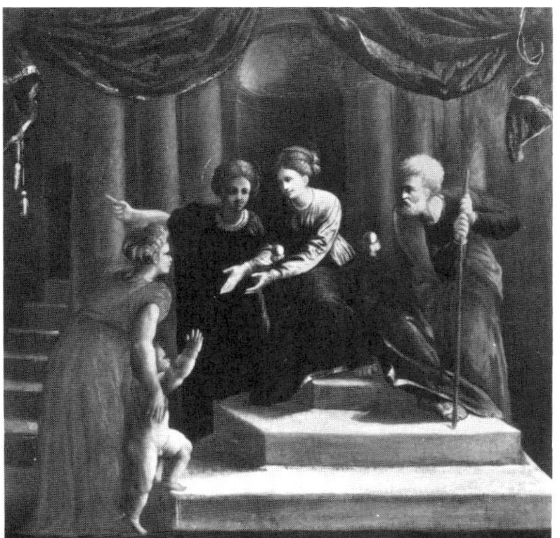

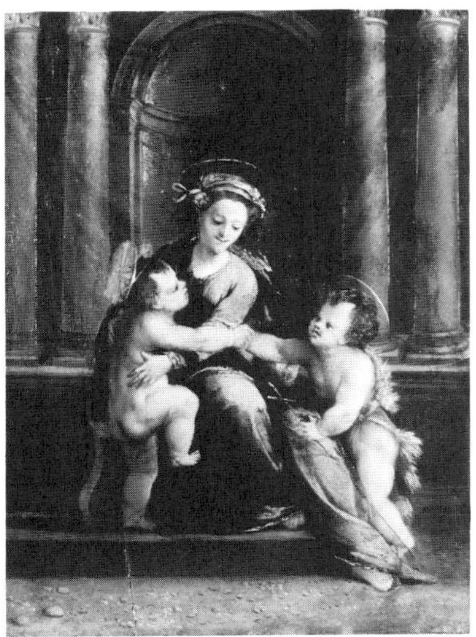

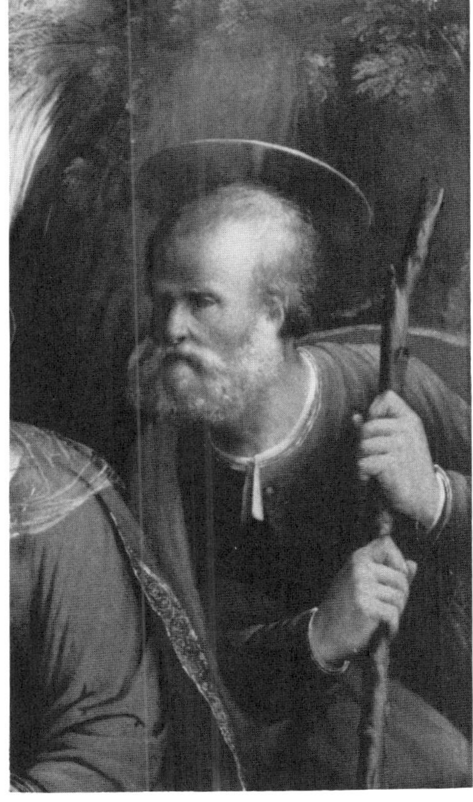

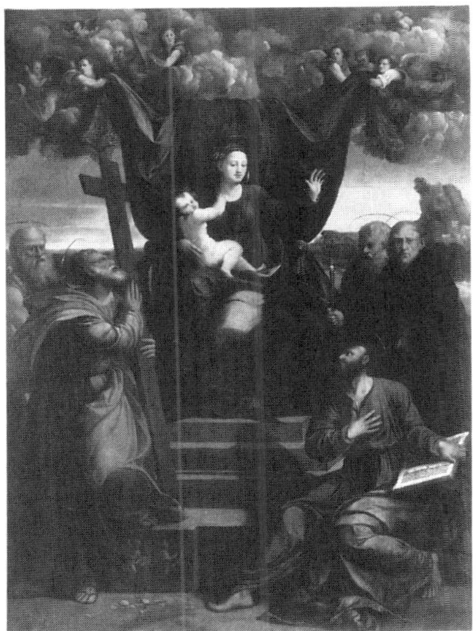

Fig. 11. Dosso Dossi
Virgin and Child with Saint Anne and Saint Joseph and Attendant
Nottingham, Castle Museum and Art Gallery
Here attributed to Sebastiano Filippi

Fig. 12. Battista Dossi
Madonna and Child with Saint John the Baptist
Warsaw, Muzeum Pałac w Wilanowie
Here attributed to Sebastiano Filippi

Fig. 13. Sebastiano Filippi
Visitation (detail)
Lendinara, Rovigo, San Biagio

Fig. 14. Battista Dossi
Madonna with Child and Saints (Arquà altarpiece)
Rovigo, Pinacoteca dell'Accademia dei Concordi
Here attributed to Sebastiano Filippi and Battista Dossi

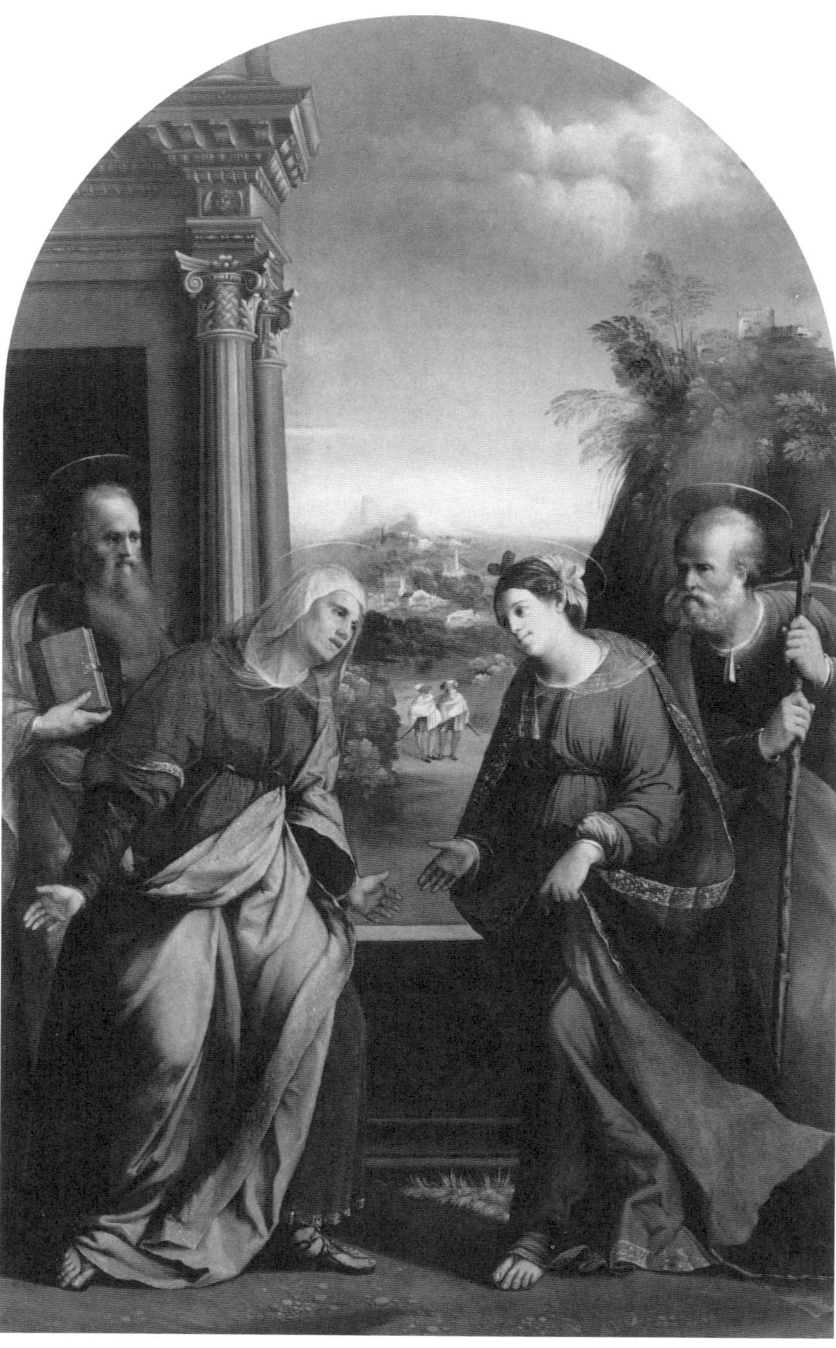

Fig. 15. Sebastiano Filippi
Visitation
Lendinara, Rovigo, San Biagio

Tolentino, on the right, seem to have been painted by the same hand that painted the "Oriental" man in the turban and the individual near him in the *Judgment of Solomon.* In truth, however, when looking at these two figures one has an odd feeling of estrangement in regard to the other figures involved in that *sacra conversazione.* They seem strangely more archaic than the others, almost as if they were fragments of an older version left in the new one, and thus the date of the painting is virtually irrelevant for them (Ballarin, on the basis of the work's style, dates it to about 1532–1533).

A useful point of comparison for these two figures, as well as for the rest of the group under discussion, may be found in an altarpiece still located in the same geographical and cultural area and which, after its recent restoration, once more demands our attention. I am referring to the *Visitation* in the church of San Biagio in the town of Lendinara (fig. 15). This work is signed and dated in capital Roman letters: "SEBASTIANUS PICTOR FACIEBAT MDXXV" (fig. 16).

This painting was described in seventeenth- and eighteenth-century sources from the Veneto region as a work by the only Sebastiano then known, namely Sebastiano del Piombo. In spite of the many doubts expressed by J. A. Crowe and G. B. Cavalcaselle, this attribution was generally accepted up to and including the publication of Giuseppe Fiocco's article of 1910.[27] The latter linked another painting (also signed and dated 1525) in the Pilastrello sanctuary in Lendinara (fig. 17) to the same artist, together with a work in the Pinacoteca dell'Accademia dei Concordi in Rovigo (fig. 18). In 1910 Adolfo Venturi cited this article but attributed the *Visitation* to a painter close to the Dosso circle, namely Sebastiano Filippi. This idea was discussed by Fiocco in his second article on the topic, published in 1925.[28] Here he was forced to perform some sleight of hand, however, because according to the documents published by Luigi Napoleone Cittadella (some of which have been lost), the artist was supposedly already dead by 1523. Fiocco tried to insinuate that Cittadella had made an error of transcription and had read "twenty-three" for "twenty-five." This same conflict between the written (or, more accurately, transcribed) documents and the figurative evidence has led many art historians, starting with Longhi in 1934 and including myself, to assume that the inscription on the altarpiece was a forgery added to a work produced by the Dossi's entourage.[29] The restoration in 1988–1989 demonstrated, unequivocally, that the signature and the date are coherent with the painting and are entirely original. Thus we are confronted with the unavoidable fact that a painter named Sebastiano, who worked in the Dossi's circle, executed an altarpiece in 1525 for the church in Lendinara. Ballarin nonetheless has continued to maintain that the inscription must be apocryphal and therefore not evidence of the true artist's name. He calls the artist who painted the altarpiece the "*Maestro della Visitazione di Lendinara,*" and attributes two paintings in the Pinacoteca dell'Accademia dei Concordi in Rovigo (usually attributed to Girolamo da Carpi) to this same hand, along with a *Female Saint* that appeared in 1995 on the Milan market.[30] This reconstruction does not appear convincing to me, for the altarpiece seems to display a style that differs from that of the two paintings in Rovigo, as well as from that of the work formerly in Milan. Further discussion of this point is, however, beyond the scope of this essay.

It seems more interesting to me to note that a new document was found in the Archivio di Stato in Ferrara during the process of checking the documents concerning Filippi that Cittadella had published.[31] This document opens everything to question once again: it is a receipt, dated 26 May 1524, for the final payment of a debt to Sebastiano Filippi—who was apparently very much alive at the time, since he accepted the five gold ducats that he had loaned to one Martino Chieregato. The witnesses were Giovanni Antonio, also known as Giovanni da Modena, and Alberto, son of Alessandro Pinzerne. If it were not for the unfortunate problem of their differing patronyms, it would be tempting to say that these two individuals could well have been the painters Giovanni Antonio and Albertino, whose names appear in several documents in the Estense records in relation to the Dossi brothers.[32]

Sebastiano Filippi, then, was still alive in 1524; his death is documented only from 1528.[33] As a resident of Lendinara, all historical probability points to him as the author of the San Biagio altarpiece, in which his remarkable artistic qualities as a member of the Dossi's circle are apparent. Although the composition of the work follows the general outlines of Garofalo's *Visitation* altarpiece, which was executed in 1518, perhaps for the church of Ostellato,[34] the Lendinara altarpiece is the work of an artist who developed during the period in which the Costabili altarpiece (p. 142) was executed.[35] The gilded fringes of the Virgin's veil, as well as (above all else) the decorations along the edges of the robe, scumbled and with red shadows, just as in the Costabili altarpiece, leave no room for doubt. The same decorative scheme is employed in the Pilastrello *Saint Peter* and the *Saint Paul* in the Pinacoteca dell'Accademia dei Concordi.[36] Sebastiano Filippi is mentioned in a document dated 4 September 1511, but only as the son of the painter Angelo, not as a painter in his own right. Filippi is referred to as a painter in at least two documents dated 25 December 1513, which were discovered by Antonio Romagnolo.[37] These documents show that Filippi completed his apprenticeship as a painter at the very time that Garofalo and Dosso were at work on the Costabili altarpiece.

In comparison to the works of Dosso of about 1525, such as the *Apollo* in the Galleria Borghese or the *Jupiter, Mercury, and Virtue* in Vienna (p. 99), the Lendinara altarpiece seems limited by an almost "*antico-moderno*" mindset. It displays the rich chromatic surfaces typical of Dosso's circle, but flattened in a subtler and minute brushwork rooted in Garofalo's art. The detail of the landscape is in this sense exemplary: it nearly crackles with small patches of color. This manner of defining the fronds of trees with small patches of color is far from both Dosso's broader and more fluid brushstrokes, on the one hand, and from Battista Dossi's more subtly inscribed brushstrokes, on the other. Yet this style is found precisely in the *Hunt of the*

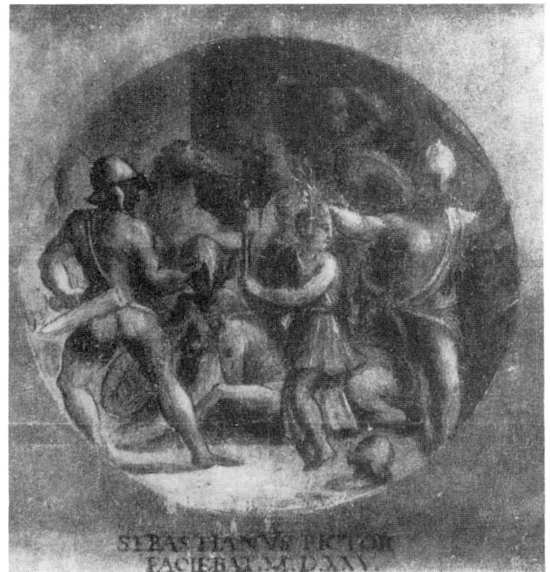

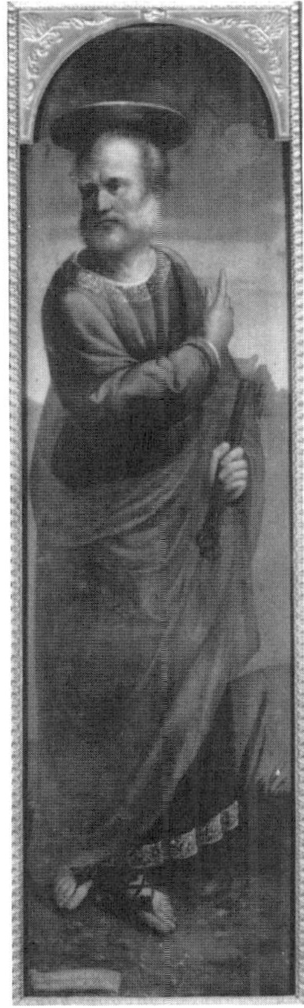

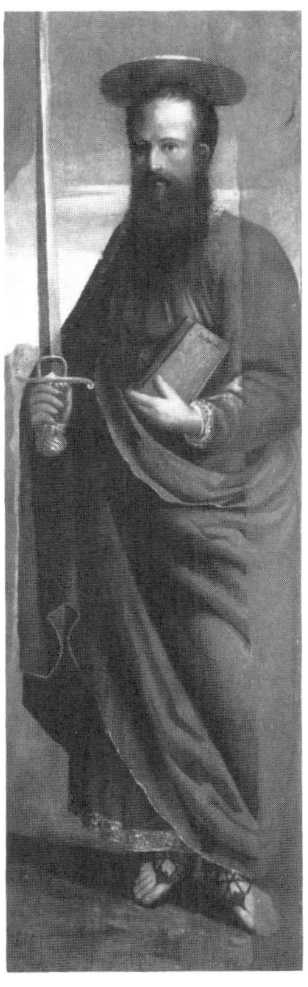

Fig. 16. Sebastiano Filippi
Visitation (detail)
Lendinara, Rovigo, San Biagio

Fig. 17. Sebastiano Filippi
Saint Peter
Lendinara, Rovigo, Santuario della
Beata Vergine del Pilastrello

Fig. 18. Sebastiano Filippi
Saint Paul
Rovigo, Pinacoteca dell'Accademia dei Concordi

Calydonian Boar in El Paso. Moreover, the rustically casual poses of the figures in the El Paso painting, like those in the *Judgment of Solomon,* reappear in the monochrome work at the center of the Lendinara altarpiece, which depicts the second martyrdom of Saint Sebastian. The same could be said for the painting of *Moses Striking the Rock.* The way in which the painter worked with formal syntheses in places such as Solomon's face, which is defined almost solely by touches of shadow in his eyes and the lines of his mouth, can also be seen in the figures of the two gentlemen strolling outside the city walls in the background of the Lendinara altarpiece. It seems worth wondering whether Filippi, as the most eminent painter active in this area, was not also commissioned to paint the Arquà Polesine altarpiece, which, following his death just prior to 1528, was almost completely reworked by Battista Dossi and some of his assistants after Battista returned from Trent near the end of 1532.

To return to the oeuvre of Battista, I do not believe that the beautiful drawing known as the *Virgin and Child with Saint Anthony of Padua* (about 1550), now in Paris in the Musée du Louvre, could possibly be his, as W. Roger Rearick and Ballarin have claimed.[38] It is unmistakably from the Veneto region and is, in my opinion, a typical work by Domenico Campagnola, as is confirmed by a comparison with his *Risen Christ* (formerly in the Skippe collection, but seen in 1979 in the possession of the London dealer Colnaghi), which can be dated to the early 1550s.[39] Nor can the *Oration in the Garden* (formerly in the Collezione Sacrati Strozzi in Florence, but now in the Pinacoteca Nazionale in Ferrara) be a work by Battista Dossi. The broader brushstrokes in the landscape, which match perfectly those in the *Three Ages of Man,* seem typical of the style of Dosso himself in about 1516.[40] The agitated and quick brushstrokes of the Allentown Art Museum's *Standard Bearer* (ca. 1517), when compared with the small panel of the *Virgin with Child and Angels* (ca. 1517, now in a private collection), allow us to see the latter as a work of Dosso's,[41] and there is no lack of connection between this latter work and the similarly sized Worcester painting.

Let us turn now to Battista Dossi's final years as an artist. The altarpiece fragment with *Four Church Fathers Discussing the Immaculate Conception,* now in the storerooms of the Bodemuseum in Berlin, certainly cannot be said to be his.[42] Given that it draws so totally on the imagery created for the ceiling of the library of the Castello del Buonconsiglio in Trent, executed in 1531–1532, it ought to be contemporary with the Arquà Polesine altarpiece and stylistically coherent with the latter. Yet in this case it seems difficult once again to find more drastic differences between two given works, although we have no ideas about an alternate attribution. Moreover, the logic of the division of labor in the Dossi's workshop required several individuals to work in a strictly interconnected way on the same painting. This tends to leave modern scholars bewildered in many cases, even when there are seemingly ironclad references in the documents. Such is the case, for instance, with the *Cleopatra in a Landscape,* formerly on the London market (fig. 19), which Ballarin has correctly identified as a painting that Battista Dossi delivered to

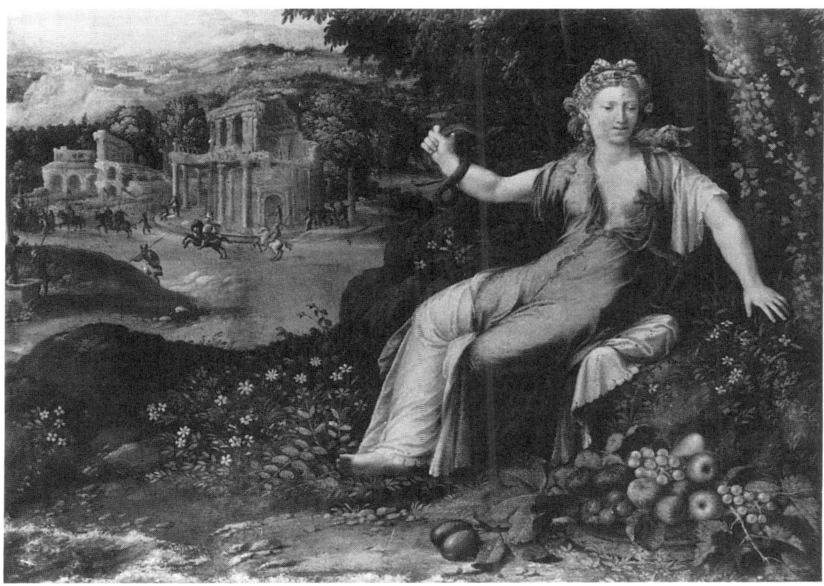

Fig. 19. Battista Dossi and workshop
Cleopatra in a Landscape
Whereabouts unknown

Laura Dianti in 1546 and for which he was paid in October 1548, a few months before his death.[43] I do not believe that there is any reason to doubt that this work forms part of a stylistic series (if not in fact part of an actual group) with the *Saint Jerome at Prayer in a Landscape* in the Musée du Louvre (fig. 20).[44] The *Venus with Amorini in a Landscape*, now in the Gemäldegalerie in Berlin (fig. 21), should also be added to these two works, especially considering its provenance, namely the collection of Vincenzo Giustiniani in Rome.[45] Although the *Venus with Amorini* is painted on wood and the *Cleopatra in a Landscape* is painted on canvas, and although the figurative field is vertically rather than horizontally extended, the virtually identical height of the two paintings (65 versus 66 cm) suggests that they once were part of the same decorative scheme. I would maintain, in fact, that the former can be identified with the "other small [painting]," inasmuch as it is opposed to the larger and consequently more expensive *Cleopatra*, "representing Venus with six putti" that is cited in the 1548 document.[46] It must be admitted that in the painting in question there are actually seven little putti, but one of them is almost entirely hidden behind the central *amorino* in such a way as to blend with him; a casual viewer of the painting might, therefore, easily mistake these two for a single figure.

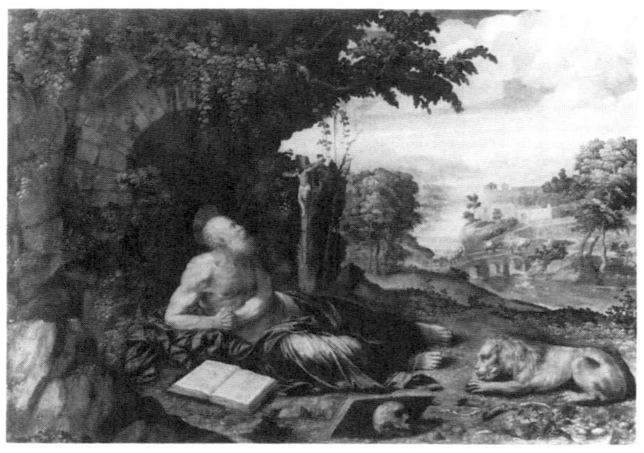

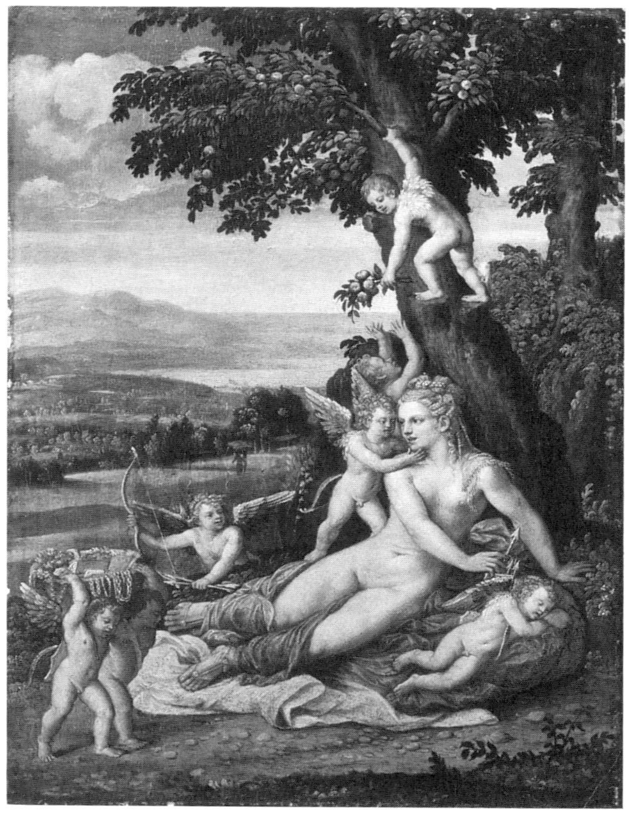

Fig. 20. Battista Dossi and workshop
Saint Jerome at Prayer in a Landscape
Paris, Musée du Louvre

Fig. 21. Battista Dossi and workshop
Venus with Amorini in a Landscape
Berlin, Staatliche Museen, Gemäldegalerie

We have, then, according to the documents, three paintings documented as having been produced by Battista Dossi between 1546 and 1548. Yet, strangely enough, these documents are contradicted by the style of the landscapes, which display no trace of the northern European influence of Patinir that we are accustomed to seeing in Battista's works. The artist's vision here is more naturalistically sweeping and realistic, in spite of the elevated point of view. Gone are the ghostly phantasms of buildings floating in the mist and vertical spurs of rocklike monoliths stuck into the ground; here instead is an undulating series of rivers, bridges, woods, castles, ancient ruins, and hills. Fronds are painted in a minute style, almost leaf by leaf, displaying elliptical touches of the brush. The lush vegetation contains cascading ivy and ferns, which never appear in Battista Dossi's other works. A comparison with the landscape of the two Dresden allegories, for which he was paid in 1544, could not display a more radical contrast.

In this case too, I do not believe that such landscapes were painted by the younger Dossi brother (although he certainly had overall responsibility for the works and perhaps painted the figures in them), but I have no other names to put forward at this time. The wooded landscape in the background of the *Saint Jerome* signed by Giacomone da Faenza (now lost) and published by Heinrich Bodmer in 1938 seems to employ a similar but not identical approach. This painting, however, was surely executed after the artist's stay in Rome from 1545 to 1551, which excludes any possible collaboration on works completed in Ferrara between 1546 and 1548.[47]

Historians still have, in short, a great deal of digging to do in order to understand better the workings of the Dossi brothers' workshop. This essay has simply sought to provide a useful starting point for such a task.

Notes

1. Giorgio Vasari, *Le vite de' più eccellenti pittori, scultori ed architettori* [1568], ed. Gaetano Milanesi, 9 vols. (Florence: Sansoni, 1878–1885), 5: 100: *"divenuto Dosso già vecchio, consumò gli ultimi anni senza lavorare, essendo insino all'ultimo della vita provisionato dal duca Alfonso."* This was reported in a more nuanced way, with a rather different meaning, in the 1550 edition of the *Lives*. See Giorgio Vasari, *Le vite de' più eccellenti architettori, pittori, et scultori italiani* [1550], ed. Luciano Bellosi and Aldo Rossi (Turin: Einaudi, 1986), 743: *"divenuto Dosso già vecchio e non molto lavorando, ebbe continuo dal Duca Alfonso emolumento e provvisione"* (Although Dosso was already old and no longer worked much, Duke Alfonso paid him a steady stipend).

2. See Creighton Gilbert, "When Did a Man in the Renaissance Grow Old?" *Studies in the Renaissance* 14 (1967): 7–32.

3. Vasari [1568] (see note 1), 5: 96: *"Quasi ne' medesimi tempi che il Cielo fece dono a Ferrara, anzi al mondo, del divino Lodovico Ariosto."* Vasari mentions the Della Sale altarpiece on page 97.

4. Amalia Mezzetti, *Il Dosso e Battista ferraresi* (Milan: Silvana, 1965); Felton

Gibbons, *Dosso and Battista Dossi: Court Painters at Ferrara* (Princeton: Princeton Univ. Press, 1968); and Alessandro Ballarin, *Dosso Dossi: La pittura a Ferrara negli anni del Ducato di Alfonso I,* 2 vols. (Cittadella: Bertoncello Artigrafiche, 1994–1995).

5. Adolfo Venturi, "I due Dossi: Documenti — Prima Serie," *Archivio storico dell'arte* 6 (1893): 131–32: *"a M.ro Dosso depintore per opere 12 de lui e suo fratello et per opere 12 de suoi gargiuni datte a lavorare quadri grandi de San Michele et san zorzo del S. n.ro Ill.mo."* Graziano Manni, *Mobili in Emilia* (Modena: Artioli, 1986), 124, reads the date as 23 March.

6. Manni, ibid.

7. Adolfo Venturi, *La R. Galleria Estense di Modena* (Modena: Paolo Toschi, 1882), 307.

8. Bernard Berenson, *Italian Pictures of the Renaissance: A List of the Principal Artists and Their Works, with an Index of Places: Central Italian and North Italian Schools,* rev. ed., 3 vols. (London: Phaidon, 1968).

9. For the entire critical discussion regarding these works, see Ballarin (see note 4), 1: 368–69 (entry no. 502).

10. Concerning all the facts mentioned here, see Amalia Mezzetti, *Girolamo da Ferrara detto da Carpi: L'opera pittorica* (Milan: Silvana, 1977), 55–56.

11. On these works, see ibid., 73–74.

12. Ballarin (see note 4), 1: 369–70 (entry no. 503); Alessandra Pattanaro, ed., "Regesto della pittura a Ferrara (1497–1548)," in Ballarin (see note 4), 1: 175.

13. Tommasino de' Bianchi detto de' Lancellotti, *Cronaca modenese* [16th c. MS], 12 vols. (Parma: Pietro Fiaccadori, 1862–1884), 5: 195: *"fatta de mane de M.ro... fratello de M.ro Dosso eximio depintore."* See also Ballarin (see note 4), 1: 361–62 (entry no. 485).

14. Adolfo Venturi, "Documenti relativi a Raffaello," *L'arte* 22 (1919): 209.

15. Ballarin (see note 4), 1: XVIII–XIX. Stefano Tumidei seems to hold the same opinion in his "Dosso (e Battista) al Buonconsiglio," in Enrico Castelnuovo, ed., *Il Castello del Buonconsiglio,* vol. 2, *Dimora dei principi vescovi di Trento: Persone e tempi di una storia* (Trent: Temi, 1996), 155 n. 34.

16. Carlo Giovannini, "Notizie inedite sull'altare di S. Sebastiano e sul presepio del Begarelli nel Duomo di Modena," in Orianna Baracchi and Carlo Giovannini, *Il Duomo e la torre di Modena: Nuovi documenti e ricerche* (Modena: Aedes Muratoriana, 1988), 223.

17. Ballarin (see note 4), 1: 316–18 (entry nos. 380, 381, 386, 388), suggests that these were done by Battista Dossi circa 1516–1517; and Tumidei (see note 15), 155 n. 34, agrees with him, although he tends toward slightly later dates.

18. Ballarin (see note 4), 1: 321–22 (entry no. 401).

19. See Ballarin (see note 4), 1: 321 (entry no. 400), for the critical history of this work.

20. On the critical history of the latter painting, see Ballarin (see note 4), 1: 335–36 (entry no. 429). Two extreme hypotheses about its date have been proposed: Henriette Mendelsohn, *Das Werk der Dossi* (Munich: Georg Müller & Eugen Rentsch, 1914), 133–34, dates the work as prior to 1520; while Jean K. Cadogan in idem, ed., *Wadsworth Atheneum Paintings,* vol. 2, *Italy and Spain, Fourteenth*

through Nineteenth Centuries (Hartford, Conn.: The Atheneum, 1991), 137–41, dates the work as belonging to the 1530s. It seems to me that the painting dates to about 1528–1530 on the basis of its treatment of the landscape, which seems inspired by that of the beautiful canvas in the Pushkin Museum in Moscow, whose figures certainly were done by Dosso's hand around 1528–1530.

21. Vittorio Sgarbi, "1518: Cariani a Ferrara e Dosso," *Paragone,* no. 389 (1982): 10–11. Mattaliano's opinion was given verbally, and I was told about it in a conversation with the owner of the painting.

22. See Finarte, *4, Vendita pubblica all'asta di opere d'arte antica, Milan, 12–13 March 1963,* lot no. 36; Carlo Volpe, "Dosso: Segnalazioni e proposte per il suo primo itinerario," *Paragone,* no. 293 (1974): 25.

23. Oliver Garnett, "A Dosso Discovery in Nottingham," *Burlington Magazine* 126 (1984): 429–30; *From Borso to Cesare d'Este: The School of Ferrara 1450–1628,* exh. cat. (London: Matthiesen Fine Art, 1984), 86 (entry no. 35 by Oliver Garnett). According to Tumidei (see note 15), 155 n. 34, both the Nottingham painting and the Edinburgh drawing related to it should be dated 1530–1535.

24. Ballarin (see note 4), 1: 318–19 (entry no. 391).

25. Gibbons (see note 4), 126, 235 (entry no. 116); Ballarin (see note 4), 1: 318 (entry no. 391).

26. For a complete accounting of the critical debate surrounding this work, see Ballarin (see note 4), 1: 355–56 (entry no. 475); and Tumidei (see note 15), 155 n. 36. Tumidei argues for a date around 1525 (p. 138).

27. Giuseppe Fiocco, "Di alcune opere dimenticate di Sebastiano del Piombo," *Bollettino d'Arte* 4 (1910): 219–24.

28. Giuseppe Fiocco, "L'arte ferrarese nel Polesine," *Cronache d'arte* 11 (1925): 121–26.

29. Ballarin (see note 4), 1: 373 (entry no. 507); Antonio Romagnolo, "La pittura nel Polesine di Rovigo 1500–1540," in Mauro Lucco, ed., *La Pittura nel Veneto: Il Cinquecento* (Milan: Electa, 1996), 420–24.

30. Ballarin (see note 4), 1: 373–74 (entry nos. 508, 509). For the two Rovigo panels, see Pier Luigi Fantelli and Mauro Lucco, *Catalogo della Pinacoteca della Accademia dei Concordi di Rovigo* (Vicenza: Neri Pozza, 1985), 109–10 (entry nos. 230, 231).

31. Luigi Napoleone Cittadella, *Documenti ed illustrazioni risguardanti la storia artistica ferrarese* (Ferrara: Tip. Domenico Taddei, 1868), 56–57. Dr. Barbara Ghelfi, one of my students at the Scuola di Specializzazione in Storia dell'Arte at the University of Bologna, was responsible for checking the documents first published by Cittadella. She alone deserves credit for the discovery of this new document, dated 26 May 1524 (see note 32).

32. Archivio di Stato di Ferrara, Fondo Notarile di Ferrara, notaio Girolamo Dal Ponte, matricola 365, pacco I, prot. 1524, carta 7:

> *Eisdem millesimo [1524] et indictione [12°], die 26 mensis maii, in domo mei notarii infrascripti, presentibus Ioanne [?] Antonio filio quondam Ioannis de Mutinensibus de contrata Sancti Petri, Alberto filio quondam Alexandri Pinzerne de contrata Sancti Apollinaris.*

(Magister Martinus Chieregatus filius quondam Francisci absoluit, liberavit Sebastianum pictorem filium quondam magistri Angeli a ducatis quinque auri, quos dictus Magister Martinus in custodia [?] dedit dicto Magistro Sebastiano, dedi prefato.

Et hanc absolutionem fecit quia dictus magister Martinus in presentia testium et mei notarii infrascripti dixit et sponte confessus fuit habuisse et recepisse. Cansans etc.)

Magister Sebastianus pictor absoluit magistrum Martinum Chieregatum a ducatis quinque auri quos dictus Martinus mutuo accepit a dicto magistro Sebastiano.

Et hanc absolutionem fecit quia dictus Magister Sebastianus in presentia testium et mei notarii infrascripti confessus fuit habuisse et recepisse.

Casans etc.

Quam confessionem etc.

(In the same year and indiction, on the twenty-sixth of the month of May, in the house of the underwritten notary, in the presence of Giovanni Antonio, son of the late Giovanni da Modena of the quarter of San Pietro, [and] Alberto, son of the late Alessandro Pinzerne of the quarter of Sant'Apollinare.

(Master Martino Chieregatro, son of the late Francisco, has absolved [and] released Sebastiano the painter, son of the late Master Angelo, from [a debt of] five gold ducats, which the said Master Martino gave in custody to the said Master Sebastiano, [and which] I gave to the aforesaid.

And he has made this release because the said Master Martino, in the presence of witnesses and of the underwritten notary, stated and voluntarily acknowledged that he had had and had received [repayment]. Annulling etc.)

Master Sebastiano the painter has released Master Martino Chieregato from [a debt of] five gold ducats which the said Master Martino received on loan from the said Master Sebastiano.

And he has made this release because the said Master Sebastiano, in the presence of witnesses and of the underwritten notary, acknowledged that he had had and had received [repayment].

Annulling etc.

Which acknowledgment etc.)

The sentences that I have placed in parentheses, "Magister Martinus Chieregatus... etc.," were struck by the notary, who realized that he had switched the names of the parties, and then rewritten more concisely. I am grateful to Adriano Franceschini for his authoritative advice regarding this document.

33. Cittadella (see note 31), 57.

34. For this painting, see Ballarin (see note 4), 1: 287 (entry no. 299); and Anna Maria Fioravanti Baraldi, *Il Garofalo, Benvenuto Tisi, pittore (c. 1476–1559)* (Rimini: Luisè, 1993), 133–34 (entry no. 64).

35. On the new date for this work, see the documents discovered by Adriano Franceschini, "Dosso Dossi, Benvenuto da Garofalo e il polittico Costabili di Ferrara," *Paragone,* nos. 543–545 (1995): 110–15; as well as his essay in this volume. On the consequences of this discovery for our understanding of Dosso's early years as a

painter, see Peter Humfrey and Mauro Lucco, "Dosso Dossi in 1513: A Reassessment of the Artist's Early Works and Influences," *Apollo* 147 (1998): 22–30.

36. On these two works, see Antonio Romagnolo, ed., *La Pinacoteca dell'Accademia dei Concordi* (Rovigo: Accademia dei Concordi, 1981), 54 (entry no. 15); and Fantelli and Lucco (see note 30), 111–12 (entry no. 233). The argument put forward in the latter for Camillo Filippi as the painter of the work depended upon the impossibility of attributing it to Sebastiano Filippi, who—according to Cittadella's transcription—was dead by 1523, and thus I no longer find it convincing. I wonder now whether the *Baptism of Christ* in the Accademia dei Concordi, which has already been linked on several occasions to Sebastiano Filippi's son Camillo (who was, in turn, the father of Bastianino), is the work of the same hand that painted the *Flight from Egypt* in the Niedersächsisches Landesmuseum in Hannover, which Ballarin (see note 4), 1: 354 (entry no. 467), attributed—unconvincingly, to my mind—to Battista Dossi and dated circa 1527–1530.

37. Romagnolo (see note 29), 421. I wish to thank Antonio Romagnolo for graciously allowing me access to these documents prior to publication.

38. Ballarin (see note 4), 1: 319 (entry no. 394); Rearick's attribution is handwritten on the mount of the drawing.

39. A. Santagiusta Poniz, "Disegni tardi di Domenico Campagnola, 1522–1564," *Arte Veneta* 35 (1981): 67, 70; and Mauro Lucco, "Il Cinquecento (Parte prima)," in Camillo Semenzato, ed., *Le pitture del Santo di Padova* (Vicenza: Neri Pozza, 1984), 162.

40. On the critical history of the work, see Ballarin (see note 4), 1: 316–17 (entry no. 382).

41. Ballarin (see note 4), 1: 318 (entry no. 390).

42. Ballarin (see note 4), 1: 363 (entry no. 487).

43. Ballarin (see note 4), 1: 370–71 (entry no. 504). The document was published by Venturi (see note 5), 224 (doc. 341, dated by typographical error as 1543 instead of 1548). Tumidei (see note 15), 157 n. 95, agrees with this identification.

44. Ballarin (see note 4), 1: 371 (entry no. 505), observes that it is unlikely that the painting in the Musée du Louvre could be identified with the work mentioned in the document, because it would then follow that it was the same size as *Cleopatra* and that the painter would have received the same sum for it. The Louvre painting is considerably larger than the *Cleopatra*.

45. *Gemäldegalerie Berlin: Gesamtverzeichnis* (Berlin: Staatliche Museen zu Berlin, Preußischer Kulturbesitz, 1996), 41 (cat. no. 350), 433 (pl. no. 1900).

46. Quoted in Ballarin (see note 4), 1: 370 (entry no. 504): "*Un altro [quadro] picolo dove glie suso una Vener con sei putini cioè amor fatto da giuro oltra mar.*"

47. [Heinrich] Bodmer, "Contributo alla biografia e allo sviluppo artistico di Iacopone da Faenza," *Melozzo da Forlì* 16, no. 3 (1938): 125–28; Felton Gibbons, "Jacopo Bertucci of Faenza," *Art Bulletin* 50 (1968): 357–62.

Part III

Court Culture in the Age of Dosso

Music in Ferrara and Mantua at the Time of Dosso Dossi: Interrelations and Influences

William F. Prizer

The two major centers of courtly musical activity in northern Italy during the life of the painter Dosso Dossi were precisely the two courts at which Dosso himself was active: Ferrara and Mantua. New genres and styles of music were developed at these two small courts, and, despite their size, they were among the more important musical centers of Europe during Dosso's lifetime. Dosso himself showed considerable interest in musical subjects in his works, and H. Colin Slim has demonstrated that he had a firm grasp of the roles of music in mythology and of the instruments and performance practices of his time.[1] The brilliant musical cultures of Ferrara and Mantua therefore form important backdrops to Dosso's work and thought. Ruled respectively by the Este and the Gonzaga dynasties, the courts were tied both through political expediency and by marriage: Leonello d'Este had married Margherita Gonzaga in 1435, and in 1490 Francesco II Gonzaga married the young Isabella d'Este, daughter of Ercole I d'Este. Neither court can be understood without knowledge of the complex interrelations and influences between the two.

The purpose of this study is to trace briefly the nature of music and musical patronage at the two courts and to sketch some aspects of the relationship between the two. Two caveats are necessary, however. First, I cannot discuss the music of either court in detail within the confines of a single essay. I have accordingly adopted the strategy of emphasizing a series of what might be called "defining moments" in the history of the two centers, moments that decisively changed either the direction or the quality of musical life. Second, I am heavily indebted to Lewis Lockwood of Harvard University, who has almost single-handedly given us our understanding of musical life in Ferrara in the fifteenth and early sixteenth centuries.[2] I must begin my survey some twenty years before the birth of Dosso, because it was then that the patterns of patronage and musical life were set; these patterns were to endure, although with significant changes, to the end of the Renaissance.

It is clear that Ferrara was the leader as a musical center during the fifteenth century, far outshining Mantua. Although his predecessors Leonello and Borso d'Este had maintained important musical establishments, Ercole I's rise to power in 1471 as the first Estense to begin his reign with the dual titles of duke of Ferrara and duke of Modena is undoubtedly a defining moment for the musical life of Ferrara in particular and for that of northern Italy in general. With Ercole, Ferrara entered perhaps its greatest phase, and it could be argued that it was he, along with his contemporary Galeazzo Maria Sforza at Milan,[3] who set the patterns for musical patronage for the rest of the Italian Renaissance. Ercole maintained and even strengthened the three basic groups of musicians responsible for secular music already present under Borso: the corps of trumpeters, the wind band of shawms and trombones (known collectively as the *pifferi*), and the string and keyboard players who were also often the singers of secular music.

Most important was Ercole's addition of a chapel (*cappella*), that is, a choir of singers for the performance of sacred music. This was by far the largest single group of musicians; in 1475 the chapel already had twenty-five members.[4] The expense of the chapel was more than that of all the other groups combined. In 1476, for example, Ercole spent 6,746 lire *marchesane* on his musicians. Of this huge sum, the singers of his chapel received 4,068 lire *marchesane,* whereas all other groups received a total of 2,678 lire *marchesane.*[5] Although he was forced to disband the chapel during the wars with Venice in the early 1480s, Ercole reestablished it immediately after the situation calmed: in 1484, there were nine singers in the chapel; in 1485, there were fourteen; and in 1486, there were at least eighteen members.

There was almost always attached to the chapel at least one major composer who was responsible for providing new works for the ensemble to sing. In 1475 two prominent composers were in residence: Johannes Martini, from the Brabant, and Johannes Brebis, a Frenchman. Ercole later hired two of the greatest composers of the entire Renaissance: Jacob Obrecht, who was at Ferrara from 1487 to 1488 and from 1504 to 1505, and Josquin Desprez, who was in residence from 1503 to 1504 and whose music appears as one of two scores depicted in Dosso's *Allegory of Music* (p. 231).[6]

Ercole also employed a wide variety of musicians who were responsible for secular music. In 1475 there were seven trumpets, three shawms, and two trombones among the *pifferi,* and eight musicians responsible for secular chamber music. The most important of these was undoubtedly the lutenist and improviser Pietrobono, who had been employed by Leonello and who sang lyric and narrative Italian verse to his own and another string player's accompaniment. This duo, the lutenist and his *tenorista,* formed the basic ensemble for the performance of Italian secular vocal music throughout the second half of the fifteenth century. Although it was essentially an oral rather than a written tradition, it is clear that Pietrobono was regarded as its outstanding representative.[7]

In the later years of his reign, Ercole hired new musicians and increased their duties, partly as a result of his deep interest in the theater. From 1486, he began annual productions of a series of classical comedies and sacred plays, the former during carnival and the latter during Lent.[8] His musicians played an integral part in these presentations, both during the increasingly elaborate *intermedi* to the comedies and as providers of music on stage during the dramas themselves.

One document, a letter from Ermes Maria Sforza and Giovanni Francesco da San Severino to Ludovico Sforza, seems worthy of mention here, since it not only provides detail on the kinds of music included in the *intermedi,* but also sums up many of the ways in which music was used to glorify particularly important moments at the court of Ferrara.[9] The letter describes the festivities attendant to the wedding of Alfonso I d'Este, first son of Ercole, to Anna Sforza in February 1491, an event that linked the dynasties of the Este and Sforza families. First, the bishop of Ferrara celebrated a solemn nuptial mass in the *cappella di corte,* accompanied by Ercole's choir. Toward sunset, everyone went to the *sala grande* of the palace for a ball, undoubtedly to the sounds of the ducal *pifferi.* Later Plautus's *Menaechmi* was staged. Between the acts were three *intermedi.* In the first, several men performed a *moresca,* a costumed, mimed dance, probably accompanied by the *pifferi.* The second consisted of two parts: Apollo sang elegiac verses to the accompaniment of his lira da braccio and then the nine muses sang several songs to the accompaniment of a lute. Both parts must have been performed by ducal string players and singers. In the third *intermedio* several men dressed as rustics danced another *moresca,* accompanied by a pipe-and-tabor player. At the end of the comedy, Menaechmus appeared and directed one of the trumpeters, assuredly another of Ercole's musicians, to announce a decree. Afterward was a dinner, for which the string players and singers surely must have performed as well. Thus all the elements of Ercole's musical staff were brought together to celebrate this significant event: the chapel, the *pifferi,* the secular singers and string players, and even the pipe-and-tabor player and one of the trumpeters.

Late in his reign, Ercole's musical staff looked much as it did in 1475: in 1500, for example, there were eleven trumpets, four shawms, and two trombones, twenty-nine singers and an organist in the chapel, and five other instrumentalists—three string players and two pipe-and-tabor players (*tamborini*)—for the court dance.[10] Some of the members of the choir must surely have done double duty as performers of secular music; in fact, one singer, Don Tomaso Fiamingo, is specifically listed as "*contrabasso a le violete.*" Granted this notice, an important element is nevertheless missing from the records. By 1500 the transition of Italian secular vocal music from an unwritten, improvised tradition to a written one was already well underway. The frottola, the new written genre of Italian lyric verse set to music, was built on the oral tradition of Pietrobono and his contemporaries, although it gradually moved beyond it, as we shall see. Pietrobono had died in 1497, and neither in this record nor in any other roster of Ercole's staff is there a single listing of a musician known to us as a frottolist. It seems likely that Ercole remained uninterested in this new music, which developed in his old age, and that his deepening religious sentiments caused him to concentrate on the singers of his chapel. Nonetheless, Ercole supported an impressive musical organization. When he died in early 1505, he had built at Ferrara what was arguably the finest musical establishment in Italy, one that fostered the most forward-looking sacred music of the day.

The situation at Mantua during the Quattrocento was very different, and it can be handled briefly. Although there were trumpets, shawms, and a small number of secular singers and string players at Mantua throughout the fifteenth century, there is little evidence of either a chapel for the performance of sacred polyphony or the presence of a known composer. It is possible that this condition is to some extent illusory, the result of lacunae in the documentation, but it is apparent that Mantua, at least musically, was a satellite court to Ferrara and Milan throughout most of the fifteenth century.

There can be no doubt that the single defining moment for the expansion of musical life in Mantua was the arrival of Isabella d'Este at court in February 1490. Neither can there be any doubt that, in the short term, the ensuing escalation was based on what Isabella had experienced at Ferrara. Her arrival was followed almost immediately by a rapid intensification of attempts to raise the quality of music at court, mostly through her extensive contacts in her native city. In the first years of her reign, the new marchesa sent musicians to Ferrara, presumably to study Ferrarese repertory unknown in Mantua. She requested that Johannes Martini, leader of her father's choir, be sent to Mantua to continue her voice lessons and that the keyboard player Gerolamo da Sestola also be sent to give her lessons. Isabella requested music and instruments from Ferrara, and she used Ferrarese musicians and courtiers as her agents in finding new musicians. Already in 1491, she enlisted the help of Martini and two Ferrarese courtiers to find a male soprano, and earlier in the same year she wrote a safe-conduct for Johannes Ghiselin, called Verbonnet, a northern European composer resident in Ferrara, to travel to France to find musicians for her court.[11]

Isabella was one of the major patrons of music of her age, and court correspondence reveals that music at court and her own performance quickly became her central concerns. Extraordinarily, she also established her own musical household. This was virtually new to the peninsula at the time: previous generations of women had employed pipe-and-tabor players who could teach the necessary graces of court dances, but they had not maintained their own self-contained staff.[12] Isabella changed this, having singers, string players, and keyboard players in her own employ, in addition to the traditional musicians associated with the dances. Perhaps her most important appointment was Bartolomeo Tromboncino, one of the two major frottolists of the day and a lutenist of considerable fame, although Isabella had other frottolists in her employ, at various times, as well.

Isabella maintained an active correspondence with the major poets of her day. She requested their verses, had her musicians compose written settings of them, and sent the songs back to them. She sent her musicians to perform at other courts and took them with her on her frequent trips to other cities in northern Italy. Thus Tromboncino performed in Casale Monferrato in 1499 and in Ferrara as a part of Isabella's entourage in 1502. These two elements, in fact, suggest the great historical significance of Isabella's patronage: she was the major patron, in some ways the principal nourisher, of the frottola. This new genre was essentially a lute song, that is, it was performed by a solo singer to the accompaniment of a lute or other instruments on the lower parts. Under her influence the frottola changed from a simple setting of Italian *poesia per musica* to a vehicle designed to set the much more subtle and elegant verse of Petrarch and his early Cinquecento imitators. At least partly under Isabella's influence, too, the frottola spread from Mantua to Ferrara and other northern Italian centers, and eventually the frottola reached Rome, Naples, Florence, and Siena.

Isabella's undoubted importance as a patron of music has tended to eclipse the patronage of her husband, Francesco, who has been viewed essentially as a military figure. At another court it would be normal to assume that the ruler had his own musicians, but the impression made on historians by Isabella's strong personality has caused Francesco's patronage to be overlooked. This traditional picture should be modified in at least two ways. First, as significant as Isabella's patronage was, it was restricted. There is no trace of any wind players in her service, nor any notice of a chapel for the performance of sacred music, nor any hint of an interest in the chanson, the secular music of France and the Low Countries that had been so prevalent at Italian courts throughout much of the fifteenth century and would continue to be popular in the first decades of the sixteenth. This was due partly to the strictures of Italian Renaissance society and its view of the place of women, but it is also apparent that Isabella was uninterested in any music that she herself could not perform. Although she used her patronage as a way of establishing her own self-image and of achieving that *fama* that was so important to the male nobility of the Italian Renaissance, Isabella was essentially a sponsor of private music for her own performance and the enjoyment of invited guests.

Second, Isabella's husband, Francesco, was also an important supporter of musical activity at court. He too was a patron of the frottola. He had employed Tromboncino before Isabella's arrival at court in 1490, and by 1494 he had hired the second major frottolist, Marchetto Cara, for his staff. Indeed, the earlier works of both frottolists tend to have the stamp of the tastes of their respective patrons. Tromboncino, in Isabella's services, is the most important figure in the move from *poesia per musica* to the more elegant Petrarchan verse. Cara, on the other hand, although a skillful formalist in his early works, tended to set simpler verse apparently more to Francesco's liking, pieces like "Forsì che sì, forsì che no," which is based on a Gonzaga motto, found also on the ceiling of one of Francesco's rooms in the Palazzo di San Sebastiano.[13]

Francesco, however, was the sole patron of public music in Mantua. He was the employer of the shawm band and, influenced by Ercole at Ferrara, the presenter of classical comedies at court.[14] Furthermore, it was Francesco who established the first successful court choir at Mantua. In 1510 the members of the Ferrarese chapel were released because of financial problems attendant to the war of the League of Cambrai, and Francesco hired them virtually en masse and even borrowed music from Ferrara for them to sing. Although he later lost many of these singers to the chapel of the music-loving Pope Leo X, he maintained a choir throughout the rest of his reign.[15] In sum, the vital musical scene at Mantua was the result of not one but two important patrons, and to ignore Francesco's determined sponsorship of music, although it was surely influenced by Isabella's passion for the art, is to have an incomplete picture of the musical life of the court.

A similar situation is true of Ferrara at the time of Dosso. After the death of Ercole d'Este, a basic change took place in musical activity at Ferrara. Although his son and successor, Alfonso I, was a major patron, musical life in Ferrara became more fragmented after 1505 and must be considered in light of the patronage of other members of the Este family, that is, Alfonso's wife, Lucrezia Borgia, and his brothers, Cardinal Ippolito I and Sigismondo.

Alfonso maintained the patterns established by his father, supporting the Ferrarese chapel at its former strength in the early years of his reign and moving immediately to find a new *maestro di cappella* to replace Jacob Obrecht, who had died of the plague shortly after Ercole. Alfonso hired one of the major composers of his day, Antoine Brumel, who arrived at court in 1506. Alfonso also supported the court shawms and trumpets, as befitting the reigning duke, and continued as a patron of the theater and its music as well. He was not as fortunate as his father, however, for, as we have seen, he was forced to disband his chapel in 1510. Several singers returned later, but the size of the choir was greatly reduced, to fewer than ten members in any given year.

A particularly significant member of the chapel was Jean Michel, whom Alfonso himself hired in Savoy in 1502. As Lockwood has shown, he was a member of Alfonso's choir for many years, was the principal copyist of music for both Alfonso and his brother Sigismondo, and acted as an agent for procuring French music at court. Sigismondo, virtually unknown as a patron of music before Lockwood's work, kept a small number of singers and keyboard players and spent much of his time collecting music by Jean Mouton and other French composers.[16]

Although Alfonso shared Sigismondo's preference for French music, the other members of the family assured a balance in Ferrarese musical life. Lucrezia Borgia, who came to the court in 1502, established her own musical staff, probably in imitation of her rival Isabella d'Este. Her bias was decidedly toward native Italian music, although she also showed a fondness for secular music in Spanish, her native tongue. In 1507 (see table 1, p. 305) she had six musicians in her employ, several of whom came to her from Mantua. Among these were Bartolomeo Tromboncino, apparently hired away from Isabella; Paolo Pocino and Dionisio, both also from Mantua; Niccolò da Padova, who had come with her from Rome; and a woman singer, Dalida de'

Putti.[17] Tromboncino, Niccolò, and Dionisio were composers of frottole, as was perhaps Pocino.

Ippolito d'Este, too, was a patron of frottolists, having the third of the great triumvirate of composers of this genre, Michele Pesenti, in his service from at least 1506 and adding Tromboncino to his staff by 1511.[18] Even more than the frottola, however, Ippolito was interested in instrumental music and the French chanson. Lockwood has shown that he kept a staff of instrumentalists in his employ, and his payment registers bear ample testimony to the many string and keyboard instruments he commissioned. These he kept in a *camera della musica,* constructed in 1508. Ippolito's room is thus one in a line of rooms at court designed specifically for music: Ercole had a *camera della musica* by 1481, and Alfonso had a similar room constructed in 1502 or 1503. Isabella, of course, put much of her energy into the building and decoration of similar rooms in Mantua.[19]

By 1506 Ippolito had in his service the important lutenist Giovanni Maria Giudeo. His major coup, however, was his hiring in 1515 of Adrian Willaert, who could well be the composer of the other of the two musical scores depicted in Dosso's *Allegory of Music* some five years later, although Slim has shown that this composer was more likely a minor master at the Ferrarese court.[20]

These early Cinquecento patterns of patronage and the personal preferences of the members of the Este family can be seen clearly by examining the forces for music in Ferrara in a typical year (see table 2, p. 305). In 1516, Alfonso had a small chapel of eight singers plus an organist. Among them was Antoine Colebault, called Bidone, the virtuoso singer whose style is contrasted to that of Marchetto Cara in Castiglione's *Il libro del cortegiano,*[21] and Jean Michel, the music copyist of both Alfonso and Sigismondo. The most important new figure among Alfonso's musicians, however, was Maistre Jhan, who was in Ferrara from 1512 until 1538.[22] He later served as *maestro di cappella* and was the composer of a long series of artful motets for the court, among which was the anti-Protestant *Te Lutherum damnamus,* based on the Te Deum and perhaps directed at the pro-Protestant sentiments of Renée of France.[23] Maistre Jhan was also one of the earlier madrigalists: his "Hor vedete, madonna" was included in the earliest printed book of the genre, the justly famous *Libro primo de la serena* of 1530.

Surprisingly, there are only two instrumentalists listed in Alfonso's employ. Michele Schubinger, a German shawm player, had long been in the service of the Estense, although by 1516 he seems to have been functioning as a string player and instrument repairer rather than a wind player.[24] The other player, Agustino della Viola, was a member of a dynasty of Ferrarese musicians of the same name. He was the father of the more famous Alfonso della Viola, composer of music for Ferrarese dramatic presentations and of two books of madrigals, among which are settings of the poetry of Ludovico Ariosto. This lack of string players is puzzling, particularly since Alfonso d'Este was himself a viol player of some ability. He, like his sister Isabella, learned the new instrument in the last years of the fifteenth century, and he performed during an *intermedio* to a comedy at his own wedding in 1502.[25] It is likely that the singers of the chapel also performed secular music for his entertainment,[26] but for the forces for instrumental music we must look to Ippolito's musicians. In 1516 he had a chapel of six singers and an organist, the most important of whom was Willaert, mentioned previously.[27] Other musicians in his employ included Alessandro Demophonte, a minor frottolist; Dalida de' Putti, who had been in Lucrezia Borgia's service; and two groups of musicians—string players and wind players—capable of providing varied types of instrumental music. Also present were the instrument builders Gian Baptista da Brescia and Alessandro da Modena.

In 1516 Sigismondo had only one musician in his service (although in other years he had as many as five).[28] This musician, Jacques Colebault, was later, and for the majority of his career, in the service of Cardinal Ercole Gonzaga in Mantua and was known accordingly as Jacquet of Mantua. Jacquet seems to have worked principally as a music copyist for Sigismondo. Lucrezia's payment register for 1516 is not extant, although we can infer that Dionisio da Mantova was in her service in this year as well.

None of these courts was as impressive as that maintained by Ercole I at the height of his reign, but together they represent the forces for the performance of a variety of music, including the sacred polyphony of major northern composers like Maistre Jhan, Willaert, and Jacquet. These courts also employed an ample number of performers for French and Italian secular vocal music and instrumental music. The combination of the diverse musical staffs at important events is seen on several occasions in Ferrara. In 1513, for example, Lucrezia Borgia was given a banquet by Antonio Costabili. The visitors were welcomed by the *pifferi* of Alfonso d'Este. At the beginning of the dinner, members of his choir sang psalms "*in voce bassa,*" and during the meal itself the guests were entertained by lutes, viols, and cornetts; presumably these instrumentalists were in the service of Ippolito and Lucrezia herself.[29]

Musicians from various members of the family also performed at later banquets. During carnival of 1529, for example, Ercole II gave a banquet for 104 guests, including his wife, Renée of France, his father, Alfonso d'Este, his aunt Isabella d'Este, and his brother Ippolito II d'Este, in the great hall of the Castello. The meal was preceded by a performance of Ariosto's *La cassaria* and by music for select guests. Each course of the banquet was accompanied by different music, as described by the court chef Cristoforo da Messisbugo. During the first course, Dalida de' Putti and four others sang a work by Alfonso della Viola, accompanied by five viols, a harpsichord with two stops, a lute, and tenor and bass recorders. During the second course, four people sang madrigals, perhaps either those of Maistre Jhan or those of Alfonso della Viola himself, even though Alfonso's works were not published until 1539 and 1540, respectively. The third course was accompanied by a polychoral dialogue for two choirs of four voices each; each choir was accompanied by lute, viol, flute, and trombone. During the fourth course, another composition of Alfonso was performed, this time by five members of the duke's chapel, accompanied by five viols, a violin, and several wind instruments—a dolzaina, a crumhorn, two tenor recorders, and a mute cornett, as well as an organ with several stops. During the fifth course, five trombones and a cornett played a purely instrumental piece, and for the sixth course, the diners were entertained by Angelo Beolco (Ruzzante) and his troupe, who sang villotte, rustic songs in Paduan dialect. The last course featured a piece for five voices accompanied by five viols and other instruments. After the meal four flutes played while the guests received their traditional gifts, four trumpets sounded to announce the end of the banquet, and then the *pifferi* played for a dance until dawn.[30]

This represents a wide variety of musical genres, ranging from purely instrumental music to purely vocal madrigals, with combinations of the two and with rustic, bawdy villotte as well.[31] The variety of musicians required was equally broad, and can be matched with some certainty to the musical retainers of the aging Alfonso I. The payment register for 1529 is not extant, but those from 1528 (see table 3, p. 307) and 1530 are. The following were included for 1528: the trumpeters who announced the beginning and end of the banquet; a chapel of eight singers, a group that matches the number required for the polychoral work of the third course; Alfonso della Viola, who composed the music for the first and fourth courses; the *pifferi* who played for the dance; and miscellaneous string players required for much of the music. Some of the string players would probably have played wind instruments as well, although the *pifferi* were expected as a matter of course to double on various wind instruments.[32] An addition in 1528 was "Cesare dal cornetto," a player whose skills were called for in the music for the fifth course.

Dalida de' Putti, the woman who had been in service to Lucrezia and Ippolito I, was still present; also performing were members of the court chapel and various wind and string players, drawn without doubt from musicians serving different members of the family. Two other musicians listed are particularly important for music historians, since both were composers whose whereabouts had not been known for this year. "Julio da Modena" is the standard indication for Julio Segni, Modenese keyboard player, harpist, and one of the early composers of the instrumental ricercare. He had been in Ippolito I's service from 1506 to 1513 and was later to become an organist at San Marco in Venice.[33] Also present is "Zoane Maria dal gitarino" (player of the soprano lute), undoubtedly the same as the virtuoso lutenist and composer Zoane Maria, variously known as Zoane Maria Giudeo, Zoane Maria Alemano, or Zoane Maria de' Medici. He too had been in Ippolito I's service, and he also served popes Leo X and Clement VII in Rome.[34]

One further point can be drawn from table 3. Even without considering the inflationary pattern of the early sixteenth century, it is clear that Alfonso was spending considerably less than his father on his musical establishment.

In 1476, Ercole had spent 6,746 lire *marchesane* on his musicians' salaries.[35] In 1528, Alfonso budgeted 3,080 lire *marchesane*, or less than half what his father had spent.[36] This represents a savings of over three thousand lire *marchesane*. The majority of this seems to have been the result of a reduction of the size in the chapel, from the twenty-nine members under Ercole in 1500 to the much smaller number listed in table 3, but the reality remains that Alfonso was spending almost a thousand lire *marchesane* less on his entire musical establishment than Ercole had spent on his chapel alone (4,068 lire *marchesane*). Alfonso's total budget, in fact, was only slightly more than Ercole had spent on his wind and string players (2,678 lire *marchesane*).

As in Ferrara, the next generation of patrons in Mantua would also effect major changes. Federico II, who succeeded his father in 1519, would turn more to Rome than Ferrara as a model for his musical establishment, as he did with his recruitment of Giulio Romano, a student of Raphael. The documentation on Federico's patronage is particularly fragile, but it would seem that he made the recruitment of musicians a major part of his trip to Rome in August 1522. Although the ostensible purpose of the journey was to speak with the pope about military matters, he also made arrangements to buy an alabaster organ that had belonged to Leo X, and immediately after his visit Michele Pesenti, who had been one of Leo's personal musicians, appears in Federico's service, as does the important foreign composer Andreas de Silva, who had been a member of the papal chapel under Leo.[37] It is likely that Federico hired the French composer Jean Lhéritier during the same trip: Lhéritier left his post in the church of San Luigi dei Francesi in Rome in August 1522, while Federico was in the city, and was definitely in his employ in 1525.[38]

Federico's brother Cardinal Ercole Gonzaga would become the major patron of sacred music in the city from the 1530s. In his role as administrator of the cathedral of San Pietro, he took an active role in its musical life, hiring new adult singers and young clerics and watching after their needs. To strengthen the forces for the performance of sacred music, he kept adult singers and clerics on his own payroll and also concerned himself with those who were paid by the cathedral chapter. The choir of San Pietro was thus made up of two distinct elements. One was that for which the chapter of the cathedral was responsible for paying, and the other that for which Ercole himself paid.

The central figure at San Pietro was clearly Jacquet of Mantua, who worked in the cathedral from at least 1534 until his retirement in 1558.[39] Jacquet was one of the principal composers of the post-Josquin generation, and he produced a large body of sacred music for Mantua. He functioned as *maestro di canto*, or singing teacher, to the young clerics in the cathedral, as *maestro di cappella*, and as composer-in-residence, always in the pay of Ercole himself rather than the chapter. In these roles Jacquet would have taught the clerics chant and polyphony, conducted the rehearsals of the choir and performed with them at their services, and composed new works for their use. George Nugent has discussed in detail the chapel's general duties.[40] These included mass each Saturday in the Chapel of the Madonna de' Voti, and mass at the high altar on Sundays and feast days. Weekdays were occasions for low mass, although, according to Nugent, motets may have been sung even then. Given the amount of music that Jacquet composed for the service, the choir must have performed vespers throughout the year and have sung polyphony at mass, vespers, and matins during Holy Week.

An analysis of the third generation of patrons in Ferrara, represented by Duke Ercole II and his family, awaits the publication of the research of Jessie Ann Owens of Brandeis University. We know that Maistre Jhan was Ercole II's *maestro di cappella* until 1538 and that Alfonso della Viola and his brother Francesco served him as well.[41] The payment register for 1542, the year of Dosso's death, shows a chapel of two chaplains, ten singers, and the organist Jacques Brumel. There are also several string players and the standard *pifferi,* now including players of the cornett, which had to some extent replaced the shawm as the standard instrument of the ensemble (see table 4, p. 308).[42]

One further point needs to be made. Although the documentation does not allow confirmation for all Ferrarese and Mantuan patrons, it is clear that the great majority were themselves amateur musicians of some accomplishment. In Ferrara, Ercole I sang, Alfonso sang and played lute and viol, Ippolito I played harpsichord, and Lucrezia Borgia sang and played harp and lute. In Mantua, Federico and Ercole Gonzaga had both received musical training as boys, and Isabella was clearly the outstanding amateur musician of her day. She sang and played lute, vihuela de mano, lira da braccio, viol, harpsichord, and organ. Musicianship was an important element of patronage: had patrons not had these abilities, their sponsorship would not have been nearly so well informed, nor could they have impressed their own musical tastes so clearly on their personal staffs.

The interrelated patterns of musical life in Ferrara and Mantua are thus clear. They were set originally by Ercole I in the 1470s. Thanks to Ercole's energetic patronage, Ferrara became perhaps the most important Italian center for music in the late fifteenth century. The musical scene there became more fragmented in the early sixteenth century, when Alfonso, Ippolito, Lucrezia, and Sigismondo each had a specialized musical staff. Ferrara, however, was the major influence on music in Mantua during the late fifteenth century. Isabella d'Este brought to the city her father's passionate interest in music, instilled in her as a girl, and without her Mantua would not have been the major center it became. She created a new musical environment at court that, through her patronage of Italian secular music, reciprocally influenced Ferrarese musical life. There, too, thanks to Lucrezia Borgia and Ippolito d'Este, the frottola flourished, largely through musicians trained in Mantua. Through Isabella's example, her husband Francesco made the support of other kinds of music a central concern. Their sons in turn supported music at a high level, with musical staffs that continued to rival those of Ferrara.

Notes

1. H. Colin Slim, "Dosso Dossi's Allegory at Florence about Music," *Journal of the American Musicological Society* 43 (1990): 43–98, esp. 48.

2. Lewis Lockwood, *Music in Renaissance Ferrara, 1400–1505: The Creation of a Musical Center in the Fifteenth Century* (Cambridge: Harvard Univ. Press, 1984). This is the capstone of Lockwood's studies of music in Ferrara; other studies of his are cited below.

3. For a survey of music in Milan, see William F. Prizer, "Music at the Court of the Sforza: The Birth and Death of a Musical Center," *Musica disciplina* 43 (1989): 141–93, and the earlier literature cited there. A general introduction to music at the northern Italian courts is idem, "North Italian Courts, 1460–1540," in Iain Fenlon, ed., *The Renaissance: From the 1470s to the End of the Sixteenth Century* (Englewood Cliffs, N.J.: Prentice-Hall, 1989), 133–55.

4. ASMO, Bolletta, no. 7 (1475). The following abbreviations are used here for archives: ASMI: Archivio di Stato di Milano; ASMN: Archivio di Stato di Mantova; ASMO: Archivio di Stato di Modena. All documents from ASMN stem from the Archivio Gonzaga. All those from ASMO are found in the Camera Ducale.

5. William F. Prizer, review of *Music in Renaissance Ferrara,* by Lewis Lockwood, *Journal of the American Musicological Society* 40 (1987): 98–99.

6. Slim (see note 1), 43–98.

7. On Pietrobono, see Lewis Lockwood, "Pietrobono and the Instrumental Tradition at Ferrara in the Fifteenth Century," *Rivista italiana di musicologia* 10 (1975): 115–33; idem (see note 2), 95–108; and William F. Prizer, "The Frottola and the Unwritten Tradition," *Studi musicali* 15 (1986): 3–37. The whole practice of an unwritten tradition was first proposed in Nino Pirrotta, "Music and Cultural Tendencies in Fifteenth-Century Italy," *Journal of the American Musicological Society* 19 (1966): 127–66.

8. See, among other studies, Egidio Scoglio, *Il teatro alla corte Estense* (Lodi: Biancardi, 1965); Anna Maria Coppo, "Spettacoli alla corte di Ercole I," in Università Cattolica del Sacro Cuore, Istituto di Filologia Moderna, *Contributi: Serie storia di teatro,* vol. 1 (Milan: Società Vita e Pensiero, 1968), 31–59; and Lewis Lockwood, "Popular Religious Spectacle at Ferrara under Ercole I d'Este," in Maristella de Panizza Lorch, ed., *Il teatro italiano del Rinascimento* (Milan: Edizioni di Comunità, 1980), 571–82.

9. Letter of 14 February 1491. ASMI, Carteggio Sforzesco, busta 1473, lettera no. 94; published in Pietro Ghinzoni, "Nozze e commedie alla corte di Ferrara nel febbraio 1491," *Archivio storico lombardo,* anno 11 (1884): 751–53.

10. ASMO, Memoriale del Soldo, no. 21 (1500). These figures, and those for the previous table, differ slightly from those in Lockwood (see note 2), 327, 319–20.

11. See William F. Prizer, *Courtly Pastimes: The Frottole of Marchetto Cara* (Ann Arbor: UMI Research Press, 1980), 5–10, for a list of documents concerning new musicians in Mantua during the 1490s.

12. On this point see William F. Prizer, "Renaissance Women as Patrons of Music: The North Italian Courts," in Kimberly Marshall, ed., *Rediscovering the Muses: Women's Musical Traditions* (Boston: Northeastern Univ. Press, 1993), 186–205.

13. See Renato Berzaghi, "Francesco II e Vincenzo Gonzaga: Il Palazzo di San Sebastiano e il Palazzo Ducale," *Paragone,* no. 485 (1990): 62–73 and plates 34–37. Cara's "Forsì che sì" predates the construction of the palazzo; it was published in 1505. See also Claudio Gallico, *"Forse che si forse che no" fra poesia e musica* (Mantua: Istituto Carlo d'Arco per la Storia di Mantova, 1961).

14. On Francesco's patronage of the shawm band, see William F. Prizer, "Bernardino Piffaro e i pifferi e tromboni di Mantova," *Rivista italiana di musicologia* 16 (1981): 151–84.

15. On Francesco's *cappella,* see William F. Prizer, "La cappella di Francesco II Gonzaga e la musica sacra a Mantova nel primo ventennio del Cinquecento," in *Mantova e i Gonzaga nella civiltà del Rinascimento* (Mantua: Mondadori, 1977), 267–76; and idem (see note 11), 14–23.

16. Lewis Lockwood, "Jean Mouton and Jean Michel: New Evidence on French Music and Musicians in Italy, 1505–1520," *Journal of the American Musicological Society* 32 (1979): 191–246. Alfonso's hiring of Jean Michel is documented in Prizer (see note 3), 103–4.

17. William F. Prizer, "Isabella d'Este and Lucrezia Borgia as Patrons of Music: The Frottola at Mantua and Ferrara," *Journal of the American Musicological Society* 38 (1985): 8.

18. Ippolito's musicians have been discussed in Lewis Lockwood, "Adrian Willaert and Cardinal Ippolito I d'Este: New Light on Willaert's Early Career in Italy, 1515–1521," *Early Music History* 5 (1985): 85–112; and idem, "Musicisti a Ferrara all'epoca dell'Ariosto," in Maria Antonella Balsano, ed., *L'Ariosto, la musica, i musicisti: Quattro studi e sette madrigali ariosteschi* (Florence: L. S. Olschki, 1981), 7–25.

19. In 1481 Francesco Sicco d'Aragona wrote to Federico I Gonzaga that Eleanora d'Aragona had taken Chiara Gonzaga to the *"camara de la musica,"* where she was shown the musical instruments kept there. ASMN, busta 1229, fol. 215; partially published in Lockwood (see note 2), 145. In the same year, there are payments to painters and others for the decoration of *"la camara de li istromenti."* ASMO, Munizioni e Fabbriche, no. 15, 69r; published in Thomas J. Tuohy, *Herculean Ferrara: Ercole d'Este, 1471–1505, and the Invention of a Ducal Capital* (Cambridge: Cambridge Univ. Press, 1996), 414. Alfonso's *"camarin della musica"* is documented in ASMO, Libri Amministrazione Principi, no. 35 (1503–1505), fol. 0v (8 February 1503): *"Illustrissimo Signore Don Alfonso d'Este per conto de le fabriche del camarin da le muxiche che fa fare sua Signoria"*; see Adolfo Venturi, "Pittori della corte ducale a Ferrara nella prima decade del secolo XVI," *Archivio storico dell'arte* 7 (1894): 305. I am indebted to Luisa Ciammitti for the reference to Venturi. There is no documentation that Isabella's *studiolo* and *grotta* in Mantua were in fact *camere della musica,* although their iconographical schemes are overwhelmingly musical.

20. Slim (see note 1), 57–58.

21. Baldassare Castiglione, *Il libro del cortegiano, novamente rivisto* (Venice: Giouanni Paduano, 1538), 27–28; and, idem, *The Book of the Courtier,* trans. Charles S. Singleton (Garden City, N.Y.: Anchor/Doubleday, 1959), bk. 1, chap. 37, 60:

> Consider music, the harmonies of which are now solemn and slow, now very fast and novel in mood and manner. And yet all give pleasure, although for different reasons, as is seen in Bidon's manner of singing which is so skilled, quick, vehement, impassioned, and has such various melodies that the spirits of his listeners are stirred and take fire, and are so entranced that they seem to be uplifted to heaven. Nor does our Marchetto Cara move us less by his singing, but only with a softer harmony. For in a manner serene and full of plaintive sweetness, he touches and penetrates our souls, gently impressing a delightful sentiment upon them.

22. On Maitre Jean, see Alfonso dalla Viola, *Primo libro di madrigali: Ferrara, 1539,* ed. Jessie Ann Owens (New York: Garland, 1990), xi.

23. George Nugent, "Anti-Protestant Music for Sixteenth-Century Ferrara," *Journal of the American Musicological Society* 43 (1990): 228–91.

24. Insofar as I am able to tell from the extant documentation, there was no established ensemble of *pifferi* during this period. They are not mentioned in 1516, nor is any fixed group listed until the later 1520s. Michele is documented as a string player and instrument repairer in ASMO, Guardaroba, no. 140, fols. 17r, 23v, and passim.

25. For Isabella's and Alfonso's learning the viols, see William F. Prizer, "Isabella d'Este and Lorenzo da Pavia, 'Master Instrument Maker,'" *Early Music History* 2 (1982): 104–5.

26. *"Anco il Prencipe [Alfonso] stesso averebbe il verno innanzi cena suonate di Vivola, ma un cotal Cameriere, un Cappellano privato de' suoi, e passato quel tempo non solo avanti, ma anco dopo la cena, cantato dui o tre mottetti, Canzone Francese, ed altri, come spesse volte l'istate alla Villa ed al Boschetto mentre si cenava i musici averebbono cantato quattro o sei Canzone molto leggiadre."* Quoted from Angelo Solerti, "La vita ferrarese nella prima metà del secolo decimosesto descritta da Agostino Mosti," *Atti e memorie della R. Deputazione di Storia Patria per le Provincie di Romagna,* ser. 3, 10 (1891–1892): 182. The passage is translated in Lockwood, 1985 (see note 18), 100.

27. The designation of "chapel" for these musicians is my own. Here and among his other musicians, it is often difficult to decipher the function of those in his employ. I have attempted to do so through payment registers surrounding the chapel for 1516. For a slightly different list of Ippolito's musicians in 1516, see Lockwood, 1981 (see note 18), 19.

28. Lockwood (see note 16), 198 n. 21.

29. Prizer (see note 12), 190.

30. The music of this banquet, of 24 January 1529, and the others described by Messisbugo, are discussed in Howard Mayer Brown, "A Cook's Tour of Ferrara in 1529," *Rivista italiana di musicologia* 10 (1975): 216–41; a full list of all the music is included there on pp. 239–40. In the modern edition of Messisbugo's *Banchetti, composizioni di vivande e apparecchio generale,* ed. Fernando Bandini (1549; reprint,

Venice: Neri Pozza, 1960), the full description of the 24 January banquet is on pp. 41–52. For a painting by Lorenzo Zacchia perhaps associated with Ruzzante and his troupe, see H. Colin Slim, "Two Paintings of 'Concert Scenes' from the Veneto and the Morgan Library's Unique Music Print of 1520," in Fabrizio Della Seta and Franco Piperno, eds., *In cantu et in sermone: For Nino Pirrotta on His Eightieth Birthday* (Florence: L. S. Olschki, 1989), 155–74. Significantly, the painting depicts the villotta, "Venite, donne belle," by Ruffino Bartolucci, who worked in Padua.

31. On the villotta and the popularizing music of the northern Italian courts at this time, see William F. Prizer, "Games of Venus: Secular Vocal Music in the Late Quattrocento and Early Cinquecento," *Journal of Musicology* 9 (1991): 3–56.

32. *Pifferi* doubling on other wind instruments is discussed in Prizer (see note 14), 160–62.

33. H. Colin Slim, "Julio Segni," in Stanley Sadie, ed., *The New Grove Dictionary of Music and Musicians,* 20 vols. (London: Macmillan, 1980), 17: 105–6. See also idem, ed., *Musica Nova: Accommodata per cantar et sonar sopra organi et altri strumenti, composta per diversi eccellentissimi musici. In Venetia, MDXL* (Chicago: Univ. of Chicago Press, 1964).

34. ASMO, Bolletta de' Salariati, no. 40 (Giornale), fol. 61v. Zoane Maria appears only in the Giornale, under the date 24 December 1528, not the normal Bolletta (no. 39). For this reason I have not included his name in table 3. This is the last known reference to the lutenist. See H. Colin Slim, "Gian and Gian Maria, Some Fifteenth- and Sixteenth-Century Namesakes," *Musical Quarterly* 57 (1971): 562–74; and Prizer (see note 7), 17.

35. See p. 291.

36. The actual figure spent by Alfonso was somewhat less than this because some musicians were not present every month of the year. The figure of 3,044 lire *marchesane* represents the amount that Alfonso must have budgeted for the year in order to keep his musical establishment at full strength.

37. Pesenti is listed in Leo's services in 1521 (Biblioteca Apostolica Vaticana, RS 1745, fols. 241r–v). I am indebted to Professor Richard Sherr for this reference. De Silva appears in Mantua by December 1522, when Federico requires his *maestro di camera* to give him twenty ducats and twenty lengths of damask, probably for livery (ASMN, busta 2965, libro 21, fol. 51v).

38. On Lhéritier, see Leeman L. Perkins, *The Motets of Jean Lhéritier,* 2 vols. (Ann Arbor: University Microfilms, 1965); and idem, "Jean Lhéritier," in Sadie (see note 33), 10: 710–11. See also Hermann-Walter Frey, "Die Kapellmeister der französischen Nationalkirche San Luigi dei Francesi in Rom im 16. Jahrhundert," *Archiv für Musikwissenschaft* 22 (1965): 272ff. and 23 (1966): 32ff. Lhéritier is shown to have been in Mantua in William F. Prizer, "A Mantuan Collection of Music for Holy Week, 1537," in Andrew Morrogh et al., eds., *Renaissance Studies in Honor of Craig Hugh Smyth,* 2 vols. (Florence: Giunti Barbèra, 1985), 1: 613–25.

39. The basic work on Jacquet of Mantua has been done by George Nugent in his *The Jacquet Motets and Their Authors,* 2 vols. (Ann Arbor: University Microfilms, 1973). See also Iain Fenlon, *Music and Patronage in Sixteenth-Century Mantua,* 2 vols. (Cambridge: Cambridge Univ. Press, 1980–1982), 1: 45–73.

40. Nugent, ibid., 1: 98–99, 102–3, 107–8. See also his review of *Archivalische Studien zur Musikpflege am Dom von Mantua, 1500–1627,* by Pierre M. Tagmann, *Journal of the American Musicological Society* 24 (1971): 476.

41. Alfonso is last listed among the Estensi musicians in 1539 (ASMO, Bolletta dei Salariati, no. 49, fol. 73v [for 24 December 1539]); Francesco disappears after 1535 (idem, no. 46, fol. 49v [6 September 1535]).

42. The list of musicians for 1542 is partly published in Walter Weyler, "Documenten betreffende de Muziekkapel aan het Hof van Ferrara," *Vlaamsch Jaarboek voor Muziekgeschiedenis* 1 (1939): 93–94. The trumpeters, unlike the other musicians, are listed in the series of Memoriali del Soldo rather than the Bollette dei Salariati. The Memoriale is not extant for 1542, and I have therefore adopted that for 1541.

Table 1. Musicians in the Service of Lucrezia Borgia in 1507[a]

Dionixio da Mantoa, deto Papino [frottolist]
Nicolò da Padoa cantore [frottolist and lutenist]
[Bartolomeo] Trombonzino cantore [frottolist and lutenist]
Rizardetto tamborino [pipe-and-tabor player]
Pozino cantore
Madonna Dalida [de' Putti] cantore

[a] Source: ASMO, Libri Amministrazione Principi, No. 1135. Here and throughout the transcriptions of the payment registers, I have left musicians' names in the original orthography of the documents. In the body of the text however, I have normalized them to the standard spellings in the literature.

Table 2. Musicians in Ferrarese Service in 1516

Alfonso I[a]

Trumpeters

Steffano da Montepulziano
Barachino
Filipo Maria del Rosso
Antonio d'Arcquà
Domenego de Jacopo da Bologna
Nicolò de Raganello

Chapel

Antonio Colobaudi, dito Bidon, cantore
Foriero [Furibon] cantore (released on 31 March)
Francesco de Lorene cantore (begins on 1 September)
Metre Gian cantore et ducale cameraro
Janes Pezenin cantore
Simon [francese] cantore
Zoane Griveo cantore
Zoanne Michiele cantore
Antonio da l'organo

Table 2, continued

Instrumentalists

Augustino de la Viola
Michiel [Schubinger] piffaro

Ippolito I[b]

Chapel

Adriano [Willaert] cantore
Aloise Benaria francese cantore
Aloixe Podreglia cantore
Francesco d'Asti cantore
Gian Lourdello cantore
Juschini [Doro] cantore
Zoane Baptista da organo

Other Musicians

Alexandro da Verona de Pre Michele [string player?]
Alexandro [Demophonte] da Bologna [frottolist and lutenist]
Madonna Dalida de' Puti [singer and Ippolito's mistress]
Zoanne Jacomo da Vicenza [string player]
Gerardo Franzozo [wind player]
Baptista Gritti da Verona musico [flute]
Zoanne Jacomo da Bressa musico
Bartolomeo Tamborino
Signoria musico [flute player]
Janes de Pre Michele
Francesco Zoppo musico
Afranio de' Conti [string player]
Maestro Zoan Baptista da Bressa [organ builder]
Maestro Alexandro da Modena [harpsichord builder and player]

Sigismondo[c]

Jaches cantore [Jacques Colebault, later called Jacquet of Mantua]

Lucrezia Borgia[d]

Papino [Dionixio] da Mantova chantore (1517)

[a] Source: ASMO, Memoriale del Soldo, No. 41 (1516); Bolletta de' Salariati, No. 27 (1515). The *piffero* ensemble is not present. The Bolletta, which lists trumpeters, is not extant for 1516. I have therefore adopted the Bolletta from 1515.

[b] Source: ASMO, Libri Amministrazione Principi, No. 796 (1516); No. 791 (1514–1524); Guardaroba, No. 140 (1516).

[c] ASMO, Libri Amministrazione Principi, No. 1472

[d] Source: Payment Registers from 1509 through 1516 not extant. ASMO, Libri Amministrazione Principi, No. 1132 covers the period 1517–1520.

Table 3: Musicians in Service to Alfonso I, 1528, and Their Salaries[a]

Name	Monthly Salary	Annual Salary
Trumpeters		
Barachino tronbeta	L. 16	L. 192
Felipo Maria tronbeta	L. 16	L. 192
Nicola de Raganello tronbeta	L. 12	L. 144
Zoane Antonio tronbeta	L. 7	L. 84
Hieronimo da Raganelo tronbeta	L. 7	L. 84
Jacomo de Raganelo tronbeta	L. 7	L. 84
Subtotal		L. 680
Pifferi		
Marco piva[b]	L. 3	L. 30
Domenego piva	L. 3	L. 36
Francesco Maria piva	L. 3	L. 36
Pelegrino piva	L. 3	L. 36
Cesaro piva	L. 3	L. 36
Lucha piva	L. 3	L. 36
Cexaro dal cornetto[c]	L. 3	L. 6
Subtotal		L. 216
String Players, Vocalists, and Chapel		
Zoan Michiele cantore	L. 18	L. 216
Zoane Gravio cantore	L. 18	L. 216
Janes cantore	L. 18	L. 216
Metre Gian cantore	L. 15	L. 180
Simon cantore	L. 7	L. 84
Francesco cantore	L. 7	L. 84
Alfonso da la Viola	L. 13	L. 156
Julio da Modena	L. 18	L. 216[d]
Agustino da la Viola	L. 27	L. 324
Afranio de Conti	L. 12	L. 144
Francesco da la Viola	L. 8	L. 96
Zoane Jacomo da Bressa	L. 3	L. 36
Antonio Capello cantore	L. 18	L. 216
Subtotal		L. 2,184
Total		L. 3,080

[a] Sources: ASMO, Bollette de' Salariati, No. 39 (1528, Bolletta) and No. 40 (1528, Giornale)

[b] Through October.

[c] November and December only: fol. 54v (7 November), "In locho de Marcho."

[d] Actually only January through August: L. 144.

Table 4: The Musicians of Ercole II in 1542[a]

Trumpeters
- Felippo Maria trombeta
- Girolimo Raganello
- Jacomo trombetta
- Rainaldo Rafanelo trombeta

Chapel
- Antonio de Sassi
- Don Antonio francese
- Don Antonio Maria Furlano [cappellano]
- Costanzo heremita cantore
- Enrigh de Campis cantore
- Francesco cantore
- Don Francesco capelan
- Giannes cantore
- Pavarello cantore
- Zoanne Gravio
- Zoane Michiel cantore
- Zoanne Millemille
- Jaches [Brumel] organista

Pifferi
- Antonio dal cornetto
- Francesco Maria piffaro
- Michiel Ferra[rese]
- Zoan Francesco trombone
- Nicolò trombone

String Players
- Zoan Francesco Rodengo
- Antonio Rodengo
- Antonio di Rivaroli
- Afranio di Conti

[a] Source: ASMO, Bolletta dei Salariati, No. 51 ("Zornale de la Bolletta"); Memoriale del Soldo, No. 71 (1541; trumpeters only)

Humanistic Culture and Literary Invention in Ferrara at the Time of the Dossi

Luca D'Ascia

Lucian of Samosata was well known to Ferrara's humanistic culture from the first half of the fifteenth century on.[1] Guarino Veronese, with his translation of *Musca,* revived the sophistic genre of paradoxical praise that was later to become widely popular in the sixteenth century. Guarino's version of *Calumnia,* which dates back to the second decade of the fifteenth century, instead provided a classical example of ekphrasis. Sandro Botticelli's humanistic iconography was to take its inspiration, as is well known, from descriptions of Apelles's masterpiece, and the rebirth of ekphrasis encouraged allegorical painting among Ferrara's artists. I do not plan to discuss the Lucianic tradition in Ferrarese culture; rather, I will look at the literary output stimulated by the free imitation of the Greek writer's work.

Leon Battista Alberti was at the source of this trend. He was at home in many places, but he lived in Ferrara during the very years (1438 and 1441–1442) that were to prove decisive for the Lucianic revival. Guarino's *Musca* is dedicated to him, among others. In his treatise on painting, *De pictura,* Alberti translated Lucian's ekphrasis in *Calumnia* in competition with Guarino. Above all, however, Alberti was inspired by Lucian's model in his *Intercenales,* or "dinner pieces." Although its chronology (from about 1428 to 1445) remains uncertain, some later pieces may possibly have come from Alberti's period in Ferrara. A manuscript of the *Intercenales* circulated in Ferrara and was in the possession of the humanist Pandolfo Collenuccio of Pesaro.[2] The latter wrote his *Apologhi* in Ferrara between 1494 and 1499; Beatus Rhenanus called them more brilliant even than Lucian's works.[3]

Another humanist with close links to Ferrara, Niccolò Leoniceno, translated into the vernacular a part of Lucian's corpus and included in it one of Alberti's dinner pieces, "Virtus." Leoniceno was Celio Collenuccio's rival in the polemic concerning Pliny's errors in medicine and Calcagnini's teacher. Matteo Maria Boiardo introduced his own vernacular version—or reworking—of Lucian's *Timon* on the stage in 1491. Antonio Cammelli (nicknamed "Pistoia"), a Tuscan writer with links to the court of Ferrara, also drew inspiration from Lucian's dialogues; he dedicated his *Sonetti faceti* to Isabella d'Este. In the years that followed, Erasmus's influence intermingled with Alberti's and Lucian's in the dialogues, *apologi,* and declamations of Calcagnini. The latter, in his dialogue *Equitatio,* represented Ludovico Ariosto as certainly nostalgic for the *serio ludere* (serious play) of erudite humanistic games, but also captivated by the *pulcherrime ambages* (lovely diversions) of the transalpine literary material so popular at the Estense court.[4] The chivalric genre was not incompatible with learned fantastic and satirical creations, however, as was shown by Ariosto's reuse of Alberti, which brought to a fitting close the history of "Lucianism" in Ferrara during the very same years in which Dosso was active there.

It seems worth noting here, in taking a closer look at some of the episodes in this history, a characteristic trait of the Lucianic genre, namely its function as a bridge between moral philosophy and figurative representation. All of the above-mentioned authors found the weightiness of the treatise form to be uncomfortable and felt the need to transmit particularly subtle ethical teachings in unusual forms that would strike the imagination and act concretely on the senses. Writers in the Lucianic mold wished to teach an ethic of "prudence" and of *exemplum,* rather than abstract norms. Some, like Alberti, rejected Cicero's stylistic authority,[5] while others, like Calcagnini, criticized Cicero's philosophy while favoring Lorenzo Valla's Epicureanism and Erasmus's "folly." These writers kept an anticlerical and antimonastic thrust alive in their works, while studiously avoiding taking sides with the enemies of the papacy. The programmatic "lightness" of the Lucianic genre allowed for periodic outbursts of nearly irreligious nonchalance. Writers after the manner of Lucian aspired, moreover, to address moral discourse to a specific audience with an intent that was largely encomiastic, but also subtly critical through its screen of irony. Such was the case of cantos 34 and 35 of Ariosto's *Orlando furioso,* which exposed the mechanism of poetic adulation. Lucianic invention was merged here with the mythological fable, in which court society—while making recourse to a slender etiological pretext—presented itself behind a transparent allegorical veil.

The success of the Lucianic genre coincided with the blossoming of court theater, which involved such important figures from Estense diplomacy and bureaucracy as Niccolò da Correggio, Matteo Maria Boiardo, and Pandolfo Collenuccio. The Lucianic revival thus acquired an intrinsically theatrical dimension. The physical and immediately apparent traits of the characters were foregrounded and exaggerated through emphasis on their physiognomy (the true source of all caricature), whether the texts involved were mythological intrigues or allegorical descriptions.

Frequent references to fictitious works of art often accompanied this visibility of ethics (if we may call it that) in the Lucianic texts. The descriptions of allegorical temples and the moral paintings they contain were the source of the sixteenth-century genre of the "gallery." Writers following Lucian's model supplied information for the construction of emblematic images charged with recondite meanings, thus emulating the great master of ancient ekphrasis. These images could be transposed to an exotic scenario such as Brahmin India in the "Picture,"[6] but they could also be applied to objects for everyday use in order to heal *aegritudo* (the symbolic and therapeutic rings found in "Anuli"). To what degree these literary images were realized in the figurative arts is a problem that remains open to interdisciplinary research.[7] Here I will merely point out some particularly significant texts as confirmation of the continuity of a genre that was programmatically in competition with painting.

Alberti's vast body of Lucianic writings appears resistant to any sweeping definition. If Lucian's aim had been to reconcile Socratic dialogue and ancient comedy (which had not yet acquired realistic conventions), Alberti—both in *Momus o, del principe* and in *Intercenales*—sought to add a vigorous narrative vein that he derived from the traditions of the Italian novella. In defining his *Intercenales* to Paolo del Pozzo Toscanelli in the proem of the first book, Alberti insisted upon the elements of therapeutic laughter and invention, but left open the question of its literary form. Among the forty-two convivial texts of his book, there coexist completely realistic (except for the highly stylized typology of the characters' psychological attitudes) novellas ("Amores"), narratives crossing the allegorical with the popular ("Naufragus"), Aesopian anecdotes ("Bubo," "Lacus," "Lupus," "Lapides," "Pertinacia," and "Aranea"), anecdotes taken from municipal and family history ("Hostis" and "Felicitas"), exotic and mythological anecdotes ("Nummus"); consolatory dialogues ("Erumna," "Pupillus," and "Anuli"), comic dialogues closely resembling those of Plautus ("Servus," "Oraculum," and "Vaticinium"), and, finally, a more properly Lucianic "core group" of fantastic-allegorical dialogues with a strong visual dimension ("Fama," "Suspitio," "Somnium," "Fatum et fortuna," "Cynicus," "Discordia," "Nebule," "Defunctus," and—in a category of its own—"Religio"). I will discuss here this last group of texts, along with the ekphrasis "Picture," which seems to have left the most lasting mark on Ferrarese culture.

"Suspitio" is in fact the development of a single image—that of Calumny growing like a huge cabbage until severed from its roots by Truth's knife.[8] Alberti's iconography is quite different from Botticelli's rather composed painting. Alberti preferred the representation of the hybrid, of abnormal and monstrous developments and, in general, of a moral bestiary rather uncommon in Italian fifteenth-century figurative culture. Only when Hieronymus Bosch's work had had its effect on northern European painting could Battista Dossi's *Dream* (Dresden, Staatliche Kunstsammlungen, Gemäldegalerie Alte Meister) supply an example of the grotesque that might be compared to Alberti's. "Picture" and "Fama" are linked by the common structural motif of the allegorical temple; in the former, it is that of Good and Bad Fortune, while in the latter it is that of Fame.[9] In "Picture" Alberti sought to render dynamically the chain of virtues and vices, seeing them above all in terms of their social consequences: good government and bad government—of the soul or of the state (it is hard to separate them)[10]—face each other on opposite sides of the temple. The first series of images may usefully serve as an example: the figure of Envy has a monkey on its shoulder that is slashing Envy's face, the figure of Calumny is vomiting fire from its mouth, the figure of Indignation has the temples of its forehead in flames, the figure of Enmity has a broken horoscope in one hand and drags a stone tied to its foot, and the figure of Misery sheds tears that drill holes through its own feet. Alberti renewed traditional iconography through painstaking research into fleeting and enigmatic details that would stimulate the recondite acumen of the connoisseur. His ekphrasis would thus seem to anticipate the kind of *ante litteram* "Mannerist" taste that is often attributed to fifteenth-century Ferrara.[11]

Another group of texts, one with greater philosophical ambitions, is centered around the critique of superstitious and corrupt religion that had caused political turmoil. Alberti's search for figurative concreteness often succeeded in these dinner pieces as well. "Religio" challenges the sort of utilitarian devoutness that holds that "God ought to make golden cabbages grow in one's vegetable garden." Another motif that is used with parody in "Virtus" is employed by Dosso in his famous painting *Jupiter, Mercury, and Virtue* (p. 99), now in Vienna. In "Virtus" Jupiter takes care of butterfly wings (in Dosso's canvas he is shown actually painting them) while Virtue can find no rest on earth. Alberti would seem to suggest that God identifies himself with Fate and *eimarmene,* while man ought "to excite his own virtue in himself" rather than merely pray. Other dinner pieces emphasize the social consequences of an undignified concept of the gods, who have been reduced to the *servi currentes* of humankind, and of the superstition that derives from that concept.

"Cynicus" is doubtless Alberti's most violent piece of writing against the vices of the secular priests and monks.[12] The fantastic invention of this dinner piece, in taking up the Pythagorean doctrine of metempsychosis, allows the writer to symbolize through bestiary-like imagery the typical vices of various social groups. Ecclesiastics, for example, are forcibly reincarnated as donkeys and tyrants as birds of prey.[13] In "Nebule," on the other hand, Alberti compares two different kinds of ambition:[14] that of the condottieri in secular life, and that of the fathers of the Council of Basel in ecclesiastical life. Mercury, on the border between these two worlds, observes men's battles from above, while Jupiter, in the ecclesiastical Heaven, enjoys the clash between clouds as they struggle to choose a king. Another general council of priests is to be found at the center of the dinner piece "Nummus." Alberti returns to the parodic motif of the learned ecumenical meeting,[15] where this time the participants agree not to put aside religious differences but to recognize money as the only true god. In "Discordia" the theme of ambition to be first and foremost is dressed up as a mythological fable in which the gods discuss who Discord's father is.[16]

The more properly "philosophical" thematics of "Religio"—the relationship between *eimarmene* and human initiative—is transcribed into figurative language in "Fatum et fortuna." Alberti presents this dinner piece as a moral "painting."[17] This allegory interested Ariosto for its figurative richness, which was derived from visionary literature. Indeed, the River of Life—which catches human beings in its currents while they try with various means to avoid ending up on its shoals or on the banks of Death that lie on both sides—reappears at the beginning of canto 35 of *Orlando furioso,* in which "the river of Oblivion" is set against "the temple of Immortality."[18] In Alberti, however, no allusion to immortality gained through literature is to be found. This is a significant absence. The Platonic and even Origenist philosophical background of Alberti's dinner pieces is greatly reduced in Ariosto.[19] In Alberti's text, the souls leave the mountain (symbolizing their celestial and divine condition) in a long procession to assume a body. Represented as sparks of the divine fire, the souls now must, in their new and shadowy form, face the struggles of earthly existence. Alberti offers, in short, a sweeping picture of human life that stands out in the *Intercenales* for its grave tone and lack of parodic elements. The autobiographical ending would suggest an overcoming of the work's pessimistic vision of the inevitable unhappiness of the man of letters.

"Fatum et fortuna" also stands apart from the other dinner pieces for Alberti's almost self-parodic rewriting of it in "Somnium." "Fatum et fortuna" is the knowledge-filled vision of a philosopher very close to Alberti; "Somnium," on the other hand, is the degraded vision of an idle man of letters and critic of Alberti, whose highest aspiration is to "rave as he pleases."[20] The land of dreams to which the philosopher Libripeta-Niccoli travels is the kingdom of false knowledge (and of true stupidity), where the presumptuous book lover can fully express his contempt for his contemporaries. "Somnium" is a satirical text that ridicules the same figurative motifs presented so solemnly in "Fatum et fortuna."[21] Ariosto's imitation in his *Orlando furioso,* in the famous episode of Astolfo on the moon in cantos 34 and 35, thus blends together two related texts by Alberti, juxtaposing the positive perspective on the cult of the *artes* ("Fatum et fortuna")—which, for Ariosto, is evidently expressed in the celebration of poetry—with the pessimistic awareness of universal folly ("Somnium"). The acrimonious satire of an individual "sewer sagacity" becomes in *Orlando furioso* an instance of generic and even cheerfully self-ironic moral reflection.[22]

Ariosto's subsequent reading of this in the speech of Saint John (in canto 35, octaves 18–30), however, calls into question the reliability of writers and thus the true virtue of famous individuals as well. Saint John's lesson seems in this way to propose a completely original view of literature and the court that has no precedent in Alberti's work. What holds for the *Orlando furioso* also holds true, in general, for the history of the Lucianic genre in Ferrara. Alberti's formal and thematic cues and his utilitarian moral thought and partially heterodox philosophy are reworked and transformed, yet the real addressees of these fantastic and paradoxical inventions are always those who subscribe to the culture of the Estense court.

At the end of the fifteenth century, Pandolfo Collenuccio, a jurist from Pesaro, began to follow forcefully in Alberti's footsteps. Although he had received his doctorate of law in Padua rather than in Ferrara, Collenuccio reflected the interests of Ferrarese humanism, which were scientific and encyclopedic in scope rather than rhetorical and literary.[23] As was the case for Alberti, Collenuccio combined Lucianic invention and a taste for the unusual and original with scientific and utilitarian empiricism.[24]

The example provided by Alberti's *Intercenales* certainly encouraged Collenuccio to renew the genre of the moral fable by stepping back from the Aesopian model. The fusion of the ancient (Lucian) and the modern (Alberti) is one of the most remarkable achievements of Collenuccio's work. His *Misopenes* reuses, with some variations, the fundamental structure of Lucian's *Vitarum auctio:* Chrysium and Sophia, gold and knowledge, are auctioned off. Numerous jokes about the omnipotence of gold and the best way to use it are taken from the conversation between Hermes and Pluto in *Timon.* The fundamental theme of the moral fable, however, derives from Alberti—namely the buyer's complaint that although he once loved knowledge, his love had given him nothing but unhappiness, economic losses, and physical and moral suffering, and so, thoroughly disillusioned, he had to turn to the power of money. Collenuccio develops one of the most common themes of Alberti's work, one that can be seen in (among others) the dinner pieces "Pupillus," "Erumna," and "Anuli." This is the saturnine intellectual's indictment of Nature and Fortune, whom he blames for the fact that "useful" studies do not bring with them any personal *utilitas.* The moral dialogue acquires a deeply subjective and autobiographical dimension that is absent in Lucian (or at least not so pronounced). Collenuccio concludes his *Misopenes,* moreover, with an ironic palinode in which the buyer, after having drawn straws, purchases Chrysium. This is far different than the Stoic medicine of the consolatory *declamatio* administered in large doses by Alberti.

Alberti's presence is even more visible in the two compositions by Collenuccio titled *Agenoria* and *Alithia,* both of which draw their inspiration from the medieval tradition of the allegorical struggle of the virtues and the vices. In composing the general structure of these two moral fables, Collenuccio must certainly have had Alberti's "Virtus" in mind. This was, after all, the most popular of the *Intercenales,* as witnessed both by the number of surviving manuscripts and by the fact that it was included in the corpus of Lucian's works. In his deployment of specific moral themes, however, Collenuccio drew more on *Momus* than on "Virtus," for the former seemed to legitimate to a greater extent satirical developments and polemical references to contemporary reality. His *Alithia* even takes its protagonist directly from Alberti's *Momus.* As the god of sincerity and blunt frankness, Momus helps the forces of Truth win their battle against Hypocrisy. The heroic presentation of the figure of Momus, who is described as *acer, durus,* and *pugnax,* is doubtless derived from Alberti. But Collenuccio takes no account of the comic connotations of this sort of heroism, which in Alberti's writings stem from the lack of proportion between the character's ambition and his true ability. His Momus is neither a rebel nor a dissimulator—the two poles between which the psychological *varietas* of Alberti's protagonist oscillates—but rather is frank and courageous. This fable has the kind of positive ending that cannot be found in Alberti's Lucianic writings.

Collenuccio's work is devoid of Alberti's sharp pessimism and instead uses a sort of secular moral thought, articulated in allegorical form. The humanist-diplomat spares Church doctrine although he exalts the active life founded on work, a stable place of residence, and a sense of civic duty—all of which he counterposes to the contemplative model. Following a procedure somewhat reminiscent of Valla's, his *Misopenes* takes aim at philosophers' contemplation and reduces it to pure visual satisfaction, stripping it of its aura. In *Agenoria* the critique of contemplative idleness is focused more specifically on the mendicant friars' lifestyle, at once ascetic and vagabond, restless and parasitic.[25] As often was the case in the fifteenth century, the attack on the friars is carried out through the figure of the cynical philosopher. This discourse becomes even more explicit when Collenuccio brings Hypocrisy herself into the conversation; she urges her listeners to exploit the psychological and psychagogic power of religion for their own purposes.

Collenuccio's *Apologhi,* like Alberti's works, employ a mythological and Lucianic allegorical framework to make acceptable, surreptitiously, a rather generic, and therefore not particularly risky, satire. This is one of the leading reasons for the genre's success during the Renaissance. It is beyond the scope of this essay to address the question of whether Collenuccio's anticlericalism might have had some real resonance in the culture of Ercole I's Ferrara, which was, after all, devout and traditionalist as well as disciplined and bureaucratic.

Collenuccio simplified Lucian and, above all, Alberti by reducing the thematic and stylistic variety of their works. But Collenuccio's true originality resides not so much in the content of the moral fables as in his efforts to adapt Lucian's poetics of laughter to the requirements of courtly sensibility. Nominated *Consiliarius Ducalis* (ducal counselor) in 1491, Collenuccio entered into the Este circle on a fixed basis. His *Apologhi* are thus aimed at a specifically Ferrarese audience and attempt to mediate between court culture on the one hand, and humanistic and philological culture on the other. In his *Specchio di Esopo,* Plautus and Lucian are presented as good courtiers who help the storyteller—the author's alter ego—make his entrance into the king's palace.[26] Like Alberti in the proem to the fourth book of the *Intercenales,*[27] Collenuccio also insists on the utility of a humble and flat style devoid of all rhetorical excess. The style, he remarks, should be *salutaris* rather than *blandus.* The poetics of the *Intercenales* are, however, translated precisely in courtly terms. The Aesop appearing in the *Specchio* is a court jester and *fou glossateur* who amuses his lord with his intelligent sense of humor and, with the aid of the weapons provided by ridicule, exposes the ignorance of so-called learned men.[28] Not for nothing are Collenuccio's Aesop and

Hercules reminiscent of carnival, in which even the prince may enjoy seeing himself counterfeited (since his authority is not at stake). The *Apologhi* are themselves a carnivalesque game of unmasking Fraud, Hypocrisy, and Vanity and an indirect presentation of Truth (which is ironically dissimulated by the texts' modest style and allegorical trappings).

Pistoia's Lucianic dialogue, which serves as a proem to the corpus of *I sonetti faceti,* was composed in 1501, and it thus followed Collenuccio's *Apologhi* by only a few years' time. In the former, however, we perceive a different historical atmosphere: in spite of the text's clever homage to Isabella,[29] the unconditional faith in the Estense court that characterized Collenuccio's *Bombarda, Misopenes,* and *Specchio di Esopo* is gone. Although it indulges in digressions, Pistoia's brief work expresses the political and religious uncertainty caused by the early Italian wars and the decline of Lorenzo the Magnificent's Florence. Furthermore, as Erasmo Pèrcopo has convincingly shown, the author was influenced by Giovanni Pontano's *Charon,* which strongly suggested—in an almost pre-Machiavellian way—that the Italian crisis was due to the sins (political, not religious) of Italy's princes. The diverse nature of this theme, which could be found not only in Ferrara but throughout Italy, and which referred specifically to contemporary events rather than to some sort of general moral idea, required a different kind of formal approach. Pistoia lacked both Collenuccio's allegorical density and his precise use of figurative details. The dialogue's infernal setting was taken directly from Lucian and Pontano, without reference to the allegorical encyclopedism that was characteristic for Ferrarese culture. Despite Pistoia's unquestionable (but often parodic) appeal to Dante's authority, this setting breaks up into a series of autonomous "inventions" that are represented in summary fashion. Pistoia made recourse to Lucian's form as a model of conversational pleasantness that could connect autobiographical allusions, sharp bites with his cynical tooth, and the often provocative claims of his bizarre philosophy. The eschatological background provided by Lucian's writings, while not necessarily burlesque, and in any event not subjected to any form of dogmatic control, allowed authors to insinuate heterodox philosophical hypotheses in moments of political and social crisis (such as the "horoscope of religions").

Pistoia's prefatory epistle to Isabella d'Este begins with a meaningful defense of poetic "figments," the only form through which one could possibly satisfy the natural desire to know the life beyond. Pistoia set himself the task of renewing this tradition, which had been all but forgotten, by following, of course, Dante's lead (the poet claimed in the *Commedia* to have actually descended into Hell). Like Dante's trip to Hell and beyond, Pistoia's Spirit set out on an educational journey that would consecrate his authority as a comic poet. But this journey was to be "without a guide," in a polemical gesture aimed at useless and verbose scholastic education: nature, animals, and poets are to him, instead, far greater teachers than are philosophers. As it was for Alberti and Collenuccio, Pistoia's vigorous reaffirmation of the empiricism of practical men was a fundamental *topos* of the Lucianic genre. Here, however, it was also taken to have secular and courtly overtones rather than exclusively academic ones. Another point of convergence with Collenuccio is found in Pistoia's vigorous anticlericalism, which stemmed from his basic skepticism in regard to all positive *leges.*[30]

Pistoia's text allows us to glimpse the evolution of the Lucianic genre from fifteenth-century allegorism to the sixteenth-century "pleasant dialogue." The satirical, extemporaneous, and whimsical dimension of this kind of writing—whose masters were Niccolò Franco and Anton Francesco Doni in the sixteenth century—prevailed over Alberti's allusive density and Collenuccio's constructive solidity. The Ferrarese Lucianic tradition was combined in Pistoia's work with the rather different sort of playfulness espoused by Pontano. It was especially close to the tradition of pranks and wordplay (including the religiously unorthodox sort) that flourished in Lorenzo the Magnificent's Florence. This was, in any case, part of a general trend: during the reign of Alfonso I, Celio Calcagnini's writings were to display greater prudence and subtlety than Collenuccio's, along with a greater virtuosity and a more nuanced skepticism.

Like Pandolfo Collenuccio, Calcagnini was a typical representative of a culture combining philological and scientific erudition with paradoxical and courtly whimsy. He knew Alberti's and Collenuccio's work[31] and used it to express the fundamental themes of his ethical vision. His perspective could be called "prudential," for he possessed a keen sense of the relativity of situations as well as a sense of diffidence in regard to absolute ethical norms. In regard to natural man, Calcagnini praised the concreteness of impulses and the empirical evidence of common sense; his openness was, however, balanced by a strong awareness of the necessity of masks in social life. His style of thinking may be illustrated by two texts that are very different in terms of their genre and stylistic level, namely the *Disquisitiones aliquot in libros Officiorum Ciceronis* and his apologue in defense of carnival.

Calcagnini used historical and philological methods to compare Panetius's lost work (a "source" of Cicero) with Aristotle's *Ethica Nicomachaea.* In so doing, however, he called into question Cicero's version of Stoicism. It is not difficult to see in Calcagnini's aversion to absolute ethical rigor the influence of Valla's thought (although stripped of its most provocatory and "Epicurean" elements). The *Moriae encomium* had, at the beginning of the sixteenth century, renewed the controversy begun by Valla. The image of the Stoics as giants at war with nature was at the center of the declamation *Quod Stoici dicunt magis fabulosa quam poetae* (that the Stoics say things more incredible than do the poets), which bore the marks of both Plutarch's and Erasmus's influence. This text constituted the link connecting "serious" criticism of the rigidity of philosophy with Calcagnini's Lucianic writings, which offered a whimsical and empirically tangible alternative that was at once icastic and allusive.

Calcagnini reversed, in an Erasmian fashion, Collenuccio's naive and schematic moralism. Momus, the prototype of the Stoic philosopher, was no longer the defender of truth, as he had been in *Alithia*. Rather, as in the ancient Greek source texts, he was once again the god of cursing, unable to appreciate nature's true beauty and perfection.[32] As a part of a literary game intrinsic to the Lucianic tradition, Calcagnini rejected the ideal of the *homo fenestratus* whose thoughts and feelings were transparent. The soul was not a mirror; the freedom of the will implicated self-determination and even self-concealing. Here Pico's concept of man as a chameleon comes to mind.[33] To reject Momus, the god of bitter but healthful truth, also meant to recognize the expediency of simulation, disguise, and play—in short, all of that intentional and ironically self-conscious folly praised by Erasmus in his famous work. The concept of prudence, which was central to his critique of Cicero, allowed Calcagnini to legitimate irrational and ridiculous modes of behavior (such as carnival), as long as they respected the conventions of time and place, according to a relativistic notion of decorum that presupposed alternating poles of serious civil commitment and recreation.[34]

Calcagnini's *Apologus, cui titulus personati* displays a mixture of Lucianic and Ferrarese traditions. The setting—that *"templum Volupie"* recalling similar allegorical temples in such dinner pieces as "Picture" and "Fama," as well as *Momus*—was derived from Alberti. The philological subtlety with which contemporary reality, including the names of the dances, was rewritten in a Hellenizing language displayed a debt to Erasmus,[35] as was also true for the idea of the triumph of Stupidity or Voluptuousness as a sacred spectacle.[36] The text's paradoxical argument was especially influenced by the *Moriae encomium:* life itself was a theatrical recital, and to remove one's mask would mean to bring the show to an end.[37] Clearly missing here was any form of judgment external and superior to this theatrical scene; unless, perhaps, the gods themselves could be considered as such. According to Plato, after all (Alberti had ironized this in *Momus*), the gods were pleased spectators of the spectacle of human stupidity.[38] If daily life was a "theater of the world," then carnival was the moment in which existence was recognized as a spectacle, and this spectacle was transformed from an objective and unwitting limitation of one's self-determination into an instance of freedom and whimsy.[39]

Calcagnini's imitation of Lucian and Erasmus, however, weakened the satirical and religious strength of his models and was reducible to the skeptical and relativistic wisdom of the *homo bulla*. Nevertheless, his cultural position was not abstract, but rather presupposed a precise relationship with Ferrarese culture. His Erasmian apologue for carnival was aimed at the taste and lifestyle of a clearly defined public. The occasion for Calcagnini's *Apologus* was in fact the criticism directed at Ercole II for favoring carnival. As a humanist split between university and court, between philological *otium* and diplomatic *negotia,* Calcagnini defended a culture of aristocratic amusements in which the people could also participate while maintaining an appropriate social distance. Calcagnini was at once a "serious" critic of Cicero's work as well as a sophistic apologist for carnival. He was able to be both by employing a Pythagorean rhetorical mode based on concise eloquence and by constructing a semiserious moral theater.

Besides his *Personati,* Calcagnini also composed a few other apologues closer to Collenuccio's model. These brief compositions were at once small moral treatises in emblematic form, courtly homages, and mythological fables ending with a surprising allusion to the duke or one of his dignitaries. The encomiastic element in them was at times entirely explicit, as in *Gigantes,* the etiological fable *Lineleon,* or *Absentia.* In these minor apologues, however, the cryptic language of moral allegory sank into stereotypical and predictable mannerisms. The encomiastic and courtly dimension remained, for the most part, in the background and was manifest chiefly in the dedicatory letter and the high degree of visual imagery within the text itself. The descriptive virtuosity of these apologues seemed to demand the presence of a spectator, as if they were the script of an allegorical masque. *Somatia* was the most notable example of this figural allegorism. Calcagnini integrated the Platonic theme of the soul's race, dragged by vices harnessed like bucking chargers, with a brilliant description of the city of the body and its legislation, which was a sort of reverse Utopia.

Calcagnini's taste for the emblematic image also constituted a point of contact between the *Apologi,* whose audience was the court, and the doctrinal dialogues that were aimed at a humanistic public. The dialogue between Ancylometus and Mnemon in *De memoria* examined, through the use of the Socratic method, the problem of the importance of memory for the art of oratory. This dialogue ended with the description of an imaginary painting found in the temple of Fortune: in order to obtain Immortality, orators call on Posterity, whose iconography is contaminated with that of Occasion.[40] This fictitious ekphrasis conferred authority while sanctioning the position of the Socratic interlocutor Ancylometus (of the convoluted mind), with which the author identified. In another apologue, *Equitatio,* Calcagnini also sought to mix philological and erudite subject matter with Lucianic pleasantness. His literary schema followed the model of a discussion during a symposium (as practiced by Athenaeus and Macrobius), but was animated by its open-air setting. The discussion, regarding difficult antiquarian issues, concerned the *Realien* of the ancient world. It did not take place inside an academy, however, but rather, in an extemporaneous manner, during the free time of some riders on horseback. Thus once again Calcagnini managed to combine the worlds of *otium* and *negotium.* The principal argument of the dialogue was the origin of the various forms of popular superstition, which were based on ancient religious rites that often were reflected in Christian practices. This theme, obviously derived from the Lucianic tradition (*De sacrificiis*), anticipated Erasmus's arguments in the *Adagia.* Perhaps more than anywhere else in Italy, philology and wit were able to proceed in step in Ferrara, even tolerating contamination with Ludovico Ariosto's chivalric "foolishness."[41]

The fortune enjoyed by the Lucianic genre in Ferrara cannot be reduced to a series of learned anecdotes. I have tried to follow the slender threads linking fantastic-satirical-allegorical invention of the humanistic sort to more vital forms of vernacular culture, namely mythological theater and the chivalric poem (which are more vital precisely because they are more socially representative). As for the theater and the poem, in which figurative cycles greatly contributed to connecting the fabulous past to the courtly and encomiastic present,[42] the social effectiveness of the Lucianic dialogue largely depended upon the force of its imagery. The more complex and allusive the latter became, the more attractive it became for a public composed of connoisseurs who knew how to appreciate the "mystery" elegantly hidden in everyday things. Symbols charged with multiple significance communicated the dynastic certitudes as well as the intellectual anxieties of Ferrarese culture. The latter were far from negligible and ranged from Alberti's heterodox Platonism to Calcagnini's dissimulating Erasmism, to say nothing of the work of Palingenio Stellato or Celio Secondo Curione.

I do not think it right to insist too greatly on the "hermetic" and "esoteric" character of these images. Texts such as *Specchio di Esopo* or *Personati* display the elite culture's extroverted attitude, which sought to exhibit its metamorphic ability to transform the culture of the writing desk according to more popular standards. The most readable—in terms of court culture—poetic work of the sixteenth century, Ariosto's *Orlando furioso,* came from these very aristocratic and erudite circles in Ferrara, which were indifferent to any sort of bourgeois historical and philosophical vulgarization and were unreceptive to normative linguistic projects, whether in Latin or the vernacular. Such efforts certainly were not lacking in Florence, whether one thinks of Donato Acciaiuoli, Cristoforo Landino, or Giambattista Gelli. With all due allowances for Ariosto's individual genius, this fact reveals the notable coherence of Ferrarese culture. The "culture of the image" shared by both learned artists and Lucianic iconographers in Ferrara was surely one of the most important factors in this special unity and coherence.

Notes

1. Borso d'Este's library contained Lucian *"ex graeco translatus per Bertholdum"*; see Giulio Bertoni, *La biblioteca Estense e la coltura ferrarese ai tempi del duca Ercole I (1471–1505)* (Turin: Loescher, 1903), 216. Ercole I's library contained Bartolomeo Fonzio's Latin version of *Calumny, De amicitia* (also in Latin), and a vernacular version of the *Golden Ass* (also attributed to Lucian), together with other works by Lucian; see idem, 236, 244–45. See Remigio Sabbadini, *La scuola e gli studi di*

Guarino Guarini Veronese (Catania: Galati, 1896), 125, for more on Guarino Veronese's translations. Emilio Mattioli, *Luciano e l'umanesimo* (Naples: Istituto Italiano per gli Studi Storici, 1980), provides an overview of the relation between Lucian and humanism. Eugenio Garin's "Motivi della cultura filosofica ferrarese nel Rinascimento," in idem, *La cultura filosofica del Rinascimento italiano: Ricerche e documenti* (Florence: Sansoni, 1961), 402–31, remains a fundamental work on the philosophical currents found in Ferrara in this period.

2. According to Lilio Gregorio Giraldi in his version of Plutarch's *Pythagorica praecepta mystica;* see Garin's note in Leon Battista Alberti, *Intercenali inedite,* ed. Eugenio Garin (Florence: Sansoni, 1965), 77 n. 1. In examining the *Convelata* from a manuscript *"perscriptus manu Pandulphi Collenutii"* (copied out in Pandolfo Collenuccio's hand), Giraldi realized that it could not have been by Plutarch. It was, in fact, one of the twenty-five dinner pieces written by Alberti that Eugenio Garin rediscovered in 1964 in a codex in the Dominican monastery in Pistoia. There is, moreover, no proof that the manuscript copied by Collenuccio was the same as the Pistoia codex.

3. See Pandolfo Collenuccio, *Operette morali: Poesie latine e volgari,* ed. Alfredo Saviotti (Bari: Laterza, 1929), 345 n. 1 (dedicatory epistle by Beatus Rhenanus, addressed to Jakob Spiegel, prefacing the Strasbourg edition of the *Apologhi* [Argentorati: In aedibus Matthiae Schurerii, 1511]): *"Accipe igitur, suavissime Iacobe, lepidissimos illos Pandulphi* Apologos, *sua festivitate etiam Samosatheum Lucianum superantes"* (Receive, then, most pleasant Jakob, these most charming *Apologhi* of Pandolfo, surpassing in their wit even Lucian of Samosata).

4. See Gennaro Savarese, "Il progetto del poema tra Marsilio Ficino e 'adescatrici galliche,'" in idem, *Il* Furioso *e la cultura del Rinascimento* (Rome: Bulzoni, 1984), 15–37.

5. See Alberti (see note 2), 64; Leon Battista Alberti, *Dinner Pieces,* trans. David Marsh (Binghamton, N.Y.: Medieval & Renaissance Texts & Studies, 1987), 127:

> *In aliorumque scriptis pensitandis ita sumus plerique ad unum omnes fastidiosi, ut ea Ciceronis velimus eloquentie respondere, ac si superiori etate omnes qui approbati fuere scriptores eosdem fuisse Cicerones statuant. Inepti! . . . At enim varia res est eloquentia, ut ipse interdum sibi Cicero perdissimilis sit* (In evaluating others' writings, we are without exception so fastidious that we expect them to match Cicero's eloquence, as if all the excellent writers of an earlier age thought themselves Ciceros. Fools! . . . Eloquence is so varied that even Cicero is sometimes very un-Ciceronian).

6. See Alberti (see note 2), 13; Alberti (see note 5), 54:

> *Apud gymnosophistas philosophos vetustissimos, cultu virtutis et sapientie laudibus celeberrimos, templum fuisse ferunt bone maleque Fortune, quod quidem omni ornamentorum copia, opumque varietate esset refertissimum* (In the land of the gymnosophists, the very ancient philosophers celebrated for their pursuit of virtue and their renown for wisdom, they say there was a temple dedicated to Good and Ill Fortune, which was filled with a vast quantity of ornaments and variety of riches).

7. Some interesting remarks on this point may be found in Claudia Cieri Via, "Il tempio come 'locus iustitiae': La pala Roverella di Cosmè Tura," in Giuseppe Papagno and Amedeo Quondam, eds., *La corte e lo spazio: Ferrara estense,* 3 vols. (Rome: Bulzoni, 1982), 3: 577–91. This study examines Alberti's treatises, rather than his dinner pieces.

8. See Alberti (see note 2), 22–23; Alberti (see note 5), 62–63:

> FAMA. . . . *Audistin rem execrandam? Ex ipso foco, virginibus adstantibus et ignem foventibus, caulum exortum esse herbe virentissime, que quidem, ipso temporis momento ut apparuit, e vestigio mirabile dictu ad cubiti altitudinem excreverit, foliaque complura omnibus ignota prelonga et admodum patula, miris omnium generum coloribus expicta, diversas in partes explicuerit* (RUMOR. . . . Have you heard the terrible news? While the virgins were tending the fire, the stalk of a hardy plant sprang from the middle of the hearth. At the very moment it appeared —wondrous to say!—it grew to the height of a cubit, and sent forth many leaves in all directions. Unfamiliar to anyone, these leaves were very long, quite broad, and speckled with wondrous colors of every sort).

9. Alberti's literary justification of ekphrasis in "Picture" is worth quoting here. See Alberti (see note 2), 13; Alberti (see note 5), 54: "*Nam nos qui legerit, cum delectabitur picture varietate, artificisque ingenio, tum se ad vitam cum ratione degendam aliqua apud nos adinvenisse grata et amena, ni fallor, congratulabitur*" (The reader will not only delight in the paintings' variety and the artist's invention, but will be grateful, I believe, when he finds in our work pleasing and enjoyable counsels for living wisely). Unlike "Picture," "Fama" is a satrical text; like "Somnium," it targets the character Libripeta-Niccoli, who represents—in an allegorical and grotesque key—the "sacrifice" of those false erudites aspiring to literary prestige. Here there are no descriptions of works of art, but the whole text is emphatically stagelike and is rich in visual details taken from the sphere of "low bodily culture."

10. For Alberti, who was very familiar with Plato's *Republic,* there existed a basic analogy between the parts of the soul and those of the political collectivity, and the form of the ideal city reflected this analogy.

11. On the "courtly style" in the visual arts, see Werner L. Gundersheimer's overview in his *Ferrara: The Style of a Renaissance Despotism* (Princeton: Princeton Univ. Press, 1973), 91–105.

12. See Alberti (see note 2), 36; Alberti (see note 5), 75:

> CYNICUS. . . . *Atqui agunt id quidem, non quo sese dictis et exhortationibus ad virtutem excitent, sed ut moltitudinem fallant verbis et vultu quoad sese opinionem bonam proseminent: nequissimique et omnium sordidissimi, aures adeo habent obtusas, ut, cum de religione propalam declamitent, ipsos sese nequaquam audiant* (CYNIC. . . . Yet they constantly rehearse such pious admonitions, not in order to rouse others to virtue by their precepts and exhortations, but rather to trick the masses, by their sermons and semblances, into disseminating a favorable opinion of them. But these most corrupt and sordid men have ears so deadened that they can't even hear their own public harangues on religion).

13. In the end, the cynical philosopher, who has taken on the function of the accuser, must also change himself into a gold-winged fly. But this is only a seemingly negative fate for him if one thinks of Alberti's paradoxical praise of the fly in *Musca,* his imitation of Lucian's *Encomium of the Fly.*

14. But also two different types of discourse, namely, an explicitly historical discourse on condottieri, and an allegorical and cryptic discourse about the Council of Basel. Contarino points this out in Leon Battista Alberti, *Apologhi ed elogi,* ed. Rosario Contarino (Genoa: Costa & Nolan, 1984), 96 n. 18.

15. Alberti was able to follow the Council of Basel's first sessions, which were held in Ferrara. The council was to lead to the declaration of unity of the Greek and Latin churches.

16. Alberti's fiction (Mercury and Argos seek Justice, who has been called upon to judge) recalls the opening of the episode about Discord in Agramante's camp in Ludovico Ariosto's *Orlando furioso* (canto 14, octaves 81–82). Michael is the Christian equivalent of Mercury, while in Ariosto's poem Silence and Discord herself are the objects of the search. Ariosto's anticlerical swipe here—the goddess of quarreling is never absent from the monasteries—is not derived from Alberti, but seems to agree rather well with the raillery of the dinner pieces. There is a reference to "Discordia" as a "source" of canto 14 of the *Orlando furioso* in Leonzio Pampaloni, "Le *Intercenali* e il *Furioso:* Noterella sui rapporti Alberti-Ariosto," *Belfagor* 29 (1974): 317–25, esp. 324.

17. See Leon Battista Alberti, *Opera inedita et pauca separatim impressa,* ed. Hieronymo Mancini (Florence: Sansoni, 1890), 142; Alberti (see note 5), 27: "*E vestigio expergiscor ac mecum ipse hanc visam in somniis fabulam repetens gratias habui somno, quod ejus beneficio Fatum et Fortunam* tam belle pictam *viderim*" (I awoke at once, and, as I recalled the fable I had seen in my dream, I was grateful to sleep for showing me Fate and Fortune *so nicely depicted*) (emphasis mine).

18. See the careful comparison of the texts in Pampaloni (see note 16), 319–23.

19. See Alberti (see note 17), 137; Alberti (see note 5), 23:

> PHILOSOPUS. . . . *Nam ut primum in fluvium umbrarum quaeque descendisset, ita illico infantum ora et membra induisse videbantur, ac deinceps, quo longius fluvio raperentur, eo illis quidem aetatis et membrorum personam adcrevisse intuebar. Cepi idcirco rogare: Et quod, inquam, o umbrae, si quid noscis humanitatis, aut si quid uspiam estis ad humanitatem propensae, quando humanitatis est homines rerum instructiores reddere, dicite, quaeso, quale sit huic fluvio nomen.*
>
> *Tum umbrae in hunc modum referunt: Erras, homo, si quales tibi per oculos corporis videmur, nos umbras putas. Sumus enim coelestes, uti et ipse tu quidem es, igniculi qui humanitati debemur* (PHILOSOPHER. . . . As soon as each shade had entered the river, it seemed at once to take on an infant's face and limbs. Then, the further the river carried the shades, the more I saw their age and members increase. So I began to ask: "If you know anything of humanity, O shades, or are in the least inclined to human feeling, since it is humane to enlighten human beings, please tell me the name of this river."
>
> The shades replied in this fashion: "You err, O man, if you think we are shades

because we appear so to your body's vision. Like you, we are celestial sparks destined for human life").

They suggest that the narrator not push this inquiry too far by looking into the question of the origin of souls: *"Desine, inquiunt, desine, homo, istiusmodi dei deorum occulta investigare longius quam mortalibus liceat"* (Cease, O man, cease searching into the secrets of the gods deeper than mortals are allowed). The presence of Origenist thought in Florentine culture during the first half of the fifteenth century (as documented by Matteo Palmieri's *Città di Vita*) should not be overlooked here.

20. "Somnium" includes biting satire of the character named Lepidus, who in the dinner piece "Corolle" also seems very close to Alberti himself. See Alberti (see note 2), 26; Alberti (see note 5), 67: *"LEPIDUS. Ergo tu, qui te philosophum haberi optas, posteaquam mutam huc usque omnem etatem duxisti tuam, hanc laudis occasionem non deseres. Primum hoc quidem philosophandi munus recensendo somnio suscipies"* (LEPIDUS. Since you desire to be thought a philosopher, you have hitherto led a life of silence, but you won't miss this chance to win praise. By relating this dream, you'll perform your first act of philosophizing).

21. The allegorical scene in "Somnium" is similar to that of "Fatum et fortuna": at the foot of a very high mountain where human destinies are forged, there flows a river *"quem aiunt excrevisse lachrimis lugentium et calamitosorum hominum"* (said to swell with the tears of wretches and mourners). As in "Fatum et fortuna," this is the river of life, subject to the whims of fortune, but the parody is quite obvious. For example, the grotesque and repugnant *"vetule"* (crones) used as rafts to get across the river of life in "Somnium" take the place of the ships (which are called empires) and the planks (which are called liberal arts) used in "Fatum et fortuna." Another figurative detail common to both texts are the *"vesciche"* (bladders); these symbolize flatterers in "Fatum et fortuna," while in "Somnium" they represent political power. "Somnium" emphasizes the vision's grotesque and expressionistic details. For instance, the *"scopuli"* (projecting rocks) of "Fatum et fortuna" are transformed into the *"vultus mordaces"* (biting faces) of the slanderers and bearers of false witness that dwell in the river of life. For "Fatum et fortuna," see Alberti (see note 17), 141; Alberti (see note 5), 23–27. For "Somnium," see Alberti (see note 2), 25–28; Alberti (see note 5), 66–69.

22. Recall that the verses *"Chi salirà per me, madonna, in cielo, / a ritrovare il mio perduto ingegno?"* (Who will rise for me, my lady, to heaven / To recover my lost wits?) (*Orlando furioso,* Canto 35, octave 1, verses 1–2) are derived directly from Alberti's Libripeta-Niccoli, who remarks in "Somnium":

> *[S]ed quod mirere primum illic partem non minimam mei cerebri offendi: eam quidem quam vetula quedam a me amata emunxerat; quod si licuisset, non enim fas est illinc aliquid auferre, hanc dextram capitis partem vacuam modo atque inanem replessem.* (But more astounding, I found there a large part of my brain, which a crone I once loved had swindled from me. If it had been permitted (it is forbidden to carry anything off), I would have filled the right side of my head, which is hollow and empty).

For this brutal satire of Niccoli, as well as for the expression "*cloacarium prudentiam*" (sewer sagacity), see Alberti (see note 2), 25–28; Alberti (see note 5), 66–69.

23. On Collenuccio's biography, see the still-useful work by Alfredo Saviotti, *Pandolfo Collenuccio, umanista pesarese del sec. XV* (Pisa: Nistri, 1888; reprint, Rome: Studio Bibliografico A. Polla, 1974).

24. For Alberti's *intarsio* poetics, see Roberto Cardini, *Mosaici: Il "nemico" dell'Alberti* (Rome: Bulzoni, 1990). Cardini (4–7) analyzes the aesthetic implications of the passage in the *Profugiorum ab aerumna libri* (in Leon Battista Alberti, *Opere volgari,* ed. Cecil Grayson, 3 vols. [Bari: Laterza, 1960–1973], 2: 160–62) in which Alberti compares his own work to that of artists who make mosaics. Collenuccio considered his own *Apologhi* to be a model of cryptic and allusive moral philosophy, requiring considerable interpretative cooperation on the part of the "alert" reader. See Collenuccio's *Responsio et declaratio nonnullorum locorum in Apologis nostris: Ad meum Cesarem Napeum,* in Collenuccio (see note 3), 350:

> *Omnia enim mysteriis plena sunt, et nullum est verbum frustra positum, quin habeat acutum aliquem sensum, consideratione dignum. Continent autem hi Apologi, et ceteri quos fecimus et adhuc faciemus, omnem humanae vitae rationem intra se inclusam. Et pulchra esset atque utilis et iucunda philosophia, si in scholis per doctum hominem Apologi isti legerentur* (For all things are filled with mysteries, and there is no word placed to no purpose, so as not to have some pointed sense worthy of consideration. Moreover, these *Apologhi,* and the rest which we have made and still will make, contain every matter of human life included within them. And philosophy would be beautiful and useful and pleasing if these *Apologhi* were read in the schools by a learned man).

Alberti also employed the term mysteria in discussing rings inscribed with moral maxims. See Alberti (see note 17), 229; Alberti (see note 5), 213: "*Explicanda igitur haec sunt* mysteria" (Then we must explain these *mysteries*) (emphasis mine). Nicola Tanda's interpretation in a hermetic key seems to me lacking in substance; see his *Pandolfo Collenuccio: Il dramma della "Saviezza"* (Rome: Bulzoni, 1988), 49–89, esp. 66, 73–75.

25. "*Uxor, aula, navis, ager*" (marriage, court life, commerce, agriculture) are in fact the four things from which Hypocrisy's followers wish to abstain, when taken with the necessary restrictions; see Collenuccio (see note 3), 12:

> *Non enim usque adeo fugienda sunt, ut si aliena uxor (modo dapsilis sit) aut credulus rex opinionisve captator (modo largus sit) in retia incidant, illi arcendi sint* (For they [marriage, court life, commerce, agriculture] are not to be shunned to such an extent that if another man's wife (provided that she is generous) or a king who is credulous or is one who courts favorable opinion (provided that he is munificent) should fall into [one's] snares, they must be repulsed).

Marriage, court life, commerce, and agriculture represent the principal occupations of the active life. Collenuccio's "secular" ethics, with its *pars construens,* is summarized in the instructions that Zeus gives to the divinities assisting humanity:

> *Ad probitatem in primis se homines instruere, bonas artes inducere, ad recta studia cohortari: rem familiarem curare, publicam formare, componere: militarem disciplinam exercere,* religionem deorumque cultum, eum scilicet qui spiritu et veritate continetur, ostendere, *iura conscribere, magistratus creare, praesto omnibus esse, per quae civitas bene beateque gubernari possit* (For men to prepare themselves for uprightness especially, to establish good skills, to exhort to right endeavors: to attend to family affairs, to direct [and] order public affairs: to exercise military discipline, *to exhibit the reverence for and worship of the gods that manifestly rests upon spirit and truth,* to draft laws, to create magistracies, to be ready for all things through which a state can be well and prosperously governed) (emphasis mine) (19).

26. See Collenuccio (see note 3), 94:

> ERCULE. *Che fa il re, o Blacico? Saria tempo di salutarlo?* BLACICO. *Io non so. Questa mattina tempestivamente rivide le sue munizioni e li tormenti e machine belliche di bronzo, le quali con summa diligenza e perizia in molta copia ha fatto fabbricare; e ora passeggiando con dui soi cortesani ragiona, Plauto da Sarsina e Luciano da Patrasso* (HERCULES. What does the king, O Blacycus? Would it be time to greet him? BLACYCUS. I do not know. Early this morning he reviewed his munitions and catapults and bronze war machines, of which with great diligence and skill he has had a great number made; and now he talks things over while walking with two of his courtiers, Plautus of Sarsina and Lucian of Patrasso).

Collenuccio anticipates Castiglione, for whom Plato and Aristotle were masters of "courtliness." The qualities attributed by Collenuccio to these two ancient writers are also typically "courtly," and represent a commonsense attitude free of all prescriptive rigidity:

> BLACICO.... *Sono omini d'ogni mano, dotti, acuti, umani, faceti, pronti, eleganti, destri et esperti, che con tanta dolcezza dimostrano le condizioni de la vita umana e insegnano costumi e virtú, che chi con loro pratica, pare a pena che mal omo possa essere* (BLACYCUS.... They are men of every quality, learned, intelligent, human, witty, ready, elegant, skillful, and expert, who with such sweetness show the conditions of human life and teach customs and virtues that, for those who follow them, it barely seems possible to be a bad man) (94).

27. See Alberti (see note 2), 24–25; Alberti (see note 5), 65–66: *"At nos rara hec delectant, que inter lautiores cenas ditiorum quam me esse profitear scriptorum, veluti in pulmento subamare interdum herbe, sint non reiicienda"* (For myself, I take pleasure in rare subjects which, like piquant herbs in an appetizer, should not be excluded from the lavish dinners of writers who I confess are richer than myself).

28. See Collenuccio (see note 3), 91:

> BLACICO. *Al re parla in modo che tu vòi, Esopo, ché (come ho detto) è instrutto di sapienza. Ma da li uscieri e da' ministri oziosi ti guarda, perchè tu parleresti nel canneto. Spaccia pur lor col riso, come la Volpe tua la mascara del mimo* (BLACYCUS.

> Speak to the king as you wish, Aesop, for (as I said) he is a learned man. But keep away from his ministers and officials, because you would be wasting your breath. But wear a smile when with them, like the fox does, and put on a mime's mask).

And further:

> *Allora udito questo, tanto riso si levò ne la turba, che fu cosa mirabile, parendo a' circunstanti che 'l fusse ben fatto, comeché a le gran falsitadi et errori miglior rimedio non sia che porvi al riscontro una espressa e gran busia* (Having heard this, a remarkable laughter rose from the crowd, for it seemed to bystanders that the thing was well done, since the best method for dealing with great falsehoods and errors is to confront them expressly with another big lie) (93).

29. Pluto and Persephone appreciate Pistoia as a fool (see, for example, Collenuccio's *Specchio di Esopo*) but refuse to allow his spirit to enter into the kingdom of the dead until he has settled his debt to Isabella, namely, he must collect and distribute his *Sonetti faceti*. See Antonio Cammelli, *I sonetti faceti,* ed. Erasmo Pèrcopo (Naples: Jovene, 1908), 19, 37–38.

30. See Cammelli (see note 29), 44:

> CHARON. *Non guardare chi cum più belle parole dica il vero, ma chi, seguendo la sua openione et il suo stile, migliore operatione produce. . et universalmente quelle discipline et quelle leggi, sotto le quali gli huomini sono migliori, a quelle che questo non fanno, sono da preporre;* et de qui prova la christiana legge et tutte le altre; *ma il tuo parlare mi ha tratto ad ragionare di cosa, che nè a te udire, nè a me dirne spectava* (CHARON. Pay no heed to those who seem to speak the truth with the most lovely words, but rather to those who, following their own opinion and style, produce the best results . . . and everywhere such disciplines and laws through which men may be at their best should be preferred to those which do not lead to this outcome; *and this is the proof of Christian law and all others;* but your speech has led me to talk of things that it was neither for me to speak of nor for you to hear) (emphasis mine).

31. Calcagnini's literary work has until now only been touched upon in the Ariosto literature. For a recent synthesis, see Claudio Moreschini, "Per una storia dell' umanesimo latino a Ferrara," in Patrizia Castelli, ed., *La rinascita del sapere: Libri e maestri nello studio ferrarese* (Venice: Marsilio, 1991), 168–88. Calcagnini's knowledge of Alberti's work is apparent in his letter to the Hungarian ecclesiastic Ferenc Perényi, *"episcopus Varatiensis,"* as Franco Bacchelli has kindly pointed out to me. This undated letter must be from 1518, given the letters that precede and follow it. The letter, which seems to be a dedicatory epistle from Calcagnini's *Encomion pulicis,* contains a genealogy of the genre of *spoudoghelaion* (serious playfulness) which includes *"Leo Baptista in cloaca et Momo, Erasmus in Stultitia, Pandulphus Collenutius in Bombarda et Misopono, Jacobus Sadoletus meus in Laoconte"* (Leon Battista Alberti author of "Sewer" and "Momus," Erasmus author of "Stupidity," Pandolfo Collenuccio author of "Bombarda" and "Misopenes," and my Jacopo Sadoleto author of "On the Statue of the Laocoön"). See Celio Calcagnini, *Caeli Calcagnini Ferra-*

rensis, protonotarii apostolici, opera aliquot (Basel: Per Hier. Frobium & Nic. Episcopium, 1544), 88. The *"elogio della cloaca"* (praise of the sewer) is an obvious reference to Alberti's "Somnium"; *"cloacaria prudentia"* (sewer sagacity) represents in synecdochal fashion the entire corpus of the *Intercenales.* Alberti's name also appears in the inventory, included in a legal document dated 29 May 1541, of the 1,187 works that Calcagnini willed to the monastery of San Domenico in Ferrara (Archivio di Stato di Modena, Archivio Privato Calcagnini, capsa 95, num. provv. 190, fasc. 32). In this inventory, which describes Calcagnini's books rather briefly, Alberti is mentioned once in general terms (c. 3v) and once as the author of *De re aedificatoria* (c. 8r). Although this inventory does not allow us to determine whether Calcagnini owned a copy of the *Intercenales,* it confirms his interest in the first and foremost of Lucian's fifteenth-century imitators.

32. See Calcagnini (see note 31), 479:

> *Et tamen si Dis placet, magni isti et admirabiles philosophi caeteros insectantur, aliorumque decretis oblatrant. Quin et naturae scita contumeliose rescindere conantur, affectus frustra, immo cum maximo mortalium malo datos asserentes, neque iram cotem virtutis, neque ambitionem glorie invitamentum existimantes. Perturbationes enim esse quasdam animi aegritudines. Nullam autem esse vel tantillam aegritudinem, quae iure laudari mereatur. Haec profecto sunt ijs simillima quae poetae de Momo conscripserunt. Momum enim quendam fuisse dixit Hesiodus Nocte et Somno prognatum, hominum ac deorum contemptorem. Hic quom non posset recte facta veris probris coarguere, confictis calumniis cavillabatur. Nam et fenestratum homini pectus, et bobus in armis cornua, et meliores Veneri crepidas esse oportere praedicabat. Quod si aequa trutina rem libraveris, et ipsos Stoicos Momi discipulos agnosces, et Somno ac Nocte satos profitebere: quom non modo obscura, sed somniculosa etiam atque adeo caligantia proloquantur* (And yet, if it pleases the gods, those great and admirable philosophers censure the rest and rail at the doctrines of others. And furthermore they insolently try to annul the decrees of nature, declaring that dispositions have been given to no purpose, nay rather, with the greatest harm of mortals, thinking neither that wrath is the grindstone of virtue nor that the desire for glory is an allurement—that, indeed, certain emotions are sicknesses of the mind—that, moreover, no sickness, however little, is deserving of being praised justly. These things are assuredly very similar to those that the poets have written about Momus. For Hesiod said that there was a certain Momus, born of Night and Sleep [and] a despiser of men and gods. Since he was not able to assail with true reproaches things rightly done, he criticized with fabricated charges. For he declared that a man should have a windowed breast, and that oxen should have horns on [their] shoulders, and that Venus should have better sandals. But if you weigh the matter in a fair balance, you will recognize even the Stoics themselves as disciples of Momus, and you will declare them born of Sleep and Night: since they utter things not only obscure but also sleep-inducing and very dark).

Another interesting reference to Momus may be found in a brief dialogue between Mercury and Diogenes in which Momus criticizes Zeus for his predilection for actors and vagabonds, a transparent allusion to the excessive influence of the mendicant friars in affairs of the Church; see Calcagnini (see note 31), 637.

33. See Calcagnini (see note 31), 620–21:

> *De qua re ab ipsis mundi incunabulis et primogenia hominis origine, Momum illum (ut accepimus) Somni et Noctis filium, sed inter deos imprimis perspicacem apud Iovem expostulasse accepimus: deosque increpasse, qui tam varium et versipelle animal rerum humanarum administrationi praefecissent: neque illi speculam saltem ullam adaptassent in pectore, unde animi, id est veri hominis arcana perspicerentur. Sed frustra Momus querimonias seu mavis accusationes illas suas attulit. Nihil enim credendum est non sapienter ac exacte a deo optimo maximo atque a natura institutum: quando expedit hoc habitu hominem esse conditum, quo et voluntatem liberam, suique mancipij habeat, et sapientiae munia non invitus exerceat. Meliore tamen conditione, si vera fateri volumus, personam hanc in Volupiae ac sacri genij gratiam sumimus, quam eximere possumus quom lubet, et palam nos profiteri* (Concerning which, from the very infancy of the world and the original coming into being of man, we have heard that the well-known Momus (as we have understood) is the son of Sleep and Night but that he found fault among the gods, especially in the presence of perspicacious Jupiter: and that he chided the gods who had placed so changeable and dissimulative a being in charge of the administration of human affairs: and had not even fitted any window in his breast, through which the minds, namely, the secrets of the true man, might be discerned. But in vain did Momus bring those complaints, or, if you prefer, accusations. For it is not to be believed that anything was instituted unwisely or imprecisely by the best [and] greatest god and by nature: since it is expedient for man to have been placed in this condition, wherein he may have free will and be master of himself and may exercise the duties of wisdom not unwillingly. But in a better condition, if we wish to acknowledge the truth, we take up this person into the favor of Volupia and of the sacred genius, which we can remove when it pleases [us to do so], and [we can] declare ourselves openly [when it pleases us]).

Calcagnini alludes here to a speech by Lycinus in Lucian's *Hermotimus* (20), which was echoed by Collenuccio in his *Specchio di Esopo* (see note 3), 97, where strangely the idea is attributed to Socrates: "*Però seria ben stato (secondo Socrate) che li omini per natura avuto avessino una finestrella nel petto, per la quale potuto avessino, ai bisogni, ne l'intrinseco ancora esser veduti*" (But it would have been good (according to Socrates) for men to have been born with a little window in the breast, through which their most intimate thoughts could be seen when necessary).

34. See Calcagnini (see note 31), 618: "*Omni enim in re agunda, praecipuum esse consilium, ut tempori et decoro inserviatur*" (For in doing everything, the most important advice is that one must defer to the state of the times and to what is suitable).

35. See Calcagnini (see note 31), 616–17:

> *Nec iam templum mystas capit, sed urbe tota discursant omnes recursantque, choreas et amores exercentes implexe pueris puellae, senes iunioribus: anus ipse denique repubescunt et in medio choro chordaca vel gymnopodiam vel tretanelo*

repraesentant (Nor does the temple now receive *mystae,* but in the whole city they all rush back and forth, occupying themselves with dances and lusts, girls intermingled with boys and old people with young: the old women themselves at length grow young again, and in the midst of the dance they display the cordax or *gymnopodia* [barefoot movement] or *tretanelo* [lyre-jangling]).

See also the comments of Erasmus's Folly (Desiderius Erasmus, *Opera omnia Desiderii Erasmi Roterodami,* vol. 4, part 3, *Moriae encomium* [Amsterdam: North-Holland, 1969], 88; idem, The Praise of Folly *and Other Writings,* ed. and trans. Robert M. Adams [New York: Norton, 1989], 17):

> *Itaque sublato illo [Momo], iam multo licentius ac suauius nugantur dii.... Tum et Silenus ille senex amator, tèn kórdaka saltare solitus, una cum Polyphemo tòn tretanelò, Nymphis tèn gymnopodìan saltantibus* (And so, in the absence of Momus, the gods revel much more freely and carelessly, "taking all things lightly," as Homer says, now that they have no censor.... There is Silenus, that dirty old man, who likes to do the "belly-dance" while Polyphemus "jangles his lyre" and a chorus of "barefoot nymphs" caper about).

Folly later observes,

> *Sed multo etiam suauius, si quis animadvertat anus longo iam senio mortuas adeoque cadaverosas, ut ab inferis redisse videri possint, tamen illud semper in ore habere, phos agathón: adhuc catullire atque, ut Graeci dicere solent, kaproun* (But it's even more macabre to think of the old women in the last stages of senility and so cadaverous that you'd think they'd been pulled out of the grave; yet they never cease repeating "life is good," while they're constantly in heat, or, as the Greeks put it, "rutting like a goat") (108/31).

36. See Calcagnini (see note 31), 617:

> *Tum Aphrodisius aeditimus dee: erat enim et ipse proximus dum Chronius ea loquebatur: cave sis, inquit, cave obsecro mi Chroni, ne tu has interpreteris insanias, que Volupie dee* sanctissima sunt mysteria *parata ad vegetationem animorum et humani generis instaurationem* (Then Aphrodisius, sacristan of [the temple of] the goddess—for he himself was also very near while Chronius was saying these things—said, "Take care, if you please, take care, I beseech you, my Chronius, not to explain these frenzies, *which are very sacred mysteries* of the goddess Volupia prepared for the enlivening of minds and for the renewal of the human race") (emphasis mine).

Erasmus ends the *explicit* of the *Moriae encomium* (see note 35), 194/87: *"Quare valete, plaudite, vivite, bibite, Moriae celeberrimi mystae"* (Clap your hands, live well, and drink deep, most illustrious disciples of Folly).

37. See Erasmus (see note 35), 106/29:

> *Siquidem peruerse facit, qui sese non accommodet rebus praesentibus foroque nolit uti.... postuletque ut fabula iam non sit fabula. Contra vere prudentis est,*

cum sis mortalis, nihil vltra sortem sapere velle cumque vniuersa hominum multitudine vel conniuere libenter vel comiter errare. At istud ipsum, inquiunt, stulticiae est. Haud equidem inficias iuerim, modo fateantur illi vicissim hoc esse vitae fabulam agere (The perverse man fails to adjust his actions to the present state of things, he disdains the give-and-take of the intellectual marketplace, he won't even acknowledge the common rule of the barroom, drink up or get out—all of which amounts to demanding that the play should no longer be a play. On the other hand, the truly prudent man reflects that since he is mortal himself, he shouldn't want to be wiser than befits a mortal, but should cast his lot in with the rest of the human race and blunder along in good company. But this, they say, is folly. I can hardly deny it, but let them confess also that this is the way the play of life is staged).

38. See Calcagnini (see note 31), 617:

An tu non audisti hanc vitam mimum esse, in qua quisque eam personam gerit, quam aut natura aut fortuna imposuit: eaque sustinenda est tantisper dum hanc fabulam, id est vitam agimus. Hoc est quod Plato hominem deorum ludum vocabat. Sed qualem ludum Di boni? Amphitheatralem scilicet et gladiatorium, in quo velis nolis depugnandum est, ut vincas aut succumbas oporteta (Or have you not heard that this life is a mime, in which each person wears that mask [i.e., plays that part] which either nature or fortune has imposed: and this must be sustained for as long as we act this play, that is, live life. It is for this that Plato called man the spectacle of the gods. But what sort of spectacle, O good gods? Amphitheatral, to be sure, and gladiatorial, in which you must fight eagerly whether you wish to or not, so that it is necessary that you prevail or succumb).

39. See Calcagnini (see note 31), 617:

At hic Volupie ludus quanto dulcior et iucundior? In quo nemo ingratus hanc vel illam personam subire cogitur: sed quam sibi quisque volens atque ultro imponit, hanc induit atque exuit pro sui animi sententia. Nihil hic servile, nihil coactum, nihil invitum, plena omnia summae libertatis ac suavitatis sunt. Quare quisquis hoc Volupie theatrum aut libertatis proscenium dixerit, non est quod a quocunque coarguatur, aut male audiat (But how much sweeter and more pleasant is this spectacle of Volupia? In which no one is compelled to take on this or that part ungratefully: but each person puts on and lays aside according to the wish of his own mind that part which he willingly and voluntarily imposes upon himself. There is nothing servile here, nothing compelled, nothing involuntary, all things are full of the utmost freedom and pleasantness. Wherefore whoever called this the theater of Volupia or the proscenium of liberty, there is no reason for which he may be refuted or spoken ill of by anyone).

On the theme of the theater of the world in the *Intercenales* and in *Momus*, see Lucia Cesarini Martinelli, "Metafore teatrali in Leon Battista Alberti," *Rinascimento*, ser. 2, 29 (1989): 3–51.

40. See Calcagnini (see note 31), 598:

> *Id quod olim in Fortunae templo ex tabella mihi aeditimus significavit.... In hac tabella, inquit, hospes, votum oratorum vides, qui se optant conciliante Mercurio ab immortalitate in comitatum et familiam recipi. Ea autem immortalitas est, quae regio ornatu insignis in solio assidet. At haec non prius admissura est, quam illi se posteritati approbaverint. Haec enim una fores, quae ad immortalitatem ducunt, tuetur: et familie rationarium habet. Illa vero, inquit, posteritas est, cuius occiput tantum vides, frontem vero mortali nemini videre unquam licuit. Huic itaque ante omnia rite ac solenniter litandum est, ut votum assequantur. Litant autem illi bonis precationibus, sepia et papyro* (That which the sacristan once showed to me in the temple of Fortuna from a painting.... In this painting, he said, O visitor, you see the vow of the orators, who wish, with Mercury bringing it about, to be received by Immortality into her company and family. And Immortality is the one who, distinguished by royal attire, is sitting on a throne. But she will not admit [them] before they have rendered themselves acceptable to Posterity. For she alone guards the doors that lead to Immortality: and has the book of accounts of the family. She, he said, is truly Posterity, the back of whose head alone you see, but whose front it has never been permitted to any mortal to see. And so to her before all things they must duly and solemnly bring offerings, in order that they may gain their wish. And they are bringing offerings with good prayers, with ink, fish, and with papyrus).

The allusion to the temple of Fortune is most likely an echo of Alberti's "Picture."

41. A strong component of learned *spoudoghelaion* is also found in the work of Lilio Gregorio Giraldi, a philologist from Ferrara who was very close to Calcagnini. See Luca D'Ascia, "I 'Dialogismi XXX' di Lilio Gregorio Giraldi fra Bembo, Erasmo, Valla," *Rivista di letteratura italiana* 10 (1992): 599–619.

42. See Guido Baldassarri, "Ut poesis pictura: Cicli figurativi nei poemi epici e cavallereschi," in Papagno and Quondam (see note 7), 3: 605–35.

Science, Cosmology, and Religion in Ferrara, 1520–1550

Franco Bacchelli

Shortly after 1520, Lilio Gregorio Giraldi, a humanist from Ferrara, sent a rhetorical exercise, titled *Progymnasma adversus litteras et litteratos,* to his friend Celio Calcagnini. In this text Giraldi developed, in a half-serious and half-playful tone, the paradoxical thesis that the practice of letters and the development of the sciences were contrary to natural human tendencies and harmful to human happiness. For Giraldi, the true cause of all the startling scientific and religious innovations of the day was to be found in the single-minded refinement of expressive or (even worse) polemical devices, as human minds became lost in the labyrinth of written culture. This had encouraged the manipulation of words rather than the government of things or the discovery that some truths were less hidden and unapproachable than was commonly believed to be the case. In order to escape from this deception, he urged a return to the voice of nature in teaching, in moral philosophy, and in religion. This voice was to be variously defined as instinct, the depths of conscience, mystical experience, or an intuitive language such as that of painting. Giraldi noted, echoing here and there Erasmus's *Moriae encomium* that

> the mind well educated and formed by nature triumphs over all letters and teachings. Too much study of letters leads men to madness. Take, for instance, children: they willingly observe and enjoy being told about everything having to do with natural phenomena, and ask incessantly the reason for everything, yet they instinctively flee from school, to which they adapt only when forced to do so with a whip. What more obvious evidence could there be that the study of letters is not born from nature, but is the result of violence done to nature? ... From where did the opinions of those who say that the moon is inhabited and that there are many cities on it come from? Or, in our own time, those who say that the earth moves while the sky stands still? From where indeed, if not from an exaggerated practice of writing and reading, and an excessive turning over and over the pages of books? From where indeed, if not from the captiousness to which all this accustoms us? ... The same thing happened to those Christians who devoted themselves to doctrinal disputes rather than to contemplation, despite Saint Paul's precept warning them that "the letter kills." They lapsed into the strangest assortment of errors, to the point of placing in doubt the most secret mysteries of our religion, and the more they thought to explore these mysteries in depth, the further and more shamefully

> they fell into error.... But letters, they tell us, help us to express the sensations and thoughts of the mind. Yet does not painting perhaps do this better? Men of letters themselves employ painting when they have to speak about something that is extremely difficult to remember, or something which literary description alone cannot adequately express. They do this, by their own admission, because painting and imagery imprint in themselves and in others the forms of things more clearly and more truthfully than letters do.[1]

This praise of visual immediacy stands out from the web of provocations and paradoxes. It was written, according to Giraldi himself, after reading Giovanni Francesco Pico della Mirandola's *Examen vanitatis doctrinae gentium,* which was first published in 1520. Pico's work was a monument of skeptical antirationalist propaganda with explicit religious aims. In truth, however, the *Examen* did not spare even the certainty of sensations themselves. Rather, it clearly affirmed that these were but the expressions of the physical and subjective condition of the faculties, rather than faithful images of the forms of things. Pico's complex battle against ecclesiastical corruption and superstition and his critique of scientific dogmatism (which he alternated with a blind and fanatical persecution of witches and the devil) left few traces in the development of Giraldi's thought. Nevertheless, his long years in the Picos' court must have led Giraldi to direct his scholarly energies away from the sciences and toward collecting material for the antiquarian, literary, and mythological works that he was later to compose in Ferrara after the count's tragic death in 1533. Here I am speaking especially about the *Historia deorum gentilium* (1548)—which begins, not coincidentally, with a description of a lost painting by Cosmè Tura that represents an allegory of poetry—as well as about the *Historia poetarum* (1545).

The mythological study was particularly meaningful. It contains, first of all, a well-ordered catalog of the religious beliefs of pagan antiquity. Giraldi lists gods that presided over the natural elements and others that were linked to various phases of human life in all its forms—civil, intellectual, moral, emotional. Then he treats the literary or figurative forms with which all this had been expressed. In regard to this latter aspect, however, it should be said that the *Historia deorum gentilium* was very different from the collections of symbols that were first being published in this same period. Giraldi was not particularly interested in complicated new reflections or in new or old systems of correspondence between concepts and images. His intent was instead rigorously historical; he aimed to document the poetical and iconographical theology of the ancient peoples during the epoch prior to the invention of writing. He thus sought to grasp the presence, within the mythological traditions, of the first expressive translations of every aspect of life, whether high or low, extraordinary or everyday, which, according to him, must have occurred in a moment prior to the development of reflexive thought or any cultural contact between civilizations.

Natural enlightenment, by means of a purely contemplative sense of wonder, had come into contact with the forms of things at the dawn of humanity. It had reacted with them, creating—once and for all, and in the best way possible—those metaphors and symbols that structured, either openly or covertly, both literary communication and the pictorial language of posterity. The *Historia deorum gentilium* was an attempt on Giraldi's part to reconstruct the structure of the primitive imagination. Naturally, he was particularly interested in the representation of the divine. His attempt was analogous to the one undertaken in those same years by Agostino Steuco in his *De perenni philosophia* (1542). Unlike the latter work, with its rigorous philosophical argument upon which Giambattista Vico would later draw, Giraldi's text maintains a broadly narrative and ekphrastic character that seems always to refer to images or promote their production. This explains the mythographer Vincenzo Cartari's ample use of the *Historia* in his works explicitly aimed at painters. The period 1520–1550, during which time Giraldi was writing his works, was for Ferrara an age of literary, scientific, and artistic flowering, no less than was the second half of the fifteenth century.

I am concerned here with the final decade of Alfonso I's reign (he died in 1534) and his son Ercole II's subsequent reign of twenty-five years. During this time, which followed the critical phase of the Italian wars and the recovery of Modena and Reggio, the Estense state enjoyed a long period of peace. In 1528 Ercole II married a French princess, Renée de France, the daughter of Louis XII, but the marriage did not tie the fate of Ercole's dynasty to French politics alone: indeed, Ferrara grew closer and closer to Rome in the years that followed. The marriage was not a happy one. It was increasingly embittered not only by private disagreements but also by the duchess's increasingly evident heterodox religious beliefs. She had come to Ferrara with a retinue of more than 160 people, which constituted a small court in its own right, including artists and men of letters as well as those who served the duchess. For more than twenty years, this court-within-a-court formed a space in which French cultural and heterodox religious figures were welcome during their journeys through Italy. In March 1536, for instance, John Calvin and his friend Jean Du Tillet were guests of the duchess. The presence of this organizational center for the Reformation in Ferrara put Ercole II in an increasingly difficult position in regard to Rome, for he was a vassal of the Holy See (at least for Ferrara). Starting in the 1540s (at least), Renée not only openly distanced herself from the Catholic cult, but, while leaning toward the practice of Calvinism, she offered protection and propaganda in support of the Reformation. Rome, on the other hand, aggressively sought inquisitorial controls in such cases while progressively reducing the relative autonomy that had once belonged to all the Italian states. Hence the executions of Fanino Fanini and Giorgio Siculo in 1550–1551, the lengthy persecution of the latter's followers, and finally, in 1554, the trial of the duchess herself and her opportunistic abjuration.

But religious unrest, including the discussion of Erasmus's and (later) Luther's ideas, existed in Ferrara well before Renée's arrival. Even before the beginning of the Reformation it was customary to hear cries of protest and concerns about ecclesiastical corruption coming from Ferrara, perhaps more so than elsewhere in Italy. It was at that time normal and ordinary for people everywhere to have negative opinions of priests and monks. In Ferrara these opinions were made fiercer, both in the city and the court, by the thirty years of tension between the Este dynasty and Rome and, above all else, by the stubborn persistence of the heritage of Girolamo Savonarola—although it took on quite a different cast in Ferrara than it had in Florence. Examples abound of this widespread anticlericalism in Ferrara. Lucrezia Borgia, the wife of Alfonso I, went to mass to give thanks to God for the death of Pope Julius II. The prince and heir to the dynasty, Ercole, composed a Latin pasquinade against Leo X when only fourteen years old.[2] The pious and severe Antonio Musa Brasavola, Ercole II's personal physician, ferociously remarked in his *Examen omnium syruporum* (1538) in regard to distilled spirits that "with the help of these, Clement VII, who was almost in a coma, survived for a few days; but the good Lord, who wanted to free his flock from the clutches of such a shepherd, weakened the strength of this liquor."[3] These displays of anticlericalism were traditional enough, but only up to a certain point and up to a certain date. From the 1520s on, this form of protest "which had some time ago earned its right to a place in the Christian republic"[4] constituted at times the sole visible manifestation of a widespread turning toward the ideas of the Reformation, albeit with various degrees of involvement and curiosity.

All levels of Ferrara's very intense scientific and literary life—the court, the university (*studio*), and the bourgeois class (which had grown in size during the reign of Ercole II) linked to the bureaucracy and administration of the Estense state—were parallel to, and embedded in, this religious debate. In these same years Ludovico Ariosto was preparing the definitive edition of his *Orlando furioso,* which would appear in 1532. This version contained political and religious concerns that were absent from the two earlier versions. Calcagnini came back to Ferrara once and for all around 1520, after wandering through Hungary, Poland, and along the Russian border. Between Cracow and Buda he developed his interest in botany and geography and became familiar (in circles near to Copernicus himself) with highly important observations concerning the limits of current astronomical hypotheses. For more than half a century, Niccolò Leoniceno had been at the center of scientific discussion in Ferrara that concerned not only medicine but methodology as well. After his death in 1524, his friend Giovanni Manardo continued the struggle for the rebirth of Greek medicine for a few more years. Manardo, who died in 1536, spent his final years preparing the definitive edition of his *Epistulae medicinales* (1540), where he continued to attack astrological medicine and took a position in favor of the possibility of human life in the torrid equatorial regions, which some Aristotelians continued to deny.[5] Antonio Musa Brasavola was a pupil of both of these physicians. Between 1530 and 1555 (the year of his death), he radically renewed scientific knowledge of traditional pharmacopia and medicinal herbs. Brasavola and his somewhat older friend Calcagnini were among the duke's most intimate counselors in the choice of professors for the university, and they were in touch with scholars and scientists from all over Europe.[6]

The spread of literature expressing religious dissent dates from the 1520s and 1530s. The works of Erasmus and Luther were read, not only by great scholars but (to a greater or lesser extent) by everyone, in a search for a new spirituality and as a protest against Rome. Schoolmasters were extraordinarily active in the capillary dissemination of these texts, especially those written by Erasmus. Members of a singular class of intellectuals, the schoolmasters of the period—some of whom worked at a high scientific level—wandered through towns and cities (like some physicians and surgeons) in search of a better job and held an uncertain social position on the margins of poverty.[7] They lived in a continuous state of conflict, at once tragic and comic, between their grand ambitions and their actual social achievements. Precisely because of their status as proudly rootless individuals, they were able to observe and live more fully than others not only the gap between the current social order and the exemplary classical models of equality that daily they had to explain to their pupils, but also the gap between the modern religious marketplace with its devotional formalism and the pure faith and charity taught by the scriptures (to which Luther and Erasmus were to make ample reference). Thus the schoolmasters tended to develop an internalized religiosity that was skeptical of the magical nature of the sacraments and that was no longer bound to ceremony, specific places for worship, or rules and prohibitions. They participated in a no-holds-barred polemic, moreover, against the warmongering of the Italian princes, while protesting—perhaps somewhat generically, but vigorously—against the social order, which they saw as structured by domination and force. This social order seemed simply unjust when compared to classical morality and to the New Testament. These readers sought to discover in Luther's writings a previously unknown religious radicality and an interpretation of the scriptures that predated any theological or canon-law distortions. They could turn, instead, to the seemingly more cautious and milder writings of Erasmus, where they could find a combination of religious and social protest, especially the *Colloquia* (definitive edition, 1533), which Calcagnini admired greatly and which were widely used as textbooks in schools throughout the duchy.

The dialogue in Erasmus's *Colloquia* involved men and women, soldiers, monks, students and courtiers and thus evoked with great simplicity a possibility of Christian life pervading every moment of existence and involving lay people and the members of religious orders equally, with equal duties for all. The *Colloquia* proposed a joyful practice of Christ's teachings—let us recall that Christ represented, for Erasmus, the true Epicurus—in which it was no longer possible to oppose a group of sacred acts to a group of secular ones. In Erasmus's writings, then, religious propaganda was joined successfully with an exhortation to a certain ordering of human and social relations that went beyond questions of etiquette. These relations, whether between superiors and inferiors, or husbands and wives, bore the marks of sweetness and affection. Often, indeed, these dialogues transmitted above all else a sort of grace and a sense of sacrality rather than specific doctrines. But this sense of sacrality was never solemn; it was instead linked to the simplest occurrences in life, and this was a component that made a special impression on Italian readers, precisely because the words of the humanists had not always suggested this possibility of an existence imbued with *humanitas* and spirituality at the same time. The *Colloquia,* in short, proposed a whole style of living. Yet they appeared on the eve of the establishment in Italy, as well as elsewhere in Europe, of a ritual that regulated inequalities and social roles (characteristic of periods of religious heteronomy), as expressed both in the language and in the sign-systems of society and the court. Instead of morality and the teachings of the Gospels, this ritual of inequalities insisted on the importance of honor, distinctions, and priorities.

Luther's work also attracted immediate interest in Ferrara. Calcagnini, Pellegrino Morato, and surely also Brasavola were among the first readers of Luther there. The position at which they finally arrived in regard to the German reformer's work is paradigmatic of their differences in cultural background and social position. Morato was drawn ever more enthusiastically toward Protestantism, whereas Calcagnini and Brasavola, after an initial period of enthusiasm for Luther as a scourge of the Church, moderated their position. Frightened by Luther's unwavering theological positions and his break with Rome, they preferred an Erasmian outlook instead, replete with political cautiousness and fear in regard to the development of a religious movement that could attract and stir up the uneducated lower classes. Calcagnini remarked in a letter of 1525 to Erasmus that, at the beginning, "Luther earned much admiration, because he criticized intrepidly and almost impudently the customs of our age . . . and I must say the truth: that man, who later on was to reveal himself to be false and a turncoat, deceived me and yet I had thought him to be a gentleman."[8]

By 1538, when Calcagnini sent Morato his famous letter on religious dissimulation,[9] the times—and his attitude—had changed. In this letter Calcagnini called on his humanist friend to refrain from public discussion of the crucial problems of Reformation theological thought. Was this a simple request—directed at both himself and his friend—to hide radical theological thought, for the sake of prudence, and to avoid confusing simple minds? Or was it a warning to keep in mind the inessential nature, for the *negotium salutis,* of the resolution of matters such as justification and predestination? Probably it was all of these at once. In his letter Calcagnini, typically enough, insisted above all on the belief that no theological *curiositas* ought to chill a solid and diligent practice of Christianity. He did not at all believe, moreover, that the scholastic theology practiced by the friars could offer a way to overcome the contrast between faith and works, between predestination and freedom of the will, between Paul's words, in which he spoke in such a

Manichaean (as Calcagnini termed it)[10] way of the radical corruption of our nature while insisting on the merits of Christ alone, and James's words, which seemed so close to Pelagianism. According to Calcagnini, theology could only dramatize and sharpen the contrast between the two requirements for salvation, which had, instead, to be mediated. The dramatization of that contrast was to take the shape of an abstract comparison of concepts that could have tragic consequences at the personal and social level. The point was not to try to discover how faith and works could be reconciled through a montage of disparate scriptural verses or through logic, nor was it to grasp how the will, with its structure, could or could not pay homage to Christ's teachings. Calcagnini concluded instead that one ought to adhere to the spirit of the scriptures, recognize what they urge us to do, and attempt to put it into practice without delay.

Calcagnini himself, however, acknowledged in this regard the existence of the very same theological difficulties that Luther had raised, although the perspective in which he saw these aporias was rather different. The fact that Christ had given men his precepts simply presupposed that we had some possibility of following them, but in a way that could be explained neither with human reason nor with theology (which was composed largely of human reason). Calcagnini understood, in short, that the tools of classical Platonic and Aristotelian philosophy, as well as the principle of causality which had implicitly been taken from this philosophy by scholastic theology, could only construct a mechanics of will that tended inevitably toward a rigid determinism. And the latter, however imperceptibly, ended by substantiating in theological discussions what Saint Paul was believed to have argued.

In 1524 Erasmus published his *De libero arbitrio diatribe sive collatio*, and Calcagnini wrote his *Libellus elegans de libero arbitrio ex philosophiae penetralibus* in response (the work was published by Froben in Basel in 1525). The Dutch humanist had gathered together all the biblical passages that could support the idea of free will and had "balanced" them against those supporting the opposite idea that was found in the various writings of Luther, Philipp Melanchthon, and Andreas Rudolff-Bodenstein (Karlstadt) from the early years of the Reformation movement. Calcagnini similarly offered to his readers a brief survey of the problem in ancient philosophy. I do not know if it can be claimed, as Silvana Seidel Menchi has done, that he "took on the task of writing the *Libellus* in order to forestall any accusation of Lutheranism," given his relationship with the typographer Zoppino, who falsely printed and circulated texts by Luther and Nikolaus von Amsdorf under Erasmus's name in 1526. I instead believe it to be quite true that, as she asserts, "Calcagnini's little book suffers from a glaring conceptual inconsistency."[11] This inconsistency, however, was perhaps not wholly involuntary. Calcagnini knew full well—perhaps even better than Erasmus—that natural reason found itself in grave difficulty in its efforts to demonstrate the freedom of the will. If anything, it could only show that to which all were agreed, such as the fact that certain sinful suggestions usually failed to affect well-built and well-educated reason and will. Thanks to his lengthy philosophical and dialectical experience, Calcagnini sensed that those same forces (whether derived from the cosmos, our surroundings, or our passions) that led us away from or inhibited the observance of Christ's precepts could, when brought together and turned entirely against the will, ultimately triumph over it. In short, he saw clearly that there was no a priori nucleus in the mind that was absolutely strong in itself and beyond outside influence; the struggle between the will and stimuli was a contest in which the former was no more and no less than a force among other forces. Even grace, when it was thought of as a surplus of supernatural force given to the natural power of the will (as simplistic sorts of theology commonly held), became nothing more than one of the agents of the sublunar world, whose intervention merely confirmed the impotence of the will.

In his brief treatise, Calcagnini made what was at the time a surprising claim. Remarkably, he asserted that Aristotle and the Platonic philosophers were rigorous determinists.[12] Neither Aristotle nor the Neoplatonists had ever been clear on this point, but this remark allowed Calcagnini rightly to recall once again that the conceptual heritage of these two doctrines converged in a rigidly deterministic construction of moral and psychological reality. In one passage in the treatise he traced, in only a few words, an acute and striking diagnosis of the situation, showing that in Italy there existed a tradition, rather more philosophical than religious, that had gone so far as to depict freedom as a state of imperfection when compared to necessity. This was a transparent allusion to Marsilio Ficino's system, which resolved the problem of the soul's motion toward the good strictly through an exchange between two types of necessity, namely a movement from the type of necessity exercised by Fate (which is the worse of the two) to the more structuring type of necessity that is part of Providence (which is clearly the better of the two). The *Libellus* could thus be considered an anticipatory text that documents for us the sensation that the first part of Luther's *De servo arbitrio* (published in 1525) must have subsequently caused. In Luther's treatise the arguments of the ancient philosophers were quickly but vigorously summarized precisely in the aforementioned sense. This is confirmed by the theologian Ambrogio Fiandino's subsequent reading of Luther's book. His interpretation completely lost sight of Luther's theology of original sin and turned it almost into a parallel text for a work of a quite different sort, namely Pietro Pomponazzi's *De fato* (written in 1520, first published posthumously in 1567), which was at that time beginning to circulate underground between Bologna and Padua.

This helps to explain Calcagnini's reaction, for he was concerned with earthly matters, especially the educational and civic consequences of the new philosophy. His concern was increased by his awareness of the poverty of the arguments that could be used to oppose Luther not only as a theologian but also as a philosopher. Although he was convinced that the scriptures—when cited in fragmentary form by those involved in the debate, as often happened in such cases—offered supporting evidence for both theses, he nonetheless believed that Erasmus had succeeded in discovering that which should be most important to a Christian, namely a certain number of incontrovertibly clear passages in the Bible (which was the voice of God) that could be used to contradict Luther's examples. The disappointing conclusion of the work, which almost seemed intent only on avoiding theology and difficult philosophical issues, can be found in Calcagnini's remarks that "the Christian must have faith that God will never send against our free will forces so great as to annihilate it" and that "in arduous and impossible things, for God it is rather magnificent that mankind simply had been able 'to will.'"[13] This was a weak enough answer to Luther's efforts to forestall any recourse both to free will and a simplistic interpretation of those verses of the Bible that expressed precepts and implicated possibilities for carrying them out. As Luther put it, with a very precise doctrine of the corrupt state of nature in mind, "Christ had commanded impossible things" from us, a remark taken up by the heterodox in contemporary Bologna.[14] Calcagnini's counsel to Morato to resort to dissimulation was a result of his distorted understanding of Luther's thought, as well as his diffidence toward the moral and religious utility of theological probing. It seemed to respond to two concerns: first, persecution by the religious authorities (but there was a rather small chance of this in 1538); and second, and more important, a refusal to radicalize the religious debate in front of ignorant people, in order to prevent it from spreading and sinking down to the level of artisans and nuns.

This was, moreover, not the first time that Calcagnini had counseled prudence. Before he returned to the consideration of the religious problems of Christianity sometime around 1520, most likely because of Erasmus's influence, and before he, in self-interest, took religious orders, he had been an elegant, cultivated, and skeptical man of arms and a diplomat. Toward the beginning of the century he wrote a text in hexameters praising complete dissimulation—the unpublished "Simulatae virtutis defensio," addressed to Gaspare Sardi—in which he provided a piece of advice in the form of a pseudo-New Testament saying, "*si non caste, tamen caute*" (if not chaste, then cautious—later to be repeated by Castiglione), which he attributed to Christ himself:

> Let him who is able to simulate and who converts black things into white entrust the sails of life to the gods. All things follow with easily moving foot, provided that he does with cautious mind whatever he does that should be concealed under night; and so the doctrines of the sanctified Christ teach: "Either avoid sins or cover them under sleep-bringing night." . . . This then is the chief point: He who wishes to pass his life well must learn that it is necessary to simulate compliance with law boldly.[15]

Here dissimulation was to serve to hide practices contrary to current morals, rather than mask religious dissidence. In a subsequent, unfinished "*silva*" titled "Coelii secta" (written around the beginning of the sixteenth century), however, Calcagnini launched a daring attack on Christianity and its doctrine of the creation of the world. In this text we encounter words that perhaps would reappear only in the libertine literature of the late sixteenth century:

> Do not fear the empty dreams of frightful death.... It is vain superstition to keep invoking the powerful divinities: let not even thunderbolts sent through the air deceive you!... Those following the dogma of Christ attribute a beginning to the world, which they believe him to have made out of nothing, having assumed the name Jesus: for so great a power is reported of him. But you, O most distinguished Plato, long before sang of true things.... Behold the Roman priests, who indeed acknowledge that there is a god who possesses the highest power over men and heaven, but they worship him in the wrong way, not denying his existence but calling him a man and giving him fictitious names. As they tell it, he created the heavens, the earth, and the stars; they imagine that he had not physical [or, material] substance, but that his power alone, which was supreme, made it: nothing more foolish than that has ever been heard; there is no one so rash as to utter such words from his own foolish mouth.[16]

This was, naturally, an expression of Calcagnini's youthful disbelief, which was to vanish without a trace from the posthumous collection of his writings printed in Basel in 1544 by his friend Brasavola. Every so often, however, he let slip some hint of intolerance toward the impulsive and turbulent religiosity of certain individuals. In one printed work he significantly remarked that "religion is a good thing, but the more fanatical it becomes and the more reasons that it lines up behind it, the further it falls into superstition."[17] There can be few doubts, then, that Calcagnini himself was referred to in Calvin's "*plurale pro singulari*" *prothonotaires delicatz.*[18]

Naturally enough, this way of dealing with the religious demands evoked by Luther's writings, like those of Erasmus, seemed disappointing to Morato. The latter expected from those works an answer to the question of how it was possible not only to conduct oneself in a balanced moral fashion but also to set one's own life into Christ's life. Thus Calcagnini's religion was, for Morato, pure ice, an ice from which Celio Secondo Curione's influence would rescue him. Curione, who taught briefly in Ferrara in 1541, influenced Morato to pursue another path. "When my salvation was in danger," Morato later recalled to the humanist (already in exile outside of Italy),

> and, abandoned by everything and everyone, I saw myself as colder than ice itself, you were sent to me by God, for when you came to Ferrara you sought me out while overlooking much greater patrons who desired to have you with them.... At that time I was nibbling Paul's and John's letters and the other scriptures, rather than reading them, but your living voice and your spirit, with which all of you burns and with which you illuminate others, moved me, penetrated me, and

> ultimately heated me so vigorously and effectively, that I can now live not in myself, but as Christ in me and myself in Christ.... You made me into fire itself from the cold being that I once was.[19]

Brasavola, Ercole II's chief court physician, had a somewhat different attitude toward the question of religion. Brasavola was at once more passionate and more determined not to avoid certain thorny issues, and his great scientific work was more specialized and less amateurish. As has already been said, he studied with Leoniceno and Manardo; like all Ferrarese doctors of this period, he was also a good scholar of ancient Greek. Brasavola did not, however, continue to wage his teacher Leoniceno's struggle, although he deeply revered him. He found that his master's biased humanist claim for the superiority of Greek medicine over that of the Arabs or Pliny was overly abstract and did not always correspond to practice and experience. Leoniceno's polemic had ultimately turned into a tedious and endless discussion concerning merely methodological and dialectical questions of general medical and biological theories. Hence Brasavola throughout his life felt an aversion to that discussion, and he made the decision to devote himself instead to a positive and experimental study of medicinal herbs and the medical virtues that they contained. Like others of his generation, he saw the urgent need for a renewal of anatomy and the practice of surgery rather than theory, and he opted for the positive, patient, and demanding work of cataloguing plants, researching systems for extracting active curative elements from them and finding ways to prevent the various components from neutralizing one another's beneficial effects.

Wary in part of old and new dogmas, Brasavola sought to avoid speculation and useless quarrels in his chosen field, but he naturally never missed the chance to emphasize the shortcomings of both the ancient and modern medical traditions in all other aspects of medicine, including anatomy, where his pupil Giovanni Battista Canani was making a major contribution during this same period. In this sense it could be said that Brasavola embodied to some degree the skepticism expressed by Giovanni Francesco Pico in his *Examen*. More than his medical contemporaries, he was sharply conscious that medicine sometimes works blindly and by chance. He saw, moreover, that there was as yet no satisfactory system for linking external symptoms to the functioning of internal organs. Although he respected some parts of ancient and venerable general theories, he held to his own prudent *empiria* and placed his faith above all in a correspondence between medicinal essences and the purely external and symptomatic appearance of illnesses. This correspondence had, of course, to be proven through an accumulation of successful and unsuccessful case studies. Brasavola did not believe at all in the influence of the stars on diseases, which had been one of the chief sources available to physicians for explaining them. Indeed, physicians in Ferrara sided unanimously with Giovanni and Giovanni Francesco Pico and had a strong aversion to astrology.

The negation of the stars as a cause for sickness—that is, the end of the search for heavenly causes—typically brought with it a renewed interest in near and proper causes. Illnesses originated not in the skies but, rather, on the sublunary level. That is to say, they were to be sought in habits, food, climate, hygienic conditions, and atavism. This was, in other words, a methodological process similar to the one through which Calcagnini had expressed his doubts to Giovanni Francesco Pico about the cases of women who had been believed to be victims of demonic possession. He claimed that the cause of their problems was not witchcraft, but hysteria and melancholy.[20] Brasavola's rejection of astrology was also explicit in his explanation of syphilis. Moralistic analyses of the disease had made particular use of the theory of astral influence: given that the stars were instruments of God, it was through these (as second causes) that he had sent this scourge to punish this century's sins of excess. Brasavola's confutation of this thesis may seem to us surprisingly contemporary, if we recall the claims of today's fanatics about the even more terrible disease that afflicts our world:

> they say that this disease is God's revenge for the intemperate excesses of the men of our age... but, given our sins, all diseases ought [then] to be of divine origin. But if God is angry only with the lustful, why isn't he also angry with usurers, thieves, blasphemers, and murderers, whose sins are far worse than those of a man who, perhaps unmarried himself, makes love with an unmarried woman? To practice sensual love is natural for each and every one of us, whereas murdering, breaking and entering, stealing, and blaspheming all strike me as rather being against nature. And if God was so displeased with men for having sexual contact, he could simply inhibit the mechanism of the erection. And those who say that this is God's revenge still have to explain to me what wrong was done by fetuses who are attacked by this disease while still in their mother's womb.[21]

Here as well we can see Brasavola's greater sense of coherence in matters of religious belief. The entire passage offers a warning about overestimating the sinfulness of sexuality (although this would nonetheless continue to spread throughout the culture). Ercole II's physician had not only solid humanistic training, but an excellent education in logic—as was normal for doctors in this period—and theology. Thanks to his education, he was prepared to subject contemporary debates to critical scrutiny even more thoroughly than could his friend Calcagnini. He was also able, however, to appreciate and approve of Erasmus's attacks on dialectical "subtleties" and the useless discussions of scholastic theology that had little to do with Christ.

All of Brasavola's works reflect the influence of Erasmus, especially the *Colloquia,* even in their literary form. Brasavola's works, not only the moral pamphlet *Quod mors nemini placeat* (1544), a realistic and powerful description of dying and of different kinds of fear of death, but also his vernacular "Vita di Cristo" (unpublished), as well as almost all of his pharmacological writings, are written in the form of dialogues. Usually these dialogues involve the author and an old pharmacist representing the *senex* (an old man). Before discussing medications, they hold a long conversation about religious, social, or political topics. The introduction to *Examen omnium syruporum* is like an extension of Erasmus's *Colloquia* about marriage, and it constitutes a noteworthy document regarding the defense of feminism in Italy in this period. This defense had its origins in Erasmus and Agrippa von Nettesheim, as well as in the new vernacular literature that followed the lead of Petrarch and Pietro Bembo. In this delicate dialogue, the youthful Brasavola shows the old man (who represents the older generation, fierce and misogynist) the new attitude of confidence and tender abandon with which wives should be treated. He speaks touchingly of the beginning of his married life and violently criticizes the ancient and modern custom of wife beating.[22] Likewise, at the beginning of the *Examen omnium catapotiorum,* the physician tells the old man about his youthful religious experience, the meditative technique through which he learned to combat his passions, and the spiritual process that led him not to make too much of the external practices of religion (with its devotion to objects) on the one hand, and disputes about the worthiness or unworthiness of human works and efforts on the other.[23]

Brasavola was a friend to religious dissidents such as Jacob Ziegler and the Sinapii brothers, and he certainly read Luther's work with interest and curiosity. Moreover, like all of his educated and sensitive contemporaries, he felt a deep aversion to priests and monks—an aversion that, as a subject of the Estense house, he felt even more keenly—and was greatly scandalized by ecclesiastical corruption. On the other hand, his medical works and in particular his "Vita di Cristo" reveal the extent to which he shared a trait of the Italian religious tradition that was typical of culturally trained lay individuals. If he protested against the current conditions of the Church, he also felt a certain diffidence in regard to the revolutionary messages of ancient and modern reformers, especially if they were monks. This sense of diffidence was motivated not only by prudence and political considerations but also by his own theological knowledge, which he employed in competition with and in polemics against religious figures. In Brasavola's case, his knowledge included all of scholastic doctrine, but went beyond it as well, thanks to his perfect intimacy with the terms of the contemporary debate. His attitude was not a new one, and it allowed him to feel perfectly at ease in responding to the repeated calls made by Erasmus to think of Christ at all times and to put into practice his teachings, which was, Erasmus argued, the task of every baptized Christian, not only those who had taken vows. "This is not something," Brasavola remarked, "that belongs exclusively to that new kind of friar that people commonly call 'Capuchins.'"[24]

Erasmus's sense of independent religious initiative stands in contrast to Brasavola's sensibility, as seen in this description of the old pharmacist's personal journey toward the imitation of Christ. The latter represents the age-old Italian tendency to leave the care of the sacred to ecclesiastics and seems almost to prefigure the subordination of faith to Church control and regulation during the Counter Reformation. On the other hand, however, that same religious initiative takes place under the auspices of the even older cultural and spiritual tradition embodied by Savonarola, the Dominican friar and native of Ferrara. It is not in fact by chance that, in the *Examen omnium catapotiorum,* the physician names his uncle, Giovanni Brasavola, as his teacher of spirituality. The latter was, in the early years of the sixteenth century, the editor of some of Savonarola's sermons.[25] In his commentary on Hippocrates, Antonio Musa Brasavola himself called the friar *"Divus Hieronymus,"* with its unquestionable meaning of "Saint Girolamo Savonarola."[26] Savonarola's name was put to ambiguous use in this period (Luther himself referred to him), but he was a figure to reckon with in the area under Ferrarese influence. For a group looking for its precedents, Savonarola could stand as the fountainhead (prior to Luther and Erasmus) of respectable and consistent religious critique and protest, which nonetheless was wary of a complete rejection of the system of papal authority and the sacraments.

Brasavola defended ecclesiastical celibacy, precisely making reference to this tradition. He called for rigorous chastity for priests, and he saw in Luther a censor of customs who had overstepped the limits of his mission. Luther had also stained his hands with the terrible heresy of considering the pope not to be authorized to issue indulgences. In the "Vita di Cristo," Brasavola wrote that

> Luther began by speaking about the evil customs of the administrators of the Church and the evil habit of indulgences and the extortion of money for the pope's luxuries and his nepotism in regard to his children and relatives with the pretext of building the new Saint Peter's. . . . The Greeks opened their ears to these things from him, which were true. Seeing that these truths had induced the minds of men to believe him, he then began to add falsities under this aegis, saying that the pope could not give indulgences and other similar things of which the world is full.[27]

In spite of this traditionalism, sometimes one is forced to admit that Brasavola, unlike Calcagnini, arrived at the most radical and daring conclusions, even by way of Erasmus's own writings. For instance, at the beginning of the *Examen omnium catapotiorum* he comes to the belief—which he picked up in Erasmus's *Modus confitendi* (1524)—that although confession to priests was certainly quite convenient and resembled similar healthy pagan practices, it was not *"de iure divino"* (of divine law).[28] This observation is typical, among other things, of someone inclined to seek justification for the sacraments in the scriptures. In the *Quod mors nemini placeat,* Brasavola made a claim that almost smacked of certain medieval heresies. There he pointed out that the consecration of the host depended on the personal purity of the individual presiding over the rite, rather than on his status as a priest: "nothing is more holy and more healthy than the Eucharist, if it has been consecrated by a chaste priest with a concentrated mind, just as there is nothing more harmful and contaminated by sin than if the host has been consecrated by a mind thinking of shameful things."[29]

This remark may seem rather surprising at first, coming as it does from a theological expert like Brasavola. Nevertheless, it could be considered as a development of Erasmus's thought, in its emphasis on the importance of the fervor of fraternal love with which the host is to be taken, rather than its magical transformation into Christ's body (since this could not be noticed by either the giver or receiver of the host). In the same way, it may seem surprising—especially in light of the post-Tridentine development of theology—to read Brasavola's remark in his "Vita di Cristo" that the pope and the cardinals are part of the Church only if they are good and honest Christians:

> Popes and cardinals ... in our day are usually the worst of all. But the Church is the congregation of true Christians united as one. If the pope and the cardinals are true Christians and come together as one, then God is among them and that is the Church; but if they are guilty of sin, then the devil is among them and that is not the Church, because only the congregation of the good ones in the name of God is the Church.[30]

Claims such as this can easily be connected to the most radical version of Savonarola's thought regarding the pope's authority, as found in his *Prediche sull'Esodo* (1498). Brasavola's distrust in either Rome or in an uncontrollable movement from below as capable of carrying out the reform of the Church is widespread in his works. It can be traced back, I believe, to the various *Lettere ai principi* (1498) then attributed to Savonarola. Brasavola's hopes were directed, apocalyptically, at the healthy celestial scourges—including, first and foremost, Luther's reforms—and, above all, at the work of the princes. In regard to the heretics, however, he turned once more to Erasmus's thought, according to which these heretics should be "convinced rather than conquered":

> the popes ought to preach ... this is the pope's principal duty ... but they do not do so ... because they are not like Peter, that is to say, the vicar of Christ, except in name and in privilege, but not in their works. The pope's first duty is to be a fisher of men, namely of souls ... but they more readily attend to earthly than to heavenly things, and their evil examples and actions have been the ruin of a large number of Christians. Tell me who was the cause of the Lutheran plague, if not the enormous vices of the popes and prelates? ... Now they think only of accumulating money and promoting their children and relatives and no longer remember their duty; they no longer fish.... At the present time, Peter's net is torn asunder and the fish get free and go where they will in the sea: the Lutherans have gotten out of the net, and they spread among the Christians, and no one corrects them by trying lovingly to persuade them with reasons and with disputations.... O poor Peter, your ship is in great danger, your net is torn asunder and already many fish have gotten out of it. O Christ our leader, look to, look to your vicars. Send the flaming sword, wait

> no longer, the members are rotting and putrefying and falling off your body. Correct them and make them good.[31]

Brasavola was, in short, a man of order, and so it is likely that he was among those who inspired Ercole II's prudent politics in regard to Rome, from the end of the 1540s on. His concerns for the dynasty and his diffidence toward radical, visionary, and anarchic religious movements were uppermost in his mind as a result of the circumstances of the public burnings that occurred in 1550–1551 and the trial of Renée in 1554. His theological positions probably remained unchanged, but the same could not be said for his view of politics that concerned the Church. In all likelihood, Brasavola was the author, in 1554, of the University of Ferrara's pronouncement in favor of the Jesuits,[32] and he was probably behind the duke's decision to take public teaching out of the hands of the lay teachers, whom he mistrusted, and to give it instead to the Society of Jesus, to which the duke's personal confessor belonged. Perhaps Brasavola considered the Jesuits simply a force for Catholic reform; perhaps, as reformer of the university, he saw them as providing better and less confusing secondary instruction. Or perhaps, at that date, he was hoping that the Jesuits would pursue the Erasmian project of mildly convincing heretics to change their minds—a hope that the Dominicans and the Inquisition, with their bloody systems, did not offer him. Neither his humanistic education nor his religious beliefs would have allowed him to abandon hope in such a dialogue. Even someone such as Giambattista Cinzio Giraldi, who was no friend of Brasavola's, could subscribe to this same position in a letter of 1562 to Egidio Foscherari, bishop of Modena:

> It is not in our interest to force so stupidly men of such great virtue and science into exile, and to thrust them violently to despair of their own salvation, since they can see no better prospects, and to revenge themselves by displaying the full force of their dialectical and theological skills.... If only this sickness of heresy, which has now spread everywhere, had been treated with mild medication, rather than with fire and iron! It would not have attained such strength by now.[33]

Notes

1. Lilio Gregorio Giraldi, *Opera omnia,* 2 vols. (Basel: T. Guarino, 1588), 2: 423–27:

> *l'ingegno bene educato e formato dalla natura la vince su tutte le lettere e su tutti gli insegnamenti. Anzi troppe lettere portano gli uomini alla pazzia. Si prendano ad esempio i bambini: essi osservano volentieri e godono di sentir raccontare tutto ciò che appartiene ai fenomeni naturali, e chiedono incessantemente il perchè di ogni cosa, ma fuggono istintivamente la scuola, cui si adattano costretti unicamente dalla frusta. Quale indizio più manifesto di questo che lo studio delle lettere*

non nasce dalla natura, ma è frutto di una violenza ad essa fatta?... Infatti da dove, se non da un soverchio esercizio dello scrivere e del leggere e da un troppo volger e rivolgere i libri, da dove, se non dalla capziosità a cui tutto ciò abitua, sono venute fuori le opinioni di coloro che dicono che la Luna è abitata e che vi sono molte città o, ancora, di coloro che ai nostri tempi sostengono che sia la terra a muoversi e che invece il cielo stia fermo?... La stessa cosa è successa a quei cristiani, che, contro il precetto di S. Paolo che li avvertiva che "la lettera uccide," si sono dati alle dispute piuttosto che alla contemplazione: essi sono caduti nei più strani e svariati errori, tanto da porre in dubbio pure i più riposti misteri della nostra religione e da cadere tanto più vergognosamente in errore, quanto più credevano di indagarli in profondità.... Ma le lettere, ci dicono, ci aiutano a manifestare le sensazioni ed i pensieri dell'animo. Ma questo non lo fa' forse meglio la pittura? Della quale si servono i letterati stessi quando devono parlare di qualcosa che difficilmente la memoria ritiene, di qualcosa ad esprimere la quale la descrizione letteraria non basta. E questo, per loro stessa dichiarazione, lo fanno perchè la pittura e le immagini più chiaramente e più secondo verità, che le lettere, imprimono in se stessi e negli altri le forme delle cose.

2. I am referring here to the "Epigramma in Leonis decimi pont. max. mortem per Ill. Herculem, Alphonsi ducis Ferrariae primogenitum," published in Erasmo Percopo, "Di Anton Lelio Romano e di alcune pasquinate contro Leon X," *Giornale storico della letteratura italiana,* no. 28 (1896): 88–91.

3. Antonio Musa Brasavola, *Examen omnium syruporum* (Venice: Officina di San Bernardino, 1538), c. 72r: *"con l'aiuto di essa Clemente VII, quasi in coma, sopravvisse alcuni giorni; ma il buon Dio, che voleva liberare il suo gregge dalle grinfie di un tale pastore, fiaccò le virtú di tale acqua."*

4. Adriano Prosperi, "L'eresia in città e a corte," in Marianne Pade, Lene Waage Petersen, and Daniela Quarta, eds., *La corte di Ferrara e il suo mecenatismo, 1441–1598* (Modena: Edizioni Panini, 1990), 272: *"che si era guadagnata da tempo diritto di presenza nella repubblica cristiana."*

5. See, concerning this last problem, Giovanni Manardo, *Epistolarum medicinalium libros XX* (Basel: M. Isingrin, 1540), 76–83 (bk. 7, 1).

6. Calcagnini owned one of the finest private libraries in Ferrara, which he willed to the monastery of San Domenico in Ferrara. My friend Luca D'Ascia has rediscovered the catalog of Calcagnini's collection that Tiraboschi saw in the eighteenth century. This list of 1,187 volumes is part of a legal document in which a Dominican of Ferrara, the Inquisitor Fra Girolamo Papino, attested to having received the entire library from Calcagnini's executors on 29 May 1541 (Archivio di Stato di Modena, Archivio Privato Calcagnini, capsa 95, num. provv. 190, fasc. 32). In Calcagnini's imposing collection were practically complete sets of Erasmus's and Valla's works, along with texts by Cusano, Savonarola, Hutten, Reuchlin, Capitone, Melanchthon, Ecolampadio, Zasio, Zwingli, Lambert, Agrippa, Aonio Paleario, Machiavelli, and others. Calcagnini owned copies of the *Summario de la Santa Scrittura,* Palingenius's *Zodiacus vitae,* the then unpublished *De incantationibus* by Pomponazzi (1520; first published 1567), and Alberti's *De re aedificatoria.* He possessed another volume containing

works by Alberti which we would very much like to identify as the codex of the *Intercenales* used by Ariosto. Calcagnini also helped Henry VIII of England to gather contemporary Italian theological and legal opinions that were favorable to his divorce from Catherine of Aragon. See Aurelio Roncaglia, "La questione matrimoniale di Enrico VIII e due umanisti italiani contemporanei," *Giornale storico della letteratura Italiana,* no. 110 (1937): 106–19.

7. See, on the schoolmasters, Silvana Seidel Menchi's fundamental chapter, "Scuola di grammatica, scuola di eresia," in idem, *Erasmo in Italia, 1520–1580* (Turin: Bollati Boringhieri, 1987), 122–42.

8. Desiderius Erasmus, *Opus epistolarum Des: Erasmi Roterdami,* vol. 6, *1525–1527,* ed. P. S. Allen and H. M. Allen (Oxford: In typographeo Clarendoniano [Oxford Univ. Press], 1926), 117 (no. 1587).

9. Celio Calcagnini, *Opera aliquot,* ed. Antonio Musa Brasavola (Basel: G. Froben, 1544), 195–96. See also, concerning this letter, Albano Biondi, "La giustificazione della simulazione nel Cinquecento," in *Eresia e riforma nell'Italia del Cinquecento: Miscellanea I* (Florence: Sansoni, 1974), 61–65.

10. Calcagnini (see note 9), 195.

11. Seidel Menchi (see note 7), 96: *"che il libretto del Calcagnini soffre di una palese inconsistenza concettuale."*

12. Calcagnini (see note 9), 398.

13. Calcagnini (see note 9), 399: *"si assunse il compito di scrivere il Libellus per mettersi preventivamente al coperto da una accusa di luteranesimo";* and, *"il cristiano deve confidare che Dio non invierà mai contro il suo arbitrio forze tali, da annichilarlo";* and, *"per Dio, nelle cose ardue e impossibili, è abbastanza magnifico che l'uomo 'abbia voluto.'"*

14. *Apologia fratris IOANNIS MARIAE VERRATI Ferrariensis* (Bologna: V. Bonardo & M. Antonio da Carpi, 1538), c. 3r–v: *"che Cristo aveva comandato cose impossibili."*

15. The two poems are anonymous but wholly in Calcagnini's handwriting; they appear in one of Gaspare Sardi's notebooks (the first of the poems is dedicated to him), Cod. Est. Lat. 174 Alpha 0.6.15, cc. 117r–122v, in the Estense Library in Modena. Here I include the full text of "Simulatae virtutis defensio":

Perdita quum tantum sint et rubigine tincta
saecula nostra, prius ferrato sordida nexu,
crede mihi, Guaspar, pauci bene vivere norunt.
Qui probus esse cupit, simulet: sic iudicat omnis,
ut videt, atque animi nunquam discludere nodos
nititur. Is superis committat carbasa vitae,
qui simulare potest et nigra in candida vertit.
Omnia succedunt facili pede, dummodo cauta
mente gerat, quaecunque facit sub nocte tegenda;
atque ita praecipiunt sacrati dogmata Christi:
"Aut peccata cave aut tegito sub nocte sopora."
Quisquis non sua furta tegit, me iudice multum
desipit: hic ars est, homines ut fallere possis.

Nec tamen huic obstat summi sententia Tulli:
"Qui simulat vulpis similis est fraude nocentis."
Tempora non florent quondam veneranda Catonis,
is vivit regnatque diu, qui probra negare
audet, ut a nullo possit super aethera duci.
Consilium Nasonis adest, qui talia suadet:
"Non peccat, quicunque potest peccasse negare.
Quis furor est, quae nocte latent, in luce fateri?"
Pacifici accedunt his aurea verba diserti:
"Ut se tempus habet, sic vitae est tempus agendum."
Haec igitur summa est: qui vult bene degere vitam,
noscat, ut audacter legem simulare necesse est.
Talia cur dicam, nosti, suavissime Guaspar.

(Since our ages are so greatly ruined and imbued with rust, dirty on account of a formerly ironclad obligation, believe me, Gaspare, few know how to live honorably. He who wishes to be upright should simulate: everyone judges as he sees, and never strives to separate the difficulties of the mind. Let him who is able to simulate and who converts black things into white entrust the sails of life to the gods. All things follow with easily moving foot, provided that he does with cautious mind whatever he does that should be concealed under night; and so the doctrines of the sanctified Christ teach: "Either avoid sins or cover them under sleep-bringing night." Whoever does not cover his own deceits is in my opinion very foolish: cunning is in the ability to deceive men. And yet the opinion of the most distinguished Cicero does not oppose this: "He who feigns is like a fox that does harm by deceit." The once venerable times [or circumstances] of Cato do not flourish; he who dares to deny [his] shameful acts, so that he cannot be drawn by anyone above the light of day, lives and reigns for a long time. Helpful advice is offered by Ovid, who recommends as follows: "He sins not, who can deny having sinned. What madness is it to confess in the daylight things that lie hidden in the night?" Similar are the golden words of the sagacious Pacificus: "As the time is, so must one's time of life be passed." This then is the chief point: He who wishes to pass his life well must learn that it is necessary to simulate compliance with law boldly. You know, Gaspare, why I say such things).

16. Calcagnini (see note 15); the passage reads:

Ne vos terrificae paveatis somnia mortis
vana, canisque tribus pandens latratibus ora
ne sit causa metus vobis, nutusque deorum
difficiles, nec fausta satis sua numina dantes,
et simulachra sonis non respondentia vestris;
lethaeaeque domus magnis ne pectora curis
vestra agitent atque umbrae, quas volitare per auras
dicitis infestare suo ac vestra ora volatu
saepius horrificam fingentes murmure vocem.

Vana superstitio divos vocitare potentes:
ne vos decipiant et fulmina missa per ethram!...
Principium mundo Christi dant dogma sequentes,
quem struxisse putant simulato nomine Iesu
ex nihilo: illius nam tanta potentia fertur.
Ast tu vera, Plato, iam dudum, summe, canebas....
[e]cce sacerdotes latii, qui nempe fatentur
esse deum, cui summa hominum est celique potestas,
sed perverse colunt hunc, quem non esse negarunt,
quemque hominem dicunt, cui nomina ficta dederunt.
Ut memorant, caelum, terram atque astra creavit,
materia caruisse volunt, sed sola potestas
id fecit, quae summa fuit: quo stultius ullum
non fuit auditum; non est temerarius usque,
talia verba suo qui insano ferret ab ore.

(Do not fear the empty dreams of frightful death, and let not the dog opening his mouths with three barkings [i.e., Cerberus] be a cause of fear to you, and the hard commands of the gods giving their unpropitious orders, and effigies that do not answer your sounds [i.e., prayers]; and let not the Lethean abodes disturb your breasts with great cares, and the shades which you say flit about through the air [i.e., the upper world, versus the lower, Lethean world just mentioned] and disturb your faces with their flying, often making a terrifying sound with their rushing. It is vain superstition to keep invoking the powerful divinities: let not even thunderbolts sent through the air deceive you!... Those following the dogma of Christ attribute a beginning to the world, which they believe him to have made out of nothing, having assumed the name Jesus: for so great a power is reported of him. But you, O most distinguished Plato, long before sang of true things.... Behold the Roman priests, who indeed acknowledge that there is a god who possesses the highest power over men and heaven, but they worship him in the wrong way, not denying his existence but calling him a man and giving him fictitious names. As they tell it, he created the heavens, the earth, and the stars; they imagine that he had not physical [or, material] substance, but that his power alone, which was supreme, made it: nothing more foolish than that has ever been heard; there is no one so rash as to utter such words from his own foolish mouth).

17. Calcagnini (see note 9), 318: "*La religione è una buona cosa, ma più si fa fanatica e si arricchisce di ragioni, più precipita nella superstizione.*"

18. Carlo Ginzburg, *Il nicodemismo: Simulazione e dissimulazione religiosa nell'-Europa del '500* (Turin: Einaudi, 1970), 164.

19. Celio Secondo Curione, *Selectarum epistularum libri duo* (Basel: T. Oporinus, 1553), 315–17:

quando la mia salvezza era in pericolo tanto che abbandonato da tutto e da tutti io mi vedevo più freddo del gelo stesso, ecco tu mandato da Dio, venendo a Ferrara, ti dirigesti proprio a me tralasciando altri ben più grandi patroni che ti ambivano.

> *... Io allora, più che leggere, sbocconcellavo le lettere di Paolo e Giovanni e le altre scritture, ma la tua viva voce e lo spirito, di cui tu tutto ardi e del quale irradi gli altri, mi mossero, mi penetrarono e mi riscaldarono finalmente così vivacemente ed efficacemente, che io posso ora riconoscere le mie tenebre e posso non io vivere, ma Cristo in me ed io in Cristo.... Mi hai fatto da freddo che ero, il fuoco stesso.*

20. Calcagnini (see note 9), 112.

21. Antonio Musa Brasavola, *Examen omnium loch* (Venice: Juntas, 1553), c. 195r:

> *Dicono che questa malattia è la vendetta che Dio prende della lussuria degli uomini di oggi... ma dati i nostri peccati tutte le malattie dovrebbero essere di origine divina. Ma poi, in sostanza, se Dio se la prende solo con i lussuriosi, perchè non se la prende anche con gli usurai, i ladri, i bestemmiatori e gli omicidi, che peccano in modo ben peggiore di colui che, magari non sposato, fa all'amore con una non sposata. Esercitare la venere è naturale per ognuno di noi; ammazzare, scassinare, rubare, bestemmiare mi risulta invece che siano piuttosto contro natura. E poi se a Dio tanto dispiacesse, che gli uomini avessero contatti sessuali, potrebbe inibirgli il meccanismo dell'erezione. E poi, ancora, mi dicano questi tali, che male hanno fatto i feti, che sin dal ventre materno sono attaccati da questa malattia?*

22. Brasavola (see note 3), cc. 1r–3v.

23. Antonio Musa Brasavola, *Examen omnium catapotiorum* (Basel: G. Froben & N. Episcopio, 1543), 1–21.

24. Brasavola (see note 23), 16: "*non è cosa che si addice solo a quel nuovo genere di frati che il volgo chiama cappuccini.*"

25. Brasavola (see note 23), 13.

26. Antonio Musa Brasavola, *In octo libros Aphorismorum Hippocratis et Galeni* (Basel: G. Froben & N. Episcopio, 1541), 302: "*Albertus Savonarola Divi Hieronymi frater.*"

27. Antonio Musa Brasavola, "Vita di Cristo," Biblioteca Universitaria di Bologna, ms. 1862, 3: c. 40r:

> *Comenzò prima Luthero a parlare delli mali costumi delli administratori della giesia et delle male consuetudine circa le indulgentie et dello extorquere dinari per suoi luxi et aggrandire suoi figli o nepoti sotto pretexto della fabbrica de Santo Pietro.... A queste cose li Greci aprirno le orechie, le quali erano vere. Vedendo che havevano cum queste verità indutti li animi delli huomini a credergli, comenciò poi aggiungere sotto questo falsitade, come che il Papa non potesse dare indulgentie et altre simile cose delle quale ne è pieno il mundo.*

The Bologna codex is the copy that was made for Laura Dianti, Alfonso I's second wife.

28. Brasavola (see note 23), 18.

29. Antonio Musa Brasavola, *Quod mors nemini placeat* (Lyons: S. Grifio, 1544), 50–51: "*Nulla è più santo e più salutare dell'Eucarestia, se l'ha consacrata un prete*

casto con animo raccolto; così come nulla v'è di più nocivo e immondo se è stata consacrata con animo che pensava alle cose turpi."

30. Brasavola (see note 27), 1: cc. 48v–49r: *"gli Papi et li cardinali... a' nostri tempi sogliono esser peggiori de tutti. Ma la giesia è la congregatione de' veri cristiani in uno. Se 'l Papa et li Cardinali sono veri cristiani et convengono in uno, in mezo loro è Dio et quello è la giesia; ma se sono rei in mezo loro è il Diavolo et non è giesia, perchè sola la congregatione de' boni nel nome di Dio è la giesia."*

31. Brasavola (see note 27), 2: c. 254v:

> *a convincere più che a vincere... li Papi doveriano predicare... questo è il suo principale officio... non lo fanno... perchè non sono Pietri, cioè vicarii de Cristo se non di nome et di godere, ma non di oprare. Lo primo officio del Papa è essere piscatore de huomini cioè de anime... ma più presto attendono a cose terrene che a la celeste et li loro mali exempli et gesti sono stati la ruina de una gran parte de' cristiani. Dimme chi è stata la causa della peste luterana, se non li vitii enormi delli papi et prelati?... Adesso non pensano altro che ad accumulare dinari et a fare grandi li suoi figlioli et nepoti et non se recordano più dello officio suo, non pescano più.... Al presente è rotta la rete de' Pietro et escono li pesci et vanno per il mare: sono usciti della rete li lutherani et per li cristiani se spandono et niuno è che cun ragione, cun disputatione amorevolmente persuadendo gli corregga.... O povero Pietro la tua nave è in grande periculo, la tua rete è rotta et già sono usciti multi pesci da essa. O Cristo capo provedi, provedi alli tuoi vicarii. Manda la spada ignita, non expectare più, che le membra non si marcino, non si putrefazzano, non cadino dal tuo corpo. Correzeli, falli buoni.*

32. See Daniello Bartoli, *Dell'istoria della Compagnia di Gesù,* in idem, *Opere,* 50 vols. in 8 (Florence: Lorenzo Ciardetti, 1829–1837), 9: 156–58.

33. As cited by P. R. Horne, "Reformation and Counter-Reformation at Ferrara: Antonio Musa Brasavola and Giambattista Cinthio Giraldi," *Italian Studies,* no. 13 (1958): 82. The complete text of Giraldi's letter may be found in the Biblioteca Universitaria di Bologna, cod. 1621, second part, c. 8v–10r: *"Non ci conviene costringere così stoltamente ad esulare uomini dotati di tanta virtù e scienza e spingerli violentemente, non vedendo essi una prospettiva migliore, a disperare della propria salvezza e a vendicarsi mostrando tutte le forze del loro ingegno dialettico e teologico.... Magari questo morbo dell'eresia, sparso ora dappertutto, fosse stato curato con miti medicamenti piuttosto che col ferro e col fuoco! Ora esso non avrebbe acquistato questa forza."*

Part IV

Collecting Dosso

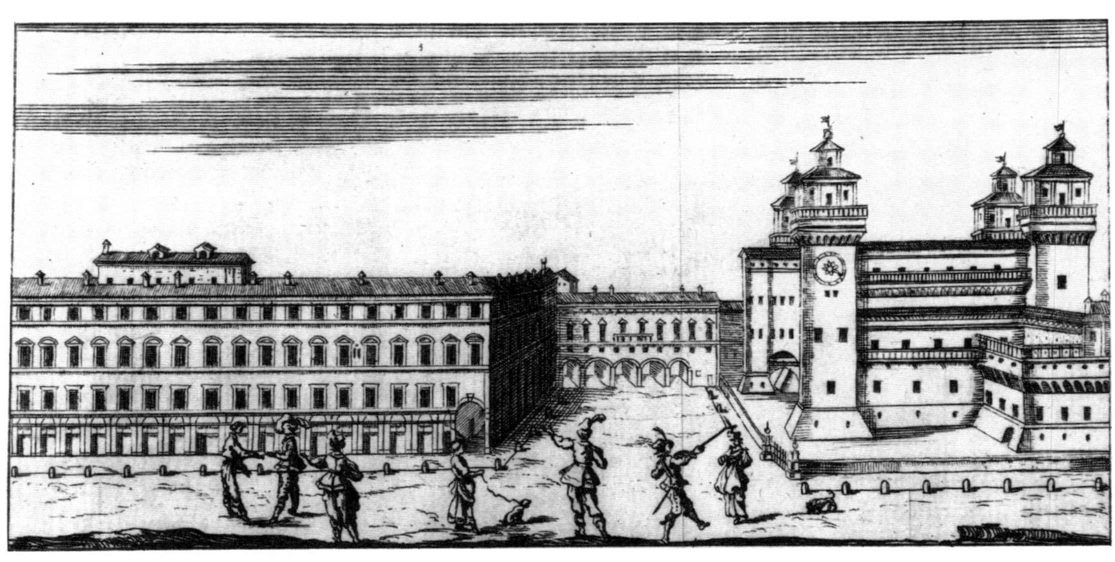

Fig. 1. View of the Piazza del Castello
Left to right: Palazzo di Corte Vecchia, Via Coperta, Castello Estense
From Antonio Frizzi, *Guida del forestiere per la città di Ferrara* (Ferrara: Francesco Pomatelli, 1787)

From Ercole I to Alfonso I: New Discoveries about the *Camerini* in the Castello Estense of Ferrara

Jadranka Bentini

The covered, elevated corridor connecting the Castello Estense to the Palazzo di Corte Vecchia, a structure known as the Via Coperta (fig. 1), has long been recognized as one of Renaissance Italy's most imporant artistic complexes. The site of Duke Alfonso I d'Este's private apartments, or *camerini,* the Via Coperta housed, among other things, antique medals and sculptures, a number of marble reliefs by Antonio Lombardo, and the famous series of Bacchanals by Giovanni Bellini, Titian, and Dosso Dossi. Dosso's frieze representing stories of Aeneas and other works by the two Dossi were also found in these rooms. Yet for all that is known about the paintings and sculptures in the Via Coperta, the original arrangement of the *camerini* within it has never been established with precision.

Until now, hypotheses about their disposition depended almost exclusively on a valuation (*stima*) of the possessions of Cesare d'Este, which was drawn up by Alfonso Benmambri on 17 April 1598.[1] This document, however, has not provided sufficient evidence for an accurate reconstruction of the Via Coperta. Studies of the documents of the Camera Ducale Estense for the fifteenth and sixteenth centuries also have thus far failed to aid in reconstructing this famous corridor, and comparative analysis of the present-day architecture of the Castello has likewise proven inadequate to the task. Now a number of conclusions may be drawn, following the study of the apartments in the Castello Estense (fig. 2, A), which was carried out at the request of the Ministero per i Beni Culturali e Ambientali and the Amministrazione Provinciale di Ferrara. Through the information revealed by a first study of the restoration work in the Castello, together with a reconsideration of the documents, we may establish a clear picture of the historical transformations of the *camerini* in the Via Coperta.[2]

The linking of the Palazzo (the ducal palace of Ferrara) and the Castello Estense by means of an elevated corridor running above the adjacent piazzas occurred early on. We know that work on covering the street between the court and the castle was already underway in 1471, during the reign of Ercole I, following the late Borso d'Este's wishes. The documents speak of the old corridor *"che avanzava sopra li cuppi"* (that ran above the roofs), which elsewhere is called *"secreta":* it was a type of simple wooden bridge linking

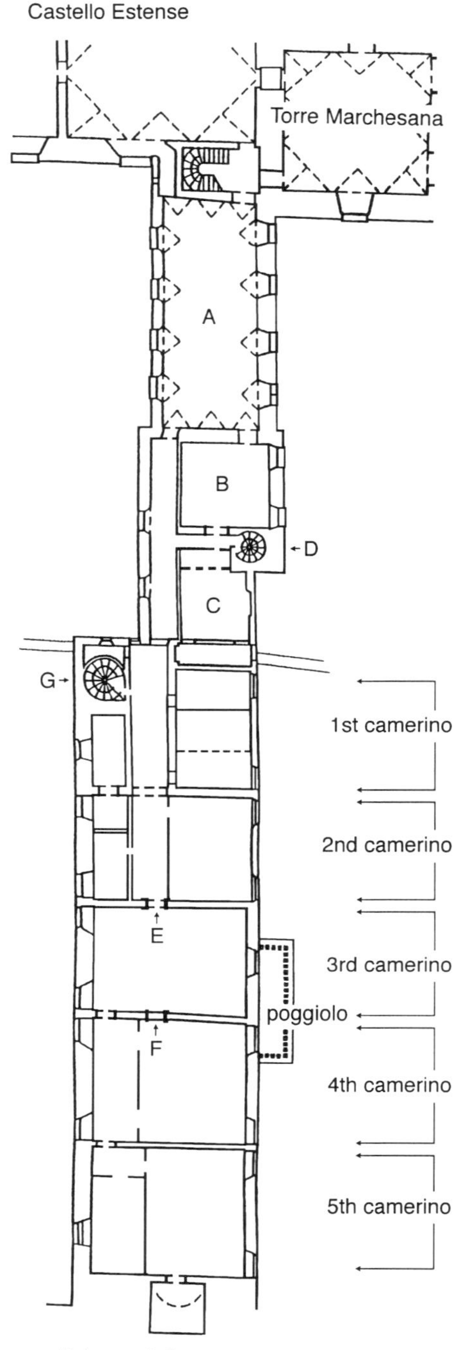

Fig. 2. Reconstruction of the floor plan of the rooms of the Via Coperta, Ferrara

the two buildings.[3] Expense accounts deal with the support structures (made of reeds) for the vaults of this new building, as well as for the wood needed for a *poggiolo*. This was a little balcony surmounted by a cornice, on which was painted a coat of arms with four fields. Two of these represented the labors of Hercules and the other two displayed the ducal arms. The braces supporting the cornice were painted red, and a carved and painted frieze ran below it. These were all the work of "master Grando" (a painter elsewhere repeatedly referred to as "Hercule," hence, Ercole Grandi).[4]

The new corridor passed over the butcher shops, which had been rebuilt along with the ducal stables in accordance with a true urban plan for the area between the Corte Vecchia and the Castello, toward the church of San Giuliano. This plan called for paving the piazza off the north wing of the building, onto which the entrance to the castle opened at that time.[5]

The room adjacent to the *poggiolo* had two windows with glass panes. On the shutters were painted the ducal arms and the diamond *impresa*. The painter of these works was again Ercole Grandi, who also painted the entire inside as well, decorating it with thirty-three small square panels with ducal arms and devices, recalling the paintings on the shutters, which alternated with square panels in feigned marble. The interior of the room was decorated with painted architectural motifs. Below the ceiling was a large lacquered cornice of gilded tin, and below that a colored mock cornice. These cornices were supported by corbels decorated at the center with spindle-shaped motifs in gilded tin and were highlighted by the interplay of red and green.

The entire Via Coperta structure was surmounted by forty-eight merlons. Twenty-one, those over the butcher shops and facing the Lions' Gate, were double; these were finished in 1471 with friezes and *"fornimenti all'antica"* (decorations in the ancient style). Eighteen merlons were found on the back side, above the storage room for firewood. Another of Hercules's labors was depicted on the vault of the butcher shops. The corridor, which was articulated as a series of rooms, could be entered from either the Palazzo or the Castello.

The documents of 1505, in which work *"nella fabbrica sopra la via coperta"* (in the building over the covered street) is mentioned, may be interpreted as recording the demolition of some interior walls of the old building and a first expansion of the preexisting structure, work dating to the reign of Ercole I. One floor was raised, it seems, judging from a document dated 20 June 1505; the pertinent passage reads: *"per aver desfato et refato et alzato tuti li muri de le stantie se fate in la via coperta"* (for having torn down and rebuilt and raised all the walls of the rooms that were in the Via Coperta).[6]

We know that in 1507 Alfonso I had the pilasters and vaults of the Via Coperta enlarged in order to support the weight of his study, which was shortly to be provided *"di preda viva"* (marble; literally, with living rock). This room had once been Ercole I's study (fig. 2, third *camerino*). In 1515 work began on a new *galleria*, which probably replaced the structure called *"la pontesela de Castello che va li Camerini"* (the connecting bridge from the castle that goes to the *camerini*).[7] This *galleria* should therefore be identified as the large room over the moat (fig. 2, A) found between the Torre Marchesana and the two rooms called *anditi* (vestibules) in the documents (fig. 2, B and C). Between these two vestibules was a spiral staircase, heretofore unknown but clearly visible in the floor plan, that led to the upper level; it was subsequently closed off (fig. 2, D).[8]

The Via Coperta was likely constructed in two different phases, as evidenced by the height of the ceilings in the *anditi* and the *galleria* in respect to that in the *camerini*, and the narrowing of the whole structure, starting from the *anditi* and leading toward the Torre Marchesana. We do not know what was in the *galleria*, which originally probably included a colonnade. The room was perhaps intended for the display of antiquities, statues, and small bronzes. A document from 1517 would seem to confirm this: in it is recorded the duke's purchase of a large quantity of medals and statues, and it mentions his wish to form a collection of small bronzes in the antique style.[9] Nor do we know what was found in the rooms called the *anditi*, but we can now say with certainty that Alfonso's *camerini* may be identified with the five "telescoping" rooms of the Via Coperta (fig. 2, the first, second, third, fourth, and fifth *camerini*).

In the course of preliminary work before the restoration was begun, a lintel and jambs of cut stone, belonging to a skillfully made doorway, were found where there was once the entryway to the third *camerino*. The lintel displays clearly, in Roman capital letters, the dedicatory inscription "ALFONSUS III DUX," or "Alfonso, the third duke," meaning Alfonso I d'Este. I maintain that this was where Antonio Lombardo's door leading to Alfonso's study was located (fig. 2, E). Dosso painted his famous tondo—a work now divided into two works known as *Poet and Muse* (London, National Gallery) and the *Laughing Youth* (Florence, Fondazione Roberto Longhi)—for the ceiling of this room, and the doors were decorated with *"varie teste antiche e moderne de sculptori"* (various heads, ancient and modern, by sculptors), as the Este-Gonzaga correspondence for the year 1518 informs us.[10] In the wall across from the doorway was another, identical doorway, which today is behind plaster (fig. 2, F). Another doorway must have been located in the fourth *camerino*, giving access to the fifth *camerino*, which was adjacent to the Palazzo di Corte Vecchia. Today this doorway no longer exists.

Vasari likely saw Titian's *Tribute Money* (Dresden, Staatliche Kunstsammlungen, Gemäldegalerie Alte Meister) on the door of the third *camerino*, a work that was later kept with the medals in the first *camerino*, which some scholars believe to have been Alfonso I's bedchamber.[11] This first *camerino*, in which Dosso's nine rhomboids were located, still communicates directly with the Via Coperta by way of a spiral staircase (fig. 2, G). The doorway that led to the second *camerino*, however, can no longer be found, inasmuch as the entire wall, for the width of the room, was knocked down. Nevertheless, two ceiling supports, made at a later date, point today to the original division of the rooms.

Indeed, the exact location of Alfonso I's study, which was born from the transformation of what had once been Ercole I's study, is reconfirmed by what was uncovered during the attempts to clean the walls. Under the modern coat of plaster, which is decorated with friezes, two earlier layers of decoration were found. The first belongs to the eighteenth century and was executed during the restorations done when Ferrara was part of the Papal States. The second, which lies beneath the first, is much older and has late fifteenth-century motifs painted in the green and red tones mentioned in Ercole I's documents.

Notes

1. Alfonso Benmambri's *stima* was discovered by Amalia Mezzetti, who published her findings in *Il Dosso e Battista ferraresi* (Milan: Silvana, 1965), 135ff. There has been a great deal of scholarly speculation about the *camerini* in the Via Coperta. Besides Mezzetti's writings, see Charles Hope, "The 'Camerini d Alabastro' of Alfonso d'Este," *Burlington Magazine* 113 (1971): 641–50, 712–21; Dana Goodgal, "The Camerino of Alfonso I d'Este," *Art History* 1 (1978): 162–90; Dana Goodgal, "Titian Repairs Bellini," in Görel Cavalli-Björkman, ed., *Bacchanals by Titian and Rubens* (Stockholm: Nationalmuseum, 1987), 17–24; Charles Hope, "The Camerino d'Alabastro: A Reconsideration of the Evidence," in Görel Cavalli-Björkman, ed., *Bacchanals by Titian and Rubens* (Stockholm: Nationalmuseum, 1987), 25–42; and the valuable study by John Shearman, "Alfonso d'Este's Camerino," in *"Il se rendit en Italie": Etudes offertes à André Chastel* (Rome: Editioni dell'Elefante, 1987), 209–29. A more recent study is Wendy Stedman Sheard, "Antonio Lombardo's Reliefs for Alfonso d'Este's *Studio di Marmi:* Their Significance and Impact on Titian," in Joseph Manca, ed., *Titian 500* (Washington: National Gallery of Art, 1993), 315–57. For an overview, see the collection of documents and rich bibliography published in the first volume of Alessandro Ballarin, *Dosso Dossi: La pittura a Ferrara negli anni del Ducato di Alfonso I,* 2 vols. (Cittadella: Bertoncello Artigrafiche, 1994–1995). See also Grazia Agostini and Anna Stanzani, "Pittori veneti e commissioni estensi a Ferrara," in *La pittura veneta negli stati estensi* (Modena: Artioli, 1996), 19–56.

2. As of 1998, work on the Castello aimed at discovering and restoring the original arrangement of the rooms and the early sixteenth-century decorations was still underway. In the case of the private apartment, today occupied by the *prefetto,* exploratory studies will be done but the rooms will not be returned to their original layout. Architects Carla di Francesco, from the Soprintendenza per i Beni Architettonici di Ravenna, and Marco Borella, from the Amministrazione Provinciale di Ferrara (which owns the castle), are directing the work. All the new documents to which I refer in this essay were transcribed by Costanza Cavicchi, who also edited the architectural drawing of the reconstructed plan of the rooms. A systematic study of documents related to the castle included a global reading of the archives belonging to the Camera Ducale Estense, Fondo Munizioni e Fabbriche, for the years 1471–1553. This study, funded by the provincial government and carried out by me, focused on assembling a "Ferrarese" archive from the collections of documents now found in the

Archivio di Stato di Modena. Adriano Franceschini, in his monumental *Artisti a Ferrara in età umanistica e rinascimentale: Testimonianze archivistiche,* vol. 2, *Dal 1472 al 1492* (Ferrara: Gabriele Corbo, 1995), orders the archival evidence according to a chronological progression of "monographic" entries on artists and artisans, which is useful for reconstructing artistic activity in Ferrara between 1472 and 1492.

3. Archivio di Stato di Modena, Camera Ducale Estense, Fabbriche e Villeggiature, mandati sciolti, 29 August 1471: *"questa sia la spesa che andaria a fare una via coperta che se partisse dale Stancie de la V. S. in Corte che andasse ne la via coperta vecchia de Chastello vecchio sopra la becharia del Lione"* (this is the expense for building a covered street starting from Your Lordship's rooms at the court and running into the old covered street from the old castle over the butcher shops near the Lion). See also Archivio di Stato di Modena, Camera Ducale Estense, Fondo Munizioni e Fabbriche, Memoriale R.7, 1471, c. 65, 107r.

4. Archivio di Stato di Modena, Camera Ducale Estense, Fondo Munizioni e Fabbriche, Memoriale R.7, 1471, c. 113r.

5. Ugo Caleffini, "Cronica de la ill.ma et ex.ma Casa de Este," ed. A. Cappelli, *Atti e Memorie della R. Deputazione di Storia Patria per le Provincie Modenesi e Parmensi* 2 (1864): 267–312. Caleffini's entry for 20 September 1474 reads:

> *Fu fornito de essere facto la becharia nova de dreto da Castel vechio in ferrara deverso San Zuliano de le mura de la tera. La quale era suso la piaza del dicto Castello per mezo la via coperta da li volti, che va in Castello. La quale becharia fece fare il Duca herchole. Et fu fornito ad essere selegato la piaza da quel lato de dicta becharia* (Plans were made for the new butcher shop, from behind the old castle in Ferrara toward [the church of San Giuliano] by the earthen ramparts. This gave onto the said castle's piazza by means of a covered street with vaults leading into the castle. This butcher shop was built by Duke Ercole [I]. And it was planned in order to link that side of the piazza by means of the said butcher shop).

Moreover, another covered street, leading toward San Domenico, must still have been in existence in 1581, as Thomas Touhy argues in his *Herculean Ferrara: Ercole d'Este, 1471–1505, and the Invention of a Ducal Capital* (Cambridge: Cambridge Univ. Press, 1996), 60–62. Touhy's argument is built upon a careful reading of the available documents and of Ugo Caleffini's chronicle.

6. This document is cited in Hope, 1987 (see note 1), 40 n. 34, and in Goodgal, 1978 (see note 1).

7. Archivio di Stato di Modena, Munizioni e Fabbriche, R.48, 31 December 1507, c. 141r: *"Spexa del studio di preda viva che fa fare el Ducha nostro sopra la via coperta"* (Expenses for the marble study that our Duke wishes to build over the covered street). Regarding the bridge, see 31 December 1510, c. 46r; 31 March 1512, c. 22r; and 1524, c. 30.

8. See the text and documentary appendices of Goodgal, 1978 (see note 1). Goodgal's hypothesis regarding the *galleria* and the *camerini* seems close to the truth in light of measurements and discoveries made during the present restoration. Currently the room is decorated with nineteenth-century imitations of grotesques and vignettes representing the myth of Hercules. It seems likely that the *galleria* was painted in the

1570s, during the reign of Alfonso II, and that the entire decorative scheme was revised in the nineteenth century. This conclusion is based on the study of ceiling designs that were drawn by Pirro Ligorio for the Castello, which are now found in the Archivio di Stato di Modena (in the Fondo Stampe e Disegni, but originally in the Fondo Munizione Ducale); these drawings represent tales of Hercules quite similar to those now visible. During the period in which the papal legate lived there, the castle's frescoes were largely destroyed and the Salone dei Giochi was repainted with architectural perspectives on the walls, as a drawing by Romolo Liverani shows; see Adriano Cavicchi, "Appunti su Ligorio a Ferrara," in Jadranka Bentini and Luigi Spezzaferro, eds., *L'impresa di Alfonso II: Saggi e documenti sulla produzione artistica a Ferrara nel secondo Cinquecento* (Bologna: Nuova Alfa, 1987), 137–50.

9. See Adolfo Venturi, "Il gruppo del Laocoonte e Raffaello," *Archivio storico dell'-arte* 2 (1889): 107; and Alessandra Pattanaro, ed., "Regesto della pittura a Ferrara (1497–1548)," in Ballarin (see note 1), 1: 131.

10. Pattanaro (see note 9), 1: 134, which summarizes the documents dealt with by Hope, 1971 (see note 1), and Goodgal, 1978 (see note 1). We cannot yet specify exactly where the original windows (eleven in number, because the estimates called for twenty-two window benches) were located; currently there are eighteen windows that serve to illuminate service rooms.

11. See William Hood and Charles Hope, "Titian's Vatican Altarpiece and the Pictures Underneath," *Art Bulletin* 59 (1977): 534–52.

The Dossi in Modena in the Seventeenth Century

Albano Biondi

Today Adolfo Venturi's *La R. Galleria Estense in Modena* is still a useful reference for anyone interested in the Dossi brothers' paintings in the holdings of the Estense court, which moved from Ferrara to Modena in 1598. Venturi's book makes ample use of the writings of Giovanni Battista Spaccini, a chronicler of city life in Modena in the late 1500s. Francesco Scannelli's *Il microcosmo della pittura* refers to the period of the reign of Francesco I, duke of Modena, and supplies information on the number and quality of the paintings by the two Dossi that were transferred to Modena.[1] But the works of the Dossi brothers already had attracted considerable attention during the reign of Duke Cesare I, precisely because they could be reused in decorating the interior of an old castle that was to become the home of the Estense court. The so-called *quadretti a Paese* (small landscape paintings) were of particular interest. Masdoni wrote to the duke on 12 March 1608, offering advice on how to reuse these works; he remarked that "these small paintings will be most beautiful for decorating with admirable ornament a *camerino* or two, like the one in the former Duke Alfonso's Palazzo Vecchio."[2] But the Dossi's works were also well suited for outdoor display during triumphal processions on ceremonial occasions; thus Duke Cesare wrote to Masdoni to have him send some of the Dossi's paintings "because they are needed for the bride's entry,"[3] referring to Isabella of Savoy, who was coming to Modena as the wife of his eldest son, Alfonso. In general, the Dossi's works helped to keep alive the imaginative passions of sixteenth-century Ferrara—as embodied in its grand poetry and figurative arts—in seventeenth-century Modena. This was accomplished through temporary festive displays, as the following example demonstrates.

On 22 December 1636, the Diet of Ratisbon approved Emperor Ferdinand II's proposal to elect his son Ferdinand as king of the Romans. This opened the way for the younger Ferdinand, who was already king of Hungary and Bohemia, to be later named emperor. This in fact quickly came to pass with the death of Ferdinand II on 14 February 1637. The news of the nomination, which was by no means a given, reached the vassal court of Modena on 1 January 1637. It had been anxiously awaited, for there had been no more sensational imperial election than this one "since the Roman Imperium [...] became a part of the House of Austria."[4] A contemporary described "the precious announcement of the long-awaited Election of the

King of the Romans" as "the arrival of this Dove that forecast, after a flood of blood, the hoped-for peace of Christendom."[5]

The "flood of blood" referred not only to the German wars. In the Po valley, Francesco I (who was allied with Spain) was at war with his brother-in-law Odoardo Farnese of Parma and his cousin Vittorio Amedeo of Savoy (who were in league with France). This was a source of sadness among the women at court, where Maria Farnese wept over the hostilities between her husband and her brother. In this context, the outcome of the Diet's deliberation, by lending certainty to the future imperial election, seemed to promise Italy the prospect of peace. A solemn Te Deum was sung in the cathedral of Modena, with Bishop Alessandro Rangoni presiding and with sumptuous baroque furnishings covering the bare Romanesque severity of the architecture. Once the religious ceremony (*"la parte dovuta alla pietà,"* the part due to piety) was finished, His Highness set himself to mark "such an excellent event" with public celebrations. Tournaments—both on horseback and on foot—were planned "in order to confirm the Estense court's reputation, going back many centuries, as the true school of the chivalric arts."[6] Gerolamo Graziani was assigned the task of conceiving the tournament and then, later on, recounting it. His *Relatione de i tornei a cavallo et a piedi rappresentati dal Serenissimo Sig. Duca di Modana nell'elettione dell'Invittissimo Re de' Romani Ferdinando III* (Account of the tournaments on horseback and on foot held by His Most Serene Lord the Duke of Modena on the election of the Most Invincible King of the Romans Ferdinand III), dated 26 January 1637 in Modena, was printed by the Stamperia Ducale (ducal press). This was the first important assignment in ekphrastic art to be given to Graziani, a court poet and later, after Fulvio Testi's tragic death (for reasons of state), Francesco I's secretary. He would compose other accounts of festivities and tournaments in later years, culminating in the sensational *Trionfo della Virtù* of 1660.

For the imperial celebration of 1637, the Dossi brothers' landscape paintings, with their vegetal metamorphoses and woodland festivities, were employed to evoke the freshness and lightness of the countryside in contrast to the rigors of the freezing northern Italian winter. A "theater" for the tournament, constructed in the castle's great courtyard, was "arranged in the form of a quadrangle."[7] The grandstand for Her Most Serene Ladyship, the princes and princesses, and so on, was built in front of the ducal palace, and the Dossi's paintings were hung on its facade. The following passage restores to us a moment of splendid life (in a pertinent context) for works that are now perhaps lost:

> The facade of the courtyard was covered with those truly great paintings that are celebrated works of the Dossi brothers, who were the Protogenes and the Apelles of their age. These paintings were hung in a long, orderly row, and represented many people transformed into plants, as sung by Ovid's famous pen. Some of them showed various woodland festivities with such artistic skill that Nature almost

> blushed with shame, although she was covered with snow; it was as if Art were striving to equal Nature herself, like a rival, making viewers wishfully take, amid the rigors of winter, these delights of spring to be real.[8]

Graziani goes on to describe "the other two sides of the theater" as grandstands for the public, decorated "with the most lovely carpets and the finest tapestries ever produced in Persia or Flanders."[9] The author of this narrative, it should be recalled, speaks of the Dossi's works as paintings, not tapestries. In the theater the spectators witnessed the burning of statues representing Jealousy, Scorn, Hate, and Malice, which had obstructed the successful outcome of the Diet's deliberations. Then the whole world paid homage to the vassal court of the empire, accompanied by splendid speeches and exquisite music. The world was personified by four female figures (Europe, Asia, Africa, and America) representing its four main parts, who had already been seen in Modena in 1599 for the funeral rites honoring Philip II of Spain. Then ceremonial carriages representing Prudence, Strength, Valor, Courage, Honor and Glory were paraded. The court nobility, including the Bentivoglio, Rangoni, Tassoni, Campori, Coccapani, Malvasia, and Molza families (among others), staged daring mock fights (including pistol duels) between "defenders" and "challengers." The duke himself took part in these exercises in the role of Hector, and his son Rinaldo took the role of Achilles. These went on until Glory recognized all to be equal in valor and, together with Europe, brought the celebrations to an end, singing songs of praise to the empire.

In later years there were other ceremonial spectacles of this sort, invented and narrated by Graziani, but the 1637 event was among the most memorable. Gamberti evoked it on the occasion of the funeral of Francesco I, praising (in his *Idea di un prencipe et eroe christiano*) the duke's "magnificent doings," such as "theaters, military entertainments, equestrian competitions, jousting, tournaments on horseback and in the open field." "For the election of Ferdinand III, King of the Romans," he exclaimed,

> there were extremely wonderful fireworks in the courtyard of the ducal palace, during which—by means of flying missiles—four large statues, representing Hate, Envy, Malice, and Scorn, were ignited and transformed into flaming pyres. There was also a noble tourney in which, after the entrance of Glory in her triumphal carriage filled with musicians, defenders and challengers from the four parts of the world fought with one another, in new kinds of skirmishes and wondrous clothing.[10]

And it was the Dossi brothers' compositions that formed the backdrop for this theater dedicated to imperial glory.

Notes

1. Adolfo Venturi, *La R. Galleria Estense in Modena* (Modena: Paolo Toschi, 1882; reprint, Modena: Panini, 1989); Giovanni Battista Spaccini, *Cronaca di Modena, anni 1598–1602,* ed. Albano Biondi, Rolando Bussi, and Carlo Giovannini (Modena: Panini, 1993), with volume 2 forthcoming; Francesco Scannelli, *Il microcosmo della pittura* (Cesena: Neri, 1657; facsimile reprint, Milan: Labor, 1966).

2. Venturi (see note 1), 118: *"questi quadretti saranno bellissimi a fornir con mirabile ornamento un Camerino o due, simile a quello del Palazzo Vecchio del già Signor Alfonso."*

3. Venturi (see note 1), 117: *"perché se ne vuol servire nell'occasione della venuta della sposa."*

4. Girolamo Graziani, *Relatione de i tornei a cavallo et a piedi rappresentati dal Serenissimo Sig. Duca di Modana nell'elettione dell'Invittissimo Re de' Romani Ferdinando III* (Modena: Stamperia Ducale, 1637), 4: *"da che la potenza Romana [...] fu introdotta nella Casa d'Austria."* Reprinted in Girolamo Graziani, *Varie prose e poesie* (Modena: Soliani, 1662), 141.

5. Graziani, 1637 (see note 4), 5–6: *"il pretioso annuncio della tanto bramata Elettione del Re de' Romani.... l'arrivo di questa Colomba che prediceva dopo un diluvio di sangue la sospirata pace alla Christianità."*

6. Graziani, 1637 (see note 4), 6: *"per confermare il credito conseguito da molti secoli addietro che la Corte Estense sia la vera Scuola dell'Arte Cavalleresca."*

7. Graziani, 1637 (see note 4), 6: *"ridotto in forma d'un quadrangolo."*

8. Graziani, 1637 (see note 4), 6–7:

> *Dirimpetto coprivano la facciata della Corte quelle superbissime Pitture celebri fatiche de i Dossi, che furono i Protogeni e gli Apelli della loro età. Queste, distese con lungo e bell'ordine fingevano molte persone trasformate in piante, decantate et espresse dalla famosa penna d'Ovidio, e parte mostravano vari trattenimenti boschereccі con tal pregio dell'Arte che vergognosa arrossì quasi la natura, benché coperta di neve, al paragone dell'emula, che fe' da riguardanti vagheggiar per vere, tra i rigori del verno, le delitie della Primavera.*

9. Graziani, 1637 (see note 4), 6–7: *"gli altri due lati del Teatro"; "de i più gravi tappeti e de i più fini arazzi, che habbia tessuti la Persia o lavorati la Fiandra."*

10. Domenico Gamberti, *L'idea di un prencipe et eroe christiano in Francesco I d'Este, di Modona, e Reggio duca VIII...* (Modena: Soliani, 1659), 213–14: *"fatti di magnificenza... Teatri, Feste d'Arma, Barriere, Giostre del Saracino, Campi aperti e Tornei";* and, 220:

> *Per l'elettione di Ferdinando III, Re de' Romani, dentro il Cortile del Ducale suo Palagio, oltre ingegnosissimi fuochi arteficiati, con cui per volanti razzi si accesero quattro grandi statue, dell'Odio, dell'Invidia, della Malignità e dello Sdegno, divenute ardenti pire a se stesse, rappresentò un nobile Torneo, in cui, dopo il luminoso corso fatto dal carro trionfale della Gloria, abitato da' Musici, combattettero i Mantenitori e Venturieri delle quattro parti del Mondo con novità di scaramucce e vaghezza di abbigliamenti.*

Collecting Dosso: The Trail of Dosso's Paintings from the Late Sixteenth Century Onward

Burton Fredericksen

In 1983 the J. Paul Getty Museum acquired from the marquess of Northampton a large mythological canvas by Dosso Dossi (p. 84) that, since its first exhibition in 1894, has been generally recognized as one of his most important works. The subject has remained mysterious, but most perplexing of all is its provenance: no one has any idea of where it was for the first three and a half centuries of its existence.[1] More recently, in 1989, the Getty Museum acquired a second, even larger, canvas that had been discovered in a small town in upstate New York. The subject has been interpreted as an *Allegory of Fortune* (p. 101), and it has been reasonably deduced as having been painted for Isabella d'Este in Mantua, but excepting a note on the reverse, which tells us that it was in the Litta collection in Milan at the beginning of the last century, its whereabouts before the 1980s are equally unknown.[2] If we believe that Dosso was an artist of the first rank, then we must ask ourselves how such paintings can exist without having caught anyone's attention until very modern times, and why more than half of his extant paintings have no provenance prior to the nineteenth century.

Surveying the provenance of Dosso's paintings is made relatively easy by the fact that Dosso and Battista were primarily active in one city, Ferrara, and for one family, the Este. Aside from brief periods in Mantua, one can assume that most of their paintings were painted in Ferrara and that those examples of their work that left Emilia before the last decade of the sixteenth century were probably gifts from the duke. Both of the Dossi were occasionally "lent" to patrons in other cities, notably to Francesco Maria della Rovere to work in Pesaro and to Cardinal Bernardo Cles to decorate the Castello at Trent, but neither episode is known to have produced paintings other than frescoes. There are a few records of payments for portraits executed for sitters outside the Este family, such as the two made in 1524 of the young daughters of Isabella d'Aragona, who was residing at the court in Ferrara, but none of these records refer to subject pictures.

A review of Dosso's paintings that were collected, as opposed to commissioned, must necessarily begin with the annexation of Ferrara into the papal states in 1598, which brought about the partial dispersal of the Este collections. While various associates of Clement VIII began requisitioning paintings, including many of the best pieces, to take to Rome, Cesare d'Este and other members of the family carried as many items as possible to Modena, where their court was reestablished and the remainder of the collection reinstalled in new quarters. Documentation is incomplete, but at least fifty pictures by Dosso and his brother were still included in the ducal collections in the seventeenth century, among them large mythological canvases as well as many smaller, decorative landscapes that apparently had no "subject." The 1685 inventory of Cesare Ignazio d'Este, for instance, lists thirty-nine paintings attributed to Dosso, including eighteen such landscapes, as well as "*Un Paese con sopra un fagiano al naturale, pernici, e uccelletti*" (a landscape with a life-size pheasant, partridges, and small birds).[3] No such bird pictures by Dosso are known to survive, but further examples are found in other inventories, and either he or members of his studio must have painted them. Other pictures by Dosso in Cesare Ignazio's inventory that have been lost included a *Mars, Venus, and Vulcan,* and a *Triumph of Solomon.* Some of the Este paintings were also taken to Rome by members of the family. At the time of his death there in 1624, Cardinal Alessandro d'Este is recorded as owning two works by Dosso, a *Stoning of Saint Stephen,* and a painting described only as "*Una Fortuna in tavola*" (a Fortune on panel).[4] Most of Alessandro's pictures returned to Modena after his death, but some were willed to others and remained in Rome.

At mid-century Francesco I was adding to the Modena collection, although he asserted he was not looking for pictures by the Dossi. Upon being offered paintings from the Savelli collection in 1650, he responded in a letter that he already had plenty of paintings by the Dossi and did not need more. He wanted instead to acquire a Raphael, suggesting even the *Madonna* at Foligno (now in the Pinacoteca Vaticana), which was still in its original location. His suggestion may, in fact, imply a more profound taste for Dosso than he may have recognized, since, as has been suggested by several scholars, Dosso may have played a role in painting the landscape of Raphael's Foligno *Madonna.*[5]

In 1748, the best of the ducal paintings in Modena were sold to Augustus III of Saxony, including seven paintings by Dosso and Battista. With the exception of one destroyed in World War II and a portrait that seems never to have arrived, they remain in Dresden to this day. Their history is well known and need not be repeated, except to note that although all of them had presumably been executed for the Este and had remained with the family for two hundred years, by the time of the sale three of them had been reattributed to Garofalo.[6]

Some of Dosso's pictures were obtained by local Ferrarese collectors after the devolution and did not leave Emilia. The most important of these collectors was undoubtedly Roberto Canonici, whose testament and inventory of 1631 and 1632 list five paintings by Dosso, including two *Madonnas,* a *Portrait of Alfonso I,* a *Sibyl,* and a genre scene depicting "*Un Frate con due donne, et un buffone (che) stanno mirando un conigiio bianco e rosso, che stà sopra una tavola*" (a friar with two women and a jester admiring a white and red rabbit that is on top of a table).[7] At least three of the pictures by Dosso have survived: one *Madonna* is now in the Pinacoteca Civica Inzaghi at Budrio, while the so-called *Portrait of Alfonso I,* as well as the *Sibyl*—apparently a copy of the painting in the Hermitage in St. Petersburg—are now in private collections.[8] The curious genre picture is untraced. Girolamo Baruffaldi tells us that the family still owned seven pictures by Dosso *"di finissimo gusto"* (of the most refined taste) at the beginning of the next century.[9]

It has recently been demonstrated that Canonici also owned the large Bacchanal now in the National Gallery in London and generally attributed to Dosso, which Canonici believed to be by Paris Bordone.[10] By 1665 it had somehow come into the Gonzaga collection at Mantua where it was reattributed to Dosso. In the following century it was sold to Marshal Schulenburg in Venice and apparently was brought to England during the 1770s, undergoing many changes of attribution en route.[11] The detailed description in Canonici's testament leaves no doubt that it is identical with the London canvas, and while one might now question whether Dosso was its author, its attribution to Paris Bordone is certainly wrong and serves to remind us that by the seventeenth century even local Ferrarese tradition was fallible.

There were other collectors in Ferrara about whom we still know relatively little. Baruffaldi records the names of three who owned paintings by Dosso. Conte Bonifacio Bevilacqua had two decorative canvases painted in gouache that depicted scenes from the story of Alcina and Ruggero; unfortunately both had been damaged by water and poorly restored. Baruffaldi also mentions that his own father, Nicolò, owned a number of Dosso's portraits, and he briefly refers to Conte Achille Taccoli, who had many paintings by Dosso that, unfortunately, he does not name.[12]

Recent research in the Ferrarese archives has shown that in the eighteenth century a large number of individuals in Ferrara still claimed to own one or more paintings by Dosso, and a certain Giovanni Leccioli supposedly had as many as twelve.[13] Most of these cannot be identified, and their subjects, generally Madonnas, saints, or portraits, do not permit us to determine much about the accuracy of the attributions to Dosso. One of them, an allegorical figure of Abundance (fig. 1), listed in the collection of Giacomo Bartoli in 1740, is probably a painting later in the collection of the Cini family which appears to be by Battista Dossi.[14]

The example of Giovanni Battista Costabili, the early nineteenth-century Ferrarese collector who most prominently represented the local tradition, may serve as an indication of the reliability of the attributions to Dosso found in Ferrarese inventories. Costabili's catalog of 1838 included twenty-two paintings by Dosso; of the few that have been identified, only one is still accepted as his.[15] Since the name of Dosso was also one of paramount importance to Ferrarese collectors of the eighteenth century, this perhaps led in some cases to optimistic attributions.

There can be no doubt, however, that beginning in 1598, many of Dosso's most beautiful paintings, and those most representative of his work, left

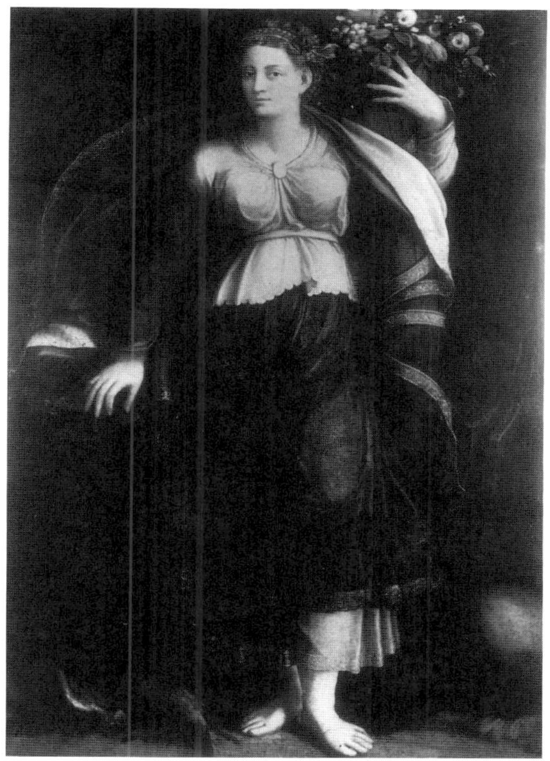

Fig. 1. Battista Dossi
Allegory of Abundance
Venice, Collezione Vittorio Cini

Ferrara for Rome. The first to leave were those acquired by Cardinal Pietro Aldobrandini, the pope's nephew, who not only inherited the collection of Lucrezia d'Este but also was able to requisition a number of pictures from Este residences. Thirteen works by the Dossi are listed in the cardinal's inventory of 1603, including twelve by Dosso and one by Battista.[16] The inventory of Lucrezia d'Este, drawn up in 1592, also contains twelve works by Dosso, but they are not the same ones that belonged to Aldobrandini just eleven years later.[17] Only one of them, a *Noah's Ark with Many Figures,* can be identified in both documents with certainty; six others can be matched more tentatively. The remaining five either had already lost their association with Dosso or were no longer in the collection. It appears that at least a few of Lucrezia's pictures had already been dispersed, probably given away.[18]

Most of the thirteen Aldobrandini paintings are still found in an inventory begun in 1709 and completed in 1710, drawn up after the death of

Giovanni Battista Pamphili Aldobrandini.[19] They probably remained part of the collection until at least mid-century, when some pictures are known to have left. Unfortunately, after that date very few of the group can be traced with absolute certainty. One of them, described in inventories as "*Un ritratto d'una donna vestita alla moresca*" (a portrait of a woman dressed in Moorish style), has often been identified with the so-called *Dido* by Dosso now in the Galleria Doria-Pamphili. The association, however, is far from certain. Similarly, because the Aldobrandini paintings were eventually merged with those of the Borghese in 1769, a *Nativity* (fig. 2) in the Galleria Borghese has been assumed to have come from the Aldobrandini.[20] It is described in earlier inventories as "*Una Natività del Signore con la Gloria sopra*" (a nativity of the Lord with the Glory above), and although there are other paintings of this subject by Dosso, it can plausibly be connected with the Borghese picture because the inscription on the scroll held by the central angel at the top begins with the word *Gloria*.[21] If correct, this would apparently be the only Aldobrandini painting by Dosso that definitively remained in the Borghese collection.

Other pictures in the Aldobrandini group have been associated with extant paintings now in various collections, although there are often discrepancies in the dimensions. These include the *Entry into the Ark of Noah* at the Rhode Island School of Design in Providence, the *Jousting Tournament* in the Pinacoteca Nazionale in Ferrara, and the *Madonna and Child with the Infant Baptist and Saint Francis* that was recently on the art market.[22] Two other paintings can be found in the Aldobrandini inventories until at least about 1665 may be added to these: the small painting of Saint Jerome (p. 228), whose whereabouts is unknown, might be the painting described as "*San Geronimo in tavola piccola come si dice di mano del Dosso*" (Saint Jerome on a small panel said to be in Dosso's hand), and *The Temptation of Christ* (fig. 3), sold at Christie's in 1949, could well be the picture described as "*Un Christo tentato dal Demonio*" (a Christ tempted by the Devil).[23] This leaves, however, at least six paintings that cannot be identified with any extant painting, including "*Un quadro grande di più Dei*" (a large painting of many gods), described elsewhere as including Vulcan, "*con un montone, un camaleonte, et un'armatura*" (with a ram, a chameleon, and a suit of armor). Because of its size (7 *palmi* high) and theme, this appears to be the missing painting from Alfonso's *studiolo*. Another large painting, depicting Saint George, is also lost.[24] Because of their origins, the attribution of these paintings to Dosso is likely to have been correct.

With a few exceptions, Dosso's paintings in the Aldobrandini collection appear to have been relatively small and generally less impressive than those acquired by Cardinal Scipione Borghese. The details of Borghese's acquisitions are still unclear, but it appears that earlier assumptions that he received the majority of his paintings directly from Ferrara are incorrect. A recently discovered inventory made shortly before Scipione's death in 1633 is the earliest known documentation of this collection and the only one that accu-

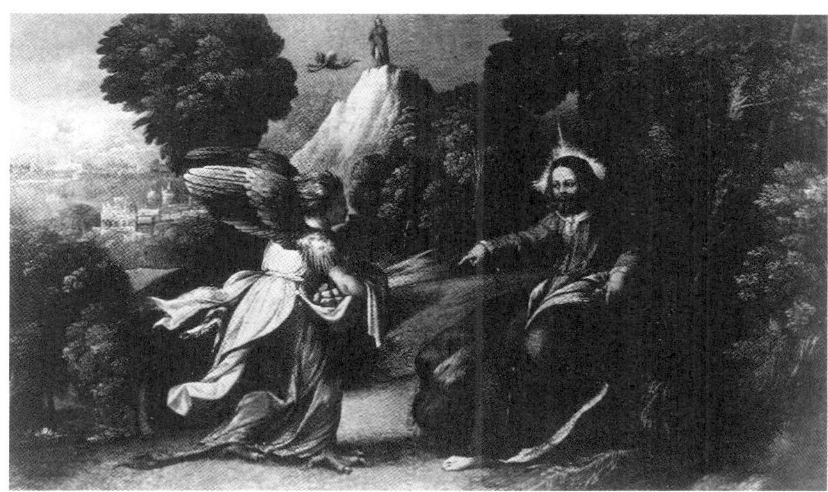

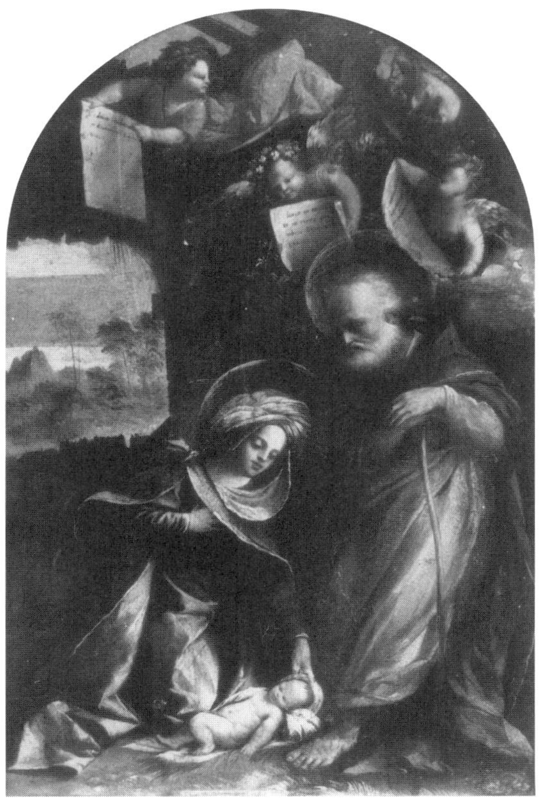

Fig. 2. Dosso Dossi
Nativity
Rome, Galleria Borghese

Fig. 3. Battista Dossi
Temptation of Christ
Whereabouts unknown

Fig. 4. Dosso Dossi
Saint Catherine of Alexandria
Rome, Galleria Borghese

rately reflects his activity. The document remains to be studied, but it apparently lists just eight paintings by Dosso and lacks many of the best-known works that one associates with the Borghese collection, including the *Enchantress Circe* (or *Melissa;* p. 235) and *Apollo and Daphne,* which only entered the collection somewhat later.[25] At least two of the rhomboid pictures from the Castello at Ferrara were present in Scipione's collection, however, although they must have left it later in the century.[26] By 1650, when Giacomo Manilli described the collection, the number of paintings by Dosso had climbed to fourteen, and in the inventory of 1693 there were nineteen.[27] This can only mean that most of the paintings were acquired from other collectors and not directly from Ferrara. Whatever their earlier provenance, these paintings included some of Dosso's most beautiful pieces.

Ten of the nineteen paintings described in 1693 were from the series of horizontal pictures depicting the story of Aeneas that Vasari recorded as having decorated the *studiolo* of Alfonso I. Three still exist: *The Sicilian Games* (Birmingham, Barber Institute of Fine Arts), *Aeneas in the Elysian Fields* (Ottawa, National Gallery of Canada), and *Aeneas and Achates on the Libyan Coast* (Washington, National Gallery of Art). A fourth has recently been discovered. It appears that the entire series must have left the Borghese collection sometime during the eighteenth century. Of the remaining nine paintings, six can be identified with paintings still in the Galleria Borghese: *Apollo and Daphne, Saint Cosmas and Saint Damian, The Holy Family with the Infant Baptist, The Story of Callisto, The Enchantress Circe* (or *Melissa*), and the *Landscape with a Bizarre Procession* that is now attributed to Girolamo da Carpi. The three other paintings listed—a *Head of Christ,* a *Portrait of a Man in Red,* and a *Madonna and Child* dated 1515—can no longer be identified.[28]

Manilli's 1650 description of the Villa Borghese includes other paintings by Dosso that do not appear in the 1693 inventory. One was the large ceiling tondo from the Camera del Poggiolo in the Castello at Ferrara, now extant in just two fragments: the *Poet and Muse* in the National Gallery, London, and the *Laughing Youth* in the Fondazione Roberto Longhi, Florence. Another painting mentioned by Manilli was a *Saint Catherine of Alexandria* (fig. 4), which is still in the Borghese collection but is not found in the 1693 inventory under Dosso's name. There is some reason to think, however, that it is the item described as a work of Leonardo da Vinci in the later inventory, since the description, dimensions, and possibly even the inventory number still inscribed on the painting correspond very closely to the entry.[29] If the painting is by Dosso, this would be an example of his authorship having been lost, but the issue has been complicated by the new inventory of about 1633, which supposedly describes the painting as a copy after Dosso by Cesare d'Arpino.[30]

There is yet a more prominent example of how the perception of Dosso's style was fading. The *Tubalcain,* or *Allegory of Music* (p. 231), now in the Museo della Fondazione Horne, Florence, appears in Manilli's book of 1650 as the work of Dosso, but it is found in the 1693 inventory as by Giorgione.[31] This was undoubtedly the most important of Dosso's works to have left the Borghese collection, albeit under another name. Like the others that departed, presumably some time in the eighteenth century, it was again recognized as Dosso's only in the present century.

A third cardinal's collection, that of Carlo Emmanuele Pio di Savoia, also originated in Ferrara and absorbed many Emilian pictures before being taken to Rome in 1626. Just two years before its transfer, an inventory was made that listed six pictures said to be by Dosso, and at this relatively early date the attributions probably reflected accurate tradition.[32] A later inventory of 1689 has fourteen pictures listed under the names of both Dossi, many of which might be important, if they could be found.[33] They include a large *Landscape with a Feast of the Gods* (6 × 8 *palmi*), a *Landscape with the*

Judgment of Paris (6 × 6 *palmi*), a *Rape of Helen* (6 × 8 *palmi*), and a *Tarquinius Attacking Lucretia* (4 × 3½ *palmi*), among others. One cannot assume that the fourteen paintings were by either brother, but two of them have been identified as theirs: a *Madonna and Child with Saint George and a Bishop Saint,* now in Bergamo at the Accademia Carrara, where it is attributed to Battista, and, especially, the large Holy Family by Dosso now in the Pinacoteca Capitolina in Rome, where the best of the Pio paintings came to rest. These lend some credence to the other attributions in the collection, although some were certainly wrong.

One painting in the Pio collection, listed in 1689 as *A Sleeping Nymph and Cupid Observed by a Satyr* by Dosso, was purchased in the late eighteenth century by Gavin Hamilton and then sold to Sir William Hamilton as a work of Palma Giovane. Although the painting cannot be traced after 1824, judging from an engraving made of it (fig. 5), the attribution to Dosso appears at least questionable.[34] Another entry in the same inventory describes a *Portrait of a Woman as Saint Margaret* "believed to be by Dosso" which can be confidently identified as the *Portrait of a Woman as Saint Margaret* by Savoldo, now in the Pinacoteca Capitolina.

In 1750 Benedict XIV selected and purchased 126 paintings in the Pio collection for the Museo Capitolino in Rome. Just one work was cataloged as Dosso's: the portrait we now attribute to Savoldo. The only painting in the group currently accepted as the work of Dosso, the large *Holy Family* that Carlo Emmanuele Pio acquired some time before 1624, had been reattributed to Palma Vecchio.[35] This is another indication of how, even in Rome, the perception of Dosso's style was deteriorating.

Another Roman collection that had its origins in Ferrara was that of Cardinal Giulio Sacchetti, papal legate to Ferrara between 1626 and 1631. Because the seventeenth-century inventories of the collection are still unpublished, it is difficult to discuss its history, but in the eighteenth century it still included some Ferrarese paintings, among them several attributed to Dosso.[36] In 1726 the marchese Matteo Sacchetti owned a *Madonna and Child with Angels* by Dosso—described as a student of Titian—as well as another of 4 × 3.11 *palmi* depicting "*Quattro Donne che contrastano*" (four women who are quarreling).[37] In an inventory made at mid-century, when a large portion of the collection was acquired for the Museo Capitolino, the dimensions of the latter were given as 3 × 3 *palmi.*[38] This is probably the rhomboidal painting now in the Collezione Vittorio Cini in Venice (fig. 6), often referred to as *Riso, Pianto, Paura, and Ira* (laughter, crying, fear, and wrath), a title given it by Vincenzo Camuccini in the mid–nineteenth century. The identification is strengthened by the presence of the next item in the same inventories, described as "*Due mezze figure, d'un huomo, e d'una donna, che s'abbracciano*" (two half-figures of a man and a woman who are embracing). No author is given, but the dimensions are identical to those of the other painting, and it is most probably the rhomboid now in the Dobó István Vármúzeum in Eger, Hungary (fig. 7). These two paintings are evidently the

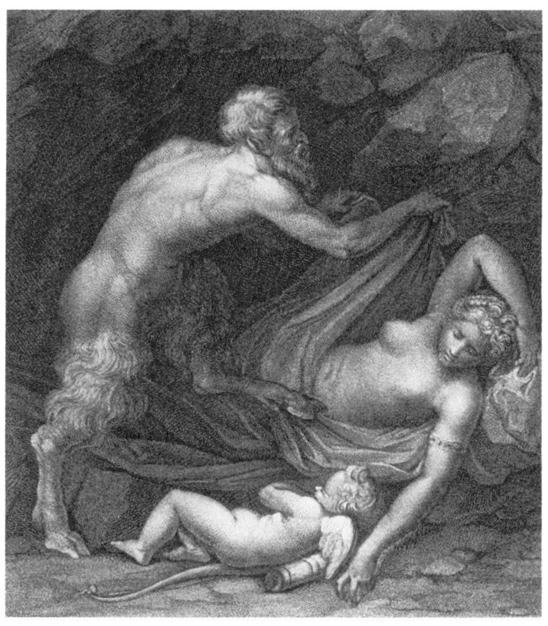

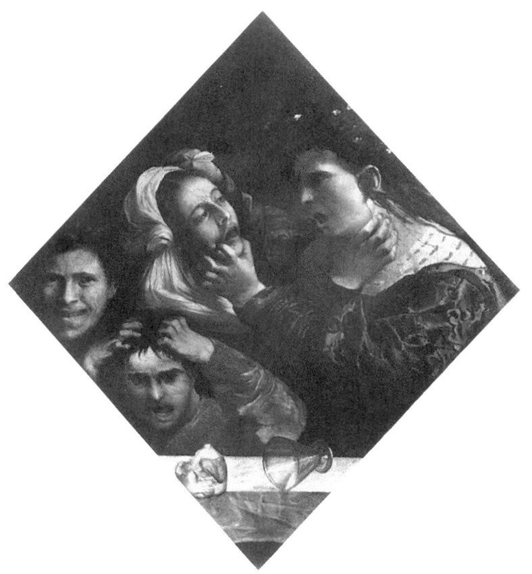

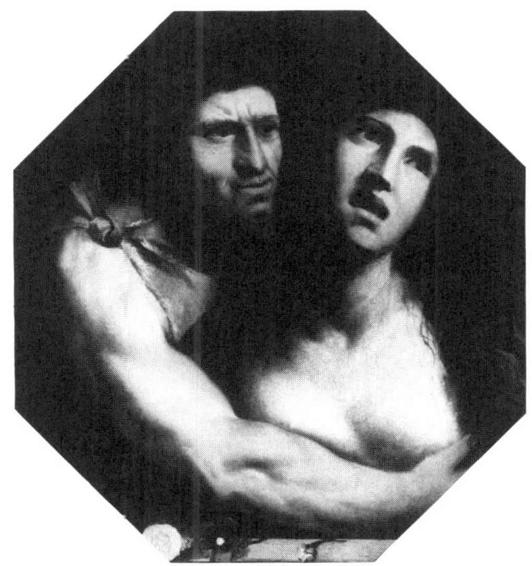

Fig. 5. Giuseppe Perini (after Palma Giovane)
Jupiter and Antiope
From Gavin Hamilton, *Schola italica picturae* (Rome, 1773)

Fig. 6. Dosso Dossi
Rhomboid (four brawling figures)
Venice, Collezione Vittorio Cini

Fig. 7. Dosso Dossi
Rhomboid (faun and nymph)
Eger, Dobó István Vármúzeum

ones mentioned above that appeared in the Borghese inventory of circa 1633. Both were among those acquired for the Museo Capitolino in 1748 but were missing some time later.[39] Since one of them, the Cini painting, belonged later to Camuccini, who was intimately involved with the development of the Capitoline collections, it is possible that it was he who removed them.

As Ferrara was absorbed into the Papal States, works of art continued to be siphoned off while the number of collections in Rome boasting Ferrarese pictures continued to rise. In the course of the seventeenth century virtually every major Roman family claimed to own one or two paintings by Dosso. In 1610 a Savelli inventory listed three pictures by Dosso, a *Venus,* a *Nativity* and a *Head of a Sibyl,* and a painting of animals and birds was listed in an inventory of 1631, another indication that Dosso must have painted a number of such pictures as decoration.[40] What is probably the same painting is also found in the earlier inventory, albeit without attribution. The entry reads "*Due quadri grandi sopra le porte. In uno un pavone, et altri uccelli, e l'altro di paesi con fantasime*" (two large pictures over the doors. In one is a peacock and other birds, and in the other, landscapes with phantasms). To this a note was added: "*Il quadro con le fantasime al Card. Borghese*" (the painting with phantasms to Cardinal Borghese).[41] This last reference is presumably to the *Landscape with a Bizarre Procession* in the Galleria Borghese, thought at the time to be by Dosso. Apparently Scipione Borghese acquired it from the Savelli family.

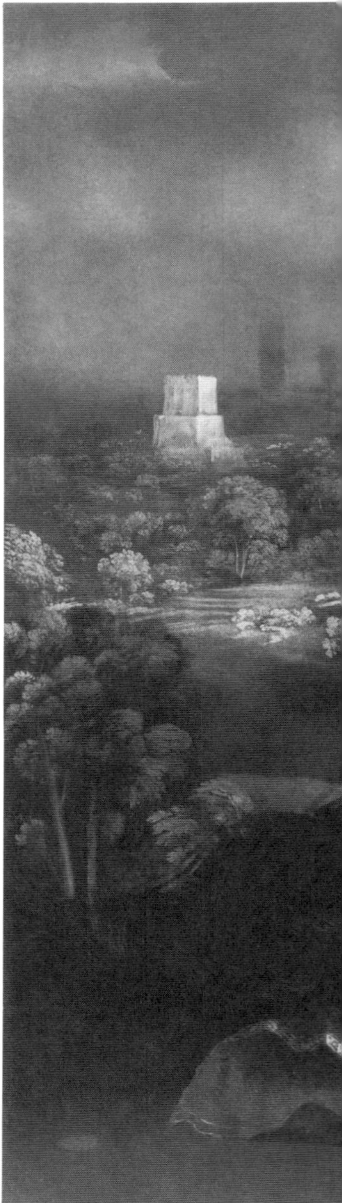

Somewhat later the Savelli family succeeded in acquiring Dosso's large altarpiece, *Saints John Evangelist and Bartholomew,* which had been taken from the cathedral of Ferrara before 1611 and replaced with a copy by Scarsellino. In 1650 the Savelli collection was put up for sale and Dosso's altarpiece was given the second highest valuation, second only to another large altarpiece, the *Assumption of Christ* by Garofalo, and five times as high as paintings by Gentileschi that had been commissioned by the Savelli.[42] These paintings by Garofalo and Dosso were then purchased by Flavio Chigi and passed to the Galleria Nazionale di Palazzo Barberini in Rome at the beginning of the twentieth century.

It has not been previously noticed that other paintings passed from the Savelli family to Flavio Chigi. This is apparently true of both the *Sibyl* and the *Venus* mentioned above. The latter is certainly identical with one of the same subject in the Chigi inventory of 1692, described as showing Venus sitting, nude, while Cupid sleeps.[43] By combining the information from both inventories, it is possible to identify it with the painting now in the Nelson Shanks Collection (fig. 8) whose dimensions correspond closely to those given in the document.[44]

The much more prominent collection of Cardinal Ludovico Ludovisi had a large number of pictures from Ferrara, some of which had been acquired with the help of Cardinal Aldobrandini. His inventory of 1623 lists twenty-two paintings by Dosso, and a posthumous inventory made a decade later added five more.[45] A number of these paintings were evidently decorative in

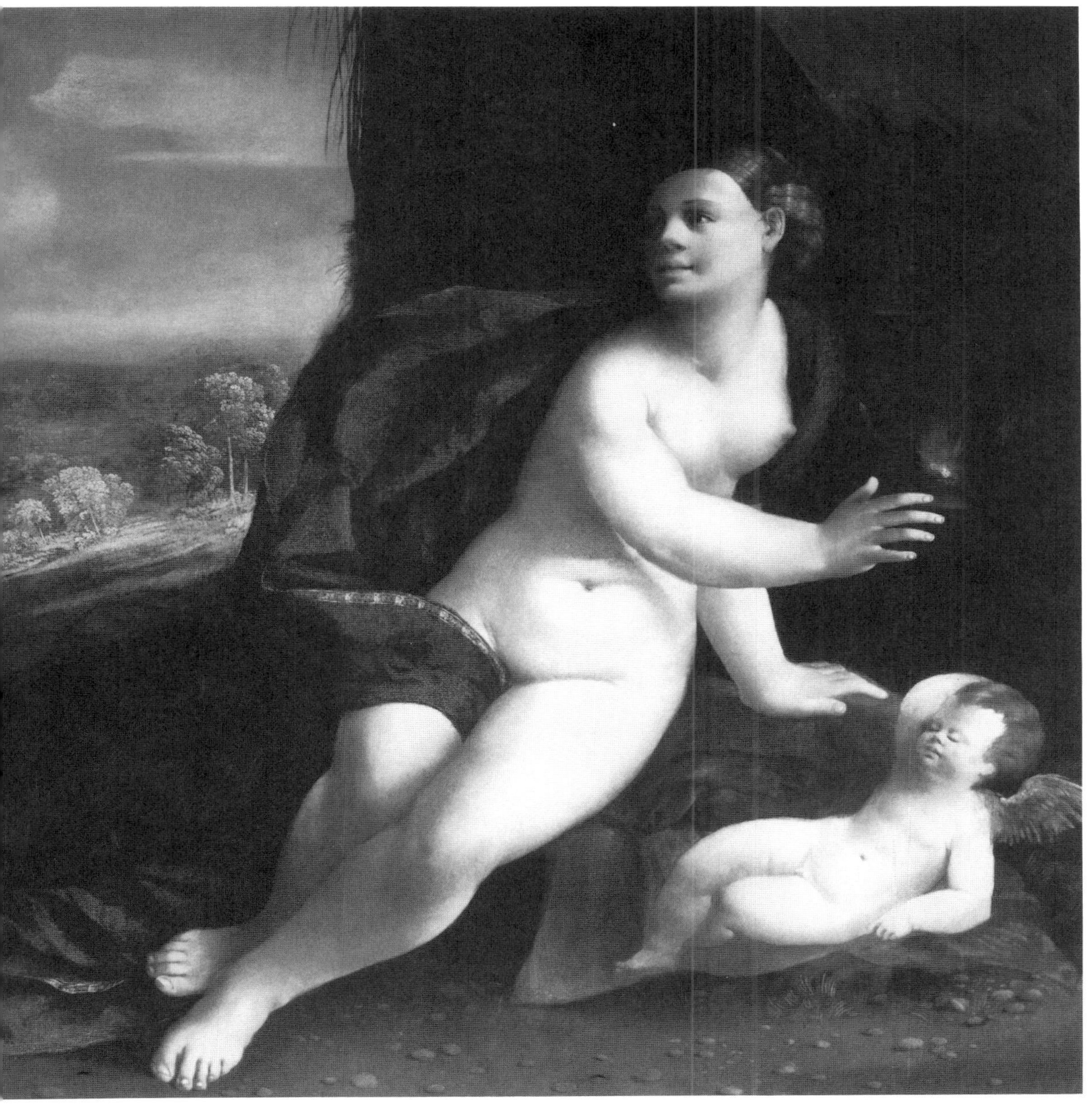

Fig. 8. Dosso Dossi
Venus and Cupid
Andalusia, Pennsylvania, Nelson Shanks Collection

nature. Twelve are described as panels with dancing putti, whose dimensions were just 1 *palmo* high but 6 *palmi* wide—proportions that clearly indicate decorative works. These panels probably were removed from an Este palace. The inventory contains a few landscapes and some religious pictures, including another *Martyrdom of Saint Stephen.* The most important entry, however, describes a large panel 10 *palmi* high that, according to the 1623 inventory, depicted *"Un orfeo con la lira in mano"* (Orpheus playing the lyre); in the inventory of 1633 it is listed as *"Un Apollo con la lira in mano"* (Apollo playing the lyre).[46] This is most probably the *Apollo* now in the Borghese collection (it was called *Orpheus* in Borghese inventories as well), which evidently passed from Scipione Borghese to Ludovisi and returned to the Borghese collection only after having belonged to yet a third collector, Cardinal Luigi Capponi (see note 25). Unfortunately, the later history of the Ludovisi collection is little understood, and the remaining pictures by Dosso have not been identified.

According to an inventory made in 1638, the collection of Vincenzo Giustiniani is supposed to have contained six paintings by Dosso, but here too all have been lost.[47] Two of them, a *Saint Jerome* and an unlikely *Profile Portrait of Petrarch,* were engraved before being sold to Frederick Wilhelm III of Prussia at the beginning of the nineteenth century, so we at least have an image of these paintings (figs. 9 and 10). It is highly unlikely that the portrait was painted by Dosso, and Dosso's authorship of the *Saint Jerome* appears at least doubtful.[48] Another Giustiniani painting that went to Berlin, an early *Madonna and Child with Two Saints,* was recognized as Dosso's only in 1931. In 1638 it was thought to be by Sebastiano del Piombo.[49]

A final, and in some ways perhaps the most instructive, indication of Dosso's presence in Roman collections is found in the records of the Barberini family. Because of an unusually high number of published inventories and other documents, one becomes aware of how frequently works entered and left Barberini collections, either by purchase or by gift. Two works by Dosso are listed in 1623 and 1626, a picture of *Christ and the Samaritan Woman* and a *Battle Scene*, and in 1636 a *Portrait of Ariosto* was received and then almost immediately given away to an Englishman named Montague. By 1644, however, the collection of Cardinal Antonio Barberini contained six new paintings by Dosso, most of them secular works. Subsequent inventories each had similar numbers of paintings by Dosso, but not always the same items. At the time of Antonio's death in 1671, a part of his collection was willed to his brother Cardinal Francesco Barberini, including two large Bacchanals by Dosso, while a second part, including yet another pair of large scenes from the *Life of Bacchus,* were given to his nephew Maffeo, prince of Palestrina. These and other pictures in the collection do not reappear in subsequent inventories, but some remained well into the next century, and in many cases probably much longer. Only a *Reclining Venus,* now in a private collection, and the *Saint Lucrezia* in the National Gallery of Art in Washington, have been identified: both belonged to Cardinal Antonio.[50]

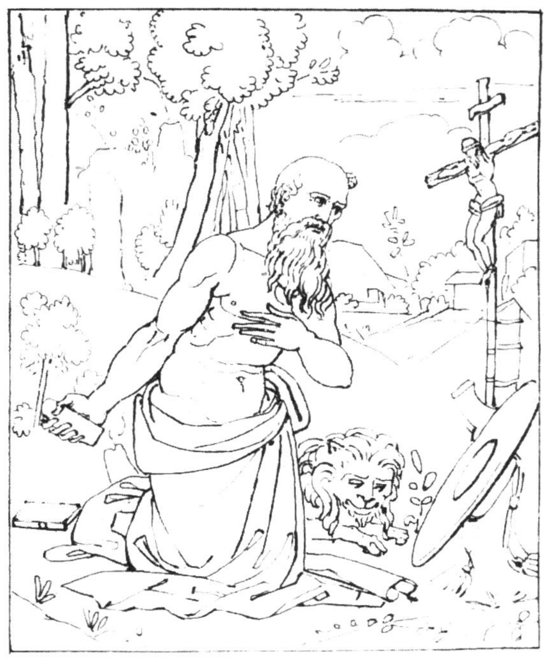

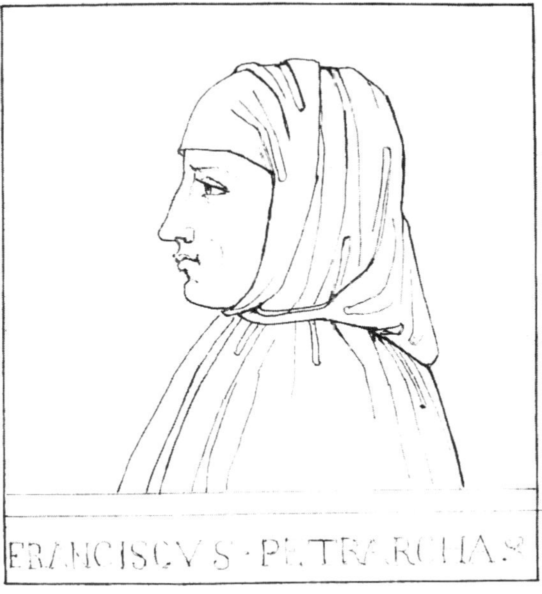

Fig. 9. Thérèse Eléonore Lingée (purportedly after Dosso Dossi)
Saint Jerome
From C. P. Landon, *Galerie Giustiniani, ou, Catalogue figuré des tableaux de cette célèbre galerie* (Paris, 1812)

Fig. 10. Thérèse Eléonore Lingée (purportedly after Dosso Dossi)
Profile Portrait of Petrarch
From C. P. Landon, *Galerie Giustiniani, ou, Catalogue figuré des tableaux de cette célèbre galerie* (Paris, 1812)

These are but the most prominent of the Roman collections that had, or claimed to have, more than an occasional work by Dosso. Many others had individual works, most of which are no longer identifiable. The collections included those of Costanzo Patrizi (inventoried in 1624), Giuseppe Pignatelli (1647), Camillo Pamphili (1648), Francesco Angeloni (1652?), Cardinal Francesco Albizzi (1682), Lorenzo Onofrio Colonna (1679), Marcello Pignatelli (1686), Cardinal Giuseppe Imperiale (1691), Cardinal Savio Mellini (1692), Abate Giuseppe Paulucci (1695), and Lelio and Paolo Falconieri (1696). The list is certainly far from complete and ignores completely the eighteenth century.[51]

Clearly Rome was by far the best place to see works by Dosso, but individual works are recorded in other Italian cities as well. No doubt a number of his pictures were in Mantua, although the Gonzaga inventory of 1627 includes only one under his name.[52] After the purchase of the Mantuan collection by Charles I, some of the previously anonymous pictures appeared in the English inventories as the work of Dosso. Because of this they will be discussed below in the context of English collections.

Bolognese collectors might have been expected to have acquired important works by Dosso, but a survey of Bolognese collections has turned up very little of consequence. Seven collectors there are recorded as owning at least one or two pictures by Dosso during the seventeenth and early eighteenth centuries, but none is identifiable and none appears to have been of unusual consequence.[53]

As far as can be determined, seventeenth-century Tuscan collectors claimed to own even fewer pictures by the artist. The only known example is the *Allegory of Hercules* (often referred to as a *Bambocciata* or *Stregoneria*) now in the Galleria degli Uffizi in Florence, which was purchased in 1665 by Leopoldo de' Medici from Giannotto Cennini of Siena. The same painting, described as *"un ritratto de' buffoni de' Duchi di Ferrara... indubitato de' mano de' Dosso et originale"*(a portrait of the jesters of the dukes of Ferrara... unquestionably by Dosso's hand and original), is also recorded in the collection of Roberto Cennini, marchese of Castiglioncello del Trinoro, in 1660. It was evidently the best of a small group of pictures that Cennini was hoping to sell in Rome.[54] In the same group were Bacchanals by Dosso, supposedly copied after paintings by Titian, which were considered much less valuable. Very little is known about Cennini's collection, but it may have derived from Cardinal Francesco Cennini (1566–1645), who was closely associated with Scipione Borghese and who was papal legate in Ferrara from 1623 to 1627.[55] Leopoldo de' Medici owned another painting by Dosso, the *Nymph Chased by a Satyr* now in the Palazzo Pitti, which was first recorded in Florence in 1675 as a work by Schiavone; later it was identified as Giorgione's.

In Naples just one painting is recorded in the seventeenth century, a *Madonna with Saints Martha and Mary Magdalen,* listed in the collection of Gianfrancesco de Ponte, marchese of Morcone, as early as 1614.[56] The situation did not change significantly in the next century with the arrival of the Farnese collection, which never included many Ferrarese pictures and possessed just one small *Madonna* that carried Dosso's name.[57] The collection also contained the *Portrait of a Woman* now in the Musée Condé in Chantilly, sometimes referred to as *Laura Dianti,* but it was listed as a work of Giulio Romano while in the possession of the Farnese family.[58] The situation was only slightly different in Genoa. Gian Vincenzo Imperiale's inventory of 1648 included three paintings by the artist, and the collection of Giovanni Battista Balbi in 1658 and 1663 included a *Rape of the Sabines.* None of the works in Genoa can be identified.[59]

In Turin we know of two collections so far that supposedly included paintings by Dosso, the earliest of which, that of Amedeo Dal Pozzo, listed a single *Madonna* in 1634.[60] More interesting is the inventory of Carlo Emmanuele I, drawn up in 1635, a year after his death, which included eleven paintings either by Dosso or said to derive from him— *"vien da Dosso."* Five were portraits (one of which is said to be a copy of a painting of Alfonso I by Titian), two were depictions of the Madonna with saints, one was a *Saint Jerome,* and another is described only as a large *Battle.* The most intriguing is an allegory, described as *"Donna ignuda sedente sopra un mondo con cornucopia, et altra figura d'huomo. Vien da Dossi da Ferrara. Mediocre"* (Nude woman sitting on top of a globe with a cornucopia and another figure of a man. Derives from Dossi of Ferrara. Mediocre).[61] Although the dimensions are not given, clearly this describes the composition of the Getty allegory. However, as pointed out previously, the description as "mediocre" and the use of the phrase *"vien da Dossi"* implies that it was perhaps only a copy. Altogether five of the eleven pictures associated with Dosso were referred to as "mediocre." None of the group can be identified now, and it is possible that some of them were destroyed in a fire in 1659 that is known to have consumed many paintings.

Most surprising is the almost complete lack of pictures by Dosso in Venice. Ottavio Fabri is recorded as owning a painting by him in 1604, but its subject is not known, and the inventory of Michele Pietra in 1656 lists *"Un quadro d'historia"* (a historical painting), which is said to *"vien da I Dossi."*[62] The only exception to this rather bleak representation is the painting of *"Giove che dipinge farfalle"* (Jove, who is painting butterflies), which was in the collection of the Widmann family in 1659; presumably this is the splendid *Jupiter, Mercury, and Virtue* (p. 99) now in Vienna, which did not leave Italy until the late nineteenth century.[63] It is still not known how this painting came to the Widmanns, but for two centuries it seems to have been the only major example of Dosso's work in the Veneto, although one should not forget that during the eighteenth century the Bacchanal now in the National Gallery in London was in the Venetian palace of Marshal Schulenberg.

Until Napoleonic times Dosso's paintings were generally concentrated in just two or three locations in Italy, so it is not surprising that very few reached other parts of Europe before the mid-nineteenth century. The earliest record of an exportation north of the Alps concerns a painting of a satyr and a nymph given to Rudolph II by Vincenzo Gonzaga and carried to Prague by Hans von Aachen in 1603.[64] Rudolph is reported to have liked the gift very much and to have asked for another by the same artist, but there is no indication that another was ever received. This *Satyr and Nymph* has been occasionally identified with the painting in the Palazzo Pitti, but this seems very unlikely.

Most of the other paintings by Dosso found in the north were in England. The first we know of is the splendid *Saint William,* now in the Royal Collection at Hampton Court, which is recorded as having been the subject of an exchange between the second marquess of Hamilton and Charles I in 1620. It was not attributed to Dosso, however, and seems to have been considered a work of either Giorgione or Sebastiano del Piombo.[65] Three other paintings by Dosso still in the Royal Collection were also acquired by Charles, but all were thought to be by other artists at the time of their acquisition. The *Portrait of a Man with Five Rings* is first recorded in the 1630s as the work of Sebastiano del Piombo, and the *Soldier with a Girl Holding a Pipe,* received as a gift from Cardinal Francesco Barberini in 1635, is recorded as by Giorgione.[66] The third was the large *Holy Family* acquired with the Gonzaga collection in 1627. In the Gonzaga inventory it is left anonymous, but it had earlier been referred to as the work of Parmigianino. By the time Charles's collection was dispersed between 1649 and 1651, however, the *Holy Family* had been recognized as Dosso's, an indication that someone with a knowledge of Dosso's style had seen it and recommended the change.[67]

The records of the various sales of Charles's collection reveal that the king had owned ten or eleven other paintings attributed to Dosso, none of which have been traced.[68] At least seven had religious themes, including a *Nativity,* an *Adoration of the Shepherds,* a *Circumcision,* a *Temptation of Saint Anthony,* and three listed as *Saint Jerome.* The *Circumcision* was probably the painting by Garofalo now in the Musée du Louvre (see below), and although it cannot be proven, there is a very good chance that the *Temptation of Saint Anthony* can be identified with the painting by Savoldo (fig. 11) now in San Diego.[69] Among the paintings with secular subjects were a *Venus and Cupid* and one described as a naked woman riding on her husband, evidently Phyllis and Aristotle. A *Phyllis and Aristotle* is recorded in the Mantuan inventory of 1627, although without an attribution; given the rarity of this subject in Italy, it must be the same painting.[70] Unfortunately it cannot be found.

Another of the untraced pictures from Charles's collection is described as a "Landscape with a Witch, by Dorse de Ferraro." In a list of pictures at Nonesuch in 1639, the same painting is described as "A Landscape of Enchantments" by "Dorsey," with an indication that it had come from Mantua.[71] And in the Mantuan inventory it is described as *"Un Paese con una Maga che sta facendo figure sopra la terra"* (a landscape with a sorceress

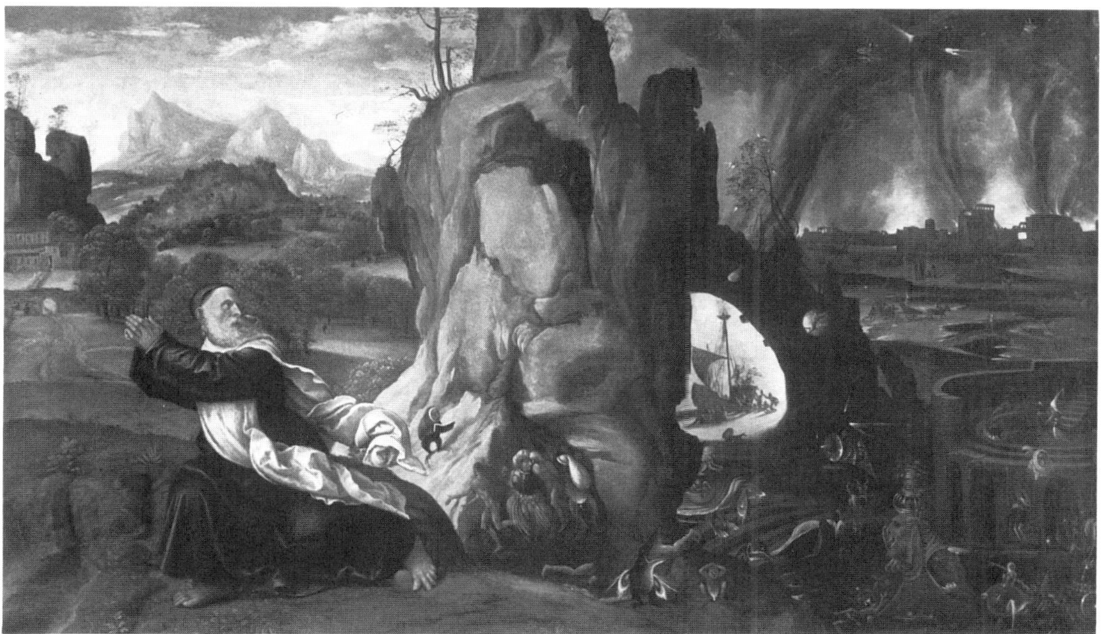

Fig. 11. Giovanni Girolamo Savoldo
Temptation of Saint Anthony
San Diego, Timken Museum of Art

making figures on the ground).[72] It is just possible, although far from certain, that this is the painting of Circe now in the National Gallery of Art in Washington (p. 235). If the Washington painting did indeed come from Mantua, this might support an early dating.

Lord Arundel also claimed to own one painting by Dosso, an *Adoration of the Magi* that he took to the Netherlands, where it is documented in the 1650s.[73] It is the only painting by the artist known to have been in Holland during the seventeenth century. In the early eighteenth century a certain Jean van Beuningen in Amsterdam owned a painting of Mars and Venus that is no longer identifiable.[74]

It is not known whether any authentic painting by Dosso arrived in France before the nineteenth century. An inventory made in Paris in 1638 after the death of the maréchal de Créquy shows that he owned a panel with *The Head of the Young Christ* by Dosso, which has since been lost.[75] In 1643 the collection of Cardinal Richelieu included a *Vulcan Surprising Venus and Mars* which was 3 × 4 *pieds* in size, but it too cannot be traced.[76] In 1661 Mazarin's inventory listed a *Portrait of a Man*, which remains unidentified.[77] Finally, Charles Lebrun's 1683 inventory of Louis XIV's collection lists three paintings by Dosso, none of them actually his. A *Circumcision* acquired from Everhard Jabach was in reality by Garofalo. (This is probably the same painting sold from Charles's collection and mentioned above; it is now in the Musée du Louvre.) A *Nativity* (Paris, Musée du Louvre) also from Jabach was by Lotto; another from the same source, *Christ in the House of the Pharisees* (Paris, Musée du Louvre), is now recognized as the work of Bonifacio Veronese.[78] This perhaps indicates that the attributions to Dosso found in other seventeenth-century northern collections may have been equally unreliable.

In central Europe Dosso's work must have been almost completely unknown. The major exception is found in Archduke Leopold Wilhelm's Viennese inventory of 1659, which contained six pictures thought to be by Dosso, including a *Saint John Evangelist,* two small panels with the heads of Adam and Eve, a *Profile Portrait of a Woman with Red Hair,* and an odd subject described as *King Miniatus with Eight Martyrs*.[79] The first of these, in the Kunsthistorisches Museum in Vienna, is now cataloged as the work of Palma Vecchio, and the profile portrait is found in the Szépmüvészeti Múseum, Budapest, listed as a minor Tuscan piece.[80] The others are untraced. The only certain picture by Dosso in Leopold Wilhelm's collection was the beautiful *Saint Jerome,* also in the Kunsthistorisches Museum. Leopold must have acquired this painting in Brussels before 1651, since it appears in David Teniers's painting of the gallery inscribed with this date.[81] It was brought to Vienna a few years later. About the same time the Fürstenberg collection in Salzburg received a small panel by Battista which, according to an inscription on the back, was a gift from Pope Alexander VII Chigi.[82] However, we have no idea what it was called at the time, and it cannot be identified in Chigi inventories.

There is no record of any painting by Dosso having gone to Spain, and none is found there now. In an inventory of 1682, one finds that the collection of Don Gaspar de Haro y Guzmán, the seventh marqués de Carpio, included five paintings by Dosso, which he probably acquired in Rome and was taking to Naples. Some of his paintings are noted as having come from the Savelli and Pio collections, although none of the pictures by Dosso, which included three depicting the Holy Family, a portrait, and a depiction of Cupid and Psyche, is so marked. After Carpio's death in Naples in 1687 some of his paintings went to Spain, while others stayed in Italy. There is no record of what happened to those by Dosso.[83]

By the end of the seventeenth century, many of Dosso's paintings that did not belong to the older collections—and many of those that did—had been confused with the work of other artists, most often Giorgione or other Venetian painters, and eighteenth-century attributions were increasingly unreliable. The public auctions in England and France, which often reflect the general perception of an artist and his oeuvre, only occasionally included minor works attributed to Dosso until well after the middle of the nineteenth century. With the rediscovery of the Ferrarese school of painters in the 1840s and 1850s, a clearer view of Dosso's works began to emerge. Nonetheless, the appearance 150 years later of major pictures, such as the Getty *Allegory of Fortune*, whose existence was previously unsuspected, continues to remind us of how much is still left to be discovered.

Notes

1. Los Angeles, J. Paul Getty Museum, acc. no. 83.PA.15. Alessandro Ballarin, *Dosso Dossi: La pittura a Ferrara negli anni del Ducato di Alfonso I*, 2 vols. (Cittadella: Bertoncello Artigrafiche, 1994–1995), 1: 348 (entry no. 453), as *Story of Pan*. The first record of the painting is its inclusion in Burlington Fine Arts Club, *Exhibition of Pictures, Drawings and Photographs of Works of the School of Ferrara-Bologna, 1440–1550* (London: Burlington Fine Arts Club, 1894), 52 (no. 56), as *Vertumnus and Pomona*. It has often been conjectured that the painting was purchased by Charles Compton, third marquess of Northampton, in Italy during the 1850s. It now seems more likely that it is identical to one lent by Robert P. Nichols to the British Institution in 1859 as *Jupiter and Antiope* by Dosso. In fact, the painting has often been interpreted as representing this subject, and the third marquess is known to have bought paintings in England as well as Italy. The picture is not mentioned in the description of Nichols's collection published in 1857 in Gustav Friedrich Waagen, *Galleries and Cabinets of Art in Great Britain* (London: J. Murray, 1857), 239–41, so it appears that Nichols must have acquired it between 1857 and 1859. Nor did it appear in the Nichols sale held at Christie's on 30 April 1875, so presumably he had sold it by then. Nichols owned other Ferrarese paintings, including the small *Temptation of Christ* probably by Battista (but listed as Dosso in the sale of 1875; see note 23), and an *Adoration of the Shepherds*. Research on his collection is still in progress. See Luisa Ciammitti's essay in this volume for a new interpretation of the *Mythological Scene*.

2. Los Angeles, J. Paul Getty Museum, acc. no. 89.PA.32. Ballarin, ibid., 1: 349 (entry no. 456). Acquired at Christie's, New York, 11 January 1989, lot no. 192. It was reported to have been found by the anonymous owner in a small town in upstate New York. A label on the reverse indicates that the painting had once been in the Litta collection, and Christie's tentatively identified it with an item described as "*Due figure allegoriche, Scuola piacentina*" in an unpublished inventory of the Litta collection that is said to date from around the beginning of the nineteenth century. Research in published or publicly accessible documents relating to the Litta family collections has so far failed to confirm or elaborate on this.

3. Published in Giuseppe Campori, *Raccolta di cataloghi ed inventarii inediti* (1870; reprint, Bologna: A. Forni, 1975), 309ff.

4. Published in ibid., 57ff.

5. Compare Campori (see note 3), 161.

6. The most recent account of the Dresden purchase is in Johannes Winkler, ed., *La vendita di Dresda*, trans. Germana Baleni (Modena: Edizioni Panini, 1989). The missing portrait is discussed on page 76. The three attributed to Garofalo are *Aurora, The Dream*, and *Saint George*, although the latter's companion *Saint Michael* was still considered to be by Dosso.

7. Canonici's inventory of 1632 is published in Campori (see note 3), 105ff. See also Emanuele Mattaliano, "Il *Baccanale* di Dosso Dossi: Nuove acquisizioni documentarie," in Joseph Manca, ed., *Titian 500* (Washington: National Gallery of Art, 1993), 359–65.

8. The *Sibyl* is discussed by Ballarin (see note 1), 1: 341 (entry no. 438), fig. 174. For the *Portrait,* which certainly does not depict Alfonso, see 1: 364 (entry no 489), fig. 224. The attribution of the latter to either brother is highly doubtful. It was later in the Costabili collection (see note 15).

9. Girolamo Baruffaldi, *Vite de' pittori e scultori ferraresi,* 2 vols. (Ferrara: D. Taddei, 1844–1846), 1: 248.

10. Compare Mattaliano (see note 7), 359ff.

11. Compare Martin Eidelberg and Eliot W. Rowlands, "The Dispersal of the Last Duke of Mantua's Paintings," *Gazette des beaux-arts,* ser. 6, 123 (1994): 250–51.

12. Baruffaldi (see note 9), 1: 267, 286.

13. Andrea Faoro and Lucio Scardino, eds., *Quadri da stimarsi . . . : Documenti per una storia del collezionismo d'arte a Ferrara nel Settecento* (Ferrara: Liberty House, 1996), 74–87. One of the Leccioli paintings, a *Madonna,* is later found in the Costabili collection (see note 15).

14. Ibid., 68 (entry no. 13). The Cini painting was first published by Amalia Mezzetti, *Il Dosso e Battista ferraresi* (Milan: Silvana, 1965), 49, 102 (entry no. 120). Felton Gibbons, *Dosso and Battista Dossi: Court Painters at Ferrara* (Princeton: Princeton Univ. Press, 1968), 257 (entry no. 168), rejected the connection with either of the Dossi brothers.

15. For a recent discussion of the Costabili collection, see Jaynie Anderson, "The Rediscovery of Ferrarese Renaissance Painting in the Risorgimento," *Burlington Magazine* 135 (1993): 539–49. Another useful article is Andrea Ugolini, "Rivedendo la collezione Costabili di Ferrara," *Paragone,* no. 489 (1990): 50–76. Emanuele Mattaliano's research on the collection, unfortunately interrupted by his premature death, is to be published in the near future. The contents of the collection are best described in Camillo Laderchi's *Descrizione della quadreria Costabili* (Ferrara: Tipi Negri alle Pace, 1838). The paintings attributed to Dosso and Battista there are nos. 108–29. In addition, nos. 268–71 are connected with the school of Dosso and no. 383 is considered a good copy after Dosso. Finally, no. 503, a *Portrait of Margherita Gonzaga* by an anonymous Italian artist, is listed in subsequent catalogs of the collection in 1871 and 1872 as Dosso's. With a few exceptions, these paintings have not been identified. The only fairly secure item is no. 109 depicting Saint John the Baptist, which was acquired by Lord Wimborne and most recently was in the Gnecchi collection in Genoa (Ballarin [see note 1], 1: 333–34 [entry no. 425]). No. 110, the *Flight into Egypt,* has been tentatively identified with the painting formerly in the Harck collection, Schloss Seusslitz (Ballarin [see note 1], 1: 352–53 [entry no. 464]), but this is rather doubtful. No. 117, the *Portrait of Annibale Saracco* (Ballarin [see note 1], 1: 322–23 [entry no. 405]), also acquired by Lord Wimborne and later belonging to Tancred Borenius, while accepted by some writers as the work of Dosso, is very problematic. No. 116, the so-called *Portrait of Alfonso I* (Ballarin [see note 1], 1: 364 [entry no. 489]), which had come from the Canonici collection (see note 8) and passed to Henry Layard, is

probably not by either Dosso or Battista. A portrait supposedly depicting a young Estense prince (no. 115), apparently still in the Wimborne collection, clearly is even more implausible (Gibbons [see note 14], 249 [entry no. 137]). Of the remainder, it is worth noting that no. 108, a *Baptism,* is said to come from Fusignano, presumably based on references to such a work in the earlier literature. However, the Fusignano *Baptism* is still in Fusignano and differs in composition. Costabili also had at least one painting, a *Madonna* (no. 123), from the Leccioli collection (see note 13).

16. Published in Cesare d'Onofrio, "Inventario dei dipinti del cardinal Pietro Aldobrandini compilato da G. B. Agucchi nel 1603," *Palatino,* new ser., 8 (1964): 15–20, 158–62, 202–11.

17. Published in Paola Della Pergola, "L'inventario del 1592 di Lucrezia d'Este," *Arte antica e moderna,* no. 7 (1959): 342–51.

18. The six that can be tentatively identified in both inventories are a *Nativity,* a *Saint Jerome,* a *Madonna,* the *Pietà, Christ at Gethsemane,* and a *Saint George.* In addition, Lucrezia d'Este's inventory lists three more paintings of Saint Jerome by Dosso, as well as one of an old man and a *Saint Anthony.* While most of these could possibly be identified with anonymous paintings in the Aldobrandini collection, no depictions of Saint Anthony by any Italian artist are found there.

19. Still unpublished; a photocopy is in the archives of the Getty Provenance Index.

20. Rome, Galleria Doria-Pamphili, inv. no. 220.

21. D'Onofrio (see note 16), 160 (entry no. 107).

22. Ballarin (see note 1), 1: 294 (entry no. 329), 336 (entry no. 430), 319–20 (entry no. 395).

23. Ballarin (see note 1), 1: 304 (entry no. 351), 317 (entry no. 383). For the *Saint Jerome,* see D'Onofrio (see note 16), 159 (entry no. 88). The 1603 inventory does not include the dimensions, but the 1665 inventory describes it as *"alto p[iedi] due incirca,"* which corresponds very well to the painting in question. For the *Temptation of Christ,* see D'Onofrio (see note 16), 161 (entry no. 124). In the 1603 inventory, this painting was attributed to an anonymous Flemish artist, but the later inventories assign it to Dosso. The dimensions in the 1665 inventory were *"alto p[iede] uno incirca."* This painting, first published in Gibbons (see note 14), 228 (entry no. 103), was formerly in the collection of Robert P. Nichols of Brighton, who probably owned the mythological painting at the J. Paul Getty Museum (see note 1) as well.

24. The composition of Vulcan and other gods and goddesses is found in D'Onofrio (see note 16), 162 (entry no. 154) (listed in the 1665 inventory as no. 153). The *Saint George,* described as being five *palmi* high, is no. 155.

25. I am grateful to Anna Coliva for information about the inventory from circa 1633. *The Enchantress Circe* (or *Melissa*) is found in Giacomo Manilli, *Villa Borghese fuori di Porta Pinciana* (Rome: Per Lodouico Grignani, 1650), 82, and so had entered the collection between 1633 and 1650. The *Apollo and Daphne* has recently been found to have entered the collection in 1659 as a gift from Cardinal Luigi Capponi (see Anna Coliva, "La Collezione Borghese: La storia, le opere," in idem, ed., *Galleria Borghese* [Rome: Progetti Museali, 1994], 123 [entry no. 56], referring to the unpublished document found by S. Schütze), although there are indications that it already

belonged to Cardinal Scipione Borghese in 1612 (see Paola Della Pergola, *Galleria Borghese, I Dipinti,* 2 vols. [Rome: Istituto Poligrafico dello Stato, 1955], 1: 30 [entry no. 35]) and was in the collection of Cardinal Ludovico Ludovisi in 1623 and 1633 (see note 45). It appears probable that the painting did indeed pass through all of these collections before settling once more in the Borghese.

26. Mezzetti (see note 14), 81–82 (entry no. 42), 135, 137, suggests that the two rhomboid paintings now in the Dobó István Vármúzeum in Eger, Hungary, and the Collezione Vittorio Cini in Venice (entry nos. 42 and 215) belonged to the paintings acquired by Scipione Borghese from the Castello in Ferrara in 1608, although there was no specific description of them. I am told that they are listed in the newly discovered inventory of circa 1633, but I do not have any details. They are apparently the same paintings that were later in the Sacchetti collection (see note 39).

27. Manilli (see note 25). The 1693 inventory is published in Paola Della Pergola, "L'inventario Borghese del 1693," *Arte antica e moderna,* no. 26 (1964): 219–30; no. 28 (1964): 451–67; no. 30 (1965): 202–17.

28. The three missing pictures are nos. 87, 124, and 639 in the 1693 inventory; see Della Pergola, ibid., no. 26 (1964): 224, 225; no. 30 (1965): 211.

29. In Manilli (see note 25), 97, as Dosso, *S. Caterina Martire.* No. 134 in the 1693 inventory (Della Pergola [see note 27], no. 26 [1964]: 226), described as *"un quadro in tela di tre palmi con una S. Caterina che tiene un libro in mano del N° 250 con cornice dorata di Leonardo de Vinci"* (a painting on canvas 3 *palmi* long with a Santa Caterina who has a book in hand of No. 250 with a gilded frame by Leonardo da Vinci), would appear to correspond to the Galleria Borghese's current inventory no. 142, the *Saint Catherine* generally accepted as the work of Dosso, which, in fact, seems to have the remains of the figure 250 inscribed in the lower right-hand corner. However, Della Pergola (idem, 230) associates this entry with current inventory no. 195, a painting of Saint Catherine by a follower of Luini, and does not find the painting by Dosso in the 1693 inventory at all. The painting in the style of Luini, which depicts the saint with both a palm and a book in her hands, also appears to fit the description less perfectly.

30. Coliva (see note 25), 123, has indicated that she thinks the painting is a copy after Dosso and has informed me that the newly discovered inventory of circa 1633 explicitly describes it as a copy of Dosso by Cesare d'Arpino. Although Arpino was very closely associated with Scipione Borghese and was still alive at the time of the inventory, I find it very difficult to believe this painting is his. If it is a copy—of which no original is known—then it is a highly successful imitation of another artist's style.

31. Della Pergola (see note 27), no. 28 (1964): 459 (entry no. 338). The correct association was first made by Ballarin (see note 1), 1: 327 (entry no. 414).

32. Published in Laura Testa, "Un collezionista del Seicento: Il cardinale Carlo Emanuele Pio," in Jadranka Bentini, ed., *Quadri rinomatissimi: Il collezionismo dei Pio di Savoia* (Modena: Artioli, 1994), 98–99.

33. The 1689 inventory of Cardinal Carlo Pio di Savoia was discovered by Luigi Spezzaferro and will be published in the near future. He has kindly allowed me to quote from it. Many of the same paintings appear—generally without the artist's name—in an earlier inventory made of the collection of Cardinal Carlo Emanuele Pio

di Savoia in 1641, published by Francesca Cappelletti and Laura Testa, "Ricerche documentarie sul *San Giovanni Battista* dei Musei Capitolini e sul *San Giovanni Battista* della Galleria Doria-Pamphilj," in Giampaolo Correale, ed., *Identificazione di un Caravaggio* (Venice: Marsilio, 1990), 85–92. Some, but not all, are still present in the inventory of Principe Francesco Pio di Savoia drawn up in 1724; this inventory has been published by Cappelletti and Testa (92–101); and by Sergio Guarino, "L'inventario Pio di Savoia del 1724," in Bentini (see note 32), 119–29.

34. The painting appears in the 1724 inventory (see note 33) as an anonymous work before being sold to Gavin Hamilton sometime prior to 1773, when an engraving by Giuseppe Perini was published in Hamilton's *Schola Italica Picturae.* The legend on the engraving attributes it to Palma Giovane, and the painting was apparently sold under this name to Sir William Hamilton. Put up for sale at Christie's in 1801 as part of Hamilton's collection, it subsequently appeared in a series of London sales. It disappeared from view after a sale held at Christie's on 30 March 1824, when it was sold to "Taylor." For a résumé, see Ian Jenkins and Kim Sloan, *Vases and Volcanoes: Sir William Hamilton and His Collection* (London: British Museum Press, 1996), 276 (entry no. 173).

35. Sergio Guarino, "La Pinacoteca Capitolina dall'acquisto dei quadri Sacchetti e Pio di Savoia all'arrivo della *Santa Petronilla* del Guercino," in Sergio Guarino, Patrizia Masini, and Maria Elisa Tittoni, eds., *Guercino e le collezioni capitoline,* exh. cat. (Rome: Edizioni Carte Segrete, 1991), 57 ("Stima de Quadri prescelti appartenenti all'Eccellentissima Casa Pio," entry no. 35).

36. The Sacchetti inventories have been transcribed by Sergio Guarino and will be published in the near future.

37. Giulia de Marchi, *Mostre di quadri a S. Salvatore in Lauro (1682–1725): Stime di collezioni Romane,* ed. Giuseppe Ghezzi (Rome: Presso la Società alla Biblioteca Vallicelliana, 1987), 471, 480. I am told by Sergio Guarino that the Madonna (*Christo con fulmine in mano con la Madonna ed angeli;* Christ with a thunderbolt in hand with Madonna and angels) has been found in the Vatican collections and is presently being restored.

38. Guarino (see note 35), 47 ("Inventario de Quadri della Casa Sacchetti," entry no. 20).

39. Guarino at one time indicated that the rhomboid with four figures was still in the Capitoline collections in 1817; he has since concluded that neither painting is documented there after 1750.

40. The 1610 and 1631 inventories are published in Luigi Spezzaferro, "Un imprenditore del primo Seicento: Giovanni Battista Crescenzi," *Ricerche di storia dell'arte,* no. 26 (1985): 71–73.

41. This painting appears in the 1610 inventory as no. 17 and in the 1631 inventory as no. 39. Ibid., 71, 72.

42. Campori (see note 3), 162.

43. The 1692 inventory of Flavio Chigi's collection remains unpublished, but a transcription exists in the Getty Provenance Index. The *Sibyl* is described as "*Un Quadro in tela di 3 palmi, con cornice tutta dorata et intagliata con una mezza figura d'una Sibilla mano del Dossi*" (A painting on canvas, 3 *palmi*, with completely gilded

frame and engraved with a half-figure of a sibyl, hand of Dosso). The painting of Venus and Cupid, described in the 1650 list of Savelli paintings as *"Una Venere con l'Amorino in tela per traverso palmi 6 e 7 in circa de' Dossi, D. 60"* (A Venus with putto on canvas approximately 6 by 7 *palmi* by Dossi, D[ucati] 60), is listed in the Chigi inventory as *"Un Quadro Tela d'Imperatore cornice tutta dorata, con una Venere ignuda à sedere, con un Amorino, che dorme, e Paese, mano del Dossi"* (A canvas with completely gilded frame, of a nude Venus sitting, and a putto who is sleeping, with a landscape, hand of Dosso). Chigi had other paintings attributed to Dosso, including two male portraits, a *Holy Family with Saint John,* a portrait of a woman, a portrait of a youth, and a copy of a half-length *Saint Catherine.*

44. Ballarin (see note 1), 1: 355 (entry no. 471), where it is attributed to Battista. Dimensions: 135 × 160 cm.

45. For the earlier inventory, see Carolyn H. Wood, "The Ludovisi Collection of Paintings in 1623," *Burlington Magazine* 134 (1992): 515–23. The later inventory is found in Klara Garas, "The Ludovisi Collection of Pictures in 1633," *Burlington Magazine* 109 (1967): 287–89, 339–48.

46. This painting is listed in the 1623 inventory as no. 205 (Wood, ibid., 521) and in the 1633 inventory as no. 24 (Garas, ibid., 340).

47. Luigi Salerno, "The Picture Gallery of Vincenzo Giustiniani," *Burlington Magazine* 102 (1960): 21–27, 93–104, 135–48. The paintings by Dosso depicted a young peasant woman (*"una contadina giovane"*), the *Adoration of the Magi* combined with the *Massacre of the Innocents* and the *Flight into Egypt,* a composition with the heads of two sibyls, a *Portrait of Petrarch, Christ Disputing in the Temple,* and *Saint Jerome;* see ibid., 138 (entry nos. 75, 76), 141 (entry no. 88), 143 (entry nos. 153, 154), 144 (entry no. 182).

48. C. P. Landon, ed., *Galerie Giustiniani* (Paris: Chaignieau Aîné, 1812), figs. 59, 69. Silvia Danesi Squarzina, "The Collections of Cardinal Benedetto Giustiniani. Part I," *Burlington Magazine* 139 (1997): 783, has recently indicated that the *Saint Jerome* has been found in the deposit of the Neues Palais at Potsdam; it appears as no. 39 in the postmortem inventory, dated 1621, of Benedetto Giustiniani.

49. Salerno (see note 47), 138 (entry no. 70). The painting is no. 50 in the postmortem inventory, dated 1621, of Benedetto Giustiniani; see Danesi Squarzina, ibid., 784.

50. All of the Barberini material mentioned here is found in Marilyn Aronberg Lavin, *Seventeenth-Century Barberini Documents and Inventories of Art* (New York: New York Univ. Press, 1975). The *Reclining Venus* is published by Ballarin (see note 1), 1: 340–41 (entry no. 436).

51. The Patrizi inventory (which includes two portraits by Dosso), the Giuseppe Pignatelli inventory (a portrait of a woman), the Angeloni inventory (a *Nativity* as well as a *Christ at Gethsemane*), the Albizzi inventory (a *Holy Family* and a *Saint Jerome*), and the Paulucci inventory (one *Madonna* and a second attributed to either Dosso or Titian) will all be published shortly by Luigi Spezzaferro. The 1648 inventory of Camillo Pamphilj, in which is found a version of the Modena *buffone,* described as *"una mezza figurina di un buffone, che ride con una pecora in braccio"* (a half-figure of a jester who is laughing with a sheep in his arms), will be published by

Giovanna Capitelli along with other Pamphilj inventories. The inventory of Lorenzo Onofrio Colonna is published in Eduard A. Safarik, *Collezione dei dipinti Colonna: Inventari 1611–1795* (Munich: K. G. Saur, 1996), 122ff. Lists of pictures belonging to Marcello Pignatelli, Cardinal Giuseppe Imperiale, Cardinal Savio Mellini, and Lelio and Paolo Falconieri are all found in de Marchi (see note 37).

52. Alessandro Luzio, *La galleria dei Gonzaga venduta all'Inghilterra nel 1627–28: Documenti degli archivi di Mantova e Londra* (Milan: L. F. Cogliati, 1913), 134 (entry no. 673): *"Un quadro sopra l'asse dipintovi una Madona circondata da Angeli et pastori con cornici di noce di mano di Dosso"* (A painting on wood depicting a Madonna surrounded by angels and shepherds with walnut frame, hand of Dosso).

53. A large number of Bolognese inventories have been transcribed by Raffaella Morselli and will be published in 1998. They contain just eight paintings attributed to Dosso and one copy. Four are portraits, including one of Gonella, and five depict saints.

54. Found in a series of letters from Cennini to Michelangelo Vanni (son of Francesco Vanni) in 1660, which are transcribed in Ettore Romagnoli, *Biografia cronologica de' bellartisti senesi, 1200–1800 [i.e. 1100–1800]: Opera manoscritta*, 13 vols. (circa 1835; reprint, Florence: Edizioni S.P.E.S., 1976), 10: 53–66. I am indebted to Andrea De Marchi for this reference.

55. The familial connection between Francesco and Roberto Cennini has not yet been determined. For a biography of the former, see *Dizionario biografico degli italiani* (Rome: Istituto della Enciclopedia Italiana, 1960–), 23: 569–71.

56. Gérard Labrot, *Collections of Paintings in Naples, 1600–1780* (Munich: K. G. Saur, 1992), 50.

57. Naples, Museo e Gallerie Nazionali di Capodimonte, inv. no. 72. Ballarin (see note 1), 1: 296–97 (entry no. 335).

58. Chantilly, Musée Condé, inv. no. 43. Ballarin (see note 1), 1: 350 (entry no. 457).

59. For Imperiale, see Renato Martinoni, *Gian Vincenzo Imperiale, politico, letterato e collezionista genovese del Seicento* (Padua: Antenore, 1983). The Balbi inventory was published in Piero Boccardo and Lauro Magnani, "La committenza," in Federica Lamera, *Il palazzo dell'Università di Genova* (Genoa: Università degli Studi, 1987), 81.

60. The inventory of Amedeo Dal Pozzo will be published in 1998 by Arabella Cifani and Franco Monetti.

61. Alessandro Vesme, "La regia Pinacoteca di Torino," *Le Gallerie nazionali italiane; Notizie e documenti* 3 (1897): 53 (entry no. 465).

62. Fabri's collection is described in Francesco Sansovino, *Venetia città nobilissima e singolare... ampliata dal M. R. D. Giovanni Stringa* (Venice: Altobello Salicato, 1604), 259–60, quoted in Michel Hochmann, *Peintres et commanditaires à Venise (1540–1628)* (Rome: Ecole Française de Rome, 1992), 206. The inventory of Michele Pietra is published in Simona Savini Branca, *Il collezionismo veneziano nel '600* (Padua: L. S. Olschki, 1965), 134ff.

63. Fabrizio Magani, *Il collezionismo e la committenza artistica della famiglia Widmann, patrizi veneziani, dal Seicento all'Ottocento* (Venice: Istituto Veneto di

Scienze, Lettere ed Arti, 1989), 25. In the nineteenth century the painting was in the Barbini collection in Venice.

64. Adolfo Venturi, "Zur Geschichte der Kunstsammlungen Kaiser Rudolf II," *Repertorium für Kunstwissenschaft* 8 (1885): 12.

65. John Shearman, *The Early Italian Pictures in the Collection of Her Majesty the Queen* (Cambridge: Cambridge Univ. Press, 1983), 89–90 (entry no. 82).

66. Ibid., 89 (entry no. 80), 90 (entry no. 83).

67. Shearman (see note 65), 90 (entry no. 81).

68. Oliver Millar, ed., *Abraham Van der Doort's Catalogue of the Collections of Charles I,* vol. 37 of the Walpole Society (London: Walpole Society, 1960); and Oliver Millar, ed., *The Inventories and Valuations of the King's Goods, 1649–1651,* vol. 43 of the Walpole Society (London: Walpole Society, 1972).

69. The *Temptation of Saint Anthony* is found in a list of paintings at Nonesuch in 1639, where it is described as "A landscept of St Anthon: temptacon, don by Dorsey, Ma[ntuan] peece" with the dimensions of 3 ft. 9 in. × 5 ft. 1 in. (see Millar, 1960, ibid., 188). (I am unable to find it among the pictures sold when the Royal Collection was dispersed a few years later.) This presumably corresponds to entry no. 518 in the Gonzaga inventory of 1627, which is the only painting of this subject, other than two by Jan Brueghel (entry no. 562, valued at 60 lire; and entry no. 578, valued at 240 lire), to be found there (see Luzio [see note 52], 125, 126, 129). It is described as *"Un quadretto sopra l'asse dipintovi tentationi di S. Antonio con cornice fregiata d'oro"* and valued at 6 lire, which is rather low. The dimensions in the 1639 inventory indicate a fairly large painting and correspond approximately to the San Diego painting if one assumes the frame was included. The chief reason for the identification, however, is the fact that Italian artists very rarely depicted this subject during the sixteenth century, and virtually no other candidates exist. See, for instance, A. Pigler, *Barockthemen: Eine Auswahl von Verzeichnissen zur Ikonographie des 17. und 18. Jahrhunderts,* 2nd ed., 3 vols. (Budapest: Akadémiai Kiadó, 1974), 1: 420, which lists works depicting the temptation of Saint Anthony by Tintoretto, Farinati, Veronese, Zelotti, Padovanino, Palma Giovane, and Antonio Campi. The latter is an upright composition, and none of the others are likely. Moreover, we have already seen an instance of a painting (the Capitoline *Saint Margaret*) by Savoldo—whose name was scarcely known outside the Veneto—that had passed previously as the work of Dosso. It is also noteworthy that when it was in the Gonzaga collection the painting hung in a gallery with the two paintings of the same subject by Brueghel. No. 578 by Brueghel, described in the 1627 inventory as "*S. Antonio tentato di diverse fantasme,*" could have served as the source for the unusual Brueghelian iconography of the San Diego painting.

70. In a list of pictures at Somerset House sold in 1649, it is listed as no. 19, "A Naked woman rydeing on her husband, by dorsy"; see Millar, 1972 (see note 68), 299. It would correspond to no. 241 in the Gonzaga inventory of 1627, *"Un quadro dipintovi Aristotile cavalcato da sua moglie iniuda"* (A painting depicting Aristotle riding on the back of his nude wife), valued at 120 lire; see Luzio (see note 52), 106.

71. Millar, 1960 (see note 68), 187 (entry no. 20); and Millar, 1972 (see note 68), 194 (entry no. 134).

72. Luzio (see note 52), 108 (entry no. 253, valued at 60 lire).

73. Mary L. Cox, "Notes on the Collections formed by Thomas Howard," *Burlington Magazine* 19 (1911): 286.

74. Gerard Hoet, *Catalogus of Naamlyst van Schilderyen,* 3 vols. (1752–1770; reprint, Soest, The Netherlands: Davaco, 1976), 1: 201 (entry no. 29).

75. Jean-Claude Boyer and Isabelle Volf, "Rome à Paris: Les tableaux du maréchal de Créquy (1638)," *Revue de l'art,* no. 79 (1988): 31 (entry no. 127).

76. Honor Levi, "L'inventaire après décès du cardinal de Richelieu," *Archives de l'art français* 27 (1985): 63 (entry no. 1011).

77. Gabriel-Jules, comte de Cosnac, *Les richesses du palais Mazarin* (Paris: Renouard, 1884), 300 (entry no. 984).

78. Arnauld Brejon de Lavergnée, *L'inventaire Le Brun de 1683: La collection des tableaux de Louis XIV* (Paris: Editions de la Réunion des Musées Nationaux, 1987), 140–41 (entry no. 63), 171 (entry no. 114), 316 (entry no. 291).

79. Adolf Berger, "Inventar der Kunstsammlung des Erzherzogs Leopold Wilhelm von Österreich," *Jahrbuch der kunsthistorischen Sammlungen des allerhöchsten Kaiserhauses* 1 (1883): lxxix–clxxvii.

80. Vienna, Kunsthistorisches Museum, inv. no. 57; and Budapest, Szèpmüvèszeti Mùzeum, inv. no. 809.

81. Petworth House, National Trust, inv. no. 76; illustrated in Annalisa Scarpa Sonino, *Cabinet d'amateur: Le grandi collezioni d'arte nei dipinti dal XVII al XIX secolo* (Milan: Berenice, 1992), 85.

82. Ballarin (see note 1), 1: 316 (entry no. 380).

83. The Carpio inventories are available in Marcus B. Burke and Peter Cherry, *Collections of Paintings in Madrid, 1601–1755,* 2 vols. (Los Angeles: Provenance Index of the Getty Information Institute, 1997), 1: 437–53, 462–83, 726–86, 815–77.

Biographical Notes on the Contributors

Franco Bacchelli has studied the philosophical and scientific debates current in Renaissance Italy under Eugenio Garin and Nicola Badaloni. Upon completing his dissertation on the concept of space in the writings of Francesco Patrizi da Cherso, he will receive his doctorate in the history of science from the Museo della Scienza, Florence. In 1997 he finished a critical edition of Marcello Palingenio Stellato's *Zodiacus vitae,* and his article "Ficino, Pico e Pierleone da Spoleto traduttori di testi cabbalistici" will appear in 1998.

Andrea Bayer is assistant curator in the Department of European Paintings at the Metropolitan Museum of Art. Her scholarly interests in the Italian Renaissance period center on the prints, drawings, and paintings of the Venetian and northern Italian schools. She has published a number of reviews and articles and has contributed to the exhibition catalogs *Giambattista Tiepolo; Jusepe de Ribera, 1591–1652; A Caravaggio Rediscovered: The Lute Player;* and *Alessandro Bonvicino, Il Moretto.* She is a coordinating curator for the exhibition and catalog *Dosso Dossi.*

Jadranka Bentini heads the Soprintendenza per i Beni Artistici e Storici of Modena and Reggio Emilia. Her many scholarly and professional activities are dedicated to the conservation of objects from the artistic patrimony of Italy. The volumes she has edited include *Bastianino e la pittura a Ferrara nel secondo Cinquecento* (1985), *L'impressa di Alfonso II: Saggi e documenti sulla produzione artistica a Ferrara nel secondo Cinquecento* (1987), and *La Pinacoteca Nazionale di Ferrara: Catalogo generale* (1992). Presently she is writing on the Este family and the history of collecting.

Albano Biondi conducts research on the Renaissance and the baroque period. His areas of interest are humanism, political history, and the history of cultures and *mentalitès,* and his publications range over topics from astrology to meat packing. Among the works that he has translated from Latin into Italian are Giordano Bruno's *De magia* (1986), Marsilio Ficino's *De vita* (1991), and Giovanni Francesco Pico della Mirandola's *Conclusiones nongentae* (1995). He is professor of early modern history at the Università di Bologna.

Jane Bridgeman is an independent scholar and freelance lecturer based in London. Her principal research interest is the investigation and interpretation of dress and ceremony as cultural phenomena in Italy and Spain during the Middle Ages and the Renaissance. Recent articles include "Dress in Southern Europe, Fourteenth to Sixteenth Centuries" (1998), "'*Condecenti e netti* . . . ': Beauty, Dress and Gender in Italian Renaissance Art" (1998), "'*Pagar le Pompe*': Why Sumptuary Laws Did Not Work" (in press).

Luisa Ciammitti is curator at the Pinacoteca Nazionale in Bologna, a post that she has held since 1978. Her publications canvass fifteenth-century Italian sculpture, art collecting in Italy during the Renaissance, and the lives of Bolognese women of the seventeenth and eighteenth centuries. She has been a research associate at the Getty Research Institute for the History of Art and the Humanities and has lectured at the Davis Center for Historical Studies at Princeton University and at the Kimbell Art Museum in Fort Worth, Texas.

Luca D'Ascia has published the monograph *Erasmo e l'umanesimo romano* (1991) and articles on several other Renaissance authors. Formerly a visiting lecturer in Italian literature and culture at the University of Bielefeld, he is a *ricercatore* at the Scuola Normale Superiore, Pisa. He is currently preparing an annotated edition of Leon Battista Alberti's *Intercenales* and a study that explores the influence of Erasmus in Italy.

Andrea De Marchi studied with Luciano Bellosi and worked for the Soprintendenza per i Beni Artistici e Storici of Pisa prior to becoming a *ricercatore* at the Università di Lecce. In addition to the monograph *Gentile da Fabriano: Un viaggio nella pittura italiana alla fine del gotico* (1992), he has published articles on Italian paintings and illuminated manuscripts of the fourteenth to sixteenth centuries. He has collaborated on exhibitions about Domenico Beccafumi, Francesco di Giorgio, and the *pittura di luce* and is one of the founders and editors of the journal *Nuovi Studi*.

Adriano Franceschini is a retired elementary school teacher, a paleographer, and a medieval historian. For over fifty years, he has steadily conducted research in archives in Ferrara and elsewhere, producing an extensive body of work that has been invaluable to scholars both in Italy and abroad. His most recent publication is *Artisti a Ferrara in età umanistica e rinascimentale: Testimonianze archivistiche* (1993–1997).

Burton Fredericksen serves as director of the Provenance Index of the Getty Art History Information Program and as senior curator for research at the J. Paul Getty Museum. He is the author of *Masterpieces of Painting in the J. Paul Getty Museum* (1980; 3rd ed. 1995) and the editor of two ongoing book series for the Provenance Index: *Index of Paintings Sold in the British*

Isles during the Nineteenth Century (with Julia I. Armstrong and Doris A. Mendenhall) and *Répertoire des tableaux vendus en France au XIX*[eme] *siècle* (with Benjamin Peronnet).

Vincenzo Gheroldi is an *ispettore storico dell'arte* for the Soprintendenza per i Beni Ambientali Architettonici of Brescia, Cremona, and Mantova and lectures on the history of artistic techniques at the Università di Bologna-Ravenna. He has recently published two monographs, *Ricette e ricettari* (1995) and *Le vernici al principio del Settecento: Studi sul Trattato di Filippo Bonanni* (1995).

Michel Hochmann focuses his studies on sixteenth-century Venetian art history, French Renaissance architecture, and Italian art theory and art collections. He is the author of *Peintres et commanditaires à Venise, 1541–1628* (1993) and of the exhibition catalog *La Stanza delle Muse* (1995), and he collaborated with Bernard Jestaz and Philippe Sénéchal on *L'inventaire du palais et des propriétés Farnèse à Rome en 1644* (1994). He is director of studies for the history of art at the Académie de France in Rome.

Peter Humfrey is professor of art history at the University of St. Andrews and the author of numerous books, articles, and reviews on Italian Renaissance art and artists. His monographs on Cima da Conegliano, Carpaccio, Lorenzo Lotto, and Venetian altarpieces are widely cited, and *Painting in Renaissance Venice* (1995), his introductory work for the nonspecialist, has been translated into French and Italian.

Mauro Lucco has centered much of his scholarship on Venetian and northern Italian Renaissance painting. An associate professor of the visual arts at the Università di Bologna, he is the editor of *Il Quattrocento* (1989–1990), *Il Trecento* (1992), and *Il Cinquecento* (1996), all for Electa's Pittura nel Veneto series, and a co-organizer with David Alan Brown and Peter Humfrey of the exhibition *Lorenzo Lotto, Rediscovered Master of the Renaissance.* His publications include the monograph *Giorgione* (1995) and the catalogue raisonnè *L'opera completa di Sebastiano del Piombo* (1980).

Alessandro Nova teaches art history at the J. W. Goethe Universität, Frankfurt. A specialist in the Italian Renaissance, he is the author of *The Artistic Patronage of Pope Julius III, 1550–1555* (1988) and *Girolamo Romanino* (1994), as well as *Michelangelo, architetto* (1984), which has been translated into French and German. He is now working on a book about the Franciscan patronage of the *sacri monti.*

Steven F. Ostrow has written and lectured widely on the history of Italian art from the sixteenth through the eighteenth centuries. He is associate professor of art history and department chair at the University of California, Riverside, and the author of *Art and Spirtuality in Counter-Reformation Rome: The Sistine and Pauline Chapels in S. Maria Maggiore* (1996). Currently, his research focuses on Gianlorenzo Bernini and on the monuments of Renaissance and early baroque Rome.

William F. Prizer is professor of musicology at the University of California, Santa Barbara. An authority on the music of Renaissance Italy and France, he has written extensively about courtly musical life in northern Italy and about the development of musical forms such as the lauda and the frottola. He has also published critical editions of music by Josquin Desprez and Guiseppe Torelli.

Giovanni Romano writes and lectures about Renaissance and early modern art in Italy. A professor of the history of modern art at the Università di Torino, he has collaborated on many works about various Piedmontese museum collections. His monographs include *Casalesi del Cinquecento: L'avvento del manierismo in una città padana* (1970), *Studi sul paesaggio: Storia e immagini* (1978; 2nd ed. 1991), and *De Mantegna à Raphaël: Vers le portrait moderne* (1996).

Salvatore Settis is director of the Getty Research Institute for the History of Art and the Humanities and professor of the history of classical art and archaeology at the Scuola Normale Superiore, Pisa. His monograph *La Tempesta interpretata: Giorgione, i committenti, il soggetto* (1978; 3rd ed. 1982) has been published in six languages, and he is the author of numerous articles and prefaces. In addition to directing several book series, he currently serves on the editorial boards of eight journals. He was the editor of *Memoria dell'antico nell'arte italiana* (vols. 1–3, 1984–1986) and is currently the editor of *I Greci: Storia cultura arte società* (vols. 1–2.2, 1996–1997; vols. 2.3–4, forthcoming).

Craig Hugh Smyth is professor emeritus of fine arts at Harvard University. He has served as director of the Institute of Fine Arts at New York University and of the Harvard University Center for Italian Renaissance Studies, Villa I Tatti, in Florence. His publications include *Mannerism and Maniera* (1963; rev. ed. 1992), *Bronzino as Draughtsman* (1971), *The Repatriation of Art from the Collecting Point in Munich after World War II* (1988), and collaborative studies with Henry A. Millon on Michelangelo and St. Peter's.

Illustration Credits

14 Reproduced by courtesy of the Trustees, The National Gallery, London.

20, 21 Photo: Soprintendenza per i Beni Artistici e Storici, Mantua. By permission of the Ministero per i Beni Culturali e Ambientali and the Museo Diocesano di Arte Sacra "Francesco Gonzago," Mantua.

22 Photo: Negative C8445, Gabinetto Fotografico Nazionale. Courtesy Istituto Centrale per il Catalogo e la Documentazione, Rome.

23 Photo: Negative C8446, Gabinetto Fotografico Nazionale. Courtesy Istituto Centrale per il Catalogo e la Documentazione, Rome.

24 Photo: Soprintendenza per i Beni Artistici e Storici, Mantua. By permission of the Ministero per i Beni Culturali e Ambientali and the Museo Diocesano di Arte Sacra "Francesco Gonzago," Mantua.

26, 28, 29 Courtesy of the owner. Photo: Dipartimento Discipline Artistiche dell'Università di Torino (40 percent research funding from the Ministero dell'Università).

42 Courtesy Graphische Sammlung Albertina, Vienna.

45 Courtesy Kunsthistorisches Museum, Vienna.

46 The Royal Collection © Her Majesty Queen Elizabeth II. Photo: Royal Collection Enterprises, Photographic Services, Windsor.

49 Negative: Gosudarstvennyj Muzej A. S. Pushkina, Moscow. Photo: Pinacoteca Tosio Martinengo, Brescia.

50 Photo: Copyright © Cameraphoto-Arte, Venice.

53 By permission of the Houghton Library, Harvard University.

64 Photo: Soprintendenza per i Beni Artistici e Storici, Modena and Reggio Emilia. By permission of the Ministero per i Beni Culturali e Ambientali.

65 Photo: Alinari/Art Resource, New York.

66 Photo: Soprintendenza per i Beni Artistici e Storici, Modena and Reggio Emilia. By permission of the Ministero per i Beni Culturali e Ambientali.

69 Photo: Massimo Velo, Naples. Courtesy Soprintendenza per i Beni Artistici e Storici, Naples.

70 Courtesy Graphische Sammlung Albertina, Vienna.

73 Photo: Conservation des Musées, Ville d'Angers. Copyright © Musées d'Angers.

84 Courtesy The J. Paul Getty Museum, Los Angeles.

85 Computer reconstruction: Yvonne Szafran. Courtesy Paintings Conservation Department, The J. Paul Getty Museum, Los Angeles.

88 Courtesy Musée du Louvre, Paris.

93, fig. 5 Photo: Soprintendenza per i Beni Artistici e Storici, Mantua. By permission of the Ministero per i Beni Culturali e Ambientali.

93, fig. 6 Courtesy "L'Erma" di Bretschneider, Rome.

94 Courtesy Kunsthistorisches Museum, Vienna.

95, fig. 8 Courtesy Library of Congress, Rare Book and Special Collections Division, The Lessing J. Rosenwald Collection.

95, fig. 9 Photo: Soprintendenza per i Beni Artistici e Storici, Modena and Reggio Emilia. By permission of the Ministero per i Beni Culturali e Ambientali.

96, fig. 10 Courtesy Soprintendenza per i Beni Artistici e Storici, Rome.

96, fig. 11 From *418. Kunstauktion: Gemälde alter und neuerer Meister, Porzellan, Mobel, Bildteppiche und Antiquitäten, Dorotheum Wien, 27. bis 29. März 1933*. Courtesy Dorotheum Wien.

96, fig. 12 Courtesy Soprintendenza per i Beni Artistici e Storici, Rome.

99, fig. 13 Courtesy Kunsthistorisches Museum, Vienna.

99, fig. 14 Courtesy Beinecke Rare Book and Manuscript Library, Yale University.

100 By permission of the Castello del Buonconsiglio, Monumenti e Collezioni Provinciali, Trent. All rights reserved.

101 Courtesy The J. Paul Getty Museum, Los Angeles.

102 Courtesy The Getty Research Institute for the History of Art and the Humanities, Research Library, Los Angeles.

112, 114 Photo: Vincenzo Gheroldi.

117, fig. 4 Photo: Vincenzo Gheroldi.

117, fig. 5 Drawing: Vincenzo Gheroldi.

118, 121 Photo: Vincenzo Gheroldi.

122, fig. 9 Photo: Sotheby's, London.

122, fig. 10 Courtesy Soprintendenza per i Beni Artistici e Storici, Bologna.

125, fig. 11 Courtesy SCT Enterprises and The Courtauld Gallery, London.

125, fig. 12 Photo: Vincenzo Gheroldi.

128 Courtesy National Museums and Galleries of Wales.

142 Photo: Alinari/Art Resource, New York.

154, fig. 1 Courtesy Staatliche Museen zu Berlin Preußischer Kulturbesitz.

154, fig. 2 Courtesy Soprintendenza per i Beni Artistici e Storici, Florence.

156 Photo: Henri Bron, Montpellier.

157 Photo: Finarte, Milan.

160 Photo: Andrea De Marchi.

162 Photo: Soprintendenza per i Beni Artistici e Storici, Mantua. By permission of the Ministero per i Beni Culturali e Ambientali.

165, fig. 8 Photo: Soprintendenza Beni Artistici e Storici, Siena and Grosseto. By permission of the Ministero per i Beni Culturali e Ambientali.

165, fig. 9 Photo: Soprintendenza per i Beni Artistici e Storici, Mantua. By permission of the Ministero per i Beni Culturali e Ambientali.

165, fig. 10 Courtesy The National Museum of Western Art, Tokyo.
166, fig. 11 Photo: Mario Brogiolo, Brescia.
166, fig. 12 Photo: Andrea De Marchi.
169, fig. 13 Courtesy Museo Poldi Pezzoli, Milan.
169, fig. 14 Photo: Andrea De Marchi.
178 Courtesy Philadelphia Museum of Art: The John G. Johnson Collection.
179 Photo: Copyright © Soprintendenza alle Gallerie, Naples.
180 Photo: Antonio Idini, Rome.
182, 183 Photo: Jane Bridgeman.
184 Reproduced by courtesy of the Trustees, The National Gallery, London.
186, 187 Photo: Jane Bridgeman.
188, fig. 15 Photo: Jane Bridgeman.
188, fig. 16 Photo: Fotostudio Rapuzzi, Brescia.
191 Photo: Jane Bridgeman.
200 Courtesy Soprintendenza per i Beni Artistici e Storici, Bologna.
203, fig. 2 Courtesy Kunsthistorisches Museum, Vienna.
203, fig. 3 Reproduced by courtesy of the Trustees, The National Gallery, London.
205, fig. 4 Courtesy Soprintendenza per i Beni Artistici e Storici, Parma.
205, fig. 5 Courtesy Musée des Beaux-Arts et d'Archéologie, Besançon, France. Photo: Charles Choffet, Besançon.
206 Albrecht Altdorfer, *Saint Christopher Seated by a River Bank*. Rosenwald Collection. Copyright © 1997 Board of Trustees, National Gallery of Art, Washington.
208, fig. 7 Albrecht Dürer, *The Flight into Egypt*. Rosenwald Collection. Copyright © 1997 Board of Trustees, National Gallery of Art, Washington.
208, fig. 8 Courtesy The J. Paul Getty Museum, Los Angeles.
211 Photo: Alinari/Art Resource, New York.
212, fig. 10 Gift of The Samuel H. Kress Foundation, Lowe Art Museum, University of Miami, inv. no. 61.026.000.
212, fig. 11 Courtesy North Carolina Museum of Art, Raleigh, Purchased with funds from the North Carolina Art Society (Robert F. Phifer Bequest).
214 Courtesy Soprintendenza per i Beni Artistici e Storici, Parma.
222, fig. 1 Distemper on canvas, 446 × 243.8 cm. Photo: Fotostudio Rapuzzi, Brescia.
222, fig. 2 Engraving, 23.7 × 40.5 cm (Bartsch 14.104.117). The Metropolitan Museum of Art, Purchase, Joseph Pulitzer Bequest, 1917, acc. no. 17.50.90. All rights reserved, The Metropolitan Museum of Art.
222, fig. 3 Engraving, 29.5 × 44.5 cm (Bartsch 14.197.245). The Metropolitan Museum of Art, Rogers Fund, 1919, acc. no. 19.74.1. All rights reserved, The Metropolitan Museum of Art.
223 Oil on canvas, 247 × 479 cm. Photo: Fotostudio Rapuzzi, Brescia.

224 Oil on canvas, 157 × 127 cm. Courtesy Philadelphia Museum of Art: Purchased with the George W. Elkins Fund.

225 Engraving, 21 × 11.6 cm (Bartsch 14.296.393). The Metropolitan Museum of Art, The Elisha Whittelsey Collection, The Elisha Whittelsey Fund, 1949, acc. no. 49.97.137. All rights reserved, The Metropolitan Museum of Art.

227, fig. 7 Oil on canvas, 211 × 140 cm. Courtesy Gemäldegalerie Alte Meister, Staatliche Kunstsammlungen Dresden.

227, fig. 8 Engraving, 21.1 × 13.4 cm (Bartsch 14.155.192). Gift of Mrs. T. Jefferson Coolidge. Courtesy, Museum of Fine Arts, Boston. All rights reserved.

228, fig. 9 Engraving, 12.8 × 8 cm (Bartsch 14.211.265). The Metropolitan Museum of Art, The Elisha Whittelsey Collection, The Elisha Whittelsey Fund, 1949, acc. no. 49.97.90. All rights reserved, The Metropolitan Museum of Art.

228, fig. 10 Oil on canvas, ca. 40 × 30 cm. Photo: Negative E6434, Gabinetto Fotografico Nazionale. Courtesy Istituto Centrale per il Catalogo e la Documentazione, Rome.

228, fig. 11 Engraving, 24.4 × 17.8 cm (Bartsch 14.83.95). The Metropolitan Museum of Art, The Elisha Whittelsey Collection, The Elisha Whittelsey Fund, 1949, acc. no. 49.97.30. All rights reserved, The Metropolitan Museum of Art.

231, fig. 12 Oil on canvas, 160 × 168 cm. Photo: Alinari/Art Resource, New York.

231, fig. 13 Engraving, 18.2 × 12.3 cm (Bartsch 7.524.18). Courtesy Ashmolean Museum, Oxford.

232 Oil on canvas, 108.5 × 163 cm. Photo: Museo Nazionale di Castel Sant'Angelo, Rome. By permission of the Ministero per i Beni Culturali e Ambientali.

235, fig. 15 Engraving, 35.7 × 26 cm (Bartsch 7.73.57, Hollstein 60). The Metropolitan Museum of Art, Fletcher Fund, 1919, acc. no. 19.73.65. All rights reserved, The Metropolitan Museum of Art.

235, fig. 16 Dosso Dossi, *Circe and Her Lovers in a Landscape*, oil on canvas, 100.8 × 135.1 cm (39⅝ × 53½ in.), Samuel H. Kress Collection, copyright © 1997 Board of Trustees, National Gallery of Art, Washington.

235, fig. 17 Oil on canvas, 176 × 174 cm. Photo: Alinari/Art Resource, New York.

236, fig. 18 Oil on canvas, 77.5 × 111.8 cm. The Metropolitan Museum of Art, Maria DeWitt Jesup Fund, 1926, acc. no. 26.83. All rights reserved, The Metropolitan Museum of Art.

236, fig. 19 Woodcut, 13.4 × 10 cm (Bartsch 8.81.63, Hollstein w.88). The Metropolitan Museum of Art, The Elisha Whittelsey Collection, The Elisha Whittelsey Fund, 1950, acc. no. 50.592. All rights reserved, The Metropolitan Museum of Art.

242 Photo: Soprintendenza per i Beni Artistici e Storici, Delle Marche and Urbino. By permission of the Ministero per i Beni Culturali e Ambientali.
248 Photo: Clemente Castelbarco Albani.
249 Photo: Mario Carrieri.
250 Photo: Clemente Castelbarco Albani.
253 Photo: Copyright © Michele Alberto Sereni, Pesaro.
264, 267 Courtesy Gemäldegalerie Alte Meister, Staatliche Kunstsammlungen Dresden.
268 Courtesy Soprintendenza per i Beni Artistici e Storici, Modena and Reggio Emilia.
271 Archive of Mauro Lucco.
272, fig. 8 Battista Dossi, *The Hunt of the Calydonian Boar*, after 1520, tempera on wood, 15⅜ × 31 in. El Paso Museum of Art; Gift of the Kress Foundation.
272, fig. 9 Archive of Mauro Lucco.
273 Photo: Carlo Volpe, Bologna.
275, fig. 11 Courtesy City of Nottingham Museums; Castle Museum and Art Gallery.
275, fig. 12 Courtesy Muzeum Pałac w Wilanowie, Warsaw. All rights reserved.
275, fig. 13 Photo: Dino Marzola, Rovigo.
275, fig. 14 Courtesy Pinacoteca dell'Accademia dei Concordi, Rovigo.
276 Photo: Dino Marzola, Rovigo.
279, figs. 16–17 Archive of Mauro Lucco.
279, fig. 18 Courtesy Pinacoteca dell'Accademia dei Concordi, Rovigo.
281 Archive of Mauro Lucco.
282, fig. 20 Photo: Copyright © Photo RMN. Courtesy Agence Photographique de la Réunion des Musées Nationaux.
282, fig. 21 Courtesy Staatliche Museen zu Berlin Preußischer Kulturbesitz.
358 Courtesy The Getty Research Institute for the History of Art and the Humanities, Research Library, Los Angeles.
360 Drawing: Antonio Lombardo. Courtesy Amministrazione Provinciale, Ferrara.
373 Courtesy Fondazione Giorgio Cini.
375, fig. 2 Courtesy Soprintendenza per i Beni Artistici e Storici, Rome.
375, fig. 3 Photo: A. C. Cooper, London.
376 Courtesy Soprintendenza per i Beni Artistici e Storici, Rome.
379, fig. 5 Courtesy The Getty Research Institute for the History of Art and the Humanities, Research Library, Los Angeles.
379, fig. 6 Courtesy Fondazione Giorgio Cini.
379, fig. 7 Courtesy Heves Megyei Múzeumi Szervezet, Eger, Hungary.
381 Courtesy Nelson Shanks Collection, Andalusia, Pennsylvania.
383 Courtesy The Getty Research Institute for the History of Art and the Humanities, Research Library, Los Angeles.
388 The Putnam Foundation, Timken Museum of Art, San Diego.

Index

Page numbers in italic refer to illustrations.

Issues & Debates

A Series of the Getty Research Institute Publications and Exhibitions Program

Julia Bloomfield, Thomas F. Reese, Michael S. Roth, and Salvatore Settis, *Editors*

In Print

Otto Wagner: Reflections on the Raiment of Modernity
Editor: Harry Francis Mallgrave
(Hardback, $55.00—ISBN 0-89236-258-8)
(Paperback, $29.95—ISBN 0-89236-257-X)

American Icons: Transatlantic Perspectives on Eighteenth- and Nineteenth-Century American Art
Editors: Thomas W. Gaehtgens and Heinz Ickstadt
(Hardback, $55.00—ISBN 0-89236-246-4)
(Paperback, $29.95—ISBN 0-89236-247-2)

Art in History / History in Art: Studies in Seventeenth-Century Dutch Culture
Editors: David Freedberg and Jan de Vries
(Hardback, $55.00—ISBN 0-89236-201-4)
(Paperback, $29.95—ISBN 0-89236-200-6)

Censorship and Silencing: Practices of Cultural Regulation
Editor: Robert C. Post
(Paperback, $35.00—ISBN 0-89236-484-X)

In Preparation

Nietzsche and "An Architecture of Our Minds"
Editors: Alexandre Kostka and Irving Wohlfarth
(Paperback—ISBN 0-89236-485-8)

Dosso's Fate: Painting and Court Culture in Renaissance Italy
Edited by Luisa Ciammitti, Steven F. Ostrow, and Salvatore Settis

Designed by Bruce Mau Design Inc., Bruce Mau with Chris Rowat
Coordinated by Suzanne Petralli Meilleur
Type composed by Archetype in Sabon
Printed and bound by Thomson-Shore, Inc., on Cougar Opaque
Cover printed by Pheonix Color Corp.

Issues & Debates
Series designed by Bruce Mau Design Inc., Toronto, Canada